THE LION AND THE EAGLE

*War and the State: The Transformation of British Government
1914–1919* (editor)

Britain, America and the Sinews of War 1914–1918

*The First Privatisation: The Politicians, the City and the
Denationalisation of Steel*

Morgan Grenfell 1838–1988: The Biography of a Merchant Bank

'Goodbye, Great Britain': The 1976 IMF Crisis (with Alec Cairncross)

Deutsche Bank in London 1873–1998 (with Manfred Pohl)

The United States and the European Alliance since 1945
(editor with Melvyn Stokes)

Troublemaker: The Life and History of A.J.P. Taylor

The Short Oxford History of the British Isles: The British Isles since 1945
(editor)

Old World, New World: The Story of Britain and America

Is This Bottle Corked? The Secret Life of Wine (with Michael Bywater)

THE LION AND THE EAGLE

The Interaction of the British and American Empires 1783–1972

Kathleen Burk

BLOOMSBURY PUBLISHING
LONDON · OXFORD · NEW YORK · NEW DELHI · SYDNEY

BLOOMSBURY PUBLISHING
Bloomsbury Publishing Plc
50 Bedford Square, London, WC1B 3DP, UK

BLOOMSBURY, BLOOMSBURY PUBLISHING and the Diana logo are trademarks of
Bloomsbury Publishing Plc

First published in Great Britain 2018

Copyright © Kathleen Burk, 2018
Map illustrations copyright © Martin Lubikowski, ML Design, 2018
Final map illustration copyright © Michael Jewess, 2018

Kathleen Burk has asserted her right under the Copyright, Designs and Patents Act, 1988,
to be identified as Author of this work

A catalogue record for this book is available from the British Library

Library of Congress Cataloguing-in-Publication data has been applied for

ISBN: HB: 978-1-4088-5617-8; eBook: 978-1-4088-5618-5

2 4 6 8 10 9 7 5 3 1

Typeset by Newgen KnowledgeWorks Pvt. Ltd., Chennai, India
Printed and bound in Great Britain by CPI Group (UK) Ltd, Croydon CR0 4YY

To find out more about our authors and books visit www.bloomsbury.com
and sign up for our newsletters

For Miranda
my sort of daughter

Contents

List of Maps   viii
Preface and Acknowledgements   ix

Introduction: What is an Empire?   1
Chapter 1 Imperial Clashes Over the Border, 1783–1815   11
Chapter 2 From Sea to Shining Sea, 1815–1903   75
Chapter 3 China and the British and American Barbarians, 1783–1914   157
Chapter 4 The United States, Great Britain and Japan, 1854–1895   231
Chapter 5 The End of the (Imperial) Affair, 1895–1972   329
Envoi   435

Notes   439
Bibliography   509
Picture Credits   535
Index   539

List of Maps

Map 1   The Great Lakes Showing British Forts 1793   23

Map 2   Determining the Border between Maine and
         New Brunswick   37

Map 3   The War of 1812   57

Map 4   The Oregon Territory   85

Map 5   Border Conflicts 1816–1818   89

Map 6   St Lawrence River to Lake of the
         Woods 1817–1827   95

Map 7   Northeast Boundary from St Lawrence
         River to the Bay of Fundy   103

Map 8   The Canadian Rebellions 1837–1838   112

Map 9   The Borderlands 1837–1842   122

Map 10   The Pig War   135

Map 11   Alaska Boundary Dispute 1891–1903   146

Map 12   China   160

Map 13   Japan   235

Map 14   World   334

Map 15   Middle East   366

Map 16   The British World After 2000   436

Preface and Acknowledgements

The story of the relationship between Great Britain and the United States, seen as empires, is an exciting one, which I was unable to consider properly in my previous book on Anglo-American relations, *Old World, New World*. That book did look comparatively at the ways in which and the extent to which the two countries could and did project their powers. Nevertheless, that book also dealt with many other aspects of the relationship, and the resulting constraints on space precluded my treating the two as empires. Yet the power of the British empire, the largest that the world has ever known, is a key aspect of the history of the modern world; similarly, the rise of the American empire and the exercise of its power, particularly in concert with or opposition to the British empire, is a key aspect of the modern and contemporary world. The story of their interactions, therefore, is one without which global history cannot properly be understood.

I want to give grateful thanks to various people and institutions. First of all, I want to thank my sister Melissa Higginbotham (Lieutenant Colonel, U.S. Air Force, retired) for her help in online research. She was indefatigable in her research and found a number of historical sources that provided very useful insights into the issues of the day. She made great use of the U.S. National Archives in College Park, Maryland, finding and reading many microfilmed documents that I had not had time to look at myself, a task truly beyond the call of duty. I want also to thank Melissa and her husband, David Fuchs (who drove me the nearly two-hour journey to the Archives day after day), for putting me up, some-times for a fortnight at a time, whilst I ruined my eyes peering at roll after roll of microfilm. Those historians who concentrate on periods and topics where virtually everything is typed or printed do not realise how lucky they are. They have not truly lived until they have had to decipher handwritten diplomatic documents on dark microfilm, some of them in handwriting as bad as mine.

I also wish to thank two friends, stars of the imperial history world, Professors John Darwin and Catherine Hall, for their very early encouragement to go ahead and tackle the subject. Yet again I want to thank my group of four friends who read the manu-script chapter by chapter, as they have done for previous books (except for my book on wine) for the past two decades. They are Jane Card, David d'Avray, David French and Jeremy Wormell. Jeremy, in fact, has read virtually everything that I've written, including drafts of articles, for the past thirty years. I am extremely lucky in their willingness to scrawl their comments all over my manuscripts. I wish to thank my former PhD student, Dr Justin Brummer, for his aid in the less exciting parts of research, such as photocopying files and double-checking references, which saved me time that I could ill spare.

I want to thank my publisher, Bloomsbury, for the quite excep-tional work they put in whilst getting the manuscript through the press. There are sixteen maps in the book, and working together with the mapmaker, Martin Lubikowski, was fun. I gave him the list of geographical names, he drew the maps, we spent most of a day going over them, he made some changes, and the result is some of the clearest maps I've ever seen in a history book. Every geographical item mentioned is on a map. My copyeditor, Peter James, was extraordinary: typos were only the beginning. He caught outright mistakes and challenged any lack of clarity. I had been told that he was the best non-fiction copyeditor in London, and I can well believe it. I really want to thank the man-aging editor, Marigold Atkey, whose organisational ability, acute attention to detail, and efficiency were admirable. She located the forty images that I wanted, helped to find others when those I wanted were either unusable or unobtainable, and crawled over the floor lining them all up. Even more taxing, I suspect, was dealing with my index, which is long and a touch convoluted. Making the above possible in the first place were my agent, Bill Hamilton, who for nearly twenty years has played a significant role in fostering the development of my ideas, and Bloomsbury's commissioning editor, Michael Fishwick, who decided to take a chance on the book.

I want to acknowledge the vital necessity for many historians of the following institutions. In the UK, they are the UK National Archive at Kew, the Bodleian Library, Oxford, the House of Lords Record Office, the Guildhall Library, the British Library and the London Library. The last-named is especially wonderful, not only because of the range and number of books on the open shelves, but also because of the possibility of borrowing and taking home up to fifteen books at a time. In the US, they are the US National Archives in College Park, Maryland, the Library of Congress, the Presidential Libraries of Roosevelt and Truman, and the Princeton and Yale University Libraries.

Finally, and truly most importantly, I want to thank my husband, Dr Michael Jewess, and my daughter, Miranda Jewess Harries. One of my earlier books was dedicated to Miranda and the girl who was taking care of her for me, and Miranda told me that she wanted a book dedicated only to her. Here it is. My husband and daughter increasingly thought – and did not hesitate to tell me – that perhaps researching and writing another big book took up time that might better be spent in, say, getting some sleep. Nevertheless, I had their support, which it would have been difficult to do without. I have been lucky in my family.

NOTES FOR THE READER

A word of explanation is required about my use of Chinese place and personal names, and Japanese governmental terms. I have used the transliteration of Chinese into English as found in the 18th and 19th century documents that I used. However, I also indicate the current form in my first use of the term. For example, I use

Canton generally, but on its first use it is Canton (Guangzhou). The Japanese names in English were pretty standardised in the late 19th century. However, I have italicised less common terms such as *bakufu*, and *rōjū*, but not the more frequently used Shōgun and daimyō.

I also think that a word about the structure of the index might be helpful, in order to save the reader some time and frustration. All empires, with the exception of the American and British, are listed in alphabetical order under the main heading 'Empires'. All of the American states are grouped together under 'American states'. All bays, gulfs, oceans, rivers, seas and straits are treated in the same manner. Under 'Treaties' may be found all treaties, conventions, agreements and protocols. All 'Wars' are grouped together. Finally, Chinese emperors, Japanese emperors, and Shōguns each have separate main headings.

Introduction: What is an Empire?

Britons have a problem with their empire. They all know that there was one, but they are split between those who think that it was a good thing and those who think that it was benighted. Americans also have a problem, but it differs from that of the British: do they or do they not have an empire? Even posing the question can outrage people. A positive answer does not necessarily condemn the United States to the ninth circle of hell, but it can seem to call into question Americans' self-identity as citizens of a country devoted to the rights of men and women. Adhesion to historical reality can anger, and many Americans have, conversely, tended to see themselves as outside of, or even above, others' history. Yet, throughout most of recorded human history, empires have been the normal way of organising peoples so that they can be governed or controlled.[1] This has been true down to very modern times. The United States of America is no different.[2]

Empires have come in different shapes and sizes, with different structures and powers. A brief and basic definition is that it is a state which rules over, or has significant influence over, territories outside its original borders, without incorporating them. It might be a land-based empire, such as that of Austria-Hungary before 1918, or a seaborne empire, as was the British empire. It might be thought that the imperial power must be large, but by no criterion could either the Netherlands or Belgium be considered a large territory. It must be able to require the subordinate territory to do what it might otherwise not want to do. Empires can grow by conquest – the normal means – or by dynastic marriages, but they can also grow by purchase, as with the Louisiana Purchase, Alaska and the Danish Virgin Islands in the case of the United States. Empire can be formal, but it can also be informal, which implies economic domination or great military influence, and overwhelming cultural influence, without full political control, as with most of the twentieth-century American empire. No point in this paragraph is without controversy, since historians and commentators differ widely, and sometimes ferociously, over what an empire is and which country is one.[3] This book is not, in fact, a history of the British and American empires, either jointly or individually. Rather, the intention is to look at what happened when they interacted, particularly out on the edges where the two empires met.

In 1914 there were sixteen colonial empires. The focus in the English-speaking world in the twentieth and twenty-first centuries has been on the British empire and, increasingly, on an American empire, for the obvious reason that they were, sequentially, the most powerful. But people who concerned themselves about such matters in 1914 also recognised, and usually called them, the French, German, Belgian, Dutch, Danish, Russian, Austro-Hungarian, Italian, Spanish, Portuguese, Ottoman, Japanese, Chinese and Abyssinian empires. Granted, they were not all massively powerful, but empires they were. Spain, whom no one thought of as a Great Power, still owned, most importantly, Spanish Morocco. The Ottoman empire, or Turkey, had been 'the sick man of Europe' for a century, but it still existed. Many Danes felt uncomfortable with their country's status as an empire, and encouraged Iceland, although not Greenland, to declare itself independent. At the end of the nineteenth century, Abyssinia, or Ethiopia, which had grown by conquering neighbouring territories, was the only fully independent territory on the African continent. Therefore, one ought not to consider the American drive for empire as anything out of the ordinary.

Look specifically at the British and American empires: both were dominated by whites, both (eventually) were democracies, both supported private enterprise, both insisted that they were bringing the blessings of civilisation and good government to those who had suffered by their lack, both justified the use of force as a way of providing these blessings. There were also distinct differences. The British had created a seaborne empire, while for most of its existence the American empire was land-based. Most important of all, the British empire was a colonial empire, while the US, once it had conquered the territory from sea to shining sea and gone through its Philippines phase, was much less a colonial empire than the semi-controller of a range of client states. In the nineteenth century, the British dominated a large informal empire as well as its formal one, while the Americans had to wait until the twentieth century for theirs. The British took to extended periods of life abroad and enjoyed exercising political control over colonial territories; the Americans, on the other hand, have always seen abroad as much less desirable than home.[4] Economic interests in particular often brought them into conflict, but partly because of the similarities, and in spite of the differences, the two empires often worked together. It is impossible to understand the modern world without understanding this imperial relationship between the English-speaking empires.

The term 'empire' has, over the centuries, meant different things at different times for both the British and the Americans. When in the mid-sixteenth century England was referred to as an empire, one meaning was that it had dominion over its own territory and was not subject to another – not to France, not to Spain, not to the Catholic Church – rather than that it had colonies elsewhere. It did, of course: Wales and Ireland. By the mid-seventeenth century, a fundamental question had emerged in England: could a country possess both liberty and an empire? The touchstone was Rome: what many Englishmen saw was that Rome had combined liberty and greatness while it was a republic but had suffered tyranny after it became an empire. The two concepts, those of empire and of liberty, would be reconciled by referring to the British empire, a term increasingly used by 1740, as an 'Empire for liberty'.[5] The classical conception of the British Atlantic empire as Protestant, commercial, maritime and free flourished only from about the mid-1730s to the mid-1760s,[6] and was destroyed by the American Revolution and the loss of the thirteen colonies.

The American Founding Fathers then adopted the term 'Empire for liberty', modifying it for a time to become an 'Empire of liberty' to describe their expectations of the new country. It should be noted that, at this time, the term 'empire' had neither positive nor negative connotations; it was a term of description. In 1780, Thomas Jefferson, primary draftsman of the Declaration of Independence, referred to the US as an 'Empire of Liberty'.[7] George Washington claimed in March 1783 that the United States was a 'rising empire'; in 1786 he wrote that 'there will assuredly come a day, when this country will have some weight in the scale of Empires', referring to himself 'as the member of an infant empire'.[8] Benjamin Franklin had been strongly in favour of an enlarged British empire on the North American continent before 1776; afterwards, it was easy to substitute American for British. The term 'empire' also indicated dominion over large spaces, and this is perhaps what they primarily meant. It would be surprising, particularly once they had gained their independence from a territorial empire, if they had claimed that term for themselves.

Yet within a few years a territorial empire is what they meant. Jefferson in April 1809 wrote to President James Madison that the acquisition of Cuba plus 'the North', that is British North America (Canada), would enable the US 'to have such an empire for liberty as she has never surveyed since the creation'.[9] In October 1823, his mind unchanged, he wrote to President James Monroe that he favoured in due course the acquisition of Cuba, a Spanish colony, which he had always considered 'the most interesting addition which could ever be made to our system of States'.[10] John Quincy Adams, son of the second President, John Adams, and himself then Secretary of State, responded in 1823 to the question of the British Minister in Washington, Stratford Canning, as to whether the US had designs on Canada by declaring that 'there the boundary is marked, and we have no disposition to encroach upon it. Keep what is yours, but leave the rest of this continent to us.'[11] Again, expansion can mean just that, but expansion into territory which is already occupied is another matter entirely. Indeed, the declaration of the Monroe Doctrine in 1823, which asserted that the Western Hemisphere was no longer open for colonisation by external powers, apparently did not preclude the same process by the United States.

The Northwest Ordinance of 1787, passed when the US had been independent for nearly four years, set the stage for the way in which the US was to handle most of its continental acquisitions. During the colonial and revolutionary periods, a number of the colonies insisted that their charters extended their boundaries west to the Mississippi River or, in Virginia's case, beyond. Between 1781 and 1785, these states ceded their claims to the federal government; by means of the Ordinance, rules were set out that determined how the Northwest Territories, which comprised what are now Illinois, Indiana, Michigan, Ohio and Wisconsin, would be organised. Congress divided the land into five territories, appointed a governor, a secretary and five judges to administer each territory, and stated that once a territory had 5,000 free adult males it could establish a territorial legislature; once it had 60,000 males, it could apply for admission to the US as a state. It was this Ordinance, which produced the pattern by which the continental American empire could develop into a nation-state, that has been used by some historians as evidence that the US was never an empire.[12]

Yet the Territories were already inhabited; they were not *terra nullius*.[13] The belief that North America was *terra nullius* had been part of the English approach to that territory since the landing of the Pilgrim Fathers. As the leader of the Pilgrims, William Bradford, wrote of their decision to emigrate to the New World, 'The place they had thoughts on was some of those vast & unpeopled countries of America, which are frutfull & fitt for habitation, being devoid of all civill inhabitants, wher ther are only salvage [sic] & brutish men, which range up and downe, little otherwise than ye wild beasts of the same.'[14] This idea was carried further in the writings of the seventeenth-century philosopher John Locke, whose works were read by many of the Founding Fathers. In his *Second Treatise of Government*, he wrote that 'God gave the world to men in common; [but] it cannot be supposed he meant it always to remain common and uncultivated. He gave it to the use of the industrious and rational'[15] – and, therefore, land which was not being used properly, that is, farmed by people living under laws and organised government, could be taken and used by those who knew best how to exploit it. Thus Americans from the seventeenth century saw the land inhabited by the natives as ill held if not entirely empty, and moved in as they wished. The US was a settler colony driven by the desire for land, as would be Australia and New Zealand, and all three considered the taking of the land, and the driving out and sometimes the extermination of the inhabitants, as perfectly acceptable. In due course the expansion of the US across the continent, driving out all in the settlers' way, would be termed Manifest Destiny,[16] but calling it by a perhaps more acceptable term did not change the substance. From its earliest days, the US was a land-based empire.

A traditional activity of an empire is growth by military conquest. In this sense, American relations with the Indians, given all the Indian wars, should also be seen as part of the conquest of the continent. More straightforward, however, would be the Mexican–American War of 1846–8 (or, in Mexico, the War of the North American Invasion), by which the US gained what are now Arizona, New Mexico, California and parts of Utah, Nevada and Colorado, constituting 15 per cent of the current United States. This continued across the Pacific Ocean, with the annexation of Midway Islands in 1867 (roughly midway between North America and Asia), and in 1898 the annexation of the Hawaiian Islands and the acquisition of the Spanish territories of Puerto Rico, Guam, the Philippines and the Moro Islands. In 1900 the US gained half of Samoa and in 1903 the Panama Canal Zone.

Latin America, especially Central America and the Caribbean, received repeated attention, usually related to American economic interests. Protectorates were established: the US would sign a treaty of protection, sometimes claiming that the country needed to be protected from Europeans trying to collect debts, but primarily to promote the US's own economic and security interests. By the Platt Amendment of 1901, the US gave itself permission to intervene in Cuba from 1901 to 1934. Other treaties established protectorates in Panama from 1903 to 1977, in Haiti from 1903 to 1941 (invaded and occupied from 1915 to 1934), in

Santo Domingo from 1905 to 1941 (invaded and occupied from 1916 to 1924) and in Nicaragua from 1916 to 1970 (invaded and occupied from 1912 to 1933, except for nine months in 1925). As late as the 1980s under the Reagan administration, there was the covert aid given to the Contras against the Sandinista government of Nicaragua, and the 1983 invasion of Grenada, a member of the British Commonwealth.

Movement into South America itself would have been considerably more difficult before 1914, because it was part of the informal British empire. An informal empire, a rather fuzzy concept, refers to less direct control, and it frequently denotes economic dominance. A French agent in Colombia wrote in 1823 that 'The power of England is without a rival in America; no fleets but hers to be seen; her merchandises are bought almost exclusively; her commercial agents, her clerks and brokers, are everywhere to be met with.'[17] Britain's merchant (investment) banks organised the finance for Argentina's railways, and its economic hegemony over Chile in the nineteenth century was widely recognised.[18] But informal power needs the implicit, and sometimes explicit, support of formal power, and Great Britain was never loath to use so-called gunboat diplomacy against Latin American countries that were reluctant to meet their financial or economic obligations. Even after the end of the First World War, American banks found it very difficult to break the hold of the British banks. Importantly, it must not be forgotten that Britain also had formal colonies there. Informal empire in any part of the globe was something for which the US had to wait until the twentieth century to enjoy.

The British empire overseas began to take shape in the seventeenth century with, in particular, North America and the West Indies. By the mid-eighteenth century it began to acquire territories in India. However, the supreme global power enjoyed by the British empire for most of the nineteenth century was initially acquired as a result of the Napoleonic War. At the Battle of Trafalgar in 1805, the Royal Navy under Admiral Lord Nelson destroyed the combined French and Spanish navies. Furthermore, the French conquest of the Dutch in 1795 had rendered the Dutch navy no longer a threat (it also enabled the British to pick up the former Dutch colonies of Guyana, Ceylon and Cape Colony). So for almost a century the power of the Royal Navy was dominant. This was a very important element of Britain's power, particularly for the protection of its trade routes and of its merchant marine, the largest in the world, and of its formal and informal empires. But its informal empire was extremely important, because Britain was a commercial nation, and lived primarily by trade and the provision of services. Not only was there mastery in South America, but there was also British commercial dominance in a huge part of China. The crucial element here was the stability of the pound sterling, the world's major transaction and sole reserve currency until after the First World War. The British not only financed their own trading and international financial activities, they also financed those of many others, such as the Argentine railway system and the movement of the Southern US cotton crops to market.

Empires always worry about their borders. One concern is restlessness or turmoil across the border which might threaten their own territories, and which encourages them to expand to control the neighbouring territories to eliminate the threat. This was the case for Great Britain in India, when, for example, it tried to control Persia and Afghanistan in order to deter Russian expansion, and for the US in its continental expansion, when it tried to eliminate successive Indian tribes. The other threat is a challenge by a rival state or empire. This had been the case for the British empire in the nineteenth century, as Britain played the Great Game with the Russian empire over the control of Central Asia, and competed with the American empire in North America. It was the case for the American empire in the post-1945 period: the US wanted to contain the Russian empire's residual legatee, the Soviet Union, within its recognised borders. In this task, the US expected the full co-operation of Britain and what was left of *its* empire.

When looking at the interrelationship of the British and American empires, whether in conflict or co-operation, it is important to emphasise that like was not necessarily confronting like: they waxed and waned in different periods, and weakness confronted strength. America separated itself from a full-blown empire, an empire which, over the following 130 years, continued to expand. So did that of the United States, but the peak of its empire came considerably later, at the point when the British empire was in terminal decline. By the time that the United States stood at the pinnacle of its own power, from 1945 on, there was not a lot of the planet left to colonise. Thus the US had to be satisfied with an informal empire, but one which was supported by a range and depth of military power which, even relatively speaking, the British empire could not have begun to match in the nineteenth century. An informal empire can be denied, and whether or not the US was or is an empire continues to be a live issue in the United States. What is nowhere an issue is the death of the British empire. Even as late as the 1930s, it was not wholly obvious that it was in irreversible decline, but the Second World War sounded its death knell. Thereafter the UK withdrew from its formal empire, completing the process by 1972, with its final withdrawal from East of Suez, often to have its place informally taken by the US. Both empires were – and America's still is – being brought down by 'imperial overstretch'. Cicero perhaps put it better when he pointed out that *nervos belli, pecuniam infinitam*: the sinews of war [require] infinite money. The United Kingdom ran out of the money necessary for holding an empire; this may also be the fate of the United States.

Chapter 1

Imperial Clashes Over
the Border, 1783–1815

In 1812, the United States declared war on the British empire. In April 1813, the Americans decided to attack York (now Toronto), the capital of Canada, which was vulnerable and thinly defended. They launched an amphibious assault against the village, driving out the British. Upon their departure, the British blew up a gunpowder magazine, which killed 250 Americans, as well as depriving their comrades of a large cache of ammunition. A surrender agreement was negotiated, whereby the US commanders agreed to respect private property, permit the civil government to continue to function and allow doctors to treat the wounded. Despite the agreement, American soldiers, including some officers, broke into homes and robbed them, pillaged the church and locked up the British and Canadian wounded without food, water or medical treatment for two days. At one point the local priest rescued a woman who was about to be shot by the Americans while they were looting her house. The priest's own pregnant wife was assaulted, robbed and probably raped by a gang of American soldiers. When the Americans took to their ships, after occupying York for a week, they set fire to the Palace of Government and the Governor's house – the Canadian equivalent of the Capitol and the White House. Three months later, York was again attacked and burned. The British would respond to these and other such attacks in Washington the following year.

The 1783 Treaty of Paris, which ended the War of American Independence, had given birth to the fourth empire to share the North American continent, the United States of America. The French, Spanish and British empires were already *in situ*. The French empire disappeared from North America with the sale of Louisiana to the US in 1803, a purchase which, by a few strokes of a pen, doubled the size of the American empire. The territory of Spain in Florida was taken over by the US in 1819, and that of its successor in North America, Mexico, by 1850. This left only the British. The two remaining empires shared a common desire: to expand, and to deny expansion to the other.

During the period from 1783 to 1815, war between Great Britain and the United States was repeatedly threatened and, from 1812 to 1815, actually took place. An extremely important grievance for the US was the treatment of Americans and American vessels by the Royal Navy. Firstly, the British followed the axiom 'once a Briton always a Briton', and impressed – that is, hauled off American merchant ships – any sailors whom they believed were British. And secondly, the British claimed the right during time of war to prevent neutral ships carrying contraband – which they themselves defined – from trading with the enemy; American ships were often the victims of the British interpretation of the rights of neutrals, which was a narrow one. These issues would be a direct cause of the War of 1812.

The other important issues were the refusal of the British to evacuate seven posts (the British term) or forts which were on the American side of the 1783 treaty boundary and their putative support of Indians who were attacking American settlers attempting to move into the Indians' lands. The British believed that they needed to retain the posts for as long as possible – although they realised that they had to surrender them at some point – in order to maintain their influence with the Indian nations outraged that their lands had by the treaty been turned over to the Americans. They also needed the posts as leverage against the Americans to force them to repay the pre-Revolution debts owed by Americans to 30,000 Englishmen; they needed them to protect the Canadian fur trade, which was worth hundreds of thousands of pounds each year to Great Britain; and they needed them to help to defend their Canadian colonies from the Americans. But linked with this was the fact that it was simply not clear whose writ ran where, because there was conflict over the boundary, and it is these conflicts which are the primary, though not the sole, focus of this chapter. Some of these problems were sorted out in 1794 through Mr Jay's Treaty (or Treaty of Amity, Commerce and Navigation), but others were not: negotiations took place over what might now seem to be relatively unimportant details about the border claims of both, but which were actually vital to the interests of both. Partial agreement, and a treaty, were finally achieved only because the naval issues were deemed unsolvable at that point and put to one side.

Particularly bad stretches of the border, such as those between Maine and New Brunswick, in New York along the Niagara boundary, between Minnesota and Ontario, and just west of the Great Lakes around the Pigeon River Falls, desperately required precise delimitation. Nevertheless, even after the Jay Treaty had been signed in 1794, the agreed border was not accepted by many Americans or Canadians. Conflict continued, and in 1812 it erupted into war. Although there were a number of important factors, such as the porosity of borders and the threat of Indian warfare, the primary causes of the war as noted above were impressment and Britain's continuing violation of what the US believed were its neutral rights. This was the context of the repeated conflicts over the US–Canadian border, as both sides attempted to move into and take over territory claimed by the other. The ferocity was fed by the myriad small conflicts during the years since 1795 over parts of the border whose legality was denied by one or both sides. Most of the land battles of the War of 1812 (known as the American War in Great Britain) were fought at and over that border (although a good deal of fighting also took place in the south-eastern part of the US). Negotiations over the Treaty of Peace and Amity – the Treaty of Ghent – which ended the war were conducted for virtually the whole of 1814, although news of its signing did not reach the US until early 1815. Five of the articles pointed out the lack of agreed boundaries around islands, on land and on the Lakes, and set out arrangements for commissions to survey and decide on them. The treaty did not prevent further conflicts after 1815, but the conflicts were often, although not always, private rather than state-sponsored: men on the frontier, keen for land or timber or furs, had little regard for what Great Britain and a distant US federal government had agreed.

I

Secure borders are vital for an empire. Indeed, correct and detailed maps of these borders are a necessity for an empire,[1] not least because quite small pieces of territory, or control of the one fording place of a river or of a good harbour, can make the difference between a defensible border and one which is open to invaders, whether agricultural, commercial or military. Theoretically, the border between the United States and what remained of British North America was set out in the Treaty of Paris of 1783, by which the independence of the United States from the British empire was legally established. According to the treaty, the border was to run 'from the Northwest Angle of Nova Scotia, viz., that Angle which is formed by a Line drawn due North from the Source of St. Croix River to the Highlands; along the said Highlands which divide those Rivers that empty themselves into the river St. Lawrence, from those which fall into the Atlantic Ocean, to the northwesternmost Head of Connecticut River'. The boundary was to continue along the Connecticut to the forty-fifth 'Degree of North Latitude', along that parallel west to the St Lawrence River, and then along the middle of the St Lawrence into Lake Ontario. The boundary was to pass through the middle of Lakes Ontario, Erie and Huron into Lake Superior. The final reaches of the northern border were to extend 'thence through Lake Superior Northward of the Isles Royal & Phelipeaux to the Long Lake; Thence through the middle of said Long Lake and the Water Communication between it & the Lake of the Woods, to the said Lake of the Woods; Thence through the said Lake to the most Northwestern Point thereof, and from

Thence on a due West Course to the river Mississippi'. It then turned south along the Mississippi to the northern border of what was then Spanish Florida, and east to the Atlantic again.[2]

Unfortunately, amid all of this important, if perhaps tedious, detail, two elements were missing. First of all, no one could say for certain where these lines ran, because the topography was wholly unclear. Which river was the St Croix – there were three possibilities – and where was on or in or by the Highlands? Did a line due west from the most north-westernmost part of Lake of the Woods actually intersect with the Mississippi River?[3] No one really knew. Secondly, there was no map appended to the treaty, which might have made things considerably clearer. Imagine the whole territory for twenty-five miles on both sides of the current border, thickly covered with spruce forest and watered by unknown streams, and for sections of which there was no agreed line between the country and the colony, and the possibilities of conflict become obvious. This meant that there was all to play for, and over the next decade crises arose all along the border.

The major concern of the British was the defensibility of the border with the US, against both military invasion and the habit of American settlers of expanding into new territories – those 'pushful and procreative American pioneers'[4] – whether or not they had the legal right to do so. Great Britain was determined to defend Canada, to keep what was its own territory. (Americans would invade Canada a dozen times over the subsequent sixty years.) It had spent a good deal of blood and treasure conquering Quebec from the French during the Seven Years' War from 1756 to 1763 (called in the US, perhaps more appositely, the French and Indian War). Britain wanted to maintain control of the trading routes of the fur trappers in Quebec and elsewhere in the territory. And importantly during a time of war, and as a global naval power, it needed access to the naval stores which Canada could provide, such as timber, masts, bowsprits and pitch. Although it could still sometimes purchase these commodities in the US, albeit at prices which were possibly more difficult for it to influence, it would naturally prefer to benefit one of its colonies while keeping the funds within the empire.

One other point is worth noting: the British were not wholly convinced that the US would remain united and not fragment into a congeries of states, or even – though admittedly much less likely – return to their own empire. As John Adams, the future second President, wrote from London to a friend in Virginia in August 1785:

> There is a strong propensity in this people to believe that America is weary of her independence; that she wishes to come back; that the states are in confusion; Congress has lost its authority; the governments of the states have no influence; no laws, no order, poverty, distress, ruin, and wretchedness; that no navigation acts that we can make will be obeyed; no duties we lay on can be collected ... [and] that smuggling will defeat all our prohibitions, imposts and revenues ... This they love to believe.[5]

If the US did fragment, the British – along with the Spanish and the French – wanted to be around to pick up the pieces. Indeed, they flirted with American secession movements before the adoption of the Constitution in 1789 encouraged the development of the US into a unified country.[6]

As for the Americans, they wanted to settle new territory, to gain a larger part of the fur and other trade and generally to expand. They saw Canada as an area which would naturally become part of the US. There was a related factor. Americans wanted access to territory in the north-west that Great Britain was trying to keep as Indian territory: Britain wanted to keep its Indian allies on side by ensuring that they had their own territory, it wanted it as buffer territory between the US and Upper Canada, and it wanted it to provide a barrier to further American expansion in that direction. The Americans wanted to destroy Britain's ability to prevent an American takeover; overall, they wanted to prevent what they were convinced was the British policy of mobilising the Indians against the US. Taking over Canadian territory would eliminate this British power.

For the Americans, the uncertainty of the border was exacerbated by the British refusal to vacate their forts in the Old

Northwest, the territory from which the states of Ohio, Indiana, Illinois, Michigan and Wisconsin would be carved out. All of these forts were situated along the border at points where they could control entry into and departure from the Great Lakes. They were described nearly a century ago by the somewhat nationalistic American historian Samuel Flagg Bemis, who reflected the general American perception of the situation:

> Garrisoned by a few hundred British soldiers and supported by a horde of savage allies ... these eight forts had enabled England to protect Canada during the American Revolution. They had helped her to harass the whole line of settlements south of the Ohio and in western New York and Pennsylvania. Held in British possession at the peace, they became important military positions in the rear of the American states. They protected the fur trade. They overawed the souls of the savage allies who more and more were coming to depend on purchasing with their furs their luxuries, even their very subsistence, from the traders sheltered under the guns of the forts. Seven of the posts were on American soil south of the boundary fixed by the treaty of peace of 1783.[7]

Holding these forts for as long as possible was vital for the British and their subjects in British North America, because the Lakes were an obvious invasion route both ways. Furthermore, they helped to pacify their former Indian allies, who felt betrayed.

In this situation, it was unfortunate for the British that their Canadian defences were so weak. The population of the US was far greater than that of Canada – fourteen times larger; if war broke out, it was feared that Canada would soon be taken by American troops. In addition, the Canadian militia was composed mostly of Frenchmen, whose loyalty the British suspected.[8] On the five Great Lakes, Britain had only five gunboats.[9] And then, of course, there were all those American settlers who had already come to Canada in response to the government's offer of cheap land for those who wished to farm: were they a fifth column? In short, Britain largely depended on a few, scattered British regular soldiers and the unstable Northwest Indian Confederacy for Canada's defence.

Arguments between Britain and America over the forts began early on. In May 1785, John Adams went to London as the first American Minister to the Court of St James's; this was a curious choice, since his detestation of England was well known. On 17 June he met with the Foreign Secretary, Lord Carmarthen. He was to discuss the issue of the debts owed by Americans to Britons, and he hoped to add other topics; he was particularly keen to contract a commercial treaty opening up the British empire to American activity, such as the Americans had enjoyed before 1776. Carmarthen suggested that, since the issue of the forts seemed the most important to the Americans, they might put their arguments in writing, and discussions could begin with that. Then Adams foolishly told the Foreign Secretary that he was instructed by Congress to 'require' British evacuation of the posts; perhaps orders had already been sent for withdrawal of the garrisons? Adams' apparent assumption that Great Britain would naturally do as the Americans wished put Carmarthen on his guard, and he again asked Adams to put this requirement in writing. This he did in a memorandum. A week later, Adams met with William Pitt the Younger, the King's First (Prime) Minister, and, as Adams wrote to John Jay, then Secretary of Foreign Affairs (sic), 'as to the posts, says he, that is a point connected with some others, that I think must be settled at the same time'. The 'some others' were the debts owed to private British creditors, and it was now clear that the issues of the posts and the debts were intertwined.[10]

The British did not reply to Adams' memorandum until the following February, having spent the intervening time collecting information on the debts, both their amounts and the details of the creditors' attempts to collect them through the American courts. Adams, as it happened, had grown more optimistic, and the uncompromising British answer came as an unexpected blow. Its essential point was that the Americans had flagrantly violated the treaty (for example, by not repaying the debts and not compensating the Loyalists for their lost land and property). Treaty stipulations were mutually and equally binding on the contracting parties. It was folly and injustice to think that Great Britain alone was obliged to adhere strictly to the terms of the treaty while the US was 'free to deviate from its own engagements as often as convenience might render such deviation necessary though at the expense of its own National Credit and Importance'. When justice was done to British creditors, and the US manifested a 'real determination to fulfil her part of the Treaty', Great Britain would then co-operate in putting the 1783 treaty 'into real and compleat Effect'.[11]

Why such a cold response? The American historian Charles Ritcheson's argument is compelling: 'The explanation must lie ... in Adams' maladroit use of the debt issue and, even more rankling, in his "requirement". Here was the envoy of a government unable to make its writ run in its own land ... paying no attention at all to serious British grievances, yet "requiring" Britain to act at America's good pleasure, and demanding in the bargain a new commercial accord directly conflicting with British maritime interests. It was impudent and absurd, and, Pitt and his colleagues must have concluded, fully deserving Carmarthen's tough answer.'[12]

Relations between the two countries continued to deteriorate. While on the one hand the ratification by the states of the Constitution of 1789 implied that the US could now produce unified policies, on the other hand 'factions' played an increasing role in politics and soon developed into political parties: the Federalist, based in the north-east, was inclined to be pro-British while the Republican, based in the south and west, was inclined to be pro-French. Yet in Britain public opinion by early 1793 had shifted dramatically – wartime bitterness and feelings of betrayal had decreased, and economic links had strengthened. Trade between the two empires had expanded rapidly: by 1790, one-half of America's exports went to Britain and four-fifths of its imports came from Britain. Furthermore, in the ten years after the Revolution, the US had developed into the granary for the so-called North Atlantic triangle, of Great Britain, Canada and the West Indies. A significant proportion of the American national debt was funded by British capital. Less legally, because

US trade with the West Indies using American ships had been forbidden by the British, a great under-the-radar network of smuggling (especially of tobacco), collusion (with the British West Indies, many of whose inhabitants eagerly co-operated in large-scale smuggling) and clandestine partnerships (false registers of American ships as British) developed, angering the British government but providing profits to both the network's British and American participants. Arguably, the ultimate importance of this private Anglo-American co-operation lay in the development of a pattern of commercial intercourse which survived even the outbreak of the British war with France in 1793.[13] Nevertheless, the British government itself showed no warmer feelings towards its American counterpart. Events, however, soon forced a change in attitude.

II

In 1789, the French Revolution burst upon Europe, and soon the populace decided to carry its blessings beyond France. In 1792, French armies overran the Austrian Netherlands (today's Belgium); the following year France annexed Belgium and was poised to invade the Netherlands. On 1 February 1793, France declared war on both the Netherlands and Great Britain. What Britain wanted from the US was neutrality, but it feared American support for France – after all, France had been instrumental in the Americans gaining their independence from Britain. Indeed, France hoped to sign a new treaty with the US. In mid-March, however, word reached Washington of the execution of Louis XVI, followed in early April by the news that France had declared war on Britain. The American response, after a great deal of memorandum-writing and heated discussion, was a proclamation of neutrality by President George Washington on 22 April 1793.[14]

Over the following months, however, the US and Great Britain moved towards war, stimulated on the American side by the Indian war on its borders and by a startling example of British interference with what the Americans asserted were their neutral rights on the sea. In mid-March 1794, news arrived in Philadelphia (the then capital of the US) of an extraordinary seizure of American merchant vessels in West Indian waters by ships of the Royal Navy. A British government Order-in-Council dated 6 November 1793 and issued in great secrecy instructed commanders of royal warships and privateers to seize 'all ships laden with goods the produce of any colony belonging to France, or carrying provisions or other supplies for the use of any such colony'.[15] The idea was to trap unsuspecting ships, and thus the Order was not published in London until 26 December 1793. In the previous February, France had thrown open its Caribbean sugar islands to American vessels, while in May information had gone out that the British West Indies might be open to them as well. The combination of the British and French announcements had lured a huge proportion of the American merchant fleet into West Indian waters. When British men-of-war and privateers suddenly swooped down, some 250 American vessels were seized and 150 condemned – roughly one-half of the entire American fleet. Furthermore, the manner of capture, adjudication and condemnation of the vessels by the British authorities in the islands could be abrupt and even brutal.[16]

Of course the American reaction was one of outrage, while that of London merchants trading with the US was hardly less heated. A new Order of 8 January 1794 appeared to ease matters: it now allowed direct trade between the US and the French West Indian islands, except for contraband, yet it also reinstated the so-called Rule of the War of 1756. This unilateral British rule stated that if trade had not been allowed in peacetime, it would not be allowed by the British in time of war; in other words, since the French had not allowed the Americans to participate in the trade between France and its sugar colonies before the war, Americans could not do so now. As far as Great Britain was concerned, it was fighting against France for its liberty, and the arguments of the Americans over neutral rights were regarded as largely irrelevant.

The situation was further inflamed by the reports coming in of events in the Old Northwest, embroiled in the so-called

Northwest Indian War. This was a war between the US and a confederation of American Indian tribes for control of the territory;
under the British, this had been Indian land, with the border the
Ohio River in the west. There had been bloody conflict between
the Indians and American settlers for decades, but this war as
such stemmed from the 1783 treaty, by which Britain had ceded
to the US sovereignty over this territory, which was occupied by
many tribes, retaining only the posts. President Washington as
Commander-in-Chief had sent a (mostly untrained) army to the
territory to deal with the problem, but these troops had suffered a
series of major defeats. After a particularly bad one in November
1791, Washington asked Major-General 'Mad Anthony' Wayne,
a Revolutionary War hero, to organise, and properly train, a military force fit for purpose. It was called the Legion of the United
States, and in 1794 it set out for the Northwest Territory.

Great Britain's position in Canada was becoming increasingly
weak. In May 1793, with conflict with France looming in the West
Indies, London ordered three regiments of regular troops to leave
Nova Scotia and New Brunswick to go to the West Indies, leaving
only one regiment for those two provinces. The Governor-
General of British North America, Lord Dorchester,[17] reported
to London that, in the whole of British North America, there
were only 3,500 troops, including the above-mentioned regiment.
The frontier posts were greatly undermanned: Forts Detroit
(on the straits between Lakes Erie and Huron) and Niagara
(which, along with the posts at Oswegatchie and Oswego, controlled the navigation of the St Lawrence River, Lake Ontario
and the connection with Lake Erie) each had just over 300 men,
but Fort Michilimachinac (on Mackinac, a little fortified island
off the northern tip of the Michigan peninsula which controlled
the entrance to Lakes Huron, Michigan and Superior) had only
sixty-one, Fort Erie, at the eastern end of Lake Erie (actually on
the British side of the 1783 Treaty boundary), had only thirty-
nine, and Fort Ontario (built on high ground on the east side
of the Oswego River overlooking Lake Ontario) had fifty-four.
The fortifications themselves were in a 'ruinous' state, with
Lieutenant-General John Simcoe, Lieutenant-Governor since

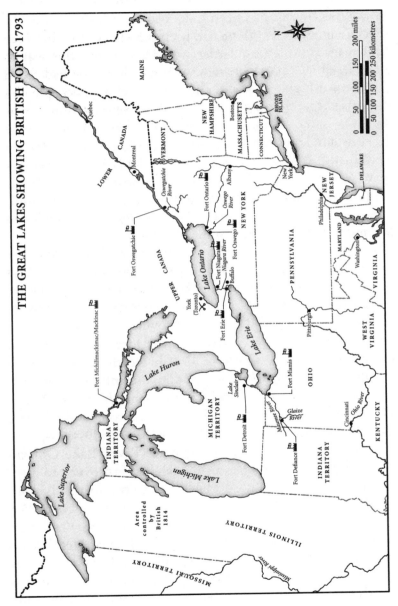

THE GREAT LAKES SHOWING BRITISH FORTS 1793

MAP I

1791 of the new province of Upper Canada, commenting that 'any Post on the Continent if attacked, must be considered as necessarily sacrificed'.[18]

Meanwhile, on 10 February 1794, prompted by the movement of Americans from Vermont into Lower Canada, and convinced that the repeated encroachments of Americans on British territory made war highly probable, Lord Dorchester made a wholly unauthorised speech to a gathering of Indians and, through them, to the seven Indian nations of Canada. He told them that because of the constant American aggression the 1783 border between the US and British North America no longer existed, and that 'from the manner in which the People of the States push on, and act, and talk on this side, and from what I learn of their conduct towards the Sea, I shall not be surprised if we are at war with them in the course of the present year; and if so, a Line must then be drawn by the Warriors'.[19] It is not difficult to imagine the reaction to this news when a version of Dorchester's speech appeared in the American press on 26 March. The reaction in England, although quieter, would be little different: he was strongly rebuked for his speech by Henry Dundas, the Secretary of State for Home Affairs.[20]

There was to be more. A week after Dorchester had made his speech in February, he instructed General Simcoe to reoccupy Fort Miamis at the foot of the Maumee River, ten miles south-west of Lake Erie and well within American territory; it had been built by the British during the war with the American colonies, but then abandoned in 1783 as unnecessary and expensive. (Dorchester's order to Simcoe to reoccupy would also be disapproved by the British government six months later.)[21] The historian Ritcheson described Simcoe as 'an energetic, feared, and effective adversary in war', but added that he was 'not a warmonger bent on revenge, as he is commonly depicted, [but rather he] believed himself weak militarily, and thus an easy prey for attack'.[22] As already noted, his position did indeed appear to be precarious. Dorchester believed that all along the frontier the Americans were engaged in 'determined aggression',[23] and he and Simcoe were both 'nearly frantic with fear'[24] about the intentions of the American General

Wayne, who was preparing a decisive push against the Indians north-west of the Ohio River. Their concern was that Wayne meant to seize Fort Detroit by force and thereby prevent contact between the British and their Indian allies; they also feared that Wayne would then persuade, or intimidate, the Indians to turn against the British. Simcoe's reoccupation of the post would present a challenge to Wayne on his putative march to Detroit. There is some evidence that Simcoe himself possibly had a second goal, which was to co-ordinate activities with the Spanish colony of Louisiana (Great Britain and Spain were allies at that point) in the event of war with the US.[25]

On 20 August 1794, Wayne defeated the Indians at the Battle of Fallen Timbers, after which he advanced to a position within range of the British guns at Fort Miamis. According to the American historian Samuel Flagg Bemis,

> Inside the fort torches hovered above the breeches of loaded cannon trained on the American cavalry. Outside the log walls stood Wayne's frontier troops, flushed with their success and indignant at the recent encroachments of the British and the aid which they believed had been furnished to the savages; for by Wayne's account the bodies of white irregulars had been found after the battle of Fallen Timbers.[26] In this warlike setting occurred the dramatic incident where only the coolness of both commanders, especially that of the British officer inside the fort, prevented a precipitation of hostilities that might have set the whole back country afire ...
>
> Colonel Campbell, the British commander, sent out a flag of truce to ask how to construe the approach of an American army to a British fort in time of peace. Wayne replied that his victory over the 'hordes of savages in the vicinity of your post' was the answer to that question. Campbell sent back word that a further move threatening the fort would be met with armed opposition – and he meant it ['I trust that if he attacks us this night he will not find us unprepared']. Wayne, with an expression of surprise that there should take place in the absence of war such a hostile act as the erection of a fort among Indians at

war with the United States, requested Campbell's withdrawal.
Campbell replied that he was under military orders only, [and]
that the question of why he was there might be left to the
diplomats. He refused to withdraw without orders. Wayne did
not attack. For three days more he kept his army on the banks
of the Maumee [River], destroying the cornfields and stores of
the Indians ... This done, he fell back to Fort Defiance, which
he had erected at the confluence of the Maumee and Glaize ...
strengthened his works there and placed himself in a position
to extinguish effectively any possible renewal of hostilities by
the Indians.[27]

Events such as these on both land and sea greatly alarmed a
group of Federalist senators from the seafaring states of the
north-east, and, on 10 March 1794, a group of them met in the
Philadelphia office of Senator Rufus King of New York (one of
the Founding Fathers). They proposed that 'an Envoy extraordinary should be sent to England to require satisfaction for the
loss of our Property, and to adjust those points which menaced a
War between the two Countries'. Two days later, they presented
their suggestion to President Washington, who delayed his decision for some weeks, but then agreed. Why? First of all, and very
importantly, news had arrived from London that the Order-in-
Council of 6 November 1793, which had trapped the American
merchant vessels in the West Indies, had been replaced by the
somewhat more liberal Order of 8 January 1794. Furthermore,
and closely related, Rufus King had learned, and had told
Washington, that Prime Minister Pitt had responded to the avalanche of complaints by London merchants about the wholesale
condemnation of American cargoes in the swoop by promising
'the most ample compensation'. A third point, also related, was
the dispatch sent by the then American Minister in London,
Thomas Pinckney, 'containing reassuring words' about the future
treatment of American ships by Lord Grenville, the Secretary of
State for Foreign Affairs. News also arrived that French revolutionary forces had captured Toulon from the Royalists (who
had been supported by the Royal Navy) on 19 December, an

event which would certainly dissuade the British from contemplating war with the US as well.[28] Finally, a letter from Alexander Hamilton, the US Secretary of the Treasury, who was known to be pro-British, suggested that the time was 'peculiarly favourable' for such a mission, and that the political parties agree that now was the time to negotiate.[29]

III

On 15 April 1794, as suggested by Hamilton in his letter, Washington offered the position of Envoy Extraordinary to John Jay, the Chief Justice of the Supreme Court. It is noteworthy that Jay had experience in negotiating with the British, as he had been one of the American negotiators for the 1783 treaty. Jay was reluctant, but, as he wrote to his wife on 19 April, 'to refuse it would be to desert my duty'.[30] Jay's instructions were dated 6 May and had been drafted by the Secretary of State, Edmund Randolph, although they were substantially based on points made by Hamilton, King and one or two other Federalists. Their prime concern was the shipping trade, and Randolph's first point was that Britain should recognise neutral rights and that 'Compensation for all the injuries sustained, and captures, will be strenuously pressed by you ... A Second cause of your mission, but not inferior in dignity to the preceding, though subsequent in order, is to draw to a conclusion all points of difference between the United States and Great Britain, concerning the treaty of peace.' It was obvious to the Americans that Britain would insist upon negotiations over the debts owed, but Jay was instructed to say that they should not be the object of diplomatic discussions, but were 'certainly of a judicial nature; to be decided by our Courts'. Of course the refusal of the British to withdraw from the posts was an issue: 'one of the consequences of holding the posts has been much bloodshed on our frontiers by the Indians, and much expense'. The third object, but one which Jay had full discretion to propose or not as he saw fit, was a commercial treaty. Randolph conceded that, given the great distance between the US and Great Britain, and 'the present instability of public events' – Britain's war with France – Jay was to consider these as recommendations only, excepting two 'immutable' cases: he was not to derogate from the American treaties and engagements with France (it was assumed that Great Britain would encourage him to do so),[31] and he was not to conclude any treaty of commerce contrary to this prohibition.[32] On 12 May 1794, Jay set sail for Great Britain, arriving in London on the 14th of the following month.

The British government had not until May understood that the peaceful relationship with the US was at risk. Shortly before Jay's arrival, however, came the reports from the Canadian governors and a mass of private and official letters and reports. Realisation dawned that, because of the increasing and ruthless depredations on American shipping, Lord Dorchester's speech to Britain's Indian allies and Simcoe's march to the Maumee River, the two countries were on the verge of war. Negotiations were vital. Yet formal negotiations were delayed for two months: when Jay presented his demand that the British compensate American shipowners for the seizures of their ships in the West Indies the previous year, Lord Grenville not surprisingly requested information and evidence, which Jay did not possess and had to request from Washington.[33]

Domestically, events in Britain were hardly tranquil. The Pitt ministry was going through a political crisis, the result of which was a reorganisation of the government. It was mesmerised with horror at the emerging catastrophe in Flanders, where the British army was on the verge of being defeated by the French. There was also the fear of political contagion from France. In Paris the Terror was in full and sickening swing, with more than 1,500 men and women guillotined in June and July;[34] radicalism, although of a paler sort, also existed in Britain, and this greatly alarmed the government. Only a small minority desired an English Revolution on the French model, but a considerable number called for parliamentary reform, and mass meetings were held. In response, the Pitt government arrested a dozen radicals and charged them with treason, Parliament suspended habeas corpus, and the militia was organised and armed. Fear of a French invasion was the main reason for the militia, but some also feared domestic rebellion, as had happened in the previous century.

Jay arrived in the midst of all of this, and on 27 June he met Lord Grenville, Foreign Secretary from 1791 to 1801. Grenville was thirty-four and well connected: his father was the George Grenville of the 1765 Stamp Act, which had begun the slide to the American Revolution, and Prime Minister Pitt was his cousin. According to the historian Bradford Perkins, Grenville was aristocratic, reserved, intensely English, cold in appearance and forbidding in personality, argumentative, dogmatic and obstinate, scornful of public opinion and awkward in dealing with colleagues and subordinates (in spite of which traits he became Prime Minister in 1806). Yet Perkins considers him the major architect of an Anglo-American rapprochement.[35] An important reason for this may have been Jay's perception of him, which was that he was 'liberal, candid & temperate'.[36] Jay himself was stuffy and long-winded, but he was also honest, and secure enough not to take umbrage nor to feel the need to score points. (Grenville knew that Jay was not trying to trick him, because the Foreign Office had the key to the envoy's cipher.)[37] The two worked easily together, they met frequently and alone, and their discussions tended towards the informal rather than the stilted.

A substantial proportion of the negotiations dealt with compensation for American shipowners and the American insistence on British recognition of the rights of neutrals. By Article VI of the final treaty, if British creditors could not obtain 'full and adequate' compensation from the American debtors, the US government itself would pay them, thereby finally settling this holdover from the Revolution. By Article VII, the British government would compensate American shipowners and merchants if their losses had arisen from irregular or illegal captures or condemnations. But neutral rights were not mentioned in the final treaty: Jay knew that Britain was not going to concede neutral rights or other restraints on its maritime power, when such concessions would damage it in the current French war. He also knew that the Royal Navy, badly in need of manpower, was not going to forgo the possibility of hauling men it considered to be British subjects off American merchant ships and on to its own warships. But these problems would not go away, and in fewer than twenty years they would contribute to the American decision to declare war on Britain.

Away from the seaboard states, the interrelated questions of the border, the posts and the Indian War were considerably more important. Jay presented Grenville with a draft treaty on 6 August which, *inter alia*, emphasised the evacuation of the posts by 1 June 1795 and proposed that the border disputes involving Maine and the upper Mississippi River be settled by mixed and impartial commissions. A few days later, Jay wrote to Grenville again, informing him that the President would be expected in his speech to Congress on the first Monday in November to include information about the negotiations; and, Jay stressed, 'he must be exceedingly anxious to insert something satisfactory and decisive relative to our negotiations'. Ships from Britain to Philadelphia and New York took six to seven weeks to make the journey: could not the materials which he had sent to him 'enable us to come to a speedy conclusion?'.[38] Grenville answered him sympathetically, but on his part emphasised that he had a 'multitude of other business' which made it impossible for him to give the negotiations with Jay his undivided attention. Jay's materials, however, had suggested to him a 'regular Projet' which he would soon send to him, 'and which may tend as I hope to bring the whole business within a tolerably narrow compass'.[39]

A fortnight later, after circulating them to the Cabinet, Grenville replied with his own draft treaties, one dealing with commercial issues and the other with legal and military disputes. Article I of Grenville's treaty stated that Great Britain agreed to the evacuation of the posts, except that the date would be a year hence on 1 June 1796 – how could the treaty be accepted and ratified by both countries, and distant trading settlements and even more distant traders be notified, in less than a year? Article I also stated that both British subjects and Indians who were southward and westward of the Lakes should have free access to and trading rights in the relevant territory.[40]

Five days later, Jay wrote to Grenville with regard to the second Article of the latter's draft treaty. Grenville had proposed a commission to deal with the River St Croix problem in the north-east, which was apparently satisfactory to Jay. However, Jay objected to stipulations setting out the north-west boundary, in that no one really knew where the Mississippi River began; currently, he pointed out, all claims were conjectures, and if the Mississippi did not intersect with a line drawn westward from the Lake of the Woods, as called for by the 1783 treaty, the conclusion must be that there was no agreed western boundary of the US. Jay continued, 'Individuals differing about Boundaries depending on the Course and Extent of Brooks or Streams, settle questions of that kind by actual Surveys. States usually and with good reason do the same. Why be content with delusive Conjectures and Probabilities, when absolute certainty can easily be had. Let a Survey be accurately made by joint Commissioners and at joint Expense.' If it appeared from this survey that it was as Great Britain stated – that 'the West Line would intersect the Mississippi' – no doubts would remain, but if the survey showed that it did not, they might consider fixing a 'Closing Line'.[41]

Several days later, Grenville wrote to the British Minister in Washington, George Hammond, informing him that, according to the 1783 treaty, the boundary in the north-west was to follow a line drawn from the Lake of the Woods due west to the Mississippi. He had no real objection to Jay's proposal of a commission to decide the matter, except that it would result in delay. However, if the results agreed with the treaty, that would end the matter; if it was found that such a line did not exist, it would be impossible to leave an 'Unascertained Boundary', and perhaps such a commission would be the way forward.[42]

Negotiations then continued over the following months, with a great deal of give-and-take. At the end of September, Jay presented Grenville with a revised draft treaty, which included a number of new provisions. One of the proposals which was not accepted, that neither country would keep armed vessels on the Great Lakes, was too radical; if Great Britain were to lose the posts, it needed the ships to protect its Canadian colonies from American invasions. Such an agreement had to wait another quarter of a century, when it emerged as a provision of the Convention of 1818. Grenville's time was largely taken up with the war against France, and in early October he put Jay off, writing that there was so much new material in his latest draft that it would take some time before negotiations could move to a conclusion.[43]

On 18 November, the Cabinet met in Grenville's office for four hours, going over the draft.[44] The following day, the two men signed the formal treaty; Grenville had delayed the government packet for over a week, in the expectation that the treaty would be concluded, and Jay, enclosing it in a rapidly scribbled eleven-page gloss, sent it off to the US the same day. By Article II, Great Britain was to withdraw all troops and garrisons from American territory before 1 June 1796; by Article III, British subjects, American citizens and Indians were free to 'pass and repass' by land or inland navigation into their respective territories; for the British, freedom to navigate the Mississippi River was reaffirmed, but the Article did not include freedom for Americans to sail into the ports, bays or creeks of Great Britain's North American colonies, thereby closing off illegal fishing and invasion routes; by Article IV, the US and Great Britain would jointly make a survey of the Mississippi to find out whether the river intersected with the westward line from the Lake of the Woods; and by Article V, a commission made up of one man nominated by the US, another nominated by Great Britain, and a third agreed upon by the two countries would be established to determine which river was the St Croix River designated in the 1783 treaty as forming part of the boundary between Maine and New Brunswick. The remaining twenty-three Articles dealt with the other issues.[45]

On the whole, the Jay Treaty finally settled certain long-standing problems between the two countries: the evacuation of the posts and the debts issue, and, a later problem, compensation for those of the ship seizures by the British which were agreed to be indefensible. Jay also fought off Grenville's proposal for a cession of enough American territory to give Great Britain access to a navigable portion of the Mississippi through Canadian territory.[46] Yet the Americans gained virtually nothing on neutral rights, the British holding more of the cards than did the Americans. On the one hand, some members of the British Cabinet feared that the Americans would aid the French, if not actively join the war against Britain. Yet Grenville himself thought that trade with Britain was too important to the Americans for them to jeopardise it; remarks by Secretary of the Treasury Hamilton, who had provided 'astonishingly gratuitous information' to the British Minister in Washington, had apparently confirmed this.[47] Grenville also believed that while a war between the two countries would be inconvenient for Britain, it would be fatal to the US. Jay himself was realistic about the concessions he could wring from the British, knowing that they would not accept any restraints on their maritime power while engaged in a desperate war with France, but he had also handicapped himself by letting Grenville know that he was eager to get a treaty agreed as soon as possible. It may also have been that Jay was simply not as good a negotiator as was Grenville. Yet Grenville represented a much more powerful country than did Jay, and Jay forbore trying to bluff, when it would have been ridiculously easy for his bluff to have been called.

The treaty was very badly received in the US. When President Washington saw it in March 1795, he decided to keep the terms secret, and thus presented it to the Senate in a secret session for its ratification; it was ratified in late June on a party-line vote, with twenty Federalists voting in favour and ten Republicans voting against. Once the terms had been made public by a leak to a Republican newspaper, however, there was a six-weeks-long uproar. 'Jay reacted to all of this ... with philosophic calm. He reportedly joked that he could, if he wanted, make his way from one end of the country to the other by the light of burning effigies of himself.'[48] Washington did not sign the treaty until mid-August. Yet when the question of funding the treaty finally came to a vote in the House of Representatives in late April 1796, the House approved the bill. Passions had died down; the removal of the British from the forts and thus the elimination of their support for the Indians would make easier the move west for thousands; and in the seaports and elsewhere the current economic boom would collapse if trade with Britain were to be cut off. At least until 1805, another Anglo-American war was never a serious possibility.

IV

In the discussions over the border which follow, four points should be kept in mind. First of all, the overall conflict was between two empires. This meant that larger concerns sometimes won out over local issues and bits of land. This was particularly the case with Britain, the greater attention of which was directed towards the French wars. As a result, Canadian interests were sometimes sacrificed. These local issues were of considerably more concern to the US, since the borders of its own land-based empire were up for grabs. Secondly, these local conflicts usually drove the resultant crises between the two empires, mainly because the local inhabitants, and the Americans in particular, often refused to accept the decisions made over their heads. Thirdly, these borders were decided bit by bit, giving plenty of opportunity for conflicts. And fourthly, although war between the two empires was repeatedly threatened, only once, with the War of 1812, did it take place. All other conflicts were eventually resolved diplomatically, by mixed and joint commissions or by arbitration.

The first problem was to determine where the border between Maine and New Brunswick[49] should run. Although but sparsely settled in 1783, by the early 1790s there were a large number of Loyalists from New England settled at St Andrews in the disputed territory,[50] while at the same time and in the same disputed territory lumbermen from Maine began to exploit the rich timber resources. This could well have led to conflict; on the contrary, thanks to a short period of amicable Anglo-American relations, the first international arbitration in modern times came to a successful conclusion. It soon paid a dividend: in July 1812, a few weeks after the US had declared war on Great Britain, men from Eastport, Maine met men from New Brunswick and decided that they did not want to fight each other; rather, with the encouragement of the British, they formed a free-port trading community on and near the St Croix River.[51]

It is useful to note the relevant part of the description of the north-east boundary of the US in the 1783 Treaty: 'From the Northwest Angle of Nova Scotia, viz., that Angle which is formed by a Line drawn due North from the Source of St. Croix River to the Highlands ... East, by a Line to be drawn along the Middle of the river Saint Croix from its Mouth in the Bay of Fundy to its Source'. The problem was, which candidate river for the River St Croix was the one which the 1783 negotiators had meant?[52] According to a former governor of Massachusetts, 'Almost every river on this Coast of Sagadahoc [Maine] has in its Turn been deemed by [the French] La Riviere de St. Croix' because 'the French, according to their Mode of taking Possession, always fixed a Cross in every River they came to'. One result of this was the discovery in 1783 by Lieutenant-Colonel Robert Morse of the Royal Engineers when he came to survey the St Croix that there were 'no less than three rivers running into Passamaquoddy Bay, each called the River St. Croix'.[53] The British first claimed that it was the Cobscook River, running into Cobscook Bay, west of and adjacent to Passamaquoddy Bay; they then moved their claim east to the Schoodiac River, while the US insisted that the correct river was the Magaguadavic, which lay further east, legal claim to which would provide Maine with a good chunk of land. The territory at issue constituted one-third of New Brunswick, territory vital, the British believed, to the survival of New Brunswick as a viable colony. For the British, there was also an important strategic issue: during the winter months, the line of communication, including the trade and military route, between the port of Halifax, St John, Quebec and the rest of Canada went through the St John River valley east of all three possibilities, and, thus, American control over the entire valley was unacceptable. For the Americans, the area was of considerable economic rather than strategic value, especially the huge forests of virgin-growth pine trees vital to the shipping and lumber industries, which were very powerful interest groups in Maine.

The 1783 negotiators had based their boundary decision on a 1755 map by John Mitchell, which was later referred to as 'little more than a geographic hoax'.[54] Mitchell had never even seen the area, but had based his map on one drawn in 1733 by Captain Cyprian Southack, a professional privateer who also produced charts for ships. Southack's map was based on a journey he had taken to Acadia in 1704. 'A delay of twenty-nine years between observation and cartography, coupled with the fact that Southack had used only log and compass to chart the coast, made his map of 1733 totally unreliable.'[55] So, the 1783 negotiators had based their decision on a 1755 map which was almost useless because it had, in its turn, been based on a map of 1733 which was almost useless. It was up to the St Croix Commission to decide which river was actually the St Croix River meant by the 1783 negotiators and thereby finally to determine the common north-east boundary of the state[56] and the colony.

The inquiry was to be carried out by a so-called mixed commission of members from both countries. The first issue was the choice of the three Commissioners. The British choice was Thomas Barclay. He had been a colonel in the British forces during the American Revolution; as a Loyalist he had been driven from his home in New York and was now the Speaker of the Nova Scotia Assembly. Ironically, he had studied law under John Jay. The American choice was David Howell, a professor of law at Brown University in Providence, Rhode Island, and formerly a member of the Rhode Island Supreme Court; he had also been a member of the Continental Congress during the Revolution. The two countries had to agree on the third choice. This might well have been problematic, but Barclay and Howell agreed to propose Egbert Benson, a judge of the New York Supreme Court. Barclay was, of course, disappointed by the choice of a second American, but otherwise the choice would have had to go to a ballot – and perhaps he could console himself with the reflection that Benson's father was the half-brother of his own mother.[57]

The discussions of the Commissioners and their decisions were based both on documents and maps and on evidence on the ground. Fundamentally, the US largely based its claim on the 1755

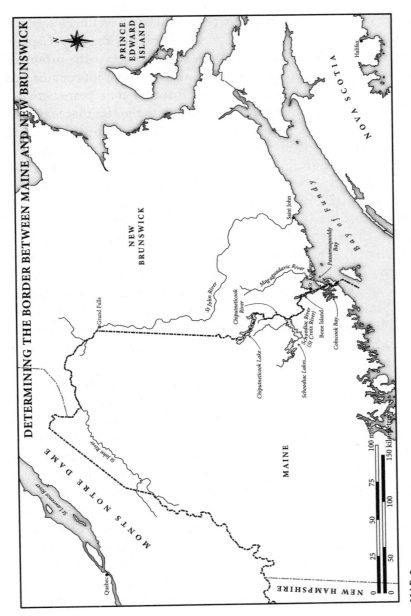

DETERMINING THE BORDER BETWEEN MAINE AND NEW BRUNSWICK

MAP 2

map, which both John Adams and John Jay agreed was the map on which they as negotiators had relied in 1783, and on oral evidence from Indians. The British based theirs on documentary evidence beginning in 1604 plus archaeological evidence. Each side had one or more agents, who were responsible for the gathering of evidence to support the respective claims; James Sullivan for the US and Ward Chipman for the British were the most active. The British also benefited from work on the ground by Loyalists from St Andrews, who feared that, if the US won their claim, the inhabitants of St Andrews would, yet again, have to leave their lands and livelihoods behind and move further north. And then, of course, there was the Passamaquoddy Nation of Indians, who complained bitterly that 'between both Countrys they are deprived of their Hunting Ground'.[58]

For those who enjoy crawling about on a map to locate the details of a claim, this particular dispute provides plenty of opportunity. The British, in tracing their claim back to 1604, argued that the river entering into Passamaquoddy Bay discovered by the French explorer Samuel de Champlain was the Schoodiac, although, and this became important, it was not then possible to say which of the many islands in the bay was the one on which Champlain and his companions wintered in 1604–5. The information was utilised in 1621 by Sir William Alexander, who by a patent from James I held territory bounded in part by the river known generally as the St Croix which was the boundary of Nova Scotia (out of which New Brunswick was carved). To rebut the British claim, the Alexander patent would have to be undermined.

Sullivan on his part argued that the Declaration of Independence had broken the social contract between Great Britain and the colonies, and that the 1783 treaty was a new beginning, rendering null and void all previous documents; the treaty was based on the 1755 map, and that had to be taken as commanding, because the negotiators had been free 'to intend whatever River they pleased by that name'.[59] The problem with this was, how would it be determined? That was the whole point of the exercise. The difficulty for Sullivan was that none of the rivers entered the bay where the map placed them. Yet, he insisted, it was the intentions of the negotiators that should prevail; because they had used the Mitchell map to agree that the St Croix was the name of the first river drawn to the west of the St John River, the name St Croix must refer to the first river that is in fact west of the St John, the Magaguadavic – and this, therefore, was the geography of the American claim. He also added oral testimony by Indians from 1764 and 1797.

Chipman for the British challenged Sullivan's premise that all should be determined by the cartographic intentions of the 1783 negotiators. Should the name, rather, describe an objective fact – that is, that there was a real 'River St Croix' out there which could serve as an agreed part of the border? Or, as he put it, 'are Maps formed from rivers or rivers formed from Maps?'.[60] One of the Loyalists from St Andrews doing detective work for the British Agent pointed out numerous errors on the Southack map, the basis for the Mitchell map, the basis for the 1783 treaty: the last of his nine points notes that Southack's 'description of St. Croix is – "small – navigable for ships & small vessels – trade – Fish of all sorts" Scudiac fits it. Magagudavic not navigable for ships more than one mile above its mouth. No trade, no fishery."'[61] The British also cast grave doubts on the veracity of the evidence taken from the Indians, on which Sullivan increasingly relied, implying that they told their questioners what they wanted to hear, and were sometimes drunk when they gave their testimony.[62] The Commissioners effectively rejected the oral testimony and returned to the 'great question' on which the British through Chipman had long insisted, that 'the decision of this honourable Board must ultimately depend, Whether the River Scoudiac was the River St. Croix of De Monts [and Champlain] in 1604?'.[63] This, again, was the foundation of the British case, because it had formed the basis of Sir William Alexander's patent to New Scotland in 1621. Therefore, the most important discovery to be made was, where was the island on which the French had camped during the winter of 1604–5? If the island could be found, the river would be known. This both sides set out to find.

In 1796, Sullivan made his attempt. As the British Agent Ward Chipman recorded: 'I found that Mr. Sullivan, as soon as he arrived at Passamaquoddy, gave out that there was an island in the mouth of the Magaguadavic river which he claims as the St Croix upon which the French had landed and built a fort under DeMonts in 1604 and hastened down to see it, but to his great mortification and disappointment, which he could not conceal upon his return[,] he could find no island there.'[64] But the British also needed to find the island, or their claim too would be tenuous. Robert Pagan, a judge from St Andrews who did not want to lose his home, in 1797 travelled to Bone Island near the mouth of the Schoodiac with a surveyor. They dug up rusty nails, charcoal and other bits and pieces. They also claimed that the pattern of ruins matched Champlain's plan as to the position of their buildings. Furthermore, the topography of Passamaquoddy Bay also matched Champlain's plan. Thus the British could argue that their evidence matched both history and geography.[65]

Compromise came on the source of the Schoodiac River, rather than on the identity of the river itself, which on 25 October 1798 was announced by the Commissioners to be the River St Croix. Its source was determined to lie in the north-west corner of Chiputneticook Lake – that is, the western headwaters of the Chiputneticook River in Chiputneticook Lake, rather than the point at which the Schoodiac joined the lakes at the southern end. The Commissioners allocated territory of roughly 3,000 square miles along the boundary of Maine and New Brunswick. This provided the British with desirable territory: St Andrews was firmly within New Brunswick, and when the due-north boundary intersecting with the St John River was included, because it ran four miles west of the Grand Falls it safeguarded a major stage in river transportation for the region. For the Americans the agreement secured the land which Maine had already granted to settlers north of the Schoodiac Lakes and west of the Chiputneticook Lake, including rich pine forests. Both sides expressed satisfaction that a dangerous issue had been resolved.[66]

Yet, arduous as the process had been, it determined only a tiny length of the boundary between British North America and the US. To sort out the identity of the St Croix had required European archivists to locate any relevant historic documents and maps, teams of surveyors to explore Passamaquoddy Bay, taking many notes, including astronomical observations, and drawing detailed maps, men taking scores of depositions and sworn testimony from witnesses, and copyists preparing multiple copies of the evidence and arguments, which were then circulated among the Commissioners, Agents and officials at the State Department and the Foreign Office. After all of this, the Commissioners had to read and digest the material, make their decision and submit it, along with maps this time, to their respective governments, which – probably thankfully – accepted the decision. After that, 'guided by magnetic readings on their compasses, surveyors had to organize parties of chainmen to run the boundary through spruce forests and cedar swamps, inscribing the landscape with monuments, witness trees, and other conspicuous boundary marks'.[67]

Remembering that the 1783 treaty had determined that the boundary would be 'formed by a Line drawn due North from the Source of St. Croix River to the Highlands; along the said Highlands which divide those Rivers that empty themselves into the river St. Lawrence, from those which fall into the Atlantic Ocean, to the northwesternmost Head of Connecticut River', it was evident that there was more work to be done. There were the various islands in Passamaquoddy Bay, about which the St Croix Commissioners did not have the authority to decide, and there was the line due north to the highlands, which lacked a decision as to exactly where they were. Furthermore, the Jay Treaty had called for a survey of the upper Mississippi, and this had never been carried out. By 1801, as a result of discussions between Sullivan and himself, the Secretary of State in the new Jefferson administration, James Madison, instructed the American Minister to London, Rufus King (who had pushed for the Jay mission) to open negotiations on the problems. The resulting King–Hawkesbury agreement would have settled some of the problems, yet in the interval between the signing of the treaty and its arrival in Washington, the Louisiana Purchase from the French in 1803 changed things significantly in the north-west, and the treaty was never ratified. The same issues were raised in fresh talks in 1806 and 1807, but they broke down, again over problems in the north-west.[68] But in general the climate had changed, first as a result of the ascension of Jefferson to the presidency, and then because of the resurgence of the British war with France from 1805. Anglo-American relations became poisonous, and within seven years the two empires would be at war.

V

Ever since the end of the American Revolution, trade had been at the centre of relations between the two countries. The British were heavy investors in US bonds, with even George III report-edly holding a substantial number in 1795.[69] Great Britain was the single most important customer of the US, with an average in the years 1802 to 1812 of 45 per cent of all American exports going to British possessions (which included India, the British West Indies and British North America); the reverse was also true, with the US receiving approximately one-half of all of its imports from the British empire.[70] This volume of trade could affect foreign policy: as Henry Dundas, now the Secretary for War, wrote to Grenville in October 1800, 'The Americans are egregiously in the wrong, but they are so much in debt to this country that we scarcely dare quarrel with them.'[71] Certainly Jefferson, Madison and many others believed that Britain was so dependent on American trade that it would agree to American demands.

A real problem for the US during this period was that it was caught between the two warring empires, Great Britain and France. Jefferson and Madison were viscerally pro-French, while at the same time the French assumed that, in exchange for their help during the American Revolution, the US would comply when they asked for American support against the British. The Jay Treaty, however, caused a spectacular dive in US–French relations: the American Minister to France, James Monroe, had assured the Directory in Paris in 1794 that the US would never sign a treaty with Britain which compromised US grievances, and the treaty had done just that. Its ratification in 1795 led to

France suspending diplomatic relations with the US, and in 1798 the Directory decreed that, if any neutral ship was found with British goods on board, both the ship and her cargo would be condemned. About 830 American ships fell victim to French warships and privateers[72] and the two countries moved into the so-called Quasi-War from 1798 to 1800. This temporarily drove the US into the arms of Great Britain, and it was during the few years after the Quasi-War that Rufus King and Lord Hawkesbury negotiated their abortive agreement over the north-east boundary. Indeed, during the war the Royal Navy had actually protected American vessels, and the two navies shared intelligence.

In 1803, the French sold Louisiana, their last territory on the mainland (which had been ceded to them by Spain in 1800), to the Americans. This removed the French as a land-based threat to the US, leaving primarily the British as the most threatening power on the continent (although there was also Spain in the Floridas, on the Pacific Coast and in much of the territory on the far side of the Mississippi River). This became even more worrying in 1805 with the resurgence of the war between Britain and the Third Coalition on the one hand and Napoleonic France on the other, with France by now controlling a substantial part of the European continent. Because of the British need to fight ruthlessly, there were continual British depredations against American commerce; to a lesser extent, there were growing tensions in the north-west of the US. The situation was exacerbated by a number of crises: the *Essex* decision, the Battle of Trafalgar and the publication of a pamphlet in London, *War in Disguise*.

The American ship the *Essex* had in 1799 carried wine from Barcelona to Salem, Massachusetts and after complying with American customs law, she set sail for Havana with the same cargo. En route, she was captured by the British privateer the *Favourite* and taken into New Providence, one of the islands in the Bahamas, where both the ship and her cargo were condemned. The British claimed that the Americans had carried out a 'broken voyage', in that the wine was really being carried from Spain to its colony Cuba, and that the ship's stopping in Massachusetts had been a subterfuge; she had thereby contravened Britain's

'Rule of 1756' by trading between a country and its colony, when the country would not have allowed it in peacetime. As noted above, this was a British imposition which had earlier caused considerable anger in the US. The decision was confirmed on appeal in 1805, with the result that the burden of proof now lay with the ship's owner, not with the ship's captor.[73] Worse, the decision was not immediately made public, and before the Americans knew what was happening, the British had seized dozens of ships engaged in the carrying trade between Europe and enemy islands.

The attacks soon increased, because on 21 October 1805, the Royal Navy, led by Admiral Lord Nelson on HMS *Victory*, defeated the French and Spanish navies at the Battle of Trafalgar. In this engagement, twenty-seven British ships of the line defeated thirty-three French and Spanish ships of the line: the French and Spanish lost twenty-two ships, which essentially destroyed the French navy, without the loss of a single British ship. This victory lessened the British need to be nice to neutrals, and they became considerably more ruthless about interfering with neutral trade and impressing sailors from American ships.

On the same day as Trafalgar took place, a pamphlet written by the lawyer James Stephen, entitled *War in Disguise; Or, the Frauds of the Neutral Flags*, was published in London. Stephen argued that most of the so-called neutral trade, particularly the American, was fraudulently sheltering enemy property. Thus 'the encroachments and frauds of the neutral flags ... [are the] channels of revenue, which sustains the ambition of France, and prolongs the miseries of Europe'. In order to deprive Napoleon of war supplies and the neutrals of their dishonest profits, Stephen urged that there be a ruthless execution of Britain's maritime code and a complete shutting down of the enemy's colonial trade as carried out by neutrals. Widely read, the pamphlet 'crystallized British opinion, [and] consolidated it behind a policy that showed little respect for neutrals'.[74] British opinion continued to back this policy, and supported the British government when from 1812 to 1814 the American War was fought.

President Jefferson was in a difficult position: how should he and the US react to the depredations of the French and the British? First of all, he believed that almost any type of peace was preferable to war. Secondly, he shared with Secretary of State James Madison the conviction that American trade was vital to Britain and that its withdrawal could be a weapon against it; he seems to have neglected the point that it was even more vital to the US. Thirdly, Republicans detested standing armies and navies, fearing them as weapons of tyranny,[75] and Jefferson was a Republican president. The upshot, of course, was that the Americans were hardly able to defend themselves, even had they wished to join the war against Great Britain. Fourthly, Jefferson still supported the traditional links with republican France, although now that France was led by an emperor who imposed vicious and predatory policies against the US (directed in particular against American trade), his faith was shaken. Nevertheless, once France had lost most of its navy, its attacks, although still exasperating, did not approach the number carried out by Britain. This devotion by Jefferson and Madison to principles which, in the abstract, might be both desirable and admirable, contributed to the absolute failure of American policies towards Britain, and would encourage the US to stumble into war with the greatest naval power in the world. These principles also nearly destroyed the unity of the American Republic.

During the period 1803 to 1815, Great Britain was convinced that it was fighting for its independence; indeed, it saw itself as the defender of the world against the man who wanted to control it. In this context, why should the US get in the way? Indeed, Britain believed that the US would also benefit from the defeat of Napoleon, given his attacks on American merchant shipping, which would only increase. On a lower level, Britain welcomed one result of its policies against neutral trading, which was that its own merchants benefited; the argument was that it needed a strong economy to finance the fight against France. British merchants did not object. Convinced of their own rectitude, neither the British nor the Americans were disposed to settle. As a result, the Americans were mercilessly squeezed between the two belligerent empires.

In November 1806 and November and December 1807, Napoleon issued a set of decrees (the Berlin and Milan Decrees) which declared a blockade of the British Isles and of British merchandise, and of those neutral ships seized by British ships; as a result, the French seizure of American ships, whether those already seized and released by Britain or other American ships, began in November 1807. The French, in fact, confiscated more American ships under the Berlin and Milan Decrees than the Royal Navy did under the Orders-in-Council.[76] Yet what was particularly infuriating to the Americans were British actions within American territorial waters, about which the Americans could do nothing. Royal Navy cruisers maintained an almost continuous blockade; indeed, off New York City the British frequently halted every ship leaving the harbour and, not infrequently, there was a queue of a dozen or so American ships awaiting inspection. There were huge number of appeals against this in the British Admiralty courts, which were supposed to apply the law impartially, but often did not.[77] Britain apparently considered that the border of its seaborne empire extended to the east coast of the United States.

British ships, desperately short of sailors, also continued to impress those seamen whom they considered to be British subjects. A difficulty for Britain was that thousands of seamen had left British ships and joined the crews of American merchantmen. Perhaps they were not keen to be shot at on the high seas; an alternative reason was that while British wages were about seven dollars a month, American shipowners paid from twenty-five to thirty-five dollars a month for much less onerous work. In 1812 the Admiralty Department claimed that at least 20,000 Britons, British even by American definition, were serving on American ships; this meant that one-half of all seamen on such ships trading abroad were British.[78]

The continual draining away of British sailors encouraged individual commanders to test, and sometimes to overstep, the limits of official British policy. After one particularly outrageous incident[79] in the spring of 1807, the US government cut off all supplies to British ships, in response to which the British stepped up their interference with American shipping. American militias then patrolled the coasts to prevent supplies reaching ships, public meetings bayed for British blood, and British officials in the US took care when venturing out of doors. Eventually the furore died down, but it was soon followed by the proclamation by the British in November 1807 of new Orders-in-Council, which have a strong claim to consideration as the most important cause of the American declaration of war in 1812.[80] The British government declared that all ports from which British ships were excluded were under blockade and foreign cargoes bound for Europe had first to be landed at a British port, where duty would be levied and a licence had to be obtained to trade with Europe. The purpose of the nakedly selfish form taken by the Orders, besides raising funds, was to gain for Britain a near monopoly of trade with the European continent. The combination of these Orders and those of Napoleon would bring international trade virtually to a standstill.[81]

VI

The response of Jefferson, supported by his Cabinet and the Congress, was to sign the Embargo Act on 22 December 1807. Its purpose was to forbid the departure of all ships from US ports, American or foreign. To be successful, such a law would require the wholehearted co-operation of Americans, because self-denial would be crucial in order to convince the British that the embargo would be continued for as long as was necessary. Precisely because he doubted that Americans would be so self-denying, Secretary of the Treasury Albert Gallatin only reluctantly supported it. He 'never forgot the value a dollar had to Americans. He knew that the nation's love for the main chance piled massive obstacles in the path of both embargo enforcement and war preparation.'[82] On the other hand, Jefferson was strongly supported by Madison, who had two long-standing beliefs about the British empire: one overestimated the empire's political and especially economic appeal within the US, supported, he thought, by the 'anglomen' (particularly in the north-east), whose adherence to the British interest would be undercut by the embargo; he further believed that the empire was vulnerable to economic pressures, making it safe to challenge it.[83] Indeed, back in 1793, Madison had written of the use of an embargo that '[i]t would probably do as much good as harm at home and would force peace on the rest of the world, and perhaps liberty along with it.'[84]

Perhaps inevitably, Gallatin's cynical view of human, or at least of American, nature proved to be more accurate than Jefferson's. In the interval between the passing of the Act and the setting up of a system to enforce it, American shipowners sent hundreds of ships to sea, while during the summer of 1808 there were numerous attempts to smuggle goods across the Canadian border to be exported via the St Lawrence River. However, it was 'only at the end of the year, as it became apparent that not war but a long embargo was most likely, and as the [domestic] political climate became more and more hostile to the whole system, did there arise the last great surge of criminality which destroyed the Embargo ... Areas contiguous to British possessions developed an unaccountable demand for goods of all sorts, a high proportion of which slipped across the border by land or water. Nineteen thousand barrels of flour reached Passamaquoddy Bay, for example, in the first week of May. Many ships found themselves forced by often imaginary bad weather or constructed circumstances to run to foreign ports for safety, sometimes all the way across the Atlantic.'[85]

As the conflict within the Cabinet over the embargo might have predicted, it tore the country apart. The government sent troops to the frontiers and gunboats and frigates up and down the east coast. They passed laws. They passed regulations. Nothing worked. Many Americans began to believe that nothing could justify the tyrannical methods used, which seemed akin to the coercive methods used by the British. As well, the flagrant violations convinced many abroad that a republican form of government was unable to govern. In January 1809, over ferocious opposition from congressional representatives from the north-east, Congress passed a law that permitted the seizure of ships which officials suspected were about to sail illegally, forbade the loading of ships without the permission of federal officials, provided for the stopping of goods travelling by road towards Canada and authorised the increased use of force on sea and by the militias on land. This all showed how pervasive were the violations of the embargo, how authoritarian Jefferson was prepared to be to enforce it and how weak the American government actually was.[86]

In short, the embargo was a thunderous failure. Napoleon was untroubled by it, since the Royal Navy had already stopped most trade with Europe, and he hardly cared any more about the French colonies – he had already sold Louisiana to the Americans. The British suffered much less economically than did the Americans: the embargo ended American trade with France and it enabled Britain to capture a near monopoly of trade with neutrals. It also allowed the import of British goods into the US, as long as they were carried in foreign ships. Unemployed sailors began to return from American to British ships. Indeed, the British government viewed the whole episode with scorn, since it demonstrated that the US could bluster rather more than it could implement a policy. In a contest of British and American wills, the Americans gave way. But, most of all, the whole exercise destroyed American unity. The north-east was in virtual revolt,[87] and the unenforceable law only encouraged contempt for the government and federal law-making. Appropriately, the embargo was repealed on 4 March 1809, the day Jefferson's term as President ended. It had failed profoundly, but so did all of the other American attempts over the subsequent three-and-a-half years to bring Britain to heel. In the end, their failure would drive the US to declare war.

VII

In the west and the Old Northwest, people were more concerned with the Indians than with American trade, although the British were blamed for the problems in both areas. Rumours sped along the frontier in the west that there would soon be another Indian war beyond the frequent instances of violence by both sides. It was believed by the Americans that Indians who had crossed into Canada were receiving subsidies from the British, who were encouraging them to attack the Americans. The former was true but the latter was not. The British subsidised the Indians because if there was to be another war with the US, the Indians would probably not remain neutral, and in that case the British wanted them on their side. It is also worth remembering that the Indian tribes did not conform to British–French–American-imposed borders, but traversed back and forth across them, and this meant that the British dealt with Indian representatives on both sides of any putative border. Certainly the British had economic and diplomatic relations with most of the villages in the Mississippi and Ohio River valleys.

The Governor of the Indiana Territory, General William Henry Harrison, in 1809 by means of the Treaty of Fort Wayne 'convinced' some of the Indian leaders to cede nearly three million acres in the Old Northwest.[88] Tecumseh, chief of the Shawnee tribe, who with his brother in 1805 had begun to create a new Indian league or confederacy, was outraged that some of the Shawnee had been excluded (those included would receive a form of payment for the land lost), and he travelled south to try to convince other tribes to join. Harrison gathered together a mixed force of regulars and volunteers, dashed north and defeated the Indians at the Battle of Tippecanoe on 7 November 1809. News of the battle quickly spread, and because conflict with the Indians had tended to accompany conflict with the British, the conviction grew among Americans that the British supported the Indian military alliance. As a result, many were determined to drive the British out of Canada and attach it to the US. Indeed, during the War of 1812, Tecumseh fought and died at the Battle of the Thames on the side of the British.

The western disaffection was partly responsible for the emergence of a more militantly anti-British attitude and rhetoric in Congress, signalled by a group of Republican congressmen from the southern and western states referred to as the War Hawks, who made up about one-third of the House of Representatives. They were intensely nationalistic and supported an expansionist Republic which was willing to defend its interests, by war if necessary. Yet, important though their rhetoric was in raising Anglo-American tensions even further, western problems arguably played a lesser role than the Orders-in-Council in nudging the US towards a declaration of war.

In Great Britain, for most of the period from 1809 until the advent of war, American activities seemed relatively unimportant, with the exception of irritated complaints about the volume of American complaints. Too much was going on domestically, and militarily elsewhere. The summer of 1809 saw the fall of the Portland ministry, after a crisis lasting two months; the Duke of Portland finally resigned as Prime Minister at the beginning of September (he had had a stroke). For three weeks, there was no effective government, thanks to conflict between possible successors. Spencer Perceval, Chancellor of the Exchequer in the Portland ministry, became Prime Minister in October 1809, but when he finally presented his list of Cabinet members the public response was to wonder at the collective lack of talent and experience.[89] Thereafter, the ministry had to worry about the cost and results of the campaign against France in the Iberian Peninsula led by the future Duke of Wellington. Taking place at the same time were the colonial campaigns, which were prompted either by enemy weakness or by strategic necessity; however, as, one by one, French or Dutch colonies, such as Cape Colony in southern Africa, were picked off, they were transformed into sources of raw materials and markets, and Britain increasingly supplanted Spain and Portugal in the Latin American trade.[90] Domestically, the return of George III's insanity in 1810 led to a virulent Regency Crisis, focused on the question whether Parliament should restrict the powers of the Prince Regent to exercise the royal authority, a debate which continued until February 1811, when Parliament passed the Regency Bill.[91] Above all, there was the vital need to keep together a varying coalition of allies with Russia at its heart who would and could fight Napoleon.

During this whole period, successive ministries in London believed that the US was too cowardly, too disorganised and too greedy to fight and that there was thus no need to make concessions. Furthermore, the desirability of making concessions was nil compared to the overwhelming necessity of maintaining every weapon against Napoleon which the country possessed. What began to modify this approach was that, from the end of 1810, Britain began to suffer from the worst economic depression the country had experienced since 1797. This was caused by a combination of a series of bad harvests, inflation triggered by the printing of paper money to finance the war, and the strains of rapid industrialisation, with its concomitant glut of goods in factories and warehouses arising from the reduction in trade with Europe and the US. Production in Lancashire dropped by 40 per cent. Imports from the US declined sharply; more importantly, while in 1810 roughly 17 per cent of British exports had gone to the US, in 1811 it was less than 5 per cent. From 1810 until 1812, trade declined by a quarter. In the spring of 1812, a series of riots swept through the Midlands.[92]

On 5 November 1811, in his annual Message to Congress, President Madison called on Congress to begin military preparations. Early in 1812, news of the so-called War Hawk Congress and of Madison's Message began to arrive in London, and this allowed the Opposition in Parliament and its supporters outside to emphasise the threat to Great Britain. In response to the news, the government ordered that three regiments be sent to Canada, but the War Office so little anticipated that they would be needed that they instructed the Canadian commander to return two of them for service elsewhere if and when the threat of war in North America receded.[93]

But it did not recede. Through a series of steps on both sides, the two countries edged, stumbled, strode into war. There were protests against the Orders-in-Council by those British interest groups on whom the disruption of the trade with the US had made a great impact: manufacturers from the Midlands,[94] opponents of the war outside Parliament (also called liberals), merchants with interests in the American trade, a section of the press, and many, both inside and outside Parliament, who thought that Britain did not need another war, since it would only divert men and supplies from the fight against Napoleon. Yet the government held firm:[95] conciliation might be interpreted as giving in to the intolerable Americans as well as betraying the maritime rights vital to the safety of the realm.

Prime Minister Perceval, a model of inflexibility, gave no sign that he was willing to compromise on the issue, and it took his assassination on 11 May 1812 to begin to break the logjam. The new ministry under Lord Liverpool was driven by these domestic considerations, not by fear of the US, to repeal the Orders on 16 June. Meanwhile, in the US, it was believed that the point of decision had now been reached: if the US wanted to maintain its honour and regain the respect of other countries, it had to declare war – although, it must be said, war fever hardly swept the country. Indeed, the war was to see significant internal dissent, with New England in particular again practically in a state of revolt. On 1 June, President Madison recommended a declaration of war against Great Britain, and on the 18th Congress agreed. The Orders-in-Council had been repealed in London on the 16th, although this was not announced until a week later. When news of the declaration reached London, the government assumed that once Washington learned of the repeal, the US would withdraw the declaration. But the Americans did not, to say the least, trust the British, and they refused. For the British, war with the US now began in earnest, although as they were still locked in their conflict with a triumphant Napoleon – June also saw his invasion of Russia, which most believed would succeed – the American War was very much a secondary consideration.

VIII

The Americans had declared war, but preparations for it had been minimal – why? First of all, they were confident of their local superiority, given that the British garrisons in Upper and Lower Canada numbered only 7,000 in 1812 and that the war on the European continent would preclude the sending of reinforcements necessary to enable the provinces to withstand an American attack. And secondly, as noted above, although Americans distrusted standing military forces, and so had hardly any available, their lack was not seen as important. Republicans, including Madison and Jefferson, had great faith in the power of a citizen militia fighting for family, home and country against regular forces.

How did the two forces compare?[96] The US Navy was largely composed of professional officers and experienced voluntary seamen, with most of the sea captains under forty and keen to fight, but it possessed only sixteen operational vessels for use on the high seas.[97] By contrast, the Royal Navy was the largest and most powerful in the world, but it had fewer fighting-fit vessels than was ideal. The French were still something of a threat on the seas, and Britain's global responsibilities meant that its crews were often ill-trained and partly impressed, under strength and sailing in relatively badly built vessels, often constructed from inferior timber. The armies both had a mixture of line and light (mounted) infantry, along with artillery and cavalry; both drew on civilian militiamen (the US called out 450,000 during the war). The US army seemed larger, with an authorised strength of 35,600, but at the outbreak of the war only 13,000 had actually enlisted, and most were untrained recruits. However, there was scope for a rapid increase: the US had a population of 7.5 million, while Upper Canada, destined to be the primary object of American desire, had a population of only 70,000–80,000, and although many were former Loyalists, many others were part of a recent and continuing stream of American immigrants. Indeed, Upper Canada was being transformed into a predominantly American province, not least by ties of economic interdependence.[98] The British forces had stronger leadership and better training. Most of the American generals were around sixty years old, and had been appointed because they had experience in the Revolutionary War and were Republicans, with the result frequently an ageing political appointee. Yet importantly, the Americans enjoyed internal supply lines, while those of the British extended to the West Indies or across the Atlantic.

What were the war aims of the two empires? The answers have been a matter of much conjecture among historians.[99] For the US, the matter seems to have turned on the question as to whether or not they wanted to conquer Canada for keeps or to conquer it and use it as a bargaining chip to make the British stop behaving badly on the high seas.[100] The conquest of Canada would also deprive the Indians of supplies and support and thereby eliminate them as a barrier to western expansion. And since the US went to war primarily because of the British attack on its sovereignty by impressing its citizens and attacking its trade, and because it knew that it was not a match for British sea power, attacking Canada was the only route to victory the Americans had. But arguably, the overarching reason the US went to war was to defend the country's honour and sovereignty against the perceived arrogance of the British; it was also important that it had repeatedly threatened war, and American credibility was now in danger. For the British, the war had three aims. The supreme factor was the war with France, and while it was still being fought, everything else had to fit within that context; therefore, they wished to eliminate any American ability to aid France. A second aim was to defend Canada against the Americans and to retain it as part of the empire; this would also take it out as a factor in the war. And thirdly, it is probable that London also intended to teach the Americans a lesson, to know their place and not to interfere with the empire. Thereafter, trade and other relationships could resume. The Americans wanted the British to treat them as international equals and the British wanted the Americans to realise that they were not.

There were three main battle areas. One was the south, which centred around the Creek (Indian) War. The second was the Atlantic coastline, which the British blockaded, and where they would in 1814 carry out naval and amphibious attacks. The war on the seas was connected, but it was relatively unimportant. And the third, which is the focus in this chapter, was the border between the US and Canada. One historian has argued that 'The War of 1812 pivoted on the contentious boundary between the king's subject and the republic's citizen.'[101] Great Britain was not convinced that the American Republic would remain united; the Canadian border would be more defendable, and access to the Mississippi River would be more certain, if the Canadian border were further south than it was, and the uncertainty might facilitate this change. On the other hand, Americans tended to assume that, sooner rather than later, Canada would become part of the US. The common point of both of these expectations was that the border could seem to be temporary and easily changeable. Therefore, it was worth fighting over.

The US took the offensive, because it was vital to take over Canada before the British could mobilise their resources. There would be eight attempts in all in 1812, 1813 and 1814, but what with mediocre leadership and the armies' lacking a staff or a supply system, in only one did they succeed in occupying British territory for more than a short period; this territory, in south-western Upper Canada, would, in fact, be handed back in the peace treaty. The original strategic plan was for a three-pronged attack. The first prong would be across the Detroit River to the British Fort Amherstberg near Detroit, a fort which was deep in Indian-held territory in Upper Canada, and the defeat of which, the Americans expected, would shake the Indians' faith in the power of the British empire. The second was to cross the Niagara River to take Queenston Heights, which was intended to cut the province in half and demoralise the population. The third prong was to be launched along the Champlain corridor across the St Lawrence River to Montreal, which kept open the St Lawrence River. This would divide the defenders, and the taking of Montreal would, the Americans assumed, cut off supplies and reinforcements from Britain and thereby guarantee the fall of Upper Canada. To support the fight for Canada, the US Navy and American-licensed privateers were to attack ships of the Royal Navy and British merchant ships. For its part, Britain embarked on sea and land offensives, first by tightening the blockade of the east coast so far as this was possible before the defeat of Napoleon released a significant number

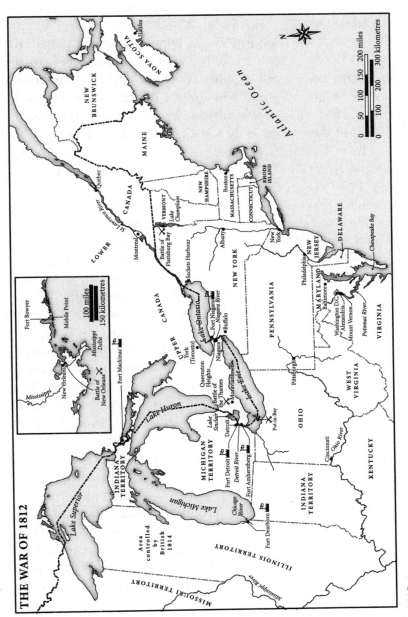

THE WAR OF 1812

MAP 3

of ships, while attacking American naval and merchant vessels, and secondly by attacking by land over the border from Canada. Both navies fought to gain control of the Great Lakes.

The first US invasion of Canada, led by General William Hull in July 1812, was a spectacular failure. He had been sent months before with troops and supplies to Ohio so that the defenders would be caught off guard. However, a British patrol intercepted the plans. His forces were in any case hardly in the shape necessary to carry out these plans: they were a combination of regulars and militia from several states, which meant that a number of separate command structures had to work together but did not, and when it was time to cross the border 200 Ohio militiamen refused, on the grounds that they were prepared to fight only within the US. When the Americans arrived in Canadian territory, Hull issued a proclamation saying that he had come to liberate the locals from the tyranny of Britain, adding that anyone found fighting with Britain's Indian allies would be executed. However, when news arrived of the movement of British forces against him, he panicked, despite his superior numbers and despite the disgust of most of his officers, and retreated with his forces – larger than the British forces – to Fort Detroit. There Hull 'panicked again and quickly surrendered his army, the fort, along with enough arms and supplies for an entire campaign season, the Michigan Territory, and sixteen hundred Ohio militia who were not even at the fort'. The Americans also lost or abandoned Forts Mackinac (the British had replaced Fort Michilimachinac with Fort Machinac (Map 1)) and Dearborn on the Great Lakes, and within a matter of weeks 'the entire Northwest frontier of the United States collapsed'.[102]

In October 1812 came the second attempt to invade Canada. This force was led by General Henry Dearborn, a former Secretary of War under President Jefferson, 'often confused and complacent', followed, more or less, by a mixed force of regulars and militia, though not the New York militia, which also refused to cross into Canada. Those who crossed the Niagara River attacked Queenston Heights, but the absence of the New Yorkers forced the Americans to surrender to the British once the latter's reinforcements arrived. Dearborn's own force of 8,000, which was meant to implement the main attack on Lower Canada, instead accepted a British offer of a ceasefire. The American government overruled him and rejected the British offer on the grounds that it would give the British time to prepare their defences. As for the third part of the plan, the invasion of Lower Canada and the conquest of Montreal, 'Dearborn meandered his way northward in late autumn, scrapping his battle plan when some of his militia refused to cross into Canada and the weather turned cold.'[103] It was a farce. In both Great Britain and the US, the campaigns were discussed and spat upon; contempt was expressed by both publics, with the Americans incandescent with rage at the humiliation. Hull was court-martialled and condemned, but Madison reprieved him from execution. What made matters worse was that it had been taken for granted that the invasion and conquest of Canada would be a doddle; Jefferson had written to a friend on 4 August 1812 that 'The acquisition of Quebec ... will be a mere matter of marching, and will give us experience for the attack of [that is, on] Halifax the next, and the final expulsion of England from the American continent,'[104] and he was hardly alone in his views.

The Americans were more successful the following year. For political reasons – the pro-war Governor of New York, Daniel Tompkins, was up for re-election and needed movement on the Canadian front – it was decided to attack York (now Toronto), the capital of Canada, which was vulnerable and thinly defended. On 27 April 1813, the Americans launched an amphibious assault against the village, driving out the British and seizing a large quantity of supplies.[105] However, they failed to attack two ships – one had left shortly before the attack and the British burned the other – while upon their departure the British blew up a gunpowder magazine, the 'Grand Magazine', which killed 250 Americans. A surrender agreement was negotiated, whereby the US commanders agreed to respect private property, allow the civil government to continue to function and permit doctors to treat the wounded. The Americans, in a violent and cold–blooded manner, entirely ignored the agreement. When the Americans withdrew, after occupying

York for a week, they set fire to the Parliament Buildings and the Governor's house[106] – the Canadian equivalent of the Capitol and the White House. Three months later, York was again attacked and burned.[107] The British would take their revenge for these and other such attacks the following year.

During 1813, the American campaigns in the York–Niagara and Montreal regions came to nothing, but they had some military success in south-western Upper Canada, driving the British and the Indians led by Tecumseh from Ohio territory back into Canada. They also won, at the Battle of Put-in-Bay on Lake Erie, one of the decisive battles of the war. The British dominated the Great Lakes, with a squadron of freshwater ships on Lakes Ontario and Erie, and the Americans needed to break this hold. The twenty-seven-year-old Oliver Hazard Perry was sent to Sacket's Harbor on Lake Ontario in March 1813 to take command of the squadron and to build some ships for it.

Captain Robert Barclay arrived in June to take command of the British squadron. Desperate for men, he commandeered footsoldiers from Fort Erie, and then tried to blockade Perry. On 31 July, by which time he had nine warships, Perry saw that the British had disappeared from the mouth of the harbour; he got his ships out and they dropped anchor at Put-in-Bay on Gibraltar Island in Lake Erie. By this time, the British squadron was short of men and supplies, but the Americans prevented reinforcement. In the end, the British had six ships with 440 men, of whom ten in each ship were trained sailors; against this were the Americans' nine ships with 530 men, a larger proportion of whom were trained sailors. The Americans' firepower was almost twice that of the British. At dawn on 10 September, American lookouts reported that the British fleet was in view, and Perry sailed out to engage them. It was close-fought and bloody. Four hours later, the commander and deputy of every British ship had been killed or wounded, and the 'murderous raking fire' of the Americans had tipped the balance. Late in the day, Perry wrote to General Harrison that 'We have met the enemy and they are ours – two ships, two brigs, one schooner, and a sloop.'[108]

Perry then ferried General Harrison and his army of 3,500 men, including 250 Indians from the Ohio country, across Lake Erie. They caught the British and their allies, including Tecumseh, at Moraviantown, where they defeated them on 5 October at the Battle of the Thames. Tecumseh himself was killed, and with him the leadership of the Indian Confederation. Within six weeks of this destruction of British power, however, the term of service (which tended to be six months) of many of the western militiamen expired, and they went home. This somewhat limited the possibilities of a further advance.[109]

When in the east the term of service of many American militiamen expired in December 1813 and they departed for their homes, the British decided to push forward, obliging the Americans to retreat back across the border to consolidate their forces. En route, the Americans pursued something of a scorched-earth policy, turning the people of Niagara out into the snow and burning their houses, while the following day American artillery near Queenston destroyed part of that village by firing red-hot cannonballs to set it on fire. The tactical argument was to prevent their use by the British. The new British commander in Upper Canada, Lieutenant-General Gordon Drummond, aged forty-one and a veteran of campaigns in both Egypt and the West Indies, had orders to exploit American weaknesses; he was also determined to avenge the destruction wreaked on the British North Americans. He crossed the Niagara River, defeated the American garrison at Fort Niagara and drove the Americans out of the region completely. Over the next several days, the British torched the settlements on the American side of the river. Drummond captured Buffalo, destroyed four ships of the Lake Erie squadron which was wintering there, and then returned to Canada. There continued to be sporadic fighting on the northern frontier for the remainder of the war, but in the end the Americans won a crucial battle: their victory on 11 September 1814 at the Battle of Plattsburg Bay on Lake Champlain stopped a British invasion force intending to slice the Union in two.[110]

IX

By the end of 1813, the Americans had regained most of the lost territory in the west, destroyed for ever the possibility of an Indian homeland in the Ohio territory and occupied part of south-western Upper Canada. On the oceans, they had won three morale-boosting frigate-to-frigate duels: the USS *Constitution*, after making a dramatic escape from a British squadron in July 1812, on 19 August defeated HMS *Guerrière* in a bloody encounter (it was primarily an artillery duel, with the ships running side by side); on 25 October the USS *United States* defeated and captured the British frigate HMS *Macedonian*; and on 29 December the *Constitution* defeated HMS *Java* off the coast of Brazil.[111] These victories, especially those of the USS *Constitution*, were vitally important for American morale, not least in providing heroes. Yet Andrew Lambert points out that if the focus is on three other frigate battles, the story is very different: 'On 1 June 1813 HMS *Shannon* captured the USS *Chesapeake* off Boston in less than fifteen minutes, in an action of ferocious intensity, fought with astonishing skill and courage on both sides. On 28 February 1814 HMS *Phoebe* took the USS *Essex* at Valparaiso, Chile, in a strikingly one-sided action. Finally, on 14 January 1815, the USS *President* was taken off Sandy Hook by HMS *Endymion* in a pursuit battle that pitted the American flagship ... against a smaller British opponent.'[112]

It is undeniable that the US Navy, on the whole, was no match for the Royal Navy. With the onset of war, the latter had to protect convoys from American frigates and privateers, but, even more important, it had to blockade the US coastline in order both to destroy America's trade and to prevent its naval operations. Early in 1812, there were seventy-seven British warships off the American coast and in the Caribbean, while by early 1813 the number had risen to 105. Indeed, a very important part of the naval conflict for both countries was the use of their warships against merchant ships.[113] The US Navy seized 165 British vessels and some troop transports, and the Royal Navy captured 1,400 merchant vessels and privateers. Both sides licensed privateers, but with mixed success. The Americans licensed 526, of which 207 took a prize and 148 were captured or destroyed; the British privateers, most of them from the Maritime provinces of Canada, took several hundred American ships, many of them coastal traders. In the Galapagos Islands during the summer of 1813, the British whaling industry was devastated by the USS *Essex*, which captured all of the ships known to be in the area, but was then, as noted above, defeated by the frigate HMS *Phoebe*. Out on the oceans, American privateers captured nearly 1,400 merchantmen, although nearly 750 of them were then recaptured by the British.[114]

The greatest impact on the ocean war was the Royal Navy's blockade of the Atlantic coast, which began with twenty ships and ended with 135. From the beginning of the war until May 1814, New England was exempted: the British Army required American grain, and the Americans were happy to ship it in vessels licensed by the British. Once Napoleon had abdicated, however, and the supplies were no longer needed, New England was blockaded as well; by the end of May, the blockade extended the entire length of the Atlantic coast. There were two major impacts of the blockade. One was to paralyse the US Navy, since it was extremely difficult for American warships to leave port. The second was to destroy America's international trade: in 1811 the value of American exports and imports totalled $192 million, but in 1814 the value fell to $31 million; customs revenues, which provided the primary income of the federal government, fell from $13 million to $6 million. By 1814, according to Carl Benn, only one ship out of twelve even dared to leave port. By contrast, Great Britain's international trade grew from £91 million in 1811 to £152 million in 1814.[115]

Beginning in February 1813, the Royal Navy and British troops launched raids in the Chesapeake Bay region, not least because it was the source of many of the privateers – the British referred to Baltimore as a nest of pirates. Resistance on the whole was patchy, and they destroyed military and industrial property and captured many ships. If the Americans resisted by opening fire, the British often torched American property or plundered. If the Americans stayed at home, they were generally left alone and were paid for the supplies taken by the British.

The following May, the British increased the pressure. On 20 May 1814, Lord Bathurst, the Secretary for War and the Colonies, instructed Major-General Robert Ross, a veteran of the Peninsular War against the French, 'to effect a diversion on the coasts of the United States of America in favour of the army employed in the defence of Upper and Lower Canada'. The force was not intended 'for any extended operation at a distance from the coast', nor was Ross to hold permanent possession of any captured district. Furthermore, '[i]f in any descent you shall be enabled to take such a position as to threaten the inhabitants with the loss of their property, you are hereby authorized to levy upon them contributions in return for your forbearance,' but the US government's munitions, harbours and shipping were to be taken away or destroyed. The nineteenth-century American historian Henry Adams was later to write that Ross's troops 'showed unusual respect for private property'.[116] Whether it was a useful diversion for the British Army in Canada is problematic. There was repeated fighting and a number of battles on either side of the frontier, but the end result was that the Americans had failed in their attempt to capture Upper Canada, whether to use it as a counter at a future peace conference or to annex it.

It has normally been assumed that the British torched part of Washington in revenge for the Americans' double destruction of York. There is some evidence for this, although it is ambiguous. Sir George Prévost, by then the Governor-General of Canada, wrote to Vice-Admiral Sir Alexander Cochrane on 2 June 1814 suggesting that he should 'assist in inflicting that measure of retaliation which shall deter the enemy from a repetition of similar outrages' as had taken place in Canada. On 18 July, therefore, Cochrane issued an order to the blockading squadrons 'to destroy and lay waste such towns and districts upon the coast as you may find assailable'. The army, however, apparently paid little attention to the order, as far as private property was concerned, but governmental property was fair game.[117]

In August 1814, the British landed 4,000 men near Washington, firing a twenty-one-gun salute as they sailed down the Potomac River past Washington's tomb at Mount Vernon. This began a five-month assault on the American coast, taking in, for example, Washington, Alexandria and Baltimore, before moving to attack the Gulf Coast in the autumn, arriving at Mobile Point in September and climaxing with the Battle of New Orleans in early January 1815. On 11 February that year, in the final battle of the war, the British took Fort Bowyer in preparation for a move on Mobile; on the following day, however, news of the peace treaty reached them.[118] For Americans, because of their defeat at Washington and victory at New Orleans, this period is the only part of the war which has burrowed itself into the historical memory. And because news of the peace treaty arrived in Washington around the same time as news of the victory at New Orleans, the Americans claimed victory in the war.

X

Desultory attempts at beginning peace negotiations had been going on for most of the war, centred around a Russian mediation proposal. Great Britain refused to accept any proposal involving Russia, although in February 1813 Madison did so, having learned of Napoleon's defeat in Russia and fearing that this could free British resources. Peace Commissioners were appointed by Madison, on the assumption that the British would not decline the Russian offer,[119] but they did. Finally, in November 1813, Lord Castlereagh, now the British Secretary of State for Foreign Affairs, wrote to James Monroe, now the American Secretary of State, offering negotiations, although neutral rights were not to be a subject for discussion. This did not stop Madison and Monroe from accepting the offer: news of American defeats on the Niagara frontier and of Napoleon's defeat at Leipzig had arrived just before Castlereagh's offer, and it was accepted in January 1814.[120]

There were to be five American peace Commissioners. The chairman was John Quincy Adams, who had been Minister to the

Netherlands, Portugal, Prussia and Russia (his current post) and would become Minister to Great Britain immediately after the negotiations, Secretary of State from 1817 to 1823 and the sixth President from 1828 to 1832. He was highly intelligent, probably the most experienced diplomat America possessed at that point, pugnacious, self-righteous and a man of towering intellectual pride. The second Commissioner was Albert Gallatin, the Secretary of the Treasury, and the peacemaker, particularly between Adams and Henry Clay, the third Commissioner; he was also good at reconciling the innumerable drafts of notes and reports, a never-ending task and not without head-aching difficulty.[121] (According to Henry Adams, 'All Gallatin's abilities were needed to fill the place. In his entire public life he had never been required to manage so unruly a set of men' as the American Commissioners.)[122] Clay, the Speaker of the House of Representatives and a War Hawk, 'was ever the beguiling and affable politician',[123] who combined a responsible attitude to the negotiations with a penchant for card playing. The fourth Commissioner was James A. Bayard, a former senator from Delaware; he was a member of the Federalist Party, but he had nevertheless supported the war. His coolness and tact were as important in settling disputes among his colleagues as in negotiations with his opposite numbers. The fifth and final Commissioner was Jonathan Russell, the former Chargé d'Affaires at the American Ministry in London and the newly appointed Minister to Sweden; he wielded less influence than the others. The Commissioners grated on each other and some-times quarrelled, but they did not let their differences show to the British. In any case, they were as one in defence of American interests, although they sometimes differed over just what those interests were.

The Commissioners received their instructions from Monroe about what they should demand. Great Britain was to abandon some of its claims to belligerent rights on the seas – for example, no blockade would be legal if there was no adequate force to back it up, and the rights of neutrals were to be respected. Impressment – 'this degrading practice' – must cease, 'our flag must protect the crew, or the United States cannot consider themselves an independent Nation'; in exchange for this, President Madison was willing to exclude all British seamen from American vessels and to surrender those who had deserted in American ports.[124] Making an optimistic bid, the Commissioners were instructed 'to bring to view, the advantages to both Countries which is promised, by a transfer of the upper parts and even the whole of Canada to the United States'.[125] Fundamentally, however, their object was 'to secure to the United States ... a safe and honourable peace',[126] with the emphasis on the honourable. The suggested venue for negotiations moved from the Tsar's offer of St Petersburg, which Britain did not want, to Castlereagh's suggestion of London, which the Americans did not want, to Göteborg in Sweden in response to the Americans' wish for a neutral venue, but which was too cold for both sides, and finally to Ghent in Belgium for convenience. Adams and Russell arrived on 24 June 1814, and were soon joined by the other three Commissioners.

The British delegation arrived six weeks later. The first member was Admiral Lord Gambier, a veteran of forty-five years in the Royal Navy, whose experience included the Revolutionary War; he was expected to defend Britain's belligerent rights, but he appears to have played a relatively minor role in the negotiations. Bayard thought him a 'wellbred, affable and amiable man'.[127] (He was also the President of the English Bible Society and prayed a lot.)[128] Secondly, there was the thirty-one-year-old Dr William Adams, a blunt and sometimes witty Admiralty lawyer, who was an authority on maritime rights. As things transpired, he earned his pay. The third was Henry Goulburn MP, Under-Secretary for War and the Colonies. He was the most active of the negotiators, but because he apparently doubted whether the Americans really wanted peace, he often held to a more rigorous line than, strictly speaking, his superiors wanted. (Henry Adams was later to write, rather contemptuously, that 'he had as little idea of diplomacy as was to be expected from an Under-Secretary of State for the colonies'.)[129] He also sometimes engaged in public arguments with the Americans, and especially with Adams, himself a short-tempered and highly argumentative man. This last point comes from an American historian;[130] it would be equally possible to call Goulburn unfailing in defending British interests, not least against the ferociously disputatious Adams. Aged twenty-eight, he had been crucial in directing the British war effort against the Americans, leaving Lord Bathurst free to deal with the French war. He later had a distinguished political career, becoming both Chancellor of the Exchequer and Secretary of State for Home Affairs. The positions of the three members of the British delegation, and the ages of two of them, were substantially below those of the Americans, but the more senior British diplomats were fully occupied at Paris and Vienna.[131]

The starting point of the instructions Castlereagh sent to the British delegation, dated 28 July 1814, was to require the acceptance of *uti possidetis,* which meant that each belligerent would keep the territory it held at the end of the war; Gallatin had already written to Madison on 13 June to warn him that 15,000 to 20,000 British regulars were on their way to America, and that the best that could be expected in the treaty was the *status quo ante bellum* – that is, the state of affairs before the beginning of the war. The British expected that victory would enable them to annex to Canada substantial parts of the northern American territories. The Americans were also required to concede at the outset as a *sine qua non* that the interests of the Indians of the Old Northwest should be included, and that territory should be assigned to them with boundaries guaranteed by both the US and Great Britain. There were other points, particularly that the Americans should no longer fish in British waters nor land and dry fish on British territory, but these were the three major conditions for a peace treaty.[132]

The first meeting of the two delegations took place at 1 p.m. on 8 August 1814. After the usual civilities, Goulburn laid out the points which the British wished to discuss; the Americans did the same the following day. The British then made more specific demands; the Americans recognised that their answers to these demands – that they could not accept them – would end the negotiations. The British on 20 August sent an official Note containing their demands, and the Americans sent it to Washington; they then sat up until 11 p.m. on the 24th, drafting and redrafting their answer, which they assumed would end the chances of peace, at the same time as Washington was burning. On the 25th, they sent it to the British Commissioners and began making their arrangements to return to the US.[133] However, they remained at Ghent, but over the following two months negotiations went on at a slow pace, as the British hoped for news of victories. Nevertheless, during this period, two issues which had hitherto been central to each side's demands disappeared. Both sides agreed not to mention impressment, but the second issue, what to do about the Indians, occupied nine weeks. The eventual outcome was that, although the British gained an agreement to ensure 'lenient'[134] treatment of their Indian allies, in effect they abandoned them when they heard that, at the Battle of the Thames (where Tecumseh had met his end), some of their allies had changed sides and fought for the Americans.

Castlereagh in Paris received letters from Goulburn describing the negotiations. He was annoyed that Great Britain had been put into the position of appearing to be engaged on a war of conquest – rather than picking up territories as a reward of victory – and that negotiations were breaking down over that point. As he wrote to Lord Liverpool, 'are we prepared to continue the war for territorial arrangements; and, if not, is this the best time to make our peace, saving all our rights, and claiming the fisheries, which they do not appear to question (in which case, the territorial questions might be reserved for ulterior discussion); or is it desirable to take the chance of the campaign, and then to be governed by circumstances?'[135] – that is, claim as much as the victory would allow? Prime Minister Liverpool shared Castlereagh's disapproval: as he wrote to the Duke of Wellington, 'It is very material to throw the rupture of the negotiation, if it is to take place, upon the Americans.'[136] Yes, the Americans should be humbled, but not so that the public would learn that the breakdown was caused by clumsy British negotiators overreaching themselves.

Public opinion in Britain was already a worry, because support for the war was fragile and opposition could easily grow. The country had been at war for sixteen years, and people were tired of it. Taxpayers were especially weary: from 1812 to 1815, government expenditure totalled £550 million – between March and November 1813 alone, Britain had paid out more than £11 million in subsidies to various European allies – and while all believed that it had been necessary to fight Napoleon, why spend even more to achieve conquests in America? Was it worth it?[137] By November 1814, according to Nicholas Vansittart, the Chancellor of the Exchequer, 'Economy & relief from taxation are not merely the War Cry of Opposition, but they are the real objects to which public attention is turned.'[138] The Prime Minister agreed, chafing under the 'prodigious expense' of a war in which there was little chance of a sweeping victory. 'We must expect ... to hear it said that the property-tax is continued for the purpose of securing a better frontier for Canada.'[139] The Cabinet first met to discuss the negotiations on 3 November. By the end of that month Vansittart was convinced that 'to the final issue of the War, provided it be not dishonourable, the country is very indifferent'.[140]

During the whole period of the negotiations, Britain was urgently trying to defuse crises, particularly over Poland, which might drag it into another European war, this time with Russia as the enemy rather than the ally. There were also threats to the life of Wellington, who was then the British Ambassador in Paris, and, partly to get him out of Paris and partly to rescue the American situation, the Cabinet offered him the chief command in America. He did not refuse, but neither did he anticipate much success: there were enough British troops, but the lack of naval superiority on the Great Lakes was a crucial weakness, since without it the Americans could not be prevented from invading Canada nor could the British press southwards. He also told ministers bluntly what he thought of their claims to *uti possidetis*:

In regard to your present negotiations, I confess that I think you have no right from the state of the war to demand any concession of territory from America ... you have not been able to carry it into the enemy's territory, notwithstanding your military success, and now undoubted military superiority, and have not even cleared your own territory of the enemy on the point of attack. You cannot then, on any principle of equality in negotiation, claim a cession of territory excepting in exchange for other advantages which you have in your power.[141]

Wellington's advice ended the Cabinet's lingering hope of strengthening the Canadian border by annexing some American territory.

The final conflict – one which nearly reduced Adams and Clay to blows in the privacy of their hotel – was over access to the British fisheries off north-eastern Canada for the Americans and the right to navigate the Mississippi for the British, rights which had been coupled together in the 1783 treaty. Adams absolutely refused to admit that the Americans did not have a 'natural right' to continue to fish in British waters and to dry fish on British soil, as they had done when subjects of the empire. This was of interest only to Massachusetts (of which Maine was then a part), but, significantly, it had been Adams' father John who had fought to get it in the earlier treaty. He was unlikely to sign any treaty which did not admit this right. For his part, Clay violently opposed a continuation of the British right to navigate the Mississippi; he, with most western inhabitants, believed that it was Canadian traders who had encouraged Indian attacks on settlers, and he swore that he would sign no treaty which contained such a clause. The patience and skill of Gallatin over the following month saved the situation for the Americans, while the eventual flexibility of the Cabinet and Bathurst did the same for the British: in the end, neither issue formed part of the treaty.[142] It was signed on 24 December 1814.

Considering the high, and low, principles over which the two empires had gone to war, the Treaty of Ghent was practically empty. There were only ten substantive articles. Article I stated that all lands and possessions were to revert to the *status quo ante bellum*, except for the islands claimed by both countries in the Bay of Passamaquoddy of Jay Treaty fame, which were to remain as they were at the end of the war until a decision on their future could be taken. Article II required the cessation of all hostilities and Article III provided for the return of all prisoners of war. Article IX dealt with the Indians: both the British and the Americans were to stop fighting with them and both were to return to them the lands and possessions they had possessed in 1811 before the war began. This, of course, all hinged on the Indians' not attacking the Americans or the British. By Article X, both countries agreed to promote the abolition of the slave trade; as Britain had abolished it in 1803, this was clearly directed at the US.

Articles IV through VIII were entirely devoted to sorting out the undetermined border between the two empires – appropriately enough, given that the war had in many respects been a 'borderlands' war.[143] The Articles were devoted to setting out the means by which the border delineated in the 1783 treaty could finally be given a form on which the two could agree. Each section of the undetermined boundary had its very own Article, but the methodology was the same. A board of two Commissioners, one each from Great Britain and the US, was to go through the same procedures as had the Commissioners after the Jay Treaty. In these cases, instead of a third Commissioner, if the two Commissioners could not agree, the matter 'may be referred to such friendly Sovereign or State ... [which] shall decide', and whose decision was 'to be final and conclusive'. This stored up trouble for the future.

And that was it – nothing on impressment or neutral rights, nothing on ceding lands in either direction, nothing on fisheries or navigation down the Mississippi. Nevertheless, it seems clear that although the United States had not 'won' the war, neither did it lose the peace. After all, by 1814 the US was internally divided, militarily weak and nearly bankrupt, and without Britain's need to fight for its own liberty and independence the outcome of both war and negotiations would almost certainly have been different. The United States' great triumph was that it had survived and remained a united country. If impressment had not been eliminated by treaty, if Britain had not agreed to respect neutral rights, nevertheless it was clear to Adams that, if there were to be another war and Britain tried to enforce the same regulations, the US would by then be strong enough to prevent it from doing so. Essentially, the two had checkmated each other. Yet, as noted above, the US saw the war as a great victory against the most powerful country in the world.[144] The Americans were thus a match for any country and essentially unconquerable, and pride, patriotism and hyperbole blossomed accordingly. For Britain, there was relief from the millstone of an American war. Lord Liverpool's ministry could now concentrate on the European threat, which was fortunate, since the Battle of Waterloo was shortly to take place.

As for the activities of the two empires on the North American continent, during this period very little had been settled, in spite of one war and two treaties. Indeed, conflict continued – who can forget the Aroostook (Lumberjack) War of 1839 over disputed territory in northern Maine or the Pig War of 1859 on San Juan Island near Vancouver? Even the Treaty of Ghent Commissioners had to turn to a Sovereign Arbitrator because of their inability to agree. Yet the remainder of the nineteenth century saw the majority of the land disputes between the two empires settled by diplomacy – although for the Oregon Territory it was a close-run thing. This was largely due to two main factors: first of all, both believed that, in Winston Churchill's formulation, jaw-jaw was better than war-war, particularly when their two countries so resembled each other in ethnicity and law; and secondly, neither would have been able to defeat the other, so war was a waste of time and money. Nevertheless, as the US tried to expand to the north, the south and the west, Great Britain tried to hem it in, at least as far as the north and north-west directions were concerned. As the next chapter will show, there were a number of acute danger points, but war, as opposed to skirmishes, was averted.

Chapter 2

From Sea to Shining Sea, 1815–1903

'Good fences make good neighbors.'[1]

On the night of 13 December 1853, Charlie Griffin, a British subject, with a band of Hawaiian shepherds and 1,300 sheep, landed on San Juan Island, which was a few miles east of Vancouver Island. They set up a sheep ranch, Belle Vue Farm, and built a sheep wharf; the enterprise prospered. In due course, men from the Washington Territory came over to raid, claiming that the island belonged to the US, not to Great Britain. There were other incursions, all with the same argument. In 1855, Lyman Cutler, a tall, fair-haired, fiercely independent and belligerent frontiersman from Kentucky, built a hut within a mile and a half of Belle Vue Farm for his Native companion and himself; he then, in the middle of the sheep run, dug up a third of an acre and planted potatoes. By all accounts, he was neither particularly hard-working nor a farmer: his ramshackle fence went around only three sides of the field. Belle Vue Farm owned forty pigs, including the most favoured of all breeding pigs, the black Berkshire. This breed loved to root in mud and dirt for whatever food could be found. One of these boars had wandered over to root in Cutler's potato patch and Cutler had threatened to shoot it if it returned. According to the story, Cutler declared to Griffin, 'Keep your pig out of my potatoes,' and Griffin shot back, 'It's up to you to keep your potatoes out of my pig.'[2] A pig soon returned in the middle of the night, and Cutler, outraged, shot it. This was the beginning of the great Pig War.

And still the border was the issue. Why? From the American side, it was a combination of a desperate need for security, a greed for land and its resources, and hatred. True, Great Britain had 'lost' the War of American Independence and had come to a draw over the War of 1812, but it was still the only global power and was a perceived threat to the US. The strategic answer for the Americans was, sooner rather than later, to absorb the Maritimes (Nova Scotia, Prince Edward Island and New Brunswick), Lower Canada (Quebec province) and Upper Canada (Ontario). At the same time, the Americans wanted the land for their farmers and the timber to fell and sell to build houses, bridges, ships and whatever else was required for development and defence. And crucially, much of the population had a visceral hatred of the British and wanted them off the continent.

For the British and the colonists of British North America, many of these desires were shared. They, too, wanted to expand into territory rich with land, timber and furs. They also wanted a port in the west to facilitate trade with China and the east, a desire shared by the Americans. Both wanted to control lines of communication and defensive points against the other. For the Canadians, indeed, security was crucial. They wanted security against the thrusting Americans, who tended to assume that land in a wilderness was up for grabs. This was complicated by a significant admixture of immigrants from the US in Canada, who had moved to the north in response to an earlier offer of land by colonial authorities keen to increase the population. As a result, it is estimated that they outnumbered Canadians by ten to one. During the War of 1812, they had often been feared as a fifth column; after the war they could still be a threat because they wished to import American ideas or habits of democracy to a Canada which remained under the administration of the imperial power. Yet because many of the immigrants to Canada had been Loyalists fleeing the US during and after the Revolution, the idea of coming under the suzerainty of the US government was not necessarily a welcome one.

The context was the urge of both empires to expand and to prevent the expansion of the other. In many areas it was complex and

messy, particularly on the north-eastern border between Maine
and New Brunswick. On the American side, much of the expansion was driven by those on the periphery rather than by the
government in Washington. This was complicated by the fervent
belief, particularly in Maine, that the state and its citizens should
be the determining factor, and that it was the duty of the federal
government to support them; few in the state thought that foreign
policy should be left to the President and Congress if they did
not agree with the state's 'rights'. The political and cultural context in the US during much of the nineteenth century was a fervent and pervasive Anglophobia, fostered by a press which never
doubted who was in the right and said so in an unbridled manner.
Unconstrained party politics was a significant contributing factor.
It was fortunate that vocal power was, repeatedly, not matched by
military power.

The two empires expanded areas of conflict while trying to
work out ways of preventing it. The Treaty of Ghent had laid
out the problems, and it set out the solution: surveying by both
empires, the ascertaining of where each thought the true border
ran, and the decision to be taken by a mixed commission. If it was
impossible to come to a decision, then there was to be an arbiter.
It was a civilised plan, and the intention was to obviate the need
to fight over the boundaries. Sometimes it worked, but there were
times when it did not. Fortunately, negotiations carried out epi-
sodically over the century eventually prevailed. The hoped-for
prizes varied. On the Great Lakes, it was the power of the two
navies to prevent invasion by the other side. In the north-east,
especially on the Maine–New Brunswick border, it was timber
and farmland for the Americans, security for the Canadians and a
military road for the British. The tensions here could be explosive.
They led to the so-called Aroostook War in 1839, also called the
Lumberjack War (because of their brawls) or the Pork and Beans
War (because that was what the lumberjacks ate). There was also
the *Caroline* incident in late December 1837, which grew out of
the Canadian Rebellions, and its dangerous sequel, the MacLeod
trial in 1840–1, over which Great Britain threatened war. In the
west, the goals were very great, control of the Oregon Territory,

encompassing Oregon, Washington and British Columbia, and of the mouth of the Columbia River, the key to trade between North America and the Far East. A pendant to these conflicts was control of an island in Puget Sound, originating in the depredations of a boar, and leading to the Pig War of 1859. An epilogue many years later, the decision in 1903 setting out the border between Alaska and Canada, aroused political uproar in Canada over its final 'betrayal' by Great Britain.

For the British and the Canadians, much of their activity was defensive, as they tried to prevent the Americans from spilling over into the Canadian colonies to cut the timber and settle on the farmland. Indeed, the period following the Treaty of Ghent was the most active period of fort building in Canadian history.[3] It should, however, be noted that this 'trespassing' worked both ways, with Canadian timber men and farmers sometimes ignoring American claims to territory. In the Oregon Territory, what fundamentally decided the matter was a combination of American fecundity, the inability of the US to fight Great Britain and the British desire not to fight with the Americans. Britain wanted to keep what it considered its own but not to claim what it could not defend. As a seaborne empire, it had interests around the globe; the riches of Canada could not compare to the riches of India or China. On the other hand, the bombastic Americans should not be allowed to bellow their way into the acquisition of British territory.

It was a curious situation. The Americans wanted to surge into and take over Canadian territory, but did not possess, and refused to produce, the military force necessary to do so. Public opinion willed the end but not the means. In Britain, public opinion was not anti-American in the way that American public opinion was ferociously anti-British. There was disdain by some, and, yes, hatred or condescension by many, but there was support for the US from part of the population. Of course Britons backed their country when the Americans, time and time again, tried to muscle into British territory, but at other times they were indifferent to the US. They were curious, they sometimes felt a kinship for this wayward child of Great Britain, many appreciated the democratic ideals of the US, and, in short, they preferred not to fight it, not least because conflicts with the European Powers repeatedly threatened. Indeed, by the end of the nineteenth century, it was recognised by British political, naval and military decision-makers that it would be impossible, save by the devotion of unimaginably huge resources, to win a war with the US; in fact, it would be difficult even to put up a serious defence of Canada. Therefore, if the US could not fight, and the British preferred not to fight, there was only one way to solve the problems of the border, and that was to negotiate. This was not easy.

I

The British were always going to be at a disadvantage. First of all, there was time and distance when supplies or reinforcements were required; the US had merely to mobilise and march to the border. Secondly, there were major geographical obstacles. The rivers providing the lines of communication, supply and attack from the sea were frequently impassable, not least because from at least December to April they were frozen. In good weather, large vessels could travel from the sea up the St Lawrence River to Quebec and in favourable conditions on to Montreal. Thereafter, only flat-bottom craft could navigate the rapids of the upper St Lawrence – and then they reached Niagara Falls. In short, warships could not reach the Great Lakes from the sea, and the Lakes had to be held for both offensive and defensive purposes, a conviction shared by the Americans. The alternative of an overland route was not attractive: in the winter of 1813 it had taken a regiment based in New Brunswick nearly four weeks to march on snowshoes from Fredericton to Quebec, a crow-flying distance of some 200 miles.[4] Nevertheless, a military road would soon be considered vital. And thirdly, the main military force was made up of regulars, and the expense of stationing them in Canada was not insignificant. The difficulty was that a Canadian militia, undependable as well as relatively lightly trained, was not always a source of strength. Of course, American militias had not performed particularly well during the War of 1812, but they could be trained and they were close.

Because both countries believed that control of the Great Lakes was vital, both intended to maintain naval fleets on them. As already noted, ships for the Lakes had to be built on the Lakes, and from 1812 through 1814 there had been 'tremendous competition in naval construction'; at the end of the war, in fact, the two empires were engaged in a naval arms race, especially on Lake Ontario.[5] However, immediately after the end of the war, Congress bowed before a gust of economy. It completely wiped out the naval forces on the Lakes: President Madison was to sell or lay up all of the armed vessels except those necessary to enforce the revenue laws, and even those were to be, according to the enabling Act, 'divested of their armament, tackle and furniture, which are to be carefully preserved'.[6] Construction was also halted on all ships currently being built.

The British were rather more accustomed to financing the building of ships. Their strategy was to build forces on Lake Champlain, Lake Ontario and the upper Lakes, but even in Britain there was a reduction in spending – after more than twenty years of war, the British taxpayer insisted on a lightening of the burden. Even so, funds were provided by Parliament, in spite of these increasingly urgent calls for economy. The US Minister in London, John Quincy Adams, reported that the British government seemed to be determined not to cut but actually to increase the armaments on the Lakes.[7] The result would be an overwhelming British advantage that, it was feared, would leave the US vulnerable.

If the US was not going to build, the only alternative was to negotiate an agreement which would limit the British right to build and maintain a fleet on the Lakes. Accordingly, in November 1815, Secretary of State James Monroe raised the matter with the newly arrived British Minister to Washington, Charles Bagot.[8] He also instructed Adams to take up the matter in London, where he was to propose that the US and Britain come to 'such an arrangement respecting the naval forces to be kept on the Lakes by both governments, as will demonstrate their pacific policy and secure their peace'. His idea was to limit the number of ships on the Lakes, the smaller the better.[9] Adams called on Castlereagh on 25 January 1816 to open the discussions. In principle, Castlereagh was a strong proponent of peace between the two countries, writing that 'there are no two states whose friendly relations are of more practical value to each other, or whose hostility so inevitably and so immediately entails upon both the most serious mischiefs'.[10] However, he was also clear-eyed about the realities of power, having spent the year dealing with the Congress of Vienna, where European and international issues of great importance to Britain were being decided. Those points at issue between Britain and the US were of lesser importance. Adams proposed the reduction of armed vessels on the 'Canadian Lakes', because the US was alarmed by the increase in the number of British vessels since the peace. Castlereagh responded that it would be absurd to keep 'a number of vessels parading around the Lakes in time of peace'. Yet, he pointed out, Britain was the weaker power there, because if war was declared the US could just pounce, without Britain having the opportunity to build up its own armaments. However, he agreed to present the proposal to the Cabinet.[11] In short, Castlereagh recognised, as presumably did Madison and Monroe, that a power vacuum on the Lakes could only benefit the Americans.

Adams heard nothing further for six weeks, at which point, and not in the best of moods, he called on Castlereagh on 9 April. Here Castlereagh told him that the British government agreed to the American proposal, except for some vessels 'for conveying troops occasionally from one station to another'. Adams, however, told Castlereagh that he had no power to agree to any such proposal, and that it should be made directly to the US government in Washington by Bagot. In the meantime, building on the Lakes would halt.[12]

This was unlike Adams, who rather preferred to conduct negotiations himself. But he had been caught by surprise by Castlereagh's willingness to accept any reasonable American proposal, given that it would weaken Britain's ability to defend Canada; Secretary of State Monroe and President Madison fully shared his suspicions. Because Bagot did not receive Castlereagh's instructions until July, he had to put off serious negotiations; Madison then became more suspicious and threatened that, unless Britain gave up its rumoured building programme, which had in fact been pretty well suspended, Congress would almost certainly order new ships to be built – which Bagot must have realised was an empty threat. Even after Bagot's instructions arrived, suspicion continued; the British wanted a vague and somewhat ambiguous agreement while the Americans wanted to tie down the British with a formal one.[13]

Negotiations continued over the following two hot and humid months, during which Bagot nearly collapsed from the heat. The concerns expressed by Monroe to Bagot on 2 August related to the 'useless' expense of maintaining the two fleets and the multiple dangers of collisions between them. He therefore suggested that each side could have one vessel no larger than 100 tons and carrying one eighteen-pound cannon on Lake Ontario, one vessel of the same size on Lake Champlain and two further ones of the same type on the 'Upper' Lakes (lakes unspecified). All other armed vessels should be dismantled and no others built on the shores of those Lakes.[14] Bagot had no power to accept the proposals without referring them to London,[15] which, strangely, again aroused Monroe's suspicions; perhaps he thought that Bagot was merely evading and delaying. Bagot and Monroe had agreed that they would exchange information on the numbers and types of ships each maintained on the Lakes, and on 4 November Bagot provided this information.[16]

The whole process seemed all too dilatory to the Secretary of State. But the reason for the delay was simple: the members of the British Cabinet were all on holiday. In fact, it was not until January 1817 that Castlereagh, 'with embarrassed apologies',[17] forwarded the British government's agreement to the proposals. Three months later, on 28 April, Bagot and the acting head of the State Department, Richard Rush, exchanged 'Notes Relative to Naval Forces on the American Lakes',[18] that is, the Rush–Bagot Agreement, which embodied virtually unchanged the American proposals of 2 August. The US now engaged in dilatoriness, and it took another year for the Senate to approve it; President Monroe had delayed until 6 April 1818 before presenting it to the Senate for its approval, which was given the same month.

The Agreement had a chequered career. Indeed, the historian C. P. Stacey has pointed out that, during every period of active Anglo-American antagonism, both countries circumvented the Agreement. In 1838, after the Canadian Rebellions the previous year, the British commissioned gunboats to be built on the Lakes to protect Canada against the large-scale border-filibustering activities (invasions by a group from a country with which their own country is at peace) carried out by American sympathisers. In 1842–4, the Americans built on the upper Lakes the gunboat USS *Michigan*, the first iron ship in the US Navy, which remained ready for action for most of the century. During the Oregon crisis of the late 1840s, the British government assisted the private building of three steamers on condition that they could be used as warships.[19]

During the early years of the 1861–5 American Civil War, 'the Americans had had to take so many measures on the lakes that in September [1864] they ... admitted that the lakes agreement was in virtual suspense'.[20] The federal government then gave notice in late October that year to terminate the Agreement because it wanted to put ships on the Lakes in order to counter Confederate raids, a desire triggered by the so-called St Albans Raid of 19 October 1864. During this episode, a number of Confederate soldiers, who had escaped from Unionist prisons and made their way to Canada, crossed the border into Vermont, and at St Albans robbed several banks to provide funds for the Confederacy. The British worried about their own neutrality and the Americans about the threat from the north.

However, on 8 March 1865, William Seward, the Secretary of State, wrote to the British government to say that the US was not, after all, going to terminate the Rush–Bagot Agreement, but was 'quite willing that the convention should remain practically in force'. Yet in September came reports from the British naval attaché in Washington that the Americans were still putting so-called 'revenue' vessels on the Lakes in violation of the 1817

Agreement. There was not much that the British and Canadians could do about this, given that the British government did not want to spend the money to build a navy on the Lakes.[21] In 1892 pressure from American shipbuilding interests on the shores of the Lakes made the question of terminating the Agreement a live political issue in the US. However, when the US government learned of the Canadian opposition to termination, the proposal was quietly dropped. In 1906 the Americans again raised the question of modifying the Agreement, 'but after a discouraging response [from the Canadians, it] had been allowed to sleep once more'.[22] Yet the Americans continued to move ships between the Lakes and the sea, as they had done since 1890. The Canadian government disliked this, but it reluctantly acquiesced for fear that the US would then give notice to terminate the Agreement. The Canadians, as always, preferred to have some sort of barrier between their country and American power, be it ever so insubstantial.

What can be said about the Agreement is that while relative military stability on the Lakes did not lead to improved Anglo-American relations, it did remove a flashpoint, in that for nearly seventy years both countries felt some constraint about putting armed ships on the Lakes. This saved a huge amount of money for both countries as well as, most likely, preventing incidents which would have threatened such amicability as there was between the two.

II

Armaments on the Lakes had been perceived as a direct threat by both sides, but there was another problem pregnant with future difficulties. This was the border from just west of the Lake of the Woods, north of today's Minnesota, to the Pacific. The problem was that, for more than a thousand miles, there was no boundary at all between what became the provinces of Manitoba, Saskatchewan, Alberta and British Columbia and the future states of North Dakota, Montana, Idaho and Washington. This

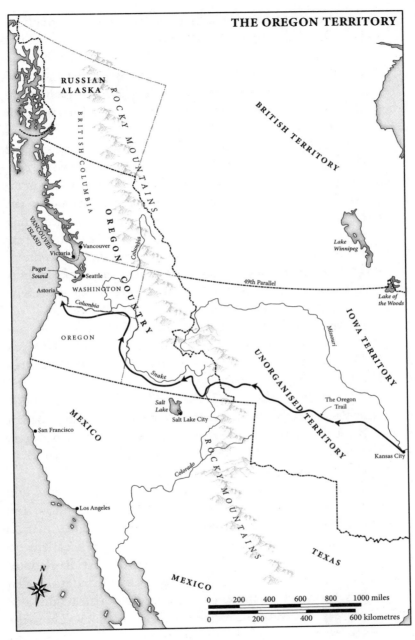

THE OREGON TERRITORY

RUSSIAN ALASKA

BRITISH TERRITORY

ROCKY MOUNTAINS

BRITISH COLUMBIA

OREGON COUNTRY

VANCOUVER ISLAND

Victoria
Vancouver
Columbia
Puget Sound
Seattle
Astoria
WASHINGTON
Columbia
OREGON

Lake Winnipeg

49th Parallel

Lake of the Woods

IOWA TERRITORY

Missouri

Snake

UNORGANISED TERRITORY

The Oregon Trail

Salt Lake
Salt Lake City

MEXICO

San Francisco

ROCKY MOUNTAINS

Colorado

Kansas City

Los Angeles

TEXAS

MEXICO

N

| 0 | 200 | 400 | 600 | 800 | 1000 miles |

| 0 | 200 | 400 | 600 kilometres |

MAP 4

opened up the whole area to conflicting claims and violence, and, beyond the local destruction and distress, the countries them- selves might be drawn into war. This was particularly the case at the western end in the Oregon country (comprising today's Oregon and Washington states and most of British Columbia), where Britain did not recognise any American claims and was determined to push the Americans south of the Columbia River, and where the Americans were just as determined to expand. The issue was complicated by being intertwined with con- tinuing American complaints and claims over the fisheries in the north-east, the question of compensation for slaves taken and freed during the Revolution, negotiations over a commercial treaty, control of a small settlement, Astoria, at the mouth of the Columbia River, American anger at the continuing British claims of the right to impress seamen, and American claims of a right to trade with British colonies.[23] All of these were issues dealt with in the negotiations leading to the Convention of 1818. Yet it was a messy beginning, given rampant American nationalism and suspicion of Great Britain, the need for Castlereagh to give pri- ority to European affairs, and – as the list above makes clear – a complicated meshing of topics.

The issue at hand, however, is the border. On 3 January 1818, after the Rush–Bagot Agreement had been signed but before it had been ratified by the Senate, the American Minister to London, Richard Rush, handed to Castlereagh a set of proposals for negotiation. Rush was as anti-British as the next American, but he did not feel the need to proclaim it publicly, nor would it have been a terribly useful piece of baggage in London, and he and Castlereagh worked together well enough. They met on 1 February and touched on all of the topics, but Castlereagh then had to concentrate on European matters. As Rush later wrote, 'He had the whole European relations of Britain at that time in his hands, with those of the continent also to discuss' (the Congress of Aix-la-Chapelle was imminent). Thus the Foreign Secretary turned the negotiations over to others.[24] In July, President Monroe, wishing to strengthen the American negotiating team, instructed Albert Gallatin, Minister to France, to join Rush in London. On 27 August, negotiations began in earnest.[25]

Rush spoke truly when he later wrote of the negotiations that 'the subjects were multifarious. All demanded attention; some, copious discussions. These, with the documents at large, the protocols, the projets and counter-projets, debated and modified by the scrutiny of each side, would present a mass of matter through which the diplomatist or politician might perhaps wade; but be little attractive to anyone else.' Suffice it to say, then, that 'neither side yielded its convictions to the reasoning of the other. This being exhausted, there was no resource left with nations disposed to peace, but a compromise,' and on 20 October 1818 Rush and Gallatin transmitted to John Quincy Adams, now Secretary of State, the text of the Convention which they had that day concluded with the British negotiators.[26]

The negotiators agreed to extend a commercial convention of 1815 regulating Anglo-American trade and to make a temporary settlement of the fisheries question; they also agreed compensation for the slaves and an arrangement over the Columbia River. The most important decision, however, was to draw the Canadian–American boundary from the Lake of the Woods to the 'Stony Mountains' (the Rockies) along the 49th parallel. At the outset, Gallatin had made a suggestion of major importance: to delimit the claims of both the US and Great Britain to the Oregon Country by drawing the border along the 49th parallel all the way to the Pacific. The British refused, since they would lose the southern tip of Vancouver Island and Puget Sound; the result was an agreement on joint occupation for ten years. The American offer could be seen as extraordinary, because it would limit American claims, but there are two possible explanations: the first is that a number of Americans, including President Monroe, anticipated that the Oregon Country would constitute an independent republic, since it was so distant from the US, and arguing over a border was therefore not worth the effort; the second was the assumption that American settlers would in due course flow into the area and therefore, as Rush put it, 'time is, for the United States, the best negotiator'.[27]

III

It was clear in 1815 that the most urgent problem needing to be settled after the end of the War of 1812 was to establish a boundary between the US and British North America, with the most difficult issues being those which dealt with the border east of the Lake in the Woods to the Atlantic Ocean. There had been two wars between the US and Great Britain in the previous forty years, and the colonies of British North America had been caught up in both; on the face of it, there was little to prevent a third. Indeed, on at least one occasion war seemed likely to break out. Certainly an agreed border did not prevent a number of attempts by Americans to take Canadian territory for themselves. The situation was complicated by the combination of a weak US federal government and fevered claims of states' rights, a conflict which would be resolved only by the outcome of the Civil War. In the meantime, Maine in particular was repeatedly a pain to both the US government and Great Britain for nearly thirty years, until the signing of the Webster–Ashburton Treaty in 1842.

Articles IV through VII of the Treaty of Ghent set out the issues to be resolved. Article IV dealt with the ownership of the islands in Passamaquoddy Bay; Article V dealt with the north-east; Article VI covered the point from the head of the Connecticut River to Lake Superior; and Article VII completed the boundary from Lake Superior to the Lake in the Woods. The boundary from the Lake in the Woods to the Rockies had been settled in 1818, and that from the Rockies to the Pacific Ocean was left to the future. The War of 1812 was in everyone's mind, and bits of land or the shore of a river or a lake could provide a strategic advantage to the occupier. There were to be independent commissions for each of the first two Articles, while a third was to deal with both Articles VI and VII. The British government appointed as Commissioners Thomas Barclay for Articles IV and V and John Ogilvy for the latter two. The US appointed John Holmes for Article IV, Cornelius P. Van Ness for Article V and Peter B. Porter for the latter two. The idea was for work on the

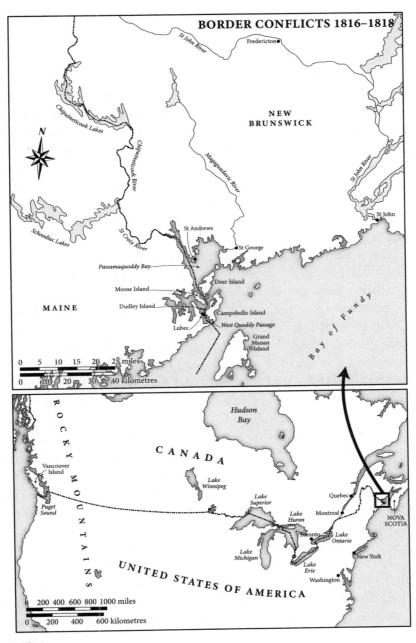

BORDER CONFLICTS 1816–1818

St John River

Fredericton

NEW
BRUNSWICK

Chiputneticook Lakes

Chiputneticook River

Magaguadavic River

St John River

St John

Schoodiac Lakes

St Croix River

St Andrews

St George

Passamaquoddy Bay

MAINE

Deer Island

Moose Island

Dudley Island

Campobello Island

Lubec

West Quoddy Passage

Grand
Manan
Island

Bay of Fundy

0   5   10   15   20   25 miles

0   10   20   30   40 kilometres

ROCKY MOUNTAINS

Hudson
Bay

CANADA

Vancouver
Island

Lake
Winnipeg

Puget
Sound

Lake
Superior

Quebec

Montreal

Lake
Huron

Toronto

Lake
Ontario

NOVA
SCOTIA

Lake
Michigan

Lake
Erie

New York

UNITED STATES OF AMERICA

Washington

0   200 400 600 800 1000 miles

0   200   400   600 kilometres

MAP 5

first three Articles to begin immediately, followed by the last as soon as possible.

This was one of the earliest examples of the use of arbitration, rather than fighting or direct negotiations, to settle problems. Using arbitration, of course, was a good thing, but the choice of a joint commission as the means was an invitation to later political or diplomatic conflict. The joint commissions were made up of two Commissioners, one from each side; if they could not agree, the matter would be referred to a 'friendly Sovereign or State', according to the Treaty of Ghent, who would act as an umpire and whose decision would be final. This attempt to preclude any future disagreement would prove to be a less than adequate solution.

The pressure on land beyond the borders was strongest in the north-east. Article I of the treaty had determined that all lands in possession of the two sides would be restored to their original owners, with the exception of the islands in Passamaquoddy Bay. These were claimed by both sides but occupied by British forces during the war, and they were to remain in British hands until the boundary was decided and the treaty enforced. They were the subject of Article IV of the treaty and provided the first problem to be tackled.

The two Commissioners, Colonel Thomas Barclay for Great Britain and John Holmes for the US, met at St Andrews, New Brunswick on 23 September 1816. Barclay had been a prominent Loyalist during the Revolutionary War who had elected to remain in North America rather than move to Great Britain. In due course he became Speaker of the Nova Scotia assembly and then British Consul in New York. His children had married into powerful families on both sides of the Atlantic. He had been officially engaged in the Maine–New Brunswick boundary question since the St Croix Commission in 1796 (see pp. 34–42). He was aided by Ward Chipman, who as Agent was in charge of the gathering of the evidence to support the British claims. Chipman was also a prominent Loyalist, in his case from Massachusetts, a brilliant student at Harvard and a founder of New Brunswick. Even more important was the fact that he had been the 'masterful'

British Agent for the St Croix Commission 'whose researches determined the outcome'.[28]

John Holmes at age forty-three was considerably younger than Barclay. He had been admitted to the Massachusetts bar in 1799 and was active in local politics in the Maine District of Massachusetts. His election to Congress in 1816 might well have undermined his concurrent position as Commissioner.[29] In 1820 he would play a significant role in the establishment of Maine as a separate state. James T. Austin, the Agent who would head the American team, was only thirty-two. He had been admitted to the Massachusetts bar in 1805. It was possibly not unimportant that in 1806 he had married the daughter of the prominent Federalist Elbridge Gerry (of gerrymandering fame). Austin sat in the state legislature from 1812 to 1832. He and Holmes were both able men, but they were inexperienced when compared to the British team.

On the face of it, the issue was uncomplicated: to determine the boundary from the mouth of the agreed-upon St Croix River out through Passamaquoddy Bay into the open waters of the Bay of Fundy. (At least the terrain was known and no one had to hack his way through a forest.) The American claim was to all of the islands in Passamaquoddy Bay plus the island of Grand Manan in the Bay of Fundy, which was off the coast of Maine. The British claim was that all of the islands in the bay had traditionally been part of Nova Scotia, and had not passed to the US in the Treaty of Paris in 1783; they would argue in particular for Grand Manan Island, which had a large Loyalist presence and was considered by the British to be part of New Brunswick. Yet 'By their position and means of communication with the mainland, these islands are all naturally within the territory of the United States; but the controversy in 1816 did not at all relate to what ought to be their ownership. The dispute was the purely legal one'[30] as to whether these islands, or any of them, came within the exceptions mentioned in the Treaty of 1783. The treaty stated that all of the islands south of the River St Croix and along the coast of the US were to belong to the US, 'excepting such islands as are now, or heretofore have been, within the limits of the said provinces of Nova Scotia'. However, Barclay warned Castlereagh that, while there was a good claim to the Passamaquoddy islands, 'I am apprehensive it will be difficult ... to support with equal evidence His Majesty's claim to the Island of Grand Manan in the Bay of Fundy, an island of far more national importance than any of the others.'[31] A 1621 charter referred to the circumference of the island, but the 1763 boundary of Nova Scotia as described in that charter went only to the northern shore of Grand Manan, barely touching it, and thereby neglecting to include a reference to the inclusive 'circumference' of the earlier charter. This weakened the claim of the British and became the legal basis of the American claim, on the grounds that the omission of 'circumference' had been deliberate.[32] A daring manoeuvre by Barclay would save it for the King.

The Board of Commissioners met on 3 June 1817 for several days, looked at all of the evidence submitted, questioned the Agents and requested that the Agents submit their responses for a meeting on 25 September. Barclay was worried, confiding to Castlereagh midway through the June meetings his fear that agreement could not be reached on the islands, and telling him that he had 'encouraged' Chipman to introduce certain documents before the Board, 'founded more on the effect it may produce on the mind of the friendly Power to whom the case may be referred ... than on the weight they would carry with the Commissioners in the present stage of the discussion'.[33]

Barclay did not, in fact, want the question to go to arbitration for fear that Grand Manan Island would either be split or awarded in its entirety to the US. He wrote eloquently to Castlereagh in late October that if it went to the decision of the friendly Power it would be 'a matter of doubt, to whom it would decide the island of Grand Manan to belong – that this Island is of more value to His Majesty, in point of Territory, than all the Islands in the Bay of Passamaquoddy; and, in a military and naval point of view, of much greater importance in that it commands the North West side of the Bay of Fundy, is immediately opposite that part of the American Coast where the waters, which pass into and out of the Bay of Passamaquoddy, at a place called West Quoddy Passage, and – that His Majesty, by being possessed of this Island, would have it in his power, in the event of a war, to prevent American Privateers from sheltering themselves in that Passage, and to protect the Province of New Brunswick and that part of Nova Scotia which lies in the Bay of Fundy' – the Sovereign's decision could seriously damage Britain's strategic interests only three years after the end of the war.[34]

On the American side, Austin similarly wrote to Adams that it was unlikely that the Commissioners would agree, and asked for another session of the Board to be arranged 'so that he could reply to the British case, largely for the presumed benefit of an arbitrator'.[35] After an exhaustive debate, the two Agents asked for time to gather new evidence and prepare new arguments to be presented in the spring of 1818.

Barclay now decided to indulge in a little brinkmanship. Holmes did not want the decision to be put off, because if the decision was not taken by 1 December he would have to resign either his position as Commissioner or his newly won seat in Congress. Furthermore, if he did resign his commission before the decisions were taken, a new US commissioner would have to be appointed and the whole thing would have to be re-argued. In that case, Barclay feared, any new commissioner would not 'possess the Candor and Discrimination I had in every instance experienced in this Gentleman'.[36] Barclay told Holmes that he had made his decision, but that he would not like to deny the Agents their request, which angered Holmes. The two met in private on 6 October and Barclay presented what he called an ultimatum. Great Britain would give up all claims to Moose, Dudley and Frederick Islands in Passamaquoddy Bay in exchange for the US giving up claims to the other islands and to Grand Manan. Moose, Dudley and Frederick had little value for New Brunswick, and Moose had been settled by Americans, while Grand Manan, Barclay averred, was of great importance to Britain and had recently been settled by Loyalists. Holmes 'appeared astonished' that the British even thought of making a serious claim to Great Manan, but Barclay told him that either he agreed to the offer or the matter would go to arbitration. 'I told him, he had my ultimatum,' Barclay wrote to Castlereagh, 'an ultimatum I had brought myself with much

difficulty to offer.'[37] It took Holmes until 9 October to agree to
Barclay's offer. On 30 June 1818, the transfer of Moose, Dudley
and Frederick Islands to the US took place – Moose Island was
already inhabited by Americans and Dudley and Frederick Island
were, according to Barclay, small and useless rocks[38] – while New
Brunswick kept Deer, Campobello and Grand Manan Islands.

The British hardly bestirred themselves to turn over to the
Americans the territory which had been deemed theirs. Months
later, the American Minister in London found it necessary to point
out to Castlereagh that no authority appeared to have been given 'to
the British minister in Washington, [or to] the governor general of
Canada, or [to] any other officer of this government in America' to
put the decision into effect. Therefore, the American government
earnestly requested that the British government issue 'orders to
the commanding officer on Moose Island to deliver up possession'
to the Americans.[39] Diplomatic language can be a wonderful
mask for emotions.

                                IV

Meanwhile, Article VI was being tackled. This required the
surveying of the area from the St Lawrence River to the end of the
furthest west of the Great Lakes, Lake Superior. This was a huge
amount of virtually unknown territory a thousand miles long,
covering lakes, rivers and forests. It was also an area of strong
contention, because French and British Canadian fur trappers had
been a dominant presence there. Indeed, the British alliances with
the Native peoples in that area had been a trigger for the War of
1812. The Americans' hold on their territory was very fragile, in
spite of sporadic attention by fur traders and the US Army. The
surveying alone would take four seasons, from 1817 to 1820.[40]

The British and American Commissioners were appointed for
the work on both Articles VI and VII, to provide some continuity
of experience. (Article VII covered the line from the end of Lake
Superior to the Lake of the Woods.) The British had appointed
John Ogilvy. Born in Scotland, he had emigrated to Canada in

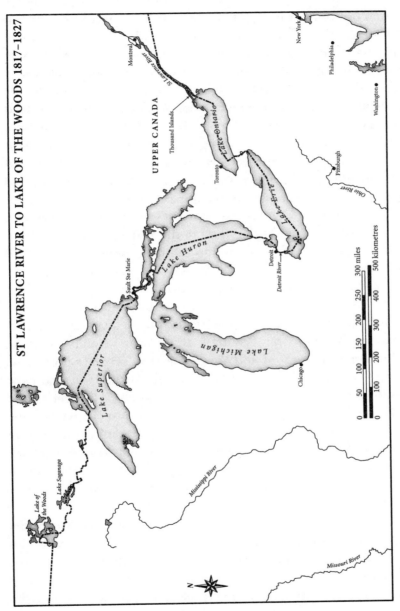

ST LAWRENCE RIVER TO LAKE OF THE WOODS 1817–1827

MAP 6

1790 at the age of twenty-one, becoming involved in the fur trade. Six years later, he became a partner in a firm which earned great profits not only in the fur trade, but in the transatlantic carriage of both goods and passengers. 'The fur trade was in a very turbulent and competitive state'[41] north and west of the Great Lakes, and Ogilvy and his firm began trading goods south and west of Lake Michigan in American territory. In 1814, a wealthy man, he sold out his interests in the fur trade. By all accounts, he was both a shrewd businessman and a conciliator. He was also a hands-on participant during the surveying, going out in a bark canoe himself daily to check on the work. It seems clear that the British were fortunate in having as their Commissioner a man with such experience in the fur trade in the upper Lakes.[42]

The American Commissioner was General Peter B. Porter, a member of the New York militia in the War of 1812. A native of Connecticut, he had gone to Yale and then moved to New York as a lawyer, settling in Black Rock (now part of Buffalo). He had ended the war as a major-general, later being elected to Congress, from which he resigned to become Commissioner. Dr John J. Bigsby, the British Secretary and medical officer for the Boundary Commission dealing with Articles VI and VII, wrote in his memoir, *The Shoe and the Canoe*, that 'on one occasion, we went to a pleasant dinner at Black-Rock, at the large and commodious house of the American Commissioner ... the very house which was sacked a few years before by the 41st British Infantry [300 regulars and forty militia]. The soldiers fell principally on the larder and cellar, and were not disappointed, as an eye-witness informed me. Although a grievous act of barbarity, the affluent American general could speak on the subject with the greatest good-humour.'[43]

Each team included three surveyors, including a trigonometric surveyor. Surveying parties set to work immediately, travelling by boat and canoe and sleeping in tents, although there was still snow in mid-May. And it was not just land and large lakes which were due to be surveyed; there was also, for example, the intricate task of mapping the Thousand Islands of the upper St Lawrence. The specialist nature of this work on such difficult terrain required the leadership of surveyors of some quality. Relatively little seems to be known about David P. Adams, the principal American surveyor, other than that he was competent.[44] On the other hand, the British surveyor, David Thompson, was a man of some reputation. Born in poverty in London in 1770, he went to the Grey Coats charity school in Westminster, where he received some education in mathematics. Apprenticed to the Hudson's Bay Company at the age of fourteen, he was sent out to Manitoba, where he trained as an astronomical surveyor. During his years in the fur trade, he explored and mapped western Canada and the northern US from Lake Superior to the Pacific, and by the time he settled in Quebec in 1811 he had completed the most accurate map in existence of that territory.[45] David Adams was to describe him as 'a gentleman, whom for his rectitude of heart, honesty of disposition, integrity of character and abilities in his profession, I shall ever hold in the highest estimation'.[46] Sadly, Thompson was to die in poverty.

When groups of hearty men, separated from family, spend years in the wilderness, sexual tension, dissension and illness can, and did, strike. To deal with the first, men sometimes took what were known as 'country wives': a fur trader, for example, would take a Native woman as a common-law wife. David Thompson had done so (he and his wife later married and were together until his death in 1857).[47] As for the second, there was certainly recurrent dissension within the American team.[48] The Agent, Colonel Samuel Hawkins, believed that he had responsibilities and powers which the Commissioner, Porter, believed belonged to himself. President Madison decided in Porter's favour, and Hawkins soon left.[49] He was replaced by Major Joseph Delafield. Born in New York in 1790, he was a lawyer; he had fought in the War of 1812, ending the war a major. He had joined the Commission in 1817; in 1820 Porter wrote to John Quincy Adams that he was 'gratified in having ... the assistance of Major Delafield, whose intelligence, habits of business, and correct deportment have rendered him very useful'. He was clearly a welcome relief to Porter after the hostility between Hawkins and himself. In May 1820, Adams appointed Delafield Acting Agent.[50] Later there was increasing conflict between David Adams and his assistant, William Darby; in the end, Porter fired Darby.[51]

The British team apparently worked together rather more amicably, but both saw men coming and going. Bigsby wrote, for example, that

> [s]everal of the surveyors, although in high spirits at first with their good salaries and new mode of life, soon left us, subdued by toil and exposure. I have in my eye now one gentleman of considerable energy, sitting by the half hour on a bare rock in the sun, wiping his perspiring face, and in angry contention with a cloud of mosquitoes. He soon went away. Another resigned because work was begun at four o'clock in the morning, or, as he called it, in the middle of the night.[52]

As for illness, Lake Erie proved to be a killer. The marshes at the west end of the lake were the source of a 'bilious fever', which was probably malaria. The surveying of Lake Erie was to be carried out in the same manner as that of Lake Ontario, with the parties working separately on both sides of the lake, and everyone in both parties fell ill. It was the British party which suffered the worst calamity, the death of Ogilvy after a fortnight's illness, and of two others. According to Porter, writing to John Quincy Adams on 30 September 1819, 'There is now in the British camp, but one Surveyor and one man fit for duty, and the condition of our own is but little better.'[53] Most fell ill the following year as well, but at least no one died.

Who was to succeed Ogilvy? His death was very disruptive, given that there had already been numerous changes of personnel as a result of sacking or resignation. In October 1819, Colonel Barclay proposed his youngest son Anthony, and in January 1820 Anthony was duly appointed by Castlereagh.[54] Born in 1792, he had been appointed Secretary to the Article IV Commission in 1816 (whose work was now completed), and was therefore very experienced (no one then particularly worried about nepotism). Indeed, a colleague praised his 'great diligence, ability, and firmness of purpose', and said that 'he of all men was enabled, by previous education and quiet amenity of manner, to cope with the eager and exacting temper of American diplomatists, and to make good the right thing'.[55] He took over the position in June 1820.

Work progressed reasonably efficiently, and Barclay expected that the survey of this part of the boundary would be completed in the following season. He did, however, point out to Castlereagh that '[t]he whole Country above alluded to is but little inhabited, very rough, and wild, being still for the most part in its pristine state: consequently it presents every obstacle which can be encountered, with little means of subduing any.'[56] Late in the summer, both parties were surveying Lake Huron; by that time, the only man left who could take astronomical readings accurately was the Briton David Thompson, and he carried this out for both the British and the Americans (according to Delafield, some of the Americans were occasionally a touch suspicious of his impartiality). The weather, however, continued to be a challenge: often calm in the mornings, by noon winds were very strong and changeable. The food, sadly, was unchanging – primarily pork and bread and whiskey – and the mosquitoes were always there.[57]

By September 1821 the work was pretty well completed, with the data compiled by November. The Commissioners met in New York City on 12 November, and consulted together for almost four weeks, arguing over the boundary and the ownership of the islands. Four informal guidelines shaped their decisions: 1) the boundary would always be a water line and would not divide any islands; 2) where there were several channels, the most navigable would be the line; 3) where there were several navigable channels, the line would follow the largest body of water; and 4) where there were several channels, the line closest to the centre of the waterway would be chosen, provided that good navigation was left to both parties. Land hardly figured in the calculations. Following these sensible guidelines, they reached agreement on most of the boundary from the St Lawrence through Lakes Ontario, Erie and Huron, all the way to the Sault Ste Marie. Unfortunately, they came to an impasse over three wholly insignificant islands in the Detroit River. In the end, the British, with conditions, ceded the ownership of the islands to the Americans.[58]

V

Article VII focused on the border from Lake Superior to the Lake of the Woods. There were no illusions about the difficulty of the task: Bigsby wrote to Barclay in June 1823 that the land west of Lake Superior was 'sterility itself, an assemblage of rocky mounds, with small intervals of marsh'; as for the weather, at the end of June, there were still small blocks of ice on the lake, not to mention fog and storms. Porter was no more sanguine, describing it to John Quincy Adams in February 1822 as 'a totally wild & uninhabited country, affording no means for the comfort or even subsistence of persons engaged in this service and a climate so cold and unhospitable that a small portion only of the year can be employed in active duties'.[59] Thompson remained the British surveyor; at fifty-two, he was more than twice the age of the newly appointed principal US surveyor, the twenty-four-year-old James Ferguson, and infinitely more experienced. (The question must arise: why did the Americans keep appointing such young and relatively inexperienced men to such responsible positions?)

Thompson and his group made good progress in the wilderness, which one member of the party ascribed to his habit of 'dealing fairly with Native people' – Thompson did, of course, have a Native wife. When they 'came upon some Indians occupying a quiet cove', Thompson knew that it would have been offensive to pass them by without notice, and so they landed and 'exchanged the pipe of peace. Our astronomer [Thompson], well accustomed to the manners of the Indians, always made a point of treating them with that punctilious decorum they so much love.'[60] He also, according to the same member, showed concern for the morals and souls of his men, who apparently trusted his knowledge and experience of the wilderness. He 'was a firm [Protestant] churchman; while most of our men were Roman Catholics. Many a time have I seen these uneducated Canadians most attentively and thankfully listen, as they sat upon some bank of shingle, to Mr. Thompson, while he read to them in most extraordinarily pronounced French, three chapters out of the Old Testament, and as many out of the New, adding such explanations as seemed to him suitable.'[61] Perhaps they were indeed religious; perhaps they appreciated the change from work.

During the summer of 1822, the American party surveyed and mapped along the lakes and rivers as far west as Lake Saganaga (in which were counted 289 islands). To their surprise, they discovered that 'the water route west from Lake Superior was not simply a single river but extended from lake to lake, connected by impassable waterfalls and rapids',[62] which required repeated stops and trudges by land (called land portages) until the next useful stretch of water. By the autumn, Delafield felt able to report to the Secretary of State that they had identified a good portion of the boundary and he was sanguine about its acceptance by the British.[63] This was not to be the case.

By the autumn of 1824, the British government was increasingly worried that Britain's interests would be severely damaged by what was emerging as the possibly correct boundary. It staved off a decision by insisting on a resurvey of the Lake of the Woods, but, except to the British, the result was not conclusive. By 1827, the decision on the boundary had still not been taken, and Barclay was instructed by the Foreign Office in January 1827 that, if the Americans did not agree to a compromise which he had proposed to them, he should close the Commission, and the British government would refer the matter to the arbitrating State or Sovereign to decide.[64]

The ability of the British government to consider anything so distant as the Canadian–American boundary was overwhelmed that year by a series of political crises. In February, the Prime Minister, Lord Liverpool, suffered a serious stroke; his successor, the Foreign Secretary George Canning, died in August, his succession having split the Tory party. Lord Goderich became Prime Minister; his Cabinet soon fell apart and he was succeeded in January 1828 by the Duke of Wellington. Nor had things been particularly calm in the US for several years. The presidential election of 1824 had four candidates. John Quincy Adams took office as President in March 1825, but he had won neither the popular nor the electoral vote. (Adams had 114,023 popular votes and eighty-four electoral votes; Jackson had 152,901 popular votes and ninety-nine electoral votes, while Crawford and Clay, the other two candidates, together garnered seventy-eight electoral votes. Since no one had a majority in the Electoral College, the decision was thrown over to the House of Representatives.) The man Adams defeated, Andrew Jackson, together with Martin Van Buren (both future presidents) and the Vice-President, John C. Calhoun, pulled together most of the opposition into the new Democratic Party and worked to destroy the administration's ability to accomplish anything, an exercise in which they were impressively successful. When Adams' ham-fisted attempt to force Great Britain to allow American trade with its colonies resulted in the suspension of all trade between the British West Indies and the US after the spring of 1827, any possibility of compromise between the US and Britain was destroyed. The issue would be resolved only by the negotiations leading to the Webster–Ashburton Treaty of 1842.

VI

The duty of the Commissioners dealing with Article V, the Article which caused by far the most conflict between the two countries, was to determine the north-eastern boundary from the Bay of Fundy to the St Lawrence River: this encompassed a line from the source of the St Croix River all along the contested Maine–New Brunswick–Lower Canada border to the point where the 45th parallel met the St Lawrence River. The Commissioners were Barclay for the British, with Ward Chipman and Ward Chipman Jr as his Agents, and Cornelius P. Van Ness of Vermont for the Americans, with William C. Bradley as his Agent. Both of the Americans were only thirty-four, again a generation younger than Barclay and Chipman. Van Ness had been born into a prominent Dutch family in New York; his father had been a general in the War of Independence. He was called to the bar in 1803, but left for Vermont in 1806, where he later became a US district attorney and later still a collector of customs. 'He cultivated good

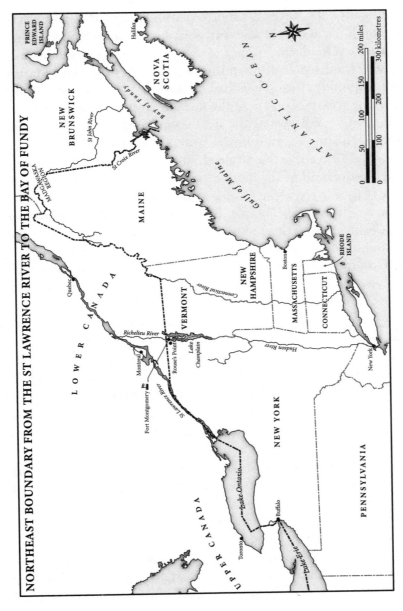

NORTHEAST BOUNDARY FROM THE ST LAWRENCE RIVER TO THE BAY OF FUNDY

PRINCE EDWARD ISLAND

Halifax

NOVA SCOTIA

NEW BRUNSWICK

St John River

MADAWASKA REGION

St Croix River

MAINE

Quebec

L O W E R   C A N A D A

Richelieu River

Montreal

Fort Montgomery

St Lawrence River

Rouse's Point

Lake Champlain

VERMONT

Connecticut River

NEW HAMPSHIRE

MASSACHUSETTS

Boston

RHODE ISLAND

CONNECTICUT

Hudson River

New York

NEW YORK

Lake Ontario

Toronto

Buffalo

Lake Erie

U P P E R   C A N A D A

PENNSYLVANIA

ATLANTIC OCEAN

Gulf of Maine

Bay of Fundy

N

0   50   100   150   200 miles

0   100   200   300 kilometres

MAP 7

relations with the Madison administration, and his appointment as commissioner arose from that connection.' Bradley, a lawyer and linguist – he knew French, German, Latin, Greek, Hebrew and Arabic – and twice a member of Congress, was also appointed by President Madison.[65]

Their task was infinitely more difficult than sorting out Passamaquoddy Bay. They had to identify five landmarks set out in the treaty of 1783: 1) the due-north line from the source of the St Croix River; 2) the north-west angle of Nova Scotia; 3) the highlands separating the waters that flowed into the St Lawrence from those that drained into the Atlantic; 4) the north-westernmost head of the Connecticut River; and 5) the 45th parallel of latitude from the Connecticut River to the St Lawrence. From the beginning, Thomas Barclay doubted that it would be possible to agree on the north-west angle of Nova Scotia or on the position of the head of the Connecticut River.[66] (He was correct.) The Commissioners' task was extremely complicated: exploring, surveying and mapping the terrain took four seasons from 1817 to 1820, a tedious portion of it carried out in pouring rain. But it was vital, because otherwise it would be impossible to determine just what territory was being discussed. The task was made almost impossible by Maine. It had become a state only in 1820, and the politicians, newspapermen and 'ordinary' people fought tenaciously to keep all of the territory which they considered to be their own, whether or not it was also claimed by Great Britain. It would, in fact, take a quarter of a century before agreement on this section of the border was reached.

The Americans assumed that the due-north line from the mouth of the St Croix River extended beyond the St John River to the brow of the St Lawrence, which would give them possession of the 26,000 square miles of the upper St John Valley, basing this on maps published in London in the 1790s. This alarmed Barclay, who wrote to Castlereagh in May 1818 that any American claim north of the St John River would cut off communication between the provinces of Nova Scotia and New Brunswick on the one hand and Upper and Lower Canada on the other, a situation which had not been intended by the 1783 treaty. This was important to the

British, because of the requirement for the road to enable troops to be sent to the interior from Halifax if necessary.[67] By the end of the 1818 surveying season, there was growing dissension between the British and American surveyors about how the topography of the area at issue agreed with the treaty. The summer surveying of 1820 would be the last chance to find each side's topographical evidence, not least because Congress was increasingly objecting to the expense of the whole enterprise.[68]

A real problem which developed over the three years was the gradual disappearance of amicable relations between the British and American Commissioners and Agents. At one point, someone (unspecified) stole the papers and equipment of a surveying team. Tensions were heightened when Americans moved into the disputed but British-claimed region of Madawaska and proclaimed it American territory.[69]

Near the end of the 1820 surveying season, an issue promising real diplomatic conflict arose. The two surveying parties reached the area called Rouse's Point on Lake Champlain. This is at the northern end of the lake, where the body of water narrows and from which the Richelieu River flows north towards Montreal. These narrows formed a strategic area, because whoever had military control could control the passage of men and boats north or south on the lake – an issue of importance given that the War of 1812 had ended only four years before. The US government had built a stone fort, Fort Montgomery, on one side after the war and was building a second one. It was therefore with some amazement and even disbelief that the British and American surveyors discovered that both of them placed the 45th latitude over 3,000 feet further south of the line earlier assumed to be correct. This meant that the two US forts were well within Canadian territory. To say the least, this would complicate matters.

Another important issue which encouraged emotion on both sides was the north-westernmost head of the Connecticut River, because it would form the boundary between Lower Canada and New Hampshire and because of the aforementioned timberland. During the last war, a great deal of amicable smuggling between the two sides had taken place, but after the war nationalist emotions hardened on both sides and there was considerable tension in the area. Surveying it was also a challenge. For the British, by mid-November 1820 'supplies were running out, and the party was forced to make tea out of the bark of grey birches; [the surveyor] had run out of paper and was keeping his journal on strips of birch-bark'.[70] Most of the necessary surveying was finished during the 1820 season. The Board of Commissioners met the following August, and it rapidly became obvious that there would be no agreement: the differences were too great. If a boundary line could not be agreed, the issue would have to be left to the arbitration of a friendly sovereign. The British suspected that, rather than go to arbitration, the Americans would propose that a new treaty should be negotiated covering the boundary from the St Croix River to the north and west of the St Lawrence. Both Barclay and Stratford Canning, Bagot's successor as Minister to Washington, wrote to alert the British government.[71]

They were correct. Adams wrote to Rush in London instructing him to propose such negotiations, because it would be difficult to find a sovereign in which both governments could 'repose equal confidence'.[72] Barclay had an alternative, and plausible, explanation. The issue of the north-eastern boundary affected the vital interests of five states, Maine, New Hampshire, Vermont, New York and Massachusetts (which had claim to a portion of the 'wild lands' in Maine). No state would agree to give up any territory it considered to be its own, and thus, '[t]here is not the slightest chance of any new commission or negotiation coming to a more satisfactory result than the present with regard to the rights in dispute, and the very nature of the political institutions of the United States seems to forbid a compromise of territorial rights. Any attempt at negotiation, therefore which is not to end in yielding the territorial claims of the States interested in the different parts of the Boundary would appear to be vain and illusory.'[73]

Furthermore, '[a] great deal might also be said as to the inexpediency of entering into negotiations on the present occasion from the utter want of candor and good faith, which is apt to mark the conduct of the Officers of the United States in Their transactions with foreign Powers. Their principle on all occasions seems to be merely to gain advantage, no matter by what means.' (He gives as an example the contretemps over Rouse's Point and the 45th parallel, which both countries' surveyors had deemed to be in British territory, a detail which the US Agent apparently tried to deny.)[74] Therefore, '[i]f the American Government should make an overture for negotiations, and it should be thought advisable not at once to close the door to discussion, I hope I may be pardoned for suggesting that under all the circumstances of the case, it should be required of that Government in the first instance to make distinct propositions in writing, to be well considered, before any new course is acceded to by His Majesty's Ministers.' (An official in the Foreign Office put three lines in the margin next to this paragraph.) He recommended referring the matter to a foreign Power.[75]

On 10 October 1822, Adams himself proposed to the British Minister in Washington, Stratford Canning, a possible compromise: Great Britain would gain title to the land necessary for a military road linking New Brunswick and Quebec and the US would gain 'an equivalent accommodation in territory'.[76] The British were wary, and Adams himself soon drew back. In July 1823 Adams instructed Richard Rush, still the American Minister in London, to begin negotiations on several subjects, one of which was the north-east frontier. Adams wanted retention of Rouse's Point with its fort (now called Fort Blunder) and he wanted American navigation rights on the St Lawrence River. These negotiations also faded away. Of course Adams disliked and distrusted the British; but possibly more important was the fact that he planned to run for President in the 1824 election, and he could not afford the opposition of Maine and Massachusetts. There were further negotiations in London from November 1824 to the autumn of 1826 between the new American Minister, Albert Gallatin, and William Huskisson, the President of the Board of Trade. They also were unsuccessful, and, after eighteen 'tiring and difficult sessions',[77] there seemed to be no alternative to referring the matter to a State or Sovereign, as set out in the Treaty of Ghent.

VII

The question as to which State or Sovereign should be nominated had arisen as soon as agreement seemed unlikely. Adams favoured the Tsar of Russia, although Gallatin was instructed in 1826 to propose also the President of Colombia, the King of Prussia, the King of France, the King of Württemberg and the Duke of Saxe-Weimar (a curious conglomeration). By February 1828, the mixture had changed to the Tsar, the King of Denmark and the King of the Netherlands; this was also curious, since Gallatin had learned in 1826 that the Tsar did not want to be involved, not least because Adams had objected to the Tsar's ukase in 1823, which had claimed for Russia the Pacific coast down to San Francisco Bay. In 1827 London had proposed the King of the Netherlands, but Adams had objected: the King was a cousin of the King of Great Britain and an honorary general of the British Army. By June 1828, however, Adams was facing another presidential election, and in addition he was probably tired of the whole border issue – he had more important political problems at home – and he agreed to the King of the Netherlands as the arbiter.[78] On 1 April 1830, the complete submissions of both countries were presented to the King.

The quiet, thoughtful approach expected of the King was noisily interrupted in the summer. In 1814, the Powers at the Congress of Vienna had united the Protestant, Dutch-speaking Netherlands with Catholic, French-speaking Belgium (known in the early modern period as the Spanish Netherlands – hence the Catholicism) under William VI, the Prince of Orange, who was then established as William I, King of the Netherlands. The intention of the Powers was to erect a northern barrier against French expansion. The Belgians hated it – they saw William I as too authoritarian and possibly anti-Catholic. In July 1830 the July Revolution took place in France, which replaced a rigidly conservative king with a more liberal one. Inspired by this, in late August the Belgians rose, sections of the army mutinied, and within two months they had driven the Dutch out of Belgium; in October, Belgium declared independence. King William turned to Europe and especially to the British for support. Dismayed, it seemed increasingly likely to the Americans that the King would do whatever was necessary to gain and keep the support of the British. Was he still a free agent? By mid-September, the Americans had decided that he was not.[79] The whole arbitration process was seen as deeply interwoven with European Great Power politics.

On 10 January 1831 the King announced his decision. He had read all of the evidence and analysed all of the arguments, he said, and considered that three sections of the boundary posed issues. The most important, and most difficult, was the Quebec–New Brunswick–Maine boundary. In essence, he had decided that neither side had produced commanding evidence or arguments, and he therefore set out a compromise line, which ran along the most obvious natural boundary in the region.[80] Maine was awarded 5 million acres and New Brunswick and Quebec 2.6 million. As for the headwaters of the Connecticut River, the King decided that the British claim should stand. Finally, the new survey of the 45th parallel was clearly more accurate than the old, and it should stand; however, because the US had built Fort Montgomery on Rouse's Point in good faith, the boundary should extend to the fort and a radius of a kilometre around it.[81] This would meet the US government's defence concerns. It also gave Great Britain the land necessary for the military road.

There was no evading the fact that the King had not fulfilled the requirement of the Convention of 1827 (which had set the arbitration process in motion), which was to determine the correct reading of the terms of the treaty of 1783. The problem with arbitration is that as likely as not the arbiter will split the difference. But the agreement to go to arbitration implies that both sides will accept the outcome. Nevertheless, the American representative at The Hague was outraged by the King's decision, protested and argued that the US should not accept it. The British, on the other hand, had already decided before the decision was handed down that they would probably accept it, even if it set out a compromise line, and Lord Palmerston, the Foreign Secretary, accepted it immediately.[82] Bagot, who had been involved with the border controversy on and off since 1816, was pleased, writing to Palmerston that he thought the decision was a good one for Great Britain. He also thought that the US federal government would accept it, hoping that 'the possession of Rouse's Point [with Fort Montgomery/Blunder] will reconcile them to much which otherwise they would have been ill pleased with – but it will raise a storm in the District of Maine which has separate and local interests'. He went on to say that '[t]his however will be a battle between the State of Maine and the General Government with which we have nothing to do,' adding presciently, if not wholly correctly, that it might be 'one of those battles perhaps which are destined, some day or other, to dissolve the confederation'.[83] Furthermore, a question put to the British law officers received the reply that the King of the Netherlands had indeed exceeded his authority, and that the US had the right to dissent from the award.[84] What should the governments do?

President Andrew Jackson, the first President from west of the Appalachian Mountains, did not like the award, but privately thought that it should be accepted, because the 1783 treaty line was unworkable. The problem, of course, was that Maine would not accept it. Jackson tried to find a solution, but his options were limited because of his and the Democratic Party's political needs. He wanted to build a political machine in the north-east analogous to the one already constructed in the south and west, and thus he could not afford to alienate Massachusetts and Maine. He proposed that, in exchange for giving up Maine's claim to land north of the St John and east of the St Francis rivers, the state would receive one million acres of public land in the Michigan Territory. This nearly worked, but a newspaper outcry in Maine – 'OUR FELLOW CITIZENS TRANSFERRED TO A FOREIGN POWER FOR CASH OR LAND' screamed one headline[85] – undermined his plan.

Meanwhile, in Washington the Senate Foreign Relations Committee recommended the acceptance of the King's decision; however, in June 1832 the full Senate rejected the Committee's recommendation by twenty-one to twenty. The Senate then recommended to the President by twenty-three to twenty-two that he reopen negotiations with Great Britain to determine the true line. Edward Livingston, the Secretary of State, suggested to the British Minister, Charles Bankhead, that the two countries might be able to agree on a compromise line. However, he also suggested that Britain grant navigation rights on the lower St John River; but Palmerston rejected the proposals on the grounds that he could not combine boundary and navigation issues, although he was always loath to give away concessions without a due return. Maine, however, then proceeded to scupper this as well by announcing that no agreement between the federal government and Great Britain could be binding unless it was approved by a majority of the citizens of Maine when assembled in town meetings.[86]

The following year, Livingston proposed to the new British Minister in Washington, Sir Charles Vaughan, that they establish joint commissions with an arbiter to resolve disagreements. Given Maine's intransigence, he proposed a boundary running north-east or north-west from the source of the St Croix to the highlands, not due north as the Treaty had set out.[87] But Vaughan feared that any change in the line might take territory from New Brunswick, and he advised the government in London that if Great Britain submitted to 'the pretensions of the State of Maine', the US would benefit from every defect in the Treaty of Paris.[88] The American proposal was rejected, and in 1835 Palmerston withdrew the British acceptance of the King's decision.[89] Indeed, the issue would not be resolved until 1842, when a compromise was agreed as part of the Webster–Ashburton Treaty. Meanwhile, things drifted, bar minor local conflicts, until 1837, when the Canadian Rebellions, short-lived as they were in themselves, inaugurated five years of increasingly ferocious tension and conflict. This time, given the background of years of distrust, resentment, hatred and repeated local conflicts, the American roars for war would come alarmingly close to succeeding.

VIII

The Canadian Rebellions grew out of a failure of constitutional reform. The British, having partially learned their lesson with the

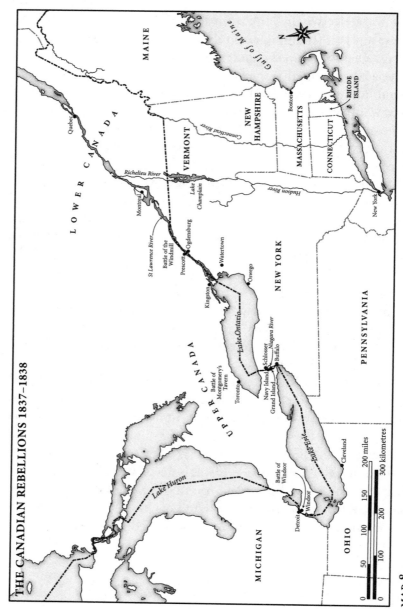

THE CANADIAN REBELLIONS 1837–1838

MAP 8

Americans, had established legislative assemblies in Lower and Upper Canada which, however, verged on the powerless. True, they were elective, but the executive councils and the governor-general were appointed, and they held the real power; furthermore, this power was exercised by oligarchies, termed the Family Compact in Upper Canada. Importantly, unlike the colonial assemblies in the American colonies, the Canadian assemblies had no power over the spending of revenues, and thus no control over the governor-general and through him the executive councils. This political framework was also not conducive to effecting proposals for reform.

Events began in Lower Canada. There was long-standing political conflict essentially between Francophone Quebecers, led by Louis-Joseph Papineau, lawyer, politician and leader of the political Parti Patriotes, and the Anglophone establishment. In the 1834 election the Parti Patriotes received 75 per cent of the vote and dominated the legislature. They petitioned London for political reforms, asking for the Legislative and Executive Councils to be responsible to the Legislative Assembly, but in March 1837 Lord John Russell for Lord Melbourne's government rejected all of the proposals: 'That part of the constitution which requires that the ministers of the crown shall be responsible to parliament and shall be removable if they do not obtain the confidence of parliament is a condition which exists in an imperial legislature and in an imperial legislature only. It is a condition which cannot be carried into effect in a colony – it is a condition which can only exist in one place, namely the seat of the empire.'[90] Therefore, there was to be no 'responsible government' for the British North American colonies. Papineau organised protests and assemblies, but when nothing resulted, men began to arm themselves and drill. On 11 November 1837 the rebels defeated a British force. However, the British soon beat them back, and some towns and farms were pillaged and ransacked. On 5 December martial law was declared in Montreal. Papineau and others fled to the US; Papineau then went on to France, where he hoped to gain French support, but in this he failed.[91]

When news of the rebellion in Lower Canada and its failure reached Upper Canada, Canadians under the leadership of William Lyon Mackenzie (a journalist, member of the Legislative Assembly and first Mayor of Toronto) and associates launched their own armed rebellion. Many of the reasons were the same – political corruption and the refusal of reforms – but it ended shortly after it began, with the rebels' defeat at the Battle of Montgomery's Tavern in what is now Toronto on 7 December. A number of the rebels fled to the US. There Mackenzie and his followers raised a band of about 200 men, mostly American citizens and mostly from Buffalo,[92] to be commanded by Colonel Rensselaer Van Rensselaer, an American citizen. They seized Navy Island on the Canadian side of the Niagara River and on 13 December proclaimed the 'Republic of Canada'. The proclamation listed the grievances against the colonial government, demanded a number of democratic rights and called for 'the distribution of the wild lands of the country to the industry, capital, skill, and enterprise to the worthy men of all nations'.[93]

It is clear why these aims would have appealed to the men along the border. First of all, there was the love of fighting for its own sake. Secondly, there was the desire to push the British out of North America. Thirdly, the establishment of a republican government appealed to the deepest urge and loyalty of many if not most Americans at the time. And fourthly, and very importantly as a context, the US was in the midst of the Panic of 1837, during which hundreds of American banks suspended payments and thousands of farmers, shopkeepers, planters, traders and speculators throughout the US went bankrupt.[94] The result was that there were hundreds of aggrieved and unemployed men along the border, who had the time to fight – and who responded to the offer of free farmland (Mackenzie offered 300 acres of 'the best of the public lands' to worthy men and, a few days later, added the promise of '$100 in silver, payable on or before the first of May next').[95] After all, many believed, they were clearly worthy, being hard-working Americans.

Navy Island had distinct advantages as a stronghold. It is surrounded by the swift-flowing Niagara River, its banks are from ten to twenty feet high, and it is about two miles above the Falls. It was also directly across from Schlosser, New York on the American side. (The island's only occupants, a widow and her son, had converted its one building into a tavern that had become a rendezvous for outlaws.)[96] The rebels needed arms, and arsenals in New York were broken into, resulting in several pieces of artillery and other arms being seized and taken to Navy Island, apparently in daylight and without serious resistance by American local authorities. Soldiers were enlisted in Buffalo. The governors of New York[97] and Vermont called for neutrality, but this had limited effect.

The turning point was the *Caroline* incident. This involved a forty-five-ton steamer from Buffalo which was licensed to transport passengers and supplies from Buffalo to Schlosser. On 29 December she arrived at Navy Island, where passengers disembarked and cargo was unloaded. She made two more return journeys from Schlosser to Navy Island, unloading passengers and cargo each time. By early in the evening, mechanical difficulties were causing the boat to run erratically, and the crew attached the ship to the dock at Schlosser with a chain. A Royal Navy officer had travelled around the circumference of the island to investigate its fortifications and had had a cannon fired at him; the same day the militia headquarters at Chippewa on Canadian soil was fired on by muskets from the American Grand Island, adjacent in the Niagara River. A horse was killed, but not the man who was at that moment riding him.[98]

Colonel Allan McNab, Colonel Commandant of British forces on the Niagara Frontier, believed that the steamer belonged to the insurgents, who were harming the colony, and he decided that the *Caroline* had to be destroyed to prevent her continuing to resupply the island. According to Captain Andrew Drew of the Royal Navy, in his report to McNab on the following day,

in obedience to your commands to burn, sink, or destroy, the piratical steam-vessel ... I ordered a look to be kept upon her; and at about 5 P.M., of yesterday, when the day was closed in, Mr Harris, of the Royal Navy, reported the vessel to me as having moved off Navy Island. I immediately directed five boats to be armed and manned with forty-five volunteers, and at about eleven o'clock, P.M., we pushed off from the shore for Navy Island, when not finding her there as expected, we went in search and found her moored between an island and the main shore.

I then assembled the boats off the point of the island, and dropped quietly down upon the steamer; we were not discovered until within twenty yards of her, when the sentry upon the gangway hailed us and asked for the countersign, which I told him we would give him when we got on board; he then fired upon us, when we immediately boarded, and found from twenty to thirty men[99] upon her deck, who were easily overcome, and in ten minutes she was in our possession. As the current was running strong, and our position close to the Falls of Niagara, I deemed it most prudent to burn the vessel; but previously to setting her on fire took the precaution to loose her from her moorings, and turn her out into the stream to prevent the possibility of the destruction of anything like American property. In short, all those on board the steamer who did not resist were quietly put on shore, as I thought it possible there might be some American citizens on board. Those who assailed us were of course dealt with according to the usages of war.

The British had three wounded, one seriously, 'and I regret to add, that five or six of the enemy were killed'.[100] The Royal Navy party then took to their boats, a huge fire on the Canadian shore acting as a beacon to guide them home across the river.[101] Unexpectedly, there was an audience for the attack, which had anticipated a British attack on Navy Island earlier that day and had gathered at Schlosser to watch. Men on the steamer had been armed: three men in the boarding party received gunshot and knife wounds, while an African-American stage driver from Buffalo, Amos Durfee, died when a ricocheting bullet went through his forehead.[102]

Rumours raced through the American side of the border like a wildfire, and the whole frontier was in commotion. Many

Americans had died – there had been a massacre – the British had been heartless, with the boarding party crying out 'G—d damn them! Give them no quarter! Kill every man! Fire, fire!'[103] – and in fostering these rumours, the newspapers were very helpful. According to the *National Intelligencer*, nearly 150 men had boarded the boat, given three cheers for Queen Victoria and killed twenty-two, while *Niles' Register* insisted that British soldiers had killed all but two or three and then sent the boat over the Falls. And so on.[104] The Governor of New York, W. L. Marcy, can only have contributed to this with his 'Special Message ... Respecting the destruction of the "Caroline"' to the Legislature, issued on 2 January 1838, when he asserted that the ship had been 'forcibly seized by a party of seventy or eighty armed men in boats ... The crew and other persons in this steam-boat, amounting to thirty-three, were suddenly attacked at midnight, after they had retired to repose, and probably more than one-third of them wantonly massacred.' These comments were taken directly from the Deposition of Gilman Appleby of Buffalo, who had commanded the *Caroline*. Marcy added that it would probably be necessary to maintain a military force for the protection of American citizens 'until an opportunity is given to the General [federal] Government to interpose with its power', so the Legislature should be prepared to pay for it[105] – always a problem in the individual states.

President Martin Van Buren was giving a dinner party on the evening of 4 January when he received news of the rebellion. He told one of the guests, General Winfield Scott, that 'Blood has been shed; you must go with all speed to the Niagara frontier.'[106] Scott had been a hero of the War of 1812, but was now perceived as pompous and vain, and was known as 'Old Fuss and Feathers'. Indeed, the future President Ulysses S. Grant, who had been an officer under Scott's command, later wrote that he 'could bestow praise upon [himself] with the least embarrassment'.[107] The following day, Van Buren issued a proclamation, stating that, in spite of the earlier proclamations of the governors of New York and Vermont, 'the excitement, instead of being appeased, is every day increasing in degree; that arms and munitions of war and other supplies have been procured by the insurgents in the United States; that a military force, consisting in part, at least, of citizens of the United States, had been actually organized, had congregated at Navy Island, and were still in arms under the command of a citizen of the United States, and that they were constantly receiving accessions and aid', and he called upon the American citizens to return to their homes. Furthermore, he stated that the laws of the US would be enforced, and that any Americans captured on Canadian soil could expect no help from the US government.[108] For its part, Congress reacted rather more hotly, and appropriated $625,000 for the defence of the northern frontier.[109]

Scott hastened north, and on 13 January he met with the American commander on Navy Island, Colonel Van Rensselaer, and told him that their cause was hopeless and that his activities as an American seriously threatened Anglo-American relations. The following day, they evacuated the island and returned to the US,[110] thereby eliminating a useful focal point and symbol of the rebellion. The fevered excitement along the border apparently abated somewhat. Possibly Scott's mission helped. Although it was pointed out to him that the US government lacked the legal authority to prevent violations of neutrality before they happened, he was nevertheless asked to use his 'influence to prevent [such] violations'.[111] At least one historian is distinctly sceptical about Scott's own perception of his duty: 'According to his own perhaps exaggerated account, [Scott] was to restore order along a frontier eight hundred miles long, enforce weak neutrality laws, and pro-tect the United States from British attacks – all through "rhet-oric and diplomacy".'[112] What he did do was to travel through much of the area promising that Washington would not allow any further outrageous British activity in the US. He also called for obedience to the law and the following of democratic procedures, and insisted repeatedly that it was the duty of the US govern-ment to deal with questions of foreign policy.[113] Although local activity continued in some places, the tension along the border continued to lessen. 'He marched before American troops at every chance, a stately military hero, over six feet tall and dressed immaculately in blue and gold uniform ... A resident of Buffalo noted the secure feeling "this yellow-plumed, gold-laced hero" gave to everyone.'[114]

The British were making their own military preparations. By the end of 1837, the government had brought 10,000 Canadian militiamen into active service and was planning to increase the number of regulars from 2,000 to 10,000. When in February 1838 news of the *Caroline* incident reached London, the government added a further two regiments. The intention was more to crush the rebellion than to conduct war with the US, since the British government at this point tended to believe that war with the US was unlikely.[115] But a new force was soon on the scene: the Hunters' Lodges. This was a secret, anti-British organisation which originated in Vermont in the early spring of 1838, but whose headquarters soon became Cleveland, Ohio, and which spread from New York to Michigan in the US and widely in Lower Canada, with a few lodges in Upper Canada. Based on the organisation of the Masonic lodges which had been widespread in the US since the days of the Revolution, it was hierarchical, with passwords, secret signs and rituals.[116] Its goal was 'to emancipate the British Colonies from British Thraldom'[117] by invading the north and assisting what the members assumed would be the uprising of the Canadians.

During the first week of November 1838, the rebels took up arms in Lower Canada. At about the same time, the Hunters from the lodges east of Oswego, New York began to come together. The plan, apparently, was for groups of Hunters to embark at different ports and to attack in different parts of Upper Canada. This, it was confidently expected, would give the great number of rebellious Canadians ample opportunity to rise in revolt. On 11 November a group of about 200 men landed at Prescott on the north bank of the St Lawrence and then marched to the nearby Windmill Point. However, all supplies were cut off by British troops, and the Canadian Hunters who had come in support were forced to withdraw. On the 16th, the stand-off came to an end when sixteen pieces of artillery were brought from Kingston. Canadian troops stopped the invaders, and of the 200 men who invaded from the US the Battle of the Windmill saw about 150 of them killed or captured, of whom about 120 were Americans.[118]

Another invasion took place near Windsor on 4 December; the Battle of Windsor had a similar outcome. 'In regard to the miserable failure of the attempts at invasion, the fact seems to be that both the Americans along the frontier and the disaffected Canadians expected the other to give more assistance than they actually did, and that each group was greatly disappointed at the showing made by the other.'[119] Interestingly, he also points out that one obligation of the Hunters was to vote for other Hunters. During the summer and autumn of 1838 the mid-term elections were in progress, and it would be natural for politicians to bid for votes by acting in ways which the organisation's large membership, at the time estimated to be between 40,000 and 200,000, would approve. This could well include encouraging the invasion of Upper Canada. However, after the elections were over – and the invasions had failed miserably – a mass meeting in Watertown, New York on 21 December 1838 called for the maintenance of peace between the US and Great Britain and for leaving the Canadians alone to choose their own form of government.[120] It was unlikely to have been the only such meeting.

Neither government wanted war. There were discussions during a two-year period about the *Caroline* affair.[121] Meanwhile the British government in early 1838 sent out Lord Durham to investigate the nature and extent of the problems which had led, and would continue to lead, to political and military turmoil in Canada. The immediate outcome would be the eponymous Report of February 1839 and the unity of the two Canadas in the Canada Union Act of 1840; eventually in 1848 the British government agreed to the principle of 'responsible government'. One can indeed argue that the Americans had helped the Canadians to achieve this. With Durham came his brother-in-law, Colonel Charles Gray, who was sent to Washington to settle some of the border issues. The two countries increased patrols on both sides of their own waters, and instituted joint patrols of the Great Lakes (ignoring for the time being the Rush–Bagot Agreement's prohibition of armed ships on the Lakes). Each recognised the other's attempts to cool the temperature. Maine, however, was about to raise it again.

IX

The perfervid anti-British atmosphere already evident on the north-eastern border was exacerbated by events leading up to the so-called Aroostook or Lumberjack War. The area at issue was referred to by Great Britain as the 'Disputed Territory'; it was referred to by Maine as Maine. It was still an issue in 1839 because neither Britain nor the US had finally accepted the King of the Netherlands' decision. The context included the continuing uncertainty over where the border ran, British security needs, the intense party conflict in Maine, a loud and vocal devotion to the right of Maine to have all of the 12,000 square miles at issue, the state's insistence that the federal government had an obligation to back Maine in all of its claims, the overwhelming need of Americans to defend their honour against Britain, and a driving local wish to make money. This conflict centred on the Aroostook Valley.

Maine wanted to encourage settlement in the state, and recognised the valley as an area of rich soil which could support a stable farming community. It was also concerned about the unauthorised logging by New Brunswick 'trespassers' to the extent, it was claimed, of timber worth $100,000 a year.[122] It therefore wanted the boundary to run north of the St John River. The British had different concerns. While they, and especially the people of New Brunswick, who were concerned in their turn by 'illegal' logging by Americans, shared the desire to exploit its rich soil and timber reserves – and certainly its economic significance had increased – more important was security. Because of the need for timber by the Royal Navy, the New Brunswick coastal settlement had always been well guarded. Because of the War of 1812, however, when the US had repeatedly tried to invade Canada, measures for defence inside the colony had assumed even more importance. As Stratford Canning, the British Minister

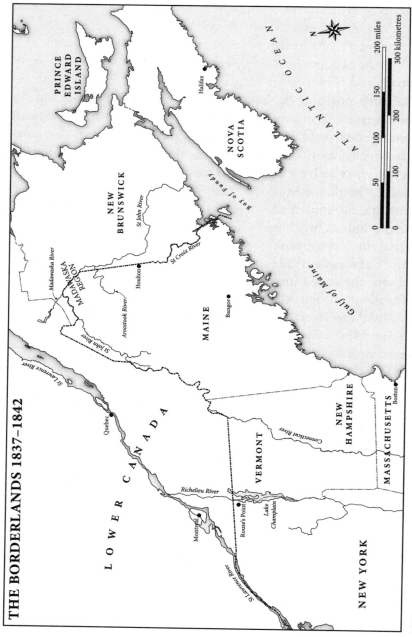

THE BORDERLANDS 1837–1842

MAP 9

in Washington, had noted probably in 1824 (the document is undated), '[t]he extent of the territory in dispute is not without some degree of interest; but the objects of real importance are, to remove the American frontier as much as possible from the line of the St Lawrence, to open direct communication between Canada and New Brunswick, and to exclude the Americans from a valuable position on Lake Champlain.'[123] As noted above, it was necessary to ensure that supplies could be brought overland from the port at Halifax to Quebec during the winter when the St Lawrence froze. Furthermore, it was vital that the tip of Maine did not separate New Brunswick from Quebec. Therefore, Great Britain wanted the border to run south of the St John River. By this time, the local Canadians and New Brunswickers also saw their honour as involved.

Early in 1837, in order to assert Maine's title to the territory, the Maine legislature ordered a census of the Disputed Territory and sent the state's land surveyor to carry it out. As soon as they heard about it, New Brunswick officials arrested him. Maine was affronted, and expected Washington to deal with Great Britain as it deserved; the response of the British government was that until the boundary had been decided by the two countries, Britain would continue to exercise jurisdiction. Maine ordered a road cut to the upper Aroostook River, which flowed into the St John River. But the British controlled the St John, thereby controlling the ability to send goods through New Brunswick to the Atlantic. Things festered.

In January 1839, a new governor of Maine was elected, the Democrat John Fairfield. He warned the legislature that the state was losing hundreds of thousands of dollars from illegal timber cutting in the area: they needed to defend the territory against Great Britain. (It is worth remembering that both American and Canadian loggers had moved into the territory and were illegally cutting the timber.) The legislature appropriated money for defence and, shortly thereafter, 200 volunteers entered the region. The head of what he called a posse was the land agent, Rufus McIntire, 'a seventy-year-old Anglophobe who was thirsting for a fight'.[124] A group of fifty Canadians promptly captured McIntire and two others in their sleep and clapped them in jail. The posse in their turn arrested a dozen trespassers, including James A. MacLaughlin, New Brunswick's Warden of the territory under dispute, and took him to jail in Bangor, Maine. The two forces arresting each other's leaders naturally set off a crisis, as Maine newspapers bellowed for revenge. Governor Fairfield called for volunteers to reinforce the posse and for support from the federal government, while Sir John Harvey, the Lieutenant-Governor of New Brunswick, mobilised the militia (the Nova Scotia Legislature, currently in session, voted £100,000 and authorised the raising of 8,000 men)[125] to confront the posse. The border appeared to be on a war footing, and in March the Lieutenant-Governor of Upper Canada, Sir George Arthur, wrote that 'I do not see how this can terminate without a *General* war.'[126]

But it did, because both sides backed off. The US government realised that it was seriously unprepared for war with Great Britain. Furthermore, the militias turned out not to be so keen as actually to fight: 'troops from New Brunswick were badly equipped and cautious, while the Maine militia found winter duty in the woods uncomfortable and saw the "trespassers" engaging in farming and lumbering despite them. Reportedly the only clash was between British and American soldiers drinking together in a tavern in Houlton, Maine, south of the crisis region.' According to Francis Carroll there were two accidental deaths in the Maine militia, one from measles and one from a shooting accident.[127] It must be said, however, that for over a year there were repeated attempts, political and military, by both sides to gain territory and push the other back, even if no one was seriously hurt.[128] For the British, given that they were concurrently involved in the first Anglo-Afghan War (1839–42), the second Egyptian crisis (1839–41) and the Opium War (1839–42), there was not a lot of attention or spare military forces left for the Canadian–American border.

Therefore, both the British and the American governments worked to lower the temperature. On 27 February 1839, the British Minister to the US, Henry S. Fox, and the Secretary of State, John Forsyth, came to an agreement by which officials in New Brunswick would release all Americans held captive and all militiamen from Maine would withdraw from the disputed territory. President Van Buren again asked General Scott to go north to persuade Maine to accept the agreement and to calm down New Brunswick. Scott found that Americans in Maine were still keen on war; furthermore, they did not like the fact that the agreement left the British in Aroostook Valley. Fortunately, Scott and Lieutenant-Governor Harvey had both been officers in the War of 1812, which drew them together, and an arrangement was reached whereby the Maine militias would withdraw, although an unarmed civil posse would stay, and the New Brunswick force would not try to drive them out. The area was divided into spheres of interest, with Maine to control the Aroostook River Valley and New Brunswick to control the Madawaska River Valley. It did not work out perfectly, but it was intended to hold the ring until the two countries could sort things out. The arrangement pacified Maine and saved Van Buren from profound political embarrassment.[129] As for Great Britain, Minister Henry Fox's dislike of the Americans had increased considerably as a result of the whole process, but Lord Palmerston told him to 'cultivate the Americans as much as you can'. Much, he pointed out, 'may be accomplished by frequent and constant intercourse with Men with whom public Business is to be transacted'.[130] Given that the British, in addition to the above-noted wars, were currently engaged in disputes with France, Russia, China and Persia, and were deeply involved in the so-called Eastern Question, it is not surprising that Palmerston was not keen to become embroiled in a dispute with the US. Fox could only obey.

X

In 1840, the *Caroline* incident was brought back into public consciousness by the reportedly drunken idiocy of a Canadian, Alexander McLeod, in a Buffalo tavern, but the incident had the benefit of strongly encouraging the British and American governments to settle once and for all the problems of the northeast. Conflict had not ceased, as Americans urged Canadian dissidents to break away and overthrow the colonial government, and raids into Upper Canada continued. The McLeod affair, with its hate-filled anti-British American response, arguably brought the US and Great Britain closer to war than at any time since 1815.

McLeod had been a deputy sheriff in Upper Canada; once the rebellions had begun in 1837, he became a secret agent for the British. Late in 1837, he fled from a mob in Buffalo after gathering information about the *Caroline*'s early activities. 'A victim of personal hatreds and patriotic malice, McLeod quickly became a habitual target for New York state law.' He was arrested in late 1840 by state officials after reportedly boasting in the Buffalo tavern that he had killed an American citizen during the attack on the *Caroline*.[131] He was charged with arson and murder, and threatened with execution if convicted.

Great Britain responded that this was a violation of international law, but it was partly its own fault. If it had stated that the *Caroline* raid had been an official act, as it had been, given that it had been led by British officers, then McLeod as a private citizen could not have been charged. Of course, it is doubtful whether this would have forestalled New York, since the belief in states' rights seemed to allow the northern states to conduct their own foreign policies. In any case, British officials strongly objected, Van Buren explained that the federal government did not have the power to intervene in a state's judicial proceedings, Congress got involved and the newspapers screamed. The British public, along with their government, were indignant, and both British and American public opinion began to feel that war would be the proper end.

The whole thing became extremely complicated, with judges in New York contradicting one another, popular leaders threatening mob attacks, the House of Representatives passing a report supporting states' (that is, New York's) rights in the affair and attacking the British approach to Anglo-American relations, the House of Lords then complaining that Congress had insulted Great Britain, and Van Buren's 'policy' of drift.[132] Lord Palmerston, the Foreign Secretary, told the American Minister in London, Andrew Stevenson, 'not officially but as a Private Friend', that 'if

McLeod is executed there must be war'.[133] To underline this, he wrote to Fox on 9 February 1841 that:

if any harm should be done to McLeod the indignation and resentment of all England will be extreme. Mr Van Buren should understand this, and that the British nation will never permit a British subject to be dealt with as the people of New York propose to deal with McLeod, without taking a signal revenge upon the offenders. McLeod's execution would produce war, war immediate and frightful in its character because it would be a war of retaliation and vengeance. It is impossible that Mr Forsyth [the Secretary of State] can wish to bring upon the two countries such a calamity, and we can have no doubt that he will prevent it. He must have the means of doing so, or else the Federal Union exists but in name.[134]

At the same time Palmerston told Fox to demand McLeod's release; if he was executed, Fox should demand his own passports and leave Washington, at the same time telling the Governor-General and the naval commanders on the American Station what had happened.[135] The American Secretary of War prepared to defend the Atlantic coast, while Stevenson in London, without consulting Washington, advised the commander of the American squadron at Marseilles to move it closer to the US. He also informed the Secretary of State of a notice at Lloyd's insurance brokers inviting bids to transport soldiers to Canada.[136]

In the midst of this in March 1841, William Henry Harrison became President (only for a month: he died from pneumonia caught while giving his two-hour inaugural address in the rain and was then succeeded by John Tyler) and Daniel Webster, who had visited Great Britain in 1839 and had many English friends, became Secretary of State. Harrison decided that while the British invasion of US territory had indeed violated America's sovereign rights, McLeod himself was not personally responsible. This would make things easier – and considering that Britain and the US were teetering on the brink of war, it was just as well. Meanwhile, McLeod's trial went on, but the prosecution's evidence so obviously lacked credibility that the jury acquitted him in less than half an hour,[137] thereby letting everyone off the hook.

The outcome opened the way for negotiations over a number of issues between the two countries, particularly the north-eastern boundary. The accession to power of Tyler and Webster was matched in Great Britain with the replacement of the Melbourne government and Palmerston as Foreign Secretary by that of Sir Robert Peel and Lord Aberdeen as Foreign Secretary. Aberdeen was mild-mannered – unlike Palmerston – hard-working and a fervent believer in amicable relations between the two empires. He decided that, rather than go through regular diplomatic channels, he would send a special mission to the US. An important reason for this then unusual approach to diplomatic negotiations was his dislike of and contempt for the British Minister. As he wrote some years later, 'the great necessity for Ashburton's mission was in consequence of our having a Minister at Washington, who although not without ability, did nothing. He passed his time in bed, and was so detested by every member of the U.S. Government that they had no communication with him, except as it was absolutely indispensable.'[138] Aberdeen finally relieved Fox of his post in 1843. Curiously, Fox remained in the US, dying of a morphine overdose in 1846.

Lord Ashburton, the British plenipotentiary, was the former Alexander Baring, head of the rich and powerful merchant (investment) bank, the House of Baring, which had huge interests in the US. Baring had lived for some years in America, managing the bank's affairs. In 1810, he had married the American Anne Bingham of Philadelphia, daughter of Senator William Bingham, and he had deep knowledge of both business and American affairs. Furthermore, he had negotiated the financing of the Louisiana Purchase from France in 1803, which had more than doubled the size of the US. Importantly, he was on friendly terms with Secretary of State Webster. He seemed ideal.[139] Although he believed that the Americans made 'troublesome neighbours' with whom 'nothing [was] more easy than to get into war ... any morning with a very good cause', he also believed that a good Anglo-American relationship was vital for both countries. Webster agreed.[140]

The negotiations began in April 1842. Ashburton had gone to the US with a very reasonable organising principle: that the disputed territory should be settled according to population. Thus if the settlers in any particular territory had for about fifty years believed themselves to be in US territory, he was prepared to leave them there and recognise the claim of the US.[141] Webster made his own important contribution to the success of the negotiations by inviting Maine and Massachusetts to send representatives.[142] He also discussed possible compromises with a number of political officials. Nevertheless, the most difficult clause in the agreement was on the northern Maine boundary: the Maine legislators were adamant about what they considered to be their rights, and Webster was reluctant to go ahead without their consent. Ashburton had every sympathy with him, writing himself that 'The Maine Legislature is a wild and uncertain Body ... but to a compromise there must be two Parties, and our [Great Britain's] other Party in this case is a jealous, arrogant, democratic God.'[143] Because of the mutual trust between Ashburton and Webster, however, the two entered, 'while in the preliminary stages of the Maine discussions, into a virtual conspiracy with each other to disarm the intransigents on that issue in each other's public and to make possible a compromise settlement'.[144]

What certainly helped to disarm them was an incontrovertible piece of historical evidence. The distinguished historian Jared Sparks of Harvard, while working in the national archives in Paris in 1841 for his books on the American Revolution, discovered a letter dated 6 December 1782 and a map sent by Benjamin Franklin to Vergennes, the French Foreign Minister. The letter said that the map marked the limits of the US and Canada as settled by the British and American plenipotentiaries during the negotiations over the Treaty of Paris. A red line on the map left all of the streams running into the St John River on the British side – which was what the British had claimed. Sparks took the map to the State Department. Webster did not show it to Ashburton, but rather asked Sparks to take it up to Maine and show it to the

Governor. As a result, Maine withdrew its claim and indicated that it would accept a compromise.

Wonderfully, the converse had happened in London. The Director of the British Museum, Sir Anthony Panizzi, had found a map drawn for British members of the delegation at the Versailles negotiations, Richard Oswald and Henry Strachey. This map also had a red line, but in this case it wholly supported the American claim. Palmerston, then the Foreign Secretary, put the map into a Foreign Office secret file, and only he and the Permanent Under-Secretary knew about it. Almost certainly Aberdeen did not.[145]

On 9 August 1842, the treaty was signed. Article I defined the frontier, and naturally it was a compromise, but one which broadly favoured the British. Roughly, the St John River became the boundary. The Madawaska settlement, which lay on both sides of the river, was divided: the northern part went to Canada and the southern part to Maine. Great Britain received only five-twelfths of the territory which it had claimed, but it was a bit more than it would have received under the King of the Netherlands' award, and it included some heights commanding the St Lawrence Valley. The US got Rouse's Point. Article III allowed non-manufactured goods from those parts of Maine through which the St John flowed to travel freely down the river as though they were from New Brunswick – an important element in the negotiations. Article IV allowed both British and American settlers to keep their land in the disputed region, if they had been in possession for more than six years, a generous application of Ashburton's principle.[146]

Back in London, a motion of thanks was voted to Aberdeen in Parliament, but the Opposition had strongly objected. Palmerston in particular was virulent, referring to the treaty as the 'Ashburton Capitulation'.[147] The disputed territory extending between New Brunswick and the Canadas afforded a 'Strong Military Position' for attack on the British empire. The United States, he concluded, had won a 'Stepping Stone' towards its ultimate purpose, 'Expulsion of British authority from the Continent of America', which it had talked about openly and endlessly since the 1780s. Most Britons, in contrast, thought that the treaty had preserved the peace.[148] Ashburton certainly hoped so. Indeed, he hoped that the settling of these long-standing conflicts would enable the US and Great Britain to conduct their affairs amicably. This, unfortunately, would not be the case: conflict over the Oregon Territory would soon lead to further threats of war.

XI

The territory at issue covered almost all of the western part of North America between California and Alaska. As described above, in 1818 the Americans had suggested that the US–Canadian border be extended to the Pacific Ocean on the 49th parallel, but the British had refused, primarily because they would lose the tip of Vancouver Island and Puget Sound. Joint occupation for ten years had been agreed, which could be denounced by either side with a year's notice. Shortly after his inauguration on 4 March 1845, President James K. Polk instructed the Secretary of State, James Buchanan, to repeat this offer of the 49th parallel as the border. The British Minister, Richard Pakenham, inexplicably rejected it, refusing even to forward it to London. Polk then withdrew the offer, gave the required notice and in April 1846 denounced joint occupation. In his Inaugural Address, in fact, he had claimed the whole of the Oregon Territory for the US.[149]

Why was there such a volte face in American policy? First of all, the idea that the US's Manifest Destiny was dominion over the entire continent had a seemingly unbreakable grip on the public imagination, and the election of 1844 had been partly fought on the issue. The Democrats' election manifesto had included the claim that 'our title to the whole Territory of Oregon is clear and unquestionable': this was trumpeted by the Senator from Ohio, William 'Foghorn Bill' Allen, as 'Fifty-four forty or fight!'[150] The Southern expansionists, particularly from the slave states, wanted Texas, and they supported the Northern expansionists who wanted all of the Oregon Territory; the obvious *quid pro quo* was to be Northern support for Southern desires. Secondly, in the early 1840s, Americans following the Oregon Trail across the plains began to arrive in droves, and by 1844 there were several thousand of them in the Willamette Valley in today's Oregon. Thirdly, the area which both countries claimed included valuable ports on Puget Sound and on the tip of Vancouver Island, and Polk was somewhat obsessive about the need for the US to gain ports on the Pacific Ocean for trade with the Far East (California, then Mexican territory, was annexed only in 1850). And finally, there was great expectation that the railways would soon reach the Pacific Northwest, thereby linking its seaports with the rest of the US.

London, on the other hand, wanted the border to run along the Columbia River, which would have placed it roughly between today's Washington and Oregon states; the US, alternatively, had offered a border between Washington and British Columbia. In November 1845, Polk heard from London that Aberdeen favoured a peaceful approach, and regretted Pakenham's rejection of the administration's proposal. This, of course, only encouraged the President's hard line. The following month, he asked Congress to extend American laws to Oregon and recommended a military build-up (this was deeply inconsistent, since his budget called for a reduction in military spending). In late January 1846, Aberdeen learned that on the 3rd of that month James Buchanan, the Secretary of State, had rejected a new offer of arbitration from Pakenham. Already disgusted with Polk's bombastic threats, Aberdeen called in the American Minister in London, Louis McLane, and 'complained of the terms and manner in which it had been declined'. He then warned him that he would withdraw his opposition to preparations 'founded upon the contingency of war with the United States'; these would be preparations 'not only for the defence of the Canadas, but for offensive operations', including 'the immediate equipment of thirty ships of the line, besides steamers and other vessels of war'.[151] Britain then began active preparations in Canada. This was just as well, considering that the previous August the Colonial Secretary, Lord Stanley, had admitted that the defences in Canada were 'sadly deficient'.[152]

Meanwhile, in Washington on 29 January 1846, a few days after receiving the warning from Aberdeen, Buchanan authorised McLane to tell the Foreign Secretary 'cautiously and informally' that while the President still claimed the whole Territory he would nevertheless submit to the Senate a new offer on the lines of that made to Pakenham the previous summer.[153] On 26 February, after receiving word of Aberdeen's sterner warning, there was an urgent Cabinet meeting; the invitation to Great Britain to settle at the 49th parallel was revived, accompanied by a private letter from Buchanan to Aberdeen, assuring him that the Senate would accept the compromise. (Polk had written in his diary on 21 February that the news from London 'was not altogether of so pacific a character as the accounts in the English newspapers had led me to believe'.)[154]

The problem for the US was that it was woefully unprepared for war. There were only 480 men on the northern frontier; even worse was the navy, with only one ship of the line, six frigates and another twenty vessels of various types. The real weakness was the shortage of steamships: the US had seven steamships, mounting some thirty-nine guns, while Britain had 141, mounting some 698 guns.[155] Polk's problem was that his party had always been against the creation of an ocean-going navy (as well as against a standing army – expensive and threatening), and thus it would be embarrassing to ask Congress for one now. And in fact it was only in December, when war with Mexico seemed imminent, that Congress provided the funds for a few ships.[156]

In London, Aberdeen produced a new proposal, accepting the 49th parallel as the border and thereby also accepting the loss of all of the future Washington state, but reserving the whole of Vancouver Island and the free navigation of the Columbia River. Consequently, the US would receive the lion's share of the Oregon Territory, including the harbours of Puget Sound. This proposal arrived in Washington on 6 June 1846, and at the end of the month Aberdeen learned that Polk had laid it before the Senate for their approval.[157] Democrats from the South were not interested in vast territories in the North, and they were keen not to break with Great Britain because they needed the British market for their cotton; as a result, the die-in-the-ditch Northern expansionists, to their fury, could not muster the necessary two-thirds vote to reject it. Indeed, more than two-thirds of the senators approved it, with no changes, and the Treaty in Regard to Limits Westward of the Rocky Mountains, or the Oregon Treaty, was signed on 15 June.[158] It seemed that there was, finally, an agreed-upon border between the two empires.

The British had now lost any chance that they might have had – and it was not large – to contain the US and, by maintaining a balance of power on the continent, to provide some protection for Canada against the ravenous Americans. Indeed, by settling with Great Britain, the US freed itself for war with Mexico, at the end of which it controlled all of the territory from Canada to today's Mexico and from the east to the west coast – from sea to shining sea.[159] What helped to save Canada from absorption into the United States was the diversion of American attention by the Civil War, along with the formation of the Confederation of Canada from four colonies, New Brunswick, Nova Scotia, Quebec and Ontario, on 1 January 1867. The perceived power of the Royal Navy still had influence. The building of the Canadian Pacific Railway two decades later would encourage Canadians to look east and west, rather than to the south. For their part, most Americans found enough land opening up in their own country to obviate any need to look to the north.

XII

There was to be an epilogue to the story of the 49th parallel, the Pig War, or Pork and Potato War, of 1859. This was one of those might-have-been wars, when open conflict at the extreme edges of the British and American empires seemed imminent, when the artillery of the Americans was focused on the ships of the Royal Navy, whose guns in their turn were pointed at the American encampment. As it happened, during thirteen years the only casualty of the war was a pig.

This was yet another conflict over a boundary, which had, yet again, been carelessly described in a treaty, in this case the treaty dividing the Oregon Territory between the two Powers. The problem was, the treaty set out the land boundary but not

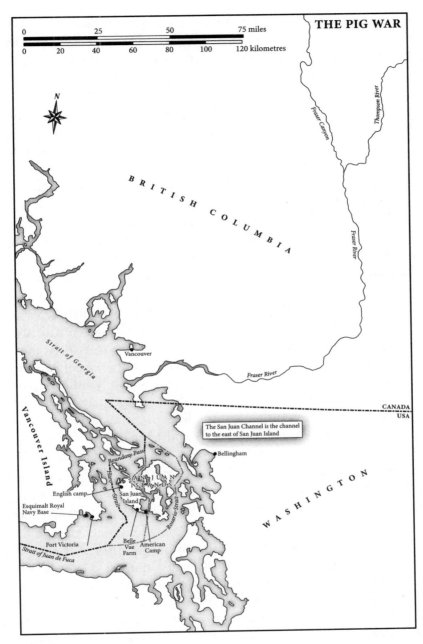

THE PIG WAR

0   25   50   75 miles

0   20   40   60   80   100   120 kilometres

N

Thompson River

Fraser Canyon

B R I T I S H   C O L U M B I A

Fraser River

Strait of Georgia

Vancouver

Fraser River

CANADA
USA

The San Juan Channel is the channel
to the east of San Juan Island

Bellingham

Vancouver Island

Boundary Pass

Haro Strait

SAN JUAN
ISLANDS

English camp

San Juan
Island

Rosario Strait

Esquimalt Royal
Navy Base

Fort Victoria

Belle
Vue
Farm

American
Camp

Strait of Juan de Fuca

W A S H I N G T O N

MAP 10

the water boundary: where did it lie between Washington and Vancouver Island? According to Article I, 'From the point on the forty-ninth parallel of north latitude, where the boundary laid down in existing treaties and conventions between the United States and Great Britain [particularly the Convention of 1818, which gave joint control to the two empires, a position confirmed by them in 1855][160] terminates, the line of boundary ... shall be continued westward along the said forty-ninth parallel of north latitude to the middle of the channel which separates the con-tinent from Vancouver's island, and thence southerly through the middle of the said channel, and of the Strait Juan de Fuca, to the Pacific Ocean.'[161] Control of this channel, which connected the (Canadian) Strait of Georgia with the (American) Straits of Juan de Fuca, had strategic significance: command could help or hinder ships from the other side, an important consideration given the continuing conflict in the north-west.

The question was, where was the channel connecting both straits? Rather like the quest for the true St Croix River in the border controversy between Maine and New Brunswick (see pp. 35–40), there were three possibilities. The Americans wanted the boundary to go through the Haro Strait, which would incorp-orate the 175 San Juan Islands into Washington state, while the British wanted it to go through the Rosario Strait, which would make the islands part of Vancouver and later British Columbia. Between the two was San Juan Island, the second largest of the group, which became the battlefield of the war. The third possi-bility, which was through the San Juan Channel between some of the islands themselves, was not very good for navigation and was only briefly discussed as a compromise.

Why was such a small island of interest to both? The British thought that possession was required in order to protect the colony and fort on Vancouver Island and the naval base at Esquimalt, the headquarters of the Royal Navy's Pacific Squadron, from the Americans. The Americans on their side wanted the island in order to protect the coast of Washington from the British.[162] James Douglas, the head of the Hudson's Bay Company and then Governor of Vancouver Island and British Columbia, was keen to take control of San Juan Island to keep it from the Americans, and from 1846 the Hudson's Bay Company, with its headquarters at Fort Victoria on Vancouver Island, began serious efforts to claim the islands. They were inappropriate for farming but quite good for grazing at the southern end, and on the night of 13 December 1853, Charles Griffin, a British subject, with a band of Hawaiian shepherds and 1,300 sheep, landed there. They set up a sheep ranch, Belle Vue Farm, and built a sheep wharf; the enterprise prospered. In due course, men from Washington Territory came over to raid, claiming that the island belonged to the US, not to Great Britain; furthermore, Washington Territory customs officials decided to test their powers, and sheep were seized and taken away on the grounds that they had been landed within Washington Territory without anyone paying import duties.[163] In 1855 American military men, including two topographical engineers, travelled around the islands to ascertain their military value.

From 1849 the British had urged Washington to join with Great Britain to establish a commission to resolve a number of issues over the recently agreed boundary, including the issue of the water boundary from the Strait of Georgia to the Strait of Juan de Fuca, but only in 1856 did Congress agree to appropriate the necessary funds. The two countries then set one up, but by December 1857 the chosen Commissioners agreed that they could not agree, and proceedings were adjourned while they reported back to their respective governments.[164] It was to be fifteen years before a settlement was reached.

In 1855, gold was discovered on the Thompson River in British Columbia, resulting in what was called the Fraser Canyon gold rush. Within a month, nearly 30,000 would-be miners had piled in, the majority being Americans, and trampled over British sovereignty. Many left, having failed to stake claims, or having discovered that high water in the canyon could cover up the (possibly) gold-holding sand bars. A few Americans then decided to try their hand at homesteading, and, not wanting to remain on British land, looked south of the 49th parallel. San Juan Island was south, and they assumed that it was part of the US; by 1859, there were a number of them there.

One was Lyman Cutler, a tall, fair-haired, fiercely independent and belligerent frontiersman from Kentucky, who was seeking his fortune but had not found it in Fraser Canyon. He built a hut within a mile and a half of Belle Vue Farm for his Native companion and himself; he then dug up a third of an acre and planted potatoes in the middle of the main sheep run. By all accounts, he was neither particularly hard-working nor a farmer: his ramshackle fence went around only three sides of his field. Among the sheep, cattle, oxen and horses owned by Belle Vue Farm were forty pigs, including, as noted above, the most favoured of all breeding pigs, the black Berkshire. One trait of this breed was a highly developed talent, and desire, for rooting in mud and dirt for whatever food could be found. One of the Berkshire boars had once before wandered from the Belle Vue barns to Cutler's potato patch to root, and Cutler had threatened to shoot it if it returned. According to the story, Cutler declared to Griffin, 'Keep your pig out of my potatoes,' and Griffin shot back, 'It's up to you to keep your potatoes out of my pig.'[165]

On 15 May 1859, Cutler awoke to the sound of laughter. Rushing outside, he discovered one of the Hawaiian herdsmen leaning against a tree and chuckling as he watched a boar rooting through Cutler's potatoes. He saw the hog 'at his old game', Cutler later wrote. 'I immediately became enraged at the independence of the negro knowing as he did my previous loss and upon the impulse of the moment seazed [sic] my rifle and shot the hog.' Later he walked the two miles to Griffin's house and offered to pay for the boar. Griffin quoted a price of $100; Cutler said that it was worth $5 and at the outside $10, adding that 'I think there is a better chance for lightning to strike than for you to get one hundred dollars for that hog.' Griffin said that the territory was British and the Americans had no right to be there; he threatened to have them removed. Cutler shouted back that this was American territory and that he had every right to live there.[166] Other Americans then hid Cutler, while Griffin reported the matter to James Douglas, now the Governor of Vancouver Island and British Columbia.

Douglas was already perturbed, having learned that the settlers in 1859 had brought a land surveyor with them to lay out lot lines in preparation for land claims. No decision on ownership of the islands had been reached, and he feared that decisions would be taken on the ground that would result in their loss by Great Britain. From the outset, he determined to control events, since the British were in possession of the island, and was urgent in his advice to London that naval and military forces be sent in order to prevent an American seizure of the territory. In due course he would need to be prevented from taking action that would exacerbate the situation. As it happened, the American commander would greatly exceed him in reckless thought, speech and action.

On 9 July 1859, Brigadier-General William Selby Harney, the American commander of the Department of Oregon, arrived by ship while touring the settlements in the area. Harney combined an eagerness for intimidation and confrontation with a serious lack of judgement. In 1846, during the Mexican–American War, his commanding officer had written of him that his actions during one episode had demonstrated 'extreme imbecility and manifest incapacity'. In fighting the Indians, another officer wrote, 'He has no more brains than a Greyhound.'[167] While many thought him reckless and feckless – he had already faced four courts martial[168] – others thought otherwise: his fellow Tennessean, President Polk, commended him as one of the 'most gallant and best officers in the service'. What was certainly the case was that he cared little for any other authority beyond his own; he was moreover fond of proclaiming that he was 'for battle not for peace'.[169] He was also an ardent expansionist and a fervent Anglophobe.[170]

Cutler was not the only American on the island who objected to the British claim of authority, and some of these complained to Harney: first of all, they had been ferociously attacked by the Natives and the Hudson's Bay Company had done nothing to protect them – an interesting charge, given that they had earlier commended the Company for protecting them against the raids – and secondly, there was the saga of the pig. They asked for troops to be sent to protect them. Harney was only too happy to comply, ordering Captain George Pickett (later famous in the Civil War as the leader of 'Pickett's Charge' at the Battle of Gettysburg, which resulted in the slaughter of half of his men) to bring sixty-six soldiers from Fort Bellingham and establish a camp on the island; Pickett's orders were to prevent the British from landing.

On 27 July 1859, Pickett and the troops arrived and set up camp very near to the Company's wharf, a distinctly provocative choice. The British feared that American squatters would soon occupy the island, and Governor Douglas, in temporary command of the Royal Navy's ships in the north-west waters, on 29 July sent a warship under the command of Captain Geoffrey Hornby. The Americans sent more soldiers and the British then sent more ships. By 10 August, there were 439 Americans with eight 32-pound cannon and some howitzers facing five British warships carrying 1,940 soldiers and sailors and mounting 167 guns.[171] Then Governor Douglas ordered Rear Admiral R. Lambert Baynes, commander of the Royal Navy's Pacific Squadron, to land marines on the island and engage the soldiers under the command of Harney. At this point the escalation was halted: Baynes's first response on hearing this was 'Tut, tut, no, the damn fools'; he then cancelled the orders from Douglas to land troops, confirming Captain Hornby's decision to keep all soldiers and sailors on board ship. His orders to Hornby were to 'Avoid all interference' with American soldiers; 'By every means in your power … prevent the risk of collision taking place.'[172] As he reportedly explained, he thought that it was foolish to 'involve two great nations in a war over a squabble about a pig'.[173] He then reported the matter to London while Harney sent a hugely exaggerated report to Washington.

The British were indignant, particularly about the seizure of the sheep and what it implied, and insisted that President James Buchanan disavow Harney's actions and order the removal of the troops: the military occupation of the island contravened the agreement to recognise the joint claim until ownership had been determined. Buchanan was in a quandary. He could not ignore Harney's violation of this agreement nor the British protest against it, since at this point, with the country in the midst of a blazing crisis over slavery, it was a dangerous time for an Anglo-American military conflict. Yet if he was seen to cave in to the

British demand, there would be uproar in Congress from those who wanted to drive the British out of North America and annex the territory. Therefore, he did what his predecessor had done and called upon General Winfield Scott to settle matters, this time in the north-west. Scott, now the US Army's General-in-Chief, was seventy-three years old, still fat, and had recently been injured by falling off his horse, but off he went. For this mission, he not only retained some of his presence, but he now also had the authority of his military position. He would later say that 'we had never been so near a war in all of our previous disputes' with Great Britain.[174]

Scott arrived at the Columbia River in the third week of October, and he immediately sent for Harney. He had had great difficulties with Harney in 1845 and 1846, when he was his superior officer, and he did not trust him.[175] This time, he believed that Harney had taken the actions he did in order to gain political points and run for the presidency.[176] The historian E. C. Coleman argues that, even though he was a member of the US Army, Harney supported the Southern cause, and worked to inveigle the US into a war with Great Britain: he believed that this would distract the North, thereby enabling the South to secede.[177] Both theories are probably correct. The Acting Secretary of War, William Drinkard, had instructed Scott to establish, if possible, a joint and equal occupation of the island; the only American military presence to remain was to be Pickett's company, whose duty would be to protect American citizens from Native raids. Scott conveyed Drinkard's instructions to Harney, which led to their yelling at each other and Harney's stamping out.

Scott sent Douglas the proposal for joint occupation with equal military forces of 100 men to protect 'their respective countrymen' from Native raids. Douglas disliked the proposal, and on his side proposed a return to the 1855 position of joint civil occupation. This went back and forth. Finally, Scott proposed that Pickett, whom Douglas disliked and distrusted, would be replaced by another, less hot-headed, officer and that Washington Territory officials would be forbidden to interfere with British subjects on the island. In return, Douglas was to reduce the Royal

Navy's presence in the neighbouring waters. Douglas reluctantly agreed to Scott's latest proposal and, in due course, only one ship remained.

Scott left the region on 11 November and arrived in New York a month later. Harney on his part reversed the orders of his Commander-in-Chief and sent Pickett back to the island, declaring that it belonged to the US. When Scott learned this, he was, understandably, intensely annoyed. Importantly, so were President Buchanan and Secretary of State Lewis Cass, who were anxious not to stumble into a war with Great Britain, and they recalled Harney to Washington and replaced him as the commander of the Oregon Department. The British were pleased. Harney was sent to command the Department of the West, but was relieved of that command in May 1861, and never received another.[178]

Pickett and his hundred soldiers returned to San Juan Island in April 1860, while on 21 March a combined force of 100 Royal Engineers and members of the Royal Marine Light Infantry had landed on the island. The Americans took up occupation of Pickett's camp in the south, which was subsequently known as American Camp, and the British established theirs on Garrison Bay in the north, which was subsequently known as English Camp. By 1 June, Pickett was fed up. 'Ever since the knowledge of the joint occupancy, the desperados of all countries have fought hither. It [the American Camp] has become a depot for murderers, robbers, whisky sellers – in a word, all refugees from justice. Openly and boldly they've come and there's no civil law over them.'[179] Merchants sold whiskey to the soldiers, who became drunk and disorderly and inclined to desert. The announcement that the British and the Americans would deal with their own citizens led a number of miscreants to claim that they were British if detained by the Americans and vice versa. In short, life in the south was frequently lawless and often in turmoil. In the north, things were much quieter: the camp buildings were strongly built, the soldiers' food was good – they grew their own vegetables and game and fish were plentiful – and discipline was observed. The twelve or so miles between the village and

English Camp forestalled most temptations, although attempts to sell whiskey were not uncommon.

The two Camps settled down and relations steadily improved. What neither realised was just how long the joint occupation would continue. The primary reason for this, of course, was the American Civil War, which began in 1861. As a result, the islands in the north-west were virtually forgotten. On the ground, there was dissension in American Camp between supporters of the North and the South. Then the soldiers were ordered to leave the camp and travel east. The order was soon reversed, but by this time Pickett had had enough. He was a Southerner, and he resigned and returned home to join the Confederate Army. On the island there were arguments between the civil authorities, the military authorities and the civilians over who really ruled the roost, there was drunkenness and there were fights, there was desertion and lawlessness. Things were much worse in the south than in the north.

As is often the case, the soldiers of the two Camps felt more comfortable with each other than with their own civilian citizens, and soon the Americans were going to English Camp to join in the celebrations of Queen Victoria's Birthday on 24 May, while the British joined the Americans in their Camp to help to celebrate 4 July. There were horse races and dances, and there were marriages. The numbers of British soldiers dwindled, what with desertions, departures and death, and they were not replaced – San Juan Island was hardly a military priority for the War Office and especially not for the Treasury – and by the end of 1866 only forty-seven British officers and men remained. On New Year's Day in 1871, English Camp welcomed many of the residents of the island to supper and a ball. In short, in this rural fastness, life went serenely on, but decisions would finally be taken to bring it to a close.[180]

During the Civil War, very serious problems had arisen between the two empires, particularly over the depredations of the Confederate ship the *Alabama*, which the British had built and (the American government claimed) helped to arm: during her subsequent career she 'captured and burned ten Union ships in the mid-Atlantic, sank the USS *Hatteras* in an engagement of only thirteen minutes in the dark in the Gulf of Mexico, turned down the coast of Brazil towards the Cape of Good Hope and then sailed around the world, capturing another eighty-two merchant ships in the process'.[181] For this, the Americans wanted vast compensation – indeed, in January 1871 Senator Charles Sumner of Massachusetts suggested that in exchange for a settlement of the claims the British should completely withdraw 'from the whole hemisphere, including the islands, and the American flag should fly in its stead'.[182] The Secretary of State, Hamilton Fish, a former Congressman and Senator from and Governor of New York State, subsequently hinted to Lord de Grey (later the Marquess of Ripon), a British diplomat, that the cession of Canada might end the quarrel. 'The English envoy contented himself with the dry remark that he did not find such a suggestion in his instructions.'[183] There were other issues, such as fisheries, the navigation of the St Lawrence, and the water boundary between the two empires in the north-west. Negotiations were held in Washington from March to May 1871, and by the Treaty of Washington a tribunal of arbitration was set up in Geneva to decide on the matters. All except the question of ownership of the San Juan Islands: by Article XXXIV, the issue was referred to the Emperor of Germany to decide.[184]

Kaiser Wilhelm set up a commission of three to determine the outcome, a professor at the University of Berlin, a councillor from the Imperial High Court of Commerce, and the Vice-President of the German High Court. After discussing – arguing? – the matter for over a year, they voted two to one to award the San Juan Islands to the US, with the international boundary to run through the Haro Strait. The Kaiser announced the decision on 21 October 1872, and it now remained only for the joint occupation to end. On 21 November the British left, after first chopping down the flagpole and dividing it among the men; a long piece was taken back to the dock as a souvenir. The Americans had rather hoped to run their flag up the same flagpole, but had to be contented with nailing it to a telegraph pole.[185] While many Canadians felt that their interests had been ignored by the British, the British and American governments were glad that the issue had been resolved.

XIII

There was one more boundary conflict between the two empires, that between Canada and Alaska, and it, too, was exacerbated by the discovery of gold. For several decades in the late eighteenth and early nineteenth centuries, disputes had arisen between the Russian and British empires along the Pacific coast from the northern point of Vancouver Island up to the Behring Strait. In 1821 the Tsar issued edicts granting to Russian subjects a monopoly over fishing, fur trading, whaling and other trading in the waters out to 100 miles from the Alaskan coast. The Russian Minister in London told Castlereagh that the purpose was to prevent any further trading operations by 'vagabonds', by which he meant American traders who were collecting furs for the lucrative Canton market in China. Britain strongly objected, and flatly refused to accept the Russian claims. Over the subsequent three years, more or less friendly negotiations were carried out, and on 28 February 1825 a treaty was signed in St Petersburg, by which the Russians ceased claiming the right to control all activity within 100 miles of their possessions along the north-west coast.[186] This was a signal British victory, but, again, the ambiguity of the maps would, three-quarters of a century later, lead to conflict.

The Anglo-Russian Convention of 1825 fixed the boundary which the US inherited when it bought Alaska from the Russians on 30 March 1867, for which it paid $7.2 million. In the 'Treaty Concerning the Cession of the Russian Possessions in North America by His Majesty the Emperor of all the Russias to the United States of America: June 20, 1867', in shorthand the Russian–American Treaty of 1867, the eastern boundary of Alaska was described in Article I as 'the line of demarcation between the Russian and the British possessions in North America, as established by the convention between Russia and Great Britain on the 28th of February 1825'.[187] In order to

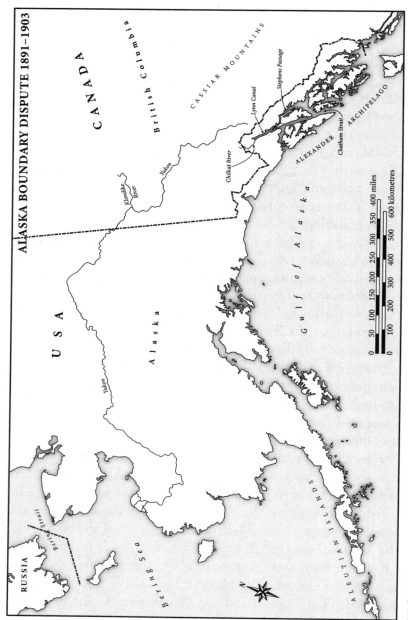

MAP II

indicate clearly the limits of Alaska, Secretary of State Seward had a map published which depicted the boundary as it had already appeared on previous maps; British cartographers accepted this line, and the British government did not object to it. However, soon afterwards, gold was discovered in the Cassiar region of British Columbia, and the question of a survey to determine the absolutely correct boundary was raised.[188] This, however, was a narrative which would continue for some years.

In June 1891, Sir Julian Pauncefote, the British Minister to the US, wrote to Secretary of State James Blaine that 'the question of the boundary ... is, at the present time, the subject of some difference of opinion and of considerable correspondence', adding that the actual boundary line could be determined only by an international commission. Blaine paid little attention to the letter until February 1892, when he had a conference with Pauncefote and three Canadian representatives, and the Canadians submitted a proposal for 'some impartial authority' to take a decision. Three days later, it was agreed that a joint survey should be made of the border between Alaska and British Columbia, which duly reported in December 1895, accompanying it with maps and photographs.[189] On the whole Canadian maps had followed the boundary as fixed by the Americans, but in 1895 the Canadian government published a map of British Columbia which set out a different, and more favourable, boundary. On 12 August 1895, this was reported to Blaine by W. W. Duffield, the Superintendent of the United States Coast and Geodetic Survey and the American Boundary Commissioner.[190] The most important point at issue at this point was the American stranglehold on the economically vital Lynn Canal, to which Canada claimed access.[191] This claim was repeatedly pressed, and it became painfully obvious to the Department of State that it was necessary to come to a settlement of the Alaskan boundary.

John Hay, the future Secretary of State, had just taken up the post of American Ambassador in London, and he reported to President William McKinley that the British government was 'manifesting a very friendly spirit towards him'. But Canada was disinclined to meet the Americans halfway, he said, and

Hay deprecated the apparent inability of the British government to ignore 'the whims of Canadian statesmen'. As far as he was concerned, the essence of the situation was this: 'It is far more to Canada's advantage than ours to be on good terms with us. Lord Salisbury [the British Prime Minister], in a private conversation the other day, compared her to a coquettish girl with two suitors, playing off one against the other. I should think a closer analogy would be to call her a married flirt, ready to betray John Bull on any occasion, but holding him responsible for all her follies.'[192] Neither country seemed inclined to appease the Canadians.

In 1896 gold was discovered near the Klondike River in Yukon. Canada demanded a much larger area, and asked for arbitration of the whole. It hoped that Great Britain would defend its claims, but even the Canadian Minister of the Interior admitted the strength of the American position. In March 1898 President McKinley and Ambassador Pauncefote (in 1893 the British government had upgraded the legation to an embassy and thereby Pauncefote from Minister to Ambassador) agreed to embark on negotiations on all outstanding Canadian–American issues, and at the end of May a Protocol was signed setting up the joint high commission. It was headed by Lord Herschell, the Lord Chancellor, appointed by London partly to keep the Canadians under control. Even the great imperialist Joseph Chamberlain, the Colonial Secretary, was tepid in his support, writing on 26 December 1898 to Henry White of the American Embassy in London that 'personally, I care very little for the points in dispute, but I care immensely for the consequential advantages of a thorough understanding between the two countries and the removal of these trumpery causes of irritation'.[193] Herschell hoped to settle the dispute by mutual concessions, but he wanted at least the appearance of not betraying the Canadians. At the same time the Americans and the British were also negotiating over an isthmian canal, and the Canadians wanted concessions on the canal to be matched by American concessions on the boundary. The British argued for this,[194] but deadlock ensued, and the Commission was adjourned in February 1899 for tempers to cool. Herschell then died.

The Alaskan boundary dominated the discussions within the Commission. The imperial representatives argued for arbitration, but the Americans rejected this on the grounds that arbitrators usually split the difference, even between just and unjust claims (ironically, this was an argument earlier made by Great Britain with regard to competing claims in Venezuela and rejected by the Americans themselves). In the end, Canada's exaggerated claims, and the British desire to strengthen relations with the Americans, led the British to tell the Canadians that the American case was unassailable, and if they delayed any further their position would only worsen.[195] The Canadians were driven to accept arbitration and everything was going well, when the Canadian Premier, Sir Wilfrid Laurier, decided that for domestic political reasons he would make further demands. The result was the end of negotiations for two years.

In 1901, Hay reopened negotiations. He suggested a binational commission in April, and the British urged the Canadians to accept it. But the Canadians delayed and insisted on neutral arbitration. This caused Theodore Roosevelt, who had become President after the assassination of President McKinley on 19 September 1901, to lose his temper – a not unusual response to having his wishes thwarted – and after more negotiations and delay he began to wonder if the British were as friendly as they seemed. He anticipated that, if gold was discovered in the disputed region, a clash would come, and therefore Britain, and especially Canada, must give way. To ensure that they would, and because clashes between American and Canadian miners were increasing in the frontier region, in March 1902 he ordered 800 cavalrymen to Alaska and, though at least partly intended for police duties, they made the intended impression, which was to convince Britain that the US meant business. To emphasise this, in May he told a member of the British Embassy staff that he was 'going to be ugly' over the question of the boundary.[196] This was followed by a raft of letters from the President and American friends of Britain warning the British government that this was the case. Roosevelt was sympathetic to Britain's plight, understanding that it could not be seen to abandon its colony, but he regarded the Canadian claims as 'untenable', declaring that 'there will of course be no compromise'[197] on his part.

There were now negotiations, a convention signed on 24 January 1903 setting up a boundary commission, Anglo-American-Canadian diplomatic manoeuvres, a crisis caused by the Senate's objection to the wording, political 'skullduggery'[198] by Senator Henry Cabot Lodge of Massachusetts as the Chairman of the Senate Foreign Relations Committee, a political brouhaha over the choice of the American Commissioners, more international suspicion and manoeuvres, more digging in of Canadian feet, and – finally – a decision on 20 October 1903 awarding victory to the Americans.[199] The US did, in fact, have a strong legal claim to the territory, precisely what, in the aftermath of the discovery of gold in Yukon, Ottawa sought to revise.[200] The Canadians, however, saw things differently, and they knew whom to blame for the outcome: as the Toronto *News* said the following day, 'Nothing is surer than that Canada has suffered incalculable loss and despoilment through the dealings of British diplomatists with Canadian interests and Canadian territory ... The Alaska treaty ... seems to be a sacrifice of Canadian interests to the paramount desire of Great Britain to cultivate the good opinion of the United States.'[201] The two Canadian representatives refused to sign the award, and the Canadians later refused to allow a mountain to be named after one of the British representatives.[202] 'There were screams of protest in England, and for years this episode provided the chief talking point for those who maintained that the Americans consistently bullied England.'[203] But after a few years, although the Canadians apparently never forgot this so-called betrayal, they had of necessity become reconciled to the decision.

XIV

The Canadian–American border was the one area where the two empires met, and where the threat of conflict between them, whether diplomatic or physical, was always present. There was an imbalance in strength, though late in this period the British began to perceive that the balance was shifting. The US had not yet the strength of Great Britain, but it was strong enough to ensure that the British took care not to annoy it unnecessarily. There was also an imbalance in intentions: the US was primarily aggressive while the British and Canadians were primarily defensive. Britain wanted to maintain its claim over Oregon north of the Columbia River, including its mouth, but the US cared more and put more effort into acquiring everything up to the 49th parallel. It had to protect its security against a hostile power, and taking over all contiguous territory was, for years, seen as the best means of attaining this safety. For both powers, then, when in 1903 the Canadian–American border was defined by treaty in its entirety, a century-long cause of Anglo-American conflict was finally resolved.

For Britain, and for Canada, this was fortunate, because by then Britain would have found it very difficult to defend its colony from the increasingly powerful United States. There are several ways in which relative power can be assessed, including economic, military and naval power, and the gradual change in the power relationships provides the context for the events in this chapter, and, indeed, in the last. First of all, there is economic and financial power, not necessarily the same thing: the ability to produce industrial goods does not necessarily imply the power to finance this production. Equally important in this context was the ability to raise taxes, both to sustain military and naval forces in peacetime and to fund the loans required to fight wars – and the ability to raise these loans was a reflection of investors' confidence in British financial strength. Throughout most of the nineteenth century, the US was a developing country, an economic and financial colony of Britain. The US exported raw materials and food to Britain, while Britain exported manufactured goods to the US. Americans were acutely aware of their inferior position. This, however, began to change after 1870, when the US experienced its own industrial revolution, and the market for British exports in the US declined accordingly. According to the historian A. J. P. Taylor, 'the test of a Great Power is the test of strength for war',[204] and in the nineteenth century the steel industry was as good a measure as any. Thus it is significant that, while in 1871 the American production of steel was very small, by the end of the century it was twice that of Britain. Where Britain did maintain its overwhelmingly supreme position was in finance. The pound sterling was the world's most important trading and only reserve currency and the City of London was the world's financial centre. Britain financed trade and the building of infrastructure around the world, not least for and in America.

Secondly, there is military and naval power. The two countries shared an aversion to a standing army, on both economic and security grounds: the Americans preferred not to waste money on an army, and they remembered that Britain had maintained a standing army in the American colonies, while the British found it difficult to shake the memory of military control in the mid-seventeenth century. Nevertheless, Britain had in effect two standing armies. One was the British Army, raised entirely in the United Kingdom. The other was the British-Indian Army, whose rank and file were recruited in India but whose officers were British, raised and trained in the United Kingdom; their duty was to police the empire. The British Army was large enough for regiments to be sent out to Canada when necessary. For the Americans, their lack of a large peacetime army meant that they depended rather more on threats, such as in 1848–9, than on military forces. The two occasions when the US Army blossomed was during the Civil War of 1861–5, when there were two armies, and after which both were largely dismantled, and the Spanish–American War of 1898, when rather more were kept in uniform, not least because, as a result of the war and America's taking over the Philippines, it had to fight a ten-year war against Philippine guerrillas.

But more important in the Anglo-American-Canadian context was the relative power of the American and British navies. Briefly, until the 1860s, Britain had little to fear from the US Navy. First of all, the Royal Navy was considerably bigger. Secondly, the combination of bases and colonies around the world made possible relatively rapid communication even before the submarine telegraph as well as the ability to concentrate forces where necessary.

And thirdly, the size, the power and the reach of the Royal Navy enabled it often to deter an enemy rather than having to fight it.[205] But this changed during the period of the American Civil War, when the Admiralty became increasingly concerned about the rapid growth of the US Navy, and in particular about the growth in the number of ironclad vessels. Britain had in 1860 launched its first such, HMS *Warrior*, and, although this class had not been tested in battle, the Admiralty were confident of its efficacy against French and American ships, including the real threat, the French ironclad. This complacency was shaken for a time with the arrival of the American ironclad, the USS *Monitor*: the latest British guns were unable to pierce her sides, and the ship could easily destroy multiple numbers of wooden ships. Furthermore, the American ironclads carried bigger guns than the British ships, which meant that, for a time, British ironclads were also at risk.[206] The result was that the ability of the Royal Navy to blockade the Atlantic seaboard and bombard the coastal cities for a time disappeared, and it was this power that had been seen as Canada's best defence.

Yet particularly worrying to the Admiralty was the pace of American shipbuilding. At the end of 1864, the US Navy had 671 ships afloat or being built, of which seventy-one were ironclads; of the Royal Navy's steam navy of 417, only thirty were ironclad.[207] Nevertheless, for some years the British were confident of retaining their lead, as the number of American ships declined, but over the next several decades a close eye was kept on the US Navy. By December 1904, the First Lord of the Admiralty, Lord Selborne, considered that nothing could be done about any threat by the US, because 'the United States are forming a navy the power and size of which will be limited only by the amount of money which the American people choose to spend on it'.[208] The British no longer considered that there might be a naval war directly with the US: the opinion of the War Office, in fact, was that 'the contingency of war with the United States should be avoided at all hazards'.[209] But there might be a war between Britain and one or more of the European Great Powers, given that there was high tension between Britain and France, Russia and Germany, and members of the Cabinet thought that it was possible that, if there was great tension between the US and Britain, the US would join Britain's enemies and the British would lose. But it should not be forgotten that the British empire was the only Power which had a string of naval bases circling the globe. This meant that the empire had a global mobility that the American empire could not match.

Naturally the Americans were concerned about the British Army and the Royal Navy, but there was a more encompassing concern, and this was the British empire. Granted that over the century the American empire had expanded from the Atlantic to the Pacific, and thence beyond the borders to Alaska on the Arctic Ocean, Hawaii in the Pacific, Puerto Rico in the Caribbean and the Philippines in the Far East, yet it seemed that wherever Americans looked, they came up against the British empire. There was Canada in North America and colonies in the Caribbean and South America, as well as informal empire in a substantial part of South America; there were South Africa, and Nigeria, the Gold Coast (later Ghana) and a number of other colonies, including those in East Africa; there were Egypt, Cyprus and Malta on and in the Mediterranean and Aden (institutionally part of India) on the Indian Ocean; there were Australia and New Zealand in the south; there were Singapore and Malaya and Hong Kong, and informal empire in China; and there were Burma, Ceylon and, very importantly, India. There were dozens of others. As the cliché pointed out, the sun never set on the British empire, and any time an American looked at a globe, he or she saw a girdle of red. Americans ached for the prestige that the British empire enjoyed: they knew that they deserved it. They felt powerful in their own hemisphere and were willing to challenge the British empire there, but in the rest of the globe, bar the Philippines, they were inferior to the British. Nevertheless, by the end of the century, while the US was developing into a potential Great Power, the British empire was under mounting pressure from the other Great Powers, Russia, France and increasingly Germany. In these circumstances, Britain looked on the US as a possible ally in an ever more threatening world, and thus, when there was a conflict, meeting the wishes of the US was normally more important than meeting those of Canada. The decision on the Canadian–Alaskan border in 1903 made this manifestly clear. But what is also clear is that at the end of the nineteenth century the British empire still had the political will to remain a global power; the United States still lacked the political will to challenge it.

The final delineation of the border also marked another milestone: on the North American continent, the United States had nowhere further to go. But even earlier in the century, American eyes had begun to look outward, in this case to the Far East. Driven by the desire for trade, the American government in the 1840s and 1850s turned its attention to China and Japan. In China, the British were already there. Japan, however, was virgin territory.

Chapter 3

China and the British and American Barbarians, 1783–1914

At dawn on 14 September 1793, Lord Macartney was introduced to the Chinese Emperor, Ch'ien-Lung. Macartney was in Peking (Beijing) as the representative of King George III, whose government wanted to establish diplomatic relations and to improve and expand commercial relations. Macartney wore his robes of the Order of the Bath over a suit of spotted mulberry velvet. The wonders of the British export trade were displayed: a planetarium, optical and magnetic instruments, Irish poplins, Birmingham metalware and Wedgwood dishes. The Embassy was received with polite condescension, and the following day taken through a succession of pavilions filled with far superior products, and then brusquely dismissed. Macartney recorded in his journal that 'Our presents must shrink from the comparison and "hide their diminished heads".'[1] The Emperor began his Edict, to be carried back by Macartney, 'We, by the Grace of Heaven, Emperor, instruct the King of England to take note of our charge.' He then commended the British monarch for his 'sincere humility and obedience', but pointed out that the Celestial Empire had not 'the slightest need of your country's manufactures'. Finally, he rejected the request for a relaxation of restrictions on trade between China and Great Britain and the appointment of a permanent ambassador.[2] Yet, within half a century, for the Chinese the world had turned upside down.

The British empire in China was an informal empire, not an 'empire of rule'. This meant that the region in question retained nominal independence, while succumbing to foreign influence. It was based ultimately on the threat or actual use of military force. This in its turn could enable preponderant influence in or the acquisition of strategically vital territories. Force also supported the use of diplomatic pressure or the imposition of key advisers in important areas of government, such as the head of the department responsible for the collection of taxes. This structure of influence normally resulted in commercial agreements favourable to the dominant power. In due course, this was the case with Great Britain. Behind its increasingly strong financial and commercial position in China there always lurked the threat of force, of so-called gunboat diplomacy, provided by the Royal Navy. It was to be naval power of an uncompromising type, backed by the land power of the British-Indian Army, that destroyed the restrictions which had shackled British trade, and opened up China to the barbarians. In short, Britain enjoyed commercial power without much political responsibility. The foreign barbarians, however, included the other Great Powers, and by the 1890s Britain found that it had to defend its position in China from these Powers, especially Russia, France and, soon, Germany – most of which *did* want to impose an empire of rule – as well as from the Chinese themselves. In this situation, Britain looked to the other commercially driven empire which was trying to establish trading relations with China, and which did not wish to take over territory, the United States.

In 1785, the first American ships landed in Canton (Guangzhou),[3] and the US early on established its decades-long position in China as competitor and sidekick of Britain, following closely behind, and insisting on any privileges and rights which Britain had obtained for itself. There were various terms for this – piggyback diplomacy, jackal diplomacy, hitch-hiking diplomacy, used both then and by later historians[4] – and it depended on the power of Britain, which possessed the naval strength in the Far East that the US lacked. The US government during the nineteenth century was even more concerned than was Britain's not to become involved in Chinese politics or the acquisition of territory; rather, it wanted to be free to trade and to spread the Christian gospel. In short, the American empire did not exist in China – but it relentlessly collected imperial pickings.

Britain was the predominant imperial power in China from the early 1800s until the 1890s. Great Power imperialism was so rampant by then that in 1890 a new word, 'imperialism', entered the *Oxford English Dictionary*. British predominance was increasingly challenged, and London looked to the US for support, and yet, although the men on the spot were mostly willing, the American government refused to become involved. There were three exceptions to this, however. One was the so-called American 'Open Door' Notes of 1898; the second was American military involvement in the ferocity of the Boxer Rebellion and its bloody suppression in 1900; and the third was the US government's attempts from 1909 to 1913 to use financial diplomacy and pressure to penetrate the Powers' spheres of interest. Otherwise, Britain had to use its own power and influence to hold its position against French, Russian, German, Austro-Hungarian and Japanese trading and military incursions. Much of this came to an end with the First World War: three of the participants ceased to be empires, one ceased to be a state at all, and the Chinese, by means of two revolutions, began to take matters more firmly into their own hands.

I

In the late sixteenth century, merchants in the City of London looked enviously on both the Portuguese and especially the Dutch for their lucrative trade in the East Indies.⁵ But trade with Asia was challenging. Costs were very high, given that both the ships able to make such a long journey and the desirable commodities were expensive; furthermore, capital was tied up for a very long period, since it could be two years before a profit was realised – if it was. The journey was fraught with difficulty and danger, what with typhoons, diseases, wars and untrustworthy governments. One

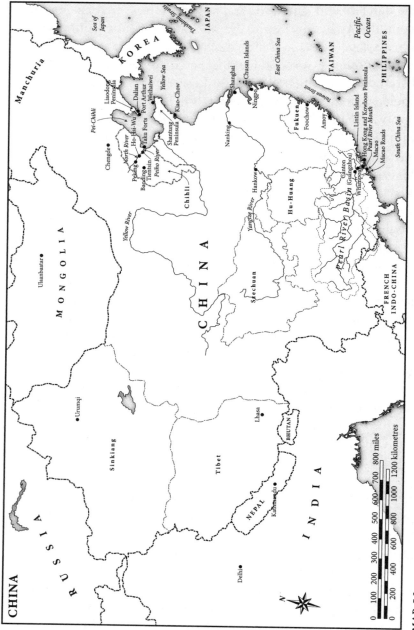

MAP 12

answer was to bring together a large group of gentlemen to share the dangers and the costs, because 'so farre remote from hence cannot be traded but by a joint and untied stock'.[6] In September 1599, a total of 101 subscribers, primarily from the London merchant community, raised £30,000 to 'set forthe a vyage ... to the Est Indies and other ilandes and countries therabouts', if they could secure from Queen Elizabeth a charter giving them a monopoly of English Asian trade. The charter for the English East India Company was finally granted in September 1600.[7]

Although the Company operated in various ports across Asia, in its first decades the concentration was on the Indonesian archipelago and India, with a position much less secure in the former – the Dutch effectively drove out the English – than in the latter.[8] English trading ships did not reach China until 1635, when the Portuguese allowed one to call in at Macao; more portentous for the future, however, was the occasion in 1637 when four English ships (not from the East India Company) forced their way into Canton against Chinese opposition and managed to acquire a small cargo. However, it was only much later in the century that the Company established a legal foothold there.

In the 1680s conditions changed. In 1684, the Emperor lifted the ban preventing Chinese ships from going to sea. He then dramatically proclaimed the opening of all coastal ports to licensed, private maritime trade and established a network of customs stations to collect taxes. The focus was on inter-Asian trade by the Chinese, but it also slightly eased trade by foreigners. In 1699 the Company established its operations at Canton, until 1842 the only port open to the Europeans. Until the end of the seventeenth century, the primary goods bought by the English were silks, along with porcelain and a small amount of tea. In 1669, only 222 pounds of tea were imported by the Company. However, in 1701, it was 121,417 pounds, in 1721 it was 1,214,629 pounds, in 1750 it was 4,727,992 pounds,[9] while by 1800 it was 23 million pounds.

For both the East India Company and Great Britain, the need to sell tea was inexorable and growing. The Company needed the money to finance its military exploits in India, against both the French and the Indians. As for Britain, by the 1780s a significant proportion of government revenue came from the excise duty on tea. Yet the need to pay the Chinese for the tea, as well as for silk and porcelain, was draining silver out of the country to an alarming extent; for example, to pay for 23 million pounds of tea required £3.6 million in silver to be remitted to China. Thus the trade with China, and the means by which it was carried out, were of real concern to both the Company and the British government.

Trade with China was by the so-called Canton system. In 1757, the Chinese government had decreed that Canton would be the only port open to foreign trade, and in 1760 detailed regulations were issued which set out the restricted times each year when foreign traders would be allowed to call in to China, where they might reside while there and with whom they might trade. There were to be no foreign wives or dependants, and the merchants' mobility was extremely limited.[10] Furthermore, they were not allowed to learn Chinese nor anything about Chinese history. The foreigners were to be kept restricted and ignorant. This was acceptable to both the Company and the British government for a time, since Canton was the port of choice, not least because it had access to the interior by means of the Pearl River system. Yet soon the restrictions grew increasingly onerous. The traders disliked the fact that foreign nationals accused of crimes on Chinese soil were tried under Chinese law by the Chinese themselves. More practically, the Company wanted a depot under its control for its goods and from where it could conduct trade.

It also disliked the Chinese organisation of its part of the trade, which has been termed 'hierarchic subordination'. Firstly, the trade was restricted to licensed Chinese monopolists, known collectively as the Cohong, who collected and then sold the tea and other goods to the foreign traders; secondly, the Cohong was subordinate to the imperially appointed superintendent of maritime customs, known to the Western merchants as the Hoppo; and thirdly, all of the imperial officials at Canton, including the local governor and the regional governor, issued orders and regulations to the Cohong, who might easily be disgraced or jailed for any non-compliance, and who then put pressure on the Western traders. The imperial officials refused to deal with the

Westerners directly, but only through the Cohong. An increasing problem was that these officials saw their positions as a means of 'squeezing' 'gifts' from the members of the Cohong, who then 'squeezed' the foreigners. Even the Emperor viewed the Canton trade as an important means of personal profit, and one duty of the Hoppo was to keep this trade open for the benefit of the Emperor. It was also a means of raising funds for imperial military campaigns, repairing the Yellow River system, and defence against coastal pirates. Thus it was careful squeezing all down the line: it had to be enough to enable all elements to make a greater or lesser amount of money, while not driving the Cohong out of business and thereby cutting off the source of these funds.[11]

In 1787, the Company and the British government decided to send a mission to China to negotiate, or extract, some improvements in the Chinese–Western trader relationship. The man chosen to lead it was Lieutenant-Colonel Charles Cathcart, MP. The reason for this choice, beyond the fact that Cathcart had lately been Quartermaster-General to the Bengal Army and was thus familiar with the trade in Asia, was given in his instructions of 30 November 1787:

> it is presumed, that a Gentleman of honorable Birth, as also a member of the Legislative Body would be most likely to have a favorable reception from a proud and ostentatious People, accustomed to think meanly of the commercial Character; the propriety of this distinction is enforced by the decided Opinion of the most respectable Persons, who have been experienced in the Company's concerns at Canton, and Witnesses of the Vexations under which they labor.[12]

Importantly, he was to be the Ambassador of the King, not an emissary of the Company.[13]

He was instructed to make his way to Peking, ideally to land at a port on the north or north-east coast, but if necessary to go by land from Canton to Peking. He was to negotiate the grant of a depot to the British to store their goods; here the resident Chinese were to remain under Chinese jurisdiction, but the

British would be subject only to their own laws. If these terms could not be obtained, he was to negotiate the best terms he could for the traders. But, 'it is necessary you should be on your Guard, against one stipulation which may perhaps be demanded of you, that is for the exclusion of the Trade of Opium from the Chinese Dominions, as being prohibited by the Laws of the Empire'.[14] These instructions betray an impressive ignorance or even arrogance. First of all, the Company, if not the government, knew that Westerners were confined to Canton: why did it assume that this unannounced mission would be allowed to land, let alone proceed to Peking? And secondly, the expectation that the Chinese would cede control over part of the Chinese empire – would the British have agreed to cede part of the British Isles to the traders of another country? – is somewhat surprising. Granted, this had happened in India, but China, unlike India, was a unified and long-established empire. The British expectations, however, were never put to the test, because in the summer of 1788, six months into the voyage, Cathcart, who had consumption, died in the Strait of Banka (Bangka). There was no one to replace him, and the ship returned home.

It was decided to send another embassy to China. However, based on recently translated contemporary Chinese documents on the Embassy, a story a bit different from the one usually presented emerges. It began in October 1792 with a letter from the East India Company to the Chinese Emperor, announcing that the King of England was sending an embassy to congratulate the Emperor on his birthday. The man appointed as Ambassador was Viscount Macartney, the most experienced diplomat in Great Britain – he had been appointed envoy to Russia in 1764 at the age of twenty-seven, and Governor of Madras in 1780. He had a cultural hinterland, having in 1779 joined Dr Samuel Johnson's circle, and he was conversant with literary London. He apparently had strong principles, a firm character and a 'powerful ambition to succeed'. He was also (as his journal shows) rather prolix. Unusually, he never enriched himself in public office.[15] In order that the mission need not be aborted this time, Sir George Staunton was appointed the Secretary of the Embassy and Minister in Macartney's absence, alive or dead. The Chinese were expected to be dazzled by the pedigree of Macartney, and, to encourage this, the whole mission was to surround itself with much ceremony and display; certainly in eighteenth-century Europe, display, ritual and ceremony were linked to the dignity and honour of the sovereign represented by the ambassador.[16] Furthermore, Macartney suggested, his Embassy should include men of scientific and artistic attainments, 'such as to impress the Chinese with the high degree of civilization attained in England'.[17] The ostensible reason for the mission was to convey the King's congratulations to his 'brother potentate' the Emperor on the latter's eightieth birthday, but the occasion was to be used to discuss future arrangements for conducting trade to the mutual advantage of the two countries.

What did Macartney hope to accomplish? According to the traditional account, his first and most important objective was to establish diplomatic relations with China. Secondly, he was to negotiate a treaty of commerce and friendship between Great Britain and China, in order to improve trading conditions for the English merchants at Canton, to gain the right to trade at other ports, such as Ningpo (Ningbo), to be able to trade directly with the Chinese without having to go through a monopoly, and, if possible, to open up new markets for British manufactures. And thirdly, he was to bring the Chinese to agree that a representative of the King could reside permanently in Peking.[18] This all seems reasonable enough, especially as the plan apparently was to negotiate and not to go in with all guns blazing. But when the British letter was translated into Chinese and the Emperor read the demands, he found them unacceptable: the British wanted to keep a permanent representative of the King in Peking, to trade at ports along the coast and in Peking, to receive tax reductions and to be given one of the Chusan (Zhoushan) Islands off the coast near the port of Ningpo as well as a base near Canton. In short, the British wanted Chinese land, economic privileges and easy access to the Chinese court.[19]

Implicit in the wish to establish diplomatic relations with China, and the desire to have an ambassador from the King reside in Peking, was the assumption of equality between the two countries, but this was not a Chinese concept. Any relationship between the Celestial Empire and a foreign country must be as one between supreme ruler and vassal. All of the barbarians outside China were obviously irresistibly attracted to the Emperor because of the power of his virtue, itself the result of his right conduct. It was taken for granted that the uncultured barbarian would recognise the superiority of Chinese civilisation and would come to 'be transformed'; in response it was the function of the Emperor to be compassionate in his 'cherishing men from afar'. They in their turn would display humble submission through bringing tribute and taking part in full Court ritual, including the full *ketou* or kowtow. In short, any relationship between China and Britain, which was referred to by Court translators as the 'Red-Haired Kingdom'[20] (the English themselves were 'red-haired barbarians of the Western Ocean'), was seen as a tributary relationship: the Celestial Empire had no equals.

Macartney and the members of his Embassy set out from London on 11 September 1792 to join his ship, HMS *Lion*, at Portsmouth. They arrived in China nine months later, dropping anchor on 20 June 1793 off Macao. They then made their way by ship up the coast to the Gulf of Pei-chihli (Bohai) and thence to Tientsin (Tianjin) at the mouth of the Peiho (Haihe) River, which was a relatively short distance from Peking itself. On 6 August, several mandarins (officials) of high rank arrived to escort the Ambassador to the Viceroy, who had been sent by the Emperor 'to compliment me [Macartney] on my entrance into his dominions, and to give proper orders upon the occasion'.[21] And so the quadrille began.

For the British, meeting the Emperor himself was vital: they would not be fobbed off with high officials. First of all, this was the only way to establish diplomatic relations. As the strongest global power, the British expected to be received as equals, although from the point of view of the Emperor and his Court – and that of every other Chinese – this was inherently unthinkable. Secondly, the British laboured under the misapprehension that because the vexations which the Western traders endured were, they thought, unknown to the Emperor, once he knew about them he would relieve the burden. He would therefore undoubtedly be willing to agree to a 'trade and friendship' treaty with Great Britain.

The main concern of the mandarins appeared to Macartney to be that he should recognise the inferior position of Great Britain to China and therefore his own inferior position to the Emperor. They knew that that the British barbarians had come as supplicants, clearly desperate for an audience with the Emperor because they were irresistibly attracted by his power and virtue, and they were bringing gifts. Thus they were representing a tributary king: how could they be equal? Macartney must therefore perform a full submission to the Emperor, and this meant the kowtow. It was described in a Chinese Court letter of 14 August 1793 by a high official as 'the ceremony of the three kneelings and the nine knockings of the head [on the floor]'.[22] 'It was performed to the shrill commands of an usher – "kneel, fall prostrate, rise to your knees".'[23] The prime concern of the Emperor and his officials, however, was not in fact the kowtow, which is seldom mentioned in the documents: it was to avoid the possible military consequences of rejecting the British demands.[24]

The entire journey to the palace of the Emperor at Peking was interlaced with repeated attempts by the mandarins to 'guide' Macartney into performing his duty – indeed, they 'pressed me most earnestly to comply with it, said it was a mere trifle'.[25] In his journal, this question of court ritual as a reflection of sovereign power is a dominant theme, presumably reflecting European practice. In his own words, Macartney was unfailingly courteous, but he was firm in his refusal. Four days before his audience with the Emperor, when the mandarins continued their attempts to persuade him,

> I [Macartney] told them that it was not natural to expect that an ambassador should pay greater homage to a foreign prince than to his own liege Sovereign ... Upon which they asked me what was the ceremony of presentation to the King of England. I told them it was performed by kneeling upon one knee and kissing His Majesty's hand. 'Why then,' cried they, 'can't you do so to the Emperor?' 'Most readily,' said I; 'the same ceremony

I perform to my own King I am willing to go through for your Emperor, and I think it a greater compliment than any other I can pay him.' I showed them the manner of it, and they retired seemingly well satisfied.

However, later in the day, the mandarins returned and said that, as it was not the custom to kiss the Emperor's hand, could Macartney not kneel on two knees instead of it? He said that he had already given his answer; that was the end of the days-long negotiation.[26]

Macartney met the Emperor three times, on 14 September at the Summer Palace in Jehol (Chengde), about 110 miles north-east of Peking and beyond the Great Wall; there again on the 18th; and on the 30th, when the Embassy paid their respects as the Emperor in procession made his way back to Peking. The first, on 14 September, was the crucial encounter: Macartney received his audience with the Emperor and presented the King's letter to him. Macartney, Sir George Staunton and the eleven-year-old Master Staunton, who had developed a remarkable knowledge of the Chinese language, set out for the Court in palanquins at 4 a.m., with the remainder of the Ambassador's escort on horseback in full uniform or livery. Shortly after 6 a.m. the Emperor arrived, announced by drums and music. As he passed in his open palanquin, Macartney and his entourage knelt on one knee while the Chinese all prostrated themselves. Once the Emperor had ascended the throne, Macartney, holding in both hands the golden box encrusted with diamonds which contained the King's letter, 'walked deliberately up, and ascending the side-steps of the throne, delivered it into the Emperor's own hands'.[27] This may seem unimportant, but actually presenting the box to the Emperor himself, rather than to the First Minister (Grand Secretary), represented another victory for Macartney in his struggle to be seen as the representative of an equal monarch. However, he received a jolt the following day when, as noted above, he was taken from pavilion to pavilion, and realised just how relatively unimpressive were the objects that he had brought from Britain.

He had tried on the 14th to arrange a meeting with the Emperor's First Minister to discuss his trade-related requests, but he found that 'though infinitely gracious and civil in his manner and expression, I could gain no ground upon him'.[28] This would continue to be the case: total evasion, encased in gracious civility.

Macartney's second meeting with the Emperor on 18 September was again at his Summer Palace, where the Emperor was marking his birthday with lavish celebrations. For most of the day before, Macartney was escorted by the First Minister, and 'I could not help admitting the address with which the Minister parried all my attempts to speak to him on business this day … I, nevertheless, found an occasion to remind him of his promise to peruse the note which I meant to send him.'[29] Macartney was having little success in trying to discuss with the Chinese the issues that were the main reason for his visit. They did not wish to discuss these with him, because the Emperor had already rejected them, and it would disturb the calm and courteous atmosphere, which was a vital element in cherishing men from afar. Not only that, it might be dangerous.

On the 18th the Embassy went to Court, at the invitation of the Emperor, to see a four-hour comedy that was greatly enjoyed by the Emperor and all of those who spoke Chinese. When finally meeting the Emperor, Macartney tried in vain 'to lead him towards the subject of my Embassy, but he seemed not disposed to enter into it'.[30] Matters had made no progress when the Emperor passed in procession on the 30th on his way back to Peking, and sent a message to Macartney suggesting politely but pointedly that he should continue on his way back home.[31]

The Edict which Macartney carried back to the King rejected every proposal made by the British. In truth, his Embassy had failed because, as is clear from the Chinese Court documents, the Chinese never meant it to succeed – even before Macartney stepped ashore, the Chinese had drafted an edict ordering his dismissal; the final version was approved on 28 September, nine days after Macartney had been received by the Emperor. Fundamentally, two different cultures and outlooks had clashed. The Chinese saw Western Ocean barbarians as warlike and dangerous and the British as the most dangerous of all.[32] According to the Emperor in the Chinese document, it was now clear that 'among the West

Ocean peoples the English were the strongest [i.e., in a pejorative sense, "brute strength"]; they not only plundered other West Ocean ships on the high seas, but were feared because of their lack of restraint ...' (the Chinese assessment of the British was pretty accurate). But it was also because they were personally untrustworthy: the Embassy had been unfailingly courteous and seemingly sincere – important to the Chinese – but, according to the historian James L. Hevia, 'it had become clear that Macartney could for a time hide his true intent behind false sincerity, a situation that made the British dangerous and perhaps, given their military technologies, capable of reckless and unrestrained applications of force'.[33]

Indeed, on the journey back to the ships, the high mandarins excelled in their treatment of the British. But this was driven by apprehension. Just before the Embassy left Peking, a letter was sent to all the coastal governors. In it the Emperor warned them that 'England is stronger and fiercer than the other countries in the Western Ocean. Since things have not gone according to their wishes, it may cause them to stir up trouble.' The governors were urged to strengthen their defences and not to give the British any excuse for military action: 'Now that country speaks of wanting us to give them a place near the sea for their trade, so the forts along the coast should not only organize a show of military force but also make defensive preparations.' With regard to the Chusan Islands, they were instructed to make advance plans 'so as not to let the English foreigners infiltrate and occupy them'. There were also a great many letters about how to get rid of the five British ships which were anchored at Chusan (the largest island after which the group was named), especially the heavily armed warship HMS *Lion*. The island provided a deep-water anchorage, which was one of the reasons that the British wanted it for a base.[34]

On 21 October Macartney discussed the Emperor's letter with a high mandarin official, and clearly conveyed something of his disappointment. The mandarin hastened to emphasise that, with the appointment of a new viceroy at Canton, things would greatly improve for the Western traders.[35] Then on 1 January 1794 Macartney received another letter from the Emperor which, the mandarin pointed out, showed his friendly disposition towards the British and promised his future favour and protection. Macartney wrote in his journal that 'These seem to be expressed in stronger terms than the former, and the Viceroy himself was particularly courteous and caressing.'[36] Clearly the Emperor's orders had been carried out.

The Chinese were both anxious and resentful. Firstly, there was massive suspicion of the Embassy, not least because of its size – seventy-seven members in all, of whom fifty-three were dragoons, infantry and artillery. Then there was dislike and contempt because of the refusal to perform the kowtow. Perhaps, the Emperor thought, they had come to spy. And finally, there was alarm when the realisation dawned of the extent of Macartney's disappointment, since they feared that he might cause trouble among the other Western traders before sailing home.[37] He had to be cocooned.

In the end, what did the Embassy accomplish? Its members were able to map what they termed the north coast of China, and they gained some knowledge of China and its approach to politics – and to foreigners. Beyond that, precisely nothing: 'the ambassador was received with the utmost politeness, treated with the utmost hospitality, watched with the utmost vigilance and dismissed with the utmost civility.'[38]

II

In doing business with China, American merchant traders were considerably behind those from Great Britain. When America had been a constituent part of the British empire, they had had full rights both in trading and in carrying goods between the American colonies and Great Britain and to all other parts of the empire. As one example, before the Revolution the American carrying trade was responsible for roughly 63 per cent of the shipping between the American colonies and the West Indies.[39] With the Treaty of Paris of 1783, which ended the war between the United Colonies of America and Great Britain, the situation changed. Granted, by an Order-in-Council issued on 26 December 1783, their goods would be admitted to Britain on the colonial terms, with lower duties on many items and others which were duty-free. But otherwise, the Americans lost all rights to direct trading and carrying goods to and from ports in the empire. The Americans were outraged: somehow, it seems not to have occurred to them that this would happen. After all, they believed they had a natural right to this trade. The British for their part were astonished: the Americans had fought to leave the empire – why should they assume that they would retain the privileges of imperial trade?

In any case, the merchants and shipowners – often the same men – had quickly to find alternative, non-British countries with which to trade, and they turned their attention to the Pacific. This was not the first American venture to the East: in 1698 the Earl of Bellomont, the Governor of New York colony, wrote in a report to the Lords of Trade and Plantations that 'I find that those Pyrates that have given the greatest disturbance in the East Indies and Red Sea have either been fitted from New York or Rhode Island, and manned from New York.'[40] Men from New York, in fact, also dispatched the first post-Revolution merchant ship to Canton. Organised by Robert Morris, who was a financier and one of the Founding Fathers, a 360-ton former privateer renamed the *Empress of China* set off with a cargo of American ginseng in 1784, which her owners hoped to trade for tea. They further hoped that the voyage would 'encourage others in the adventurous pursuit of commerce'.[41] More practically, it returned a profit of nearly 26 per cent.[42]

For Americans, as for the British, tea was still very important, although coffee would in the late 1820s supplant it as the drink of choice. By 1803, over half of the tea imported into the US was in fact re-exported to Europe. American traders were interested in a wider range of goods than were the British.[43] They faced the same difficulty as the British: how to raise the money to buy the goods. They provided ginseng – less good than that found in the Far East but cheaper – furs from the north-west coast of North America and sandalwood from Hawaii, but supplies, particularly from the latter two, soon ran out. The Chinese welcomed silver, and for some years American ships sold goods in Latin America for which they were paid in silver, and then carried the specie to China, but it could be difficult to accumulate enough. They soon shared the British conviction that the most dependable commodity they could sell in China was opium. Indeed, by the mid-nineteenth century, the British and American opium traders were to be the world's leading drug barons, operating on a scale which dwarfs more recent Latin American drug cartels.

The problem was, where to find the opium? The best was produced in India, in Bengal, but it was controlled by the East India Company. Although as already noted, American ships were forbidden to take part in imperial trade, in 1787 Earl Cornwallis, the Governor-General of India, gave instructions that American vessels should be treated with favour at the Company's settlements.[44] Certainly American commerce enjoyed great latitude in India, but only by the Jay Treaty in 1794 were American vessels formally given access to India. However, they could take goods only to and from India and ports in America – the India–China trade route was not included.[45] This rule was very laxly enforced, and American vessels carried many commodities between India and Canton. But what was rigidly enforced was the prohibition of the carriage of opium between British India and China. The Company itself did not actually carry the drug to China in its own vessels. In 1726 the Chinese Court had forbidden the smoking and importing of opium and, rather than lose access to the China market, the Company banned the shipping of opium in its ships. Instead, it auctioned the drug in Calcutta, and private British and Indian traders, what were called 'country' traders, bought it and then took it to China. This way, the Company could display its clean hands without losing profits. The Americans had to look elsewhere, and from 1805 began to carry opium from Smyrna in Ottoman Turkey to Canton,[46] a trade that they soon largely controlled. Turkish was inferior to Indian opium, but it was cheaper, and Chinese dealers frequently bought both and mixed them.

In general, until 1821 the British and American merchant traders and shipowners certainly competed, although without the rancour which might have been expected after the Wars of

Independence and of 1812. On the contrary, it can be argued that the bitter rivalry felt elsewhere, such as on the Canadian–American border, did not transfer to China, where they were all foreigners together. But an event in 1821, and its fallout, brought the American and British traders rather closer together in the way that the trade was organised.

The Chinese had tried repeatedly to end the drug trade, but the combination of the corruption of its own officials and the smuggling ability of the Western traders had rendered their efforts unsuccessful. In the autumn of 1821, however, an incident involving the Baltimore vessel the *Emily* provided the Chinese with a perfect opportunity and, indeed, drove the opium ships from the Canton (or Pearl) River. In May 1821, the *Emily* arrived in Chinese waters and anchored in Whampoa Reach, off Whampoa (Pazhou), an island some miles downriver from Canton. The ship could not be taken into Canton port itself because of her illegal cargo of opium; rather, she anchored at Whampoa and waited for the Chinese dealers to come out to her. For the next four months she remained there, selling the chests of opium to dealers who arrived in their 'fast crabs' or 'scrambling dragons' (the Chinese terms) or 'smug-boats' because of their use by smugglers or 'centipedes' because of their forty oars wielded by fierce Tanka rivermen armed to the teeth (the foreigners' terms).[47] On 23 September, following an argument, a seaman from the ship allegedly threw an olive jar at a Chinese woman, hitting her on the head and knocking her out of her sampan, a small sailing boat, and she drowned.

The captain of the *Emily*, William Cowpland, refused to follow the advice that he was given, which was to bribe the bereaved family in order to avoid the inevitable problems with the local authorities. The authorities demanded that the Americans turn the Sicilian sailor, Francis Terranova, over to them for trial. For the Chinese, whether or not he was the man who had actually done the deed was arguably of lesser importance than the concept of group responsibility: it was an American ship and therefore the American community was responsible for the death of the old woman. The Americans refused to turn him over, but an agreement was reached that the Chinese might try him for murder aboard the *Emily*, in truth a substantial concession by the Chinese. The trial unfortunately was farcical. The Chinese official refused to hear any evidence, refused to allow the charges to be translated into English and abruptly broke off the trial, declaring that Terranova was guilty and demanding that the Americans surrender him immediately. At first the Americans refused, and the Chinese retaliated by cutting off all American trade, a very persuasive weapon. The serried ranks soon collapsed: the captains wanted to remain defiant in support of the sailor, the merchants wanted to surrender him, and the latter prevailed. Perhaps, if the sailor had been an American the outcome might have been different; perhaps not. On 24 October Terranova was seized by the Chinese and taken off the ship, retried in secret and on the 28th put to death by strangling on the common execution ground.[48]

James Urmston was President of the Select Committee of the East India Company, which was made up of three or four supercargoes, or agents, of the Company in Canton. Contemptuous of American action, or inaction, in the affair, he wrote a confidential report on the episode to the Chairman of the Company's Court of Directors, who managed the Company from London. He made his opinion clear:

> The unaccountable apathy and the total absence of exertion manifested by the Americans at this place throughout the whole affair, either to assist or to save the unfortunate man who has thus fallen a sacrifice to the inhumanity and the injustice of the Chinese, has excited considerable surprise and regret to [sic] the whole foreign Community in this quarter, nor has the deplorable result produced what was certainly anticipated, the slightest representation or remonstrance, either from the American Consul, or from any of his countrymen in China, against a proceeding so summary and unjustifiable, and at once so contrary and so repugnant to every feeling of humanity and mercy.

His next sentence makes clear why the British thought that keeping control over the process of justice for those under their responsibility was vital: 'This event has completely confirmed the opinion so long entertained by those acquainted with the character of the Chinese, that no reliance whatever can ever be placed on their Professions, or their justice, when once a Foreigner is unhappily under such circumstances, directly or indirectly, thrown in their power.'[49]

Sadly for the American and other traders, and for Terranova himself, the sacrifice of the sailor was rendered useless by a subsequent incident. A Chinese man who had been a professional collector of bribes was arrested on a charge unconnected to his profession, but nevertheless he confessed everything connected to it, revealing names, ships, sums collected, quantities of opium and the methods of trade. One of these ships was the *Emily*, and she and several other ships suffered for it.[50]

An important consequence of the Terranova incident was the rapid development of a new opium-marketing arrangement called the Lintin system after Lintin (Nei Lingding) Island near Macao, the most prominent of the islands used. This involved the use of 'outside anchorages', primarily islands close to the open sea but still within the Canton river system, where 'store ships' lay at anchor. These were just what they sounded like: ships which acted as floating warehouses for the illegal cargo until it could be bought. An historian explains:

Ships arriving off the coast would stop at Lintin and transfer their opium to a store ship before proceeding upriver to Whampoa. Chinese smugglers would buy opium chits at a counting house in Canton, paying in silver. They would then present their chits and a $5 *cumsha* (gift or bribe) per chest at Lintin and receive their opium. The resident merchant charged the seller a commission on each chest sold, and the store ship usually got a demurrage fee (compensation for undue delay) as well. The dangerous and unpleasant part of the business – bribing officials, delivering the narcotic ashore, and retailing to addicts – was handled by the Chinese dealers. Of course, the whole system was made possible by bribery and the technological gap between China and the West, for an opium vessel could outshoot and outsail anything the Chinese could put on the water.[51]

This system was used by both American and non-Company British traders; Company ships, because they would not be carrying opium, could go straight in to Canton.

The period until the late 1830s was one of business competition between the British and Americans but also of social intercourse within the foreigners' enclave. Furthermore, Protestant missionaries from both countries often preached together and jointly founded benevolent organisations, co-operating 'to advance their spiritual enterprises in China'.[52] The British, however, could be quite scathing about the Americans, as over the Terranova affair, but the Americans pointed out their lack of support from the US government. As another historian recounts: '"The American Government", declared "an American" in the Canton English press in October 1830, "requires of us to submit peaceably to the laws of the country we may visit; hence we consider ourselves bound to obey the laws of China. Other foreigners may take a different view of their obligations and their governments may uphold their resistance."'[53] This did not prevent American traders from trying to get around the system: the willingness to obey the laws of China did not seem to extend to obeying the law prohibiting the smuggling of opium.

III

In 1833, the East India Company lost its British monopoly of the China trade: it was insupportable in an era dominated by the policy of free trade. This monopoly power had given it the legal and 'sole exclusive right of trading, trafficking, and using the business of merchandize into and from the dominions of the Emperor of China', a truly wide sweep. Now, as far as Great Britain was concerned, China was open to 'free trade'. This made

Chinese restrictions seem even more unacceptable.[54] A number of traders, both Company and, especially, the private or 'country' traders, decided that little was to be gained in China 'by any refinements of diplomacy' and supported what was euphemistically called a 'forward' policy:[55] just find a harbour, seize an island and enforce the opening of China fully to Western trade. There were possibly 400 million people there, and the attractions of this virtually unlimited market were as alluring then as they would continue to be over the subsequent centuries. Furthermore, many of the British thought, the common people in China would fully support the end of bureaucratic control of commerce.[56] Very important was the fact that the Chinese had not realised that the commercial equation had changed. Before, the foreigners had come to buy Chinese goods, and the Chinese could more or less control this; now, with ever-increasing force, the foreigners wanted to break into the Chinese market and sell.

One result of the end of the Company's monopoly was the appointment by the British government of a superintendent of trade in Canton. The first Superintendent, the Scottish peer William John, the 9th Lord Napier, who arrived on 25 July 1834, by his aggression triggered a crisis which rapidly escalated. The new Superintendent had a simple solution to the difficulties before him: blast the country into submission. 'The Empire of China is my own,' he confided excitedly to his diary. 'What a glorious thing it would be to have a blockading squadron on the Coast of the Celestial Empire ... how easily a gun brig wd raise a revolution and cause them to open their ports to the trading world. I should like to be the medium of such a change.'[57] Napier's aggression, which included an attempt to take two frigates upriver to Canton without permission, exchanging fire with a fort along the way and losing two British sailors, might be said to have broken most of the diplomatic rules.[58] The Chinese blockaded the foreigners' Thirteen Factories in Canton, – that is, their warehouses and living quarters – with sixty-eight war junks; in due course Napier lost the support of the merchants, fell ill, backed down and in September died.[59] From this, the Chinese deduced that a blockade would render the British helpless hostages. Such a tactic would be tried again in 1839. From this, the British deduced that the next time they challenged the system, they should have the forces at hand to back them up.

During the later 1830s, as Anglo-Chinese relations plummeted, the Americans were relatively uninvolved. Partly this was because their share of the China trade, and particularly of opium, was falling: the opening of China to free trade had vastly increased ruthless competition. But partly it was because they knew, as noted above, that the US government would not support offensive action on their part. True, the cruise of the USS *Peacock* in 1832–4 was the beginning of an almost constant US naval presence in the Far East and of a separate East India Squadron (renamed the Asiatic Squadron in 1866).[60] Yet she was not there to fight the Chinese as such: rather, it was there to protect the lives and property of Americans, both traders and missionaries. Meanwhile, the Americans watched anxiously the increasing determination of the Chinese to stop the opium trade. There was, slowly, a drift to war.

What drove the Chinese Court? First of all, there was the moral degradation: it was estimated that 1 per cent of the population smoked opium – this was four million people. Secondly, many of the gentry were addicted, as well as 20 per cent of central government officials, 80 per cent of *yamen* clerks (the bureaucracy in government offices) and a substantial part of the army. (Indeed, during the Opium War, one army of Chinese fighters was massacred partly because the commander in charge of the reserves was comatose in an opium stupor.)[61] In short, the Chinese Court were terrified that the entire government was rotten with addiction. Thirdly, there was a huge and growing export of bulk silver to pay for the opium, which had a grave impact on the Chinese currency. And finally, with the Lintin system and the inability of the Chinese to shut it down – not least because of their susceptibility to bribes – they were in danger of losing sovereignty over some of their coastal territory.[62]

By November 1836, the Chinese government, after debating whether to legalise the opium trade and gain the revenue or actually to enforce its prohibition, had finally decided on enforcement.[63] The importing and smoking of opium had, in fact, been illegal since 1726. It was perhaps time. At first the foreign merchants did not take the new Edict seriously: over the years, they had seen this before. After the Terranova affair in 1821 there had been a clampdown, but it was eventually loosened. This time, it slowly became clear, things were different. The Canton region Viceroy broke the smugglers' ring and destroyed the natives' 'fast crabs' in the Canton River. In Canton province, he sent his soldiers on house-to-house searches at night. Along the coast and, indeed, all over the empire, smokers and sellers were being seized. Finally, the Cohong merchants were 'so harassed with threats' that they ceased business altogether.[64]

In the spring of 1839 the Emperor appointed Lin Tse-hsü (Lin Zexu) as Special Imperial Commissioner. Lin Tse-hsü, the Governor-General of the Chinese province of Hu-Huang (Huguang, later Hubei and Hunan), was an accomplished administrator and bureaucrat who could get things done; he also wrote poetry in his spare time. He was a man of integrity, high morals, strong determination and impressive self-confidence, and in October 1838 he had been summoned to the Imperial Court and instructed by the Emperor to stamp out opium addiction in China. Lin changed the focus of the crackdown, from the seller and the user, to the root of the problem, the foreign importer. In March 1839, he ordered the immediate surrender of all opium brought to China, and demanded that in future 'the heads of foreign firms sign a bond assuming full responsibility before Chinese law for all ships assigned to their charge'.[65] When the foreign traders delayed, Lin retaliated.

On 24 March 1839, he ordered all Chinese servants out of the Factories, imposing a labour boycott, and leaving the 350-strong foreign population penned in for the next forty-seven days. The streets between the Factories and the city of Canton were filled with a thousand armed police, soldiers, servants and coolies, while the waterways south of the city were barricaded with a triple line of junks, thereby cutting off all trade as well as supplies.[66] (The loss of supplies was not, however, as threatening as it might sound, since sugar, oil, bread, capons and water had been smuggled in before the blockade was tightened. The greatest physical risk the foreign traders suffered was apparently 'too much food and too little exercise'.)[67] The foreign population were to be blockaded in their Factories at Canton until the opium was surrendered and bonds signed guaranteeing that their ships were not carrying any of the drug when they came to the city. Lin explained to the Emperor why he had resorted to the virtual imprisonment of the foreign traders in the Factories: 'for while the opium was on the high seas "amidst gigantic waves", the owners were in the factories within his reach'. In short, the Chinese lacked the naval power to intercept the opium ships.[68] In the circumstances, what should the British do?

In 1836, Captain Charles Elliot had been appointed Chief Superintendent of the China trade. Grandson of an earl, son of a soldier-diplomat, dazzled by Nelson at the Battle of Trafalgar, at the age of fourteen he went off to sea. In 1830 he joined the Foreign Office, serving as the 'Protector of the Slaves' in British Guinea, and emerged a fervent abolitionist. He came to China with the Napier mission in 1834. He very much disliked the opium trade, partly because of its immorality, but also because of the vulgar merchants it attracted, such as the Scots Dr William Jardine and James Matheson, and they returned the dislike and contempt.[69] But he recognised the economic need of the British government for the excise duties produced by the tea, paid for by the proceeds of the opium trade, and he also knew that his duty was to protect the British flag and British subjects at Canton. It did not help that his instructions from the Foreign Secretary, Lord Palmerston, were unclear.[70]

When the crisis at the Factories blew up in March 1839, it was Elliot who was in charge. It is also true to say that, notwithstanding the complaints of the traders, he saved the economic lives of many of them, although most were wholly ungrateful and attacked him unremittingly both during and after the war.[71] (He would be summarily replaced in May 1841 by the stolid Irishman Major-General Sir Henry Pottinger, who had served for years as a political agent in Sind in western India.) First of all, he ordered his available warships to go from Macao to Hong Kong and prepare for hostilities. He then left Macao himself for the

Factories, arriving on 24 March. Things were a bit tense – Elliot feared a massacre by the Chinese soldiers surrounding the foreign enclave – but on the 26th Lin made it clear that the British would be released when they had surrendered all of their opium, which greatly relieved Elliot. The traders were delighted. Elliot told them that the British government would compensate them for their losses (neither Palmerston nor the Chancellor of the Exchequer was particularly happy when they learned of Elliot's promise),[72] and because Lin had arrested the traffickers, not a chest of opium had been sold for five months, which left the traders sitting on a glut of the drug. The British turned over 2.6 million pounds of opium to the Chinese, and by 5 May Lin had begun to destroy it. Chinese soldiers removed it from the Factories, and Chinese sailors in war junks removed it from the store ships, which were actually in international waters. As Lin watched, the chests were opened one by one and the drug poured into the bay. He then lifted the blockade, and most of the foreigners decamped to Macao.

The turning over of the opium was important to Lin, but of even more importance was that the merchants should sign the bond. However, if a trader signed a bond, and was then caught smuggling opium, he would be executed. The British refused to sign; they would not agree to render themselves subject to the Chinese judicial system. Lin could wait: he assumed, rightly, that they would come back to trade.

Elliot knew that the British traders would be more concerned about losing their profitable trade than about exposure to the dangers of Chinese justice. He also knew that they would be especially concerned that their main competitors, the Americans, would sweep up the annual tea contracts. Therefore, he had virtually begged the American merchants to come with the British to Macao, as related by one historian, 'in the name of their future common interest. Robert Bennett Forbes, the leading North American trader, had answered in turn that, "I had not come to China for health or pleasure, and that I should remain at my post as long as I could sell a yard of goods or buy a pound of tea … We Yankees had no Queen to guarantee our losses." Once the English were out of the city, the Americans earned windfall profits.' Those British opium-free traders anchored at Hong Kong heard about this and began to fidget, and soon two of them broke loose and signed the opium bond.[73]

Palmerston had little sympathy for the traders. 'The Chinese, he said, had a perfect right to ban the trade and punish those who engaged in it.'[74] However, this was not what he said in the House of Commons on 9 April 1840, in reply to another MP: 'They [the government] were told [by the Opposition] that the Chinese government were anxious to put down this trade out of regard for the morality of their subjects ... [If so], why did they not prohibit the growth of the poppy in their own country? The fact was, that this was an exportation of bullion question, an agriculturalist interest-protection question.'[75] Palmerston was correct, in that the Chinese government were worried about the flow of silver out of the country, although the fate of the poppy farmers appears not to have been of great concern. He himself was concerned about the restrictions on British trade – the actions of the Chinese had over some months provoked petitions to the government from more than 300 commercial firms – and he was certainly furious about the blockade of British citizens and especially of Her Majesty's Consul. He was, however, probably even more concerned about the loss of revenue to the government. The millions earned from smuggling opium into China were used to buy tea to sell at home. The duty on tea levelled by the British government had, since the late 1820s, raised £3 million a year, equal to half of the yearly cost of the Royal Navy.[76] In response, Palmerston in October 1839, even before the above-mentioned debate in the House of Commons, had already ordered the Royal Navy to blockade the coast to force the Chinese to pay reparations for the lost opium.[77]

The use of force was also supported by many missionaries, who wanted all of China to be open to the impact of Christianity. As one missionary wrote, 'The body social of the Chinese is too inert, too lifeless for the whole body to be affected by a rap on the heel; it must be on the head.' In this they shared the opinion of most of the American missionary communities. One prominent American missionary, a historian writes, 'with his special insight on the role of fear and force in "God's plan of mercy," was "sure that the Chinese need harsh measures to bring them out of their ignorance, conceit, and idolatry." "Nothing short of the Society for the Diffusion of Cannon Balls will give them the useful knowledge they now require to realize their own helplessness."[78]

At the beginning of June 1840, a large British expeditionary force arrived, which included steam-powered gunboats and thousands of marines, including sepoys from India. The steamboats included shallow-draught iron steamers, which could go upriver and fire on towns which had heretofore been out of reach. Their artillery was accurate and deadly. The Chinese were very experienced at siege warfare, and held fortress positions with artillery in place and immobile, concentrating on firing at massed frontal attacks. The British, however, would land under the support of naval fire, attack from the flanks and overwhelm the Chinese. Lin sent out eighty war junks, but many of them were blown out of the water. The invaders imposed a blockade on the Canton estuary, and then attacked and took control of strategically important sites along the China coast.[79]

During the war, the British tried to continue the trade along the coast, but until they controlled the area were often driven back. In the meantime, the Americans were making money hand over fist. Having remained at Canton they, with other neutrals such as the Prussians and the Dutch, handled most of the trade, including that for British traders, sailing out and collecting the goods from ships hovering off Hong Kong and returning to Canton. Some British ships flew American colours.[80] As an unknown Briton reputedly said, 'We hold the horns, but they milk the cow.' For the Americans, this was Anglo-American co-operation of a most lucrative sort.

After a bloody war – bloody, that is, for the Chinese, as the British lost only sixty-nine men – the Treaty of Nanking (Nanjing) was signed on 29 August 1842, by which the British imposed the first of what the Chinese were to call the Unequal Treaties. First of all, China ceded in perpetuity the island of Hong Kong opposite the approaches to Canton harbour, and this rapidly became one of Great Britain's most important commercial and financial bases in Asia. The Chinese were also forced to open up to foreign residence as well as to trade the five port cities of Canton, Amoy (Xiamen), Foochow (Fuzhou), Ningpo and Shanghai; to standardise, and lower, all tariffs; and to pay a large indemnity of twenty-one million silver dollars to cover the costs of the war and to recompense merchants for their losses (who received six million of the sum). The treaty also stipulated that British officials should henceforth communicate on terms of equality with Chinese officials. On 8 October 1843, China and Great Britain signed a Supplementary Treaty of Articles at the Bogue (Humen) in the Pearl River Delta. By Article VIII, Britain was given Most Favoured Nation (MFN) status, which guaranteed that any rights and privileges conceded to other governments would automatically also apply to the British.[81]

This concession was made palatable to the Emperor by being translated into Mandarin as 'whatever favors the emperor may in the future choose to grant to the other nations he will also grant to the English'.[82] Indeed, he only finally agreed to negotiations because peace was seen as a hiatus: an emperor did not give in to force, but 'we are governed at every hand by the inevitable ... What we have been doing is to choose between danger and safety, not between right and wrong.'[83] There was no intention of carrying out the terms of the treaty, a decision which would lead ineluctably to the Second Opium War fourteen years later.

IV

The Americans in Canton reacted to the coming of what the US would call the Anglo-Chinese War by requesting that their government appoint a commercial agent to negotiate a treaty for them and to dispatch a naval force to protect American lives and property. Various congressmen interested themselves in China, while traders and missionaries urged the US government to take a more active interest in Chinese affairs.[84] What was probably crucial, however, was the information garnered by Commodore Lawrence Kearny, who arrived at Macao in April 1842 to provide the requested show of naval strength. Several weeks after the signing of the Treaty of Nanking on 29 August that year, Kearny pressed Chinese officials for the same treaty rights. To his surprise, the Chinese replied that the US would be granted equal benefits. He immediately urged the US government to take advantage of the open door.[85]

On 30 December 1842, in a Special Message to Congress, President John Tyler pointed out that the Treaty of Nanking provided for four new ports to be open to British merchants, but 'it provides neither for the admission nor for the exclusion of the ships of other nations. It would seem, therefore, that it remains with every other nation having commercial intercourse with China to seek to make proper arrangements for itself with the Government of that Empire in this respect.' He recommended that Congress appoint a commissioner to reside in China to watch over the persons and property of Americans.[86] Implicit in this was the expectation that further concessions should be wrung out of the Chinese. The question then became, whom to appoint? The answer was Caleb Cushing.

Cushing was a Massachusetts lawyer and politician and later US Attorney-General. He was a cousin of John P. Cushing, a partner in one of the most prominent of the China trading firms, J. & T. H. Perkins in Boston with its branch Perkins & Company in Canton,[87] as well as numbering among his friends and acquaintances merchants prominent in the China trade. He was a supporter of an aggressive policy in the Pacific. He was also an intense Anglophobe. He was not the President's first choice – that was Edward Everett, the Minister to Great Britain – but Everett had no desire to leave one of the premier diplomatic postings in the world for a remote and uncomfortable sojourn in China, and he turned it down. Cushing was then offered the positions of Commissioner to China and Envoy Extraordinary and Minister Plenipotentiary to Peking – the latter in case diplomatic relations were established – on 8 May 1843 and he immediately accepted the offer.[88]

What were the objects of Cushing's mission? As set out by Daniel Webster, the Secretary of State, they were essentially two.

Firstly, 'to secure the entry of American ships and cargoes into these ports on terms as favorable as those which are enjoyed by English merchants'. And secondly, to establish a diplomatic relationship of equals. Webster continued,

> [i]t is of course desirable that you should be able to reach Peking, and the court and person of the Emperor, if practicable. You will accordingly at all times signify this as being your purpose and the object of your mission; and perhaps it may be well to advance as near to the capital as shall be found practicable, without waiting to announce your arrival in the country. The purpose of seeing the Emperor in person must be persisted in as long as may be becoming and proper.

His object was to put a letter from the President into the hands of the Emperor, or, if necessary, into the hands of a high official in the presence of the Emperor.

The instructions include a statement which makes it clear that the need for equality with Great Britain was driving the mission nearly as much as was the desire to facilitate American trade: 'you will signify, in decided terms and a positive manner, that the Government of the United States would find it impossible to remain on terms of friendship and regard with the Emperor, if greater privileges or commercial faculties should be allowed to the subjects of any other Government than should be granted to citizens of the United States'. The final paragraph emphasizes this need for equality: Cushing was to conclude a treaty such as that between China and England, and 'if one containing fuller and more regular stipulations could be entered into', that would be even better.[89]

Certainly, Cushing would take seriously the permission to use threats as a negotiating tactic, although it must be said that the necessary American power to enforce these threats, and the ability to project what military power the US had, hardly existed. As discussed in Chapter 2, the US had just emerged from a near-war with Great Britain over the American–Canadian northeast border, and several years later, when the crisis over Oregon appeared to be about to break into open conflict with Great Britain, American military force was still derisory.

Cushing departed from Norfolk, Virginia on 31 July 1843 with the hopes and expectations of the US government and of American traders and missionaries on his shoulders and arrived at Macao Roads on 24 February 1844. Three days later, he moved to Macao and decided to remain there. The other choice was Hong Kong, but that might give the Chinese the idea that the US and Britain were close allies, and Cushing clearly did not want to bear this taint. Macao, however, was Portuguese and therefore, he decided, neutral territory.[90]

Unfortunately, in a situation which might have flummoxed a less determined man, Cushing realised that no one, neither the Chinese nor the Americans nor the British, wanted him there. The Chinese had made no arrangements whatsoever to receive his mission.[91] The American merchants' position was exemplified by one who wrote from Canton that 'I most heartily wish he [Cushing] were anywhere else but here and am, as well as every other American merchant here, in great fear. As Americans we are now on the very best of terms with the Chinese; and as the only connection we want with China is a commercial one, I cannot see what Mr. Cushing expects to do.'[92] The British were inclined to ridicule, as shown by press comments in London, although Sir Henry Pottinger, who had negotiated the Treaty of Nanking, wrote from Hong Kong offering to send him the official papers relevant to Britain's own commercial treaties with China.[93]

The sniggers arose from the fact that what Cushing had been sent to demand the US had already received. The Articles set out in the treaties of Nanking and the Bogue provided to the traders of the US, and of every other nation, entry 'on terms as favorable as those which are enjoyed by English merchants'. Cushing wrote to Washington on 2 March admitting that this was the case; yet Cushing's whole thrust was to equal or, ideally, better the British, and thus, when the Secretary of State read the British treaty, Cushing wrote, he would see that it rendered a US treaty with China 'more indispensably necessary'.[94]

Cushing naturally decided to forge ahead. It was entirely possible that he might be able to extract further concessions from the Chinese for the US. In any case, he still had to present the President's letter to the Emperor, an occasion which grew to assume ever greater importance. On 27 February, he wrote to Ch'ing (Qing) Yu-tsai, the Acting Viceroy of the region, that he had arrived as the representative of the United States, 'was invested with full and all manner of powers', wanted to conclude a treaty of intercourse and to establish 'permanent relations of justice and friendship' between the two countries, and was on his way to Peking to deliver a letter from the President into the hands of the Emperor; and he also expressed polite interest in the state of the Emperor's health.[95]

This elicited on 19 March an apparently perplexed reply from Ch'ing: China had concluded a treaty with Great Britain because they had fought a war; China and the US had not fought a war, so why did they need a treaty? In any case, Cushing could not go to Peking until his request had been conveyed to the Emperor and he had sent his reply.[96] This theme – Cushing's 'importunate' insistence on meeting the Emperor and the Chinese attempts to 'soothe and stop' him[97] – dominated the correspondence until early May. The general tenor of belief about the Chinese in the US appears to have been that they reacted only to threats and force. As noted above, missionaries were among those most keen to treat them in that manner.[98] The Americans fully shared the British belief that the world ought to be open to their trade, and that those countries which did not necessarily agree had to be bullied into compliance. This had been the British approach with the Opium War, and this was the American approach now, although in this case bluster alone had to do, since the single American naval ship in the area was hardly going to overwhelm the country with fear.

Cushing established his tone early on. He decided on 13 April to send the USS *Brandywine* up the river to Whampoa and he wanted to exchange twenty-one-gun salutes with the Chinese. Ch'ing objected to both, the former because it was a warship, which even the British did not send, and the latter because the Chinese did not fire salutes and the people would take fright.[99]

Cushing in reply wrote that he 'deeply regret[s], for the sake of China, that such is the fact. China will find it very difficult to remain in peace with any of the Great States of the West, so long as her Provincial Governors are prohibited either to give or to receive manifestations of that peace, in the exchange of the ordinary courtesies of national intercourse.'[100] Ch'ing responded that 'during the two hundred years of commercial intercourse between China and your country, there has not been the least animosity or the slightest insult. It is for harmony and good will your excellency has come; and your request to proceed to the capital, and to have an audience with the Emperor, is wholly of the same good mind. If, then, in the outset, such pressing language is used, it will destroy the admirable relations'[101] – in other words, do not threaten us.

The Chinese had their own interpretation of Cushing's object, and they were not far wrong. The Imperial Commissioner Tsiyeng (Qiying),[102] who carried the Emperor's authority to conclude a treaty, arrived at Macao on 16 May. He later wrote a memorial (that is, an official letter to the Emperor) explaining what 'the said barbarian envoy Cushing' wanted, which was 'to secure trade with China on the same terms ... [as] for the English barbarians. As he learns that the English barbarians have concluded a definite treaty, he also follows their example. But his request to go to Peking is really with a view to surpass the English barbarians.'[103] To prevent such a journey was, he himself believed, his primary duty. The Chinese tended to see all of the Western barbarians as more or less the same, although with different strengths, so that it did not terribly matter if the trade privileges already granted to one country were extended to all. But they would not be allowed to force their way into Peking.[104]

Cushing tried, but he finally had to face reality. The Chinese gave their final answer by Tsiyeng's hand: 'neither by land nor sea can it be permitted him [Cushing] to enter Peking, but let there be orders for him to wait for the Imperial Commissioner'.[105] As Cushing later wrote to the Secretary of State, 'with the Brandy wine [sic] alone, without any steamer ... it would be idle to repair to the neighborhood of the Pin-ho [Peiho River], in any expectation of acting upon the Chinese by intimidation, and obtaining from their fears concessions contrary to the feeling and settled wishes of the Imperial Government'.[106] Thus, on 4 July, he wrote to the Secretary of State that a Treaty of Peace, Amity and Commerce (the Treaty of Wanghia) had been signed by the Imperial Commissioner and himself: '[t]his Treaty is in all respects one eminently favorable to the United States.' It promised ties of sincere friendship and it also 'gives to the US a position alike honorable and independent in China'. He added that he thought it was more important to agree a treaty rather than let it await China's agreement to moving to Peking.[107]

Both China and the US had achieved their main aims. They could agree a satisfactory treaty in a relatively short time (Cushing and Tsiyeng themselves spent only three days in negotiations, although lower officials in addition engaged in talks) because by that time neither needed to urge the point to which the other objected. Cushing no longer fought to get to Peking and, in a rush of relief, Tsiyeng conceded to Cushing a treaty which did put the US on a level with Great Britain, at least as far as the Treaties of Nanking and the Bogue went. In addition, Tsiyeng agreed to deliver the President's letter to the Emperor himself, a concession which satisfied Cushing.[108]

As for the Treaty of Wanghia (Wangxia) itself: by Article II the US achieved MFN status, which ensured that it gained all of the privileges which Great Britain had won by war; by Articles IV and XXX, the US could station consuls at each of the five treaty ports, and they would speak and correspond with Chinese officials 'on terms of equality and reciprocal respect'; by Article XVIII, Americans could learn Mandarin from Chinese scholars, and were allowed to purchase Chinese books, both of which had been denied to them and the other foreign citizens, and against which prohibition the Americans had argued in the 1830s; and, perhaps most important, by Articles XXI and XXV they achieved extraterritoriality: American citizens would be subject to American, not Chinese, legal procedures and justice. The one exception to this, which had been requested by Tsiyeng, was set out in Article XXXIII, whereby American citizens who attempted to trade in any ports other than the five now open for foreign traders, or who dealt in opium or other contraband merchandise, were to be dealt with by the Chinese government, and the US would not protect them.[109] With regard to extraterritoriality: 'Though the Treaty of the Bogue had included a form of this protection, the British regarded Article XXI as "superior." In the "vigilant protection of their subjects in Canton," a high-ranking British authority admitted, the United States had "evinced far better diplomacy ... than we have done."'[110] Fully satisfied with what he had accomplished, on 27 August Cushing triumphantly left for home, where the treaty was passed unanimously by the Senate.

v

The twelve years after the signing of the treaty saw the Chinese doing everything possible to evade implementing the Treaty of Nanking in full. Canton was a focal point for both sides; indeed, one historian has written that the 'most knotty issue in the postwar period was the question of the British right to enter Canton'. The British would not be welcome: historically, 'Canton had a reputation for conflicts with foreigners.' In fact, during the Opium War, 'its people were subjected to British humiliation more than those of any of the other cities'.[111] The British believed that the treaty supported their right to enter. Article II in the English text reads: 'His Majesty the Emperor of China agrees, that British subjects, with their families and establishments, shall be allowed to reside, for the purpose of carrying on their mercantile pursuits, without molestation and restraint at the cities and towns of Canton, Amoy, Foochow, Ningpo, and Shanghai.' On the other hand, the Chinese text, when translated into English, reads: 'Hereafter, the Emperor of China graciously allows the subjects of Great Britain to bring with them their families to reside temporarily at the ports of the five coastal cities of Canton ... there to carry on trade without the least restraint.' For the British it provided for permanent residence in the cities, while for the Chinese it allowed only temporary residence at the ports – not in the cities.[112]

The local and regional officials and gentry may have encouraged, or at least not discouraged, the population's hatred for foreigners, but in any case it was there. 'The moment the entry question is raised,' wrote the Imperial Commissioner to Canton in 1849, 'popular anger soars to the point of wanting to eat the Britons' flesh and sleep on their skin. Persuasion is useless.'[113] The deteriorating economic situation in that area probably encouraged bandits and beggars to come into the city and there is some evidence that they were more ferociously anti-foreigner than the bulk of the population.[114] In any case, the British were not in a position to differentiate.

But even worse for British merchants, and the government, was that the expected economic benefits did not materialise. Somehow, pianos and stainless-steel cutlery were not as irresistible to the Chinese as Manchester and Sheffield manufacturers had hoped. Four new ports had been opened to join Canton: why had not exports to China increased proportionately? Indeed, in 1848, exports were less than in 1843, and the British balance of trade was again significantly in the red. The answer was not to reduce imports from China, because the government needed the import duties to finance the Royal Navy, while the government of India needed the export duties on opium shipped from India to China to fund its own expenses (by 1856, it provided almost 22 per cent of British India's total revenue). In the circumstances, increasing the sale of opium, which the Chinese would buy, seemed to be key.[115]

The conclusion must be that what drove Great Britain into a second war with China was primarily greed. There were other more peace-loving arguments put out by politicians and the press, such as bringing Christianity and the benefits of Western knowledge and civilisation to the Chinese people, but these arguments do not ring true, at least at this distance in time. Missionaries indeed had been disappointed by the lack of results after 1842; 'they, too, wanted the great hinterland of China opened up to them: to be able to live, travel, build schools and churches wherever they liked – a privilege due "to the honour of Great Britain, to the great principles of liberty, and above all to the interests of Christianity"'.[116]

What Palmerston and most of those who supported a 'forward' policy in China wanted were more ports open to trade, the right to travel and trade inland, the legalisation of opium and the right to have representation in Peking – that is, to bring China fully into the international comity of nations with its assumption of equality between countries. (The insistence that China accept this equality had, of course, driven the British government since the Macartney mission in 1793.) The 1844 US treaty had in Article XXXIV set out the right of treaty revision twelve years after its signing, a right shared by Great Britain because of the Most Favoured Nation clause in the Treaty of Nanking. The Chinese were resisting this. The historian C. A. Bayly summed it up: '[t]he men on the "periphery", be they Indian government officials or private traders, wanted to shoot their way into Chinese markets. In this they formed an unholy alliance with ministers who had long been irked by China's continued refusal to treat with Britain on the terms to which it felt itself entitled. The petty incident over the *Arrow* and the fate of its Union flag provided a pretext on which both interests could pick a fight.'[117] In fact, hotheads in Canton and Hong Kong jumped the gun and began the *Arrow*, or Second Opium, War. In this case, however, Britain was not to be the only Western belligerent.

The Americans as well were intensely annoyed, because they too had been trying to open negotiations for treaty revision. They were, of course, anxious to help the Chinese become civilised, but they also worried about the apparently unstoppable British advance in Asia. As did the British, they wanted greater access to China, especially for trade but also for missionary enterprises, and as did the British, they wanted to exercise their treaty right of entrance and residence in Canton, but they rather wanted to do some of the pushing themselves. They attempted treaty nego-tiations with China in 1856, but the results were nil. In frustra-tion, the majority of American diplomats in China wanted to use varying measures of force, but the American government 'managed with fair success to hold its agents to a policy of advancing American commercial interests through treaty revision accomplished without coercion'.[118] As a consequence, the American envoy William B. Reed, a model of neutrality, when the time came followed the French and British and shared the spoils.[119]

On 8 October 1856, the Chinese Governor of the province including Canton, Ye Ming-ch'en, arrested a Chinese-owned and Chinese-crewed pirate lorcha (a small coastal trading vessel) called the *Arrow*. However, she was registered in Hong Kong – although this registration had expired – and she flew the British flag. The British Consul, Harry Parkes, considered the arrest an outrage, and determined to use the opportunity to crush the Chinese. The Governor of Hong Kong, Sir John Bowring – 'a learned, fractious Englishman with a fine command of Latin and an ignorant impatience with China'[120] – eagerly agreed. On 29 October, British guns broke through the city walls of Canton; bombardment into January 1857 destroyed the southern part of the city. Bowring was jubilant: 'we are so *strong* and so *right* ... and we must write a bright page in our history'.[121]

Back in London, however, *Punch* magazine had a different take on the events. It wrote a parody of Bowring's letter to Parkes: 'The plain English of it is that we haven't a legal leg to stand upon, so I have ordered up Seymour [Rear Admiral Sir Michael] and the big guns.'[122] Furthermore, in both government and Opposition, as well as in the civil service, many were sickened. One example of the last-named, Frederick Rogers, who, as Permanent Under-Secretary of State for the Colonies, was the senior civil servant in that department, declared that the Chinese war was 'one of the greatest iniquities of our time', and that Bowring 'has made such a fool of himself'.[123]

In the House of Commons there was a four-day debate in late February 1857 over the Resolution proposed by Richard Cobden, a leading free-trader, which was strongly backed by William Gladstone: that Her Majesty's Government had failed 'to establish satisfactory grounds for the violent measures resorted to at Canton in the late affair of the *Arrow*'. In essence, he was calling for a vote of no confidence in the government. One of his more acidic questions, which implicitly referred to the government's call for diplomatic relations on the basis of equality with China, was 'why do we not treat the Chinese as we do the Americans? We have a reciprocal treaty with them ... I confess I have seen with humiliation the tendency in this country to pursue two courses of policy – one towards the strong, and the other towards the weak .... We have never yet acquired the character of being bullies to the weak and cowards to the strong. Why are we changing now? What would the government have done if they were dealing with the US rather than with China?'[124] In short, it was not acceptable that the government should use force to improve British commercial relations with China. When it came to a vote, the government led by Palmerston lost 263 to 247. Palmerston then called the so-called Chinese Election and, on 7 April 1857, won. War it would be, now with the strong support of the country.

However, the government had already some months earlier decided on war. Since September 1856, the British had been in secret negotiations with the French, the Russians and the Americans to build an alliance for a joint occupation, although only the French agreed (in late November) to fight; Napoleon III had decided that the French should avenge the murder of a Roman Catholic priest. By early February 1857 – even before the debate in the House of Commons – the Cabinet had already sent instructions to India to dispatch a military force to China. In April, ten days after the vote was lost, James Bruce, the 8th Earl of Elgin (son of the Earl of the Elgin Marbles), was appointed High Commissioner and Plenipotentiary to China.[125]

Elgin travelled to India, gathered troops together and then sailed to Hong Kong. On 28 December, the guns of the Royal Navy were turned on Canton, and on 5 January 1858 British and French forces entered the city, with Harry Parkes, the war-seeking British Consul, hunting down Governor Ye Ming-ch'en through the narrow streets. When he was found, 'a captain on hand "took the fat gentleman round the waist, and the coxswain twisted the august tail of the imperial commissioner round his fist"'. A month later, against diplomatic protocol, he was shipped to India, where he died a year later,[126] possibly from sickness and boredom, possibly from starving himself – stories differ.

Elgin sent word to the Chinese Court revealing what he had done, and on 8 April 1858 an Anglo-French fleet carrying troops sailed north; US Minister Reed and the Russian envoy went along. On 20 May the fleet destroyed the Taku (Dagu) forts that controlled access to Peking and moved upriver to Tientsin. The Chinese Court then sent two high-ranking officials there and in June negotiations took place. On the 18th the Sino-American Treaty of Tientsin, very close to the British one, was signed by Reed, while on the 26th the Anglo-Chinese Treaty of Tientsin was signed. (The Russians had signed theirs some days before.) It called for the establishing of diplomatic relations with resident ministers at London and Peking, although the Chinese requested that this be modified, again to keep Peking inviolate. Elgin agreed to take China's compromise proposal to London. Eleven new treaty ports were designated, and trading could continue up the Yangtze (Yangzi) River, British merchants and visitors could travel in the interior, and missionaries could preach. A tariff conference was to be held in Shanghai, which in November 1858 resulted in the legalisation of the opium trade with an excise duty on the drug. 'Last, in an article unique to the British treaty, the Qing [Ch'ing] government was forbidden to ever again use the ideo-gram *yi*, which the British translated as *barbarian*, in its official correspondence.'[127] Elgin then took the treaty back to London; formal ratification was to take place in Peking within a year. The British government appointed Elgin's younger brother, Sir Frederick Bruce, as the Minister to China.

Following their defeat, the Chinese Court ordered the refortification of the Taku forts and built a number of obstacles to prevent passage up the North River to Tientsin and Peking. Thus when the fleet under the command of Admiral James Hope, which was carrying Bruce and the new French Ambassador to Peking for the ratification, arrived at the forts on 16 June 1859, they had an unwelcome surprise. They found the river full of obstacles, which they proceeded to remove; by the 25th the gunboats had opened an initial passage and began to move towards the forts.

At this point, the Chinese opened fire with, to the British, hor-rifying accuracy. Indeed, the (unwarranted) suspicion grew that there were Westerners helping – probably Russians, it was thought.[128] Four of the gunboats were sunk with another two badly damaged, and there were nearly 500 casualties, including a badly wounded Admiral.[129]

This particular occasion saw a supposedly neutral American naval ship give some help to the beleaguered British and French. The Commander-in-Chief of the US Navy in the China Waters was Josiah Tattnall, and he was taking the American Minister, John E. Ward, to Peking to ratify the Sino-American Treaty. Their ship was the *Toey-Wan*, a little light-draught steamer which Tattnall had had to charter for the journey. They crossed the Taku Bar (sand bar) on 24 June, taking note of the thirteen gunboats anchored just out of range of the forts, and seeing that they were preparing for action, anchored out of the way. Once firing began, it soon became clear that the fleet was suffering badly. Tattnall and Ward conferred, and they decided that they should help by towing boats with British sailors from support ships to reinforce the crews of the gunboats; they saw this as repayment to Admiral Hope for aid earlier given to the Americans. The following morning the *Toey-Wan* towed two boatloads of British wounded over Taku Bar to larger British naval vessels. Tattnall sent the ship in once more under the command of the senior lieutenant 'with orders to remain at the mouth of the harbor, out of fire, and to afford all aid consistent with our neutrality'. Tattnall apparently justified his concept of neutrality with the statement that 'blood is thicker than water'.[130] Certainly the Royal Navy did not forget his help in time of dire need.

The Royal Navy battle fleet left China on 14 July 1859. The Ch'ing Court was euphoric, although the general in charge of the Chinese forces warned that the British were enraged and would almost certainly gather forces together and strike again in the north. Over the period from the late autumn of 1859 to the spring of 1860, the British and French decided on a joint expedition, and on 26 June both countries declared war on China; Lord Elgin returned to China at the head of the British expedition. This was largely made up of front-line regiments fresh from suppressing rebellion in India and was commanded by one of its heroes, General Sir James Hope Grant. Altogether he commanded nearly 11,000 troops, about one-third of them Indian.

The British and French forces landed on 30 July. They marched north through all of the obstacles, pausing on 14 August to pound the forts at Tientsin into the ground, until they reached Ho-Hsi-Wu (Hexiwu), which was situated midway between Tientsin, where the treaty had been signed, and Peking, where it was to be ratified. It was unclear who actually had the authority to deal with them, and Elgin halted the armies and sent Parkes and Wade, acting as his interpreters, to speak to Prince Yi at Tungchow (Tongzhou). Things were not settled satisfactorily, and Parkes and his entourage withdrew to mark out an encampment for the allied armies, where they found Ch'ing troops in fortified positions and Mongolian cavalry scattered throughout the area. Prince Yi said that the Ch'ing troops would not be withdrawn until peace was settled. The Ch'ing Court then learned that the Tientsin prefect had been detained by the British, and the Prince ordered the arrest of Parkes and his entourage of more than thirty men, in spite of their supposed diplomatic immunity. They were questioned under torture in Peking's Board of Punishments, a regimen which focused on slicing men to death bit by bit, including the use of tourniquets to prolong the experience.[131]

Elgin immediately moved forward, fought field by field, and finally defeated the Ch'ing forces. The Emperor, Prince Yi and the Chinese general fled to another stronghold, the Mountain Resort at Jehol, 110 miles north-east of Peking. With negotiations at an impasse, Elgin and the military forces moved on Peking. They reached the Old Summer Palace, a few miles from Peking, on 7 October, and the French and then the British forces began to loot it. Elgin told Prince Kung (Gong), the Emperor's half-brother who had been left to deal with matters, that either the Chinese surrendered by the 13th or the allies would break in and storm the city. Prince Kung surrendered.

Over the following few days Parkes, what was left of his entourage and what was left of the bodies of the nineteen who had been tortured to death arrived at the allied camps. Among the dead was the correspondent of the London *Times*. Elgin considered their treatment an 'atrocious crime', protested to Prince Kung and decided to punish the Ch'ing leadership, but not the people. Since they could not get their hands on those responsible, it was decided to destroy an imperial palace instead. The Old Summer Palace was destroyed as a 'solemn act of retribution'. The French representative Baron Gros, however, did not agree with the choice of palace, and refused to take part in the destruction.

On 24 October, Lord Elgin and several hundred troops entered Peking, met Prince Kung, signed the Convention of Peking and ratified the Treaty of Tientsin. The Convention included clauses that confirmed the right of the British government to establish an embassy in Peking, vastly increased the amount of the indemnity that China was forced to pay and required China to cede to Great Britain part of the Kowloon Peninsula, which faced Hong Kong across the water. In addition, the Emperor was to issue a decree ordering the publication of the Treaty of Tientsin in the capital and in all of the provinces of the Ch'ing empire. The following day Baron Gros entered Peking for the ratification of the French treaty. The *Arrow* War, or the Second Opium War, or the Second Anglo-Chinese War, was now officially over.[132]

VI

The next thirty years saw the US and Great Britain marching along more or less in step. Both governments wanted to stay out of Chinese affairs as much as possible – the Americans even more than the British – while their people on the periphery put unremitting pressure on them to support their interests, possibly by diplomacy but if necessary by force. In this respect, the merchants and the missionaries were as one, although the use of gunboats in the interior was less easy than some missionaries appeared to think. There were incidents, but the British government hardly leapt to become involved. With the growth of international competition in the 1890s, however, the British government had to rethink its policy; the Americans for their part were keen to gain rights and privileges, but as usual preferred to let the British take the pressure.

The thorough defeat of the Ch'ing Court during the recent war finally convinced enough decision-makers that China must be reformed in order to strengthen itself to be able to protect the country, and the dynasty, against foreign states that were clearly trying to slice off bits of greater or lesser size. France would drive Chinese influence out of the southern tributary states such as Viet Nam, but Russia, Japan and Germany were increasingly going after parts of China itself. Until the late 1890s, the British government was not interested in a sphere of influence – although Britons in China were – and the US never really was.

After the end of the war, there were calls for reform, particularly by the higher mandarins. This reform movement, called the Self-Strengthening Movement, was essentially based on the idea that China could combine Confucianism, the essence of what it meant to be Chinese, with organisational structure and knowledge from the West, especially in science and defence.[133] This covered a number of changes, but first and foremost it meant industrialisation, to be instituted and managed by the state. The overwhelming focus was national defence: the previous two wars had demonstrated that China was no match for the foreign predators. The shock of Western troops occupying Peking, on which the Chinese had spent so much energy denying access of any sort to foreigners, had been overwhelming. Thus the emphasis was on defence and munitions industries, followed by the heavy industries such as coal, iron and heavy machinery, all of which were necessary for the production of munitions. There was the need for shipyards for the production of ships. The army and a navy needed to be rebuilt.

Secondly, there was the reform of institutions, which in this context was pre-eminently the establishment of the Chinese equivalent of a Foreign Office, the Tsungli Yamen (Zongli geguo shiwu yamen, or General Office for Administering the Affairs of Various Countries). Its first head was Prince Kung. He had negotiated the end of the recent war and fully understood the strength of the foreigners, and consequently was the leader of those reformers who were amenable to this selective borrowing from the West; they were known as the Foreign Affairs Party.[134] The importance of the Tsungli Yamen was considerable, because now that Peking seemed, to the Chinese, to be stuffed with foreigners who expected to deal with the centre of government rather than with provincial officials, such an institution was clearly necessary. (This perception that Peking was stuffed with foreigners was not that of the foreign legations themselves, housed together as they were in a self-contained compound. As the wife of the American Minister, Anson Burlingame, wrote to her father in Boston, 'There are very few strangers in Peking ... [and] we look upon all outsiders as intruders ... Sir Frederick [Bruce, the British Minister] has nicknamed all such [people] as "Gorillas", and it is the universal announcement of a stranger's arrival, that "a Gorilla has come".')[135] And thirdly, information was needed, as well as the setting up of training colleges to train interpreters and those who could understand this international law that the foreigners kept invoking. Indeed, beginning in 1872, several classes of selected young Chinese men were sent by the Ch'ing Court to the Chinese Educational Mission in Hartford, Connecticut to be 'acculturated in aspects of American life, including baseball'.[136] All of this effort would not prevent China's defeat in the 1894–5 Sino-Japanese War nor the predation of the Western countries up to 1914.

Li Hung-chang (Li Hongzhang), the single most important policymaker during the period 1879–95, was practical and direct, and stood over six feet tall – his height being of real advantage when speaking to foreigners. He was also the most important of those who looked particularly towards the US. His intention was to draw in the aid of a stronger state to help defend the frontier areas threatened by foreigners, sometimes as an ally, sometimes as an intermediary; alone of all of the Western Powers, the US posed a threat neither to the safety of the tributary states, as did France and later Japan, nor to Chinese territory itself, and it continually stated that it had no territorial ambitions – at least not until the late 1890s, when there was an occasional musing in Washington about the possibilities. (When in September 1899 Secretary of State John Hay wondered aloud to President William McKinley if the US could truly deny any interest in Chinese territory, McKinley responded, 'I don't know about that. May we not want a slice, if it is to be divided?')[137] Li believed that he could use the American devotion to commerce to manipulate the US. Furthermore, the US was clearly a powerful state, which had recently put two million men into the field during its own civil war; the ability of China to call on this would strengthen its own position immeasurably. At least until 1900, then, China repeatedly focused on the US for help. It would be repeatedly disappointed.[138]

VII

During the 1860s, Great Britain and the US worked closely together. The first US Minister to China, Anson Burlingame, received precise instructions of this nature from the Secretary of State, William H. Seward, in a dispatch which was sent to him on 6 March 1862, when he was already in China:

> Great Britain and France are not only represented in China by diplomatic agents, but their agents are supported by land and naval forces, while, unfortunately, you are not. [The US was in the midst of the Civil War.] The interests of this country in China, so far as I understand them, are identical with those of the two other nations I have mentioned. There is no reason to doubt that the British and French ministers are acting in such a way as will best promote the interests of all of the western nations. You are therefore instructed to consult and co-operate with them, unless, in special cases, there shall be very satisfactory reasons for separating from them, and in every aspect of affairs you will keep me well advised.

And a hopeful addition: 'Our domestic affairs are improving very rapidly, and I trust we shall soon be able to send a war steamer to your support.'[139]

Consult and co-operate they did – in fact, one historian has referred to 'co-operation' as 'the word of the decade'.[140] The idea of co-operation among the foreign legations in Peking was an idea fostered by Bruce from the early 1860s. The arrival of Burlingame helped to accelerate the evolution from the idea of co-operation to the Co-operative Policy, which has been described as 'a gentlemen's agreement to subordinate individual national interests to the collective progress of the West's civilizing mission, and a diplomatically brokered holiday from adventurous military expansion'.[141] The evolution was gradual, both because the four ministers from Great Britain, Russia, the US and France arrived at different times over two years, and because it was supported much more actively by Bruce and Burlingame, while the other two passively acquiesced (France supported it even less than did Russia).

The Co-operative Policy that emerged had four general principles that all four parties agreed to follow. First of all, foreign powers must respect the interests, autonomy and territorial integrity of China (within a few years, this went the way of the dodo). Secondly, foreign powers must act in concert, not unilaterally, because as a result of their treaties with China each would share what advantages accrued. Thirdly, foreign envoys and their Chinese counterparts should co-operate when addressing a grievance to achieve a fair solution. And fourthly, all sides had to accept the authority of the treaties when questions arose. Burlingame's own explanation was that 'we are making an effort to substitute fair diplomatic action in China for force'. Furthermore, the representatives were all 'men of modern ideas'. He was also encouraged by the fact that British public opinion seemed to be shifting. Quite frankly, the British public had grown tired of expensive conflicts in China. Bruce himself believed strongly that alternative means to war had to be found. For him, then, the Co-operative Policy was both practical and the right thing to do.[142]

Burlingame was vital because of his personal charm and openness. Furthermore, the 'foreign ministers met frequently at the house of Mr Burlingame as upon neutral territory, and there we discussed over our cigars Chinese policy past and present, and in our stroll, which usually closed the afternoon's confab, the policy that should be pursued in the future was the constant theme'.[143] It was also crucial that Burlingame and Bruce had a close personal relationship. Bruce was a bachelor, and he visited Burlingame and his wife almost daily. There the men would sit for hours, smoking and talking, and often the talk centred on China, the treaty system and the extent of Chinese sovereignty within the context of the treaty system. Not infrequently, afternoon talk would elide into dinner, followed by card games or poetry readings, and more discussion of current problems.[144] This personal liking did not blind Burlingame to what he saw as the contradictions in the British position – that is, calling for diplomacy but resorting to force. Nevertheless, to his surprise, he and Bruce held the same views with regard to how relations with China should be handled: as with other equal states in the international system, and by cultivating good relations with both state and people.[145]

The Ch'ing leaders certainly found Burlingame sympathetic and a man whom they could trust. When after five years his time in China came to an end, he was, to his very great surprise, asked to act as the Chinese envoy to the US and Europe: Prince Kung expected him, in Burlingame's words, to 'state China's difficulties, and inform the treaty powers of [its] sincere desire to be friendly and progressive'.[146] He accepted with pleasure, and, with an entourage of nearly three dozen, embarked on his mission, travelling at a stately pace through the US, Great Britain and Europe, giving speeches of flowing rhetoric. On 23 June 1868, in a speech at a banquet held in his honour in New York City, he declaimed that only by a policy of forbearance could China be 'brought into the comity of nations', that it was only too willing to accept reform, and that it asked only that 'those treaties which were made under the pressure of war' be given 'a generous and Christian construction'. China had made great progress, but there were those who said that it had to be grabbed by the throat, had to be forced to do what non-Chinese knew had to be done. It was, in fact, 'against the malign spirit of this tyrannical element that this Mission was sent forth [from China] to the Christian world'.[147]

Once back in Washington, Burlingame 'unilaterally assumed additional status and negotiating rights for himself in Washington, and before anyone knew it, "he has made a *Treaty with the U.S.!!*", as one British official in China noted in his journal, which, a Chinese high mandarin told him, "surprises them very much". He had no right to sign anything.' As it happened, the Washington Treaty was so anodyne that it was easily ratified: it restated US non-intervention in Chinese affairs, pledged free emigration between the two countries – which could hardly be implemented against the ferocious opposition of California and other states – and pledged each to protect cemeteries (an American missionary cemetery had been damaged by some Chinese).[148]

Burlingame reached London in December 1868, and met with the Earl of Clarendon, the Foreign Secretary, on the 26th. It was the record of this conversation which became the Clarendon Declaration of 28 December. It makes two general points. First of all, as far as Great Britain was concerned, 'there was neither a desire nor intention to apply unfriendly pressure to China to induce her Government to advance more rapidly in her intercourse with foreign nations than was consistent with safety, and with due and reasonable regard for the feelings of her subjects'. But Britain expected that China would observe the terms of existing treaties and provide 'the fullest amount of protection to British subjects' in China. The provincial governors were 'too often in the habit of disregarding the rights of foreigners'; the central government should be prepared to exercise authority over their local authorities.[149]

Interestingly, Burlingame in his reply to Clarendon added a point which they had presumably discussed on the 26th but which does not appear in the Declaration: with regard to enforcing the treaty stipulations, the two agreed that the 'exercise of force' should be used only 'to protect life and property immediately exposed'.[150] Clarendon then reassured Sir Rutherford Alcock, the British Minister to China, that Burlingame clearly understood that force could be immediately employed 'to protect life and property immediately exposed'.[151] Thus the Chinese government would know and, presumably, so would the US government that the British reserved the right to use force if necessary.

There was no real public reaction to the Declaration until the publication early in January 1869 of the instructions to British consuls and naval officers to refrain from applying local pressure and to pay due respect to the laws, feelings and usages of the Chinese people, and, specifically, that they were not to use force unless it was required to protect subjects from actual threats to lives or property. Furthermore:

> H.M. Government cannot leave with H.M. Consuls or Naval officers to determine for themselves what redress or reparation for wrong done to British subjects is due, or by what means it should be enforced. They cannot allow them to determine whether coercion is to be applied by blockade, by reprisals, by landing armed parties, or by acts of even a more hostile character. All such proceedings bear more or less the character of acts of war and H.M. Government cannot delegate to H.M. servants in foreign countries the power of involving their own country in war ... H.M. Consuls must appeal to H.M. Minister at Peking to obtain redress through the action of the Central Government.[152]

The reaction of British traders in China was incandescent. They saw obstruction by the Chinese and, believing that the Chinese reacted only to force, apparently wanted *carte blanche* for consuls and naval officers to apply it. British officials in London could see the contradiction here, even if those in Shanghai could not or would not: if what was desired was that the Chinese government take responsibility for enforcing the treaties, continually using force against them would only undermine their authority, thereby lessening their ability to do what the traders wanted them to do. The American traders supported the British traders in their attempts to get the British government to do what they wanted; they had to, since the US government would not become involved. But in general terms, from the 1860s until the end of the century, the British government followed a policy of reconciliation. There were no official attempts to grab significant chunks of territory, but there was an insidious, acquiring creep:[153] foreigners in the treaty ports refused to stay within the boundaries as set out by treaties, 'for empire was made by men who pushed boundaries and staked claims'.[154]

The so-called Old China Hands, those British traders and trading firms who had been in China for years and whose lives were tied up with the China trade, spent the remainder of the century trying to convince the government to recognise the weight of their arguments. The essentials of their 'doctrine' were consistent. They believed that it was political rather than economic obstacles which prevented the realisation of the potential of the China market. They argued that, because the Chinese empire had for long been decentralised, and the centre could not impose its orders in the provinces, the British government should deal with the local viceroys and not bother with appealing to Peking. They were contemptuous of London's official policy of supporting Peking and treating China as if it were a civilised state in the international system. They believed that 'Orientals' could never be trusted, because they would weasel out of obligations as soon as pressure was removed – so pressure should never be removed. In general, the China Hands believed that it was not international rivalries that prevented the opening up of the full China market, but the backwardness of China and the Chinese. Therefore, they cried constantly for the British government to apply a policy of 'vigor'.

In spite of the arguments for the independence of the traders, for their right to do just as they wanted without government interference, traders (and missionaries) were never reluctant to request government aid for their private ventures. As Nathan A. Pelcovits puts it, 'To the merchants, their private interests were "national interests" and the concept of laissez-faire is conspicuously absent from mercantile briefs.' This was particularly the case in the 1890s, when foreign competition threatened British economic predominance. And finally, in the face of strong opposition to it in Shanghai and Manchester – the latter the city of free trade – organised mercantile opinion strongly supported the carving out of spheres of influence. They tried to persuade the Foreign Office that only by 'effective occupation' of a British sphere would Great Britain's preponderance in the China Seas be maintained. For example, they tried in vain in 1899 and again in 1905 to convince the government to declare the Yangtze valley a protectorate, although earlier in the 1890s the Foreign Office had thought seriously about it. The China Hands never succeeded in convincing the government, and in 1905 they finally gave up the attempt.[155]

VIII

At the end of the century, Great Britain and the US shared in two events, one of little lasting importance, the other of a country-changing nature: they were the Open Door Notes and the Boxer Rebellion and its aftermath. The context was the greatly accelerating and ferocious nature of attempts by foreign countries to establish and then extend spheres of interest or even, as Russia and Japan were doing, attacking and acquiring huge tracts of territory. In 1884–5, by the Sino-French War, France had taken control of Cochin-China (Indo-China). By the Sino-Japanese War of 1894–5, China lost the tributary territories of Taiwan, Korea, Talien (Dalian) and the Liaotung (Liaodong) Peninsula, and the loyalty of a generation of their subjects, 'who howled with rage at this defeat and all it symbolized'. The Chinese had habitually referred to the Japanese as 'dwarf pirates' – from the fourteenth through the sixteenth centuries, Japanese pirates had attacked and despoiled the coast of China[156] – and the smashing of their forces by the Japanese shattered Chinese pride.[157] The social Darwinist parlance, or cant, of the 'survival of the fittest' was rapidly applied to China, and the idea that it might be about to collapse 'spread like an epidemic throughout Europe'.[158] Indeed, in A.J.P. Taylor's words, 'China had taken the place of Turkey as the pre-eminent Sick Man; and between 1897 and 1905 the future of China determined the relations of the Great Powers.'[159]

Relations among the Great Powers were fraught. The Franco-Russian Alliance of 1894 checked Germany in Europe and enabled the two alliance Powers to concentrate on extending their empires. France had two areas of concentration: in Africa and Indo-China. From the latter, it was moving to extend its influence in south-west China. For its part, Russia, with its back covered against Germany, was expanding rapidly in two directions: south towards India, towards which it was building railways, and east towards China. Its thrust was into Manchuria, over which it had significant control by the end of the century. Great Britain was threatened by Russia, both in Central Asia and the approaches to India through Persia and Afghanistan, and in Russia's further attempts to gain a warm-water port, in order to build a base for its navy. Germany wanted *Weltmacht*, or world power, and this required colonies, since it was hemmed in in Europe. It acquired part of East Africa, threatening the British railway thrust from the Cape to Cairo, and it was also pushing its way aggressively into China.

The pace accelerated in 1897, and over a period of 200 days the Powers made their grabs. In November 1897 the Germans seized the port of Kiaochow (Jiaozhou Bay); their intention was to provide a base for the rapidly developing German Navy in the expectation that, sooner rather than later, they would challenge the Royal Navy, and it would provide a sphere from which they could expand further into China. In March 1898, Russia demanded a 'lease' of Port Arthur, which would help it to tighten its grip over Manchuria, over which it already enjoyed predominant financial control. In March as well Great Britain demanded the lease of Weihaiwei harbour on the Shantung (Shandong) Peninsula to offset the German acquisition there. The British request, as it happened, was rather welcome to the Chinese, as the British would provide a counterweight to the Russians at Port Arthur.[160] (The acquisition was less welcome to the Prime Minister and Foreign Secretary, the Marquess of Salisbury, who had written to the Colonial Secretary, Joseph Chamberlain, agreeing with him that the British public would require 'some territorial or cartographic consolation in China. It will not be useful and it will be expensive; but as a matter of pure sentiment, we shall have to do it.')[161] The US refused to become involved in grabbing pieces of China, but as it was involved in absorbing its own new colony of the Philippines, a halo is not appropriate. It seemed that the partition of China was well on the way.

Great Britain still believed in free trade, as did the US. However, although both called for it, their policy emphases were different. The British believed that free trade also applied to themselves. The US, conversely, had always been a protectionist country, with very high tariffs at home; what it called for was equal entry elsewhere, without the resident political power giving advantages to one country over another – what the Secretary of State John Hay called a 'fair field and no favor'. In March 1898, Britain suggested to the US that they issue a joint call for an 'open door' in China – rather late in the day, one would have thought. However, this approach to Washington was for the British the third and least preferred option. Lord Salisbury had worked for a rapprochement with Russia, which was unsuccessful; the other option was the seizure of a naval base in northern China, which took place in March 1898 with the taking of Weihaiwei (as noted above).

The reaction of the United States should not have been unexpected: tired of being in Britain's shadow, it moved alone. After extensive discussion in Washington, Hay issued his own Open Door Note in September 1899. Writing to Salisbury on 6 September, Hay queried the British agreements with Russia and Germany, since Britain was still calling for an 'open door': Great Britain had agreed to recognise the German sphere of influence in Kiaochow and the surrounding area in Shantung, and the Russian sphere of interest, and Hay worried that the rights of the US would be imperilled. He therefore wanted Great Britain to declare that it would not interfere with any treaty port or with any vested interest of others in its so-called sphere of interest or any of its leased territory, adding that he had already received oral assurances from Russia and Germany. Salisbury replied on 30 November, agreeing 'to make a declaration in the sense desired by your Government'. Germany told the American Chargé d'Affaires in Berlin on 4 December that 'if the other cabinets adhere to the proposal of the United States Government, Germany will raise no objection', and gave its agreement in writing on 19 February 1900. France agreed on 16 December. Japan agreed on 26 December, 'provided that all the other powers concerned shall accept the same'. Russia agreed in an ambiguous fashion in a note dated 18 December 1899. Italy agreed on 7 January. On 20 March 1900, then, the US sent to the governments of all of these countries the announcement of their acceptance of the policy of an 'open door', and included copies of each of their assurances.[162]

And the result of this diplomatic initiative? The other Powers paid lip-service and their policies mostly remained unchanged, although the British were still insisting on an 'open door' in the 1920s and 1930s, albeit with little success. As Hay explained to President McKinley, 'The inherent weakness of our position is this: we do not want to rob China ourselves, and our public opinion will not permit us to interfere, with an army, to prevent others from robbing her. Besides, we have no army. The talk of the papers about "our preeminent moral position giving us the authority to dictate to the world" is mere flap-doodle.'[163]

IX

On 8 August 1898, after days of heavy rains, the Yellow River 'broke its high banks and poured its silt-laden waters down the sides of the dykes over a seven-mile stretch and out onto the farmlands below'. The banks failed further downstream, and then again in November, and as a result there was terrible flooding over thousands of square miles of farmland. A million people were displaced, thousands drowned, the crops were ruined, seed and clothes were swept away, and soon the whole area suffered famine and disease. The following year there was a terrible drought. In the rural areas, villagers had always competed for scarce resources, and were willing to fight for them. In short, violence was endemic. The situation was now even worse, because the destructive impact of the weather on farmland meant that many young men were unemployed, and thus idle and bored, always a bad combination. Increasing numbers of young men were attracted by a new combination of religion and martial arts in north-west Shantung by a group calling themselves Spirit Boxers, or 'Boxers United in Righteousness' (Yihequan). They had come together for self-protection, but they were sometimes indistinguishable from bandits, also firmly rooted in the country-side, and both groups challenged the state.[164]

But the situation developed in a new way. China had suffered horrible floods and droughts, far beyond what many had ever experienced: why were things so out of kilter? The answer seemed obvious to many: the presence of the foreigners, particu-larly the missionaries. (At the end of the nineteenth century, mis-sionaries from the US alone numbered about 1,500.)[165] This was less a general theory than one tied to local communities, given the frequent conflict between Chinese converts to Christianity with their missionary protectors on the one hand and the wider village society with its long-standing customs and institutions on the other. And now there was a new factor: the rise of a movement whose members were convinced that, because they could summon the gods to possess them, they were invulnerable to foreign bullets.

In May 1900, local Boxer bands fought and defeated Ch'ing troops at Pao-ting (Baoding) south-west of Peking, and after that the ideas of the Boxers spread to the capital and to the cities of the north China plain. The Boxers stormed towards Peking, leaving behind them dead Christians both Chinese and for-eign, and Western-owned property laid waste. With the permis-sion of the Tsungli Yamen, the legations called up small military detachments from the treaty ports in May. By June the foreign legations' compound was in a state of siege, with missionaries, particularly Americans, directing the building of fortifications. The German Minister left the Legation to speak with officials, and a Chinese soldier stepped out and shot him in the back, killing him. The Secretary of the Japanese Embassy was also murdered. The legations then requested a second detachment from their military forces, but because the Court had neither been asked for nor given permission, this second detachment was seen as an invasion. It quickly found itself bogged down, with the railway cut and strong resistance by both Boxers and Ch'ing troops. To gain some control over the situation, the foreign forces seized the forts at Taku, 'and by way of response to this unambiguous act of aggression, and emboldened by this mass loyal uprising, the court at Peking declared the existence of a state of war "in the ancestral shrines"' on 21 June 1900.[166] The foreign diplomats were given twenty-four hours to leave Peking, after which the legations were surrounded and essentially put under siege.

There was a whole group of wars fought across northern China, as the Powers responded with military forces; the south remained relatively quiescent, as the officials negotiated a 'watchful truce' with the foreign diplomats and military forces.[167] The wars were fought between Boxers and Christians, and between the Ch'ing forces with Boxer allies against the 'Eight Power' allied expeditionary force, made up of British, Americans white and black, French, Russian, Italian, German, Japanese and Austrian forces (as well as Sikhs, Bengalis, Annamese, Algerians and a British regiment of Chinese from Weihaiwei).[168] The Russians swept down through Manchuria, while German forces 'pacified' the north China countryside. The foreign troops often saw villages as nests of Boxers and wiped them out. The Eight Powers also waged 'symbolic warfare' against symbols of Chinese sovereignty and civilisation: where missionaries had been killed, for example, Europeans and Americans blew up city walls and gates and destroyed temples.[169] It was a colonial war, a racist war, a bloody war, a civil war.[170] The foreign troops prevailed; the Chinese would not forget.[171]

Now what would happen? The inevitable result appeared to be partition, but this did not take place. The antagonism and distrust between the European Powers were so great that it was feared that moves to grab territory in China would result in a conflagration in Europe itself. As Thomas Otte has pointed out, 'Germany's unification, the formation of the Franco-Russian alliance, Japan's rise to Great Power status, and the outcome of the 1894–5 [Sino-Japanese] war outside Europe had shifted the equilibrium in Europe and East Asia. Combined, they created the conditions in which the "China Question" had the potential to affect the relations between the Great Powers to an extent that the "scramble for Africa" or the Anglo-Russian Great Game [over Central Asia] did not.'[172] Nevertheless, Russia refused to give up Manchuria and, for the time being, no other Power felt able to force it to disgorge the territory. Of more practical influence was the growing recognition by the Europeans of the high cost of controlling China – and in any case, was it physically possible to do so? Then came a huge and wholly unexpected shock: in the Russo-Japanese War of 1904–5, tiny Japan smashed the Russian forces in Siberia and Manchuria, and its navy sank two-thirds of the Russian fleet in the Tsushima Strait between southern Japan and southern Korea. The rise of a fearful Asiatic Power able to threaten the European dominance in the Far East had begun.

Hay had attempted to restrain the European Powers by the Open Door Note, to negligible effect. On 3 July 1900, he sent out a second Open Door Note, calling for China's preservation both territorially and administratively. This on its own would hardly stop the European Powers. Hay continued to speak of a commonality of interests (against Russia and Germany) between the US and Great Britain in China, neither of which wanted to acquire territory,[173] but the general American antipathy towards the British, which dominated American public opinion, ruled out any suggestion of a link between the two. The US government did, in fact, wobble a bit. In November 1899, rumours triggered by the dispatch of the first Open Door Note in July 1899 had brought the Chinese Minister to the US to see Hay at the State Department. 'Under examination,' writes Michael H. Hunt, 'Hay freely admitted that the US reserved the right to claim "conveniences or accommodations on the coast of China", though for the moment such a demand was not on the cards.'[174] Doubtless the Minister was reassured.

X

For the Chinese, the period from the Boxer Rebellion to the First World War saw, first, a strong attempt by the Ch'ing dynasty with some success to institute substantial reforms, then two revolutions, the imposition of a military dictatorship and continuing rebellions in areas around the country.[175] Great Britain and the United States continued to try to increase their influence and power in China, but by relatively peaceable means. Arthur James Balfour (later the Earl of Balfour), First Lord of the Treasury,[176] Leader of the House of Commons and temporary Foreign Secretary, went to East Manchester on 10 January 1898 to give his annual speech to his parliamentary constituency. Midway through his *tour d'horizon* he set out the broad principles of British policy in China. The first principle was that:

> Our interests in China are not territorial; they are commercial ... territory, in so far as it is not necessary to supply a base for possible warlike operations, is a disadvantage rather than an advantage, for it carries with it responsibilities ... The second principle I draw is this – that inasmuch as our interest in the external trade of China is 80 per cent of the whole trade of the rest of the world put together [that is, trade not carried out by the Chinese themselves] ... we have a special claim to see that the policy of that country is not directed towards the discouragement of foreign trade.

And in the third place, 'by the very traditions of our policy ... we are precluded – and I am glad to think that we are precluded – from using any trading privileges granted to us as a weapon for excluding rivals'. In his final peroration on the subject, he insisted that 'I disdain absolutely the spirit of petty jealousy which animates too many politicians in all parts of the world.'[177] The self-righteousness of the leader is impressive. In short, Britain would combat any attempts to set up preferential trade regimes in China,[178] but the combat would be diplomatic in all its forms and financial, not military.

The US agreed entirely with Britain, but was rather less successful in its drive for influence. The Chinese government had given up its attempts to lure the US to its support. Indeed, in reaction to savage American restrictions on Chinese immigration, in 1905 a powerful protest movement grew in China which developed into a massively successful boycott of American goods both in China and in overseas Chinese communities; American trade was significantly damaged. This 'enlightened anti-foreignism' was a far stronger and more dignified weapon than violence, and far safer: 'nobody could be forced to smoke an American cigarette'.[179]

The Chinese government itself could not entirely ignore the Americans. Indeed, both the Americans and the British would take advantage of China's increasing need for funds. The defeat of Russia by Japan in 1905 seems suddenly to have triggered extensive reforms by the Ch'ing empire to modernise state and society. The 'New Policies' produced new armies, schools, police forces, modern communications, industries (China was largely agricultural) and so forth as the Chinese strove to build a modern state. In addition to this, the huge Boxer Indemnity of £67 million, plus those from the earlier lost wars, had to be paid. The government began the process of fiscal restructuring, which involved a much greater centralisation of the collecting and spending of revenues. This, however, did not produce nearly enough funds, and the government was forced to turn to the Western Powers for loans[180] – as those Powers desired. Financial privileges held by the Powers, such as the right to float a loan to finance a railway line, also facilitated contracts to supply the materials needed to build it, such as the steel for rail tracks. Bankers, merchants and businessmen, frequently organised in country groups, all jostled to gain advantage. However, it was also the case that Chinese self-confidence had revived, encouraged by the rise in national consciousness that was a strong theme of the period. As Sir Ernest Satow, the British Minister to China, wrote privately to the Foreign Secretary, Sir Edward Grey, in March 1906, 'China is no longer as ready to submit to all and every demand of the Powers as she was, and unless she gets another knock-down blow, will in the future be less and less tractable.'[181] This was to be the case in the important railway negotiations of 1909–11; neither the Europeans in 1909 nor the four-power Consortium (which included American interests) in 1911 were able to force China to accept all of their terms.[182]

China's repeated need for funds, and for infrastructure, gave rise to many opportunities for the Powers to co-operate. However, the sometimes assumed Anglo-American unity of commercial desires did not necessarily lead to commercial agreements. Indeed, it is important to underline a significant change during this period. Over the previous century, as emphasised above, Anglo-American relations in China were primarily co-operative. The US government, on the whole, was content to trot behind the British government, scooping up the advantages won by Britain through the use of force or pressure, thereby saving a great deal of money and effort. This also served to preserve a vision of itself as innocent of territorial ambitions, unlike other players in China. American territorial restraint also encouraged China to hope for some years that the US would live up to its rhetoric and support China against the other Powers, but this did not happen. With the advent of a new American administration in 1909, however, American strategy and tactics changed. Now the US government itself would become involved, rather than, as before, leaving everything to the private sector.

Trying to work with the Americans could be frustrating for the British. For example, in 1903 the Chinese government pledged that if the country itself could not raise the capital to build the Hankow–Szechuan (Hankou–Sichuan) railway, British and American capital would be given first option to participate in the loan.[183] In 1904 this information was passed to the American Legation in Beijing. The following year, on 25 July and again on 19 September, when the British Ambassador asked the Secretary of State if American capitalists wished to participate in the enterprise, the Secretary could only answer that no financial group had indicated any interest at all.[184] This was possibly because the US had an investing public which was relatively small and was unused to foreign loans, given that domestic American investments seemed safer and carried relatively high rates of interest. Consequently, the banks could not be confident that they could sell the bonds. But US political goals in China then changed, and Anglo-American commercial conflict was repeatedly the result. The American government was now interested in supporting financial and industrial enterprise in China, a change of heart that came as something of a surprise to the British.

The intentions of the US government had reversed themselves with the advent of a new administration. The Secretary of State from March 1909 to March 1913, under the new President William Howard Taft (who was elected in November 1908), was Philander C. Knox, a corporation lawyer and former Attorney-General (in Hunt's depiction, 'As a British diplomat serving in Washington acutely observed, "To him a treaty is a contract, diplomacy is litigation, and countries interested parties to a suit."'[185]) The two accepted without question a broad vision of the China market, of its 'almost boundless commercial possibilities'; as already noted, this was an assumption that was not normally shared by the British Foreign Office, to the anger and disappointment of China Hands. The priority of Washington and the Foreign Service, Taft and Knox decided, was to be the realisation of those possibilities. 'Today diplomacy works for trade,' Knox declared, 'and the Foreign Offices of the world are powerful engines for the promotion of the commerce of each country.'[186] This would lead him to manoeuvre for political as well as commercial influence in China. His intention was to work together with Great Britain, and, like that country, to utilise financial power. The US had mixed success: American bankers were not eager to be so utilised.

This announcement by the Americans that they would like to reanimate the earlier agreement was given to the British on 3 June 1909, less than three months after the arrival of Taft in the White House.[187] This intervention of the US was not welcome to the Foreign Office. Sir Francis A. Campbell, an Assistant Under-Secretary in the Office, minuted that 'we have hitherto found the Americans quite useless and unreliable in the matter of providing capital for railways in China. The Hankow-Canton line is a case in point. It was originally an American concession, but the Americans did nothing.'[188] Now the American Note arrived just as it seemed likely that China would sign a final agreement for the loan; it was seen as a high-handed attempt by the Americans to push in and share the fruits of three to four years of hard negotiations. It was clear that the US government wanted the British government to intervene and force the European banking groups to include American banks. In response, Grey set out his reasons for preferring not to do so. He pointed out to the American Ambassador in London that, given the lack of interest shown by the American banks, the British, French and German groups had decided to go ahead with preparations for a loan, that the then Secretary of State, Elihu Root, had been told this in mid-October 1905 and had made no objection, and that a copy of the Anglo-French Agreement had been sent to the US Embassy in London, with a covering letter stating that 'as the offer of a share of the loan to be reserved for American capital had not been taken up, that offer must be regarded as having lapsed'. There was apparently no reply to this letter. Furthermore, negotiations had been going on ever since, given their complicated nature, and were a matter of common knowledge. During the whole period, there was no indication of the desire of American financiers to take part. In the circumstances the US government 'will readily understand' that the British government 'would scarcely feel justified in interfering with the arrangements concluded'.[189]

The Americans insisted that the lack of response by the American bankers could not be construed as 'a relinquishment' on their part of the right to participate in the undertaking.[190] Somewhat reluctantly, the Foreign Office agreed, with an official pointing out that the British themselves would not admit that British procrastination would cancel any such right.[191] However, the Americans were on firm ground in international law, and would be able – and probably would not hesitate – to cause trouble.[192] The problem was, groups in Great Britain, Germany and France had been working together on the loan, and while the British did not mind if the Americans participated in the loan, the issue was the related construction and supply rights to build the railway. But Foreign Secretary Grey indicated that 'it will not do for us to be more Anti-American than the French & Germans',[193] and made no objection to American participation in this particular loan – known as the Hukuang (Huguang) loan – as long as this did not disturb the agreement between the three

European groups. The British were content to let the Europeans express any anti-American sentiment that might be going. They might have been less agreeable had they known that, thanks to the American intervention and the necessary renegotiations, the final agreement would not be signed until May 1911.[194]

Then things got complicated. The French had no objections to this loan, although the Germans did, but then the Russians wanted to participate, although they had no claim to do so. Because of the Franco-Russian alliance, their demand would be hard for the French to resist if the Americans were allowed in – and the more participants, the smaller the share of the proceeds for each. The Foreign Office was a touch apprehensive that Japan would also demand to be included.[195] But keeping the Americans out could be dangerous, since they could provide formidable competition, so they were let in. Besides, Grey's highest priority was to maintain good Anglo-American relations: railways in China came a somewhat distant second.

On 7 July 1909, the European groups met the Americans for hard negotiations, which rapidly reached deadlock. The Americans claimed that they were entitled to 50 per cent of the loan but reluctantly agreed to 25 per cent; they then demanded 25 per cent of another loan. The Europeans rejected this demand and the American bankers were ready to withdraw it, but President Taft ordered them not to give way. The meeting was adjourned. Then Taft did something unprecedented: in defiance of all diplomatic usage, he telegraphed a protest direct to the Prince Regent of China. Taft had thereby elevated an issue between bankers to one between governments, which would make Anglo-American relations awkward. It rapidly became clear that China would yield to the Americans in the hope that the US would then support China against the Japanese in Manchuria. There was a real danger of an American–European contest in China that would block all progress on financing and building the railways; besides, if the Americans were kept out, their demands would only increase and Japanese and Russian claims would be provoked. All in all, Grey decided, the Americans should be put on a footing of absolute equality with the British for the Hukuang loan.[196]

The Americans then caused great irritation by trying to push into Manchuria, making it very clear that they expected British support. Knox had conceived a truly breathtaking scheme for what he hoped would be the 'neutralization' of the Japanese- and Russian-controlled railways of the region.[197] Knox's tactic was to put together the so-called American Group; by contrast, the British Group was put together by the bankers and businessmen themselves. Secretary of State Hay of Open Door fame had indicated in 1902 that the way to increase American political influence in China as well as to stimulate American commerce was through investment. Knox asked four Wall Street firms, including the leading American investment bank J. P. Morgan & Company, to form an American Group to bid for loans and contracts.[198] Of course Knox wanted to increase investment, but he had a larger goal in view. He wanted to penetrate the other Powers' spheres of influence, and thereby increase American political influence.[199] This was a significant change by the US government from its normal concentration on commercial influence and the shying away from political entanglements.

By the turn of the twentieth century, these spheres of influence, or areas of economic hegemony, covered a significantly large area of the Ch'ing empire, which went far beyond the coastal enclaves. Manchuria was tacitly Russian, although Japan would soon make a lunge; Shantung and parts of adjacent north China were German; the Yangtze valley was British; Fukien (Fujian), which was across the strait from Japanese Taiwan, was Japanese; and south-east China near to Indo-China was French. William T. Rowe explains: 'Within these spheres, the appropriate power was understood to have first priority at mineral exploitation, railroad construction, and other economic development activities, and the Qing Ch'ing was pledged not to "alienate" or cede parts of that jurisdiction to any other foreign power.'[200] Looking at a map, it becomes clear why Knox wanted to penetrate these spheres.

In November and December 1909, Knox launched his project, assuring the Powers that it was no more than a plan for 'an economic and scientific and impartial administration'[201] of the railways in Manchuria. With the eager support of China, the proposal was that the participating Powers would purchase the lines from Japan and Russia and return them at least nominally to Chinese ownership. Knox was pleased with his plan: he calculated that Russia would sell out as a step towards liquidating its northern Manchurian sphere, Great Britain would support it, and China was expected to agree. The whole plan makes one wonder if Knox knew anything at all about China or about Great Power politics. In January 1910, Japan and Russia united in opposition – quite a coup for Knox, given that only four years before they had been fighting each other in a bloody war – and their British and French allies as well as Germany deferred to them. When China realised that the Americans had managed to unite Japan and Russia against it, it became alarmed. Grey was in a real bind. Once the Japanese had objected, Britain did not support the US, because a basic strategic principle of Grey's foreign policy was to maintain good relations with Japan. The Anglo-Japanese alliance gave Britain 'security with economy' in the Far East,[202] and made it possible for the Royal Navy to move a substantial number of its ships from the South China Sea to the North Sea in order to concentrate its naval power against the growing German threat.

On the other hand, an axiom of British foreign policy was to do everything possible to prevent a conflict with the US. Indeed, Britain would have very much liked an open or even tacit agreement with the US to help in maintaining the world balance of power – for Britain had some time before moved far beyond considering the European balance as its main international concern. (This would, of course, soon reveal itself to be something of a mistake.) The US, however, refused to become involved. As a further complication, in 1907 Britain had signed an agreement with Russia (though it was not an alliance as with Japan), setting out their respective interests in Central and East Asia, in order to protect the approaches to India. Therefore, when Grey had to choose between on the one hand his ally Japan and associate Russia and on the other relations with the US, he felt that at that point he had no choice but to support the former. Those involved with developing the policy in the US government were intensely bitter: they had taken it for granted that Britain would support the US. The Secretary of State railed that Britain had been foolish in not realising that its true interests lay with the US rather than with Japan.[203] It is worth pointing out in all this that, had the negotiations been left to the bankers, there would have been much less trouble and strife, because they just wanted the business to go forward.

After his Manchurian débâcle, Knox realised that he had to take a more reasonable view of what could be achieved in China, at the same time modifying his tactics. Co-operation with the Powers would now replace aggression. Following the advice of a young Foreign Service officer in Peking, he encouraged the formation of an international financial consortium, made up of the American, French, British and German Groups, in order to moderate the aggressive policies of Russia and Japan. In July 1910 the American Group met with their counterparts 'to begin a ten-month-long contest over the precise terms of the international marriage of convenience'.[204] Meanwhile, the American Group negotiated with the Chinese the terms of a $50 million combined development and currency loan, which were agreed at the end of October. The following month, against the wishes of the Chinese, Knox accepted that the British, French and German Groups would each have a portion of this loan, thereby nicely eliminating inconvenient competition of which the Chinese could take some advantage. Where China did succeed in imposing its wishes on the Powers, though with a little help from its temporary friends among them, was in preventing Knox from achieving his demand that an American financial adviser with broad powers be appointed to oversee the loan. The four groups then formed the so-called Consortium, guaranteeing each a share in all future Chinese loans; there would now, presumably, be no need for unseemly arguments, at least not over the loans. Japan and Russia were outside the Consortium because they lacked financial resources – both were exhausted from their war, and Russia had for some time been financing many of its activities by borrowing in France – but in July 1912 Knox agreed that Japan and Russia could be admitted to the Consortium. The expectation was that this would facilitate greater co-operation among the Powers;

disagreements, particularly those between Russia, Japan and the four Consortium Powers, had substantially interfered with business.[205]

And then, just as the advent of the Taft administration had changed US policy towards China, the advent of the new Wilson administration in March 1913 changed it once again. Not for the first time, nor for the last, a new American administration would upend the policies of the previous one. The new President, Woodrow Wilson, and his Secretary of State, William Jennings Bryan, believed that what the American Group were trying to do in China was immoral, and on 19 March they publicly censured the entire operation. The following day, the American Group withdrew entirely from the Chinese loan negotiations. The J. P. Morgan partners in New York were left to send their embarrassed regrets at Wilson's actions to their European banking associates.[206] The European groups continued their quest for profits.

XI

By mid-October 1911, revolution was spreading throughout much of the south, centre and north-west of China. However, as Rowe points out, 'the progress of industrial, mining, communications, educational, and other infrastructural developments did not miss a beat as a result of revolution. Neither was the foreign establishment in China much [of] a target of the disturbances, or much affected by the change of regime.'[207] Indeed, the revolutionaries on the whole made a point of not attacking the interests of foreigners (according to Assistant Under-Secretary Campbell in the Foreign Office, the revolution 'was not in any way anti-foreign',[208] although how he could be so certain from London is unclear). Britain certainly had no sympathy for the imperial regime, with Campbell reputedly regarding it as corrupt and rotten. Whether the regime was monarchical or republican did not particularly matter to the British government: as Campbell wrote in a semi-private letter to Sir John Jordan, the Minister to China, 'We [Campbell and Grey] quite agree that China today is not suited to a Republic, but if the great majority of the people are determined upon it, we can hardly obstruct. All we want is a good strong Gov't who will keep things quiet and enable us to do the maximum amount of trade.'[209] In his own dispatch to Jordan, Grey also emphasised the latter point but widened the ambit: 'What we desire to see as an outcome of revolution is a Government strong enough to deal impartially with foreign nations, and to secure order and favourable conditions for progress of trade in China.'[210] Furthermore, it was essential for Britain to be neutral, because British interests were widespread, with some in government-controlled areas in the north, but with the greater portion in rebel-dominated areas in the centre and south.[211]

The United States, too, put a premium on stability. The American Legation wanted a strongman, preferably one with reformist credentials, who could guarantee that stability. Their choice was Yüan Shih-k'ai (Yuan Shikai). He had crushed the Boxers in Shantung and later helped to commit the Ch'ing Court to wide-ranging reforms. In Chihli (Zhili) he had created a model province where opium had been suppressed, educational changes made, modern armies trained and a small degree of public participation in politics encouraged. He kept foreigners and foreign-educated Chinese close by for consultation.[212] As it transpired, Yüan would also be the British choice. After the revolution, Sun Yat-sen (Sun Yixian) was proclaimed provisional President of the new Republic of China, which incorporated all of the Ch'ing empire bar Mongolia, but he then stepped down in favour of Yüan, who was the most powerful of the Ch'ing commanders. This was a surrender not to force, but to an urgent desire to re-establish order and unity before foreign Powers took advantage of the chaos[213] – the British, Japanese and Russians had continued, and in some cases intensified, their penetrations of Tibet, Sinkiang (Xinjiang), Mongolia and Manchuria, while consolidating the positions that they already held in China.

Yüan's precarious political position and the fragility of Chinese order encouraged a certain ruthlessness. There was growing hostility between Yüan and the Nationalist Party (Kuomintang) led by Sun Yat-sen; Sun was an idealist, while Yüan was increasingly ruthless in his drive to become dictator or, ideally, a dictatorial monarch. Once elected as provisional President, Yüan rapidly began to make a travesty of the Republic. In December 1912, parliamentary elections were held, which were won by the Nationalists; they commanded more votes than the other three parties combined, which now merged into the Progressive Party and supported the Yüan government. The Nationalist victory was largely the result of the work of Jiaoren, Sung Chiao-jen (Song Jiaoren), its leader after Sun who believed that it was the responsibility of the Cabinet and the loyal opposition to check the excesses of the presidency. Since Yüan was the provisional President, Sung's victory angered him greatly, and he decided to have him assassinated. Sung was shot just as he was leaving the Shanghai railway station; somehow the assassin died suddenly in prison, and others involved in the case were poisoned or killed by various other means.[214]

In spite of their ostensible neutrality, the British threw their support behind Yüan – in Robert Bickers' words, 'aligning themselves, as was usually the pattern, behind the force best guaranteeing order and stability'. They supplied more than moral support: Yüan needed money in order to sustain his position against the Nationalists, if necessary by using force to quell any rebellion against his authority. This was provided by the Consortium (of which the now disbanded American Group was no longer a member) as a 'Reorganisation Loan', theoretically for the reorganisation of the state. Yüan used part of the funds to suppress a revolt by the Nationalists; the Loan also provided funds for the necessary bribes, for paying troops and for purchasing munitions. At Shanghai, 'the foreign staff of the Customs, the British consul, naval officials and bankers worked together to help release large sums for the Chinese navy which kept them on the government side'. The Loan was based on foreign supervision of the salt monopoly, whose supervisor would be British. In October 1913, the Treaty Powers formally recognised Yüan's government as the government of the Republic of China.[215]

As for the Americans, they fully approved. The Minister, Chicago lawyer William J. Calhoun, argued in 1911 that, in spite of the lack of certain democratic niceties, the US government should support 'Yüan's attempt to restore order' because 'he will fail unless supported, with nothing in sight but anarchy'.[216] The American Legation in Peking continued into 1914 to view him as vital for order and authority. Paul S. Reinsch, a former University of Wisconsin professor of political science with a long-standing interest in the development of the 'Orient',[217] wrote to Secretary of State Bryan in May 1914 that although 'the powers now centralized in the hands of the President are extraordinarily great' and although 'this is justly regarded as a pause in the progress towards the development of a representative form of government' – which was one way of putting it – the assumption of those powers is the only way in which 'conditions of national cohesion and internal tranquility' can be fostered.[218] In other words, given all the threats by foreign Powers, and the internal opposition and widespread bureaucratic confusion, the Chinese Republic needed a strongman. In this crisis, the British and Americans marched shoulder to shoulder. Shortly thereafter, the advent of the First World War diverted their attention elsewhere.

XII

From 1793 to 1914, the general tenor of relations between Great Britain and China, between the US and China, and between Great Britain and the US in China had a certain uniformity. All of the relationships had their basis in the Western desire for secure, open and unfettered trading conditions, and in the Chinese desire to restrict and control these conditions. On the whole, both Britain and the US were steadfast in not wishing to have the responsibility and cost of territorial possessions, beyond the right of traders and their families to live in the port cities and of their missionaries to own and use land for their missions. What spheres of interest they claimed – and the British made no positive claims until 1912 for the Yangtze valley, while the Americans never made any – were claims for economic hegemony. Both the British and Americans used force, but it was the British in two wars – with some help from the French in the second – who first broke into China and imposed their wishes on the Ch'ing Court. For the Americans, the only real instance of the use of force was defensive against the Boxers, although they also engaged in a bit of rampage during the campaign.

However, the interactions of the British and American empires was not one of serene placidity. They were frequently at odds. The Americans on the ground were jealous of the British position, and wished to increase the political and commercial strength of their own. The British for their part could be intensely annoyed by the American failure, as during the First Opium War, to act in solidarity with them against the Chinese. Both however shared occasional frustration at the unwillingness of their home governments to act forcibly in their support, whether against the Chinese government, the other Powers or each other. Many of these similarities and differences would be present in their activities in Japan.

Chapter 4

The United States, Great Britain and Japan, 1854–1895

In 1851, President Millard Fillmore asked Commodore Matthew C. Perry of the United States Navy to lead an expedition to Japan to open trade relations. Fillmore knew that Perry shared his keen wish to expand American trade and to advance the nation's prestige. They also had a larger conception of the expedition: this would be the opening move in a struggle with Great Britain for eventual control of the Pacific. Consequently, on 8 July 1853, Perry began the forced opening up of Japan to the outside world by steaming defiantly into the Bay of Edo (or Yedo, later Tokyo) with a fleet of four very large ships, two of them black-hulled coal-fired steamships – the 'burning ships' to the panic-stricken Japanese – each of the two carrying sixty-one guns and together nearly a thousand men. He was taking a letter from the President to the Japanese Emperor, requesting that Japan open its borders to the Americans. The Japanese stalled and Perry left, warning that he would return the following year with many more ships.

The Japanese fortified the harbour, but this failed to prevent the arrival of the Americans in February 1854 with a considerably larger force. Perry had been instructed by the US State Department to 'do everything to impress' the Japanese 'with a just sense of the power and greatness' of the US.[1] Consequently he brought with him huge quantities of champagne and vintage Kentucky bourbon to lubricate the wheels of diplomacy, a pair of Colt six-shooters and a scale model train to display US technological achievement. He employed Chinese 'coolies' and African Americans to show the command of white over colour, and he used uniforms and pageants as manifestations of American cultural supremacy. It is probable that American power rather than American culture convinced the Japanese to deal with Perry.

Why should the US, or Great Britain, care whether or not Japan was open to the world? What made it worth all the effort? The opening of Japan was certainly of greater concern to the US in the mid-nineteenth century than it was to the British. First of all, until the discovery of oil in Pennsylvania in 1858, and indeed for some time thereafter, the US was illuminated by lamps filled with whale oil. Hundreds of American whalers roamed the Pacific Ocean, and in times of bad weather a ship in the North Pacific or the Sea of Japan could crash on to the shore of Japan itself. It was not unusual for the Japanese to fire on the ships, to refuse to help them and to hunt down and imprison or kill the sailors. The Americans wanted to protect the whalers. Secondly, the Americans wanted Japan to be open to trade. At this point, however, China was of more importance in this context than Japan. Americans were deeply involved in the China trade, including the trade in opium, and with the advent of steam navigation they needed coaling stations between Honolulu and Shanghai; Japan would provide a convenient coaling stop, as well as a place to take on food and water. But it was not just trade in goods that was firing the imagination: rather, it was the possibility of steamship routes circling the globe and carrying people as well as goods. Indeed, by early 1849, there was a proposed new steamship route between San Francisco and Shanghai.[2] Americans had moved west to the Pacific Ocean following their Manifest Destiny: why should they stop there, when the Pacific was surely destined to be their lake? And finally, there was the always-present anti-British drive. Breaking into Japan for the Americans was a way of breaking into the world of the Powers, first economically and commercially, and then internationally. Domestically, the US remained an economic colony of Great Britain;[3] in Japan it might be on equal terms.

Great Britain, on the other hand, was primarily interested in opening up Japan to trade. The British came to China from the west, and already controlled a number of coaling stations for refuelling and restocking. Their merchants, red in tooth and claw, wanted to expand from China into Japan, which was only nine hours' steaming away. Considering 'imperialism' as a policy, the British government had little or no interest in establishing either political control or spheres of interest as far as Japan was concerned, although this did not preclude some of the British officials in Japan from treating the Japanese as though they were a lesser breed. The British government was quite happy for the US to take the lead initially in Japan: the Americans would bear the cost and do the work, and the British would benefit.[4] It was quite enough having China on its plate. As Foreign Secretary Lord Malmesbury made clear in July 1852 when commenting on rumours of Perry's forthcoming expedition: 'Her Majesty's Government would be glad to see the trade with Japan open; but they think it better to leave it to the Government of the United States to make the experiment; and if that experiment is successful, Her Majesty's Government can take advantage of its success.'[5] Besides, Japan was a very speculative prospect, possessing few economic attractions compared with China.

The arrival of both the US and Great Britain in Japan in the 1850s coincided with the beginning of the end of the power of the Tokugawa clan, which had already lasted for three centuries and was steadily growing weaker. This clan provided the Shōgun (also called the Tycoon or Tykoon or Taikun), the political ruler of Japan, whose government or administration was called the *bakufū*. (This word referred to the battle headquarters of the military leader during the wars of conquest, and literally meant 'government behind the curtain'.) The Shōgun lived in Edo. There was, however, also an emperor (the Mikado), who resided in Kyōto and was considered the spiritual leader of the country. What happened during the period between the arrival of the Americans in 1854 and the Meiji Restoration in 1868 ('Meiji' meant 'enlightened peace') was the elimination of the Shōgun and the 'restoration' of the Emperor (whose predecessors and their courts had lived in seclusion for hundreds of years) to political, as well as his existing spiritual, power. This was a political process that was not wholly caused by the drive by the Western powers for the opening up of Japan, since there was already great internal opposition to the Shōgun, but the Western influence was certainly crucial and was frequently used as a handle on which to hang political opposition to the Tokugawa Shōgun and especially to the *bakufū*.

From around 1625 until forced by the US to change in 1858, Japan had fended off approaches by foreign merchants, allowing only the Chinese and, to a limited extent, the Dutch to engage in trade. By 1641, the 'seclusion policy' was fully imposed: Tokugawa policy was driven by the need for domestic political security, and foreign trade and foreign aid might benefit a disgruntled daimyō.[6] (The word 'daimyō' refers both to the head of a clan and to the territory or domain belonging to the clan. Context is all.) Even less than China did Japan need goods from abroad; even more than China was it united against the barbarians – and 'united' was the operative word. But this unity rapidly weakened as the Shōgun and his advisers tried to decide how to react to the foreigners, and those outside the magic circle often reacted angrily to the Shōgun's policies. With the Meiji Restoration in 1868, the approach that was adopted was to open up to the Westerners, learn what you could and in due course become strong enough to drive the foreigners out. In the end, the Japanese settled for containing them.

I

In the popular American imagination, it was Admiral Perry who was the first to open up Japan to the outside world. A veil hides the previous official attempt by an officer in the US Navy to convince the Japanese that the Western, civilised, part of the globe had much to offer, not least trade. Of course there had been earlier foreign contacts – Japan was not 'hermetically sealed'[7] off from the rest of the world – but they were primarily merchants. The Dutch had been established traders in Japan since at least the early seventeenth century, but in 1641 they were forced into very constraining circumstances. The Japanese had constructed

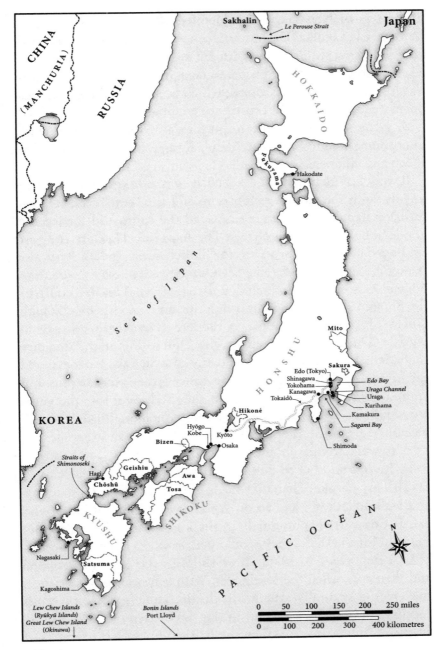

MAP 13

in the Bay of Nagasaki a tiny (600 feet by 200 feet) fan-shaped artificial island called Deshima, which was connected to the mainland only by a stone bridge with Japanese guards stationed on it. The roughly twenty Dutch permanent residents and their black slaves had to stay on this island, which was surrounded by a high board fence constructed on its stone embankments and painted with signs warning people to stay away. Japanese guards and interpreters also lived on the island, along with a few pigs, cows, sheep and chickens.[8]

It was less than idyllic. Indeed it was boring. Ships arrived in July with the summer monsoon, and the crews remained on board as Japanese labourers unloaded the cargo and loaded the goods bought by the merchants. The ships sailed back to the port of Batavia (now Jakarta) in the Dutch East Indies with the November monsoon, leaving the Dutch residents to resume their normal existence. This included a regular visit to the court of the Shōgun in Edo. There is a description of a visit by the high Dutch officials on Deshima in the late seventeenth century to Shōgun Tsunayoshi, written by the Dutch doctor in residence there, which makes clear the contempt in which the Japanese held the foreigners: 'after the usual obeysances [they were required to approach the Shōgun crawling on their bellies across the audience Hall of a Thousand Mats][9] ... Bingosama [the Lord of Bingo] welcom'd us in the Emperor's [Shōgun's] name and then desir'd us ... to walk, to turn about, to dance, to sing songs ... to be angry, to invite one another to dinner ... I was desired once more to ... take off my peruke. Then they made us jump, dance, play gambols and walk together'[10] and so on, for four and a half hours. It was exhausting as well as humiliating, but if it was necessary to remain in Japan for the trade, they would perform.

It is important to notice how skilfully the Japanese isolated and then controlled the foreigners. With centuries of experience, they would naturally attempt to do the same in the nineteenth century, and much of the tension in the early months and years after the Americans, and then the British, French, Prussians and others arrived, stemmed from the Japanese determination to continue their policy of isolation and control and the determination of the Western powers to defeat it. The foremost threat came from Russia: in the sixty years before Perry the Russians repeatedly probed from the north, their depredations causing particular apprehension in the early 1800s.[11] The Japanese were overwhelmingly agreed on the imperative of keeping foreigners out and themselves in. This was of course partially to protect the country, although few if any of them understood its relative military weakness, but of equal importance was the need to preserve Japan's identity and its way of life. Unfortunately, the concerted pressure of the Western nations on Japan to open coincided with the growing weakness of the Shōgun's political authority.

Few in the outside world understood the different foci of power in Japan and how they interacted. It is necessary to go back briefly to the period from 1467 to about 1605, the 'Age of Warring States', when the country was the scene of numerous wars between rival daimyō (there is no plural in Japanese, so daimyō can stand for one or many). These were essentially warlords, each with his own domain, who took part in a changing web of alliances made and broken. This period was brought to an end by Tokugawa Ieyasu, the warlord who triumphed over all and unified Japan.[12] Those who held the clan name Tokugawa, whether by birth or adoption, would alone be able to become the Shōgun. 'Shōgun' translates as military commander or general,[13] and from the time of Tokugawa Ieyasu to 1868, Japan was ruled by a warrior aristocracy.

By the mid-nineteenth century, the system established in the seventeenth century had become ossified. The situation was undoubtedly complicated, but the history of Japan during the second half of the nineteenth century provided the context for the interactions of Great Britain and the US in Japan, and they make little sense without some awareness of it. As noted above, in Kyōto resided the Mikado, the 'spiritual' Emperor. He invested the Shōgun with his office, but the Shōgun kept watch over him by means of his representative at the court. In Edo lived the Shōgun, who held the political authority and power; it was to him that the daimyō swore allegiance. However, by this time affairs of government had pretty well passed out of his hands and into those of the *rōjū*, a council of elders made up of five senior ministers; the term was also used for an individual member.[14] This introduces another complication. By the end of the Tokugawa period in 1868, there were 258 daimyō. Of these, twenty-one were part of the Tokugawa clan, which included the three cadet branches called the Three Families (Gosankē) from which a shōgun was chosen if there was a failure in the direct line.[15] One hundred and thirty-nine were known as *fudai* lords (hereditary vassals of the Tokugawa), descendants of those who had supported Ieyasu early in his career, and only they could hold office in the *bakufū*, and thus only *fudai* lords could be part of the ruling council. The other ninety-eight daimyō were headed by *tozama* or 'outside' lords, those who had come late to the support of Tokugawa Ieyasu or had been beaten into submission. They were not allowed any position or office in the *bakufū*. Not surprisingly, it was from their ranks that opposition to the Tokugawa primarily arose. It was also the case, not wholly coincidentally, that the *tozama* lords were the source of much, though not all, of the opposition to opening up the country to the barbarians. They gathered around the Emperor as the centre of opposition to the Shōgun. The foreigners were sometimes caught in the middle.

II

The opening up of China as a result of the Opium War naturally brought Japan into view.[16] On 15 February 1845, US Congressman Zadock Pratt proposed in the House of Representatives that 'immediate measures be taken for effecting commercial arrangements with the empire of Japan and the kingdom of Corea', and urged that 'a judicious embassy, characterized by the justice which should ever sway our government, will succeed in establishing intercourse with Japan and Corea that may be largely beneficial to the American people'.[17] Later that year, Alexander Hill Everett was sent to China as the United States' first Commissioner to China but with instructions also pertaining to Japan; however, he fell ill and had to be left in Rio de Janeiro, from where he returned to the US. He had been a passenger of Commodore

James Biddle, captain of the *Columbus*, a ship of the line, which was accompanied by the sloop *Vincennes*; when Everett proved to be too ill to continue to China, he transferred his credentials and instructions to Biddle. Biddle was, first of all, to exchange ratifications of the Treaty of Wanghia with the Chinese government (see pp. 191–2); his second duty was to establish permanent US consulates in as many of the four treaty ports north of Canton as he saw fit. In the end, only Shanghai had enough trade to justify a consul.[18] And finally, his instructions from Secretary of the Navy George Bancroft were that he should then continue to Japan, taking 'the utmost care to ascertain if the ports of Japan are accessible': in other words, was Japan open to trade with the US? He was to '[p]ersevere in the design, yet not in such a manner as to excite a hostile feeling or a distrust of the Government of the United States.'[19] In short, he was to inquire, not to demand.

The only port open to foreigners was Nagasaki, but Biddle feared that the Dutch would hamper him, in order to ensure that they retained their monopoly of trade. Accordingly, the two ships sailed into the lower harbour at Edo on 21 July 1846. A Japanese officer with a Dutch interpreter immediately came on board and asked him why he had come to Japan. When Biddle told him, he was instructed to put his request in writing, forbidden to come on shore and forced to wait for six days. The two ships were surrounded by hundreds of armed barges, and for the first two days Biddle allowed the Japanese to swarm on board and look around. This was perhaps stupid, since a number of them were samurai or 'two-sword men', each wearing one long and one short sword; the American sailors would have been ill matched. On the 27th, a Japanese message bearer came with a response to Biddle's letter from the 'Emperor', in fact from the Shōgun, who 'positively refuses the permission you desire. He earnestly advises you to depart immediately, and to consult your own safety by not appearing again on our coast.'[20]

This was a note reeking with antagonism. Nevertheless, Biddle had been instructed not to arouse any hostile feelings among the Japanese, and he therefore accepted the rebuff, responding that the US wanted a trade treaty with Japan only if that country also

wanted one. He had asked, and he had been told. It remained only
to depart when convenient for both parties.[21] Things, however,
soon turned nasty. He later explained to Secretary of the Navy
Bancroft that he had been asked to come to a nearby junk to meet
the Japanese message bearer. He refused, and sent his interpreter
to tell the Japanese, demanding that the letter be brought to his
flagship. Unaccountably, within the hour he changed his mind
and, not warning the Japanese, according to his biographer, he
' "went along in the Ship's Boat in my uniform. At the moment
I was stepping on board a Japanese on the deck of the junk gave
me a blow or a push which threw me back into the boat." The
shaken and furious commodore demanded that the offender be
arrested and at once returned to the *Columbus*. The Japanese
officers hurriedly followed him and protested that they had not
known that he was coming to visit them. They assured him that
the one responsible for the outrage was a mere "common soldier" who had acted on his own initiative. He would be "severely
punished."' Biddle emphasised the enormity of the outrage, but
the Japanese manifested severe anxiety and apprehension. Biddle
had been instructed not to excite a 'hostile feeling' and soon
decided to drop the matter.[22]

There were mixed reactions to the event both then and later.
Some approved of his forbearance: after all, he had an armed
fleet there, so surely the Japanese did not think he had shown
weakness, but the candour and justice befitting the American
Republic. One who approved of his 'prudent and judicious conduct'[23] was the Secretary of the Navy. Others, however, including
many of his diplomatic, commercial and naval contemporaries,
thought that Biddle's acceptance of the insult had been inept and
had given a very bad impression of America to the Japanese, who
had interpreted it as weakness and as displaying a lack of dignity. Certainly the British thought that this 'gratuitous insult' by
the Japanese did much to weaken their original impression of the
power of the American ships.[24] A Japanese observer wrote in the
early twentieth century that 'Commodore Biddle's mission was
worse than a mere failure. It had the effect of lowering the dignity
of his country in the mind of the oriental.'[25] Whether or not this

was true, it made such an impression on the mind of Commodore Matthew C. Perry that when he embarked on his own voyage to Japan he determined that by his actions and demeanour he would force the Japanese to respect and, if necessary, to fear him.

When Perry was asked by President Fillmore to lead the expedition, he was told that he could have any available ships, appoint his own officers and spend any reasonable amount of money on equipment and presents for the Japanese.[26] Sadly for Perry, not all that was promised arrived – in particular the number of ships that he had expected – but the hoped-for prize and glory were worth his making the best of things. Perry himself drafted the objectives of his journey, which were incorporated as government policy in the official letter of instructions dated 5 November 1852. They were 1) to 'effect some permanent arrangement for the protection of American seamen and property wrecked on these islands, or driven into their ports by stress of weather', 2) to gain permission for American ships to enter their ports to obtain supplies and, if damaged, to refit them, 3) to gain permission to establish a coal depot on one of the islands, ideally on one of the principal ones, but at the least on one of the small uninhabited ones, and 4) to gain permission for US ships to enter one or more of their ports to sell or trade their cargoes.

C. M. Conrad, the Acting Secretary of State, then pointed out that it was quite clear, from past experience, that arguments were useless, unless they were supported by 'some imposing manifestation of power'. Perry was therefore to take his whole force to the point on the coast that he deemed best, to make contact with the government and, if possible, to see the Emperor in person and to deliver to him the letter from the President that he was to take with him. If, however, after exhausting every argument and means of persuasion the Japanese government still refused any relaxation of its system of exclusion or any assurance of humane treatment of shipwrecked American seamen, 'he will then change his tone, and inform them in the most unequivocal terms ... that if any acts of cruelty should hereafter be practiced upon citizens of this country, whether by the government or by the inhabitants of Japan, they will be severely chastised'. However, he was reminded that, because the President had no power to declare war, he should limit his use of violence to cases of self-defence of the vessels and crews, 'or to resent an act of personal violence offered to himself, or to one of his officers'.[27] That appears to have given permission for most contingencies.

While sailing to Japan, Perry turned his mind to the urgency of securing 'one or more ports of refuge and supply to our whaling and other ships'; should the Japanese government object to the granting of such ports upon the mainland, 'and they cannot be occupied without resort to force and bloodshed', then it would be necessary for the squadron to 'establish places of rendezvous at one or two of the islands south of Japan ... and by kindness and gentle treatment conciliate the inhabitants so as to bring about their friendly intercourse'. His choice, he wrote to Washington on 14 December 1852, would be the Lew Chew (Ryūkyū) Islands, whose sovereignty was disputed by Japan and China. He then continued with a not unfamiliar justification: 'the occupation of the principal ports of those islands for the accommodation of our ships of war, and for the safe resort of merchant vessels of what-ever nation, would be a measure not only justified by the strictest rules of moral law, but what is also to be considered by the laws of stern necessity; and the argument may be further strengthened by the certain consequences of the amelioration of the condition of the natives'.[28] Of course.

On 15 February 1853, Edward Everett of the Department of State replied to Perry's dispatch, saying that he had consulted the President, and the President had agreed that it was highly desir-able, even necessary, to secure one or more ports 'of refuge of easy access'. The President agreed with Perry that the Lew Chew Islands would be the best to approach, both because of their pos-ition (in the East China Sea south of Japan and facing China) and because of the 'friendly and peaceful character of the natives'. But they must see that the coming of the Americans 'is a benefit, and not an evil to them'.[29]

Perry decided to visit these islands on his way to Japan: he had heard much of their disinclination to wage war, and he could easily obtain the supplies he needed and probably permanent access without too much effort. Samuel Eliot Morison points out that Perry decided that 'a call there could be a sort of dress rehearsal for his main mission, as well as a means of securing a coaling station if Japan refused to grant one'. He also understood the strategic value of the Great Lew Chew Island, now known as Okinawa. Great Britain had already established bases at Singapore, North Borneo and Hong Kong, and thus could control every entrance to the China Seas from the west. An American-controlled port at Great Lew Chew Island would, he thought, enable the US Navy to control access to the China Seas from across the Pacific, and thereby balance British power in the Far East.[30]

The squadron arrived at Great Lew Chew Island on 26 May 1853. Then began a dance. Of course the islanders did not want these visitors and did what they could to discourage them by shutting up their shops, having spies follow the Americans around and fending off Perry's requests to see the rulers. They were polite, Perry found, but suspicious of foreigners and evasive. They used procrastination as a weapon: they were otherwise unarmed. When the Regent of the Lew Chew Kingdom (the ruler was a young boy) finally came on board Perry's ship, his entourage were reserved and grave, until Perry announced that he would return the visit at the royal palace, at which point there were horrified protests. Perry replied that he intended to visit the Regent in the palace on 6 June and 'would expect such a reception as became his rank and position as Commander of the Squadron and diplomatic representative of the United States'.[31] While awaiting the day of the visit, Perry set in motion an expedition to explore the interior. The Americans tried to outstrip their guides by quick marching, but the guides always managed to run ahead to tell the islanders to disappear.

Perry soon decided that visiting the Regent was not enough and insisted on meeting the Queen Mother and the heir. He took with him more than 200 sailors and marines, two pieces of artillery and the ship's band, which played 'Hail, Columbia' as they arrived. The palace was up a hill, and Perry believed that it would be undignified for him to walk, so he had his men build him a sedan chair. Although Perry's biographer emphasises that he was firm not arrogant, dignified not conceited, imperious not imperialistic,[32] it is, of course, possible that the islanders found it difficult to discern the differences. During the visit he managed to extract vague assurances that American vessels in distress would be allowed to call in in safety and not be molested. This accomplished, Perry decided that he would give the islanders time to realise how wonderful the Americans were and forgo suggesting a treaty with the Kingdom until a later date.

As his squadron had to remain on the island while awaiting a shipment of coal from Shanghai, he decided to take a ship and visit the Bonin Islands to the south-east of Japan, arriving at Port Lloyd on 14 June. He was searching for more 'points of refuge' and coaling stations, as well as possible stopping places for steamships from the Sandwich Islands (now Hawaii). While there, he bought a parcel of land from an inhabitant for future use as a coal depot.[33] However, there was a problem: which country exercised sovereignty? The 'most prominent claimant is the queen of England, with no other right, however, than that which may have grown out of the performance of a ceremony (perhaps not expressly authorized by his government) by Captain Beechey, commanding the English surveying vessel "Blossom," who, in 1827, formally took possession of the group and gave English names to all of the islands'. However, four years before, 'a Captain Coffin, whose nationality is not mentioned, but from the name the probability is that he was an American, visited the group, and gave his name to one of the islands'.[34]

One possibility would be to propose that Port Lloyd might be considered a free port under the flag of either the US or Great Britain or a local flag (unspecified). It would be of the highest importance to American trade with China and, opportunely, few English vessels crossed this part of the Pacific. And then the hope emerges: 'Should the department, however, deem it desirable for me to take possession of the islands in the name of the United States, I will do so and adopt the best means of holding them.'[35] Some months later, Perry received the answer from the President to the seizure of that or of any other island: no.[36]

III

On 8 July 1853, Perry's squadron of two warships towing two sailing sloops of war steamed into the Bay of Edo and anchored off Uraga in line-of-battle. (Uraga is, very roughly, about eight statute miles north of the entrance to the bay, now Tokyo Wan, and Edo twenty-seven miles further north.) It was clear to the Japanese that they were foreign ships because they were black,[37] but what was new was that they were burning ships, or so it seemed from the belching black smoke. It was a total surprise and it was frightening. But the *bakufū* ought not to have been surprised, because they had been warned. In 1852 the Dutch at Nagasaki had sent them an official letter warning that the Americans were coming to Uraga to present a letter from their President to the Emperor, and word had arrived from Okinawa that they were on their way. The *bakufū* recipients decided that it was a ruse by the Dutch to get more business and did nothing. In any case, Edo Bay was supposedly so well fortified that no other stranger would dare enter (as it happened, earthern forts equipped with smooth-bore guns were all that the bay had for defence).[38] Of course, Commodore Biddle had sailed in, but Abé Masahiro Ise no-kami, Daimyō of Fukuyama and presiding member (*shuza*) of the *rōjū* (the Shōgun's Council), had certainly dealt with Biddle successfully; naturally this second visitor would be no more difficult to send back home. No one, however, dared to tell the Shōgun of the arrival of the Americans.[39] People were terrified: no one had ever seen the powerful 'burning ships' before. Bells tolled and people streamed out of Edo and the surrounding villages, carrying their goods with them, to hide further away.

According to Perry's 'Note referring to events', which was sent back to Washington in August, he had decided that he would not request 'those acts of courtesy which are due from one civilized nation to another', but would demand them. He also decided that he would deal only with the highest dignitaries in the empire and, indeed, would make himself exclusive and exacting, which would gain the respect of 'these people of forms and ceremonies'. Perry therefore refused to see a number of the officials who came to his ship, but turned them over to his officers. He had also repulsed the many Japanese samurai from the numerous guard boats who attempted to climb into the ships, and warned that if those boats did not leave the vicinity he would turn the guns on them. This worked.[40]

A higher official, the Governor of Uraga, came the following day. Interestingly, the *bakufū* when dealing with foreigners sometimes made temporary promotions and sent lower-ranking officials with higher-sounding names, a way of keeping the foreigner in his lower place.[41] It would be surprising if this had not been such an occasion. The official insisted that Nagasaki was the place where communications with foreigners took place (the continuing reference to Nagasaki made Perry bristle during the remainder of his mission, leading him to refuse automatically anything relating to it). After a long discussion, Perry told him that 'if the Japanese government did not appoint a suitable person to receive the documents addressed to the emperor, I would go on shore with a sufficient force and deliver them, whatever the consequences might be'. At this point, the Governor said that he would send a communication to Edo asking for further instructions, but that the answer would take four days; Perry, of course, said that he would require an answer in three.[42]

The decision to receive the President's letter was taken only very reluctantly. The *rōjū* noted that it included a paragraph stating that 'If your imperial majesty is not satisfied that it would be safe altogether to abrogate the ancient laws which forbid foreign trade, they might be suspended for five or ten years, so as to try the experiment. If it does not prove as beneficial as was hoped the ancient laws can be restored. The United States often limit their treaties with foreign States to a few years, and then renew them or not, as they please.'[43] Perhaps this was marginally reassuring.

Washington had instructed Perry to exhaust every argument and means of persuasion before changing his tone to a more threatening one. In his reports to Washington, Perry implies that he was always the soul of firm courtesy. However, Japanese documents give another account, and it is clear that Perry did not exhaust every argument. According to the historian Marius B. Jansen,

> At the very outset of the talks he sent some white flags to the Japanese negotiator together with a harsh personal letter. Failure to meet his demands, he warned, would bring on a war that Japan would most assuredly lose, and in that case the white flags of surrender would be useful. In this bit of bravado he was probably acting beyond his instructions, and since it gives a rather different picture of his achievements than he might have wished, he quietly omitted all mention of this letter from his official and personal reports.[44]

While the Americans awaited the return of the Japanese official with the expected agreement to receive the President's letter, Perry on the morning of 9 July sent a surveying vessel from each ship, all four flying white flags, to take soundings of the harbour and Strait of Uraga. In case they met with resistance, he told the officer in charge of the surveying party, Lieutenant Silas Bent, not to go beyond the range of the warships' guns. When asked by the Governor of Uraga what they were doing, they told him that they were surveying the harbour; 'he said it was against the Japanese laws to allow of such examinations, and he was replied to, that, though the Japanese laws forbade such surveys, the American laws command them, and that we were as much bound to obey the American as he was the Japanese laws'.[45] This was, of course, a lie: Perry's instructions asked him to do so,[46] but such instructions do not normally pass as laws.

One question must be, why did the Japanese not try to prevent this? There were twenty forts along the bay, most of them concentrated on the Uraga narrows, and all of them with guns. The fear in the *bakufu*, however, was that the Americans planned to act as the British had done in China and carve out an enclave to act as their Hong Kong, and they were not convinced that they could prevent it. Therefore, no one was to fire on the boats for fear that the Americans would use it as an 'incident' allowing them to grab some land.

Two days later, the survey boats were sent higher up the bay, accompanied by one of the warships, the USS *Mississippi*. Perry again: 'I had purposely sent the Mississippi and the boats on this service, being satisfied that the very circumstances of approaching nearer to Yedo with a powerful ship would alarm the authorities and induce them to give a more favorable answer to my demands.' The Governor of Uraga came out to his ship – Perry assumed to find out what the boats and ships were doing – and Perry 'directed that he should be informed that unless the business which brought the squadron to these waters was arranged at this time, I should return in the ensuing spring with a larger force, and, as the anchorage in front of Uraga was not convenient or safe, I was desirous of seeking a more favorable situation nearer to Yedo, which would make our communications with that city more convenient'.[47]

On 13 July the reply from Edo arrived: a distinguished personage had been appointed by the Emperor to receive the letter and carry it back to his sovereign, but he had no power to enter into discussions. That was acceptable to Perry. At dawn on the following day, his two warships weighed anchor and steamed the short distance to Kurihama. The Americans arrived in great force, with their ships and boats in a single long line, and after disembarking, all of the soldiers and sailors who could be spared stood in formation (about 400). Perry with his staff of twenty-five and accompanied by two very tall black orderlies marched between the ranks to the pavilion where the reception of the letter was to take place. The display was to impress the Japanese, but Perry was aware of the thousands of soldiers lining the bay; he estimated the number as from 5,000 to 7,000, 'composed of cavalry, artillery, infantry, and archers; some of the infantry with flint muskets, others with match-locks'.[48] Indeed, according to the diary of the Court physician, Dr Ito, the mobilisation to meet the invader was almost complete: 'the entire western shore of Edo Bay was crowded with troops, every town and village had a garrison, and the roads were congested with gun carriages, carts hauling arms and provisions, laden pack horses and porters carrying heavy burdens slung on poles'.[49] The spectacle which greeted the Americans was stunning and colourful, with the pennants, the colours of the samurais' uniforms and the long *baku*, a curtain behind which more troops were hidden. Morison describes it as 'a muster representing the gallantry and chivalry of medieval Japan'.[50]

As demonstrated by the forces on display, neither side trusted the other in the least. When the American steamers anchored on the beach, they had springs on their cables so as to bring a full broadside to bear in case of attack. The Japanese in their turn concealed ten samurai under the floor of the reception hall with orders that, if the visitors attempted any violence, they were to rush out and kill Perry and his staff. The two Japanese dignitaries were seated on 'campstools', and rose and bowed as Perry advanced. They spoke not a word during the proceedings, accepted the letter from the President, gave a receipt, rose, bowed and left.[51]

The reluctant, indeed forced, acceptance of the letter carried by Perry was made very clear by the receipt from the Emperor, in reality from the Shōgun:

> It has been many times intimated that business relating to foreign countries cannot be transacted here in Uraga, but at Nagasaki; nevertheless, as it has been observed that the admiral in his quality of ambassador of the President would feel himself insulted by a refusal to receive the letter at this place, the justice of which has been acknowledged, the above mentioned letter is hereby received in opposition to the Japanese law. As this is not a place wherein to negotiate with foreigners, so neither can conferences nor entertainment be held. Therefore, as the letter has been received you can depart.[52]

Perry responded with contempt, as he wrote to the Secretary of the Navy:

> To show these princes how little I regarded their order for me to depart, on getting on board, I immediately ordered the whole

squadron underway, not to leave the bay as they doubtless expected, but to go higher up, having determined to examine the channel towards Yedo, being satisfied that the employment of so large a force in surveying service and so near the capital, and in waters hitherto unknown to foreigners, would produce a decided influence upon the pride and conceit of the government, and cause a more favorable consideration of the President's letter.[53]

He moved all four of the ships up Edo Bay in a line abreast, running lines of soundings across the bay. The following day he steamed further up to a point seven miles from Edo. 'I might have gone still higher', he wrote, 'but was apprehensive of causing too much alarm, and thus throwing some obstacle in the way of a favorable reception at court of the President's letter, which I had delivered only the day before, and which was probably then under consideration; and, thinking that I had done enough to work upon the fears of the emperor, without going too far in my experiment, I caused the ship to rejoin the squadron.'[54]

On 17 July the squadron left Edo Bay, Perry having told the Japanese that he would return in the spring for their answer. He clearly felt that he had to give his reasons to the Secretary of the Navy, J. C. Dobbin, in order to pre-empt any criticism. First of all, he did not have enough water or provisions to last more than a month, and he confidently expected the Japanese to delay for longer than that. Secondly, the disturbed state of China required one or more of his ships to go there. And finally, 'considering that not a single vessel which had been promised by the department should immediately follow me had yet joined my force, and being without the presents sent from the United States ... I was glad to have a good excuse for consenting to wait until the ensuing spring for the final answer of the Japanese government.'[55] As it happened, this pre-emption did not work, Secretary Dobbin writing that in consideration of the vast expense and the great need for the ships for other important purposes, it was 'much to be regretted' that action had been postponed until the following spring.[56]

Secretary Dobbin and through him the President received Perry's 'Note of events', which was dated 3 August 1853, and read it 'with much interest', Perry was told in the Secretary's dispatch of 14 November. Their reaction was not, perhaps, as fulsome as he might have wished. The President 'desires to impress you with his conviction that the great end should be attained, not only with credit to the United States, but without wrong to Japan ... your mission is one of peaceful negotiation, and ... no violence should be resorted to except for defence.' He was to remember that Congress alone had the power to declare war, so he should be prudent. Of course they had every confidence in his judgement and patriotism, but their suggestions that he not employ violence or intimidation had 'been called forth by a portion of your interesting notes, in which you express some hope of success in the spring by operating on the fears of the Japanese, but speak, at the same time, of the number of the batteries already erected on the shore "to expel the Americans"'. They continued to quote from his dispatch:

> Doubtless many others will be erected before the ensuing spring for the same object; but with the force I shall have, and especially with the aid of the Vermont, I shall not be deterred from penetrating to the very head of navigation in the bay, and within three or four miles of Yedo, perhaps within gun-shot. It is very certain that the Japanese can be brought to reason only through the influence of their fears, and when they find that their sea-coast is entirely at the mercy of a strong naval force they will be induced, I confidently hope, to concede all that will be asked of them.

He was then told that he was not to have the *Vermont*, the three-decker ship which he had expected to use to overawe the Japanese, because, he was told, the navy did not have enough sailors to man it without removing them from other ships.[57] Not terribly subtle.

The squadron then sailed to China, where Perry ran into two difficulties, one to do with the Bonin Islands, the other over the control of his ships. Sir George Bonham, the Chief Superintendent of Trade at Hong Kong, was rather curious about what Perry had been doing at the Bonin Islands, and the two discussed the matter on 21 December. What particularly piqued his curiosity was the report that Perry had 'purchased ground from a resident there for a coal depot, for the use of the government of the United States of America'. It was, naturally, far from his intention to dispute the right of any person to purchase land on the islands, but it was generally understood that the group of islands was some time before taken possession of in the name of the British government. Perry responded with the somewhat lame excuse that the transaction was one of a strictly private character: he wanted to withhold the only suitable position in the Port Lloyd harbour for a coal depot from 'the venality of unprincipled speculators, who might otherwise have gained possession of it for purposes of extortion'. His whole purpose was to secure ports of refuge and supplies in the north Pacific, and it mattered little who owned the islands, as long as their ports were open to all. After all, would that not be a good thing?[58] Apparently the topic was dropped, but presumably it was understood that no coal depot would be created without the permission of the British government.

The other contretemps was more protracted and considerably more critical to Perry. Essentially it was a struggle for control between Perry as Commander-in-Chief, US Naval Forces, East Indies, China and Japan, and Humphrey Marshall, the American Commissioner to China. The Taiping Rebellion, essentially a bloody civil war in 1850–64 between the Ch'ing dynasty and a Christian millenarian movement, the Taiping Heavenly Kingdom, was engulfing China. Shanghai, where many American and other foreign merchants had their businesses, was under threat, as were some of the other treaty ports. Marshall wanted some of Perry's ships to remain and pass under his command to protect the Americans. Perry thought that Marshall was wildly overemphasising the danger and insisted that he needed all of his ships for the expedition to Japan. The Secretary of the Navy had written a discouraging dispatch on 28 October 1853 in response to Perry's earlier complaints that he had not received the number of ships that he had been promised, pointing out that

> [t]he mission in which you are engaged has attracted much admiration, and excited much expectation. But the present seems to be a crisis in the history of China, and is considered by many as throwing around China, at least, as much interest and attraction as Japan presents. To have your name associated with the opening of commercial intercourse with Japan, may well excite your pride; but to be identified, also, with the great events that we trust may yet transpire in connection with China, may be well esteemed a privilege and an honor.[59]

This was quite a slap, and it did not bode well for future arguments. Perry and Marshall carried out a protracted, stiff correspondence, all of which was sent on to Washington. Marshall departed, but the arrival of a new Commissioner, R. M. McLane, lit a spark of rebellion in Perry. Writing in some exasperation to the Secretary from Hong Kong on 14 January 1854, he complained that '[o]n the eve of getting under way for Japan, with all my arrangements made to leave in an hour, and a large portion of my force actually gone', the dispatch dated 28 October 1853 from the department arrived and instructed him to detach one of his steamers and place it at the disposal of McLane. He was furious, and wrote to the department that it would be 'highly injurious' to his plans, which he had already begun to carry out. If the department knew the damage this order caused it would revoke it, 'but as it is my duty to obey, though it cannot be done at this moment without serious consequences to the success of my mission, I will detach one of the steamers from the Bay of Yedo, and send her to Macao. Although Mr. McLane may not find a steamer waiting for him at Macao when he arrives, I will order her to the coast of China the moment I can do so consistently with the public interests.'[60] And off he sailed. (As it happened, it did arrive in Macao before McLane.) In short, he disobeyed his instructions. His assumption must have been that in the time it took – in those pre-cable days – for dispatches to be sent, answered and returned, his reputation at home, and the great success that he expected to gain in Japan before the department could respond, would amply protect him.

Perry had told the Japanese officials that he expected to return to Japan in the spring, but the activities of the Russians convinced him to accelerate his departure. Russia had long been aware of the strategic advantages that would be gained by being the first foreign Power to establish bases in the Japanese islands. When the Americans announced in June 1851 their intention to negotiate a treaty with Japan, the Russians decided to organise an expedition of their own to pre-empt the Americans. In 1850 the Russian naval centre had been moved from Okhotsk to Petropavlovski, and this made Sakhalin Island, relatively close to Russia and very close to Japan, of new importance. The outbreak of the Crimean War in March 1854 meant that access to bases in Japan, which would help them to attack British and French merchant and warships around China, became of greater urgency. Therefore, when Perry had set out for Japan, a small squadron of four ships of the Imperial Russian Navy under the command of Vice-Admiral Count Poutiatin was dispatched to Japan.[61]

Poutiatin had spent three months at Nagasaki in an effort to convince the Japanese to sign a treaty, but 'he effected nothing'. His ship reached Shanghai at the end of November, and when in due course he met Perry, he 'openly avow[ed] his desire to join my force and enter into full co-operation with me', the two squadrons returning to Japan together. Perry of course declined. In addition, he learned that the French Commodore of the frigate *Constantine*, then lying at Macao, had received sealed orders from Paris and suddenly put to sea. Since it was common knowledge that the *Constantine* was to have sailed to Shanghai with the French Minister and his wife, this was intensely suspicious.[62] Consequently, Perry decided that, instead of waiting for the spring, when the weather would be considerably less stormy, he would depart as soon as possible. He gathered his ten ships together – rather more than the four he had commanded on the earlier visit to Japan – and steamed out of Shanghai on 14 January

1854. After a stop at Great Lew Chew Island, he wrote to the Secretary of the Navy on the 25th strongly suggesting that his squadron take it over.

Washington was horrified:

> Your suggestion about holding one of the Lew-Chew islands 'upon the ground of *reclamation for insults and injuries committed upon American citizens* [their emphasis] ... should the Japanese government refuse to negotiate or to assign a port of resort for our merchant and whaling ships,' is ... embarrassing. The subject has been laid before the President, who, while he appreciates highly the patriotic motive which prompts the suggestion, is disinclined, without the authority of Congress, to take and retain possession of an island in that distant country, particularly unless more urgent and potent reasons demanded it than now exist. If, in future, resistance should be offered and threatened, it would also be rather mortifying and expensive to maintain a force there to retain it. Indulging the hope that the contingency may not arise to occasion any resort to the expedient suggested, and that your skill, prudence, and good judgment may enable you to triumph over the ignorant obstinacy of the Japanese without violence, it is considered sounder policy not to seize the island as suggested in your dispatch.[63]

Perry would not receive this answer to his wish until the summer. Presumably, then, he retained this sense of entitlement when he arrived at the Bay of Edo on 13 February 1854; certainly some of his actions suggest that this was the case.

IV

Meanwhile, in Japan the proposals in the President's letter caused a storm of opposition. Abé, leader of the *rōjū* (the Shōgun's Council), had broken with all precedent: after the Americans had departed he sent the letter to all the daimyō, all high officials and even to some commoners. It was the duty of the *bakufū* to deal with foreigners, and Abé's action was the first crack in the wall around the *rōjū*. As one Japanese historian has written,

> the convening of all the Daimyos for discussing the nature of the reply to be given to the President of the United States was an entire departure from the traditional policy of the Yedo Government. The authority invested in the Shogun by the Emperor was absolute and autocratic. The departure thus made clearly demonstrates the magnitude of the disturbed state of the whole country over the grave problem of admitting foreigners. The Government of the Shogun was fully aware of the strong opposition existing against opening the country, and would not dare take the whole responsibility upon its own shoulders.[64]

Abé had hoped to achieve a consensus, but only a handful of the daimyō favoured a policy of opening up Japan: most of the rest wanted to fight. From the beginning the opposition was led by the senior prince of Mito, Tokugawa Nariaki, member of one of the Three Families of the Tokugawa Blood, and one of the strongest and ablest of the daimyō.[65] Those who favoured opening up believed that 'Japan must have ocean-going vessels, and these cannot be procured in a moment ... and [she should] lose no time in furnishing herself with powerful men-of-war and with sailors and gunners capable of navigating and fighting these vessels. In short, the wisest plan is to make a show of commerce and intercourse, and thus gain time to equip the country with a knowledge of naval architecture and warfare.'[66] The most important of these was Ii Kamon-no-kami Naosuké, *fudai* daimyō of Hikoné, who thought that they should accept the American demands and thereby buy time to prepare for a future confrontation. It would fall to him in due course to implement this policy, and he in turn would fall under an assassin's sword.[67]

Abé seems to have lost little time in constructing defences: batteries were built at Shinagawa to guard the approaches to Edo; defensive preparations were made along some of the coasts; the daimyō were invited to build and arm large vessels; cannon were set up and troops were drilled. 'But all of these efforts tended only to expose their own feebleness, and on the 2nd of November, 1853, instructions were issued that if the Americans returned they were to be dealt with peacefully.'[68]

And return they did, the squadron first rendezvousing at Lew Chew and then steaming into the Bay of Edo on 13 February 1854. Naturally the significantly increased size of the squadron initially aroused apprehension among the Japanese as to whether Perry had come to negotiate or to invade, but it soon became clear that his intention was the former. The first conflict arose on the day of arrival over where the negotiations would be held. For the Japanese, their priority was to keep the Americans out of Edo and they strongly urged that they be held at Uraga, where they were already building a 'treaty hall', or at Kakamura. Perry, however, was dead set on Edo and demanded that the negotiations be held there, refusing the two suggestions because the harbours were too exposed for safety. The *rōjū* told the Commissioners to resist at all hazards Perry's demand: if it were accepted the *bakufū* would be deemed incapable of defending the capital and would probably be overthrown. Perry finally realised that to insist would seriously endanger the regime, which he had no wish to do. They finally compromised on Yokohama, which was both decently away from Edo and had a magnificent harbour.

Then came the conferences, both formal between Perry and the imperial Commissioners and more informal between less grand officials and Perry's officers. There were three formal conferences, for which Perry landed with pomp and circumstance. He proposed that the 1844 Treaty of Wanghia between the US and China be used as the basis for the new treaty, but, not wanting a trade treaty, the Japanese refused. They presented their own series of propositions founded on Perry's letters, which then formed the basis for the negotiations. During the negotiations gifts were exchanged, Perry having brought over two telegraph instruments and a reduced-size locomotive, along with tender, cars and rails, as well as a wealth of other gifts – including a quantity of spirits, of which the Japanese had rapidly become very fond.[69] According to one historian, 'Lieutenant Preble, who

played host on the quarterdeck, gives a lively description of the
main banquet, in which he had been instructed to make the guests
eat and drink as much as possible. After they had worked through
champagne, Madeira, cherry cordial, punch and whiskey, Preble
mixed up tomato ketchup and vinegar "which [he later wrote]
they seemed to relish with equal gusto".[70] It is also clear that
Preble's comment expresses no little contempt. Indeed, the interpreter appointed by Perry, Samuel Wells Williams, wrote in his
diary that 'I do not at all like the way in which this nation is
spoken of by the commodore and most of his officers, calling
them savages, liars, a pack of fools, poor devils; cursing them
and then denying practically all of it by supposing them worth
making a treaty with. Truly, what sort of instruments does God
work with!'[71]

The negotiations were not rapid. One American historian of
an older school explained that 'Anyone who has tried to find
an address in a remote part of Tokyo will appreciate how much
patience one needs to deal successfully with the Japanese; how
long the explanations and excuses take with a people who use
a hundred words in a polite circumlocution where a Westerner
would use two words abruptly.' Perry exhibited a modicum of
patience, 'but once, according to the Japanese interpreter, he
lost his temper and said "if his proposals were rejected, he was
prepared to make war at once; that in the event of war, he would
have fifty ships in nearby waters and fifty more in California,
and that if he sent word he could summon a command of one
hundred warships within twenty days"',[72] a bluff of monu-
mental proportions.

Perry did not understand and could not abide Japanese diplomatic tactics, which they would continue to use against the
Western Powers for some years. Lacking military weapons
able to overbear the Americans, their weapon was negotiation
supported by procrastination. Perhaps it was absolutely necessary that every decision had to be referred back to, and eventually
agreed to, by the Shōgun in Edo, but the assumption must be that,
even if it were not necessary, it still provided one of the delaying
tactics designed to wear the foreigner down.[73] This had succeeded

with the Russians the previous year – Admiral Poutiatin and his squadron had spent a fruitless three months in Nagasaki, arguing for a Russo-Japanese treaty, before departing for China – and it might well work with others. It is also important to remember that the Japanese government had to keep the balance between supporters and enemies within Japan. Its success or failure in the negotiations with Western Powers would severely affect this balance.

Perry eventually gained Japanese agreement to the humane treatment of shipwrecked sailors and access to supplies and coal. He then turned to trade: why would the Japanese not permit commerce? It was, after all, the exchange by a country of what it had for what it lacked, which brought great profit and wealth. The Japanese negotiator replied that Japan produced what it needed. Furthermore, 'if the commodore had come to Japan to have greater value placed on human life and to seek assistance for ships, "you have attained your purpose. Now, commerce has to do with profits, but has it anything to do with human life?"' Outmanoeuvred, Perry agreed that 'Commerce brings profit to a country, but it does not concern human life. I shall not insist upon it.'[74] This would be left to Townsend Harris, the first Consul-General (American or otherwise) to Japan.

On 31 March the Convention of Kanagawa was signed. This provided for the opening of the port of Shimoda immediately and that of Hakodate in a year's time for coal and supplies; all ships had to land there unless they were in distress or shipwrecked. Good treatment for shipwrecked Americans was promised as well as assurances that the restrictions suffered by the Dutch and Chinese at Deshima would not be imposed. Trade under temporary Japanese regulations was to be allowed, as well as most-favoured-nation status, by which the US would receive the same rights as those granted to any other foreign country. After eighteen months an American consul or agent could be appointed to reside in Shimoda, provided that either of the two countries thought it necessary.[75] Disagreements would arise later, due to the fact that in the English-language version if either country wished for it a consul would be sent, while the Japanese-language version said that if both countries wished it, one would be appointed. The American interpretation would prevail.

Before returning home, Perry decided to indulge himself in a remarkably arrogant manner: a visit to Edo in his ship, a gesture which could well have destroyed the carefully cultivated goodwill. Perry 'felt a compulsion to steam near enough to view the castle [of the Shōgun] at close range' and to fire a twenty-one-gun salute in honour of the Emperor. Hayashi, one of the Commissioners, tried to dissuade him, but to no avail. On 10 April the two remaining ships travelled up Edo Bay towards the capital. The interpreter Einosuke and two other officials who had come on board to say farewell begged him to turn back, Einosuke warning him that if they fired the salute he would throw himself into the cannon mouth, while his colleague gave his cloak and long sword to the purser's son, retaining the short sword to disembowel himself. Furthermore, Perry was told, if Edo were profaned, Hayashi and two other negotiators would be compelled to commit suicide, 'out of shame for not having kept the barbarians out'. At this point, Perry recovered his senses: he took out his telescope, exclaimed how clearly he could see Edo, said 'Having now seen Edo, let us go,' and turned his ships away.[76] After calling in at Shimoda to see if it was suitable – he decided that it was – and after extracting the Treaty of Naha (Naha was the major city on Great Lew Chew) from the Lew Chew Islands on 11 July 1854, he turned to other duties.[77]

V

Great Britain was much less interested in Japan than was the US, and certainly felt less need to bestir itself for it. The British already had predominant influence in China, and the actions of the government in Japan for most of the nineteenth century were largely conditioned by Britons' experiences in China.[78] They assumed that there were few differences between Asian countries. There is a distinct theme, particularly in the press, that Japan had no right to prevent other countries from sharing in its riches: the *Edinburgh*

Review in October 1852 declared that 'The compulsory seclusion of the Japanese is a wrong not only to themselves, but to the civilised world ... The Japanese undoubtedly have an exclusive right to the possession of their territory; but they must not abuse that right to the extent of debarring all other nations from a participation in its riches and virtues.'[79] On the whole (with the occasional exception – see below), it would be the interests in Japan of British merchants that were of prime concern. The US, on the other hand, came later on the Far Eastern scene; it had substantial economic interests in China, not least in the opium trade, but relatively little diplomatic or military influence. Many of those Chinese who were involved in or aware of these affairs treated the US with some contempt, seeing the Americans as running behind the British, picking up what the British had secured, but taking no lead themselves. In 1845, following the Opium War, a British fleet from the East India Station had been brought into Chinese waters to protect British rights and interests under the Treaty of Nanking. There was soon a permanent squadron on the China Station and, consequently, the weight of British power, in particular that of the Royal Navy, meant that within a very few years Britain ineluctably became the most important of the foreign Powers dealing with Japan, regardless of the fact that the US had seniority.

There had been early attempts to establish a trading relationship, with British merchants opening a factory (trading centre) in 1613. However, the Dutch had already been there for four years, and they essentially forced its closure in 1623. For one thing, they constantly cut their prices to drive English goods from the market, but more importantly the Dutch controlled the seas and for some years the only English ships which arrived were brought in as Dutch prizes. In the early nineteenth century, interest revived, but for the East India Company as for others with funds to invest, the likely reward did not justify the effort.[80] The British government was certainly uninterested. For a short time in the aftermath of the Opium War, there was a modification of this position, but its reconsideration would probably not have taken place without the support of Foreign Secretary Lord Aberdeen and a government led by Sir Robert Peel whose members were 'very desirous of availing themselves of any opportunity of opening new markets for all important Articles of our Manufacture by commercial arrangements with foreign powers upon principles of mutual advantage'.[81]

The Foreign Office responded to the arguments of Sir J. F. Davis, Superintendent of Trade in China, that it would be a valuable move to visit Japan, with a gunboat, and negotiate with its government a treaty of amity and commerce. Over the years 1845–6, the Foreign Office considered the proposal, but in July 1846 the project was discontinued: there was already rivalry with other Powers, although this was of less importance than naval strength. Of particular concern was the fact that parliamentary grants for the Royal Navy were too small for enough ships to be manned on the China Station – Perry would have the same problem with congressional parsimony – and, as noted above, Davis believed that a show of force was a requirement for its success,[82] a belief shared by Perry.

It was the news of Perry's success that reawakened interest at the Foreign Office, in particular given the apparent ease with which he had gained a treaty.[83] However, it was the outbreak of the Crimean War in 1854 with the British, French, Austrian and Ottoman empires against the Russian empire which set the scene for the Stirling Convention, the first ever Anglo-Japanese treaty. Rear Admiral Sir James Stirling was the Commander-in-Chief of the East Indies and China Station and came to the China waters for three reasons: first of all, a Russian squadron was known to be in the vicinity (there were Russian bases at Kamchatka and the Sea of Okhotsk), and his duty was to find and defeat it; secondly, he wanted to secure an undertaking that Japan would observe an equally 'neutral' stance towards British and Russian warships that might enter Japanese ports during the war (Japan found this difficult because of long-standing relations with and some fear of Russia); and thirdly, he wanted to obtain the right to visit Japanese harbours, partly to discover if the Russians were using them to shelter, and partly to secure supplies and fuel.[84] Stirling would later argue that he and his squadron came to Nagasaki, arriving on 7 September 1854 with his flagship HMS *Winchester* and three other ships, to negotiate with the Japanese government for these permissions, because it was part of his responsibility. He was apparently not interested in commercial matters.

From the very beginning there was intense confusion, largely because of the lack of any halfway competent translators on either side.[85] As a result, Stirling found it virtually impossible to make clear to the Japanese just what he wanted. Having just dealt with Perry, the Japanese assumed that the British Admiral would demand at least the same concessions in terms of the opening of ports; he was wholly unable to put across his desire to have a purely military agreement. The Japanese were considerably more apprehensive about Great Britain than about the US, since they were familiar with its activities in India and even more know-ledgeable about the recent events in China. Their idea was to con-cede as little as possible but enough to satisfy the British, and Stirling sailed away with a treaty opening the ports of Nagasaki and Hakodate to British ships, but no commercial agreement. Nevertheless, Stirling believed that the Convention provided sig-nificant advantages in his operations against the Russians, since it opened both Nagasaki and Hakodate as ports of call and supply to British warships as well as merchant vessels. Certainly during 1855 the Japanese ports were being used as bases for operations against the Russians.[86]

Stirling was at least the equal of Perry in his arrogance and assumption that the Japanese would not have any choice but to agree to his demands. In spite of his signing of the Anglo-Japanese Convention, which included an Article VII stating that once the Convention had been ratified 'no high officer coming to Japan shall alter it', he soon went back to Japan with a list of the changes he wanted made and demanded that the Japanese accept them. On his return in October 1855 to exchange ratifications, he also presented what he called a 'liberal Explanation' of the terms of the Convention, but which was, in fact, a demand for consider-able changes both in the treaty and the port regulations. When the Japanese refused a rapid acceptance of his demands, 'he then stormed out of the conference-room with the parting threat that he would immediately notify his government that the treaty had been broken by Japan'. Their fear of the use he might make of his eleven ships induced the Japanese to accept some modifications,[87] but it is difficult to imagine that a British admiral would try the same techniques in, say, Paris or Washington.

VI

Townsend Harris, the first Consul-General to Japan, had a somewhat mundane background for his future position. Born in 1804 in New York State, at the age of sixteen, as his elder brother's junior partner, he helped to open and thereafter run a shop selling chinaware in Manhattan. He was bookish, teaching himself three European languages to enable him to read their literature; but he also enjoyed being part of the New York militia, took part in New York politics as a member of the Tammany machine, and at his request was appointed to a seat on the Board of Education. In short, by the time he was in his early forties, he was well on the way to a moderately successful career in business and politics.

This was all upended with the death of his mother, with whom he lived and whom he adored, and who died at the age of eighty-three. He took to drink, and while he continued to run the business, friends admitted that he was 'noticeably under the influence of liquor in the afternoons when all respectable business men were cold sober and clear headed'. The shop rapidly lost money, and his brother decided to take it over, writing to Townsend from London and condemning him as the black sheep of a respectable family. Fortunately, he did not learn of the drinking until he reached New York.

Before his brother could arrive and repeat his strictures to his face, Harris took ship in May 1849 and embarked on a trading expedition to the Far East. By Christmas 1850 he was in Manila and the following year in Penang, and thereafter continued to travel widely. He sailed from port to port, buying goods in one place to sell at the next or carrying freight for other merchants. During his travels he visited Singapore and Calcutta, Ceylon and Burma,

Borneo and Siam, New Zealand and North China, picking up a knowledge of Malay along the way. He met dozens of consuls, for which his languages proved very useful, and he lived in Hong Kong for a time. In short, it seems probable that there were few diplomats or consuls who had such a broad acquaintance with the Far East as Harris. Moreover, by report he ceased to be a problem drinker, and, in general, he appears to have revitalised his life.[88]

He had visited virtually every country in the Far East except for Japan, and when Perry's expedition was announced his interest was aroused. Perry anchored at Shanghai on 4 May 1853 on his way to Japan, and Harris approached him to offer his services. To his irritation, Perry politely declined, as he had declined the hundreds of other offers and requests. Harris seems already to have decided that he wanted a more permanent position, and had applied for the position of American Consul at Hong Kong or Canton; instead, he was appointed to the position at the treaty port of Ningpo, probably the least desirable consulship in China. His response was to appoint a vice-consul and then return to Washington.

The treaty negotiated by Perry was proclaimed on 22 June 1855, and Harris arrived in New York on 27 July, and continued immediately to Washington. The treaty called for the appointment of an American consul to reside in Shimoda, and Harris and his friends and supporters set to work. The Secretary of State, W. L. Marcy, had said that 'to the victor belong the spoils', and Harris was, everyone said, a faithful Democrat. Significantly, he also had the support of Commodore Perry and Senator William Seward of New York, a future Secretary of State.[89] Harris found the wait agonising, and on 4 August he wrote to President Franklin Pierce from his Washington hotel room: 'I have a perfect knowledge of the social banishment I must endure while in Japan, and the mental isolation in which I must live, and am prepared to meet it. I am a single man, without any ties to cause me to look anxiously to my old home or to become impatient in my new one:– You may rely, Sir, that I will not ask for leave to visit my friends, or resign the place for reasons of dislike to the country, but will devote myself, zealously, to the faithful discharge of my duties.'[90]

There was one final concern: his gender and marital status, because the Japanese had apparently insisted that they wanted no women in Shimoda. President Pierce was obliged to appoint a bachelor, 'and of the good Democratic bachelors, Harris was undoubtedly the most worthy and the most suitable'. He was appointed the same day.[91]

He arrived at Shimoda a year later, on 21 August 1856. Accompanying him as his secretary and interpreter was Henry Heusken of New York. Born in Amsterdam in 1832, Heusken had emigrated to the US and become a naturalised US citizen. It was a member of the Dutch community in New York City who had introduced him to Harris. Because the Japanese had for centuries restricted trade to the Chinese and the Dutch at Deshima, Dutch was virtually the only Western language any Japanese knew (as Stirling had discovered to his frustration). Heusken would become reasonably competent in Japanese, and Harris sometimes loaned him out to others in the diplomatic community.

From the first meeting between Harris and the Japanese on 25 August, it was clear to Harris that they did not want him, they saw no need to have him, and they would do everything they could to prevent his establishing a consulate at Shimoda, or anywhere else for that matter. When it was clear that he was going to stay, they put him in a broken-down temple. Even when it had been cleared and Heusken and Harris had settled in, as Emily Hahn recounts, 'Life in it was a long battle against unwelcome guests such as mosquitoes – "enormous in size" – crickets that sounded like a miniature locomotive at full speed; bats; an "enormous *tête de mort* spider, the legs extended five and a half inches as the insect stood"; and large rats "in numbers, running about the house."'[92] Harris' journal has some wonderful descriptions of the dance between the American and the Japanese. He gave the subordinate officials a letter for the Governor of Shimoda – he discovered later that there were in fact two governors or *bugyō* and two vice-governors – and a letter from Secretary of State Marcy addressed to the Minister of Foreign Affairs in Edo. Heusken had already translated them from English to Dutch; they had now to be translated from Dutch to Japanese. This cumbrous method of communication slowed matters down considerably, doubtless to the satisfaction of the Japanese.

On 26 August, Harris met with a vice-governor as well as a 'superior' (in fact the chief) interpreter from the office of the Minister of Foreign Affairs, Moriyama Yenosuke: 'My interview was long and far from satisfactory ... They did not expect the arrival of a Consul, – a Consul was only to be sent when some difficulty arose, and no such thing had taken place. That Shimoda was a poor place and had been recently desolated by an earthquake; that they had no residence for me; that I had better go away and return in about a year, when they hoped to have a house ready. The Treaty said that a Consul was to come if *both* nations wished it; that it was not left to the simple will of the United States Government.'[93] As noted earlier, the two languages provided different versions. On 1 September, Harris and Commodore James Armstrong (the captain of the USS *San Jacinto*, which had brought Harris to Shimoda) met with the two *bugyō* and their deputies. As Harris describes it:

> ... I was asked what was the secret object of my Government in sending me to Japan. I answered that I knew nothing beyond the fact of my appointment and our treaty rights ... They then run over all the old objections, and civilly ask me to go away; and, on my declining to do so, they asked the Commodore if he had no power to take me away. This was answered by saying that he was a military man. His orders were to bring the Consul General to Shimoda and land him there, and then his part was done. They asked would he take a letter from the Japanese Government to the American Government explaining their embarrassed position, and asking for my removal. The Commodore answered that all communications for his Government from the Japanese would of necessity come through the Consul General.
>
> Next, would the Commodore write to his Government, explaining the reasons why the Japanese refused to receive the Consul General? This question, covering as it did a positive intention to refuse me, excited much surprise and received a

positive negative. I was then asked, would I forward a letter from the Japanese Government to the American Government? I answered I would if it was written by the Minister of Foreign Affairs. Would not the Governor of Shimoda do as well? He had full powers to treat with me; therefore it was the same thing. I replied that it might be the same thing to them, but it was not in our eyes. Would I write to my Government asking for my own removal? This was declined. It was now twelve o'clock – two mortal hours having been frittered away in renewing and twisting the foregoing into all possible forms ... I should remark that at tiffin time I was told [by the Japanese] the boats were ready to go to the frigate to bring off my luggage, and asked if they should go. I answered in the affirmative. Now this fact took place during a discussion in which they had, in fact, declared they would not receive me, and it convinced me they were acting a part in which they did not even hope to succeed.[94]

Harris became increasingly frustrated by the Japanese method of negotiation. He kept catching them out in dissimulation and downright lies, and, although on the whole he kept his temper, he finally lost it. On 10 September,

[m]en are here working on various matters for my house. Had a *flare-up* with the officials, who told me some egregious lies in answer to some requests I made. I told them plainly I knew they lied; that, if they wished me to have any confidence in them, they must always speak the truth; that, if I asked anything they were not authorized to grant, or about which they wished to consult, simply say they were not prepared to answer me, but to tell lies to me was treating me like a child, and that I should consider myself as insulted thereby; that in my country a man who lied was disgraced, and to call a man a liar was the greatest insult that could be given him; that I hoped they would, for the future, if they told me anything, simply tell me the truth, and that I should then respect them, which I could not do when they told me falsehoods.[95]

This may have been the occasion when he picked up an object and threw it against a wall. After that, in fact, friendly relations steadily increased, Harris writing in his journal on 22 October that the 'Japanese officials are daily becoming more and more friendly and more open in their communications with me'.[96]

Those Japanese officials who dealt with Harris were in an unenviable position. They were inexperienced in dealing with foreigners and knew little if anything about Western diplomatic procedures. Indeed, as the early historian J. H. Gubbins has pointed out, Harris 'was the first foreign agent to deal on equal terms with the Government of Japan', and in that capacity 'he had to bear the brunt of obstruction so ingeniously and constantly exercised that had he not been plentifully endowed with patience, he must have relinquished his task in despair. He had been forced upon the Japanese. They retaliated by practically boycotting him.'[97] Furthermore, it must not be forgotten that neither knew the other's language, and it was difficult to communicate through three languages. Harris, however, had power behind him – or, at least, he hoped that he did and he certainly acted as though he did. The Japanese did not want him there, yet they also did not want to give offence. But they also feared displeasing their superiors in the *bakufū*, and apprehension, and sometimes even terror, were evident.

Harris had two objectives when he came to Japan: he wanted to be received at Edo as the accredited representative of the United States on the basis of equality, and he wanted to negotiate and sign a trade treaty that would open up Japan for both trade and the right of Americans to reside. Their accomplishment would take no little time and effort, and in the meantime he negotiated changes in the Convention of Kanagawa that Perry had signed.

There were three men of importance with whom Harris dealt, at least one of whom became a close friend. This was one of the two *bugyō* of Shimoda, Inouye, Shinano no kami, Prince of Shinano, whose first meeting with Harris was not promising: 'I do not like the looks of the new Governor; he has a dark, sullen look, like a bandog [a large, heavy dog], and I fear I shall have trouble with him.'[98] Fortunately, things improved, and it was a great help to

Harris to have a friend in such authority, not least in facilitating his life in Shimoda and the surrounding area. He must also have helped Harris understand what was happening in Japanese politics. The second man was Hotta Bitchiu no kami, daimyō of the Sakura domain, who was Foreign Minister and Prime Minister during most of the period when Harris was negotiating the trade treaty. In October 1855 he became a *rōjū*, as described by a Japanese historian in 1876: 'Hotta Bitchiu no kami was appointed a Minister, with rank above his colleagues. It is said that this was done by the advice of the Minister Abé Isé no kami, who found the burden of state affairs too much to bear, for various portents had occurred during the last two years, and the Bakufu was driven to its wits' end by the repeated visits of the foreigners.'[99] Hotta was one of the few who supported the opening up of Japan to the outside world, working endlessly to convince the daimyō and the court to accept the treaty that he and Harris had drafted.[100] The third man was Īl Kamon no kami Naosuké, who replaced Hotta in June 1858; he was, unusually, given the title of 'Tairō', which elevated him to a position second only to that of the Shōgun himself. He would be in charge during the period when a number of foreign representatives joined Harris in Edo once they had been allowed to establish their legations there, a period which saw increasing hostility and touches of internecine warfare among the daimyō as they argued over whether to accept the foreigners or to drive them out and welcome the resulting war. He was not one of those lusting for war.

VII

By October 1856, Harris had decided that public opinion (at least in Shimoda), the increasing friendliness of the *bakufū* and his apprehension that the British would get in first meant that he should now approach the *bakufū* about the President's letter. On 25 October, he wrote to the Minister of Foreign Affairs, stating that he had a letter from the President for the Emperor, and that he had decided to travel to Edo with his secretary to present it to him.

He asked that all necessary arrangements be made, and added as a lure that he would reveal the intentions of the British government towards Japan. He was not intending to betray any confidence. When he was in Hong Kong, he had talked to Sir John Bowring, the Governor of Hong Kong and a friend of his, who told him that the British government was dissatisfied with the agreement made with Admiral Stirling, and that he, Bowring, thought that he should go to Edo with a large naval force and accept nothing short of the complete opening of Japan to the British and their commerce: that Japan should be brought into the great family of commercial nations, whether by peace or war, whichever it chose. Bowring gave him permission to tell the Japanese this.[101] Harris did not know that the Dutch had already warned the Japanese of British intentions (see below).

On 20 September 1856, Hotta Bitchiu no kami had been appointed to the position analogous to a Minister for Foreign Affairs. In his younger days he had spent time studying foreign affairs, and his intention now was to put together a clear and coherent foreign policy. He decided that it was necessary to announce the policy to be followed, and he convened a meeting of the responsible officials of government, including the *bugyō* of Nagasaki, Shimoda and Hakodate, to whom he stated the following:

> The burning of Canton by Englishmen, as reported by the Dutch captain, has received careful consideration on our part. The frequent reports rendered to us by the Dutch captain now leave little room for delay on our part ... It being now more or less clear to everybody that the treatment accorded by us to foreign people is not compatible with the needs of the times, we should guard ourselves by bearing in mind that by provoking foreigners, the Canton disaster might be experienced by us ... The treatment of foreigners should be made more liberal ...

He added that the exchange of letters, receptions and other affairs 'should be conducted in genuine sincerity so as to command the confidence of foreigners'.[102]

This would have been music to Harris' ears, had he but known it. For most Japanese who were part of the ruling elite, however, the idea was appalling, and there was fervent and widespread opposition. Hotta appears to have paid little attention to it, and as more details of what had transpired in China arrived, 'in the first month (January 25–February 22) [of 1857] ... the Bakufu thus came to the conclusion that it must do its best to preserve peace'.[103] Nevertheless, Hotta was not going to hurry to make an agreement with Harris, and therefore continued the dance. Early in January 1857, the *bugyō* of Shimoda (Harris does not say which one) told Harris that he had been directed to give Harris a verbal answer; Harris said no, that only a written reply would be acceptable. In February he received a letter from the *rōjū* saying that the *bugyō* was authorised to transact all business with Harris, including any letter to the Shōgun; no, replied Harris, only he could deliver it. Many, many interviews took place.[104]

On 10 June, when told that the two *bugyō* had full powers to negotiate, Harris suggested that the Convention of Kanagawa, which Perry had signed, should first be executed, and then they could turn to other business. Harris negotiated some improvements, such as extraterritoriality, the opening of Nagasaki for supplies and some rights of residence for Americans. It was signed on 17 June – at least something had been accomplished.[105]

On 14 August came a particularly tense meeting between Harris and, probably, the *bugyō* Inouye. As Harris described it to the Secretary of State, Inouye came with a compromise: Harris was to make the communication and Inouye would go to Edo and give it to Hotta, described as the equivalent of a prime minister. Harris said that this would dishonour the President, and the refusal to grant an audience seemed an attempt to assert a superiority over the US that could not fail to give offence. There were a number of interviews on the subject – did Harris want to ruin Inouye and his colleagues? Did he not feel friendly towards them? Finally, Inouye told him that if Harris persisted, he would be unable to meet him again in a friendly manner. This meant that he would have to commit hara-kiri, which he had said before, and Harris had made a 'playful observation'. This time, Harris said, his answer was serious: he hoped that the remark would not be repeated to him, that while he would deeply regret any misfortune, he would not be responsible for it, as his duty was only to his own government. Inouye, of course, was one of his closest friends in Japan. According to a nineteenth-century Japanese historian, the *bakufū* 'exhausted every possible art in order to dissuade him from his project. Harris, however, would not listen, and it had no resource but to give way.'[106]

On 7 September both *bugyō* met with Harris and yielded on every point that they had contested so strongly for eight months: he was to proceed to Edo, where he would have an immediate meeting with Hotta, and on the next fortunate day he should have a public audience with the Tycoon (Shōgun), when he would deliver the President's letter. They made a 'faint request' that he would prostrate himself, and he replied that when a Japanese minister was presented to the President, he could prostrate himself if he wished, but he need not. Finally, Harris assured the Secretary in his dispatch that his relations with the Japanese were 'most agreeable', that he had never been molested or annoyed, and though his house had more than twenty unlocked doors, in a year's residence there he had never been robbed.[107]

The *bugyō* had warned Harris that it would take two months for arrangements to be made, and on 23 November he and Heusken, along with a train of about 130 Japanese officers and officials, left Shimoda to travel to Edo. They arrived on 30 November, after a somewhat tiring journey: the procession climbed up and down mountains, the road on one of which was at an angle of 35°. He concluded that that was why they had put him at Shimoda: it was not the rather impressive bay, but the fact that getting to Edo was neither an easy nor a rapid journey, and it would presumably be easy to block any unsanctioned journey there. Upon his arrival he was greeted by 'my old friend the Prince of Shinano', Inoue, the bandog-faced *bugyō* of his early days at Shimoda, who showed him his suite of rooms. Harris was pleased to discover that they had installed a water closet copied from his at Shimoda; in fact, 'prior to that gentleman's visit, the government had sent privately to Shimoda to have exact copies made of his furniture, so, on reaching Yedo, he found, to his astonishment, chairs, tables, and beds, in a city where all such articles had been previously unknown'.[108]

His official duties then began. On 3 December he wrote to Hotta, enclosing a copy and translation of the President's letter to the 'Tykoon', and the following day paid him an official visit. After some time spent in courtesies and tea, he gave Hotta a copy of the address he intended to give at his audience with the Shōgun. The Minister withdrew for half an hour to have it translated; upon his return to the room, he told Harris that his address was quite satisfactory, and then handed him a copy of the Shōgun's reply, 'showing clearly that His Majesty would utter exactly what the Council would dictate'. This was exactly so, since for some years the Shōgun had been a figurehead and the *rōjū* the true centre of power. Finally, after fifteen months, on 7 December he had his audience with the Shōgun, which was entirely ceremonial. (He wrote home that he had stood upright before the Shōgun.) He then returned to his rooms and spent two days being quite ill.[109]

On 12 December, negotiations on a trade treaty began. Harris met with Hotta and eight Commissioners, two of whom had negotiated the Convention of Kanagawa with Perry. He said that with steam navigation there was growing international commercial intercourse, and Japan would have to abandon its isolation: the Western nations would one after the other send large fleets to Japan to demand the opening of the country. Therefore, it would be much better for Japan to conclude a moderate treaty with the US, which was not threatening it militarily and by which the honour of Japan would not be injured, than to be forced to conclude a harsher one with a negotiator backed by a fleet in the Bay of Edo. Referring to China, he stated that a treaty with the US could have a clause prohibiting the bringing of opium to Japan. In summary, he stated that a satisfactory commercial treaty could be based on three points: 1) the residence of a diplomatic representative at Edo; 2) freedom of trade with the Japanese, without the interference of government officers; and 3) the opening to foreigners of additional harbours.[110] This address was taken down virtually verbatim by the Japanese officials; according to Hotta,

Harris had 'very ably and eloquently elaborated on all the points that came up for discussion ... His able representation made a very strong impression on his hearers, and convinced them of the impossibility of keeping the country closed any longer.'[111]

Very little of any importance happened for a month, and on 9 January 1858 Harris decided to bring matters to a head. Inouye the Prince of Shinano called on him, and Harris complained that he had had no response at all to his very important communication to the Minister, even though he had offered to explain any points that were unclear, and that he could not submit to such treatment. He 'wound up by saying that their treatment of me showed that no negotiations could be carried on with them unless the plenipotentiary was backed by a fleet, and offered them cannon balls for arguments'. Unless something was done, he would return to Shimoda. Shinano told him to wait until the following Monday (the 11th), and he would be satisfied. On the 11th, he said that the Minister understood that he had just cause for complaint, but that the position of the government was very difficult. The government knew that what Harris had proposed was truly in the best interests of Japan – it was everybody else who had to be convinced. He ended by saying that on Friday 15 January, he would let him know the day on which he would receive their reply.[112]

On the 16th, Harris went to see Hotta for the third time; his welcome was warmer, and he thought that Hotta's smile 'was more than skin deep'. Everything had been submitted to the Shōgun, and these were his answers. Firstly, the demand for the residence of the American diplomatic representative at Edo was accepted; secondly, the right of free trade was granted; but thirdly, because three harbours had already been granted, and Japan was a small country, the number could not be increased, although if he wished Shimoda could be exchanged for another. (Harris had suggested Kanagawa or Osaka.) Harris replied that he could not make a satisfactory treaty under such restrictions: Japan had a coastline a thousand miles long with no harbours open, and because there were many American whaling ships in the Japan Sea, they needed a harbour for refuge and to resupply. He 'earnestly recommended' that they reconsider that decision of His Majesty. The Japanese replied that negotiations would begin in two days. Before then, Harris decided, he would give them a draft of his proposed treaty. He was, he wrote, anxious to take the initiative because a draft presented by the Japanese would have been difficult if not impossible to reject entirely, 'and to try to amend one of their performances would have made a piece of literary or diplomatic patchwork that would have excited the laughter of all who might have the misfortune to be compelled to read it'.[113]

On 25 January 1858, negotiations commenced. Harris describes them at great length in his journal, with occasional expressions of astonishment when he thought the Japanese were trying it on: it was too dangerous for foreigners in Edo (this probably contained some truth), the Japanese had been isolated for 200 years and would intensely dislike being open to foreigners, and, in any case, the Americans could have what had already been granted to the Dutch and Russians (three exclamation marks at the inadequacy of this proposal). The negotiations both broad and detailed continued for some days. On 3 February, the Prince of Shinano called for some private conversation: 'he said that there was an intense excitement among the old party at the Castle; that the concessions already made had greatly exasperated them, and he feared, if I persisted in insisting on Kyoto being opened and on the right of the Americans to travel in the country, I should run a great risk of losing the whole Treaty'. Harris responded that if his wishes were met on other parts of the treaty, he would meet them on those two points.[114] It is probably useful to remember that this was the first treaty of this type that the Japanese had ever made with a foreign government.

Another fortnight of intense negotiations followed. Harris seems to have assumed that the matter was close to being settled, but on 17 February he discovered from the Commissioners that, on the 11th, they had submitted the treaty to the daimyō, and 'instantly the whole Castle was in an uproar'.[115] There was an avalanche of memoranda and letters against the proposed opening up of Japan,[116] and Nariaki, the Prince of Mito and leader of the opposition, was quoted as saying to a delegation from the

The American assault on York, Canada, 27 April 1813

The British burning of Washington, 24 August 1814

Combat between the USS *Constitution* and HMS *Guerrière*, 19 August 1812

Lake of the Woods, each individual island of which had to be surveyed and mapped

John Quincy Adams, US Secretary of State 1817-25 and President 1825-29

General Winfield Scott, sent to deal with American interference in the Canadian Rebellions in 1838 and the Pig War in 1859

British attack on the American steamer the *Caroline*, 29 December 1837

Earl Macartney, leader of the Embassy to Peking in 1793

Caleb Cushing, American envoy who negotiated and signed the 1844 Treaty of Wanghia with China

Li Hung Chang (Li Hongzhang), the most important Chinese statesman of the later nineteenth century

Yüan Chi-k'ai, ruthless and dictatorial second president of the Chinese Republic

British bombardment of the treaty port of Canton during the Second Opium War

A temple in the ruins of the Old Summer Palace, destroyed by the British in October 1860 as revenge for the Chinese torturing to death of nineteen Britons

Townsend Harris, first Consul-General from any country in Japan, and first American Minister

Sir Rutherford Alcock, first British Minister to Japan. He detested Townsend Harris

8th Earl of Elgin meets with Japanese officials in August 1858 to negotiate the Anglo-Japanese Treaty of Amity and Commerce

Ïl Kamon no kami Naosuké, powerful political leader of the Tokugawa shogunate, who was assassinated in 1860

Tokugawa Yoshinobu (Keiki), the 15th and last Tokugawa shōgun

Anson Burlingame, American Minister to Japan 1861-67, and then China's envoy to Washington

Sir Harry Smith Parkes, arrogant and overbearing British Minister to Japan 1865-83

The Chōshū Five, 1863: from top left, Endō Kinsuke, Inoue Masaru, Itō Hirobumi (Japan's first Prime Minister); from bottom left, Inoue Kaoru (first Foreign Secretary), Yamao Yōzō

Samurai or 'two-sword man', circa 1860

Itō Hirobumi, one of the Chōshū Five, and four-times prime minister

Mutsuhito, the Meiji Emperor of Japan

Commodore George Dewey, commander of
the American fleet that attacked the Philippines

John Hay, Secretary of State during the Boxer
Rebellion and the Spanish-American War

The American fleet at the Battle of Manila Bay, led by Commodore Dewey's flagship USS *Olympia*

2nd Earl of Selborne, First Lord of the Admiralty, reconfigured British naval deployment and strategy

Sir Robert Craigie of the Foreign Office warned of the danger of war with the US

General Sir Edmund Allenby entering Jerusalem on foot through the Jaffa Gate

Henry J. Morgenthau, Jr, Secretary of the Treasury   Cordell Hull, Secretary of State

In the front are President Franklin Roosevelt and Sir Winston Churchill, whilst in the back, left to right, are Ensign Franklin Roosevelt, Jr, Captain Elliot Roosevelt, General H.H. Arnold, Air Vice-Marshall Sir Wilfred Freeman, Sir Alexander Cadogan, Permanent Under-Secretary of the Foreign Office, Vice-Admiral Ernest J. King, and General George C. Marshall

Henry L. Stimson, Secretary of State 1929-33, Secretary of War 1911-13 and 1940-45

King Ibn Saud (Abdul Aziz ibn Abdul Rahman ibn Faisal ibn Turki ibn Abdullah ibn Muhammad Al Saud)

Sir Ivone Kirkpatrick, Permanent Under-Secretary of State at the Foreign Office, supported both the defence of the Buraimi Oasis and the attack on Egypt over the Suez Canal

Chancellor of the Exchequer Harold Macmillan
pausing before a meeting about Suez

" And now I want some for sending
to the States with plenty of holly and
not too much about good will ! "
1.xii.56

Cartoonist Osbert Lancaster's response
to the Suez Crisis

Prime Minister Gamal
Abdel Nasser on his
arrival back in Cairo
from Alexandria,
where he had
announced that the
Suez Canal was Egypt's

Demonstration in Trafalgar Square, London against the British invasion of Suez

Secretary of State John Foster Dulles and President Dwight D. Eisenhower deploring the nationalization of the Suez Canal in a television broadcast on 3 August 1956. They would equally deplore the reaction of Great Britain, France and Israel in November

Prime Minister Harold Wilson and President Lyndon Johnson in acrimonious discussion over Vietnam

Roy Jenkins, Chancellor of the Exchequer 1967-70, who thought that Great Britain harboured 'outdated imperial pretensions'

Minister of Defence Denis Healey, who set in motion the British military withdrawal from East of Suez

The last days of the empire: Sir William Luce, Political Resident in the Persian Gulf 1961-63, reviewing the Trucial Oman Scouts

The B-2 or stealth bomber, symbol and instrument of American power

shōgunate, 'Let Bitchu [Hotta] and Iga commit hari kiri, and decapitate Harris at once.'[117] It had not been strictly necessary to submit the treaty, because ever since the establishing of the shōgunate the rule had been that it controlled all political and military activity without the need to consult the Imperial Court. In this case, however, the proposal was so revolutionary and the elite apparently so divided that the *bakufu* believed that it would be very dangerous not to consult – it was clear that the prejudice against the barbarians was so great that the power of the *bakufu* might well not survive. It turned out that they therefore wished to delay the treaty until a member of the *rōjū* could go to Kyōto to get the approval of the Mikado, the 'Spiritual Emperor', believing that as soon as this approval was secured the daimyō must withdraw their opposition. All of this, he was told, would not take more than two months, if that long. On 18 February, both sides agreed that the treaty would be signed in sixty days' time if not before. In the meantime, Harris suggested, they could complete the treaty and have it ready for signature. This required further days of tedious negotiations.[118]

On 27 February, Harris fell ill; by 2 March his condition was serious and he asked to be taken back to Shimoda by boat. At that point he had a severe nervous breakdown, and his secretary Heusken had to nurse him day and night. Interestingly, even after all the diplomatic arguments and conflict, the Japanese authorities demonstrated their liking and respect for Harris: the *rōjū* wrote anxious letters, while the Shōgun himself – or his minders, the *rōjū* – sent presents and dispatched two of the imperial physicians to keep watch over the patient.[119]

On 15 April Harris left Shimoda for Edo for the signing of the treaty on the 21st, but, to his dismay, he then received a letter from Hotta saying that the signing had to be postponed, because he had not yet returned from Kyōto. Harris waited for a month, and then learned via a message from Hotta that the Heavenly Sovereign Kōmei had informed him that 'the draft was unacceptable because "to revolutionize the sound laws handed down from the time of Ieyasu would disturb the ideas of our people and make it impossible to preserve lasting tranquility"'.[120] This probably meant that unless and until the daimyō gave their consent, the Mikado would not: the Emperor's court, the centre of anti-for-eigner feeling, was now part of the decision-making process, thanks to Hotta. Harris agreed to a second postponement until 4 September, but he imposed the condition that no treaty with any other Power should be signed until thirty days after the signing of the American treaty (the Dutch were currently in Edo seeking a new treaty). On 1 June Hotta returned to Edo from Kyōto.[121]

VIII

On 23 July 1858, the USS *Mississippi* arrived at Shimoda with news of the success of the British in suppressing the Indian Mutiny and of the military success of the British and French in China, where the Chinese had essentially been beaten to their knees, and which had resulted in the oppressive and individual treaties of Tientsin being signed between China and Great Britain, France, the US and Russia. Harris also learned that Lord Elgin and Baron Gros, the British and French plenipotentiaries respectively, would very shortly arrive in Japan with a large fleet, and that the Russian Admiral would arrive at Shimoda in two to three days. Harris had already told the Japanese that it would be less humiliating for them to sign a treaty which had been peacefully negotiated with the Americans than to be forced to do so by the European Powers, and he hurried to warn them. (The Dutch, in fact, had also alerted them and, given the long relationship between the two, this warning may have been as important as that of the American.) On the following day, he wrote a letter to Ïi Naosuké, who had taken over responsibility for foreign affairs from Hotta, to the effect that, fresh from their triumphs in India and China, the British with a fleet of thirty to forty vessels (it turned out to be three), along with the French (with their own three vessels), would probably arrive in Edo at any moment. Without the treaty between the US and Japan being signed, the English would insist on greater freedom for themselves in Japan. The treaty with the Americans should be signed without delay.[122]

The next day, the USS *Powhatan* under Commodore Josiah Tattnall plus a supporting vessel arrived (and the day after, two Russian ships). Harris explained the situation to Tattnall, and the Commodore became as anxious as Harris that the American treaty be signed before the descent of the Europeans. Harris knew that it would take at least twelve days for him to receive an answer by land, and he had the Commodore take him up the Bay of Edo, arriving at Kanagawa at 1 p.m. He immediately wrote to Hotta, telling him why he had come, and enclosing a copy of his letter of the 24th. This galvanised the Japanese, a special conference was called, and the majority advocated signing the treaty at once. Ii argued for delay until he could gain imperial approval, but the majority of the *rōjū* were extremely apprehensive about the threat, and Ii finally accepted their arguments. At midnight on the 28th, a Japanese steamer brought the Prince of Shinano and the Prince of Higo, the Commissioners who had negotiated the treaty with Harris. They tried to persuade him to postpone the signing of the treaty; Harris answered that he had merely given them his candid advice, and he could just return to Shimoda to await 4 September. He wrote a letter at their request to the effect that he thought that the British and the French would accept the treaty, and that if there were any problems he would be a friendly mediator. The Commissioners went back and translated the letter, and then returned at 3 p.m. and signed the treaty. The Commodore hoisted the two flags – the red ball of Japan and the 'flowery flag' of the US – and gave a twenty-one-gun salute. Harris on 2 August wrote in restrained triumph to Sir John Bowring that 'Lord Elgin and Baron Gros will find their work all done to their hands when they arrive, and that a large fleet was not required as a demonstration.'[123]

Meanwhile in China, the Earl of Elgin and Kincardine decided that, during a hiatus in the negotiations with the Chinese government, he should visit Japan. Because he had only a fortnight to spare, it was to be an exploratory visit, with no expectation of negotiating a treaty. Indeed, in W. G. Beasley's words, 'Most members of the mission seemed more interested in shopping than diplomacy, while the tone of the account given by Oliphant,

Elgin's secretary, even suggests that the discomfort of Shanghai's summer heat had something to do with the decision to escape for a few weeks from China.'[124]

On 11 August, Lord Elgin arrived at Shimoda with a squadron consisting of the steam frigates HMS *Furious* and HMS *Retribution*, the gunboat HMS *Lee* and a pretty steam yacht intended as a present for the Shōgun. Harris and Elgin met and their discussion was of 'the most agreeable kind'. Harris gave Elgin a great deal of information about the state of affairs in Japan and handed him a copy of the treaty. An offer which Elgin accepted most gladly was the loan of Heusken, since without an interpreter he would accomplish very little. On the 12th the ships set off for Edo, steaming up the bay, and, in the exultant words of Captain Sherard Osborn of HMS *Furious*, 'up out of the sea, and out of the mist, rose ... temples – the Imperial palace – Yedo itself curving around the Bay – all for the first time looked upon from the decks of a foreign man-of-war!' In their excitement, however, they did not forget to train all of their guns on the Japanese vessels in the harbour as well as on the huge batteries at the water's edge. He continued: 'an English squadron and an English Ambassador were now off the capital of Japan, the bearers, it is true, of a message of goodwill, but yet to show, in a way not to be mistaken, that the hour had arrived for Japan to yield to reason, or to be prepared to suffer, as the Court of Pekin had done, for its obstinacy'.[125] The British were later to claim that Harris had cheated, in a sense, by using the threat of the British to gain his treaty; certainly he used the threat of British force, but from the comments of Captain Osborn, who had taken part in the Opium War in China, Harris was perhaps not wholly wrong.

Once anchored in sight of Edo, Elgin officially informed the *rōjū* that he had come to negotiate a treaty with them and would do so in Edo; after the necessary arrangements had been made (virtually the same as those made for Harris), he entered Edo with great pomp and ceremony on 17 August. Unlike Captain Osborn, Elgin wanted to get on with the Japanese and not use force to carry out his instructions. He had been told to base a treaty on that of Tientsin, but he did not have the necessary time, and thus the American treaty became the model. The only differences were a lowering of the tariffs on cotton and woollens from 20 per cent to 5 per cent, and the insertion of a most-favoured-nation clause; Harris himself should probably have tried to include this clause in the American treaty. The date when the treaty would come into effect was changed from 4 July 1859 to 1 July 1859: 'as Baron Gros later told the Japanese commissioners, Lord Elgin did not wish to mention a date "which would recall a painful epoch for England"'.[126] The treaty was signed on the 26th, and the steam yacht presented to the Japanese as a gift from Queen Victoria to the Shōgun.[127] On the 27th, Elgin sailed back to China. It had been a particularly busy period for the Japanese. Negotiations for three of the treaties took place at the same time, for all of which the American treaty was used as a basis, and very few changes introduced; the Dutch signed on 18 August, the Russians on the 19th, the British on the 26th and the French on 7 October.[128] Legally, Japan was now well and truly open to the world.

IX

For the next ten years, Japan was repeatedly in turmoil, with frequent periods of violence and a final coup by the supporters of the Imperial Court, leading to the Meiji Restoration in 1868. During this period, the diplomatic representatives of the US and Great Britain, as well as those of the other Powers, tried to implement the treaty provisions, all the while pushing against the sometimes successful resistance of the Japanese. Indeed, the Powers were caught up in the turmoil, representing as they did the devils with whom – the resisters believed – the Shōgun and the *rōjū* had worked to betray the true Japan. Harris and the first British Minister, Rutherford Alcock, at first worked together, but by the end of Harris' time in Japan the two were wholly estranged, and Alcock certainly detested Harris.

Politics in Japan at this point were centred around the growing conflict between those who owed loyalty to the Shōgun and the *bakufu* and the increasing numbers who were drawn to the Emperor, led, as noted above, by Nariaki, the retired Prince of

Mito. What was termed 'Mito learning' stressed the importance of changing the balance of power in Japan to foster the purity of its imperial tradition. This would be done by overturning the shōgunate and centralising power in the Imperial Court. While the negotiations between Harris and the *bakufū* were taking place, there was intense conflict over who would succeed the dying Shōgun Iesada (he died in August 1858): the direct heir, a thirteen-year-old boy, or a young man of ability and substance, who would be designated the heir 'in the Chinese fashion'. He was also Nariaki's seventh son.

The successor was the direct heir, and those who had supported the alternative were punished by Ii Naosuké, now the Tairō or 'great leader' of the *rōjū*; the objectors and their underlings, who had lobbied for them in Kyōto, were hunted down and executed in the fashion of common criminals. Political responses to a shōgun had traditionally been largely left to the clan leader and his close associates, but now the supporters of the daimyō who had been punished were increasingly politicised, and disaffection and hatred spread throughout the samurai class all over the country.

Samurai theoretically followed *bushidō*, the 'way of the warrior', which emphasised that between life, particularly with dishonour, and death, the samurai always chose death. A samurai did no work – that was for the peasants and artisans, and the lowest level of all, the merchant, who made nothing – but was to concentrate on deepening his virtue and on embodying it in society. He was to give unthinking loyalty to his master, fidelity to his friends, and, above all, to devote himself to duty. In sum, he was to do his duty and make certain that others did theirs, and to use his warrior skills to enforce this if necessary.[129] These ideals had pretty well faded by the nineteenth century, and many samurai were quietly scorned as being unable to use the two swords or to ride a horse: rather, they were only good for wearing pretty clothes. But the advent of the foreigners brought an intense ethnic consciousness, and rejuvenated the 'way of the warrior' as the guiding philosophy of many samurai, particularly in those whose daimyō felt strongly about political developments. Furthermore, throughout the countryside many samurai took it upon themselves to keep a close eye on political matters in their own daimyō. This meant that the daimyō themselves 'had to keep an ear to the ground and their officials had to watch their backs'.[130]

An added element were the *rōnin*. Clan samurai received a stipend and other privileges and had a direct role in the leader's military forces. But there were hundreds, perhaps thousands, of samurai who had left their clans, often because there were too many of them to be supported, and were freelance warriors, loyal primarily to other *rōnin* who were their friends. Many felt strongly that foreigners were vermin who should be driven out of Japan. The *rōnin* were under no leader's firm control. As described by Harris, who does not seem to differentiate between clan samurai and *rōnin*, '[t]he aggregate number of these retainers and followers, all of whom are armed, is very great – it is said to be over 300,000 men – the character of this class is an important consideration; they lead a life of idleness and many of them are exceedingly dissolute; towards those whom they regard as being their inferiors, they are arrogant and aggressive, they haunt the streets in great numbers – frequently in a state of intoxication – and being always armed are not only prompt in taking offence, but ready to seek it.'[131] It was this element who tended to be the quickest to attack foreigners. Most foreigners hardly understood the political and social situation and held the *bakufū* responsible for the violence that they could not always control. During the 1860s, violence against the foreigner and against each other continued to increase.

X

Rutherford Alcock arrived in Japan in June 1859 to take up his position as British Consul-General. Born in 1809, the son of a surgeon, he studied medicine at King's College London. In 1844 he was appointed to the position of Consul at Foochow (Fuzhou) in China, one of the treaty ports, followed by consulships at Shanghai and Canton. In 1858, with the signing of the treaty between Great Britain and Japan, British representation was needed there and Alcock was appointed Consul-General.

He was unhappy. Instead of a position nearer home, 'I am now transferred', he wrote to Edmund Hammond, the Permanent Under-Secretary at the Foreign Office, 'to the most outlying region in the world ... either to die in these regions where so many have gone before me, with two or three years more service, – or be expended, as naval stores are expended – so long as wear & tear will let them hold together, with no unnecessary regard to what is to become of them afterwards.'[132] He was probably equally unhappy with his instructions, which seemed simple but would be difficult to implement: he was to insist upon fulfilment of the treaty, but to allow it to be done with all deliberate speed, making no threats and making allowances for the 'ignorance and timidity' of the Japanese.[133] Sadly, Alcock rather liked threatening to use force.

The assumption in the Foreign Office seems to have been that China and Japan were much the same, and that Alcock's experience in China would transfer easily across the Sea of Japan. There were, however, significant differences. First of all, Japan was an organised, strongly hierarchical and, normally, controlled country, wholly inward-looking, and with a government system that had ruled successfully for over 200 years; it was not falling apart and being nibbled at by Western Powers, as was China. Secondly, as already noted, Japan had thousands of two-sword men, the clan samurai and the *rōnin*, all over the country, who were always straining to fight; the Chinese government had no such trained forces. And thirdly, a major problem which rapidly arose was that Westerners were, quite frankly, used to pushing the Chinese around. When this was tried in Japan, the Japanese fought back, or, at the very least, used strong passive resistance.

Alcock shared the Western habit in the Far East of calling on military force or perhaps a simple gunboat to enforce unmet wishes; the exception here was the US, which had very few spare ships. Alcock annoyed the Foreign Office at one point by asking for part of the Royal Navy to steam over from China to enforce British treaty rights. (As far as the Foreign Office, and Parliament, were concerned, Great Britain did not need yet another war in the Far East.) He also had high expectations of the position he would occupy as the first British representative in Japan. Indeed, he promoted himself. He believed that no other representative should outrank him, and that if all were consuls-general there would be no hierarchy, except for that of seniority. Seniority gave one the position of *doyen* or leader of the diplomatic corps; in this case, it would be Harris. This could not be tolerated, not least because it would, Alcock believed, derogate from the influence he would have on the Japanese. He therefore awarded himself the title of Plenipotentiary, and wrote to the Foreign Secretary, offering his resignation if he did not approve of his temerity; in the same dispatch, he recommended that the future representative should be Minister Resident. Fortunately for him, the government chose to appoint him Envoy Extraordinary and Minister Plenipotentiary, an even higher rank than that which he had suggested.[134]

Alcock lost little time in notifying Harris about his new rank, which he held in addition to his rank of Consul-General. Shortly thereafter, Harris wrote to the Secretary of State to point out that the British government of course wanted Alcock to hold a higher rank than he did, because in a land which placed great emphasis on ranks and titles it would ensure that Great Britain exercised the 'paramount influence in the country'. Harris also reassured his superior that he would not dream of suggesting any future action to the President in this respect, 'as such suggestion might bear the appearance of a desire on my part to promote my personal interests'.[135] His modesty paid off, because by mid-June 1860, when he returned to Japan from sick leave in Shanghai, he carried the title of Minister Resident. In terms of practical power, of course, Alcock had the Royal Navy with its sailors and guns, while Harris hardly saw an American ship from one year to the next. This position would in fact worsen with the beginning of the American Civil War in 1861.

XI

One of the stipulations of the treaties was that, in addition to Shimoda and Hakodate, two further ports, Kanagawa and

Nagasaki, were to be opened to foreign shipping on 1 July 1859, the first anniversary of the signing of the British version of the treaty.[136] In January that year, Harris travelled to Kanagawa to choose the site where Americans should live. He had chosen Kanagawa, a busy town just thirty miles from Edo, because it was situated on the Tōkaidō, the highway which linked the southern areas to the capital. To build a market for Western goods, foreign merchants had to be on or near this highway, because, as one historian puts it, along it 'passed most of the pilgrims, peddlers and travellers of nineteenth-century Japan', who would spread the word about the foreigners' goods. Above all, the great trains of the daimyō, sometimes with a thousand retainers, would pass along it to and from Edo.[137] The anchorage was not of the best, but this could be improved, Harris thought, and the commercial possibilities made it worth it. However, the *bakufū* officials shook their heads: not only was the anchorage bad, but the foreigners would be in danger from all of the samurai in the trains of the daimyō. They suggested, as they had been doing for several months, that Yokohama, which had a deep-water anchorage, should be the port. In reality, they continued, Yokohama was really part of Kanagawa. But: it was five miles from the Tōkaidō and seven miles from the centre of Kanagawa; furthermore, it was separated from the Tōkaidō by three wide expanses of water without bridges, and by a precipitous hill. The only link with Japanese people was a footpath so steep as to be impassable on horseback. The *bakufū*, as is clear, traditionally kept foreigners in what might be termed a geographical prison, and Harris wanted to stop them. As he wrote to the Secretary of State, 'For that reason I placed Yokohama out of consideration.'[138]

Harris was outsmarted by the Tairō, Ïi Naosuké. The latter had accepted that the foreigners had to be admitted to Japan, but they were to be as tightly controlled as possible while the Japanese acquired Western scientific and engineering knowledge. Once they had become as militarily strong as the foreigners, they would expel them. In the meantime, they were to be corralled. To effect this, hundreds of men were set to work to turn a tiny fishing village on a mudflat into a seaport, building bridges, a road, a seafront, houses and warehouses, a customs house and a landing pier. The government offered tax relief, land and houses to Japanese merchants who would move from Edo to Yokohama; these were not substantial wholesale merchants but largely adventurers with small capital. When Harris and the new acting US Consul for Kanagawa, Eben M. Dorr, visited it in June, 'the muddy beach had become a bustling town of many dozens of buildings', with Japanese shopkeepers unpacking their stock and moving into their new homes. To add insult to injury, workmen dug out the swamp at the rear of the settlement linking the two rivers which bounded it, thereby making the muddy flat beach into an island. In short, it was a new Deshima, the man-made island connected to Nagasaki only by a stone bridge, which had penned in the Dutch traders for centuries. Furthermore, although the Japanese did not deny that the foreigners could trade at Kanagawa, they continually delayed matters while offering immediate facilities at Yokohama. Thus, even as Harris was fighting to keep Kanagawa as the true site of the Consulate, the foreign traders flowed into Yokohama.[139] Ii Naosuké and the *bakufū* had won that particular battle.

The other vitally important stipulation of the treaties was that the diplomatic representatives were allowed to have their residences in Edo. When Harris left Yokohama he travelled to Edo, where he established his new Legation near the centre in the Zempukuji Temple. Alcock, however, turned down a site offered by the Japanese which was also in the centre; rather, he established the British Legation in a large temple with extensive grounds in Shinagawa, a mile and a half away. This was apparently based on his and others' experiences in China, where 'running for the boats' was a not infrequent occurrence. Alcock told the Foreign Secretary that he had chosen this somewhat suburban site because it was 'advantageous for communication with the ships'.[140] He had already applied his China experience when he delivered his copy of the treaty to the *bakufū* by staging a parade of armed sailors through the capital. In China it might have gained respect, but it was unlikely to have done the same in Japan. Edo had, in fact, the highest proportion of samurai among the population of any city, and by this parade Alcock had humiliated them while not frightening them. This was a foolish move.

Beginning in August 1859, there were violent incidents against foreigners at the ports as samurai stabbed, hacked and generally murdered them.[141] The anger against the forced opening of the country did not abate, and with the opening of the ports to unregulated trade there was a rapid increase in economic distress. As Harris explained to the Secretary of State, Japan was a small country and only produced a small surplus of anything, and the demand for export goods had caused a huge increase in prices: at the opened ports, prices of raw silk, oil, tea, fish glue and other goods, all of 'prime necessity' to the Japanese, had increased by 100 to 300 per cent.[142] Furthermore, there were substantial problems with the exchange levels set for the currency, which eventually resulted in gold draining out of the country. The *bakufu* utilised the potential for manipulating the exchange to benefit themselves and the diplomats in a manner which, although just about legal, was certainly unethical. Alcock substantially increased his salary by this means, which a junior member of his staff, who was later the Minister to Japan, described in his memoirs as 'highly unethical'.[143] The Foreign Office later agreed, referring to his manipulation of the Mexican dollar/Japanese itzeboos exchange rate as 'indefensible', and making it clear that the loss of this privilege was not a ground for either compensation or an increased salary.[144] And then there was the arrogance of those who acted in Japan as they had in China. All in all, the numbers of Japanese who actually benefited from the advent of the foreigners was distressingly small.

XII

In 1861, the violence was also turned against the diplomats, from which both the Americans and the British suffered. To help the Prussians negotiate a treaty with Japan, Harris had loaned the Minister, Count Friedrich von Eulenburg, the services of his young interpreter, Harry Heusken. Heusken delighted in

company and in the night life in Edo, and for more than four
months he visited the Prussian Legation almost nightly, returning
home between 8 p.m. and 11 p.m. with only a few guards and lan-
tern bearers. When he had first arrived in Edo, Japanese officials
had warned Harris that the streets were very unsafe at night and
that they themselves never went out except in case of necessity,
and then they were surrounded by a large train of their retainers
with many lanterns. Harris in his turn had repeatedly warned
Heusken. The night of 15 January was rainy and dark. Heusken
was attended by three mounted Japanese officers, one before him
and the other two behind him, and four footmen bearing lanterns.
Suddenly, the party was attacked on both sides; the horses of the
officers were struck and cut, the officers fled, the lanterns were
struck out, and Heusken was wounded on both sides of his body.
Harris afterwards wrote that Heusken 'put his horse into a gallop
and rode about two hundred yards, when he called out to the
officers, that he was wounded and that he was dying, and then fell
from his horse. The assassins, seven in number[,] instantly fled,
and easily escaped in the dark streets. Mr. Heusken was brought
to this Legation about half past 9 o'clock. I immediately procured
surgical aid from the Prussian and English Legations [Alcock was
in fact the physician], and he received every possible assistance that
skill and kindness could supply, but all was in vain, his wounds
were mortal, and he died at ½ past 12 o'clock on the morning of
the 16th.'[145] He was probably hacked down because he followed
a pattern and was thus an easy target. Certainly the *bakufu* who
knocked on the door of the Legation at 7 a.m. appeared deeply
shocked.[146] Heusken was only twenty-eight.

At the end of the first week in January, according to the French
Consul-General, *bakufu* warnings of a *rōnin* attack on foreigners
had upset Alcock visibly; with the assassination of Heusken the
following week, he broke under the strain. He called a meeting
of foreign diplomatic representatives, and on 19 January, the
day after the funeral, Harris, Duchesne de Bellecourt of France,
Eulenburg from Prussia, J. K. de Wit from the Netherlands and
Alcock met in the British Legation. Alcock argued that the foreign diplomats at Edo were in danger of their lives, and that in

order to force the *bakufū* to protect them at Edo they should all withdraw to Yokohama. As a strategy this was a touch strange. Two weeks earlier Alcock had written to London that the *bakufū* wanted the diplomats to leave Edo[147] – and now, to bring pressure on the *bakufū*, he proposed that they should do precisely that. All agreed except Harris, who had spent too much time and effort gaining the right to live in Edo to give it up.

Alcock was outraged. In his twenty-six-page *compte-rendu* (summary) of the meeting, he uses the first fourteen pages to give his own views, with the dozen remaining setting out the views of the other four. Harris had been short and to the point: the foreigners should unite at Edo against the present very bad situation and not run away in fear of a future calamity. If they left they might not be able to return. If they landed troops to protect themselves at Yokohama, the Japanese might consider this an attempt at colonisation and go to war. After Harris had given his reasons for wishing to remain in Edo, John McMaster explains,

> the Prussian minister had charitably noted that perhaps the American could be excused as he enjoyed better relations with the *bakufū* and had suffered fewer indignities at Japanese hands [so much for Heusken]. To this Alcock countered that he would pass over the Prussian's remark in silence. If he included it in his *compte-rendu* he would also feel obliged to include his own opinion of Harris. This was that the American attributed to himself a special role in Japan merely because he had been there first, that he was no different from the other diplomats in his relations with the *bakufū*, that his treaty was gained solely by Anglo-French victories in China and that Harris's false view of his own influence with the *bakufū* could be flattered if the situation were not so important.[148]

This must have been astoundingly unexpected and painful.

The group minus Harris met again on 21 January; Harris had a meeting with the Japanese over Heusken and, believing that the point of the diplomats' meeting was to verify the summary, not to reopen the discussion, he thought that the Japanese meeting was more urgent. Alcock sent Harris the *compte-rendu* on the 22nd and asked him to sign it. The other diplomats then left for Yokohama on the 26th, leaving Harris the sole diplomatic representative in Edo.[149] (According to a nineteenth-century Japanese history, the *bakufū* decided that they had left 'in order to prepare for an attack with troops'.[150]) In his reply three weeks later, Harris pointed out that Alcock's personal attack on him had been omitted and he therefore refused to sign the document as a correct record. He also asked that his comments be attached to it when Alcock sent it back to his government. Alcock then wrote a long commentary on Harris' comments and asked that it be sent to the State Department. By now it was getting down and dirty, with Alcock making the sort of comments that might almost be expected from someone about to break off relations. Harris then responded with a final letter on the topic to Alcock, but in rather more restrained language.[151] Alcock wrote his own final letter on 25 February, saying that further discussion on the points at issue was profitless and that the language which Harris had used would justify his (Alcock's) declining any further correspondence on the subject.[152] This was a bit rich, considering the intemperate and even insulting language that Alcock himself had used. Everything was then sent off to their respective departments, whose officials were likely to have been a bit bemused by the correspondence.

Why did Alcock behave as he had towards Harris? Normally, the diplomats of the two countries co-operated in the Far East. One reason for such a gratuitous attack must have been that he was terrified and nervous. He was also probably intensely annoyed by Harris' opposition to his plans, believing that the latter was foolish to trust the *bakufū's* goodwill and desire to protect the foreigners, overlooking the political turmoil in which they found themselves. Harris pointed out, in an undeniably patronising comment, that they were doing their best: 'the Japanese are not a civilized, but a semi-civilized people, and the condition of affairs in this country is quite analogous to that of Europe in the middle ages. To demand, therefore, of the Japanese Government the same observance ... of justice, as is found in civilized lands, is simply to demand an impossibility.' In any case, in Western countries the governments were seldom held responsible for the non-official activities of individuals.[153] On a social note, did Alcock see Harris as a member of a lower order?

There was a clash of personalities. Alcock was pompous, proud, verbose and imbued with the assumption of British superiority, backed up by the nearby might of the Royal Navy. Harris of course resented this, and his claims of a superior ability to understand and get on with the *bakufu* was one of his few cards in a thin deck. There is also evidence that Harris had his little ways. He was, it is clear from his correspondence with Alcock, combative. He was not keen on the American merchants, finding many of them uncooperative over Yokohama, and angry at their refusal to carry his dispatches back to the US. With no regular postal service, this was a serious obstacle to carrying out his duties as representative of the US. On the other side, American merchants believed that Harris was not protecting their interests. Indeed, according to Francis Hall, correspondent for the *New York Tribune*, when Harris travelled to Kanagawa to host a dinner on Christmas Day 1860, he discovered that all of those invited had found excuses not to attend. Hall later wrote that 'Mr. Harris has alienated himself from the good will of his countrymen by his official and personal neglect of them hitherto and the refusal to meet him at dinner was a marked token of their disesteem for the man.'[154]

Another niggling pain for Alcock was, as noted above, the securing by Harris of a treaty with Japan before the British could do so, and in his memoirs he accused Harris of using British strength to benefit the US.[155] His comments are ridiculous. Harris never concealed that he waved the threat of the imminent arrival of the British and French ships as a means of playing on Japanese fears. Indeed, Sir John Bowring, the Governor of Hong Kong and a friend of Harris', had encouraged him to do so. But, more importantly, Harris was being a diplomat, securing his country's interest without the use of American military force. It was a tidy manoeuvre, and Alcock seems to have been displaying more than a hint of professional jealousy. The exchange about the *compte-rendu* certainly brought the personal relationship to an end: Harris refused to meet Alcock, and for the remaining fifteen months while both were in Japan the two men did not speak.[156] This did not, however, prevent Alcock from continuing to attack Harris in his dispatches to the Foreign Office; indeed, it probably encouraged him to do so.[157]

Alcock's long dispatch home on 26 January 1861,[158] the day of the withdrawal to Yokohama, clearly alarmed the Foreign Office, whose officials were by now familiar with his predilection to threaten. In his reply of 8 April, the Foreign Secretary, Lord John Russell, again warned Alcock not to break off relations with the Japanese, who were probably 'anxious' – and, he said, Alcock should not moderate that anxiety. But he then issued a clear instruction: '[e]xcept in a case where immediate action is required to preserve the lives and properties of British subjects, or of the subjects of foreign powers in amity with Her Majesty, it is the desire of Her Majesty's Government that the employment or even the menace of force should not be resorted to.'[159] As far as the retreat to Yokohama was concerned, after receiving no response from the *bakufu* for three weeks, those representatives had to accept that they were hardly going to be asked to return. Indeed, by their withdrawal from Edo the representatives had in fact complied with their wishes. Alcock himself realised, by the reactions of the officers on HMS *Encounter* lying in Yokohama Bay, where he had taken up residence, and of the English-language press in China, that he was not being admired for his action in defence of British rights but scorned. Furthermore, naval support was refused. It would be difficult to return without the submission of the *bakufu* to the foreigners' demands, however: what to do?

The French representative de Bellecourt suggested that they write a letter announcing a trip through the interior, which would alarm the *bakufu*, who did not want foreigners wandering around the interior of the country, and this probably stimulated a letter asking them to return to Edo. The ministers replied with a long letter full of conditions – since it was long, it was probably drafted by Alcock, who was exceedingly verbose – and the Japanese replied with a short one, accepting the conditions. They then neglected to implement them.[160] As a postscript to this episode, when Alcock wrote to Harris announcing their return, Harris replied that he was delighted, adding that 'I feel this is a subject of congratulation, and I avail myself of this occasion to state, that my good offices have not been wanting to bring about this very desirable result.'[161] Alcock's reaction may easily be imagined. It is also ironic that, after all of the difficulty and conflict, de Bellecourt soon returned to a rented house in Yokohama, Alcock and von Eulenburg departed for China for some months, and the Dutch Consul-General returned to Deshima. By the summer, Harris was again alone, his life, he wrote to von Eulenburg, 'almost as isolated as it was in Shimoda'.[162]

As it happened, when Harris and Alcock did agree, their advice elicited a roar from across the Pacific. The *bakufu* with increasing urgency had asked the Western Powers to postpone the treaty obligation allowing foreigners who were not diplomats to reside in Edo. They truly feared that a rash of murders by samurai would invite the Powers to invade. Harris and Alcock finally agreed, and recommended the acceptance of a postponement of rights of residence at Edo and Osaka and two new ports.[163] The recipient of the dispatch from Harris was William Seward, Secretary of State in the administration led by the newly elected Republican President, Abraham Lincoln. There were various layers in Seward's response. First of all, he had long believed in the expansion of the American empire to Asia, and had backed every proposal relevant to this, including Perry's expedition and the treaty with Japan.[164] Secondly, he did not like the proposed delay in Japan's treaty obligations – this was not how proper nations behaved, and should not be allowed. Thirdly, it must not be forgotten that the election of Lincoln was the signal for the outbreak of the Civil War. Harris' transmission of Japan's formal request had arrived only one day before the shocking Confederate victory at the Battle of Bull Run. Seward needed to ensure that the European Powers did not back the Confederacy; in practical terms, this meant that he would try to co-operate with them if at all possible. In this context, by far the most important relationship was that with Great Britain, both for historical reasons and because of the Civil War, during which the two countries would clash repeatedly over whether Britain would recognise the South as an equal belligerent and over Confederate commerce-raiders, a number of which were fitted out in Great Britain.[165] Fourthly, he believed in forceful action, but the war meant that American resources for this type of action were extremely limited and would soon be nil. The US needed to work with the other Treaty Powers.[166]

Seward's response to Harris' dispatch was to write on 14 May 1861 to the British, French and Dutch Ministers in Washington proposing a joint naval demonstration against Japan.[167] Seward argued that to give way on the Edo question, particularly after the murder of Heusken, would encourage the anti-foreign elements in Japan and all the ground gained by the treaties would be lost. Under the proposed convention for organising such a demonstration, each treaty nation would send steamships to the Bay of Edo. A joint Note would be presented demanding the full implementation of every provision in the treaties. A time limit would be set, the warships would return to their normal duties and on an agreed date all would return to Edo. If the reply of the *bakufū* was evasive or negative, the foreign diplomats were to be removed, and the naval commanders would begin hostilities. The *bakufū* were saved by the Powers. The Netherlands thought that any such discussions should take place at The Hague – the Dutch had been in Japan longer than anybody else, and, in any case, the Washington administration was new and untried. London would have nothing to do with it. Fortunately for Seward, he was able to retreat gracefully before he had been completely rejected by the Powers, not all of whom had dealt with the matter on 8 May 1861, when Harris' letter arrived advising that Edo remain closed.[168]

Meanwhile in Edo, the British Legation had suffered a terrific assault. After three months in China, Alcock returned to Japan, travelling overland from Osaka – a rather brave journey to undertake – and arrived back at the Legation on 5 July. It was a warm night and there was a comet overhead; eight of the staff sat up until late watching it and listening to songs from home sung by one of their number. They did not retire to bed until after midnight, and were not yet asleep when a stray dog picked up by the Secretary to the Legation, Lawrence Oliphant, which lay across his closed door, began a furious barking. This was accompanied by a scuffling, and, running out into the darkened corridor, two of the Britons were slashed at by swordsmen in masked helmets and armour. Oliphant was also seriously wounded. Expecting discovery and death at any moment, the eight men hid behind a screen in the dining room, listening in the darkness, as the assassins 'dashed into all of the rooms, slashing recklessly about them, and plunging their swords through the mattresses in the hope of transfixing a sleeper'. Fortunately, seconds from when the eight would have been discovered, their Japanese bodyguards came through the doors and counter-attacked, driving off the attackers. Some hours after it was over and he had been bandaged in order to stem his rapid loss of blood, Oliphant came out of his bedroom barefoot and, in his nightdress, tottered around the screen into the dining room. His first sight was of a man's head, and, as he walked into the room, he stepped into pools of blood, 'and feeling something like an oyster under my bare foot, I perceived it was a human eye'. Altogether fourteen people died, eleven of them the attackers, who turned out to be *rōnin* loyal to Prince Tokugawa Nariaki of Mito.[169]

Alcock retired to Yokohama and never again lived at Edo. British warships were now stationed at Yokohama, and marines protected him. (Harris, however, retained his trust in his *bakufu* guard for protection, a trust vindicated when, the following month, the American Legation was attacked and his Japanese guards drove off the attackers.) Alcock finally decided, and argued, that enforcement of the treaties would mean war. He departed for London in May 1862 on a year's leave, during which he would receive a knighthood, and on arrival repeated this advice to the Foreign Secretary. The result was the signing by Britain and Japan of the London Protocol of 6 June, which agreed to a five-year delay in the enforcement of the treaties in return for the removal of all restrictions on trade and social contact between Japanese and foreigners. Few, including some of the Japanese officials themselves, believed that the terms of the Protocol would actually be carried out. In Japan, many of the merchants were outraged by the Protocol, particularly at the failure to open

Osaka.[170] Altogether, as far as many of the American and British merchants were concerned, their representatives were distinctly unsatisfactory.

On 10 July 1861, Harris asked to return to the US. His commission dated from August 1855, he was lonely and homesick, and was feeling old (he in fact lived for another seventeen years); he finally left Edo on 6 May the following year, when the new American Minister arrived.[171] In October 1861 Robert H. Pruyn, a long-time friend and colleague of Secretary of State Seward, had been appointed Minister to Japan. Alcock would remain Minister, although not always in Japan, until 1864. Harris and Alcock had been present since the beginning of Japan's opening to the world. They had witnessed increasing turmoil and violence, a situation which would not improve for some years. The relationship between Great Britain and the US had been distinctly unbalanced during their joint tenures, but with the advent of the American Civil War, it became even more so. Seward was very Anglophobic, but the fact that the US had virtually no resources to send to the Far East meant that the US had to hew closely to the British empire, a situation that continued for some years.

XII

For Japan, the period from 1860 to 1895 was dominated first by internal conflict and violence and secondly by a drive to escape from the economic 'unequal treaties' imposed by the Western Powers. The period to 1868 saw, first of all, the local struggles for control of the Satsuma, Chōshū and Tosa daimyō. Secondly, there was an intense conflict for control of the Imperial Court and the Mikado at Kyōto and over the policies and politics of the Tokugawa shōgunate at Edo. And thirdly, there was conflict and violence – the period saw a lot of suicides, forced by authorities[172] or self-driven – as well as battles between the 'Loyalists' supporting the Imperial Court and Emperor and the so-called 'bakufu supporters' of the Shōgun for overall control of the country.

A major focus in this conflict was the policy on foreigners. The radical conservatives, whose power centred on the Imperial Court at Kyōto, wanted them expelled as soon as possible by whatever means were necessary. In this they were supported by most of the samurai. The *bakufu* for their part were fearful of the foreigners and their assumed propensity for violence and tried to carry out their treaty obligations. They planned to learn engineering and military science from them, and then to drive them out. Two of the daimyō on the western coast, Satsuma and Chōshū, had never been truly integrated into the *bakufu* system and would play important independent roles (see below). In 1868 came the 'Restoration' of imperial rule, with the Edict of January 1868 announcing a 'renewal of all things' and the Charter Oath of 5 April 1868, which promised that all classes would be involved in the administration of the state and that future policies would be based on consensus. In the midst of all of the turmoil and violence, Western diplomats attempted to hold Japan to its treaty promises. They sometimes suffered from samurai violence, but inflicted rather more them-selves, although in a less personal manner.

Robert H. Pruyn, the new American Minister, was a mid-level Republican politician in New York, having served as Speaker of the State Assembly in Albany during the mid-1850s. Essentially he was part of the wide-ranging Seward political network. He was perfectly acceptable, and were it not for the fact that the Secretary of State was determined to increase the US presence and power in the Far East, it might be suspected that Pruyn was sent to a relatively obscure and unimportant posting as part of the spoils system.[173] The one does not, of course, preclude the other. He had recently faced economic disaster, when his Albany Iron and Saw Works suffered from the onset of the Civil War. The offer of the ministerial post with its substantial $7,500 salary came at the right time, as did Harris' advice on how he might double or triple it by clever use of the extremely attractive rate of exchange.[174] During his tenure, Pruyn would keep his eyes open for ways to improve his personal finances. Unlike Harris, he made no attempt to learn much about Japan, nor does he seem to have developed any ideas about how he would comport himself. What he did do was to try to mediate between the Japanese and the Western countries. He was affable, and proud that the American merchants liked him more than they had liked Harris, but he was sharp enough to admit that this was not yet the case with the Japanese.[175]

In his instructions to Pruyn, Seward emphasised that 'it is important to preserve friendly and intimate relations with the representatives of other western powers in Japan. You will seek no exclusive advantages, and will consult freely with them upon all subjects ... In short, you will need to leave behind you all memories of domestic [the Civil War] or of European jealousies or antipathies.'[176] He wrote to him again the following month, with even more emphasis:

> Mr. Harris's dispatch of July 12 (No. 30) is before me ... I notice in Mr. Harris's dispatch some ground for supposing that a good understanding does not exist between him and Mr. Alcock, the British minister in Yedo ... I cannot too earnestly enjoin upon you the duty of cultivating the best possible understanding with those representatives, and of doing all in your power to maintain harmony of views and policy between them and yourself, because very large interests, not of our own country only, but of the civilized world, are involved in retaining the foothold of foreign nations already acquired in the empire of Japan.[177]

Pruyn concentrated on establishing good relations with his British, French, Dutch and Russian colleagues, as he repeatedly assured Seward. Indeed, only days after Harris had left Japan in May 1862, Pruyn met with the French and British ministers to discuss common problems, something which, as noted above, Harris had latterly refused to do. However, his relations with the British gradually worsened, as he disagreed with their manner of dealing with Japan: as had been Harris, he was more sympathetic with the internal pressures on the *bakufu*. Emblematic was an occasion in the spring of 1863 when he was excluded from talks attended by the other Powers. In mid-April 1863, British, French and Dutch naval officers gathered at the British Legation in Yokohama to discuss the defence of the port. Although ill in bed at the time,

Pruyn was irritated that he had been neither invited nor informed of the meeting.

> His testy note to the British chargé drew an equally brusque response ... Pointing to a previous lack of enthusiastic cooperation by Pruyn and charging that U.S. merchants were actively aiding anti-Tokugawa forces, Neale [see below] struck an equally vulnerable point in observing that the meeting had been for professional military leaders. Had even one U.S. man-of-war been in port, her commander would definitely have been invited. This caustic remark underscored the comparative weakness of the United States in Japan, a factor Pruyn had previously shrugged off but now began taking seriously.[178]

The British Chargé d'Affaires was Lieutenant-Colonel Edward St John Neale. Alcock had left Edo in May 1862, a few days after which Neale arrived to stand in his place. He had been a soldier during the 1830s in Portugal and Spain; he was later the British Consul in a number of cities in the Balkans and Greece. He was from 1860 to 1862 the Secretary of Legation in Peking after the end of the Second Opium War, and thus shared the general British approach to Japan. He had a short fuse, but he was conscientious, with moral and physical courage. A later biographer referred to him as 'probably not outstandingly intelligent, but he had common sense and his actions were usually restrained and cautious'.[179] These traits would be indispensable when he had to deal with the Namamugi Incident.

In an attempt to settle the internal conflict between Edo and Kyōto, in 1861 the Shōgun received in marriage the younger sister of the Emperor. The cost to the *bakufū* was high: they had to pledge themselves to expel the foreigners within ten years. This inspired and energised the radicals at the court and in the country to force their expulsion sooner rather than later, and this political conflict thoroughly unsettled the country. One of the leading members of the *bakufū* and backer of the marriage, Ando Nobumasa, was attacked and wounded and obliged to retire. In response, Shimazu Hisamitsu of Satsuma[180] travelled to Edo to try to compel the *bakufū* to adopt policies to stabilise matters and to encourage the two sides to reconnect. It was on his return on the Tōkaidō (the great highway) to Satsuma with an entourage of a thousand men that the incident took place. On 14 September 1862, the Briton Charles Lennox Richardson, along with two other men and a woman, were riding on the Tōkaidō when they met the entourage. Descriptions of what then happened vary, but Neale's dispatch to Lord John Russell describes it as follows: the British party were ordered off the road, but after the leading members of the cortège had passed by, 'those who followed barbarously attacked' them. While two of Richardson's colleagues were seriously wounded, Richardson himself, 'nearly cut to pieces, fell from his horse, and while lying in a dying state, one of the high officials of the cortège, borne in a chair, is stated to have told his followers to cut the throat of this unfortunate gentleman'. The lady escaped unwounded and galloped to Yokohama, where she arrived 'exhausted and fainting'.[181]

When Neale discovered that the wounded men were being looked after at the American Consulate in Kanagawa, he sent an armed cutter to collect them and bring them back to Yokohama. Meanwhile, the British Consul at Yokohama, Captain Francis 'Punch' Howard Vyse, without first contacting Neale, chaired a midnight meeting of the British and a number of other members of the foreign community. A deputation called on Neale at 3 a.m. to tell him that they had already met Rear Admiral Sir Augustus Kuper, Commander-in-Chief of the East Indies and China Station, who had just arrived from Hong Kong, and who had agreed to a meeting at the French Legation at 6 a.m. There Neale denounced the idea of attacking several hundred armed Japanese and capturing Shimazu: this would be tantamount to commencing hostilities against the Japanese government, and such a premature measure would be altogether unjustified. (The French, British and Dutch naval commanders later met to decide how the settlement should be patrolled, and it was not being invited to this meeting that had angered Pruyn.) Vyse was angered by Neale's response and insisted that a record of the proceedings be sent to London. Neale did so, pointing out the 'highly improper course which [Vyse] had followed throughout the proceedings', including urging Admiral Kuper, without consulting Neale, 'to adopt immediate coercive measures'.[182]

When Lord Russell read the dispatch, he entirely approved of Neale's actions, by implication condemning Vyse's: the action proposed 'would have been an act of war, [and the] Colonel is not authorized to make war'.[183] In a dispatch of 24 December to Neale, Russell set out the British demands. He considered that both the Shōgun and the daimyō were at fault, the former because he had not punished the murderers, who were known, and the latter because his retainers had killed and had not been punished. He demanded from the Shōgun £100,000 and an apology, and from the daimyō £25,000 for the relatives of Richardson and to those who had escaped death, and the trial and execution of the killers in the presence of British naval officers: otherwise, there would be reprisals. Neale did not entirely agree with the demands, since there was no evidence that the *bakufū* had known about it; he would first try for redress without coercion, and if that did not work he would direct the hardest blows at Satsuma, a move, he assumed, that would be looked upon by the *bakufū* with favour.[184] The demands were presented to the Shōgun on 6 April 1863.

When the Court at Kyōto heard of the demands, they decided to prepare for war. On 5 June the date for the expulsion was given, and the Shōgun was instructed that by the 25th the foreigners were to be expelled, peacefully if possible, by blood if not. At the same time, the daimyō were instructed to defend their coasts. In mid-April, one of the Shōgun's foreign ministers had met with Pruyn and formally asked him to intercede with Neale over the 'inflexible' deadline;[185] the basis was Article II of the 1858 treaty which called on the US to exercise its good offices in 'such matters of difference as may arise between the Government of Japan and any European power'. Meanwhile, the deadline for the *bakufū* to pay the indemnity had been twice extended after Pruyn had asked Neale to do so. The final deadline was 11 May, and on the night of the 3rd the Japanese residents of Yokohama began to flee the city, and supplies stopped coming in. After various manoeuvres by the Japanese on one side and Great Britain and France on the other, war seemed imminent. It was Pruyn's opinion that the Japanese would accept a foreign war, if that would avert civil war.[186] During this period, the *bakufu* first said that they would pay the indemnity at some later date, because if they paid it then it would precipitate civil war; then they said that they would pay it in instalments by 30 July; and then they announced that they could not pay the indemnity, because the Shōgun would die. This was on 14 June, the same day on which the French Minister learned about the Kyōto decision to expel the foreigners.[187] The indemnity was paid in a single sum on 24 June; on the same day the foreign representatives were handed a Note by one of the Shōgun's ministers of foreign affairs stating that 'he had been instructed by his Majesty the Tycoon [Shōgun], who is now at Miako, and who has received this order from the Mikado [Emperor], to close the opened ports and to remove the subjects of Treaty Powers, as our nation does not wish to have any relations with them'.[188] Assurances, however, were given that the Shōgun would not use drastic measures to carry out Kyōto's demand. Nevertheless, in October the Shōgun's representatives attempted to revert to the policy of expelling the foreigners, only to tell the representatives on 12 November that the policy had been changed once again, and requested the return of the earlier letter.

At the same time the daimyō of Chōshū, Lord Mori, who was one of those most eager to drive out the foreigners, inaugurated the expulsion order at the first opportunity: early on 26 June 1863, the little American steamer *Pembroke* was fired on at the entrance to the Straits of Shimonoseki; on 8 July a French gunboat was fired upon at the same place by the Chōshū ships and batteries; and on 11 July a Netherlands steam sloop was attacked. Thereafter foreign vessels avoided the Straits. On 28 July, representatives of these three countries and Neale met and resolved, as they declared to the Japanese ministers, that 'the outrages and insults' to the vessels would be resisted 'by a force the extent of which cannot at present be contemplated'. It was, however, only with the return of Alcock to Japan in March 1864 that the crisis would be resolved.[189]

Neale now decided that the conflict between Kyōto and Edo so occupied the Japanese that the way was open for action against the Prince of Satsuma for the murder of Richardson. Leaving only three vessels at Yokohama, Admiral Kuper departed with the other seven ships of his fleet to Kagoshima, the domain capital, with Neale on the flagship and most of the diplomatic mission on board the other ships; the subordinates went along to provide services, including translations. The fleet arrived on 11 August and, after three days of negotiations and naval manoeuvring, the shore batteries opened fire on Kuper's ships. Battle raged for the remainder of the day, with the cost to the Japanese the destruction of the batteries and a conflagration that engulfed over half of the town. The British also suffered badly, with the loss of thirteen men, including two captains who were beheaded by a Japanese shell, and a further fifty wounded. This was a heavy toll for a minor battle, partially caused by Kuper's utter lack of any battle plan.[190] Indeed, a Japanese historian of the period, 'after describing the action, wrote that "The land and sea strove together like a couple of bulls, until the robber vessels, unable to endure it any longer, were entirely defeated and fled in discord to the ocean." ... Captain St. John, who was present at the action, wrote: "The result of our attack on Kagoshima was to induce the Prince of Satsuma to grant our demand. He evidently was not aware how he had really driven us off."'[191]

XIII

What the battle did do was to convince Satsuma of the power of the foreigners and, as a result, they opened themselves up to their influence. As it happened, leaders of Chōshū domain had already decided that they also needed to master Western science and technology. In 1863 the domain smuggled five young noble samurai out of the country, defying the long-standing ban on overseas travel. (Interestingly, three of the five had taken part in an arson attack on the newly built British Legation in December 1862.) Chōshū was the centre of the *jōi* ('expel the barbarians') movement, which had been triggered by the signing by the *bakufu* of the four international treaties in 1858 without awaiting the approval of the

Emperor. Therefore, a prime motive of the domain was for the students to learn naval techniques 'to suppress the barbarians with the arts of the barbarians'.[192] Sending them to Great Britain, the foremost naval power of the nineteenth century, was an obvious move. They wanted to master military technology.

The Satsuma domain sent its students to London in 1865. Some of these students had strong *jōi* sentiments as well and shared Chōshū's interest in naval and military technology, but their domain government, which did not support this movement, was much more concerned with 'enriching the nation'. These ministers believed that this would be possible only if Chōshū mastered Western manufacturing technology and encouraged foreign trade. This argument gained strength after the bombardment of Kagoshima in 1863, resulting in the sending of Satsuma students to Great Britain as well.

The smuggling of the students out of Japan was facilitated by their domains' connections with British merchants. Chōshū turned to Jardine, Matheson & Company, from which they already bought ammunition; Satsuma was aided by the Scottish merchant Thomas Blake Glover. All of the students were sent to University College London (now called UCL). This was for three reasons: first of all, it taught both science and its practical applications; secondly, it was secular in character; and finally, the Foreign Office already had a connection with UCL, in that Lord John Russell occasionally wrote to the Council asking them to recommend students who might become student-interpreters in Japanese. UCL was encouraged to accept these students because the college needed the money; in addition, individual academics, such as the distinguished Professor of Chemistry, Alexander William Williamson, wanted them in order to provide cultural diversity in the college.[193]

The coming together of these students from Chōshū and Satsuma in the industrial and naval powerhouse that was Victorian Britain proved to be very important for the future history of Japan. Firstly, the two domains would be crucial in the fall of the shōgunate and the establishment of the Emperor as the political, diplomatic and military centre of Japan, known as the Meiji Restoration. Secondly, of the five initial Chōshū students (referred to in London as the Chōshū Five), one would become Japan's first Prime Minister (Itō Hirobumi) and another was a future Foreign Minister (Inoue Kaoru), both of whom had helped to torch the British Legation in 1862. Thirdly, the bonding of the students from the two separate domains, which had been enemies, helped to cement the future Chō–Sat alliance, which would dominate Japanese politics during the generation after the 1868 Meiji Restoration. Fourthly, their knowledge and appreciation of British power, as well as that of the other Japanese students who studied in Britain, facilitated the signing of the 1902 Anglo-Japanese Alliance. And finally, fulfilling the fundamental goal of the domains in sending students to the United Kingdom, on their return some of them were instrumental in transforming the Japanese educational system; in particular Mori Arinori, one of the Satsuma students, became the first Japanese Minister of Education.

XIV

The results of the bombardment of Kagoshima were greeted in London by uproar, with a great deal of criticism in Parliament and in the press. Prime Minister Palmerston and Foreign Secretary Russell were heavily attacked, and this public outrage convinced Russell of the dangers of conducting military operations in Japan except in the most dire of circumstances:[194] Japan must not become another China. This did not encourage the British to take on Chōshū, particularly since British ships had not been attacked. Alcock was due to return to Japan, and in a dispatch of 17 December 1863, Russell instructed Alcock to 'require from the Tycoon and the Daimios the execution of the engagements of the Treaty'. If Alcock and Admiral Kuper agreed, they could land marines to destroy the batteries, but only if 'their hostile purpose had been clearly proven by acts of a hostile character'. Furthermore, 'no unarmed or peaceable town should be harmed'. However, if British ships of war were fired upon, the 'fire must be returned with vigour and rapidity' – a sentence almost certainly insisted upon by the Admiralty.[195]

Alcock returned to Japan simmering with anger against the *bakufū*, whom he believed to be plotting to undermine the treaties. Fundamentally, he believed that the British empire – indeed, all foreign relations – ultimately rested on force, whether as economic or military power. The other Treaty Powers did not necessarily share the belief that all of their positions rested on the threat or use of force, and it took some time for Alcock to convince them to go after Chōshū. Pruyn, for example, knew that Washington, overwhelmed by the Civil War, hardly cared about Japan, and he threw what weight he had behind the *bakufū*. He wrote to Alcock in mid-May that any attack on Chōshū must not provoke war with Edo, but, on the contrary, 'should aid it in its difficulties, and strengthen it as far as may be safe, to enable it to resist any combination of the Daimios'.[196] Unbeknown to him, in fact, by mid-August the *bakufū* understood Alcock's determination to punish Chōshū, and adjusted their own policy approach by moving strongly against the Mikado and the Imperial Court in order to prevent an open breach between Edo and the Western Powers.[197]

Alcock later regarded Russell's instructions as justifying the joint action against Chōshū to which on 25 May 1864 he and the other three foreign representatives had agreed. Before the fleet departed, there was an unexpected interlude. Two of the Chōshū students, Itō and Inoue, had dashed back to Japan from Britain to try to mediate between their domain and the Powers. They made themselves and their object known to Alcock, who was delighted with the opportunity of entering into direct contact with the daimyō. On 21 July, two men-of-war were dispatched with the students, along with a French officer instructed to discover what he could about the batteries. Alcock had sent a long memorandum for the daimyō, and during the five days of the journey the two students and the young interpreter Ernest Satow translated it into Japanese. On the 27th the students left the ship to make their way to the daimyō; this could have been a life-threatening journey because of the 250-year-old policy of *sakoku*, which prescribed the death penalty for Japanese nationals leaving the country.[198] In the end, their attempt to mediate failed.[199] The joint expedition, which departed from Yokohama on 28 and 29 August, comprised nine British ships, four Dutch, three French and one American. As the only American ship of war in Japanese waters was a sailing ship, which would have been useless, a little American merchant steamer was chartered, on which was mounted one gun; her purpose was to carry the American flag into action and demonstrate the unity of the Powers. On 5 September the forcing of the Straits began, and over the following three days the batteries were silenced and forces were landed to spike or remove the cannon.[200] On 14 September, an agreement was reached with the representatives of the daimyō, whereby the Shimonoseki Straits would be open to foreign shipping in the future, no new forts would be built nor the old ones repaired, a ransom would be paid for the town of Shimonoseki and the expenses of the expedition would be defrayed.[201]

Russell had earlier learned about the planned expedition and sent a dispatch to Alcock on 26 July telling him that the British government 'would indeed regret the adoption of any measures of hostility against the Japanese Government or Princes even though limited to naval operations, unless absolutely required by self-defence'. The policy preferred by the British government appeared 'to be in conformity with the views, so moderately and carefully expressed by the Minister of the United States' to support those of the Shōgun's ministers and daimyō who supported foreign trade; to make arrangements with the Japanese government to protect Yokohama; to keep for the present a strong squadron in the 'Japanese Seas'; and to come to an agreement with the other foreign representatives over their common interests in Japan. The dispatch was approved by both the Cabinet and the Queen.[202] Even stronger terms were used in a dispatch of 10 August, responding directly to Alcock's of 26 May reporting the planned assault on Chōshū. He hoped that it was successful, but that 'all further operations of this kind, except under special instructions from home, will come to an end: for there is the strongest feeling in the Government, Parliament, & country against any attempt to force ... trade by measures of hostility. Even if such measures are successful, the morality of them is doubtful.'[203] Underlying this was the fact that trade with Japan represented a tiny percentage of British trade overall, and was not worth fighting for. The instructions did not reach Alcock until after the attack on the Chōshū batteries. A fortnight later, Russell recalled Alcock to London. The dispatch was short, but Russell found room to add that 'I confess I cannot perceive ... that your account gives reason to apprehend any immediate attempt to drive foreigners out of Japan.'[204] This was a pretty strong statement of a loss of faith in Alcock's judgement.

Alcock resented the implied 'censure and condemnation', insisting that only the threat of war would convince the Japanese that they had to respect the treaties.[205] Indeed, according to his interpreter, Ernest Satow (himself a future Minister to Japan), 'Sir Rutherford [had] contemplated nothing less than the complete subjugation of the Choshiu clan,' but Admiral Kuper had refused to attack the 'castle town', Hagi.[206] Alcock sent a number of explanatory and defensive dispatches to Russell; Russell sent terse replies to Alcock, and the recall remained in place. Alcock's dispatch of 28 September, however, seems to have saved him, although his recall was not rescinded. Russell wrote to him on 2 December that it was a 'successful vindication of the policy you have pursued'.[207] Alcock may have had the support of the Admiralty, and he would have needed the support of the Cabinet; perhaps the Queen was pleased to approve of his activities. When he reached London for consultations, he was praised, and then sent to China as the British Minister.[208] China was more important than Japan in the British scheme of things, and this was a distinct promotion.[209] It also gave more scope for his rather belligerent approach to foreign affairs.

XV

It will be remembered that although the Shōgun had approved the treaties of 1858, the Mikado (the Emperor) had not done so. What the Imperial Court had forced the *rōjū* (the Shōgun's Council) to agree to was that, while the treaties were temporary evils that could not be avoided, as soon as adequate armaments could be procured or produced the barbarians would be expelled and seclusion resumed. This decision of the Mikado had been conveyed to the *rōjū* on 2 February 1859.[210] Nevertheless, and this was crucial, the treaties had not been approved, that is, ratified, by the Mikado, and the pro-shogunate and pro-Mikado factions used the lack of ratification as a hook on which to hang their mutual enmity. The Mikado had not ratified the treaties and therefore they were illegal; the illegal treaties had been signed by the Shōgun, who was therefore wholly responsible for the dangerous situation – so argued those who hated the shogunate. On the other hand, the Shōgun and the *rōjū*, their supporters said, were defending Japan in the only way possible while the country was relatively weak. On 5 June 1863, the Mikado announced that by the 25th the barbarians must be expelled from the country.[211] The *rōjū* knew that it would be madness to attempt to expel the foreigners, not least because the largest fleet ever assembled in Japanese waters lay off Yokohama.[212] At this point, matters were taken out of their hands by the daimyō of Chōshū, probably the most anti-foreign of the daimyō. It was on 26 June, the day after the date for expulsion set by the Mikado, that the armed ships of Chōshū fired on the first foreign ship to come within range, the little American ship *Pembroke*. The eventual response to this was, as noted above, the destruction in September 1864 of Chōshū's armed ships and batteries. This was the signal for the Treaty Powers to force the Mikado to ratify the treaties.

The driving force behind this policy was Sir Harry Parkes, the successor to Alcock as the British Minister to Japan. The son of an ironmaster and orphaned at the age of five, at thirteen he was sent to China. He learned Chinese well enough to act for some years as translator for Alcock. He also began learning Japanese. He then became a consul himself in China, involved in the two Opium Wars; it was, in fact, Parkes who, as the Consul at Canton, had helped to precipitate the Second Opium War (see p. 195). He arrived in Japan on 24 June 1865, remaining there until he died in harness in March 1884. Depending on one's point of view, he was either just what was required to defend British merchants and their trade, and the British position in Japan overall,[213] or he was the supreme example of the negative, overbearing, hectoring and hostile approach which many British manifested towards Japan.[214]

Some strong evidence points to the latter. On 1 March 1886, Parkes' successor as Minister, Sir Francis Plunkett, reported to the Foreign Office a conversation with Count Itō Hirobumi, one of the London Chōshū Five and now Prime Minister. Plunkett had complained to Itō of what he saw as a marked preference for Germany on the part of Japan, warning that its continuance, so far from helping treaty revision, would hinder it: 'Japan can do nothing without the help of England.' Itō responded that one cause of this was 'the continuance, for years after it ceased to be appropriate, of the policy followed by Sir Harry Parkes ... Was it in human nature that, while being, as they considered, harshly and unfairly treated by the British Minister, they should not, to a certain extent, yield to the continued blandishments of the German Minister, who was as steadily inviting them to come to him for support and consolation, as the British Minister repelled them by his criticisms and advice.' Itō then admitted that 'in this respect the policy of Her Majesty's Government had entirely changed for the past two years; but the seed previously sown had necessarily thrown out roots, and they could not be eradicated at once'.[215]

After Parkes' arrival, the allies decided to mount a joint naval demonstration, and a squadron of nine British, French and Dutch ships arrived on 4 November 1865 off Hiogo in the Bay of Osaka, which was, for the Japanese, uncomfortably close to Kyōto.[216] Parkes, on behalf of his diplomatic colleagues and himself, sent a letter to the *rōjū*, emphasising, among other demands, the importance of the formal approval of the treaties by the Mikado. In Kyōto there was great excitement and anxiety. The *rōjū*, who had been summoned earlier by the Mikado, urged ratification for fear of war between Japan and the Treaty Powers. The conservatives, on the other hand, excoriated those who proposed such a course, not least because, if ratification took place, they would lose a hugely important weapon against the Shōgun. There was such a political divide in Japan by then between the Mikado and Imperial Court in Kyōto and the Shōgun and *rōjū* in Edo that civil war threatened to break out, and the position of each as to whether or not Japan should remain open to the external world was for many extremely important: on that decision, they fervently believed, rested the future safety, unity and cultural identity of Japan.

Negotiations, endless negotiations, ensued; as in earlier years, negotiation was one of the few weapons that the Japanese could wield against foreign Powers and their representatives. Soon, the patience of the latter ran out, and on 23 November each sent identical notes to the Shōgun to the effect that, if a straight reply to the letter setting out the allies' demands, particularly that the Mikado ratify the treaties, was not received by the following day, they would consider 'that its absence denotes a formal refusal of our conditions on Your Majesty's part, and we shall in that case be free to act as we may judge convenient'.[217] This threat had the desired effect, and on the afternoon of the 24th a member of the *rōjū*, accompanied by his officials, came aboard the flagship, the HMS *Princess Royal*, to announce that the Mikado had ratified the treaties.[218] In his dispatch to Russell, Parkes emphasised that the ratification of the treaties by the Mikado 'completes the validity of our position, and thus deprives the Daïmios of the principal pretext they have hitherto had for assailing the Tycoon and the Foreigners he has admitted into the Country. If they continue their contest with the former it must take other grounds, and the latter will no longer furnish the ostensible cause of contention.'[219] This is, in fact, what happened, with foreign affairs becoming much more separated from domestic politics. There were incidents against foreigners, of course, but they were not as frequent, and, as the country slid towards civil war, the foreigners were the least of the concerns of many Japanese.

XVI

Although the decline into civil war accelerated from early 1866, the roots, as must now be clear, extended back to 1854, with the advent of Perry and the increasing numbers of foreigners, and beyond. The foreigners demanded trading rights; they brought women out of seclusion and into the public eye; they practised Christianity; they interfered in Japanese politics; and, in general, they insisted on pushing the boundaries of Japanese political and social customs and mores beyond the acceptable. The Shōgun and the *rōjū* were held responsible.

The foreigners provided a popular and widespread justification for many to oppose them, although opposition to all contact was not unanimous: a significant number wished to engage with them, although more often than not it was because they wanted to become familiar with Western science, technology and military strategy to enable them, in due course, to throw the barbarians out. It should, however, be noted that numbers of Japanese, particularly in urban areas, were interested in Western clothes, culture and mores. Nonetheless, there were enough ferocious two-sword men to disrupt the even tenor of life by attacking foreigners. As a result, the foreigners brought increasing pressure on the *rōjū*, which weakened the shogunate.

Fundamentally, however, civil war was driven not so much by a wish to dismiss trouser-wearing barbarians as by the long-simmering anger of the *tozama* daimyō, those condemned never to hold office or power. The leaders here were Satsuma and Chōshū, the latter by the mid-1860s under the control of a radical anti-Tokugawa administration. For some time, they had cultivated the Imperial Court, and as conflict between Kyōto and Edo grew, they increasingly assumed the leadership of the opposition daimyō.

The negotiations for the Edo Convention on Tariffs of 25 June 1866 enshrined a 5 per cent duty for both imports and exports, as well as a number of other concessions by the *rōjū*.[220] They had been distracted during the negotiations by the need to prepare for war against Chōshū, the so-called Summer War, which broke out a few weeks later. The defeat of the *rōjū* had two important results: first of all, it signalled the effective end of Tokugawa power, not least because of the second result, which was a rapprochement between Satsuma and Chōshū, a core around which others, including some of the moderate daimyō such as Tosa (which curved around the south-eastern coast), joined to form an opposition which grew in power.[221] The death on 20 September of the young – he was only twenty years old – and ineffective Shōgun Iemochi might have changed things, but the opposition was by now too strong for his successor to overcome them.

The new Shōgun was Hitotsubashi Keiki, also known as Yoshinobu. He had been a claimant in 1858, but had lost out to the young and weak Iemochi. He became Shōgun on 10 January 1867. Aged thirty-one, he was an impressive man, and if anyone could have succeeded in maintaining the Tokugawa role it surely would have been him. He knew that the political structure would have to change in order for Japan to maintain its independence and to develop the vital familiarity with Western science, technology and culture. He wanted to unify the Mikado, the Shōgun and the daimyō into a new political system, including in particular the *tozama*, the outside daimyō. He looked for support to the Western representatives, but they could not act together, because Alcock's 1864 neutrality doctrine was still in place. Over the following year, the bases of Tokugawa support crumbled.

The new American Minister Resident, General Robert Van Valkenburgh, was a New York lawyer and politician. He had fought in the early days of the Civil War and was subsequently a member of the US House of Representatives from 1861 to 1866. He arrived in Japan in 1866, during one of the Tokugawa's military expeditions against Chōshū. He judged the new Shōgun to be 'a man of energy and ability',[222] and certainly Van Valkenburgh was one of his strongest and longest-lasting supporters among the diplomats. Parkes, on the other hand, kept his distance from the *rōjū* and increasingly supported the Mikado.

The death of the Mikado Komei on 3 February 1867 was a turning point. The new Mikado, sixteen-year-old Mutsuhito, ascended the throne on a wave of support, and over the year the imperial power grew while the Tokugawa power continued to decline, as Chōshū and Satsuma plotted for its military overthrow. Matters came to a head in October and November. In October, the daimyō of Tosa sent to the Shōgun the 'Eight Point Plan', signed by Satsuma, Geishiu (representing Chōshū), Bizen, Awa and Tosa; among the points were that the political power of the country should be returned to the Imperial Court, which would issue all decrees; that two legislative bodies should be established on the basis of popular opinion; and that men of ability among the lords, nobles and people at large should be employed as councillors. In short, 'Japan may then take its stand as the equal of all other countries.' Shōgun Keiki agreed. He had been saddled with responsibilities without the power to deal properly with them; furthermore, Satsuma was subjecting him to pressure. On 5 November, he resigned all of his powers to the Mikado. In his new position as councillor, he would expect to be *primus inter pares*. His resignation was accepted, although he was asked to continue to deal with foreign affairs.[223]

The announcement to the foreign representatives on 16 November that 'the Tycoon has hereafter no authority to confer or make arrangements with reference to any of the internal affairs of Japan' came as a huge shock. Van Valkenburgh was the first to be notified; his colleagues were notified later, Parkes late that same night. The following day two *bakufū* officials visited Van Valkenburgh and explained that the Shōgun had surrendered all of his power and authority into the hands of the Mikado, but that, for the time being, he would continue to deal with foreign affairs. Van Valkenburgh began gathering intelligence, and noted that there was a great number of men and munitions of war moving towards Kyōto.[224] Then came the crisis. On 1 January 1868, the ports of Hyōgo and Osaka were due to be opened, and because the Imperial Court were extremely hostile to this, the Western ministers decided to be there in case any difficulties arose. Van Valkenburgh arrived at Hyōgo on 23 December, where in due course six American and eight British vessels assembled. On 3 January came the palace coup, organised by officials of the opposition daimyō and Court officials: Satsuma, Tosa, Geishu and other anti-shōgunate daimyō took over the imperial palace and control of the young Mikado. A proclamation was issued in the Mikado's name accepting the resignation of the Shōgun and abolishing the office.

On 26 January, in response to an invitation from the Mikado, the Shōgun Keiki set out for Kyōto from Osaka. On the way, his forces were attacked by troops from Satsuma and other daimyō, and for four days the troops fought, until finally the Shōgun and his troops were forced back to Osaka. Hostile troops had continued to flow into the area, and at 2 a.m. on 31 January Keiki and some of the high officials of the *bakufu* took refuge on the USS *Iroquois* for two hours, until at dawn they were taken off by one of their own frigates and conveyed back to Edo. On the evening of 1 February, with fighting and the burning of villages rapidly moving ever closer to Osaka, Van Valkenburgh, with the Prussian, Italian and Dutch representatives, embarked with their suites and their countrymen on the USS *Iroquois* for Hyōgo, eleven miles distant.[225] Here they remained until 5 March, when they sailed to Yokohama.

On 14 February the Mikado officially declared war on the Shōgun; fighting between the two sides had been going on for some time, but the imperial forces now felt strong enough to overthrow the governmental structure that had lasted for over 300 years and to replace it with another. To ensure freedom from foreign intervention, the Mikado also announced that Japan 'will abide by the treaties as they stand, and that foreigners must … therefore be properly treated'.[226] On the 15th all of the foreign representatives received a request from the Mikado that they preserve strict neutrality 'in the Civil War which has broken out between the Mikado and the Taikun (Shōgun)'. On the 16th, Parkes was to meet with the other foreign representatives in order to see what powers they had to maintain neutrality. They all agreed that neutrality had to be effective, because otherwise it would be difficult to protect all of the foreign communities at the open ports. Certainly, enforcing neutrality could be difficult for some of the representatives.[227] Parkes does not say, but it is likely that he had the Americans in mind, since they were busily supplying munitions to both sides. After daily discussions among the representatives, on the 18th they declared their neutrality.[228] It was not yet clear that the imperial forces would win, given that the Tokugawa families controlled 25 per cent of the land and all of the open ports.

It was crucial for the imperial forces to act as though they were destined to win. In April the Emperor issued the Charter Oath, which blended spiritual tradition and promises of future participation in government. In June this was implemented with the setting up of a new governmental structure, which included a legislature of two houses. In September Edo was renamed Tokyo (Eastern Capital) and on 24 November the Emperor took over the castle of the shōgunate in Tokyo. This all took place while fighting was going on elsewhere and the outcome remained uncertain. As already noted, on 14 February, the imperial government had presented a formal letter to the foreign representatives announcing that the Emperor had assumed the treaty-making power and that all existing engagements would be observed. Their concerns were thereby allayed, to be disturbed primarily by attacks on their nationals, from which the French in particular suffered, notably from massacres of French sailors on 4 February and 8 March.[229] These massacres convinced the Mikado's advisers that they needed a dramatic gesture to emphasise their control – which was clearly incomplete – over unruly internal elements, and to emphasise their desire for peaceful relations with the Powers. An audience with the Mikado, whose person no barbarian should see, would meet both requirements.[230]

From the beginning Parkes took the lead among the ministers in supporting the Mikado. On 8 March, the Mikado invited the ministers to an audience at Kyōto. Parkes and the Dutch Political Agent, who had remained at Hyōgo when their colleagues returned to Yokohama, accepted immediately, and Parkes eventually talked the French Minister into agreeing. However, the Italian Minister, the Russian Chargé d'Affaires and Van Valkenburgh declined the invitation. Parkes was both contemptuous and angry, writing furiously to London that they had claimed that the time was inopportune, that they needed to get back to Yokohama, and that they did not have the equipment fit to meet a sovereign. The Russian thought (as did Van Valkenburgh) that it was a bad idea to increase the intimacy of his relations with the Mikado's government before he knew more of the position and intention of the Shōgun. According to Parkes, 'I had no hesitation in adopting a different course, for the reason that whatever the position of the Taikun might be even in the plenitude of his power, there was no question that the Mikado was the Sovereign of Japan.'[231] It was probable that, for the American Van Valkenburgh, this was not a commanding argument.[232] Probably as a gesture to the French after the massacre of their sailors, French Minister Roches was the first to have an audience with the Mikado, which took place on 23 March. Unfortunately, also on the 23rd, on their way to their audiences, Parkes and the Dutch representative were attacked by two Japanese samurai, who wounded twelve men. The Mikado's Court were shocked by this attack on their chief foreign supporter, and made complete reparation. Parkes' audience with the Mikado took place on 26 March.[233]

By the end of March, when his official credentials from the Queen arrived, matters now seemed sufficiently settled for Parkes to present them to the Emperor. The latter was temporarily in Osaka, and this would make possible a display of British naval power; Parkes wanted to impress on 'the mind of the young Mikado who will be brought for the first time in direct relations with Foreign Sovereigns, a just sense of the rank and dignity of the Queen and also of the power of the nation which is the first to offer to Japan this proof of friendship' – that is, Parkes' credentials.[234] The ceremony took place on 18 May.

Throughout the year imperial officials had tried to convince Van Valkenburgh to withdraw his support for neutrality. This took the form of insisting that he turn over to them the *Stonewall Jackson*, an ironclad ramming ship which had been built for the Shōgun, and which by itself could wipe out the Imperial Navy. However, the proclamation of neutrality also precluded Van Valkenburgh's turning it over to the Shōgun. Van Valkenburgh finally met the Mikado for the first time on 5 January 1869 and was pleasantly surprised; it was also the first time all of the foreign representatives, including Parkes, waited on the Emperor together.[235] Parkes was amply rewarded for his early support. He was invited to meet with Iwakura Tomomi, whom he referred to as the Mikado's Prime Minister. Iwakura 'acknowledged the support derived by the Mikado's Government from England's early recognition, and he invited me to speak freely with him on any points connected with their administration in which they might be guided by foreign experience. This ... gives promise of much greater intimacy in our intercourse than that which has hitherto existed.' This was an invitation of which he took great advantage in the succeeding years, until, as noted above, the Japanese finally grew tired of his interference.[236]

It took a month of intense lobbying by imperial officials and Parkes before Van Valkenburgh finally agreed to consider the withdrawal of neutrality; it was difficult for him to accept that the forces of the Tokugawa shōgunate had lost. Finally, on 9 February 1869, the withdrawal of neutrality by all of the foreign representatives took place, and Van Valkenburgh turned the *Stonewall Jackson* over to the Mikado.[237] As far as the Western Powers were concerned, Japan was now a country with a unified system of government. What it took some years for them to accept was that it should now be treated as an equal.

XVII

The years from 1869 to 1895 saw Japan grow and develop from a country which was politically independent but held under strong economic constraints by foreign Powers to a country which had extracted itself from most of these constraints. The shackles were the 'unequal treaties', those dating from 1858 and 1866, whose terms had not changed. The fact that Japan was unable to raise its tariffs in order to fund its industrial and military development was damaging. It also struck at Japanese pride. The British were the most obstinate, and here Parkes led the way. The primary concern of this section is the pressure exerted by the Japanese on the Western Powers to make them agree to renegotiate the treaties so that they would be acceptable to Japan. Great Britain finally agreed to renegotiate for a number of reasons: firstly, its recalcitrance was becoming unacceptable to the other Western Powers; secondly, there was growing fear that, if the treaties were not renegotiated to its satisfaction, Japan would unilaterally repudiate them, and this would cause a major crisis in international relations; and thirdly, it was aware, as were the other Powers, of Japan's rapidly growing naval strength, and a possible alliance with Britain was already being talked about, although not yet seriously. The context for Britain was the increasing threats from Russia, France and Germany. As for the US, it had tried to renegotiate its treaty in 1878, but had been blocked by Parkes. Therefore, once the British government had successfully renegotiated its treaty, the US was able to do the same.

Iwakura Tomomi was one of the three who had engineered the seizure of the imperial palace in January 1868. In 1871 he was appointed Minister of the Right, a position last filled in the late twelfth century, and one held by a close adviser of the Mikado. In late March 1869, he wrote a letter to another member of the regime, which one historian sees as the 'intellectual beginning of revision': '[w]e must defend our imperial country's independence by revising the trade treaties we recently concluded with Great Britain, France, Holland, America, and other countries. Currently, foreign countries' troops have landed in our ports, and when resident foreigners break our law, they are punished by their countries' officials. It can be said that this is our country's greatest shame.'[238] They could, however, do little about the situation for the next couple of years because of the need to pacify the population and to centralise control.

In late April 1871, the Vice-Minister of the Japanese Foreign Ministry presented a preliminary list of demands to Parkes. As it happened, the Japanese envisioned discussions taking from three to five years, giving them time to build up their strength. Perhaps for that reason, the Western representatives decided that they wanted treaty changes to take place as soon as possible, and both Britain and the US told Tokyo on 22 May 1871 that their countries wanted revisions. For the British, the process was about obtaining better trading conditions, and had no political or cultural importance, as revision did for the Japanese.[239] The latter decided to send a major embassy to the Treaty Powers as an initial attempt to change the way they perceived Japan. Headed by Iwakura himself, the Mission sailed from Yokohama for the US on 23 December 1871.

The Mission arrived in San Francisco on 16 January 1872, and made its way by train across the US, arriving in Washington, DC at the end of February. The warmth of their official reception may have misled Iwakura and his nearly fifty colleagues (who included Itō Hirobumi, now one of the four vice-ambassadors), because they went beyond their original intention, which was merely to outline the treaty issues that they considered most important.[240]

The Mission had its first meeting with Secretary of State Hamilton Fish on 11 March, the first of eleven which would continue until 22 July. Fish came from a socially prominent New York family, and had a long but relatively uneventful political career. He was hard-working, with an almost petty attention to detail, and he had a thorough knowledge of international law. The Japanese did not, and there were repeated misunderstandings. Furthermore, their lack of knowledge as to the precise diplomatic meanings of certain words such as 'protocol', and Fish's precise use of the same terms, led to some confusion. Things were not helped by the fact that during the period of the Mission Fish was also almost entirely absorbed by the bitter negotiations with Britain over the *Alabama* claims arising out of the Civil War.[241]

The Japanese had their own problems, a major one being that they had never clarified the line between simple discussions and formal negotiations, nor had they discussed how far such discussions were to bind Japan. In fact, even though the Mission had agreed not to begin formal negotiations over revision, Iwakura stumbled into just that, laying out what they wanted, and alerting both the US and the other Powers that he essentially wanted to upend the treaties: the Japanese wanted, among other things, the right to set tariffs freely, the end of consular jurisdiction and the cessation of the landing of foreign troops in Japan. The final mistake was to request the holding in Europe of a conference of the Treaty Powers to consider revision.

The immediate result was to alienate Fish, 'a defender of both the American tradition of aloofness from European power politics and that of the special Japanese–American relationship'; as one historian writes, 'Fish immediately rejected any participation in a European conference'.[242] In Great Britain, although Foreign

Secretary Lord Granville had initially approved of the idea of a European conference, he was soon persuaded by the British Chargé d'Affaires in Tokyo, F. O. Adams, to reverse his decision. Adams wrote to Granville that '[t]he great aim of the Japanese rulers is to make it appear that their country is the equal of all other nations ... As is natural in a country which has been long-isolated from the rest of the world, the Japanese are inordinately vain, and nothing would flatter their vanity more than to have a great Conference in Europe ... assembled, as it were, at the bidding of Japan.' On a more practical level, he pointed out that many of the matters which were to be settled could be decided only in Japan, because the mercantile community had to be consulted. (He had earlier written to the Permanent Under-Secretary that 'Iwakura's head has been turned – and he is a baby as to foreign affairs, only knowing those of his own country.')[243] Nevertheless, it was a strategic challenge to the Treaty Powers: 'Tokyo had asked too much, too quickly, without possessing the status for making such demands.'[244]

The Mission was further undercut by the American Minister in Japan, Charles De Long, who had come to the US with the Mission. He had spent hours in Japan discussing the Mission with Iwakura and, wanting to increase American influence in Japan, had encouraged the tenor of the instructions that Iwakura had received. Nevertheless, back in January 1871, he had sent Fish a letter complaining about the lack of trade between Japanese and American merchants, and blaming it on the Meiji bureaucracy, writing bitterly that 'the system of treaty ports is the great method by which this government is enabled to carry on this system of extortion against foreigners'. Fundamentally, he believed that the Meiji government was no better than that of the Tokugawa, and that a solid front of the Treaty Powers would be necessary to force Japan to change its ways.[245]

In the end the Mission left the US with little accomplished and a bit chastened by the débâcle, aware of the unfulfillable nature of the goals which had grown while they were there. They then visited Britain, where their time was primarily spent in investigating British manufacturing industry and many other political, social and cultural aspects of British life.[246] They had come to realise that changes had to be made at home beyond the driving need for scientific and military knowledge. When they met Foreign Secretary Granville, which they did on 22 and 27 November and 6 December 1872, they made it clear that Japan was eager to conform with Western legal and social norms as were relevant to the structure of the treaties. However, by surrendering the initiative, Iwakura enabled Granville to put him on the defensive by calling for unfettered internal travel for Westerners. He had no choice but to fall back on a description of the difficulties that that would entail in the rural areas, and thus its impossibility.

It was only with his second interview with Granville that Iwakura fully understood just how far the Mission had overreached and how completely it had lost the room to manoeuvre it had possessed since 1858. Granville made explicit what had been implicit in all of the negotiations between Japan and the Treaty Powers, declaring that 'the policy of the British Government was to yield the local authorities jurisdiction over British subjects in precise proportion to their advancement in enlightenment and civilization'. In other words, Granville reserved to Great Britain the right to determine Japan's level of advancement and thereby to control the terms of treaty revision. There is no record of Iwakura making any objection to this, and the assumption must be that he was forced to accept that 'considerations of power solely structured the Anglo-Japanese relationship, and that negotiation was no longer the primary mechanism of treaty relations'.[247]

After the Mission had left Britain, they visited a number of countries in Europe, meeting monarchs and statesmen, manufacturers and icons of culture. Their enormous appetites for pâté de foie gras and champagne in St Petersburg caused some amusement – at least to the Secretary to the British Embassy – although the Russians found 'the expenses of their entertainment quite enormous'.[248] Finally, in July 1873, they sailed for home, via the recently opened Suez Canal. The whole experience for Japan was important, because the five-volume report of the Mission was instrumental in transforming Japan into a modern industrial nation. As far as diplomacy went, however, virtually nothing had been accomplished.

It does seem to have been the case overall that the Treaty Powers did not entirely know how to treat Japan after 1868. It was non-white and non-European, but it had not been conquered by the Powers, nor had its territory been nibbled away. In short, it was an anomaly, and in these circumstances the Powers preferred to keep Japan in the box to which they had relegated it.

As Japan rapidly modernised, it was understood that revision of the treaties would mean international recognition that Japan was now a member of the first rank of nations. Intellectually, the treaties were now stigmatised and referred to as 'unequal' because the Japanese, both politicians and, increasingly, public opinion, saw them as labelling Japan as an inferior nation. Revision became as much a moral crusade as a political one. There were two prongs in the drive to prepare Japan to demand their revision. The first was to transform Japan into a state with modern political, judicial and social structures. The second was to develop Japan as a regional power by increasing its influence in Asia, the assumption being that this would provide leverage against the Treaty Powers.[249] The instrument was to be Korea, and the background, and sometimes foreground, to the episodic negotiations with the Treaty Powers was provided by Japanese manoeuvring and aggression.

After 1872, there were various revision proposals discussed, with the most important attempt made between the US and Japan in 1878. On the Japanese side, they were careful and worked on a bilateral basis; on the American side, Fish had been replaced as Secretary of State by William Evarts, who was sympathetic to Japan's wish to overturn the 1866 Edo Tariff Convention. The two sides reached agreement on a pact that returned tariff autonomy to Japan. The plan, however, was blocked by Parkes, who did not want British imports and exports to be subject to higher tariffs; refusing to allow autonomy, at the most he would consider a new tariff. The Foreign Minister in 1879, Inoue Kaoru, believed that Great Britain's clear ability to block the bilateral Japanese–American agreement left Tokyo with only one option: to hold a joint meeting of all of the Treaty Powers to deal with all relevant issues. There was strong support from Germany and the US, and this succeeded in forcing Parkes to agree to convening one in Tokyo in January 1882. The first round of meetings lasted until July, when Parkes forced it to close by refusing even to consider far-reaching changes to the extraterritorial and tariff clauses of the treaties.

It took four years for another conference to be held, in May 1886, after Parkes had left Japan. Germany and Britain, continuing to distrust Japanese courts, reintroduced the idea of mixed Japanese–Treaty Power consular courts, which would hear cases involving foreigners and would have a majority of foreign judges. Japanese newspapers were outraged, and they helped to whip up public opinion until the public, too, were outraged at the suggestion that Japan lacked a competent judicial system. In July 1887 the Japanese Foreign Minister adjourned the conference *sine die* until the Treaty Powers fully accepted that Japan had such a system.[250]

Inoue's successor, Ōkuma Shigenobu, decided on a flank attack, and in November 1888 he negotiated an equal treaty with Mexico. The main point for him was that Mexicans could thereafter travel freely in Japan and would be subject to Japanese law: there would be no mixed courts. His hope was that this would provide a useful precedent for future revision negotiations. During the following year, new draft treaties with Germany and the US were drawn up, but again Britain proved to be an obstacle. By this time, however, Japan had promulgated the Meiji Constitution on 11 February 1889, which also provided for the opening of the Diet (the legislature) the following year; a cabinet system had been introduced in 1885. Altogether, Japan believed that it had introduced enough 'liberal' reforms to meet the highest foreign expectations. The pressure was building and even Britain was forced finally to agree to serious negotiations.[251] Unfortunately, they came to an abrupt halt in mid-October 1889, when Ōkuma narrowly escaped assassination and the Prime Minister resigned. All parties involved now had to accept that the threat to revision no longer came from the Treaty Powers, but from public opposition to the terms proposed. The public would only accept actual and total revision, by which the Western Powers would recognise Japan's equality as a nation.

Indeed, the perception of Japan in the West had totally changed since 1858, and there were no longer any clear grounds for withholding treaty revision. Great Britain, as the strongest naval power in East Asia, had always had the final say, but, by the mid-1890s, it found that its resistance was opposed by all of the other Powers. In January 1894 Lord Rosebery, the Foreign Secretary, when presented on 27 December 1893 with a draft treaty by Aoki Shūzō, the Minister to Germany, had 'in view of the antiforeign agitation in Japan ... refused ... to entertain the question of Treaty Revision'.[252] In response, the Chargé d'Affaires at Tokyo, Sir Maurice de Bunsen, warned that repudiation of the treaties was being seriously considered. Britain finally accepted that there had to be an agreement with Japan, and in July 1894 the Treaty of Commerce and Navigation, known as the Aoki–Kimberley Treaty, was signed. Extraterritoriality would now end on 17 July 1899, although Japan would have to wait until 1911 for the agreed tariffs to end and the freedom to set its own tariffs regained. The opposition of the other Powers to Britain's continuing reluctance and their fear that Japan would simply denounce the treaties were perhaps the immediate causes of Britain's agreement,[253] but, as noted above, there were larger geopolitical threats from Russia, France and Germany with which it needed to cope. In this geo-political arena, Japan's increasingly powerful Imperial Navy might well play a part,[254] and it would be wise for the British gov-ernment to keep it on side.

As for the United States, it had for over fifteen years been attempting to come to an agreement with the Japanese but had been prevented from doing so by the British. Japanese negoti-ations with the Americans also took place in 1894. In late May, the Japanese Minister to the US, Tateno Gozo, handed Secretary of State Walter Q. Gresham a draft treaty. The American problem was the proposal in Article I that the treaty be reciprocal in all of its provisions. This would mean that Japanese and Americans would have full liberty to enter, travel and reside in both coun-tries, and would have the same privileges and rights as the natives.

The Senate would certainly not accept this.[255] The Japanese government agreed to a clause restricting this, not least because Japan itself was keen to control inward labour migration and the purchase of land by foreigners. In the midst of the negotiations the Sino-Japanese War broke out, and this slowed matters, but by 15 September negotiations resumed and proceeded without difficulty. The Japanese–American treaty was signed on 22 November 1894, although the vagaries of American senatorial politics meant that it was not ratified until the following March.[256]

XVIII

And so, by 1895, Japan was recognised internationally as a fully independent state, with which the British and American empires, and the other Powers, no longer had the right to interfere. The following thirty years would see a divergence in the relations of Japan with the two: Great Britain would move closer, signified by the Anglo-Japanese Alliance, which was signed in 1902 and renewed in 1905 and 1911; the US, conversely, would increasingly see Japan as a threat to its own aspirations for a commanding influence in the Far East. In 1895, therefore, while Japan was not a Great Power, it certainly had the economic and military potential to become one, and the knowledge that it had gained from the West, and especially from Britain, during its period of enforced dependence, had been crucial.

As for the relationship between the two empires in the Far East during this period, the Japanese experience largely mirrored that towards China. The US, if not the least of the Great Powers – that encomium perhaps belonged to Italy – nevertheless had the potential to become one of the greatest. The primary attention of Americans, however, was directed inwards towards the Civil War and the drive to command an increasing part of the continent (although by 1895 Canada and Mexico were pretty well left alone). Nevertheless, among certain sections of the political, military and economic elites and the press, the aspiration to expand economically and politically – in short, the drive to empire – remained.

As for Great Britain, it was at the height of its imperial power in the Far East during this period, although by the 1890s the maintenance of this position was becoming increasingly difficult. The US, as demonstrated by the repeated but unsuccessful attempts to renegotiate the treaties, remained subordinate to the British empire in the Far East, with seemingly little hope of challenging this position in the near future.

Chapter 5

The End of the (Imperial) Affair, 1895–1972

During the Second World War, President Franklin Roosevelt more than once urged the British to dismember their empire. He felt at liberty to make jibes, and Hong Kong was repeatedly the focus of his attention. His plan was to return the colony to the Chinese, providing that they agreed to designate it as a free port. In January 1945, he nudged the British Colonial Secretary Oliver Stanley and said that 'I do not want to be unkind or rude to the British, but in 1841 [sic], when you acquired Hong Kong, you did not acquire it by purchase.' Stanley snapped back, 'Let me see, Mr. President, that was about the time of the Mexican War, wasn't it?'[1] Given its habit of denigrating the British empire, it is something of an irony that just when the United States began greatly to appreciate its strategic value, it began to fall apart. For the Americans, this was ideologically a consummation devoutly to be wished, but it came at an inconvenient moment, given the rise of the Soviet and then Chinese threats. Be careful what you wish for.

The twentieth century saw the decline and fall of the United Kingdom as the supreme global Power and the rise of the United States to the same pinnacle. It was an unprecedented and even curious dance. Great Powers sometimes fight each other and sometimes ally with each other, but seldom does one invite the other to assume such a position. Naturally, Great Britain did not invite the US to assume a superior position: rather, it wished to co-opt American power, to be exercised with British guidance, in defence of British, and sometimes American, interests. By the Second World War, it needed American power desperately in defence of its existence as an independent country. After the war, the need to co-opt remained. For its part, the US recognised that the two Powers had sometimes to work together, as during the First World War, but it was determined to walk its own furrow and not to be 'guided' by the British. During the inter-war period it held back, as far as possible, from involvement in overseas affairs, but by the Second World War it had no choice. The war ended with the US the supreme global Power and the UK in many respects its subordinate. Yet the British empire and the American empire had still a last generation of interaction. It was brought to an end by the Americans inflicting a final crushing blow.

In 1900, Britain felt itself a beleaguered Power. Certainly, its empire extended to every continent of the world: its flag flew over 20 per cent of the earth's surface and 25 per cent of its people. It had absolutely no rival as a global Power. The size of the Royal Navy, allied with its ports and coaling stations across the globe, allowed it to project its power wherever it chose to do so. The pound sterling was the supreme international reserve and transaction currency, while the City of London was the world's leading financial centre. The Foreign Office had over a century before mastered the art of building wartime coalitions. Britain's merchant marine was larger than the merchant fleets of the rest of the world combined.[2] It hardly appeared to be in decline.

Nevertheless, its positions as an economic, naval and imperial Power were increasingly threatened. Economically, Germany had surpassed it in the production of steel, and was trying to claw its way up as an international financial power, while by 1914 the US was producing as much steel as the whole of Europe put together.[3] In naval terms, Great Britain had felt so threatened by the rapid growth of, in particular, the French Navy that in 1889 it had adopted the 'two-power standard' policy, by which the Royal Navy had to be larger than the next two threatening fleets, in this case France and Russia. The naval threat was increased substantially by the German announcement in the Preface of the 1898

Navy Bill that the intention was to build a High Seas Fleet that could match the strength 'of the mightiest naval Power'. This was required in order to achieve *Weltmacht* or world power for the German empire, a position that the Germans believed required overseas colonies. In this case, Germany was joining France and Russia in driving to expand their empires, France particularly in Africa, the Middle East and South-East Asia, Russia particularly in Central Asia and China, and Germany particularly in Africa and China, but also anywhere else the opportunity arose.

The United States in 1900 was on the way to acquiring world power but had not yet actually done so. From 1899 it had possessed Alaska, the Midway Islands, the Hawaiian Islands, the Philippines, American Samoa, the Moro Islands, Puerto Rico and Guam, so it now had an overseas or seaborne empire. But it was primarily driven by commercial considerations, the need to find foreign markets for the huge increase in manufactured goods resulting from its own industrial revolution after 1870, and for the wheat and preserved meats produced by its farmers. The American market itself was not big enough to absorb it all, and there was a real fear that, if these goods could not be sold, there would be depression, and perhaps even rural and urban uprisings. America's power at this point was primarily economic, but this was so great that, should it turn its mind to it, its naval and military power could rapidly be increased substantially. This would soon happen.

The First World War and the Versailles conference saw Great Britain expand its empire in the Middle East, when it took advantage of the break-up of the Ottoman empire. It also acquired colonies in East Africa, taking advantage of the break-up of the German empire. In both cases it would come into conflict with the United States, as President Woodrow Wilson determined to use the power of public opinion and the moral authority of the US at the peace conference to force empires to allow the self-determination of their peoples. Britain managed to evade their implications, as well as to block the attempts of the US to undermine the power of the Royal Navy. This conflict between the navies would continue into the inter-war period, contributing to the worst period of Anglo-American relations in the twentieth century.

There was another crucial outcome to the war: Great Britain as the supreme financial power was supplanted by the United States, a position which the US never lost. In order to build and maintain a navy, an army and often a coalition, a country needs funds, and from 1919 the UK never had enough: it would have spent, but could not. The US, on the other hand, for the next decade could have spent, but would not. During the inter-war period, Britain continually tried to convince the US to take on the international responsibilities commensurate with its power, especially in the Far East, but the US refused, not least because many Americans thought that the British merely wanted to use American power to defend its own empire. The British, on the other hand, tried to convince the Americans that they, too, had interests there to be defended, particularly against the Japanese, but in this they largely failed.

During the Second World War, the Americans were pulled two ways about the British empire. On the one hand, they disliked it intensely, and believed that they had a duty to force the British to give it up, especially India. On the other hand, the US government knew that the extensive territories and resources of the British empire were vital to the Allies' ability to defeat the Axis powers, a recognition symbolised by Lend-Lease. Curiously, in spite of the fact that the American government as a whole had refused to help contain Japanese expansion before the war, during the war itself the US Navy claimed as its own the war in the Pacific Ocean and the Far East, relegating the British forces largely to the land war in Burma.

After the war, the UK, burdened with a massive load of debt and with a country to rebuild, realised that it had to limit its military and naval responsibilities. Large parts of the empire, particularly the Indian subcontinent and adjoining countries, were given up. The UK had in December 1947 decided where to focus its forces: the defence of the home islands was the absolute priority, of course, but the other pillars were its sea communications to the US and the Dominions, and the Middle East. The US again saw the territories of the British empire as of great strategic value and vital to US security, and a significant amount of Marshall Aid was directed to support the British in maintaining its overseas positions.

The US also agreed with Britain on the supreme importance of the latter's maintaining its influence and even control over the Middle East, seeing this area as a British imperial responsibility. But, as British and American interests diverged, the Americans grew increasingly dissatisfied with British intentions and actions, and the defining blow came with the Suez Crisis in 1956. Thereafter, the UK during the late 1950s and the 1960s rapidly withdrew from its imperial role in Africa, as colony after colony received its independence. The US did not seriously object.

Where the US did object, and object violently, was to the British withdrawal from its bases East of Suez,[4] which included Aden, Qatar and, most importantly, Singapore. Beginning in 1968, by 1972 the process was virtually complete, with Hong Kong, Antigua, Brunei, the Falklands, Grenada, Gibraltar, the two sovereign bases on Cyprus, and islands in the Pacific and Indian Oceans and in the Caribbean the only territorial possessions of any sort remaining. Why did the US object? First of all, it did not want to be the only white Great Power in the Far East. But secondly, and more importantly, the loss of British bases in these areas caused at least a temporary rent in the American network against the expansion of the USSR and its influence. The postwar imperial role of the US was to lead, and greatly finance, the containment of the Soviet empire within its own borders, much as Great Britain had done in the nineteenth century, as it sought to contain the expansion of the Russian empire through Central Asia and down to India. The American destruction of the British empire damaged the latter's ability to act as a junior partner of the US. By 1972, it seemed that the US was, as it had wished earlier in the century, the cat that walked by himself.[5]

I

It is not possible to identify a single date when the fact that there were an increasing number of threats to the British empire was

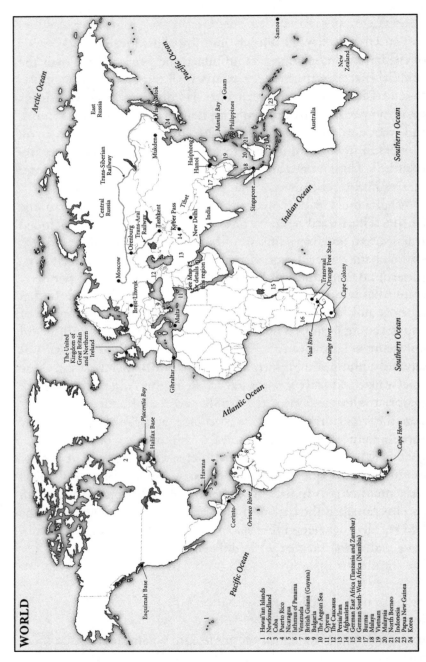

WORLD

Arctic Ocean

Pacific Ocean

Samoa

New Zealand

East Russia

Vladivostok

Guam

Manila Bay

Australia

23

Mukden

Haiphong

Hanoi

19

18

20 21

22

Trans-Siberian Railway

Central Russia

Orenburg

Trans-Aral Railway

Tashkent

Khyber Pass

Tibet

Singapore

17

Southern Ocean

Indian Ocean

Moscow

12

14

New Delhi

13

India

See Map 15 for details in this region

Transvaal

Orange Free State

15

Cape Colony

The United Kingdom of Great Britain and Northern Ireland

Brest-Litovsk

Malta

11

10

16

Vaal River

Orange River

Gibraltar

Southern Ocean

Atlantic Ocean

Placentia Bay

Halifax Base

2

Havana

4

3

Cape Horn

Esquimalt Base

Corinto

5

6

Orinoco River

8

Pacific Ocean

1 Hawaiian Islands
2 Newfoundland
3 Cuba
4 Puerto Rico
5 Nicaragua
6 Isthmus of Panama
7 Venezuela
8 British Guiana (Guyana)
9 Bulgaria
10 The Aegean Sea
11 Cyprus
12 The Caucasus
13 Persia/Iran
14 Afghanistan
15 German East Africa (Tanzania and Zanzibar)
16 German South-West Africa (Namibia)
17 Burma
18 Malaya
19 Vietnam
20 Malaysia
21 North Borneo
22 Indonesia
23 Papua New Guinea
24 Korea

MAP 14

recognised by the government in London. It is possible to cite various comments that demonstrated a growing awareness, but less often a date when the Cabinet faced the reality and took a decision that signalled a shift in ministers' world. One candidate is a Cabinet meeting on 11 January 1896, when the decision was taken to acquiesce to an American demand over Venezuela. The context was Britain's growing relative weakness in naval terms in the face of an increasing number of threats from other Great Powers. But why should the US be the lever? What was its power relative to that of Britain? And what was the geopolitical context?

The irreplaceable weapon in the conquest and maintenance of Great Britain's seaborne empire was, of course, the Royal Navy. In the 1880s, the Royal Navy had 367 modern warships, but it was soon to receive a jolt from France. Ever since 1882, when the British had occupied Egypt, the French had been implacably hostile around the globe. For several years they had been engaged on a shipbuilding programme, but the British had hardly noticed: after all, was not the Royal Navy unchallengeable? When the newspaper the *Pall Mall Gazette*, drawing on leaks from within the government, revealed in 1884 that the two navies had an almost equal number of first-class battleships, public opinion was distinctly alarmed and the Cabinet had to respond. (According to the historian Thomas Otte, the scare was generated by the Admiralty, which had been pressing for more ships since 1881.) It committed several millions of pounds to building ships and securing more coaling stations.[6] But over the decade the French threat increased, because France and Russia appeared to be moving towards an agreement resolving their differences.

This possibility rang alarm bells in London. Britain and Russia had for decades been imperial rivals in Central Asia, playing the so-called Great Game.[7] The single most important possession in the empire for Britain was India, and Russia, as it had for most of the century, clearly intended again to challenge the British position. Branches of the Trans-Siberian Railway snaked southwards towards Persia, which shared a border with western India (now Pakistan), and the British knew very well that it was intended to carry troops and supplies for military action. Britain controlled the sea approaches to India, but from 1900 the railways threatened an invasion by land (the Orenburg–Tashkent branch of what was later the Trans-Aral Railway was completed in 1906). There was also the Khyber Pass between Afghanistan and the Indian North-West Frontier, for centuries an invasion route, and since 1838 Russia and Britain had been in repeated conflict over control of Afghanistan.[8] There was tension in China, as the two countries came into economic and diplomatic conflict. In addition, Russia was also building up its fleet. If Russia and France settled their differences, and even agreed to work together, this would be a grave threat: the two navies could catch the under-strength British Mediterranean fleet in a pincer movement and cut off lines of communications if there should be a war, as well as taking control of the Suez Canal.

This threat could not be ignored, and on 7 March 1889, the First Lord of the Admiralty, Lord George Hamilton, introduced the Naval Defence Bill in Parliament. It called for a five-year construction programme, which had two main thrusts: first of all, Parliament should agree that 'the establishment [of battleships] should be on such a scale that it should be at least equal to the naval strength of any two other countries', in this case the combined navies of France and Russia; and secondly, Parliament should vote for the construction of ten battleships, forty-two cruisers and eighteen torpedo boats, as well as for other facilities. Parliament agreed, and the Act was passed on 21 May 1889.[9]

What was the condition of the US Navy? Frankly, it was pathetic. When in the early 1880s the Royal Navy had 367 modern warships, the US Navy had fewer than ninety, thirty-eight of which were made of wood, and only forty-eight of which were capable of firing a gun. In 1882, Congress provided the funds to build four modern warships, but it was a near-war with Germany over Samoa in 1889 that brought home to Americans the disturbing fact that their navy ranked twelfth in the world, below those of the Ottoman empire, the Austro-Hungarian empire and China, none of which was a celebrated naval power. The following year, Congress agreed to fund the first three US modern armoured warships.[10]

The disparity between the British and American armies was almost as great. The British Army in Europe seemed relatively small; indeed, as Otto von Bismarck, the Chancellor of the German empire, remarked, if the British Army landed on the German coast, he would send the local police force to arrest it.[11] Yet if those overseas were included, the army was considerably bigger. In 1878, for example, there were about 123,000 sepoys recruited in India and about 166,000 British soldiers recruited in Britain, about 66,000 of whom were stationed in India, making a total of nearly 290,000.[12] Those in India were used primarily in the empire for conquest or police action. Bismarck presumably took into account only the 100,000 or so left in Britain.

Compared to the British land forces, the American army was tiny. No more than the British did the Americans want a standing army, and by 1880, fifteen years after the end of the Civil War, the numbers stood at 38,000, where they remained for nearly twenty years, when the Spanish–American War of 1898 caused them to shoot up to a quarter of a million. Thereafter, the numbers never fell below 100,000, but nor did they rise very much until 1917, when the US entered the First World War. As a quick comparison, in 1890 the British (plus Indian) Army was roughly seven times the size of the American.[13]

II

The Venezuela Crisis of 1895–6 is not an episode that dominates the historical memories or textbooks of either the Americans or the British. Nevertheless, in the context of a fundamental shift in Anglo-American relations, it was extremely important: it redefined the relationship. Situated in a faraway land of which few knew anything, it arrived out of a clear sky, surprising the British government and both publics.[14] The primary question at issue was the ill-defined boundary between the country of Venezuela and a British colony, British Guiana (now Guyana), and the interest of many was aroused by the discovery of gold in 1876 in territory claimed by both Venezuela and Great Britain. Also at issue was control of the mouth of the Orinoco River. But primarily it was the point in Latin America where the two empires first clashed, and the outcome of which six years later determined control of the planned isthmian canal. Admittedly, if one looks at informal empire expressed in commercial terms in South America, Britain was overwhelmingly dominant and would continue to be so until after the First World War, at which point the prodigious economic power of the US began to tip the scales.

In 1887, Venezuela had seized a British ship and imprisoned the captain; in response, Prime Minister Salisbury sent part of the Royal Navy's West Indian Squadron to demand and receive satisfaction. Venezuela appealed to the US for help, arguing that the Monroe Doctrine was threatened, and the US offered its services as arbiter.[15] (Recall that the Monroe Doctrine had been announced in 1823 by President James Monroe, and stated that 'the American continents ... are henceforth not to be considered as subjects for future colonisation by any European powers' and any attempt to do so would be considered as 'the manifestation of an unfriendly disposition toward the United States'. In other words, the European Powers must accept that the Western Hemisphere was a US sphere of influence.)[16] Britain refused the offer of arbitration and, when the offer was later repeated in 1890 and 1891, refused again.[17] After this history of indifference on the part of the US, what had changed so dramatically by 1895 that the US not only took up Venezuela's cause, but threatened war if Britain did not do what the US demanded? The answer is a combination of an aroused public opinion responding to the work of a first-rate lobbyist, the political difficulties of the Democratic President Grover Cleveland, and the determination of the new Secretary of State, Richard Olney, to assert himself and bring Britain to heel.

In 1895, Cleveland was the target of increasingly ferocious Republican attacks, not least on what they saw as his supine response to British activities in Central and South America. With an election looming in 1896, he had to be seen as the stout defender of American interests. He was not, for example, particularly imperialistic, having refused to annex Hawaii to the United

States in 1893. Furthermore, public opinion was being whipped up, especially by a pamphlet published in 1894 entitled *British Aggression in Venezuela, or the Monroe Doctrine on Trial* (the author, William Scruggs, had been US Minister to Venezuela, but had been dismissed for bribing local politicians, including the Prime Minister).[18] Scruggs pointedly warned of a drive by the British to control the commerce and then the political life of the 'northern quarter' of Latin America. An appeal to the threat to American commercial interests was clever, since the US was acutely conscious of Britain's commercial dominance in Latin America. Indeed, the idea of encroachment on what should be America's commercial territory was a red rag, given that wherever US businessmen turned, China, the Middle East, and South and East Africa, the British already held a commanding economic position. Britain had in fact held such a position in Latin America since the 1820s: as related above, a French agent in Colombia had written in 1823 that 'The power of England is without a rival in America; no fleets but hers to be seen; her merchandises are bought almost exclusively; her commercial agents, her clerks and brokers, are everywhere to be met with.'[19]

Gunboats, however, had not hitherto had that much of a role to play. This might now change, it was feared, because Britain was strengthening its bases in the Caribbean. (Indeed, a crisis in Nicaragua later in 1895 would include the occupation by the Royal Navy of the port of Corinto from 27 April to 3 May to force the country to come to terms.) British demands relating to the territory claimed by Venezuela appeared to be part of a pattern.[20] Copies of the Scruggs pamphlet were sent to all senators and congressmen, and naturally elicited an anti-British response. They passed a joint resolution recommending that Britain and Venezuela submit their differences over the boundary to arbitration; Cleveland added his support, and on 9 April 1895 the State Department sent it to the US Ambassador in London to present to the British government.[21] Britain responded with demands that Venezuela could not accept, and there it lay for some months.[22]

The situation changed dramatically with the advent of a new Secretary of State, Richard Olney. He was a brusque and highly opinionated lawyer with a temper, who was wholly unfamiliar with diplomatic language and practices. Based on his reading of American diplomatic files and other American material, Venezuela, he decided, was clearly the injured party. Furthermore, looking over a decade's correspondence between the US and Great Britain on the matter, Olney decided that soft words had been worthless. Nevertheless, a clash between Venezuela and Britain analogous to that between Britain and Nicaragua could not be allowed because, the President feared, Venezuela would probably invoke the Monroe Doctrine again, and the US might become involved in a war with Britain. Therefore, Britain should be required to deal directly with the US. Venezuela was not asked for its opinion. Consequently, on 20 July 1895, a dispatch of some 12,000 words was sent to James A. Bayard, the US Minister, with instructions to read it out to Salisbury, who was both Prime Minister and Foreign Secretary, and leave a copy with him. On 7 August, Bayard began reading the dispatch to Salisbury, but after some time Salisbury intimated that it 'was evidently much too large and much too complicated an argument to deal with in the course of conversation', adding that it would be necessary to investigate the whole question very carefully and that it was unlikely that an early response could be provided.[23]

What was this complicated argument? The territory in dispute was big, but because Venezuela was so much weaker than Great Britain it could only hope for a peaceful settlement. For twenty-five years it had pressed for arbitration, but the British government had refused to go along with that unless a substantial part of the territory was conceded to it. The US had several times offered its good offices, Olney wrote, as 'the controversy is one in which both its honor and its interests are involved and the continuance of which it cannot regard with indifference'. To demonstrate American impartiality, the US again offered arbitration, which Olney thought would be a relatively straightforward task, turning, as it did, on 'simple and readily ascertainable historical facts'. The fundamental basis of the American position was the Monroe Doctrine, which he appeared to be extending to the condemnation of current European settlements: 'That distance and three thousand miles of intervening ocean make any permanent political union between an European and an American state inexpedient will hardly be denied' (so much for Canada). On the other hand, the states of North and South America, by their geographical closeness, similarity of governmental institutions and natural sympathy, were friends and allies. Olney then issued a stark warning:

> Today the United States is practically sovereign on this continent, and its fiat is law upon the subjects to which it confines its interposition. Why? It is not because of the pure friendship or good will felt for it. It is not simply by reason of its high character as a civilized state, nor because wisdom and justice and equity are the invariable characteristics of the dealings of the United States. It is because, in addition to all other grounds, its infinite resources combined with its isolated position render it master of the situation and practically invulnerable as against any or all other powers.

An aggressive European power on the South American continent could threaten the safety bestowed by this isolation.[24]

Later known as the Olney Doctrine, this came very close to claiming that might makes right. When revealed to the public it also, not surprisingly, infuriated the Canadians and the Latin Americans: 'If Washington won its point with Salisbury, the Chilean minister to Washington observed, "the United States will have succeeded in establishing a protectorate over all of Latin America",' and Latin American editorials referred to the 'suffocating presence of the Colossus' whose Anglo-Saxon race sought to 'found a single colonial state extending from the North to the South Pole'.[25] The history as set out in the dispatch was bad and the language intemperate, but Olney later explained that the Note was designed 'effectually even if rudely' to dispel British complacency. Its phrases were of a 'bumptious order', but the 'excuse was that in English eyes, the United States was ... so completely a negligible quantity that it was believed only words the equivalent of blows would be really effective'.[26] He was also an experienced arbiter himself. Great Britain knew as well as he did that arbiters often split the difference, and was therefore insisting on keeping land on which British citizens had been settled for some time so that they would not have to leave British jurisdiction. Olney, however, assumed that, because land which was settled had a stronger argument for award than land which was merely claimed, Britain would gain title to most of what it wanted. This would indeed eventually be the case.

Meanwhile, the British response was heavy with gravitas and ripe with the very sort of *de haut en bas* tone that might have been calculated to outrage the Americans: 'the British Empire and the Republic of Venezuela are neighbours, and they have differed for some time past, and continue to differ, as to the line by which their dominions are separated. It is a controversy with which the United States have no apparent practical concern ... It is simply the determination of the frontier of a British possession which belonged to the Throne of England long before the Republic of Venezuela came into existence.'[27] In an accompanying dispatch, based on the British, Spanish and Dutch archives and setting out the history of the controversy, Salisbury stated that Great Britain 'cannot consent to entertain, or to submit to the arbitration of another Power or of foreign jurists, however eminent, claims based on the extravagant pretensions of Spanish officials in the last century, and involving the transfer of large numbers of British subjects ... to a nation ... whose political system is subject to frequent disturbance, and whose institutions as yet too often afford very inadequate protection to life and property'.[28] In short, the answer to the demands of both Venezuela and the US was no.

The two dispatches from Salisbury to the British Ambassador to the US, Sir Julian Pauncefote, were not sent until 26 November, fully four months after Bayard had read Olney's dispatch to Salisbury. Pauncefote laid both before Olney on 7 December, and upon Cleveland's return from a duck-shooting holiday, Olney showed them to him on Sunday the 15th. After discussing the matter with Olney, Cleveland sat at his desk until dawn in the white heat of composition (he was 'mad clear through'),[29] read it to the Cabinet on Tuesday the 17th and then sent it to Congress.

He took the British as challenging the Monroe Doctrine, their declining of arbitration 'far from satisfactory', and decided that the dispute had now reached a stage where the US must determine what the true boundary was; therefore, he asked Congress to make the funds available so that the Executive could set up a Commission to investigate and report.

> When such report is made and accepted it will, in my opinion, be the duty of the United States to resist by every means in its power as a willful aggression upon its rights and interests the appropriation by Great Britain of any lands or the exercise of governmental jurisdiction over any territory after which investigation we have determined of right belongs to Venezuela. In making these recommendations I am fully alive to the responsibility incurred and keenly realize all the consequences that may follow ... [but] there is no calamity which a great nation can invite which equals that which follows a supine submission to wrong and injustice and the consequent loss of self-respect and honor beneath which are shielded and defended a people's safety and greatness.[30]

The Senate chamber rang with applause. However, in traditional diplomatic exchanges between countries, the message was a call for war, and war between the US and Great Britain might indeed have been the consequence.

There was a range of reactions throughout the country to Cleveland's message, not least of which was surprise: it was the first most Americans had heard about an Anglo-American crisis over Venezuela. Congress reacted with enthusiasm, voting the funding as Cleveland had requested. Newspapers screamed for action, Irish-American organisations shouted that they could put 100,000 men in the field, Democrats thought that it would help them in the upcoming elections and businessmen saw this as a weapon against British commercial supremacy. There were, however, chastening developments. 'The pulpit thundered against the President,'[31] stock prices plummeted on 20 December, three days after Cleveland's message, with $400 million lost in two days, and it began to dawn on people that coastal cities would be defenceless against British naval power. Canada began military preparations and to look to its own defences.

In Britain Cleveland's threat also came as a surprise, shattering the indifference of most politicians as well as the public towards the US. It certainly gave impetus to planning for the defence of Canada. Prime Minister Salisbury, however, seemed unconcerned, remarking to a Cabinet colleague that 'the American conflagration will fizzle away'. He very much disliked America and Americans, having written in 1850 that 'The Yankee, whose life is one long calculation, appears to have bombast for his mother tongue.' What he feared was not America's military and naval prowess but its democracy, presumably worried that it might be contagious. He essentially decided to wait until the crisis, which he referred to as 'Cleveland's electioneering dodge', had blown itself out.[32] This did not, however, mean that he entirely dismissed an American threat, writing on 2 January 1896 to Sir Michael Hicks Beach, the Chancellor of the Exchequer, that 'A war with America – not this year but in the not distant future – has become something more than a possibility.'[33]

Salisbury, to his anger and astonishment, discovered that his Cabinet did not support his haughty defiance, because the American crisis occurred at the same time that Great Britain was bombarded with a number of other threats. First of all, there was the Ottoman empire: the Turks in Constantinople and especially in Asia Minor were slaughtering thousands of Armenians, many in Constantinople in front of European diplomats, but others deep in eastern Anatolia. The British government sent a fleet to the mouth of the Dardanelles Strait to back up demands for reform, but it had neither the will nor the military forces to carry out a police action so far inland, and besides, it feared that Russia would take advantage of the crisis to try to seize Constantinople and the Dardanelles, which meant that Russia could then move its warships out of the Black Sea and into the Mediterranean. The Admiralty insisted that, in the new circumstances of the Dual (France and Russia) Alliance, which had been signed in 1894, it would be too risky for the Royal Navy to confront any such

Russian attempt; the Cabinet, against Salisbury's will, agreed. Then there was the crisis in South Africa, with war threatening between the British Cape Colony and the two Boer republics, the Republic of the Transvaal and the Orange Free State. The Jameson Raid, a private enterprise incursion (but backed by the Colonial Secretary, Joseph Chamberlain) into the Transvaal, had taken place on 29 December 1895 and had been a fiasco. Even worse, on 3 January 1896, Kaiser Wilhelm II of Germany sent to Paul Kruger, the President of the Transvaal, a telegram of support against Britain, couched in extremely offensive language. This was important because, first of all, Germany was competing with Britain for colonies in that part of Africa and secondly, it did great damage by setting British and German public opinion against each other's country. Then there was an unlooked-for break with the Austro-Hungarian empire. In 1887, Britain had signed the Mediterranean Agreement with that empire (and another with Italy) to maintain the status quo in the Mediterranean against Russia: in January 1896 the Austrian government refused to renew the agreement. Besides the loss of a bit of naval security, the refusal also broke an indirect link with Germany, since Austria-Hungary, along with Germany and Italy, was part of the Triple Alliance. And finally, there was growing concern over relations with Russia and France, primarily because of imperial rivalries.

In short, when the Cabinet met on 11 January 1896, the crisis with the US over Venezuela was only one concern among several. As it happened, over the previous two days *The Times* had run a series of reports, based on European newspapers, about British isolation, and the Cabinet tried to deal with several of these problems. It was agreed to try to sort out various issues with France as well as to clean up the mess left by the embarrassing Jameson Raid in South Africa. In comparison, Venezuela was small beer. Salisbury had argued that the Monroe Doctrine did not apply to the boundary dispute and that Great Britain would not negotiate with the US over the matter, but the Cabinet refused to support him – recall that he was both Prime Minister and Foreign Secretary, so this was quite a blow – and thereafter the Cabinet did not deny that the US had the right to intervene. Rather, the

Foreign Office concentrated on limiting the amount of territory which was to be submitted to arbitration. Salisbury's approach now was to play a waiting game, in the hope that the US might in some way damage its case.

The British first of all overwhelmed the Americans with evidence. In January and February 1896 Cleveland appointed the Commission to investigate and determine the boundary, and the State Department asked that Great Britain provide 'documentary proof, historical narrative, unpublished archives or other evidence' for its claims; the immediate response of the British was fully to comply.[34] But the British also temporarily blocked progress by refusing to agree that all of the territory claimed by both countries should go into the pot. The concern was the areas already settled by the British: the Colonial Secretary, Joseph Chamberlain, thought that they might contain gold, while Salisbury was more concerned about the settlers themselves, not wanting them abandoned to the Venezuelans. Furthermore, he considered compulsory arbitration a dangerous precedent for the empire, and he very much disliked such far-reaching questions being left to the decision of one foreigner (Cleveland's Commission was made up of two British subjects, two American citizens and a Russian international lawyer). Canada was alarmed as well, because if arbitration were agreed over the boundary, and territory was subsequently lost, its own border might be in some danger.[35] Salisbury's, and others', apprehensions about arbitration were difficult to assuage.

Long and sometimes desultory negotiations over the year sorted things out. The British finally agreed to allow all of the territory to be submitted, and the issue then became, for how long territory needed to have been settled to allow it to be an 'excepted settlement'; after a series of proposals back and forth, the decision was for fifty years – the British wanted forty, the US said sixty, and the difference was split. On 2 February 1897, an Anglo-Venezuelan treaty was concluded stipulating that the boundary should be decided by an arbitral tribunal; a month later Cleveland's Commission published its report on the 'true divisional line'; and the tribunal handed down its award on

3 October 1899. As Olney had rather expected, barring two substantial alterations in favour of Venezuela, the boundary in the main followed that claimed by Britain.[36]

This was indeed a turning point. For the United States, as a future Secretary of State would say about another enemy, had come eyeball to eyeball with Great Britain and the other fellow blinked.[37] Never again would Britain be perceived as such a threat. The US had established that the Western Hemisphere was its sphere of influence, and in December 1904 President Theodore Roosevelt would openly proclaim the right of the US to enforce American hegemony:

> Our interests and those of our southern neighbors are in reality identical ... While they ... obey the primary laws of civilized society they may rest assured that they will be treated by us in a spirit of cordial sympathy. We would interfere with them only in the last resort, and then only if it became evident that their inability or unwillingness to do justice at home and abroad had violated the rights of the United States or had invited foreign aggression to the detriment of the entire body of American nations.[38]

What the Chilean Minister had feared had come to pass.

III

Meanwhile, as the Venezuela Crisis was playing out, both the US and Great Britain became involved in imperial wars, the Spanish–American War, by which the US acquired an overseas empire by conquest, and the Second Anglo-Boer War, by which Britain extended its control beyond the border of its empire. In both cases the other country was practically the only international supporter that each possessed. The conflicts also signalled changes in public opinion in both countries. The Americans appreciated the practical support provided by Britain against Spain, and although there was more of a split over the Boers – the American general public mostly supported the Boers while the government and elite opinion supported the British – there was no official condemnation of the British government as there was, for example, from the Kaiser. Acceding to American demands over the next several years was made easier for the British by their growing conviction that, if and when there was trouble in the international jungle, the US was more likely to support them than side with their enemies.

In 1895, the latest in a series of uprisings in Cuba against its colonial masters led the Spanish government to send 150,000 troops under General Valeriano ('the Butcher') Weyler, who carried out brutal and largely effective reprisals. A huge wave of 'Cuba Libre' sentiment washed over the US, and in January 1898 President William McKinley decided that Spain could no longer maintain order and dispatched the battleship USS *Maine* to Havana harbour to protect American citizens and their property. On 15 February, a massive explosion sent it to the bottom, with a loss of 266 of the 354 crew. When the news reached London, not only did the British government send its condolences, but crowds gathered in front of the American Embassy to pay their respects.[39]

It is worth pausing a moment to consider the importance of this gesture, because the reverse almost certainly would not have taken place. The American public, on the whole, continued to perceive Great Britain as a competitor, if no longer precisely an enemy, and one which everywhere worked against American interests. They were in the habit of disliking, distrusting and sometimes fearing the British, and habits tend not to change unless there is a reason for them to do so. The British public, on the other hand, had for several decades been growing more pro-American – or at least less anti-American – possibly because many considered that they were all English-speaking Anglo-Saxons together, sharing British values. The US was now much less of a rough frontier country and more of a technological and economic powerhouse, which had a history and a literature separate from those of Britain, and enjoyed other accoutrements of modern civilised life. Famous British writers commented on these new feelings of closeness: in 1862 Anthony Trollope referred to 'these children of our own', in 1883 W. E. Adams to 'our American Cousins' and in 1888

Matthew Arnold to 'the English people across the Atlantic'. The apotheosis of this must have been that written by Arthur Conan Doyle, when in 1892 he had Sherlock Holmes say that 'It is always a joy for me to meet an American, Mr Moulton, for I am one of those who believe that the folly of a monarch and a blundering of a Minister in fargone years will not prevent our children from being some day citizens of the same world-wide country under a flag which shall be a quartering of the Union Jack with the Stars and Stripes.'[40]

The reaction in the US to the sinking of the *Maine* was that the Spanish were responsible, and the US raced to war. Certainly the rantings of the so-called yellow press whipped up public opinion, but McKinley was driven more by other concerns: an end to violence in Cuba, partly for humanitarian reasons but also because it indicated weakness in the US if it could not deal with bloody chaos a mere ninety miles away. He was also concerned that Cuba was diverting attention away from alarming events in China (see pp. 210–1). McKinley prepared logically and carefully for war: he had Congress appropriate funds for the army and navy, he asked for and received the support of business, and he ensured the backing of religious leaders. Then, on 11 April 1898, he sent a war message to Congress.[41] On the 29th, war against Spain was declared, and by 22 July Cuba and Puerto Rico, another Spanish colony, had been captured.[42]

Meanwhile, in the Far East, Commodore George Dewey, commander of the Asiatic Squadron of the US Navy, led the destruction of the Spanish defences of the Philippines. The squadron had three tasks: first of all, it had to destroy the Spanish fleet in Manila Bay; secondly, it had to bombard the capital, Manila, and destroy its defences, leaving it open for the US Army to land and take control; and at the same time, it had to blockade the bay in order to hold it while awaiting these land reinforcements to arrive from the States.[43] The Asiatic Squadron had been concentrated in Hong Kong harbour since receipt of a cable dated 25 February 1898, which instructed Dewey to prepare for an attack on Manila. The fleet moved to Mirs Bay outside Hong Kong, which it used for refuelling and other services for the remainder of the war. The

British authorities also allowed Dewey to maintain communication with Washington through the Hong Kong cable, which
was the only transpacific link. The US and Britain had mostly
cooperated in China, and Dewey may well have known some
of the officers in the Royal Navy. In any case, Britain supported
the US in the Philippines to the extent that neutrality allowed –
'benign neutrality' in diplomatic terms.

The order to attack Manila was finally approved by the
President on 24 April, and the squadron sailed for Manila Bay
near the end of the month. The British also helped the Americans
indirectly. Late in June the Spanish fleet left for the Philippines
by way of Suez. At Alexandria, Rear Admiral Manuel de la
Cámara asked the Egyptians if the fleet could take on water,
coal and other supplies; Egypt, however, was essentially, if not
yet legally, a British protectorate (this had to await the outbreak
of the First World War), and the British 'induced' it to refuse.
A week later the fleet returned to Spain. This was unfortunate for
Spain, because the Spanish naval force in Manila was so weak 'that
its commander, anticipating destruction, anchored his ships in
shallow water to minimize the loss of life'. On 1 May, in 'a seven-
hour bombardment of the sitting ducks',[44] Dewey destroyed the
Spanish fleet, and thereby Spanish naval power in the Pacific.

Neutral vessels arrived to watch. On 2 May, a British gunboat,
HMS *Linnet*, arrived, reinforced on the 8th by the armoured
cruiser *Immortalité*, commanded by Captain Edward Chichester,
who was to enter American myth (see below). During the ensuing
weeks, varying numbers of British (another three gunboats),
German, French, Japanese and Austro-Hungarian warships
entered or left the bay, but many, including a growing number
of German ships, remained. It was proper for the various countries to be there to rescue their nationals, given that American
and Spanish soldiers plus the Filipinos themselves would soon
be fighting, and many crowded ships left. The number of British
ships did not worry the Americans, because the British were
the largest foreign investors there and thus had a stake in what
happened; furthermore, the British were disturbed by their
mounting rivalry with the Germans, both naval and imperial,

and thus were conspicuously friendly to the Americans. It was the Germans who tried the most to interfere with the Americans during the period of the blockade. Germany sent the fleet to the Philippines not, in fact, to try to prevent the Americans from defeating the Spanish; rather, it was there to acquire the islands if the US decided not to annex them.[45]

Dewey certainly realised that the Germans were on the prowl for colonies, and he knew that their squadron at Manila was commanded by a forceful officer, Vice-Admiral Otto von Diederichs, who was something of a war hero in Germany because of his prowess in grabbing and occupying Kiaochow in China in 1897. When the first-class cruiser *Kaiserin Augusta* arrived on 12 June, followed by two more cruisers the week after, Dewey's suspicions hardly abated, but another concern was the obvious rise in Spanish morale with the advent of the Germans, whom they hoped would support them. Nevertheless, the German ships were annoying in their own right. They took soundings of the harbour, landed supplies for the besieged Spanish and refused to salute the US flag as required by naval courtesy.[46] Chichester reported to Commodore Swinton Holland in Hong Kong on 9 July that the German ships had been constantly entering and leaving Manila at night and burning searchlights and 'making flashing signals' between their ships at Manila and those further away. 'Their ways are certainly mysterious, but the American officials look on the same as a "game of Bluff",' he added. In fact, on several occasions, the Americans had to fire over the German ships to bring them to a stop.[47] Dewey finally buckled, and on 10 July threatened war. According to the German version, produced immediately after the meeting, when a German officer complained that a ship had been improperly stopped and boarded, Dewey cried out (in Thomas A. Bailey's account), ' "Why, I shall stop each vessel whatever may be her colors! And if she does not stop I shall fire at her! And that means war, do you know, Sir? And I tell you if Germany wants war, all right, we are ready ..." Admiral Dewey became more and more excited. When the phrases: "If Germany wants war," etc., began to recur, the flaglieutenant [sic] left.'

Dewey himself supplied a slightly toned-down version:

'Do you want war with us?' asked the Admiral impressively. 'Certainly not,' replied the German. 'Well, it looks like it, and you are very near it; and' – his voice rising in pitch and intensity until it could be heard in the officers' quarters below – 'and you can have it, sir, as soon as you like.' The German backed in consternation away from the Admiral, and in an awed voice said to Lieutenant Brumby, 'Your Admiral seems to be much in earnest.' 'Yes,' replied Brumby, 'and you can be certain that he means every word he says.'[48]

Dewey's and Brumby's version probably iced the cake a bit, but both versions agree that war was threatened. Whether Congress would have agreed was not, fortunately, put to the test.

On 7 August, Dewey warned the foreign ships to change their positions by noon of the 9th, so as to be out of the line of fire, and on the 13th Dewey's squadron moved into position to begin the bombardment of Manila. Shortly thereafter the two British cruisers, the *Immortalité* and the *Iphigenia* (which had arrived after *Immortalité*), circled around Dewey's fleet and came to a stop in a position roughly between the German and American squadrons in order to observe the effects of the American fire; indeed, all of the neutral navies were keenly interested in the technical aspects of the conflict. In so doing, Chichester appeared to place the British deliberately between the American and German ships in order to protect the Americans. This is the story, but there is evidently not a shred of evidence in the German documents, while Chichester himself reported that he had shifted position to get a better view.[49]

Nevertheless, nothing that the Germans could say or do checked the growth of the legend, which received sustenance from an erroneous account published the following year in Henry Cabot Lodge's *The War with Spain*.[50] Further encouragement to the legend came from the fact that, when the American flag was raised over the city, only Chichester fired a twenty-one-gun salute in its honour. Whatever the truth of the matter, 'more than any real episode, this imaginary one contributed to the belief that England was the only friend America had during the war with Spain'.[51] This belief was also stimulated by the European press, which was almost entirely critical of the US and sympathetic towards Spain. The Germans were particularly bitter. In Britain, however, the reaction to this press abuse was to stimulate a great deal of public support for the US, not only in the press, but also in the form of speeches, processions and the establishment of Anglo-American associations. According to one historian, 'It was not that Englishmen especially liked Americans, but continental ill-will had so often been directed against English imperialism that when this ill-will was turned against the United States, Englishmen felt that they and the Americans were on "the same side".'[52]

Once the war was over, the question became, how much of the Spanish empire should the US annex? More specifically, should it take the Philippines? They would provide a base for American ships both naval and merchant on the way to China and Japan, and thus were strategically vital. There was pressure from Protestant religious leaders to civilise and Christianise the natives, never mind that under the Spaniards they had been Christians for centuries (they were Catholics, the wrong kind of Christians). There was a strong imperialistic urge. McKinley was a Republican, and most Republicans were pushing for empire (under McKinley Hawaii had been annexed in 1898). And finally, if the Americans did not take them, another country certainly would,[53] and it had been made pretty clear by the Germans that it would be them. Germany and the US had already a decade earlier clashed over control of Samoa, and it would have been politically impossible, even had there been a desire for it, to allow Germany to push the US out of the Philippines.

When the question arose as to whether the US should annex the Philippines, the British on the whole supported the idea. Rudyard Kipling wrote a famous poem in support, the full title of which is usually forgotten: 'The White Man's Burden: The United States and the Philippine Islands'. Some country or other would take them over, and no more than the Americans did the British want them to fall into the hands of the French or Germans. More important was the fact that London did not believe that British and American interests would come into conflict in the Far East. As Prime Minister Arthur Balfour wrote to Senator Henry Cabot Lodge several years later, 'I agree with you in thinking that the interests of the United States and of ourselves are absolutely identical in the Far East, and that the more closely we can work together, the better it will be for us and the world at large.'[54] The islands were therefore safe in American hands.

By the time this annexation had been confirmed by treaty with Spain in February 1899, the British were sliding into war in South Africa. In 1795 the British had taken over Cape Colony from the French, who had taken it over from the Dutch, and from the beginning the Dutch settlers and their descendants the Boers were unhappy with British rule. They objected to the ending of slavery in 1833, and to Parliament's passing of the Cape of Good Hope Punishment Act, intended to stop white aggression against the natives and the grabbing of their lands. This resulted in 10,000 Boers setting out in 1836 on the 'Great Trek', moving to lands beyond the Orange and Vaal rivers. Many settled in Natal, but in 1843 the British made that a colony, and the Boers upped stakes again. In 1854, they established the Orange Free State and in 1856 the South African Republic, formerly the Transvaal. Unfortunately for the Boers, in 1867 diamonds were discovered in the Orange River, and in 1871 the British annexed the diamond area. Just to tidy things up, and through apprehension that links threatening to British colonies might be established with Germany, in 1877 they annexed the South African Republic as well, although after the First Anglo-Boer War in 1880 the British government recognised its independence. This angered British imperialists in South Africa, especially Cecil Rhodes, and thereafter he and others worked to return the Boer states to British rule by bringing them into Cape Colony. Events deteriorated over the next few years, and on 11 October 1899 the Orange Free State and the South African Republic went to war against Great Britain.

During the first three months of the war the Boers won a number of victories: the nadir for the British was the week of 10–17 December, called Black Week, when the Boers inflicted three devastating defeats. The Boers' numbers were greater and they had better equipment, besides which Britain was occupied in China (see pp. 211–3); furthermore, the British were not used to war on the plains, and their troops were of a poor standard.[55] The Boers, however, did not have the manpower to dash to the seaports and control them, and the British were able to land reinforcements. By the spring of 1900, they had defeated the Boers in battle. The Boers then turned to guerrilla warfare, and the British responded with a ruthless destruction of Boer farms and crops and the herding of the civilian population into what were termed concentration camps.[56] The war came to an end in 1902, facilitated by generous British peace terms to the Boers to encourage them to work together with the British: the fundamental reason that the British government had gone to war was not to secure more gold, but rather to secure the rights of the *uitlanders* or non-Boers and the region within the empire.[57]

The US was the only Power not to condemn Great Britain over its activities in South Africa. The use of concentration camps was widely condemned, and public opinion in the US largely supported the Boers – the Irish-Americans were particularly virulent – and the Republican convention in 1899 nearly came out in their support.[58] John Hay, the Republican Secretary of State, was one of those who moved heaven and earth to prevent this. Essentially, he was deeply Anglophiliac. The US was officially neutral, but Hay's attitudes and comments made clear his pro-British stance. He was complacent about the concentration camps – he wrote to Henry Cabot Lodge on 19 February 1902 that 'the Boer women and children are in the concentration camps simply because their husbands and brothers want them there'[59] – and rather contemptuous of the Boer request that the US intervene or mediate. He believed that British control of South Africa was necessary for the spread of civilisation, a strategy the US was already undertaking in the Philippines. Hay was almost certainly thinking in racial or cultural terms, concluding that the existence of the British empire was in America's interest because only then would civilisation and progress be ensured.[60]

In this he was supported by a wide range of the north-eastern elite, such as the future President Theodore Roosevelt, who believed that the English-speaking peoples constituted the vanguard of civ-ilisation.[61] But there were others who also supported the British, such as black religious leaders and others, because of the Boers' support of slavery; furthermore, more American volunteers fought with the British than with the Boers.[62] In spite of the support, many Americans were distinctly unimpressed by the British perform-ance in the war. The Anglophile Lodge was scornful, attributing the British defeats to 'the fact that they have been whipping hill tribes and Dervishes so long that they have forgotten how white men fight'.[63] Britain and the Boers eventually declared peace in 1902, but the awareness of its own weaknesses which the war had highlighted, and the build-up of a whole range of threats, forced Britain to embark on both a diplomatic realignment and a strategic redeployment. From these, the US was to benefit.

IV

The Spanish–American War had brought to the forefront of Washington concerns the need for an isthmian canal to connect the Atlantic and Pacific oceans. In 1850 the US and Great Britain had signed the Clayton–Bulwer Treaty, by which they had agreed that neither was to fortify or exercise control over any future railway or canal linking the two oceans via Central America. However, it did not take long for the Americans to regret this, and over the remainder of the century Congress and the Cabinet periodically called for full American control of any future canal. In 1881, for example, the Secretary of State, James G. Blaine, told the British that the treaty had to be altered, arguing that the US now had paramount interests in the area, not least because of the growth of the Pacific states, which covered an extremely large area and required easy transit from the Atlantic because of their export trade. He also informed the British government that 'England as against the United States is always wrong.'[64] Nothing began to change, however, until 1899.

What made the question of a canal crucial to the US was the long cruise the battleship USS *Oregon* had been forced to make

around Cape Horn at the tip of South America in order to reach
Manila and join in battle. In December 1898 Hay proposed to
British Ambassador Pauncefote in Washington that the two
countries should discuss modification of the 1850 treaty; the
British Cabinet agreed, and by mid-1899 the two men had drawn
up a draft convention. The principal adjustment was to concede
to the US the right to regulate and manage a canal. Hay asked
US Ambassador Henry White at the London Embassy to urge
the Foreign Office to make haste, for fear that the Senate would
obstruct it. 'In the usual reckless manner of our Senate,' he wrote,
'they are discussing the matter with open doors every day, and are
getting themselves so balled up with their own eloquences that it
is greatly to be feared they will so commit themselves as to consider themselves bound to reject any arrangement that may be
made.'[65]

The Foreign Office had its own problems, particularly with
the Admiralty. The canal would damage British naval supremacy,
because in enabling the US Pacific and Atlantic fleets to join up
it would essentially double the operational size of the US Navy.
Salisbury also objected, because he wanted the question of the
Alaskan frontier (see pp. 145–50) decided at the same time. There
the matter rested for some months, until Great Britain's cata-
strophic reverses in the Boer War drove it back to the negotiating table: the European Powers were mooting intervention and
trying to convince the US to join them, and thus it was not the
time to offend the US. Hay revived the negotiations in January
1900, and on 5 February Pauncefote signed the Convention.[66]

It was then sent to the Senate for ratification, and everything
that Hay feared came to pass. By the Davis Amendment, the
Senate insisted on an American right to fortify the canal, Hay
and Great Britain agreed to delay ratification, and in December
the Senate essentially rewrote it. Salisbury was no longer
Foreign Secretary, and his successor Lord Lansdowne, a former
Governor-General of Canada, had a much clearer idea than
Salisbury of the potential power of the US, and decided to come
to an agreement. He had already cabled Pauncefote that the
Cabinet had decided to reject the treaty if it retained the Davis

Amendment, but the expectation was that the US would come up with an alternative proposal, and this it did. The new treaty allowed the US to construct fortifications – the British knew that they could not prevent it so they might as well agree to it – and stipulated that it need not be kept open during time of war. The treaty gave the US the right to build and manage it, provided that all nations had access. The treaty conceded an important British point, which was that the same conditions and charges would apply to all, that American ships would not attract lower charges. Equitability of charges was important, because the British estimated that 60 per cent of the traffic through a canal would be theirs. On 18 November 1901 the treaty was signed in Washington, with the Senate ratifying it by an overwhelming majority a month later.[67]

This treaty was deeply significant to the relationship of the two powers. The British decision taken in January 1896 to agree to arbitration over Venezuela had been seen as tactical, but arguably it was strategic: would the Cabinet have agreed to it, even while considering the demand outrageous, had it realised that it was the first step on the path to the irrevocable passing of Britain's predominance in the Western Hemisphere? Britain had essentially agreed to American hegemony, and it would have been counterproductive, not to say useless, had it tried to prevent the US from providing the means to defend it. Little did the Cabinet know that it had set the pattern which its successors were often forced to follow.

V

The decisions so far taken in Latin America were of far greater importance to the US than to Britain: the US was a regional power, but Britain's concerns were global. It needed to protect its empire and safeguard the sea lanes, the highways for its trade and for vital imports of food and raw materials, and the pressures were becoming very challenging. To meet all of these needs, it had to consolidate its strength and its resources. Thus the period from

1898 to 1907 saw Britain carrying out both a diplomatic revolution and a strategic redeployment.

By 1900 the Great Powers of Europe were linked in two military alliances, the Triple Alliance of Germany, Austro-Hungary and Italy versus the Dual Alliance of France and Russia. Great Britain was part of neither, nor did it wish to be. Its traditional policy had been to maintain a balance of power on the continent, which meant that it temporarily allied with other Great Powers against whichever Power was trying to dominate. From the seventeenth century its greatest imperial rival in North America, India, Africa and the Far East was France, while in the nineteenth century France was joined by Russia as a rival in the Near East, Central Asia and the Far East, and was a particular threat to India. Traditionally, Germany in its various guises was more likely to be an ally than an enemy: it was a land power while Great Britain was a sea power, and so not were direct threats to each other. But from the 1890s German power and politics had been changing. German expansionists, including the Emperor, argued that part of the definition of a Great Power was to have colonies, and the Royal Navy was blocking Germany's way. The combination of German activities during the Boer War, the German Navy Bill of 1900 (the Preface of which stated that 'there is only one way of protecting Germany's commerce and colonial possessions: Germany must possess a fleet of such strength that a war with her would shake the position of the mightiest naval Power')[68] and its aggressive activities during crises in Africa, the Middle East and the Far East emphasised Britain's increasing exposure to danger and the lack of any ally.

By 1902, Great Britain was feeling beleaguered because the world was becoming unbalanced. Powerful outside Europe, it was increasingly dismissed within it, because other Powers, in particular Germany and Russia, did not believe that it would fight. For Britain, the rise of the two extra-European Powers, Japan and the US, meant that even a balanced Europe no longer protected its empire in the same way as it had done. The outcome was a reconfiguration of British relations with other Powers, including the US, by two successive foreign secretaries, Lord Lansdowne and Sir Edward Grey. At the same time, Lord Selborne, the First Lord of the Admiralty, after some years of consideration by the Admiralty and the Cabinet Defence Committee, accepted that Britain no longer possessed the naval superiority that it had enjoyed for nearly three-quarters of a century, and changed the shape and deployment of the Royal Navy to meet the new realities.

The organising principle of both strategies was to make changes on the peripheries in order to concentrate resources near the home islands. Until the latter nineteenth century, any competing naval powers were European, and the main tasks of the Royal Navy in wartime were threefold: to sweep the oceans of enemy vessels, whether warships or merchant ships; to blockade the enemy fleets in their home ports; and to attack them if they tried to escape. Britain's command of the four 'narrow seas' – the Channel, the North Sea, the Suez Canal and the mouth of the Mediterranean at Gibraltar – enabled its warships to control access to and thus to control the world's oceans. After 1880, however, European naval powers, as already noted, strengthened their fleets and new non-European naval powers rose, specifically the US and Japan. With the safety of the shipping lanes and its empire increasingly at risk, and given that by 1895 it imported four-fifths of its wheat,[69] did Britain dare to give up the attempt to maintain global dominance? Or should the decision be that the most crucial thing was to retain superiority in the home waters in order to defend the British Isles themselves, and thus accept that it no longer had the resources required to maintain global pretensions?

The first change, both diplomatic and strategic, was fundamental: Britain signed a peacetime alliance for the first time in centuries.[70] The Anglo-Japanese Alliance was signed in 1902 and renewed in 1905 and 1911. The purpose was to commit the Imperial Japanese Navy to combine with the Royal Navy to contain the other Great Powers, particularly the combined Russian and French fleets, in the Far East.[71] This allowed the Royal Navy to withdraw five battleships from the China Station and place them in the Mediterranean. The second diplomatic agreement was with France, and by the Anglo-French Agreement of 1904 (popularly known as the Anglo-French Entente), the two countries settled outstanding imperial conflicts in North Africa as well as the question of French access to the rich fishing ground off Newfoundland. In due course, the French assumed responsibility for the Mediterranean and the British were able to withdraw ships to station them in the Channel.

The negotiations with Russia were very much more difficult than those with France, because the imperial rivalry with Russia in Central Asia was more ferocious than that with France in Africa: in Central Asia, the safety of India and, to a lesser extent, Persia was at stake. India was obvious, but there were two points about Persia: first of all, it shared a border with North-West India, and secondly, there was British-controlled oil there. The latter was of singular importance, because in 1913 the Royal Navy, which already ran some of its ships on oil, decided that for the future, all of its ships would be oil-fired rather than coal-fired. The outcome was the Anglo-Russian Agreement of 1907: Persia was divided into spheres of influence, with a buffer zone between them; Afghanistan would be neutral, with British overlordship; and Tibet would remain neutral. Russia, however, saw this as a breathing-space while it built up its power after its defeat in the 1904–5 Russo-Japanese War, and so the British had constantly to keep watch on its activities.

The place of the United States in this 'revolution' is clear. Because the value of Britain's commercial interests in the Western Hemisphere was high, and the extent of its colonial possessions was larger than the territory of the US, it did not like resigning its position to the US, but it did not fear that the US would attack its colonies. Furthermore, if the latter insisted that it was in charge, it thereby took on the responsibility of keeping unruly countries in order, which could only benefit those, such as Britain, with financial and commercial interests there. So, in the face of greater dangers elsewhere, Britain accepted that the US would thereafter dominate the Western Hemisphere. By late 1907, then, the view from the Foreign Office window had changed considerably.

Relations with the US had gone through the most complete transformation, in that by means of a series of agreements, which almost without exception reflected American demands, there were virtually no points of conflict left. Furthermore, the changes in public opinion in both countries meant that their governments accepted that war between them was now unthinkable. (The advice of the British War Office, as noted above, was that 'the contingency of war with the United States should be avoided at all hazards'.)[72] In this situation, each could hope for at least neutrality from the other; indeed, from Britain the US could count on firm support in almost any contingency.

A primary reason for these changes was that the elimination of these imperial crisis points would considerably lessen the need for the Royal Navy to maintain fleets around the world. The Admiralty had concluded by September 1901 that policies had to change, and here a major reason was financial. Public expenditure on military forces in 1901 was 58 per cent of total government expenditure, of which 15 per cent was spent on the navy. By 1903, with the growing German naval threat, the navy alone would count for 25 per cent of government expenditure.[73] A major reason for this was the massive growth in the cost of the ships themselves: between 1895 and 1905 the cost of a first-class cruiser (a vessel with a long range and high speed that could scout ahead of the main battle fleet) nearly quadrupled.[74] Furthermore, because they were much larger, the ships took considerably more expensive manpower to run.

The main driver of the need for financial retrenchment was the Chancellor of the Exchequer, Sir Michael Hicks Beach. The personification of the need for rigid orthodoxy, he feared that the growth in taxation would drive Great Britain to the end of its resources. The First Lord, Selborne, thought that this was ridiculous and, in any case, Britain was nowhere near the end of its capacity to borrow, given that in March 1900 the National War Loan had been eleven times oversubscribed, while a year later a Treasury issue of Exchequer bonds had been subscribed twice over.[75] In a memorandum for the Cabinet on 16 November 1901, written in response to Hicks Beach's arguments, Selborne reminded his colleagues that 'the growth of the Naval Estimates had been caused solely by the efforts of France and Russia to establish a naval superiority over this country'. Yet he was increasingly concerned by the growing German naval threat, which the Germans themselves had spelled out in the previous year's Navy Bill (quoted above).[76] By February 1904, he had concluded that, as he told the Cabinet, 'the great new German navy is being carefully built up from the point of view of a war with us'.[77] Britain could more than match the combined navies of France and Russia, but adding the German navy to the equation put the Royal Navy, and therefore Britain itself, in peril.

On 6 December 1904, Selborne presented to the Cabinet a memorandum entitled 'Distribution and Mobilization of the Fleet'. One decision already taken in December 1903 was to withdraw from the Royal Navy's bases at Halifax (on the east coast) and Esquimalt (on the west coast), thereby handing over the defence of Canada to the Canadians themselves.[78] The threats from France, Russia and Germany were being met by a consolidation and redistribution of the fleets. The Pacific and South Atlantic Squadrons entirely disappeared. Three of the four battle fleets were concentrated in European waters, the Channel Fleet plus an Armoured Cruiser Squadron based in England, the Atlantic Fleet plus an Armoured Cruiser Squadron based on Gibraltar, and the Mediterranean Fleet based on Malta. The China, East Indies and Australia Squadrons were combined into an Eastern Fleet based on Singapore, while all but a flagship and an armoured cruiser (with their supporting smaller craft) were withdrawn from the North America and West Indies Station.

There was really nothing to be done about any American threat, because, as noted above by Selborne, in the Western Hemisphere 'the United States are forming a navy the power and size of which will be limited only by the amount of money the American people choose to spend on it'. (That same year, a British visitor to the US saw fourteen battleships and thirteen armoured cruisers being built simultaneously in American shipyards.)[79] Fortunately, there was not believed to be a threat from that quarter. And so, as a by-product of the threats from Europe, Great Britain had, after centuries, finally withdrawn the Royal Navy from the Western Hemisphere, leaving the Caribbean an American lake. This, at least, was how the Americans saw it, but the British viewed it differently: they had turned over to the Americans the task of defending the hemisphere, thereby incorporating the US Navy into the British defence strategy. But, however one viewed it, the power of Great Britain to exert virtually unencumbered influence in Latin America had ceased.

VI

The First World War was, for Great Britain, first and foremost a war to stop Germany from establishing its hegemony over Western Europe and thereby posing a mortal threat to Britain itself. But it was also an imperial war, a war to save the empire. The central concern remained India, but to save India it was vital to retain control of the Eastern Mediterranean and the Suez Canal. Russia was now an ally, and while this might not have wholly prevented threatening moves, that country had no spare resources to devote to its decades-old drive south to Persia, Afghanistan and India. Germany, on the other hand, saw the war as a means of continuing its attempts to gain colonies in the Middle East. Beginning two decades before the war but accelerating in 1902, its vehicle, as it were, was the plan to build a railway from Berlin to Baghdad.[80] Now it had two possibilities: to continue to build the railway, and to eliminate the Russian barrier and utilise the core territory of its Turkish ally to gain access to the Mediterranean. Turkey – or the Ottoman empire – had its own aspirations, that is, to reclaim control of its provinces, including driving the British out of Egypt.

Great Britain, to gain what it needed to protect the empire, had to protect what it already had, territories such as Egypt, and to rip others such as Arabia and Mesopotamia out of Turkish control in order to construct a barrier against Germany; later in the war, as it began to gain control over areas such as Mesopotamia and Palestine, the desire grew to expand the empire for its own sake. Although begun in 1914, the work was primarily accomplished during 1917–18. Britain also had to accommodate the desire of its ally France to expand its own empire into the Middle East. Another concern was the German colonies in Africa. The government of South Africa moved early to take over German South-West Africa (now Namibia) and German East Africa (now Tanzania and Zanzibar). The latter had been a British desire for some decades, blocking, as they did, the British drive for a railway from the Cape to Cairo; taking over South-West Africa was also seen as providing protection for Cape Colony. But, equally, it was vital in order to prevent the Germans from using their colonies as naval bases from which they could 'interdict Britain's imperial maritime communications'.[81]

The US would soon be seen by Great Britain as a major barrier to achieving these imperial goals. The opposition was not military, but Woodrow Wilson's ideas. For Britain, there were two overwhelming concerns: the attempt by the US effectively to destroy the powers of the Royal Navy to protect its empire during wars, and Wilson's plan to eliminate the foundation of the British and other empires by requiring that peoples have the right to self-determination. This particular fight of the British with the United States was carried out in the post-war peace conferences, which Lloyd George had foreseen: as early as June 1917, he had told the Cabinet War Policy Committee that 'he did not want to have to face a Peace Conference some day with our country weakened while America was still overwhelmingly strong'.[82] In the territorial conflicts, the British empire, in particular the white Dominions (except for Canada), jointly succeeded in defeating Wilson's plans; retaining the full power of the Royal Navy was Britain's own success.

Britain had for a century been a firm supporter of the territorial integrity of the Ottoman empire, 'the sick man of Europe', primarily against Russian aggression. It had, with France and Piedmont-Sardinia, fought with the Ottomans against Russia in the Crimean War of 1854–6, popularly remembered only for the hopeless Charge of the Light Brigade. This was not for love of the Turks: rather it was from fear of the Russian empire and its seemingly inexorable extension east, west and south. At first France took the lead, but Turkey's most ferocious anti-Russian

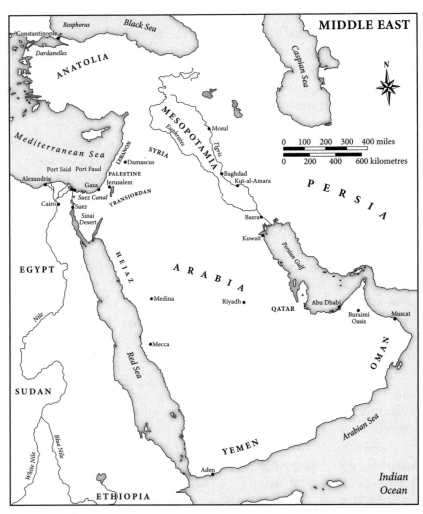

MAP 15

supporter soon became the British: they feared that, should Russia become more powerful, it would threaten the European balance of power; they also feared its clear intention to control the Ottoman empire, which would both allow an overland route to India and threaten Britain's trade in the Near East. Control of Constantinople and the Dardanelles Strait alone would enable Russia to send its warships from its bases in the Black Sea to the Mediterranean, giving it the long-desired warm-water port and, crucially, posing a dangerous threat to the Royal Navy's control of the Mediterranean. Russia was defeated, and retired from the fray for two decades to build up its resources for another push (as happened in the Russo-Turkish War 1877–8). British support for Turkey's survival as an independent entity continued until the First World War.

This support naturally disappeared when in 1914 Turkey joined Germany and Austria-Hungary as one of the Central Powers at war with the Entente Powers Great Britain, France and Russia. Now it was an enemy, and imperial conflict with Russia, before the war a major determinant of British policy, took a back seat as a geopolitical threat. Hereafter the threat would be Germany and the Ottoman empire itself. Of singular concern was that the entry of Turkey, a Muslim power, into the war would mean war against the Caliph, the spiritual leader of all Muslims in the Middle East, which could only encourage disaffection among the Muslims of India. Strategically, it also meant that the Eastern Mediterranean, and particularly the Suez Canal, was severely threatened. On 1 October, the Turks closed the Dardanelles Strait, and shortly thereafter an expedition was sent by Britain to secure the head of the Persian Gulf. The Admiralty wanted to protect its oil supplies, and the government of India, headed by the Viceroy Lord Hardinge of Penshurst, was worried about German agents penetrating eastwards through Persia and Afghanistan, given that the Germans, even before the war, had begun to encourage Muslim agitators in India and Egypt.[83] It is worth noting that the government of India made policy in its own right and, although linked to the Cabinet via the Secretary of State for India, was not bound to refer matters to London. During the nineteenth century, as one historian explains, 'it forged south Asia into a single unit for defence purposes by means of annexations, alliances and the exercise of influence, and extended that unit into the Middle East'.[84] Hardinge's main concern was the security of the Raj and the 'contentment' of its subjects.[85] The government of India also wanted to prevent the Turks from putting pressure on the friendly sheikhs of the Gulf and Kuwait, who were 'guided' by the British. On 22 November, the British entered and secured the port of Basra in order to protect the nearby oil fields. Meanwhile, on the 5th of that month, Britain and France had declared war on the Ottoman empire, and Britain annexed Cyprus (which had been leased from the Ottomans in 1878, when Russia had again fought with Turkey). The British sent military reinforcements to Egypt and on 18 December declared it a protectorate.

London then rather wanted British forces to remain where they were, but the government of India wanted to continue into Mesopotamia. The latter's appointment in April 1915 of Lieutenant-General Sir John Nixon, an aggressive commander in the Indian Army and 'a hearty cavalry soldier in his mid-fifties, a polo player and pig sticker',[86] as Commander-in-Chief of British forces in Mesopotamia signalled a new forward policy. Nixon had great contempt for the quality of Turkish forces and a singular lack of concern for the provision of suitable and adequate equipment, transport and medical facilities for his own troops. Following some early successes, he became convinced, against the advice of his field commander, Major-General Sir Charles Townsend, that Townsend's small force could advance to Baghdad with little difficulty, and in October 1915 Townsend was ordered by Nixon to take Baghdad. However, he suffered reverses, and was forced to retreat to Kut-al-Amara, where from December he was besieged by the Turks. A British relief force was repulsed, and Townsend surrendered in humiliation in April 1916. London then replaced Nixon with its own choice of commander, and Lieutenant-General Sir Frederick Maude took over the command. On 11 March 1917, having swept away the Turks in front of them by enjoying a troop ratio of four to one against the Turkish Army, the Anglo-Indian force entered Baghdad. In London, the Cabinet

War Committee had wanted a dramatic achievement on the Tigris to counterbalance military setbacks on other fronts.[87] Kut was presumably avenged; yet tactically, rather than politically, the conquest of Baghdad, 500 miles from the port of Basra whence the troops' supplies came, was not terribly useful as a staging post for further major offensives. Maude advanced another 200 miles, until by the summer of 1917 neither the British nor the Turks wanted to continue fighting, and the campaign ended with much of Mesopotamia under British control.[88]

Meanwhile, the civil and military establishments in Egypt were extremely concerned about the Suez Canal, which was subject to occasional attacks by Turkish forces. They constructed and manned an elaborate system of trenches, bunkers and barricades along both sides of the Canal. As Howard M. Sachar recounts, the Suez base was 'unprecedented in the sheer magnitude of its logistics, involving water-supply, metalled railways in the sand, floating bridges on the Canal itself, railway extensions, and entrenchment and wiring on an enormous scale ... a bottomless sinkhole for imperial resources and manpower'.[89] In the words of another historian, 'A Suez "fixation" thus came into being that was vitally to affect Britain's Imperial consciousness in the years ahead.'[90] In January 1916, Sir Archibald Murray, 'cultured, reserved and intelligent',[91] was sent out to take command of the Egyptian Expeditionary Force, and reorganised the British forces in the region. To eliminate the Turkish threat to the Canal and Egypt itself, and to conquer some spoils for the empire – by this time the idea of its expansion was driving some of the imperialists in London[92] – the Cabinet in April 1917 ordered an offensive into Palestine.

Murray led an advance into the Sinai desert, but was soundly beaten in the First and Second Battles of Gaza. In June 1917, he was replaced by General Sir Edmund ('Bull') Allenby, 'tall, with a strong, determined face',[93] a soldier of great vigour and imagination. He won the Third Battle of Gaza, the gateway to Palestine, in early November, and then continued towards Jerusalem, which the British captured on 9 December (Lloyd George had insisted that it be captured 'before Christmas'). Writes Sachar, '[t]he mayor of Jerusalem, a somewhat befuddled Arab in striped trousers and frock coat, walked out to surrender the keys of the city to a group of British mess cooks who wandered by.' On entering Jerusalem at noon on 11 December, Allenby, the thirty-fourth conqueror of Jerusalem and the first victorious Christian to set foot in the city since the Crusades, dismounted and, together with his officers and some foreign diplomats and military attachés, entered the city on foot through the Jaffa Gate. His intention was to show respect for the status of Jerusalem as the Holy City of Christians, Jews and Muslims.[94] London also wanted to demonstrate how different the British were from the Germans, whose Kaiser in 1898 had entered it riding a white horse, to enable which the Ottoman authorities had had to fill in the moat between the Citadel and Jaffa Gate.

Alongside these two campaigns, there was a third, which was to foment revolt in Turkish Arabia in order to win the Arabs over to the British side. In 1915, Husayn bin 'Ali, the Sharif of Mecca and Hashemite ruler of the Hejaz Arabs, called for an Arab revolt against the Ottoman empire. In 1916, the British came to an agreement with the Sharif, by which they would help each other to defeat the Turks. As a military leader, however, the British preferred Emir Feisal, the Sharif's third son. The British liaison officer was a former archaeologist, T. E. Lawrence. He had been working for British Military Intelligence in Cairo, and his knowledge of both the Arab people and the language made him an ideal man for the task. During the war he fought with the Arab guerrilla forces alongside Feisal's Arab army against the Turks, but his main achievement was to help to convince the Arabs to co-ordinate their efforts with those of the British.[95]

Events in the war brought about a profound change in the situation. In October 1917, the new Soviet government issued a 'Decree on Peace' which proclaimed that Russia wanted peace with all of the world's belligerents. In November, the Russian and German delegations arrived in Brest-Litovsk and began negoti-ations, culminating in the signing of a peace treaty, the Treaty of Brest-Litovsk, on 3 March 1918. Russia was now out of the war, leaving the Germans free to embark on a drive to the west to try to defeat the Entente Powers before the US, which had entered the war in April 1917, managed to get their soldiers to France. The situation in the Middle East itself was transformed. Lord Milner, a member of the Imperial War Cabinet, wrote to Lloyd George on 20 March that, with the fall of Russia, 'which used to cover our whole Asian flank',[96] there was a new war: there was no more Russian pressure on Turkey, and the Germans could now sweep around the Black Sea into the Caucasus, threatening both Persia and Afghanistan, which were buffers intended to protect India from Russia – and now from Germany.

Urgent attempts were already being made to shore up Arab support. In January 1918, Great Britain gave to the Sharif of Mecca a guarantee of his independence. Furthermore, the following July the British issued a public declaration promising complete sovereign independence to those Arab territories, that is, the Hejaz (which was also ruled by the Sharif), which had been independent before 1914, as well as those where the Arabs had driven out the Turks themselves. In addition, those territories currently under Allied occupation, Palestine and Mesopotamia (actually under British occupation), would be able to determine their own rulers. Allenby made certain that the army under Feisal took the lead in entering Damascus; in addition, he raised the Arab flag over the city and installed Emir Feisal as the military administrator.[97]

There was a fundamental difficulty with all of this unplanned-for generosity: quite simply, the British had promised the same territory to two different allies. In 1916, the British Commissioner in Egypt, Sir Henry McMahon, had promised the Arab leadership post-war independence for the Ottoman Arab provinces, but the same year also saw the signing in February of the Sykes–Picot Agreement with the French, which split the Middle East into spheres of influence: France was to get Syria and the Lebanon, while Great Britain gained Iraq, Kuwait and the Transjordan. Palestine was to be internationalised. After January 1917, however, with the war going so badly on the Western Front, the British became even more concerned: what if Germany won, retained its strength and in due course resumed its drive into the Middle East? It was vital to secure the outer defences of Egypt, and here Palestine entered the equation even more prominently than before. According to John Darwin, 'It was largely this thinking – "strategic Zionism" – that converted the British War Cabinet to the Balfour Declaration in November 1917, promising a Jewish "national home" in Palestine: a colony of Jewish settlers, fiercely anti-Turk, would help guard the approaches to Egypt'[98] in order to secure the Suez Canal. Lord Curzon 'gloomily, and accurately, predicted that whoever received the Mandate for Palestine' – which would be Britain – 'would have to keep the two groups', the Arabs and the Jews, 'from killing each other'.[99] This was to be one of Britain's most onerous responsibilities in its expanded Middle East empire.

The collapse of Turkey was unexpected and complete. It was triggered by the coincidental loss of both Palestine and Bulgaria in September 1918, the latter of which left Turkey open for its enemies to sweep through to Constantinople. The Turkish government accepted the inevitable, and on 14 October presented a request for an armistice to President Wilson in Washington.[100] In a speech given on 8 January 1918 Wilson had set out his proposed peace plan, his Fourteen Points, stating in Point XII that 'The Turkish portion of the present Ottoman Empire should be assured a secure sovereignty'; moreover, Lloyd George in January 1918 had declared that 'we do not challenge the maintenance of the Turkish Empire in the homelands of the Turkish race with its capital at Constantinople'.[101] Notably, the Ottoman imperial territories were not accorded the same assurance by either Wilson or Lloyd George, and Lloyd George certainly had no intention of letting them slide out of Allied control. On 1 October, the War Cabinet had decided to send two Dreadnoughts, the fastest and most powerful type of ship then in existence, to the Aegean to ensure that the Royal Navy was the dominating naval power in the region. Against the wishes of the French, a British admiral led the Allied, not just the British, fleet through the Dardanelles to Constantinople and into the Black Sea.

On 20 October, the Turkish government informed London that it wanted an immediate peace treaty with the British. It would allow autonomy for Mesopotamia and Palestine, but it insisted that they should remain under the Sultan's sovereignty. This was rejected and the counter-offer made that Turkey could remain independent and retain Constantinople.[102] On the 22nd, the War Cabinet agreed to inform the Italians and the French about the approach made by Turkey, but not to allow them any say in the negotiations; Lloyd George's justification was that when France had negotiated the armistice with Bulgaria, those countries had not consulted the British about the terms.[103] Understandably, the French in particular were angered, but they were essentially brushed aside with a sop given to them of their being allowed to share in the fortifying of the Dardanelles and the Bosphorus. On 31 October, the armistice theoretically began, but not in actuality until British troops occupied Mosul: the Admiralty was not going to lose control of what it saw as a vital source of oil for the fleet, one untouchable by either the French or the Americans.

In planning to extend their power in the Middle East, the British were driven by two emotions: fear and greed. They feared the possibility that in the future India would still be under threat, and thus that defences had to remain and, indeed, be strengthened. This was the age-old fear of empires, fear of what was across the border and beyond their control. There was also the fear, as emphasised above, of losing control of the oil in Iraq. The US was winning in the competition to control the oil in Mexico: it must not control the oil in Iraq as well. Britain kept it in its own hands by occupying Mosul and the surrounding territory. And then there was greed: what the British had won, they wished to keep. They were not alone in this. France felt the same, and during the final months of the war and into the peace negotiations, France, not the Arabs, was Britain's main opponent in the Middle East. In certain respects, the outcome was a draw, but they shared an opponent in Wilson. At the end, in this area if not always in Europe, they essentially won.

VII

The focus for the British now turned to fending off the Wilsonian attack on the Royal Navy and safeguarding their gains abroad.

The general apprehension of the War Cabinet was expressed by General Jan Christian Smuts, South African Defence Minister and member of the Imperial War Cabinet, in his October 1918 'Note on the Early Conclusion of Peace': he urged the Cabinet to conclude peace as early as possible, because if the war continued into 1919, Great Britain 'would have lost the first position; and the peace which will then be imposed on an utterly exhausted Europe will be an American peace'. By 1919, the USA 'will have taken our place as the first military, diplomatic and financial power of the world'.[104] It did not, but Britain still had a fight on its hands.

The conflict over naval power erupted even before the peace conference began. In Wilson's address to the Senate of 22 January 1917, in which he had set out his ideas for a future peace, he had stated that 'The freedom of the seas is the *sine qua non* of peace, equality, and cooperation.'[105] The inclusion of this principle was not surprising, given that the War of 1812 had had as one of its causes the actions of the Royal Navy in constraining the trade of the neutral United States during the Napoleonic War. He did not change his mind, and on 8 January 1918 Point II of his Fourteen Points was as follows: 'Absolute freedom of navigation upon the seas, outside territorial waters, alike in peace and in war, except as the seas may be closed in whole or in part by international action for the enforcement of international covenants.' In late October that year, Wilson's close friend and adviser Edward M. House travelled to London for discussions with the Allies. His assumption, he wrote to Wilson, was that 'England cannot dispense with us in the future,' and he was therefore confident that 'the English I think will accept your fourteen points with some modification such as ... making the freedom of the seas conditional upon the foundation of the League of Nations'.[106] He was wrong. Lloyd George told House on 29 October that 'Freedom of the Seas ... could not be accepted without qualification.' Furthermore, if it 'was made a condition of peace Great Britain could not agree to it'.[107] If it became a principle of the League of Nations, the British would refuse to accept the League.[108]

The crux was the right to impose a blockade. House threatened a separate peace between the US and Germany; Wilson added that he might go before Congress and ask whether the US should fight for the Allies' war aims; and House 'told the British privately that you [Wilson] anticipate that their policy would lead to the establishment of the greatest naval program by the United States that the world has ever seen'.[109] Lloyd George wrote reassuringly to House that the Allies would make peace on the basis of the Fourteen Points and those set out in Wilson's later speeches, but he reiterated that they could not accept the freedom of the seas without changes and qualifications. Wilson then agreed that, although the blockade power would have to be redefined, it need not be abolished. On 3 November, Lloyd George told House that he was quite willing to discuss the matter, which House took as a great diplomatic victory.[110] The British, however, believed that they had given away nothing while placating the Americans, with the result that they could now work together on other issues. Discussions on the subject died away.

Negotiations over the Middle East took considerably longer, and Wilson died before things were finally settled. The relevant point was Point XII. It began, as noted above, 'The Turkish portion of the present Ottoman Empire should be assured a secure sovereignty,' but it continued with a clause wholly unwelcome to the Turks: 'but the other nationalities which are now under Turkish rule should be assured an undoubted security of life and an absolutely unmolested opportunity of autonomous development, and the Dardanelles should be permanently opened as a free passage to the ships and commerce of all nations under international guarantees'. As far as the British and French were concerned, 'unmolested opportunity of autonomous development' was not going to happen, and the conflict between the two countries and the US was fought over whether, and how, the conundrum was going to be resolved. (It is worth remembering that the US never declared war on the Ottoman empire.[111]) Fortunately for the Allies, Wilson himself provided the answer.

The existence and nature of the League of Nations dominated the Versailles peace conference. Wilson wanted it so badly that he eventually sacrificed other issues. As he told House on 14 December 1918, he intended 'making the League of Nations the center of the whole program and letting everything else revolve around it. Once that is a *fait accompli*, nearly all the very serious difficulties will disappear.'[112] The Allies knew that he felt this, and early on the British government determined to exploit this ambition, with Lloyd George emphasising to his colleagues that the League 'was the only thing which [Wilson] really cared about', and that they should let him have his way and deal with it first, on the assumption that it would ease other matters. (The Australian Prime Minister, Billy Hughes, put it more brutally: 'Give him a League of Nations and he will give us all the rest.')[113]

It was not that the British did not support such a League: it had, in fact, been partly their idea, and its name had been suggested by Sir Edward Grey. The difficulty was that Wilson's moral and ideological approach was in sharp contrast to that of the British: although some members of the British government also strongly supported the concept, they were extremely sceptical about whether Wilson's approach would work. Steeped in the diplomatic tradition, the British were very concerned with how an international organisation would work – where was the power to lie, which countries would be members, how would collective security be enforced, and so on. Wilson believed fervently in the existence of a moral force of international public opinion, which emanated from people everywhere and which, when mobilised, was more powerful than military forces: such opinion would force governments to do the right thing.[114] The British believed in a balance of power, skilful diplomacy and the power of the Royal Navy. In fact, the Lloyd George government, both civilian and military leaders, saw the League as alien, fundamentally flawed and unworkable: the only advantage, to which Lloyd George clung, was that it might facilitate future Anglo-American co-operation.

What emerged from the negotiations was the mandate system. In the olden days, countries would gain territory by right of conquest, but in the bright new era this was felt to be unacceptable. Wilson wanted the League of Nations to assume responsibility for all of the former territories controlled by the three collapsed enemy empires, the German, the Austro-Hungarian and the Ottoman, but how to do it? Annexation or colonisation was clearly no longer appropriate; either the League should assume responsibility directly, or it should mandate other countries to do so. It was the South African General Smuts, whom Lloyd George had appointed as one of the two British representatives on the League Commission (established on 25 January 1919), who came up with the suggestion of mandates in his influential December 1918 pamphlet *The League of Nations: A Practical Suggestion*. This was arguably the most influential of all of the pre-peace conference proposals,[115] and Wilson took over the idea from it.[116]

Wilson stated that he did not approve of mandates 'for European peoples'; rather, they were for peoples who were not quite ready to look after themselves, that is, everyone in the German and Ottoman empires. Smuts had written in December, 'The peoples left behind by the decomposition of Russia, Austria and Turkey are mostly untrained politically; many of them are either incapable or deficient in the power of self-government; they are mostly destitute, and will require much nursing towards economic and political independence.' Poles and Finns would have little difficulty, but it would take longer in the Middle East. The British supported mandates, which would avoid antagonising the Americans; they could then suggest that they take over the onerous responsibility under minimal supervision by the League.[117] However, the French were angry because they would not be allowed to raise soldiers in any mandate that they might receive, important to them because their population and birthrate were lower than Germany's, while South Africa, Australia and New Zealand wanted annexations pure and simple. Wilson, however, refused to budge on this particular point. Smuts and his colleague on the League Commission, Lord Robert Cecil, came up with a proposal which was eventually accepted. There would be three types of mandates: 'A' for nations, such as those in the Middle East, which were close to self-government; 'B' for nations which would be administered by the country which had the mandate; and 'C' for territories which were next, or close, to the mandatory power, which would essentially run the territory as part of its own country – almost indistinguishable from annexation.[118]

And who was to get what in the Middle East? Wilson had resisted the allocation of the mandates, and only relented on 6 May 1919. On the following day, just before the Germans received the draft treaty, the US, Great Britain, France and Italy accepted Lloyd George's proposals for the distribution of the mandates. (Arnold Toynbee, a member the British Political Intelligence Directorate, 'one day had to hand some papers to Lloyd George after the close of some meeting on Middle Eastern affairs' and 'when he had taken the papers and started to scan them, Lloyd George, to my delight, had forgotten my presence and began to think aloud. "Mesopotamia ... yes ... oil ... irrigation ... we must have Mesopotamia; Palestine ... yes ... the Holy Land ... Zionism ... we must have Palestine; Syria ... h'm ... what is there in Syria? Let the French have that."' Lloyd George had left out the rights and wishes of the Arabs themselves.'[119]) The British concerns were, as before, the security of the Suez Canal and of the routes to India, the restriction of Russian access to the Mediterranean, thereby limiting its opportunities for gaining influence in the region, the ability to control the supplies of oil in Mesopotamia and Persia, and the prestige of controlling the Holy Land. Indeed, at the end of the war, the ambitions of the British had blossomed, and they even proposed abolishing the Sykes–Picot Agreement with the French. The French reacted with ferocity and the British retreated, but Anglo-French relations were by now abysmally low, with Clemenceau actually threatening Lloyd George with a duel.[120]

Decisions were taken in April 1920 at the San Remo conference and then forced upon the Turks by means of the Treaty of Sèvres in August. The situation was that the collapse of Turkey had been so complete that, according to Harold Nicolson, a member of the Foreign Office who took part in the conference, 'The Ottoman Empire lay at our feet dismembered and impotent, its capital and Caliph at the mercy of our guns.'[121] The Turks were to lose all of their Arabian territories. Nevertheless, Feisal did not receive, as promised by the British, control of an independent Arab nation; rather, he reluctantly agreed to accept the throne of an independent Greater Syria, while his brother Abdulla was offered the kingship of an independent Iraq (from the former Turkish territory of Mesopotamia), but he preferred Jordan. Not surprisingly, this 'independence' was limited: France received Syria and the Lebanon as mandates, while mandates for Mesopotamia and Palestine went to Great Britain (they were not, however, sanctioned by the League until July 1922). Indeed, the tide of Arab nationalism forced Feisal to fight the French, the outcome of which was the decisive defeat of the Arabs and the fleeing of Feisal in July 1920. Furthermore, concurrently with the signing of the treaty at Sèvres in August, the British, French and Italian governments settled a 'Tripartite Agreement', by means of which Anatolia, the heartland and core of Turkey, was to be partitioned between France and Italy. Although the Sultan signed the treaty, he did not dare to ratify it.[122]

Indeed, it was never ratified, but was superseded by the Treaty of Lausanne in July 1923; there was some urgency on the part of the Turks, because they wanted to get foreign soldiers out of their capital. By this time, the dynamics of power had entirely changed. The British military presence in the Middle East had ebbed away and the nationalist revolt led by Mustafa Kemal, or Atatürk, had revitalised Turkey and led to a resurgence of pride and strength, which was enhanced by the Turks' defeat in 1922 of Greece's attempt (backed by the British) to carve out its own sphere in Turkey. The Treaty of Lausanne reflected the changed reality. 'Hitherto we have dictated our peace treaties,' Foreign Secretary Curzon reflected. 'Now we are negotiating one with the enemy who has an army in being while we have none, an unheard of position.'[123] The crippling terms of Sèvres almost entirely disappeared: there was now no independent Armenia or Kurdistan, virtually all of the Turkish-speaking territories were gathered within Turkey's borders, the Straits remained Turkish, although it was now an international waterway, and there was a massive transfer of Muslim populations in exchange for Christian. Turkey was the only Central Power to have negotiated a treaty with the Allies, rather than having one imposed on it, and this is still apparently seen in Turkey as modern Turkey's greatest diplomatic victory.[124]

In this multiple collapse of empires, comparing the expectations of the British and the Americans is illuminating. The British are normally condemned for acting as empires tend to do, which is to expand by incorporating new territory. The US tends to be let off more lightly, in that rather than wishing to incorporate foreign territories into a growing American territorial empire, Wilson wanted to incorporate them into an American economic and cultural empire: they would benefit by throwing off their existing imperial chains and assuming the much lighter American ones. Of course, self-determination is much better for a people than being controlled by another, but the question could be tentatively asked, how wholly free was the freedom which the Americans intended to delimit? Yet the inspiration of the whole idea of self-determination cannot be denied.

Wilsonianism was part of an American tradition: the idea of the US as the beacon of mankind, as the leader to a more promising human condition, dates from the earliest days of the settlement of the American colonies. What was different in 1919 was the anticipation that the power of the US would enable Wilsonianism in all of its manifestations to be implemented. But it was not to be imposed by weapons: rather, the force of world public opinion would oblige the leaders at the peace conference to accept it. The self-determination of subject peoples was for many the most important of the Fourteen Points. And yet Wilson himself believed that self-determination should apply only to Europeans. Colonial peoples in the rest of the world, such as in the Middle East, needed guidance by the mandatory powers. Wilson, writes William Roger Louis, 'belonged to the tradition of colonial reform, not liberation'. It was the duty of the European Powers to guide the colonies in their political, economic and social development. Over a period of decades, or centuries, these peoples might gain the maturity which would enable them to stand on their own. Self-determination would, probably, be the eventual result.[125]

Even within the Wilsonian context, Great Britain emerged from the war in some triumph. It now had a larger Middle Eastern empire, plus the new African colonies, to join with the empire as it had stood in 1914. Yet within half a century, 'imperial over-stretch' led it to breaking point, and the empire became one with Nineveh and Tyre. As for the US, its policy remained, *mutatis mutandis*, one of putting pressure on Britain to withdraw from the empire, at least when it did not itself want to use its strategic advantages. Nor would the US cease to try to force Britain to accept parity between the Royal Navy and the US Navy, a conflict that would dominate Anglo-American relations for over a decade after the war.

VIII

A statement written in November 1901 by Lord Selborne, First Lord of the Admiralty, neatly summed up the problem for the government both then and nearly twenty years later: Great Britain's 'Credit and its Navy [are] the two main pillars on which the strength of this country rests, and each is essential to the other. Unless our financial position is strong, the Navy cannot be maintained. Unless the Navy is fully adequate for any call which may be made upon it, our national Credit must stand in jeopardy.'[126] And unless the Royal Navy was maintained, the British empire and even the safety of the realm would be at risk. During the inter-war period, both seemed under attack by the US, and Britain, having lost its position of financial predominance over the US as a result of the Great War, was also forced to surrender naval supremacy and agree to formal parity.

The growing naval rivalry between the two countries, which in one historian's phrase caused 'the worst level of Anglo-American hostility in the twentieth century',[127] was of supreme importance to Britain and only slightly less so to the US, which had fewer global interests but a widespread desire for its navy to reflect its new-found international status. The US also needed to be able to defend itself against an enemy in war, and for much of the 1920s the US Navy, in which Anglophobia was rife, thought that the enemy might be Britain. The Royal Navy, which had ended the war as still the greatest navy in the world, obviously wanted to retain that position, but there was an almost insuperable obstacle: lack of money. Even the First Lord of the Admiralty, Walter Long, admitted that if the Americans 'chose to put all their resources into the provision of a larger Navy the competition between us would be impossible, and we should in the end be beaten from the point of view merely of finance'.[128] But even if Britain was being 'beaten', on realpolitik grounds this was just about acceptable, because the assumption continued to be that the US was not a threat. The Cabinet was acutely concerned about the huge sum of government short-term debt needing to be repaid,[129] and about the costs of reconversion to a peacetime economy, and, therefore, to the dismay of many within and without the Royal Navy, decided on a one-power standard in battleships and battle cruisers with the US – that is, parity between the navies – thereby overturning a policy of decades.[130]

At the end of the war, the US was engaged on a vast building programme. In December 1918, Wilson emphasised his challenge to British naval supremacy in the Atlantic and Japanese naval supremacy in the Western Pacific, and to the British refusal to agree to 'freedom of the seas', by convincing Congress to pass the 1918 Army and Navy Act. The intent was to double the number of capital ships to forty-four battleships and sixteen battle cruisers, thereby planning for a total of over 800 modern combat ships.[131] In 1921, the new and powerful Secretary of State, Charles Evans Hughes, saw this fleet as a means to end the Anglo-Japanese Alliance, rather than purely as a way to challenge British naval supremacy. He feared that the Japanese were becoming increasingly hostile towards the US, and that the continued existence of this alliance would encourage them to mount a challenge. His strategy was to use a conference to lessen Britain's apprehension of American plans and thereby talk it into refusing to renew the alliance. Thus, on 11 July 1921, the new Republican President, Warren G. Harding, invited Britain, France, Japan and Italy to a conference in Washington to discuss arms control and security issues in the Pacific. The British Cabinet agreed. The country was in the midst of a severe depression and wished to reduce expenditure, and besides, it would be unwise to antagonise the US, but at the same time ministers authorised another four battle cruisers, which would either be built or used as bargaining chips at the conference.[132] As for the Japanese, between 1917 and 1921 they had tripled their naval budget, and post-war maintenance costs alone would soon claim almost one-third of Japan's annual budget.[133] They, too, were agreeable.

The Conference on Limitation of Armaments, or simply the Washington Conference, opened on 12 November 1921. The British had assumed that the Americans would not be prepared: stunned, they discovered that they were. As Theodore Roosevelt Jr, the Assistant Secretary of the Navy, noted in his diary, 'The plan is to spring everything, including our definite naval program on the opening day,'[134] and they did. In his opening speech Hughes, 'in a skilful and dramatic way ... led up to his main proposals', which were that the US would scrap every capital ship laid down as part of the 1916 building programme; that the British and Japanese would have to stop all capital-ship construction and scrap a large number of older vessels; and that they would all stabilise their capital-ship strengths in a ratio of 5: 5: 3, with Japan being the 3. He suggested that the way to keep this balance was to institute a capital-shipbuilding holiday for ten years and then to regulate subsequent building. The British government had already in 1919 agreed on the so-called 'ten-year rule', which was based on the assumption that 'the British Empire will not be engaged in any great war during the next ten years, and that no Expeditionary Force is required for that purpose', in an attempt to cut defence expenditure,[135] and thus its response was to accept the plan with regard to capital ships and the ratio (the so-called 'Rolls-Royce: Rolls-Royce: Ford' ratio). But Lord Balfour, the head of the British delegation, stressed in his speech the following day Britain's need for cruisers and destroyers. For their part, the Japanese naturally wanted a higher ratio.[136]

Negotiations over the subsequent months modified the proposals, although the result, as set out in the Washington Naval Treaty of February 1922, adhered to the capital-ship ratio, which became 5: 5: 3: 1.75: 1.75, with France and Italy filling the final two slots. Great Britain, however, with memories of the war still fresh, absolutely refused to accept a severe limitation on cruisers, a significant number of which were needed for the defence of its trade and sea communications and, if need be, to maintain a blockade. The American administration, unwilling to wreck the conference and happy to have achieved at least some measure of success in a naval agreement with Britain, agreed. The bottom line for the Americans, however, for which they were willing to sacrifice a stronger limitation on ships, was the abrogation of the Anglo-Japanese Treaty. This would be a real concession by Britain, because the Cabinet, on balance, wanted to keep it, as it provided a check on Japan, and relieved Britain of some responsibility for patrolling the Far East. Britain had initially proposed the renewal of the Alliance, but the leader of the Japanese delegation, Navy Minister Admiral Shidehara Kijūrō, suggested adding the US to the Alliance because he believed, rightly, that the US would oppose any extension of it. Hughes suggested that the agreement include France but not apply to China. A Four-Power Treaty linking the US, Britain, Japan and France was substituted, which provided for mutual consultation over regional security issues, and which stipulated that the Anglo-Japanese Alliance would end with the ratification of the new treaty. Usefully for Japan, it specified that the US and Britain would maintain no fortifications west of Hawaii or east of Singapore; the accord in effect 'gave the Japanese Navy parity in East Asian waters with fleets that the Anglo-American powers could station on the perimeter of the Pacific'.[137] It was signed in December 1921. (In total, the conference gave birth to nine treaties and twelve resolutions.) The limitation on capital ships, of course, stimulated the building of non-ratio ships, particularly cruisers, destroyers and submarines, but also aircraft carriers. For the US and Britain, it imposed a temporary check on their naval rivalry, although it must be said that the US Navy continued to see Britain and its empire as a potential foe and by far the most formidable. Nevertheless, according to the Foreign Office, the outcome of the conference contributed to a 'curve of good feeling between the countries'.[138] Unfortunately, just over five years later, it was crushed.

Calvin Coolidge, the Vice-President, became President on 2 August 1923 after President Warren G. Harding suffered a fatal heart attack. One of his first announcements was to declare his support for arms control, although it is not clear whether this was for moral reasons or because he was arguably the most parsimonious President that the US has ever had. On 10 February 1927, he invited the British, French, Italians and Japanese to a disarmament conference in Geneva, with the intention of applying the capital-ships ratio to cruisers and other auxiliary vessels.

The British reaction was cautious, especially the Admiralty, which was acutely conscious about the British reliance on trade. There were two main factors here. First of all, by 1927 Great Britain had recovered its dominance in shipping: its merchant shipping tonnage was almost twice that of the US and constituted more than one-third of the world's total.[139] But importantly, it was the world's largest importer, especially of food and oil; Britain was vulnerable to a blockade, as had been demonstrated during the First World War, when German submarines had been slowly strangling it. Thus the Admiralty wanted a greater number of cruisers than the Americans might desire that Britain possess or that they believed that it actually needed. The Admiralty distinguished between two types of cruiser, and this distinction was crucial in the conflict that ensued. The first was the 'Washington class', built up to the Washington Treaty's 10,000-ton limit and armed with eight-inch guns, which were ideal for fleet work, and which the Admiralty was willing to see fall within the 5: 5: 3 ratio; the second were those of less than 7,500 tons, with guns of six inches or less, which were ideal for commerce protection and blockade duties, being small and fast. The Admiralty wanted few restrictions on numbers of the smaller class.

Members of the Cabinet, however, did not agree on their approach to the conference. The delegation was led by Lord Robert Cecil, who was committed to the arms-control process – he had been an early and fervent supporter of the League of Nations – and by William Bridgeman, the First Lord of the Admiralty, a man of frequent indecision. Austen Chamberlain, the Foreign Secretary, admitted that he knew very little about the conference issues, while Winston Churchill, the Chancellor of the Exchequer, was determined to reassert the supremacy of the

Royal Navy. Prime Minister Stanley Baldwin hardly knew what he wanted.[140]

The conference officially opened on 20 July 1927. The Coolidge administration assumed that, because Great Britain had agreed to parity of capital ships, it would recognise America's right to parity in all ships, and if not, Washington could use 'America's enormous latent power to compel the British to recognize America's right to equality'. This would not be the case. Essentially, the Americans wanted fewer but bigger cruisers, while the British wanted more but smaller. The US did not have to protect thousands of miles of trade routes, as the British did; conversely, lacking the British network of naval bases around the world where they could refuel and take on supplies, the Americans wanted cruisers which could sail longer distances in case of, say, war with Japan. What was really at issue was the traditional conflict between the British intention to maintain the Royal Navy's ability to enforce belligerent rights versus the American desire to maintain neutral trading rights in time of war. Thus they could not agree on cruiser limitation.[141]

Early in the negotiations, the British government had supported its two delegates in stating to the Americans that Britain did not question their right to naval parity. Churchill, however, objected strongly, writing in June 1927 that 'It always seems to be assumed that it is our duty to humour the United States and minister to their vanity. They do nothing for us in return, but exact their last pound of flesh.'[142] He saw the conference as Britain's last chance to assert 'strategic independence' from the US, and even proposed the rejuvenation of the Anglo-Japanese Alliance. He convinced the rest of the Cabinet that they could not agree to parity, and when Bridgeman and Cecil returned to Geneva on 28 July they informed the Americans of this. The Americans immediately rejected the British proposals, and on 4 August the conference broke up in anger.

For some time all trust between the two countries was dead. Insults flew: the British Foreign Secretary called the head of the American delegation a 'dirty dog', while the US Secretary of State accused the British of going back on their word and told

Coolidge that there was no point negotiating with them. Cecil accused Churchill of causing the break, and the latter certainly welcomed the collapse of the conference. Bridgeman seems not to have fully understood what had happened. But he blamed the Americans for the breakdown, saying that they had not prepared, and in any case they had very little knowledge of cruiser limitation. Indeed (he wrote in his diary),

> The real object with which they came was to try to get 'parity' on the cheap by forcing us to give up the numbers we require for security, and also to prevent us from intercepting contraband in wartime. They hoped to get a good election cry for Coolidge by saying they had not only made a further peace move, but also twisted the British Lion's tail by making him reduce his cruiser strength. If they could have got their own proposals [for example, for parity] agreed to as they stood, they would have settled, but I much doubt if they ever meant to agree to any other terms.[143]

His analysis was not far off the mark.

The US Navy and the 'big navy party' were delighted by the breakdown, because they now had presidential support for a huge new building programme, with Coolidge asking Congress for seventy-one new cruisers, including twenty-five of the Washington class; in March 1928 Congress authorised fifteen of the latter, the largest authorisation since the end of the war. Churchill had assumed that Congress would not agree to this, but he had failed to anticipate the depth of American anger at the British manoeuvres. There was an attempted Anglo-French compromise, but the Americans by now were so antagonistic towards and suspicious of the British that the unanimous view of the White House and the State and Navy departments was that the compromise was 'sneaky and self-serving'. On Armistice Day, 11 November 1928, Coolidge publicly condemned the British and called for American naval superiority.[144]

The British government reeled. Robert Craigie, former First Secretary at the British Embassy in Washington and now the head of the American Department at the Foreign Office,[145] wrote a magisterial memorandum on Anglo-American relations which was circulated to the Cabinet the following week. His opening sentence established the problem: 'It is probably safe to say that at no time since 1920 have Anglo-American relations been in so unsatisfactory a state as at the present moment.' He then reminded the Cabinet of some home truths, and the need to maintain good relations with the US, given their relative strengths:

> Great Britain is faced in the United States of America with a phenomenon for which there is no parallel in our modern history – a State twenty-five times as large, five times as wealthy, three times as populous, twice as ambitious, almost invulnerable, and at least our equal in prosperity, vital energy, technical equipment and industrial science. This State has risen to its present state of development at a time when Great Britain is still staggering from the effects of the superhuman effort made during the war [it had suffered nearly a million casualties, 15 per cent of its total wealth and its financial supremacy], is loaded with a great burden of debt [in 1928, 40 per cent of public expenditure was used to pay interest on wartime debts and to repay capital] and is crippled by the evil of unemployment. The interests of the two countries touch at almost every point, for our contacts with the United States – political and economic, by land and sea, commercial and financial – are closer and more numerous than those existing with any other foreign State.

He agreed that dealing with the US was frustrating, but 'in almost every field, the advantages derived from mutual co-operation are greater for us than for them'. In summary, Great Britain needed to spend a good deal of time and effort in sorting out the causes of Anglo-American antagonism because, he pointed out starkly, 'war is *not* unthinkable between the two countries. On the contrary, there are present all the factors which in the past have made for wars between States.'[146]

The Cabinet took the point, and although Churchill spat and thrashed about – Coolidge was a 'New England backwoodsman' who would 'soon sink back into the obscurity from which only accident extracted him' – his dangerous lack of judgement had been fully exposed. The main hope now was that the US would again fail to build all of the authorised ships (it did fail). Prime Minister Baldwin decided that he should make a visit to the US and began dropping hints; unfortunately, he lost the 1929 general election, and it was Prime Minister Ramsay MacDonald who would visit from 4 to 10 October 1929. By that time, both sides were eager to settle the naval question. President Herbert Hoover had come up with the 'yardstick' proposal: instead of using gross tonnage to establish cruiser parity, he suggested letting the newer and more powerful American ships count for more than an equal tonnage of Britain's older and smaller ships. As a result the Royal Navy would have a higher cruiser tonnage allowance but older ships. MacDonald was quick to agree to the yardstick proposal, and, to make coming to an agreement easier, he also offered to reduce from seventy to fifty the number of cruisers to be built.[147] MacDonald's visit was extremely significant beyond settling the cruiser question: this was the first visit by either head of government to the other's country, and the Atlantic voyage was from east to west.

The US Navy did not share the view of the President and the Secretary of State, Henry Stimson, that war between the two countries was unthinkable, and worked hard to prevent any lowering of the number of cruisers to be built. Its influence, however, along with that of the big navy party, was lessening, given the lack of 'crucial anti-British oxygen'. The London Naval Conference opened on 21 June 1930. This time, however, things were very different from 1927 – importantly, a great deal of preparation had been done beforehand. The key was the cruiser yardstick: the US was allowed 323,000 tons and up to eighteen Washington-class cruisers, while the British got 339,000 tons but had to stop at fifteen of the big cruisers. The two sides also agreed on parity for submarines and destroyers. The result was the end of twelve years of intense naval rivalry. Japan, however, was kept in a distinctly inferior position. Japanese nationalists were incensed,[148] with unhappy consequences with which the US and

Britain would shortly have to deal, but the two found it almost impossible during the 1930s to agree on what to do. Furthermore, the Anglo-American naval rivalry seared the memories of many in the US Navy, and during the next war their distrust of Britain was intense, with significant influence on the conduct of the war in the Pacific.

IX

Relations between the US and Britain during the 1930s were frequently difficult and bad-tempered. A fundamental reason was that the US wanted to be a Great Power, with the attendant respect and deference, but declined to take on the international responsibilities of such a position. For a country to be a Great Power, two things are required: it must have the necessary financial and economic resources and it must possess a sustained will to power. The US had the resources, but emphatically lacked the will, as would be demonstrated in the Far East. It also wrapped itself in a complex isolationism. It left European affairs to the Europeans, regardless of what was happening there; on the other hand, it was relentlessly interventionist in Central America. The Far East was a curious combination: the US was very involved with trade in China and, to a lesser extent, in Japan – why else colonise the Philippines? – but it more than once refused to become involved with events in the region.

What was holding it back? It was, of course, experiencing a Depression that was so deep that the word was capitalised, but that was not the main reason for its lack of involvement abroad. First of all, there was its abundance of natural resources and its geographical isolation: with weak powers both north and south of the country and oceanic moats east and west, it did not feel threatened enough to encourage adventures abroad. They might contaminate the US and its people and damage what made America great. Rather than go abroad, they raised tariffs hugely to keep foreign goods out and raised the fence against immigration to keep foreigners out. An overwhelmingly important reason for its isolationist policy was the conviction held by many that becoming involved in the Great War had been a bad mistake. So: stay at home and pull up the drawbridge, and let the world – except for Central America – take care of itself without American involvement.[149]

For Great Britain, relations with the US were difficult because of the combination of contempt and despair at the latter's inaction. Britain had myriad responsibilities but declining resources to carry them out, and the US evaded what Britain saw as the obligations of power. Britain's economic situation was such that it could no longer, after September 1931, keep the pound on the gold standard – the former symbol of its economic and international power. The floating of the pound stimulated economic growth, but the tax base was still not large enough to support the military forces necessary to fulfil its responsibilities and defend its national interests. It was too close to Europe to ignore the Franco-German conflict and the rise of Hitler; the Suez Canal was too important to its empire to ignore the rise of Mussolini; and in the Far East Britain had extensive economic interests in China, a number of colonies (such as Burma, Singapore, Malaya, North Borneo and Papua New Guinea), a number of Pacific islands and the antipodean Dominions (Australia and New Zealand), all of which relied on the Royal Navy for protection. As the 1930s rolled past, it was increasingly faced with the alarming prospect of fighting a three-front war: Germany in Europe, Italy in the Mediterranean and Japan in the Far East. To its intense frustration, it could not seem to convince the Americans that their interests were also involved, that a global war could engulf them as well, and that they ought to help to prevent it. But Britain also tended to conflate its imperial interests with those of the rest of the right-thinking world, as the US itself would frequently do after 1945, and therefore it could not understand that, as far as the US was concerned, Britain just wanted help in maintaining its empire. This was out of the question.

The most important region in the 1930s for the relationship of the two empires was the Far East. The US was hardly in the same imperial league as Britain, but it possessed the Hawaiian Islands, Guam, part of Samoa and the Philippines, as well as extensive and long-standing commercial interests in China and elsewhere in the region. Nevertheless, it was an episode in the Far East that convinced many British policymakers that, in a foreign crisis, the US was worse than useless. This was the 1931 Manchurian Crisis.

On 18 September 1931, violence planned by the Japanese Army erupted in Manchuria. The Japanese Kwantung Army, a private force which guarded the Japanese-owned railways in Manchuria, blew up a few feet of track on the South Manchurian Railway near Mukden, and engaged in skirmishes with troops loyal to the local Chinese warlord, who in turn owed fealty to China's leader, Chiang Kai-shek. Regular Japanese troops were then sent from their colony in Korea, and by mid-October they controlled most of the Manchurian railway system and were fanning out to conquer the remainder of the province, which was part of China. The Japanese had thereby violated the Nine-Power Treaty (one of the Washington treaties), which guaranteed the integrity of China, as well as the Covenant of the League of Nations, of which they were a member. On 21 September China desperately appealed to the League, the members of which had agreed to the principle of collective security: if one member was attacked, the others would come to its aid. The Council in Geneva met, and urged both sides to cease fighting. Shortly afterwards, China also appealed to the US.

Great Britain was in the midst of a financial and associated political crisis: the very day of the Chinese appeal, it went off the gold standard. But even had it not been in crisis, it could have done little. As the Permanent Under-Secretary at the Foreign Office, Robert Vansittart, wrote in February 1932, 'We are incapable of checking Japan in any way if she really means business and has sized us up, as she certainly has done. Therefore we must eventually be done for in the Far East unless the United States are eventually prepared to use force.'[150] In any case, British public opinion was broadly pro-Japanese and, furthermore, some British officials thought that the Chinese had behaved so badly that it was not surprising that the Japanese had reacted violently. Certainly the Foreign Secretary, Sir John Simon, was seen as pro-Japanese. In mid-November 1931, when the Cabinet met to consider the options, its decision was that Britain could not provide military forces, and thus the only alternative was to conciliate the Japanese.[151]

Over in the US, Secretary of State Henry Stimson's first inclination was to act, but he was prevented from doing so by President Hoover, who was acutely aware of the support for isolationism. Although he thought that the US had to do something 'to uphold the moral foundations of international life', he would not even agree to economic sanctions through fear that they would lead to war. The US, of course, was not a member of the League of Nations, the Senate, against Wilson's wish, having failed to ratify the Treaty of Versailles, and thus was not bound by any of their decisions. Nevertheless, when the Council of the League met in November and December, Stimson sent the banker Charles G. Dawes, but Hoover would not allow him to join in the discussions, for fear of outraging the isolationists in Congress. Instead, he 'simply paced the lobby to show American solidarity with the League'.[152] This did not advance matters very far. American policy appeared so unfocused and lame that Stanley Baldwin, once and future Prime Minister but at that point Lord President of the Council, burst out to a friend: 'You will get nothing out of Washington but words, big words, but only words.'[153]

As it happened, Stimson was about to provide some words, but they had no impact at all. What he came up with became known as the Doctrine of Nonrecognition, or simply as the Stimson Doctrine. The key phrase was that the US 'did not intend to recognize any situation, treaty or agreement which may be brought about by means contrary to the Pact of Paris', that is, by armed aggression. On 7 January, the Doctrine was delivered to the Japanese. It contained tough words, but no action to follow it up, and the Japanese pretty well ignored it. Vansittart's assessment in the Foreign Office on 1 February was that 'It is universally assumed that the US will never use force.'[154] It was this episode as much as anything which convinced many British foreign policymakers that it would be prudent to work on the assumption that the US would shy away from standing up to the Japanese. They were correct. Very soon Japanese troops were landing in Shanghai, where both the US and Great Britain had extensive interests. Six per cent of British foreign investment was in China, with three-fifths of this in Shanghai, then Asia's greatest seaport.[155] On 5 February 1932, US and Royal Navy warships arrived to help to defend the International Settlement, which included 25,000 to 30,000 women and children. But the Japanese took the city in a bloody attack, and the British and the Americans restricted themselves to rescuing the foreign nationals. By March the conquest was complete, and a puppet government declared the independence of Manchukuo (Manchu-land).

For the remainder of the 1930s, American attention was primarily focused on domestic policy. In June 1921, Lord Curzon had commented that 'Official relations with the American Government almost ceased to exist, and for ten months we practically did no business with America at all,'[156] and although the Anglo-American relationship did not wither quite so much in the 1930s, nevertheless it was episodic, with relatively little sympathy between the two. Britain was increasingly focused on Europe, in which the US was little interested; the US was focused on protecting itself from involvement in any future war. Even the *Panay* crisis of December 1937, when a Japanese aeroplane flying along the Yangtze River in China attacked an American ship and shot its passengers in the water as they were trying to escape, at the same time as Japanese shore batteries shelled two Royal Navy riverboats, failed to lure the US government into action. Washington had had to be torpedoed into the First World War by Germany; it would require Japanese bombs and torpedoes to kick it into confronting Japan in the Second.

X

The Anglo-American relationship during the Second World War, while by general agreement the closest and most successful wartime alliance in history, was nevertheless bedevilled by widespread and apparently ineradicable American suspicions of British motives. It is, however, important to disentangle the imperial strand from the general story of Anglo-American relations during the war. The US in broad terms utilised its financial strength and military power to force the acquiescence of Britain to policies that had as their intention the post-war weakening of Britain and of its hold on its empire. It was undoubtedly the case, for example, that Henry Morgenthau, the Secretary of the Treasury, determined to weaken drastically Britain's financial power in order that the latter could not obstruct the Treasury's post-war plans: to supplant Britain as the most important global financial power and to gather unto Washington significant control over international finance. It is obvious the effect this would have on Britain's ability to act as an imperial power, but Morgenthau's intention was not specifically to attack the empire. Fundamentally, the United States from the beginning set out to replace Britain as the pre-eminent global power. Some parts of the military services, such as the General Board of the Navy, were in fact quite predatory about the matter (see below).

President Franklin Roosevelt, although he strongly believed that it was necessary to sustain Britain in the war, was, nevertheless, most likely something of an Anglophobe – or, at least, an empirephobe. According to Roosevelt's son Elliott in his book *As He Saw It* (1946), the President believed that the future threat to world peace came not from Russia, but from the European colonial powers: 'His thoughts turned to the problem of the colonies and the colonial markets, the problem which he felt was at the core of all chances for future peace. "The thing is", he remarked thoughtfully, replacing a smoked cigarette in his holder with a fresh one, "the colonial system means war.'"[157] Great Britain was the worst.[158] ' "The British", Roosevelt told Churchill, "would take land anywhere in the world even if it were only a rock or a sand bar.'"[159] On the other hand, Elliott wrote, 'I wagged my head, thinking about how well Stalin and father got along, thinking about the identity of interests that we apparently had.'[160] According to Elliott, Roosevelt had a consistent and detailed suspicion of British 'perfidy', and considered Churchill, now Prime

Minister, a 'combined buffoon and villain', who schemed to turn the Americans away from fighting Germany to fighting Russia[161] (on the face of it a curious suspicion).

Roosevelt was in line with US public opinion. Famously, in the 12 October 1942 issue of the American *Life* magazine, the editors addressed an 'Open Letter' to the 'People of England'. Americans, they wrote, still lacked a consensus on war aims, but 'one thing we are sure we are *not* fighting for is to hold the British Empire together. We don't like to put the matter so bluntly, but we don't want you to have any illusions. If your strategists are planning a war to hold the British Empire together they will sooner or later find themselves strategizing all alone.' They then 'entreated the British to forsake "Your side of the war", which included imperialism, and join "Our Side", which meant the side fighting for freedom throughout the world'. So, goodbye British empire. Equally famously, Churchill made his response in a speech at the Mansion House in London a month later on 10 November. He denied that the British wanted to acquire any more colonial territories, and then continued: 'Let me, however, make this clear, in case there should be any mistake about it in any quarter. We mean to hold our own. I have not become the King's First Minister in order to preside over the liquidation of the British Empire.'[162] Churchill's rhetoric was rather over the top, but he was presumably reacting to the self-righteousness of the editors of *Life*. His words, however, shocked many Britons as well as Americans, failing, as he did, to convey the responsibility which many imperialists felt towards the colonies, but sounding dismayingly reactionary. Moreover, there were Britons who believed that Britain should indeed give up its colonies. Churchill undoubtedly celebrated his own clarion call, but it advanced matters very little, and did positive harm.

During the war, Roosevelt repeatedly attempted to convince the UK to give up territories, particularly Hong Kong and India. The concern about Hong Kong, a major issue between Churchill and Roosevelt, arose primarily because of the President's plan that China would soon again be a Power and would help the US, the USSR and Great Britain to police the world; if Britain still held Hong Kong, it would jeopardise relations with China. He proposed that it be returned to the Chinese, provided that they designated it a free port.[163] (Churchill, on the other hand, thought that China had neither the cohesion nor the military force to be ranked as a Great Power, and was likely to lapse into civil war. He thought that the US was assuming that China would be its puppet.)

It was India, however, that rapidly became the 'major irritant' in the wartime partnership. In April 1941, the British requested that an Indian officer with the title 'agent general for India' be attached to their Washington Embassy; the Americans leapt at the opportunity and demanded as their price that the US be allowed to send a commissioner to New Delhi. The British were forced to agree. Kenyon J. Clymer argues that this was what 'precipitated increased official American interest in Indian matters', and, for the first time, the US 'considered pressuring the British to settle the Indian problem'.[164] It also meant that the US had official diplomatic relations with the government of India. Thereafter they insisted that Lend-Lease for India be sent directly to the Indian government rather than through London, and Roosevelt insisted that the government of India itself sign the 1942 Declaration of the United Nations, which bound the twenty signatories to making the maximum war effort and prevented them from making a separate peace with Germany, Italy or Japan. When the two leaders met for the first time as fellow belligerents in January 1942, Roosevelt pointedly suggested that Churchill pledge support for eventual Indian independence, adding that he had given 'much thought' to the country since it was 'an untenable burden' to Britain, and suggested a transitional government, setting out its structures and duties. 'The infuriated Prime Minister did not reply.'[165] Both attempts at 'guiding' British policy failed.

But what was successful was the use of American financial power to force the UK finally to surrender weapons which it had used to protect both its home islands and the empire, forcing it to accept 'freedom of the seas' and restrictions on its financial policies, including insisting on the pound resuming convertibility, and also to force the elimination of imperial preference, the ability of the constituent parts of the British empire to impose tariffs against other countries, while providing preferential tariffs for each other. Woodrow Wilson had told his confidant Colonel House in July 1917 that 'England and France have not the same views with regard to peace that we have by any means. When the war is over we can force them to our way of thinking, because by that time they will, among other things, be financially in our hands.'[166] It did not work then, but it certainly worked during and immediately after the Second World War.

It is notable that it was in 1941, while the US was still a neutral, that it managed to pin Great Britain down and force it to accept long-standing American desires – which soon became requirements – in exchange for American support and aid. Although the Lend-Lease Act was passed in March 1941, the detailed negotiations did not end until February 1942, and it was the Atlantic Charter of August 1941 that first set out the American vision of the post-war world. On 9 August, at Roosevelt's suggestion, he and Churchill met at Placentia Bay off the coast of Newfoundland. A number of Roosevelt's advisers feared that Britain and the Soviet Union would come to an agreement that would trade Soviet help against the Germans both during and after the war for British agreement to Soviet territorial gains in Eastern Europe.[167] (As it happens, the situation was the reverse: Churchill feared the power of a USSR unconstrained by a defeated Germany, as shown by his 'iron curtain' speech in Fulton, Missouri on 5 March 1946.) There was also the desire to tie Britain down to Wilsonian principles, such as self-determination. And there was the simple wish to meet and see how they worked together.

With HMS *Prince of Wales* nestled cosily next to the USS *Augusta*, Roosevelt and Churchill and their aides spent three days in discussions. Churchill wanted a declaration of war; Roosevelt demurred. Instead, the outcome was the Atlantic Charter, which was initiated by Roosevelt but drafted in the first instance by Sir Alexander Cadogan, the Permanent Under-Secretary to the Foreign Office.[168] The Charter promised a post-war world suffused with and dominated by the principles of self-determination,[169] non-aggression,[170] free trade[171] and the freedom of the seas.[172] It was no accident that the final two were principles which the US had been trying to force on Great Britain for a century and a half, while the first was a premier Wilsonian principle. The Atlantic Charter was a joint Anglo-American declaration of war aims; of course, it was not as welcome to the British, or as useful, as a declaration of war would have been, but it publicly tied the still-neutral US more closely to Britain.

What shackled Britain to the American requirements was the Master Lend-Lease Agreement, signed in February 1942 after eleven months' negotiations and after the US had entered the war. By the spring of 1941, Britain had been at war for eighteen months and was running out of funds to pay for vital supplies. Roosevelt had won re-election on 5 November 1940, and the hope was that he would now feel safe enough to respond positively to British arguments. Urged by Lord Lothian, the British Ambassador to the US, Churchill wrote a letter to Roosevelt which asked for help, according to one of Churchill's private secretaries, 'above all in buying munitions and aircraft on credit. It is intended to make R. feel that if we go down, the responsibility will be America's.'[173] On 9 December, Roosevelt received the letter. According to Harry Hopkins, Roosevelt's aide and confidant, the President 'read and re-read the letter and for about two days seemed unsure about what to do ... Then the following day he came up with the Lend-Lease idea.' His Treasury Secretary, Morgenthau, wrote in his diary that the President had told him that 'I have been thinking very hard on this trip about what we should do for England, and it seems to me that the thing to do is to get away from a dollar sign.'[174] There were to be no more war debts of the type that had poisoned Anglo-American relations in the early 1920s.

Nevertheless, there had to be some recompense – Congress would never agree to the scheme otherwise. Negotiations took almost a year, with the stumbling block being the question of the 'Consideration'. Countries receiving aid had to agree not to use Lend-Lease goods 'to enable their exporters to enter new markets or to extend their export trade at the expense of the United States exporters', nor could scarce materials of any kind be used to manu-facture goods for export. In other words, the Americans were deeply suspicious that Britain would take advantage of American generosity to safeguard or to expand its commercial interests at the expense of American business. Therefore, the British had to mortgage their future.[175]

Where London baulked, however, was at the American demand that Britain agree (in Article VII) to the prohibition of discrimination in either country against any product originating in the other. In other words, Britain would be required to abandon imperial preference, by which members of the British empire and Commonwealth set agreed preferential tariffs, and the Sterling Area. (The Sterling Area was a group of countries which, after most countries had left the gold standard, stabilised or pegged their currencies to the pound. In 1933, it comprised most of the empire and Commonwealth – although not Canada, Newfoundland or Hong Kong – along with more than a dozen other countries from Norway to Brazil to Japan. After the outbreak of the war, however, when Britain introduced exchange controls, most of those countries with no British connection withdrew.) Instead, it would have to embrace multilateralism, but would still face very high American tariffs. (Presumably the Americans thought that this was acceptable because there was no preference: everyone would have to pay these tariffs.) For the Americans, this would make a level field for all; for the British, weakened by war, it would unfairly open up their markets to the dominant power of American business and commerce, as well as smashing one of the primary links uniting Britain, the empire and the Commonwealth. The result might well be devastating to British industry and commerce. There were extremely tough negotiations, and there was a serious possibility that the Churchill coalition government would fragment: a majority of the Cabinet, along with Churchill, believed that the acceptance of Article VII would be tantamount to agreeing to 'intervention in the domestic affairs of the British Empire'.[176]

The State Department came up with a solution that neither excluded imperial preference, since it did not want to sell the pass, nor emphasised it: the British were told that acceptance of Article VII did not imply specific commitments about imperial preference, and they were also reassured that the US recognised that the Dominions had the right to a say in the matter, that the UK could not necessarily speak for them. Furthermore, reductions in preferences would always be linked to reductions in US tariffs. This made the Article considerably less one-sided. Roosevelt telegraphed these concessions to Churchill and the Cabinet accepted them, as did the Dominions. On 23 February 1942, the Mutual Aid Agreement was signed.[177] This brought to an end the use of Lend-Lease as the main battleground to compel the acceptance of American post-war policies: that battle would now shift to the negotiations over the 1946 American Loan Agreement, by which, in exchange for a loan of $3,500 million, the British had to agree to the elimination of imperial prefer-ence and to make sterling convertible. The latter requirement, carried out in July–August 1947, nearly destroyed the pound. Fortunately for Britain, the Americans then let up the pressure, as they realised just how economically weak Britain was,[178] agreeing to the continuation of the Sterling Area, imperial preference and discrimination against dollar-priced imports.

During the period from February 1942 to the spring of 1945, Lend-Lease was used by the US Treasury to bring Britain to a state of such severe financial weakness that the British would not, they hoped, be able to obstruct its plan to eliminate the Sterling Area, nor to prevent American domination of the international finan-cial system after the war. Morgenthau and Leo Crowley, head of the Foreign Economic Administration (which had replaced the Lend-Lease Administration in 1943), plotted to restrict Lend-Lease. The intention was to force the British to pay cash for what-ever they required that was not a war-need narrowly defined, and the straightforward intention of the US Treasury was to limit the size of the British reserves to a level which the British believed to be dangerous. What the Treasury was doing was increasing the so-called take-out, that is, specifying goods such as sugar, fish and paper for which Lend-Lease aid would not be available, and for which the British would have to pay cash. However, the British were saved from this particular wheeze in the first months of 1944 by a bureaucratic fight. It had become clear to Cordell Hull, the

Secretary of State, that if Britain were too weak, it would not be able to share in the development of what became the UN, nor would it be able to accept a multilateral economic order – to the idea of which he was utterly devoted – if it could not rebuild its reserves. Through devious manoeuvres the State Department provoked a crisis, during which either the President would have to slap down the Treasury or the British would be alerted to what the Treasury was doing to them and thus give Churchill a chance to protest to the President. The latter is what happened, and the Treasury had to agree that there would be no more take-outs.[179]

Great Britain also faced threats from the US armed services once it had cottoned on to the idea of using Lend-Lease for leverage. In September 1944, for example, General Brehon Somervell, Chief of the Supply Services, suggested that Lend-Lease be used to force the British to turn over their bases in the Pacific to the US, because the latter would need these islands after the war, given their expectation of exercising wide control over the area. (This expectation would have made Commodore Matthew Perry proud: recall that in 1851 both he and President Fillmore saw Perry's voyage to force open Japan as the opening move in a struggle with Britain for eventual control of the Pacific.) This anticipated taking of the islands was not imperialism, according to the General Board of the Navy, 'because the islands had no economic value'. Somervell also called for the conversion of the ninety-nine-year leases on bases in the Caribbean and the Atlantic into permanent transfers. Furthermore, he wanted to secure unconditional landing rights for US military, and commercial, aircraft at British bases around the world; and he wanted to prevent Britain from blocking American access to strategic materials in the Middle and Far East.[180]

The US Navy clearly felt very proprietorial about the Pacific and the Far East: it wanted to do the fighting and control the policy, and insisted that the British should stay out of it.[181] The outcome was that the British concentrated on the land war, particularly on the recovery of Burma and, figuratively, stayed out of ships. (As it happened, Roosevelt was possibly not in this particular loop. According to his son, when the President discussed the Pacific war, he asserted that '[t]he British want to recapture Burma. It's the first time they've shown any real interest in the Pacific war, and why? For their colonial empire!')[182] The loss of Singapore had convinced many not only that the British empire was morally wrong, but that the British were incompetent in running it. The US Navy generally aimed to prevent British claims to any part of the Japanese empire; furthermore, by restricting European participation in the Pacific war, the US would be in an ideal position to determine the future of the Japanese colonial empire and the European colonies occupied by Japan.[183] It did not help the British position that Admiral E. J. King, Chief of Naval Operations and Commander-in-Chief of the US Fleet, was a fierce Anglophobe, who was convinced that the British were manipulating the Americans to recover their empire. His temperament was fiery: according to his daughter, he was 'the most even-tempered man in the Navy. He is always in a rage.' Reportedly, there was one Combined Chiefs of Staff meeting over Burma when 'Brooke got nasty and King got good and sore. King almost climbed over the table at Brooke. God, he was mad.'[184] (Brooke was General and then Field Marshal Sir Alan Brooke, the Chief of the Imperial General Staff. Given that he was quite capable of taking on Churchill, King probably did not faze him in the least.) The incident seems to underline Christopher Thorne's memorable judgement that 'Anglo-American relations in the context of the war against Japan were in many respects extremely poor, and ... this in turn placed a considerable strain upon their war-time alliance as a whole, as well as foreshadowing serious difficulties to come ... Here, if nowhere else, they were only allies of a kind.'[185]

The President and the civilian branch of the US government had another plan for the disposal of Japan's and everyone else's colonies, and this was trusteeship. Roosevelt saw the continuation of empire as a cause of future wars,[186] and, as noted above, railed against European colonialism, insisting that all peoples should be able to determine their own political systems. On the other hand, he shared Wilson's and many others' belief that most colonial peoples were not ready for independence and needed guidance from the 'advanced powers'.[187] Under the mandate system, the League of Nations had done little to monitor how many of the colonies were treated by the countries which were responsible for them. According to Elliott Roosevelt, in January 1943 he suggested to his father that 'the United Nations – when they're organized – they could take over these colonies, couldn't they? Under a mandate or as a trustee – for a certain number of years'.[188] It is possible to doubt that this was the origin of the suggestion trusteeships, which he seems to imply, but perhaps this is reading too much into it.

The British use of the term 'trustee' dates back to Edmund Burke, a Member of Parliament, and his address on the East India Bill on 1 December 1783: 'every species of political dominion ... [is] all in the strictest sense a trust; and it is of the very essence of every *trust* to be rendered accountable.'[189] To whom were those who dealt with the colonies accountable? The answer was, to Parliament. Those holding the mandates from the League of Nations, however, were accountable to an international organisation. The British were willing to accept this, because they assumed that the monitoring would be tolerable. Furthermore, the idea that Britain held control of its colonies in trust for the benefit of the native populations was a continuing assumption in the official mind of the Colonial Office. From the First World War, the argument in Britain was that these populations needed to develop the customs, mores and representative institutions necessary for independence, and this was best done under the tutelage of the British. Unfortunately, not very much was accomplished: according to Peter Marshall, '[u]p to and beyond the Second World War ... Britain's imperial mission was seen less as preparing its subjects for eventual freedom than as exercising an almost indefinite "trusteeship" over them.'[190] Indeed, in 1945, the Colonial Office expected the African empire to last another sixty years.[191] Therefore, when the policy of trusteeship was strongly pushed by the Americans, it was not a foreign concept to the British. The idea was that these trusteeships would be held by the colonial powers under the auspices of the planned-for United Nations organisation. The Americans tended to assume that, by this means, they would maintain a strong influence, if not control, over developments. Trusteeships were meant to lead to independence for the various colonies, and the Americans took it for granted that they would be well placed to ensure this.

There were strong objections from at least two directions. One was the US Joint Chiefs of Staff, who objected strongly to there being international control of any sort over any of the liberated territories and especially over the Japanese mandated islands: this was to be their responsibility so that they could control them to the extent that they thought necessary for security. Their preference was for US sovereignty to permit 'full control'.[192] The other objectors, of course, were the colonial powers themselves. The British strongly objected to the responsibility being taken from a national trusteeship to an international one, that is, out of their hands and into those of an organisation over which they would have much less control than the Americans. According to William Roger Louis, a theme running through the British wartime documents is that the Americans were using 'strategic "trusteeships" as a cloak for American expansion'.[193] Not surprisingly, Churchill, and other Britons of all political persuasions, insisted that no British colony would become a trusteeship.[194] They did not.

By the end of the Second World War, then, Britain had pretty well managed to fend off American attempts to undermine British control of its empire. No colonies received their independence; Britain's empire-wide economic and financial links had not yet been fatally weakened; and no colony under British control had become a trusteeship. Ironically, what was about to happen by 1947 was the Americans' realisation that, in this new world, with the rise of the USSR as a seemingly irrevocable enemy, Britain was their most important ally, with an empire that was of great strategic value. Unfortunately, as this realisation took hold, the British empire began to crumble and fall away.

XI

As America looked out over the Brave New post-war World, it had reason to feel triumphalist. Many Americans tended to believe that they were overwhelmingly responsible for victory in the war. The fact that the USSR had done much more of the fighting against the Germans in Europe than had the US or Great Britain tended to be forgotten. Responsibility for the Mediterranean area and Italy had to be shared with the British. But the Pacific War was theirs, and this included the atomic bomb, again forgetting the role of Britain in inventing it and helping to develop it. Rather, the US strode the world as a Colossus politically, economically and militarily. There seemed to be no enemies in sight of any significance, and therefore a limited need to deal with allies, although the wartime Combined Chiefs of Staff continued to work together.

From 1943 until his death in April 1945, Roosevelt had seen the future of the world as one to be guided by the united efforts of the US and the USSR – to his mind the two liberal and reformist powers.[195] Britain, the conqueror and possessor by force of a great empire, was relegated to the sidelines. Roosevelt's successor as President, Harry S Truman, however, encouraged by his advisers, did not see the world through Roosevelt's spectacles. From 1946 onwards, apprehension as to the intentions of the USSR grew. The USSR, both as a traditional Great Power and as the centre of a communist movement that was perceived as determined to take over as much of the world as possible, threatened the US and its allies. But which allies? There were Canada and Australia, neither of which had been attacked on home territory, but they were hardly military or naval powers of great size (perhaps small but perfectly formed). The Europeans were trying to rebuild their countries. There was only one major power besides the US which had been neither invaded nor occupied nor defeated, whose economy was working, whose democratic political system was in good condition, and which still possessed a sizeable army, navy and air force, and this was Great Britain.

By the end of April 1947, Secretary of State George C. Marshall had decided that the USSR was irrevocably hostile to the US and to the capitalist West in general. Unfortunately, Europe was in terrible shape economically, and the decision was taken that the US had to help the European countries to help themselves to rebuild their economies and forge intra-European trading links.

The outcome was the Marshall Plan, by which the US provided $13 billion worth of goods over roughly three years to sixteen countries. Britain, in terms of the shape of its economy (but not of its huge indebtedness), was one of the least needful of these, if domestic factors are the focus. Nevertheless, it received the largest tranche of Marshall Aid, primarily to ensure that it could continue to occupy Germany and its empire and thereby to do its part in helping the US to defend the free world. In short, during the period from 1945 to 1947, Britain went from being, in Roosevelt's assessment, more of a threat than the USSR to the world as desired by the US, to being America's major ally against the USSR.

Conversely, since the turn of the century Britain had seldom deviated from the belief that a close relationship with the US was vital to its safety and that of its empire. In March 1944, the Foreign Office wrote in a memorandum that 'A strong American policy must ... be based not on a determination to resist American suggestions or demands, but on an understanding of the way in which their political machinery works, and a knowledge of how to make it work to the world's advantage – and our own. Instead of trying to use the Commonwealth as an instrument which will give us the power to outface the United States, we must use the power of the United States to preserve the Commonwealth and the Empire.'[196] This is a very straightforward statement of the policy that Britain had followed for decades, and would continue to follow: the co-optation of American power to augment its own in order to secure its preferred foreign policies.

And what were these policies? Basically, what were Britain's fundamental national interests? One thing was certain, and that was they had to be tailored to the resources that existed to support them. Britain could not be separate from Europe, given the advent of aeroplanes and then missiles, but after the defence of Britain itself (or, rather, of the UK – 'Great Britain' includes Northern Ireland in this discussion) and its maritime communications, priority was given to the defence of the British empire and Commonwealth. Britain would not again land soldiers on the European continent in time of war, and the Royal Air Force would normally only fly from bases in Britain.[197] By December 1947, the Chiefs of Staff had decided on the three pillars which had to be defended at all costs: the home islands, the sea communications to the US and the Dominions, and the Middle East.[198] The only way these could be safeguarded was by close co-operation with, and the co-optation of the power of, the US.

Why did the US allow its power to be co-opted? What could the British provide that made it worthwhile? The answer was, the empire and Commonwealth. According to a State Department policy statement of 11 June 1948 – while the two countries were in the midst of such acrimonious discussions over the Marshall Plan that talks nearly broke down six days later[199] – 'The policies and actions of no other country in the world, with the possible exception of the USSR, are of greater importance to us.' Consider that statement in the history of Anglo-American relations. It continues: 'British friendship and cooperation ... is necessary for American defense. The United Kingdom, the Dominions, Colonies, and Dependencies, form a world-wide network of strategically located territories of great military value, which have served as defensive outposts and as bridgeheads for operations. Subject to our general policy of favouring eventual self-determination of peoples [note that this is a subordinate clause], it is our objective that the integrity of this area be maintained.'[200] Or, as it was later put by Frank Wisner, the first head of covert operations for the CIA, in a conversation with British intelligence officer and Soviet spy Kim Philby, 'whenever there is somewhere we want to destabilize, the British have an island nearby'.[201]

Two years later, just before the outbreak of the Korean War, the importance of Great Britain and the Commonwealth to the US was reaffirmed and widened: another State Department policy paper stated that:

No other country has the same qualifications for being our principal ally and partner as the UK. It has internal political strength and important capabilities in the political, economic, and military fields throughout the world. Most important, the

British share our fundamental objectives and standards of conduct ... To achieve our foreign policy objectives we must have
the cooperation of our allies and friends. The British and with
them the rest of the Commonwealth, particularly the older
dominions, are our most reliable and useful allies, with whom
a special relationship should exist. This relationship is not an
end in itself but must be used as an instrument of achieving
common objectives. We cannot afford to permit a deterioration
in our relationship with the British.[202]

During the period from 1947 until late 1956, Great Britain was the
United States' primary ally. The US made some effort to support
Britain, occasionally when it would have, strictly speaking, been
more in its own interest not to do so. Around the world, the US
saw itself as the unquestionable leader of the free world, but in
one area, the Middle East, Washington considered that Britain
had the experience and expertise that the US itself did not necessarily command: 'We expect and depend upon the British to be
a major force in ensuring political and economic stability in the
Near and Middle East.'[203] Therefore, as part of the wall of containment around the Soviet Union, Britain was to take care of the
Middle East on behalf of the US, itself and their allies.

As already noted, one outcome of the First World War was a
major expansion of Britain's empire in the Middle East. Once the
Second World War had begun, American interest in the area grew,
primarily at that time because of the oil, and this particular focal
point was Saudi Arabia. Saudi Arabia was not part of the British
empire, Britain recognising its 'complete and absolute independence', but the British did their best to remain close to the kingdom
because its size and wealth could help to ensure regional stability,
and thereby British imperial hegemony over the Middle East.
This meant that Britain did not possess the institutional controls
in Saudi Arabia analogous to the ones it had over the other territories under its influence, but it had spent forty years developing
a relationship with Riyadh that the Americans could not begin to
match. The Americans did not really have a 'Middle East' policy
during the war, beyond wanting as much access to as much oil

as was possible. Therefore, while not arguing that all was hand-in-hand down the lane of Middle East policy, nevertheless the Americans more often than not eventually conceded that British policy was probably in both of their interests. In the end, during the Second World War, 'the prevailing consensus among a range of policy makers on the American side held that the sustained British influence in Saudi Arabia was an upshot [sic] to American oil security'.[204]

It is, therefore, a touch ironic that the first Middle East conflict on the ground between the two countries after the war involved Saudi Arabia. This was the struggle over the Buraimi Oasis. The oasis was roughly circular, about six miles across, and with a population of between 6,000 and 10,000 gathered into nine villages controlled by the Persian Gulf emirates, three by Abu Dhabi and six by the Sultan of Muscat and Oman. It was fertile and well watered, but what was crucial was its strategic position at an important crossroads, because whoever controlled the oasis controlled the approaches to Muscat and Oman. It was a useful point in the Saudi slave trade. It might also contain important oil reserves. These considerations were not unimportant to Ibn Saud, the King of Saudi Arabia, which had claimed the area since the early nineteenth century, and in August 1952, supported by the Arabian-American Oil Company (ARAMCO), he sent in troops to occupy the oasis. It was still emirate territory, not Saudi Arabia's.

This was a shock to the British, because they controlled the defence and foreign policies of the Gulf states, and it was a direct challenge to their imperial position in the Middle East. The US had a great interest in Saudi Arabia, deriving from ARAMCO's control of the oil reserves, which were the largest in the world. Washington had few direct interests in other Middle East countries, and none that compared with Saudi oil, and had therefore been reasonably content to let Britain exercise predominant influence in the area on behalf of both. This, of course, would only work if the two had reasonable confidence in each other, but this drained away during and because of the crisis: Britain was determined to retain its position, and the US increasingly became determined to replace it, or at least to require that it report to them – clear with them? – any policies or moves that might affect US interests.

It is a complicated and deeply interesting story.[205] Britain intended to remain the dominant Power in the Middle East, because it believed that its position as a Great Power depended on it. It had substantial military resources in the area, including the huge base at Suez, 80,000 troops manning the Canal, air squadrons in Iraq, naval facilities in Aden, the Arab Legion, headed by Sir John Glubb, in Jordan, rear bases in Cyprus and Malta, and the string of protectorates along the Persian Gulf.[206] Yet its power was clearly in decline, not least because of its relatively fragile economic situation, and it needed to control this area of soil for strategic reasons in order to maintain its control of the emirates. There was also the question of oil. Oil had not yet been discovered in Abu Dhabi, but there were strong suspicions that reserves lurked under the Buraimi Oasis. Britain had had a monopoly of oil in Iran, through the Anglo-Iranian Oil Company (now BP), but this had been nationalised by the Iranian government in March 1951. Britain needed the oil, because otherwise it was threatened by the loss of its independent ability to provide domestic and military energy.

Anthony Eden, the Foreign Secretary, and the Foreign Office thought that, because Britain had complied with American policies elsewhere, the US was obliged to support Britain in the Middle East. (They would learn their lesson: in 1964, their conclusion was that 'rightly or wrongly the Americans tend to convince themselves that their policies have a moral validity of their own and thus deserve our support: this limits their sense of gratitude when such support is given.'[207]) Churchill, again Prime Minister, was driven by the conviction that global Anglo-American unity was the most important factor in British foreign policy. (A relevant Foreign Office memory: 'More than one British Ambassador to the United States has quoted the story of the successful Foreign Office candidate who gave to the question: What three things matter most in the world? the reply "God, Love and Anglo-American relations".')[208] One result of that unity, Churchill believed, should be US support for the British position in the Middle East. President Dwight D. Eisenhower, on the other hand, thought that this was nothing but a ploy to use American power to maintain British influence in the Middle East. The two were clearly in agreement, just not on its desirability. Indeed, the US government's conviction that, in the midst of a Cold War, Britain could be trusted to maintain the interests of both countries in the Middle East, was coming to an end.[209] In short, the British still worked primarily with the local elites – although Eden at least was beginning to question the wisdom of this, warning the Cabinet in February 1953 that 'the methods of yesteryear' were no longer workable[210] – while the Americans wanted to build links with the nationalist rising middle classes. Worse, the British could no longer ensure the area's security against the USSR.

There was an attempt at diplomacy, but the Saudis would not leave the oasis, and an unsuccessful standstill agreement was made, with the Saudis holding the village and the British the remainder of the territory. John Foster Dulles, the American Secretary of State, recognised that Saudi Arabia was the cause of the problem, but refused to support the British position, for fear of undermining America's own influence in Saudi Arabia. After a tour in the Middle East, Dulles wrote to Eisenhower in May 1953 that Great Britain and France were 'millstones around our neck'.[211] The British out in the field could sense this. As Sir Henry Pelham, British Ambassador to Saudi Arabia, wrote on 17 December 1952, 'The Americans seem anxious to build their empire on their own, and in so far as they seek our co-operation at all ... seem to find us embarrassing partners. Their attitude reminds me of those advertisements warning against bad breath.'[212] The US urged more negotiations, and in February 1954 it seemed that an agreement might be reached. Britain wanted to set up an international oil consortium as in Iran, but ARAMCO was not keen, and began to work with the State Department; ARAMCO wanted the expulsion of other oil companies, and convinced the State Department to help. Britain, however, insisted 'that she stay in and ARAMCO stay out of Buraimi'.[213]

Events in Iran, that is, the nationalisation of the Anglo-Iranian Oil Company and the subsequent insistence by the Americans that ARAMCO take over a major part of the British concession,[214] convinced Eden, now Prime Minister, that the US was trying to push Britain out of Iran, and possibly Egypt, with the result that the British stance over the Buraimi Oasis hardened. The head of ARAMCO, insisting that his company had concessionary rights there, demanded on 3 April 1954 that the British companies discontinue their operations, or ARAMCO would hold them strictly accountable for any violation of its rights. His letter was transmitted by the US State Department. The American Ambassador to Britain, Winthrop Aldrich, reported back that the British found it insulting; the Foreign Office reply warned that neither the Saudis nor ARAMCO would be allowed in the area, a clear indication that, if necessary, force would be used.[215] Neither the State Department nor ARAMCO believed this, and ARAMCO in mid-May decided to enter Buraimi. Dulles cabled the British that ARAMCO would enter well away from the British operations, and that Britain should look the other way.

ARAMCO personnel entered the area, and the British decided to act. The Cabinet met and agreed to send a large British force to chase them out. Unwilling to face the British, the ARAMCO personnel withdrew on 8 June. They also decided that Buraimi was not worth the trouble, and implied that they had been forced to act by the Saudis. Churchill was naturally worried about the impact all of this was having on Anglo-American relations, and in late June he invited himself to Washington (over Eden's objections). There he and the Americans came to an agreement, termed the Declaration of Washington, which came up with a solution to Buraimi, as well as to problems in Egypt, Iran, Indo-China and the rearmament of Germany.[216] As announced by Eden in Parliament on 29 July 1954, Britain and Saudi Arabia would go to arbitration, a neutral zone was established, and both sides would withdraw their forces, leaving fifteen soldiers for each side.[217]

The Saudis departed, but left behind a secret organisation to continue underground activities, attempting to undermine the British in Buraimi and all around the Arabian Peninsula, from Aden to Kuwait.[218] They also interfered with the Arbitral Tribunal which had been set up in early 1953 to decide the issue – their member was the Saudi Minister for Buraimi – by attempting to instruct witnesses before their appearance. The British member, accepting that there would be no impartial solution, resigned, as did the two neutral members.[219] The British then evicted the Saudis from Buraimi on 16 October 1955, and declared the boundaries to be the same as before the Saudi occupation. This was done without consulting the Americans, who were upset and angry. Dulles knew what the Saudis were doing, and understood that Britain, for the sake of its position in the Middle East, had to accept the Saudi challenge; nevertheless, he protested against the reoccupation of Buraimi. The Foreign Office reacted badly:

> we were thrown into a rage with the Americans upon receiving two notes or messages – one telling us that we had better go back to arbitration on Buraimi because otherwise the Saudis will be very annoyed and may take us to the Security Council; and the other practically ordering us to call off the Sultan of Muscat's impending clear-up of the rebellious Imam of Oman, again because the Saudis won't like it. Kirkpatrick [the Permanent Under-Secretary in the Foreign Office] is breathing fire and has sent for the US Minister, poor man, a Mr Barbour, who is new.[220]

Barbour was on the defensive, 'nor could he give any guarantees that the United States would oppose further Saudi encroachments, even if Great Britain yielded on Buraimi. Barbour went on to explain that "the Americans wanted ... a settlement on Buraimi and Oman by peaceful means. Mr Dulles wished to do everything possible to deter the Soviets from using armed force [anywhere]. For this reason he opposed the use of force to settle any question."'[221] This did not lessen Kirkpatrick's anger:

> Sir I. Kirkpatrick asked whether Mr. Dulles really meant that no state should object to subversion from outside and use force

to restore internal order. This was a new and startling doctrine, which would be very embarrassing to the United States government if universally applied. But apart from considerations of expediency, there was the question of right and wrong. To throw a small Arab state to the wolves for the American reason, which was[,] with respect, that the Saudi government would be annoyed if we did not, was entirely wrong.[222]

According to Evelyn Shuckburgh, Eden's Private Secretary, the British reoccupation of the Buraimi Oasis was a turning point. Churchill had thought that Britain pretty well had to walk hand in hand with the United States; Eden had apparently proven that Britain could act independently of, even contrarily to, the Americans. Furthermore, the use of military force seemed to have had a salutary effect on Saudi behaviour. According to Tore Tingvold Petersen, 'Gone was Eden's measured approach to Middle East nationalism, his main concern now being to maintain British prestige and influence in the area. Thereafter, increasingly, the prime minister and his cabinet regarded military force as the solution to Great Britain's problems in the Middle East.'[223] The unfortunate result, soon, was the Suez Crisis.

XII

If there is one episode in Anglo-American imperial relations that many Britons, but far fewer Americans, know about, it is the Suez Crisis of October–November 1956. The British Cabinet, led by the Prime Minister, Anthony Eden, and the Chancellor of the Exchequer, Harold Macmillan, as well as Sir Ivone Kirkpatrick, the Permanent Under-Secretary of the Foreign Office, and 'one of the few officials within the Foreign Office who favoured intervention',[224] arguably entirely misjudged the situation, refusing to listen to, or to take seriously, those of their own civilian and military officials who tried to dissuade them from military action. The American government, in response, was merciless. It attacked the pound, refused to supply oil, shadowed the Royal Navy on its journey from Malta to Egypt and essentially ostracised the British government until it agreed to withdraw. Within a year, the two countries had patched things up, but the crisis essentially marked the destruction of Britain as an independent imperial power. Sadly, it need not have happened.

When the Americans looked at the British leaders, they were not impressed. Churchill, by the end of his premiership in the spring of 1955, had neither health nor full capability of mind, having suffered a stroke in June 1953. Anthony Eden, who succeeded him on 6 April 1955, also suffered badly from ill health and great pain. Two years before, he had had an operation to remove gallstones, during which the bile duct was damaged. His various illnesses and injuries were controlled only by the use of various drugs, and he was consequently subject to severe mood swings;[225] as his Private Secretary noted in his diary, he repeatedly made stunning and even dangerous errors of judgement.[226] One of these was when he essentially decided to act as his own Foreign Secretary by replacing Harold Macmillan with the colourless and easily controlled Selwyn Lloyd. This had repercussions. Macmillan and Dulles were good friends; Eden and Dulles detested each other.

The US government by this time no longer trusted the British to be responsible for the Middle East on behalf of both countries. Rather, it feared that Great Britain by its actions was opening the Middle East to Soviet penetration and communist subversion. The British feared nationalists, who threatened the empire; the US feared communists, who threatened the free world. The problem for Britain was that it believed control of the Suez Canal was fundamental to the maintenance of its sea communications to its South-East Asian colonies, and to Australia and New Zealand; of equal if not more importance, it was also the route for oil from the Persian Gulf. Furthermore, its base in Egypt was the centre of defence for its positions in the Mediterranean and Africa. Britain's claim to control of the canal rested on its position as the major shareholder in the Suez Canal Company, 44 per cent of whose shares had been purchased from the Egyptian government in 1876. In December 1914, Britain had declared Egypt a protectorate, but it gave the country its independence in 1922.

Nevertheless, British soldiers did not entirely vacate Egypt. In 1936 the Anglo-Egyptian Treaty ended British occupation of cities such as Cairo and Alexandria, but confirmed the British operation of the Suez Canal base, the largest in the world and the centre of British military operations outside the home islands.

After the end of the Second World War, events in Egypt moved against the British. There was increasingly violent activity by nationalist groups, both against the British themselves and against their wayward puppet ruler, the licentious King Farouk. In July 1952, a month before Ibn Saud sent troops into the Buraimi Oasis, the Egyptian Revolution, or the Free Officer coup, led by General Mohammed Neguib and a group of middle-ranking, middle-class young officers (six of whom had studied in the US), successfully overthrew Farouk and took power. From this group emerged Colonel Gamal Abdel Nasser, who became President in March 1954. Nasser had been in touch with American officials since October 1951, and he maintained close relations with the CIA, his main channel for communications with Washington. In 1953, Miles Copeland Jr, a one-time CIA employee but in 1953 a non-official 'cover operative' or spy, travelled to Cairo to meet Nasser; the two men hit it off, and Copeland apparently became Nasser's primary Western adviser. According to Copeland, he had been sent to Egypt to assess the feasibility of assassinating Nasser, 'on the tacit understanding that he would reach a negative assessment' and thus 'discourage any British attempt'. (MI6 was discussing ways of eliminating Nasser, as were parts of the US State Department and the CIA.) Hugh Wilford explains what happened next:

> Arriving in Cairo, Miles immediately confessed his mission to Nasser, whereupon the old friends began gaming out possible assassination plots. 'How about poison?' the American asked the Egyptian. 'Suppose I just wait until you turn your head and then slip a pill into your coffee?' 'Well, there's Hassan standing right there,' replied Nasser. 'If I didn't see you, Hassan would.' 'But maybe we could bribe a servant to poison the coffee before bringing it in?' 'The coffee would only kill the taster.' And so the conversation carried on – at least in Miles's recollection.[227]

A new Anglo-Egyptian Treaty was signed on 19 February 1954, by which British troops were to leave the Suez Canal Zone (which contained the base) by June 1956, although – significantly for future events – they could re-enter in the event of war or the threat of war against any Arab state or Turkey, as long as the attack was not instigated by Israel. What the British did not then know was that the treaty had been drafted in the State Department:[228] the Americans did not trust either country, but particularly the British, not to exacerbate the situation. Nevertheless, American influence may have been responsible for the existence of the clause allowing conditional British re-entry.

The Suez Crisis had manifold implications. The US and Great Britain had different defence strategies. Mention has been made of their links to different groups of Egyptians, with the British retaining their links with the old elites and the Americans fostering closer links with the nationalists, especially with the growing and increasingly important middle classes. They also worked with different groups of countries in establishing a barrier against Soviet penetration. In January 1955, the Turks and Iraqis began to hold talks, encouraged at first by the Americans, and signed a pact. By the Treaty of Versailles, as noted above, Britain had received Iraq as a mandate, and even though that had ended, it still retained treaty rights to bases there. On 5 March 1955, Egypt, Syria and Saudi Arabia signed a defence agreement. Ten days later, Britain joined the Turkish–Iraqi Pact, now called the Baghdad Pact; Iran and Pakistan later joined. At first, the intention was that the US would also adhere to the Pact, but this was during a period of attempts to mediate an Arab–Israeli agreement. If they succeeded, the Americans thought that the Israelis could then also join the pact and they would all face down the USSR together. However, once the mediation attempts failed, the Americans began to see the pact as destabilising and, to the bewilderment and annoyance of the Foreign Office, suggested that the British hold back on it. As it was now their primary defence arrangement in the Middle East, the British were not about to do so.[229] In any case, the US's closest relations in the Middle East were with Israel and Saudi Arabia, and, not surprisingly, after events leading up to Israeli independence and the conflict with the Saudis over the Buraimi Oasis, Britain had somewhat frosty relations with both.

Nasser reacted with fury to the Baghdad Pact, which promised to interfere with his project for pan-Arab unity, to be led by Egypt and himself. In September 1955, he announced the Egyptian purchase of arms from Czechoslovakia, a member of the Soviet bloc (on 26 September two high-ranking CIA officers had spent over three hours with Nasser, 'trying to find a placatory way of publicly announcing this shocking agreement').[230] Nasser pointed out that he had attempted more than once to purchase arms from the US, and that it was only when he had been refused that he had turned to Czechoslovakia. (After the 1948 Arab–Israeli War, the US and Britain had imposed an arms embargo on both sides.)[231] Allen Dulles, the head of the CIA and brother of the Secretary of State, strongly supported Nasser, seeing him as riding the wave of the future in the Middle East. In December 1955, the US and Britain agreed to help fund the construction of the Aswan High Dam, an ambitious plan to provide water to the Nile Valley. By the following year, however, Foster Dulles had lost patience with Nasser and Egypt as insufficiently pro-Western, not least because Egypt had recently recognised the communist People's Republic of China (as had Britain in 1950 but not the US), and on 19 July 1956 he withdrew the offer of finance, followed by the British. The United States' and Britain's views on Nasser and the danger he posed to their interests had largely converged; unfortunately for Britain, however, the two countries' views on how they should respond had diverged.

Nasser's response to the cancellation of the American and British offers of funding was to nationalise the Suez Canal, partly to use the tolls to finance the dam, but overwhelmingly to assert that it was Egypt's and prove that the country was entirely independent of British rule. The differing American and British responses to this opened up a chasm between the two powers. On 7 and 8 January 1952, Churchill and outgoing President Truman had had a series of four meetings. During the third meeting, Truman said that 'US–UK agreement was necessary for any settlement of Middle Eastern problems.'[232] The British had thus been alerted, and, indeed, Eden as Foreign Secretary had been at the meeting. Yet in October 1955 Eden told the Cabinet that 'Our interests were greater than those of the United States because of our dependence on Middle East oil, and our experience in the area was greater than theirs. We should not ... allow ourselves to be restricted overmuch by reluctance to act without full American concurrence and support. We should frame our own policy in the light of our interests in the area.'[233] The US wanted a peaceful solution, and Foster Dulles embarked on a number of manoeuvres and arrangements, but little came of them. He spoke more fiercely in Washington than in London, but President Eisenhower, who controlled foreign policy, time and again emphasised that the US would not support the use of force. Neither Macmillan nor Eden believed him, assuming that the US merely wished to remain in the background, not that it would undermine the whole endeavour. For example, on 25 September, while Macmillan was in the US, he had 'very private and personal' talks with Eisenhower and Dulles. 'Ike', Macmillan wrote, 'is really determined, somehow or other, to bring Nasser down.' Separately but similarly, Dulles 'went on to talk about different methods of getting rid of Nasser ... Dulles then observed that he quite realised that we might have to act by force.'[234] Although Macmillan's impression was that 'this was a positive and supportive private message from Washington, even if the public presentation was more ambivalent', Sir Roger Makins, then the British Ambassador, later wrote that Macmillan had 'misinterpreted' Eisenhower's 'cautious remarks'.[235] Nevertheless, there is reason to believe that, had the British succeeded in their Suez adventure, the US would have accepted the situation. Foster Dulles himself later asked Foreign Secretary Selwyn Lloyd, 'Selwyn, why did you stop? Why didn't you go through with it and bring Nasser down?'[236]

Yet what the British missed, or dismissed as unimportant, was the crucial fact of the US presidential election being held on 6 November. Makins had informed – warned? – the Foreign Secretary that '[o]ur relationship with the Americans in this crisis is following the pattern which has appeared on previous occasions and which is becoming more and more marked. We agree about the substance of the policy, but differ on method and timing. We press for immediate action while the Americans are inclined to move with greater phlegm and deliberation. This is the opposite of what our natural temperaments are supposed to be.'[237] Dulles had, in fact, warned Macmillan at their meeting 'that at present Suez was not playing much part in the election ... But if anything happened it might have a disastrous effect ... Could we not ... try and hold things off until after November 6th?'[238] It was no wonder that the Americans were outraged: could the plea have been any more direct?

Meanwhile, by 10 August 1956, the British government had approved Operation Musketeer, presented to the Egypt Committee of the Cabinet by the Chiefs of Staff. Its mission was to occupy Egyptian cities and overthrow Nasser, and although the plan would later be revised, getting rid of Nasser remained the primary objective. The French also wanted to oust Nasser, who was supporting rebels in the French colony of Algeria, and on 1 September they hinted to the Israelis that they would like to co-ordinate joint action. By the 24th, there was a tripartite agreement, the Sèvres Protocol. The plan was that Israel would attack Egyptian airfields – it was keen to destroy Egypt's air force – and the British and the French, on the pretext that they were separating the two sides, would then move in and take control of the Suez Canal Zone. Macmillan, then a hawk, told the Cabinet on 11 September that only force would work; conversely Foster Dulles announced in Washington that 'we do not intend to shoot our way through' the Canal.[239]

On 29 October the Israelis attacked Egypt, and thus began a rich, full week. The following day, Great Britain and France sent an ultimatum to each side, instructing them to withdraw ten miles to either side of the canal to allow Anglo-French occupation. The Anglo-French task force, due to set sail from Malta, was delayed for twenty-four hours because the US Sixth Fleet was getting in the way; once it had set sail, it was shadowed and even harassed by the Americans.[240] On the 30th, Eisenhower called a meeting with his key advisers and bluntly stated that 'he did not see much value in an untrusty and unreliable ally and that the necessity to support them might not be as great as they believed'[241] – something of an understatement. On the 31st, the British and French also attacked Egyptian airfields. There was uproar in the House of Commons, and at the UN on 1 November Britain and France vetoed a resolution calling for a ceasefire which had been proposed to the Security Council by the US. As it happened, it had been proposed by Dulles as a way of preventing an even worse resolution by the USSR.[242] On 2 November the UN General Assembly called for a ceasefire. On the 3rd Russian tanks rolled into Budapest to put down the Hungarian uprising. On the 4th the Egyptians blocked the canal, and Britain was warned by the Americans of oil sanctions against it. On the 5th, British and French paratroopers were dropped to take Port Said and Port Fuad near the northern end of the canal; on the same day, the Russians threatened rocket attacks on Paris and London, their first threat to use nuclear weapons against a Western Power. The Soviet intervention deeply concerned Eisenhower, who worried 'that the Soviets, seeing their position and their policy failing so badly in the satellites, are ready to take any wild adventure'. Foster Dulles commented that the British and French had perhaps committed a worse crime in Egypt than the Russians had in Hungary, but they would soon bow to American wishes because 'there would be a strain on the British and French and it will be economic and quickly [sic]'.[243]

The decisive date was 6 November, the day of the American presidential election. At dawn, Anglo-French troops landed in the Canal Zone, but back in London the condition of the pound was now critical. Britain had two points of extreme weakness, its oil supplies and its currency. When the invasion began, Nasser ordered the closing of the canal to halt the flow of oil, an action strengthened by the cutting by Arab nationalists of the oil pipelines from the Persian Gulf to the Mediterranean through Syria. Syria itself destroyed three of the Iraq Petroleum Company's pumping stations.[244] The US refused to make up the shortfall in oil, a decision which was to prove decisive in forcing British capitulation.[245] By 5 November, the pound and the sterling reserves were in dangerous shape. Both the British and American authorities as well as the financial markets had long regarded $2 billion as the danger point for sterling reserves; on 6 November, the British prepared to ask the US for massive assistance and, in the expectation of receiving it, they decided to ignore the crucial $2 billion point and to make propping up the exchange rate of the pound their first priority. But the expected aid did not materialise. As Richard E. Neustadt recounted in a later report, 'Secretary of the Treasury, George Humphrey, strong in government and close to Eisenhower, gave the British Treasury a virtual ultimatum: as Londoners recall it, he posed the simple choice of an immediate cease-fire or war on the pound, with not a dollar to be had for oil supplies.'[246] When Macmillan telephoned Washington, he was told that only a ceasefire by midnight would secure American support for a loan. Macmillan reported this to the Cabinet, urging that the country faced financial disaster; the Cabinet decided at 9:45 a.m. that a ceasefire would take place at midnight, and British troops stopped twenty-three miles down the canal from Port Said. But financial pressure did not cease, and as long as British and French troops were left in Egypt they would receive no help from the Americans.[247] On 30 November, the Cabinet accepted that withdrawal from Egypt was inevitable, and on 3 December the Foreign Secretary announced that British troops would be withdrawn from the Canal Zone. On 22 December, the evacuation was complete.

The Suez Crisis was a watershed in British history. It was the end of Great Britain as an independent Great Power: it was now clear that it could no longer implement any foreign policy which required the use of force without at least the acquiescence of the United States. As the Foreign Office put it in a planning paper, 'Against her opposition we can do very little (e.g., Suez) and our need for American support is a fact which we cannot ignore.'[248] The distinguished diplomat Sir Pierson Dixon was more bitter, later writing that the main result of the Suez débâcle had been that, at one stroke, Great Britain had been reduced 'from a 1st class to a 3rd class power'.[249] It is unclear whether there was any true cause and effect, but within five years Britain had made its first application to join the European Economic Community. As far as Anglo-American relations were concerned, any conclusion must be mixed. Sir Harold Caccia, the British Ambassador to Washington, wrote at the end of December 1956 that 'something has ended, and, in my view, three things: first, the sentimental attachment, in the Administration, created by our wartime experience as crusaders in arms; second, the innate trust in our longer experience of international affairs and our reputation for dependability; third, our largely unquestioned right to a special position ... Now the position is different.'[250] The US intended it to be different, and now preferred to deal with Britain and France through the machinery of NATO, the North Atlantic Treaty Organisation set up in 1949.

Yet there was one relationship that, according to Percy Cradock, Chairman of the Joint Intelligence Committee (JIC) from 1985 to 1992, remained unbroken, even during the Suez episode, and this was the intelligence relationship. 'During the Suez rift ... the two intelligence communities were closer than their political masters and it is interesting that ... the CIA representative on the JIC ... was left as the sole US–UK channel when all other communications between the two governments had been broken off.'[251] While in the US in mid-November 1956, Lloyd wrote to Eden that Harold Caccia had told him that 'Allen Dulles' willingness to continue to cooperate with us on the intelligence side is the first indication of its kind that there has been in day to day business here so far as the administration is concerned.'[252] The official history of the JIC backs this up by referring to a meeting which Caccia and Allen Dulles of the CIA both attended, when, according to Caccia, Dulles 'could not have been more cordial'.[253] By December Anglo-American intelligence relations were as strong as they had been before the crisis. Indeed, JIC (Washington) reported to London that 'collaboration with US intelligence had been in no way affected ... There has, on the contrary, been considerable evidence that the American intelligence community as a whole are anxious to reassure the UK representatives that from their standpoint the value of cooperation with the United Kingdom is permanent, whereas the recent political divergence is essentially temporary.'[254]

There were attempts by both Eisenhower and Macmillan, who replaced Eden as Prime Minister on 9 January 1957, to repair the rip in the fabric of the relationship. Macmillan, of course, was desperately eager, but Eisenhower as well moved rapidly to bring the two countries closer together again, not least because of a deterioration in relations with the Soviet Union. (Interestingly, on 1 November, the same day as the Anglo-French veto of the US resolution at the UN Security Council, Eisenhower had met with the US National Security Council, during which he told them that 'he could scarcely even imagine that the United States could abandon Britain and France'.)[255] Eisenhower launched his restorative drive in January 1957 by looking to recreate a nuclear relationship, and meeting Macmillan on the 17th, just eight days after Eden's resignation.[256] Over the longer term, in fact, Eisenhower came to regret his reaction in 1956. Some time in the 1960s, he told his former Vice-President, Richard Nixon, that his worst foreign policy mistake was his failure to support Britain and France during Suez.[257]

The question remains to be asked, what impact did the disaster that was the Suez Crisis have on the British empire? It seems clear that it did not have an immediate effect as such – stakes were not pulled up all around Africa, nor was the base at Singapore abandoned. Certainly it highlighted some alarming weaknesses, one of the most important of which was Britain's fragile economy; another was its military weakness, in that in the face of a hostile population, the loss of regional allies and Washington's veto, it had had to retreat and withdraw. Undoubtedly it meant the loss of its attempts to retain imperial dominance over the Middle East.[258] But another question occurs. There was huge uproar in Britain itself, analogous perhaps to the period in the early twenty-first century when the nation was divided over the invasion of Iraq: did this express, or herald, a feeling that the empire was no longer of value to the country? At the very least, it probably made the series of independence ceremonies which took place over the following fifteen or so years more acceptable, or at least more bearable.

XIII

When the Labour government headed by Harold Wilson came to power on 15 October 1964, it inherited from the Conservatives a financial crisis of some magnitude: while the balance of payments deficit in 1963 had been £35 million ($98 million), in 1964, thanks to an attempt by the Conservative government to go for growth, with one result a huge surge of imports, it was estimated at £750–800 million ($2.1–2.24 billion). Devaluing the pound was one obvious remedy; this would make exports cheaper and imports dearer, thereby in due course improving the balance. However, virtually the first decision of the new government was not to devalue. Wilson had been scarred by the 1949 devaluation, and he was fearful that because the last two Labour governments had had to devalue (1931 and 1949), a third Labour devaluation would encourage the markets to expect that the election of the Labour Party to office was the signal for a sterling crisis. For the Chancellor of the Exchequer, James Callaghan, it was a moral issue: if Britain devalued, it would betray the interests of the members of the Sterling Area.[259] And finally, for the Secretary of State for Economic Affairs, George Brown, it was the duty of a Labour government to protect the working classes and improve their conditions, and he believed strongly in the traditional position that devaluation hurt these very people by making food more expensive.

The amount of the deficit was published on 26 October, at the same time as the government imposed a Temporary Import Surcharge of 15 per cent on all imports save food and raw materials. This was contrary to the rules of the General Agreement on Trade and Tariffs and of the European Free Trade Area, both of which included Britain as a member, and there was an inevitable international outcry. Holders of sterling noticed this, as well as the size of the deficit, and, from this point onwards, the pound came under recurring attack.[260] To round out the situation, Labour had won the election with a working majority of only three. This meant that the government would have to call another general election sooner rather than later, which meant that money needed to be spent: both Labour's voters and the trade unions, which largely financed the party, were demanding that spending on social welfare and domestic matters be sharply increased. This then meant that cuts had to be made elsewhere, because, with the pound periodically in a tailspin, borrowing money by the government was bound to be expensive. To many members of the party, the obvious cuts were in defence spending – Britain was spending twice as much on defence as its European allies – and this would mean an enormous cut in defence commitments. The new Secretary of State for Defence, Denis Healey (who held the office for the entire six years of the two Labour governments), figuratively took out a map. It was immediately clear that there would be difficulties in giving up bases, because of Britain's responsibility to defend its dependent territories and its treaty obligations to sovereign states such as Australia, Kuwait – which Britain had rescued from an attack by Iraq in 1961 – and Malaysia. Before defence cuts could be made, Britain would have to give up the colonies to independence and negotiate treaties with the independent states.[261]

By 1966 Healey had made a number of cuts, primarily in equipment for the Royal Air Force, but he needed to make more. In the February 1966 Defence White Paper (issued just over five weeks before the general election), he announced that Britain would withdraw from the base at Aden in 1968, but the conundrum remained: there could be no savings on expensive manpower as long as Britain's commitments in the Gulf and the Far East remained. This was certainly the case while Britain was still engaged in the 'Confrontation' with Indonesia over its attempt to conquer the British dependency, Borneo. What Healey believed had to be done was to withdraw Britain from its commitments East of Suez (capitalised because it morphed from merely a geographical location into a concept) without destroying either the stability of the area or its influence in the world. There were however, countries which strongly urged that Britain remain at the posts. Malaysia and Singapore, as well as New Zealand and Australia, were deeply concerned; the latter two countries regarded this area as their forward defence zone. As Healey

himself recalled in his memoirs, 'Later, our attempts to withdraw our forces from Malta and Gibraltar were resisted by the
colonial peoples themselves.'[262] The United States was also adam-
antly against it, and, as the Vietnam War continued, its objections
became shriller. Nevertheless, more cuts had to be made, and in
the 1967 'Supplementary Statement on Defence' it was set down
that Britain would withdraw from its Malaysia and Singapore
bases by the mid-1970s, but with a continuation of a limited
British role.[263] The looming financial crisis was to undercut all of
the calculations.

The crucial consideration had undeniably become the state of
the British economy and currency. But because of political considerations, uncomfortable decisions had been repeatedly postponed and the economy lurched on, increasingly supported by
borrowed money, especially during the recurring sterling crises.
The American Embassy in London had written to Washington
on 26 May 1966 that Britain had a limited future as any sort
of international Power: perhaps the US should cease to help
and allow it to find its natural level as a 'comparatively lesser
middle state'.[264] By July 1966 the US Secretary of the Treasury
had decided that Britain's problems were by now so acute that
they threatened not only American interests but the free world's
financial system. There had been sterling crises in November
1964, July–August 1965 – the US played a critical role in
supporting the pound in those two[265] – and July 1966, before the
final crisis in November 1967.

The value of the pound was a primary American concern, and
officials worked hard to support it. Both the pound and the dollar
were reserve currencies – that is, they were major components of
the reserves of central banks around the world. But speculators
speculate, and if they succeeded in destroying the exchange rate
of the pound relative to that of the dollar, American officials
believed, they would next turn their attention to the dollar itself.
The American economy was also in difficulties, in that attempts to
pay for both the Vietnam War and the social reforms of President
Lyndon Johnson's Great Society programme – both guns and
butter – without raising taxes were causing alarming budget

deficits, immense public borrowing requirements and inflationary pressures. And if the dollar went, many Americans feared, so too would the Bretton Woods system of fixed exchange rates, thereby heralding a return to trade and payments restrictions. Hence the importance to the Americans of the pledge by Callaghan to Henry Fowler, the Secretary of the Treasury, and Al Hayes, the Chairman of the Federal Reserve Bank of New York, that he would never voluntarily devalue the pound; and hence the repeated efforts by the Americans to put together credit packages to support it.[266]

There was a second reason for American concern about the pound: the US government's determination that Great Britain should not remove its forces from East of Suez. 'East of Suez' referred to the retention of British bases, aircraft and ships, and in some cases the deployment of troops, in Singapore and Malaysia, the Persian Gulf, Aden and the Indian Ocean. By the mid-1960s, these deployments were costing £320 million a year, or 25 per cent of the British defence budget, with an additional £90 million annually spent in purchasing foreign currencies. There were 100,000 men deployed, with 55,000 fighting in Malaysia alone in the confrontation with insurgents backed by Indonesia. The US administration was genuinely alarmed at the prospect of the British departure. It valued the British bases at Singapore, which were designed for all three services to use, and at Aden, thought it useful to have the Union Jack rather than the Stars and Stripes flying in the Persian Gulf and the Indian Ocean, did not want to be the only Western – that is, white – power in East Asia, and feared that, if the British withdrew their forces, congressional pressure to withdraw America's from Germany would increase.[267]

But there was another American demand, and this related, as far as the Americans were concerned, less to British finances and more to British will. The Americans were becoming increasingly embroiled in Vietnam, as they fought alongside the dismayingly corrupt South Vietnamese government against local insurgents who were supported by communist North Vietnam. Both domestically and internationally, opposition to US involvement grew. The Americans wanted a major Power to stand alongside them, and thus they became increasingly desperate for Britain to send even a token force. But there was strong opposition to the war in the House of Commons, and in June 1966, when the US began bombing the outskirts of Hanoi and Haiphong, over 100 Labour MPs urged Wilson to make clear the government's disapproval. In the streets of Britain there were increasing numbers of anti-war demonstrators. On 27 October 1968 a crowd in Grosvenor Square tried to storm the American Embassy in what the police called 'the worst riot in memory'.[268]

Public support by the government for what might be called an American imperial war was therefore impossible. Wilson pointed out to Johnson that South Vietnamese soldiers were being trained in jungle schools in Malaysia, a medical relief team was being sent out and the British were providing policemen in Saigon. The Americans were distinctly unimpressed by this wide range of contributions and called for some British soldiers by their side. Johnson asked, bitterly, could not the British send even a token force? 'A platoon of bagpipes would be sufficient; it was the British flag that was wanted.'[269] The Americans became increasingly blunt about their disappointment. Secretary of State Dean Rusk told the journalist Louis Heren that 'All we needed was one regiment. The Black Watch would have done. Just one regiment, but you wouldn't. Well, don't expect us to save you again. They can invade Sussex, and we wouldn't do a damned thing about it.'[270]

Various defence reviews by the British government inched towards cutting back its commitments East of Suez. In talks in December 1964 between Healey and the American Secretary of Defense, Robert McNamara, McNamara had emphasised strongly the importance to the US of Britain's continuing presence in the region. As Healey told the Cabinet on 11 December, the Americans did not want Britain to 'maintain huge bases but keep a foothold in Hong Kong, Malaya, the Persian Gulf, to enable us to do things for the alliance which they can't do. They think that our forces are much more useful to the alliance outside Europe than in Germany.'[271] But eventually, according to Healey, 'hard experience compelled me to recognise that the growth of nationalism would have made it politically unwise for Britain to maintain a military presence in the Middle East and South East Asia, even if our economic situation had permitted it'.[272] And as Britain moved more towards Europe, making a second application in 1967 to join the EEC, choices had to be made. But the government was rapidly left with no choice at all as it was driven on to the rocks by a ferocious sterling crisis.

The pressure, building from the early summer of 1967, became inexorable. On 6 June the Arab–Israel War began and on the following day the Suez Canal was closed, which immediately caused a flight from the pound and other currencies into the dollar, seen as a strong, safe financial haven. The closure of the canal also held up the flow of oil, which was exacerbated by the civil war in Nigeria. Britain was forced to buy oil from the Western Hemisphere at considerably higher prices, which worsened the balance of payments and the deficit. In September, dockers in Hull, Manchester, Liverpool and London announced an indefinite strike, causing a pile-up of goods on the docks and devastating exports. In reaction, the pound weakened further, and the result was the beginning of yet another sterling crisis.

On 4 November, Wilson and Callaghan decided on devaluation, and Washington was notified. The Americans were horrified, and offered a loan of $3 billion. But it was too short-term and it came with strings attached: Britain would have to retain its commitments East of Suez and its agreement to purchase fifty F-111A strike aircraft. On 14 November the October trade figures showed the worst monthly trade deficit in British history, and sterling was again sold heavily. On the 16th the Cabinet agreed to devalue, on the 17th $1 billion was lost from the reserves, and on the 18th the pound was devalued by 14.3 per cent, thereby dropping its dollar value from $2.80 to $2.40. By the time it was announced, Callaghan had placed his resignation in Wilson's hand.[273]

The devaluation accelerated withdrawal from East of Suez. The new Chancellor was Roy Jenkins, the former Home Secretary and a confirmed Europhile, who was highly critical of the 'outdated imperial pretensions' embodied in the East of Suez role.[274] The coalition which had supported Great Britain's world role, pre-eminently Wilson and Callaghan (now Home

Secretary – he and Jenkins had traded positions), was weakened. Other changes also facilitated Jenkins' plans. In 1964, Healey had merged the three separate service departments into a Ministry of Defence. The Colonial Office had been abolished in 1966, and the Commonwealth Relations Office would go in 1968.[275] These reorganisations eliminated many political positions traditionally held by supporters of Britain's foreign role.[276]

On 14 January 1968, President Johnson 'sent a sharply worded letter to the Prime Minister ... which stated that if Britain abandoned east of Suez commitments and rescinded the F-111A order, the United States would no longer consider Britain a valuable ally in any strategic theatre, including Europe'. Wilson did not back down, even though he too was devastated by the decision. The British, he cabled Johnson, were 'sick and tired of being thought willing to eke out a comfortable existence on borrowed money'. On 16 January, 'Black Tuesday' in the Ministry of Defence, the Cabinet's decision was announced: nearly all British forces were to be withdrawn from the Middle East and East Asia by the end of 1971, although Britain would remain in Hong Kong, which provided, among other things, a valuable listening post for signals intelligence. The US administration was outraged. It was the ultimate betrayal by America's closest ally and only partner in global policing, and it came at time when the US itself was truly mired in Vietnam. Wilson emphasised that Britain was certainly not becoming neutralist; rather, it needed to find a military role which matched its resources.[277]

It was the end of an era. Great Britain, which had been a global and an imperial power for over three centuries, was now a regional power only. For many, it was extremely difficult – one Cabinet minister at the time, Richard Crossman, refers in his diary to 'breaking through the status barrier ... [and] it's terribly painful when it happens'.[278] Wilson himself regretted the move, not only because of the absolute loss of prestige, but because it signalled the end, for many years, of a close Anglo-American relationship. Countries ally because each has something to contribute to the relationship, but now it seemed that Britain had relatively little. Thanks partly to the attacks on the empire by the Americans over

the decades, when Britain finally resigned the last of its territories, the US lost many of the geographically strategic fortresses
and outposts which Britain had contributed to the alliance. The
British economy was weak, and would nearly self-destruct in the
next decade. Britain was not unimportant to the Americans, given
the NATO, intelligence and nuclear links, but in a world which
had recently held three empires, there were now only two – and
neither was the British empire. In the words of Sellar and Yeatman
in *1066 and All That*, 'America was thus clearly top nation, and
History came to a.'[279] But not for long.

Envoi

What of these two empires now? There is no British empire, but there are the British Overseas Territories: Anguilla, Ascension Island, Bermuda, British Antarctic Territory, British Indian Ocean Territory, the British Virgin Islands, the Cayman Islands, the two sovereign base areas on Cyprus, the Falkland Islands, Gibraltar, Montserrat, the Pitcairn Islands, St Helena, South Georgia, the South Sandwich Islands, Tristan da Cunha and the Turks and Caicos Islands; until July 1997, they included Hong Kong. These constitute a sizeable handful, with a wide placement on the map. The widely known epigram, that 'the sun never sets on the British empire', still lingers in the memory and the question, 'does the sun never set on the British Overseas Territories?', demands an answer. It is a touch complicated.

Formerly, it was possible to imagine the sun rising over one part of the empire and, long before the sun had set over that, the sun rising over another part. From the British Indian Ocean Territory to Pitcairn Islands, this can be readily imagined. But in the Southern Hemisphere winter, it would be touch and go whether the sun set on the Pitcairn Islands before it rose on the British Indian Ocean Territory. This is because they are 157.5° of longitude apart (the short way around) which corresponds to a time difference of ten and a half hours. Sadly, the possibility of a new epigram is stillborn.[1]

What about the American empire? The contiguous territory conquered in the nineteenth century is now firmly ensconced within

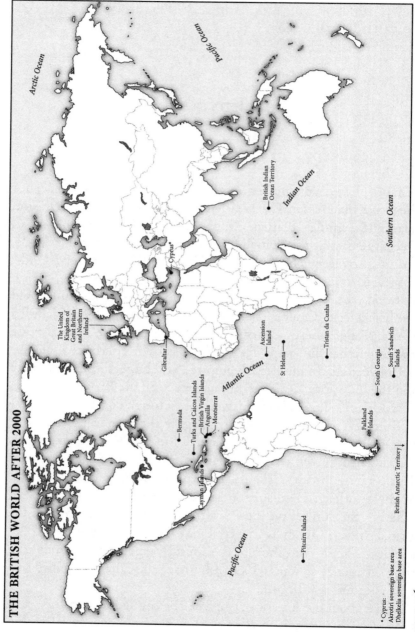

THE BRITISH WORLD AFTER 2000

Arctic Ocean

Pacific Ocean

British Indian
Ocean Territory

Indian Ocean

Southern Ocean

Cyprus*

The United
Kingdom of
Great Britain
and Northern
Ireland

Gibraltar

Ascension
Island

Atlantic Ocean

St Helena

Tristan da Cunha

Bermuda

Turks and Caicos Islands
British Virgin Islands
Anguilla
Montserrat

South Georgia

South Sandwich
Islands

Cayman Islands

Falkland
Islands

British Antarctic Territory

Pacific Ocean

Pitcairn Island

* Cyprus:
Akrotiri sovereign base area
Dhekelia sovereign base area

MAP 16

the nation-state, but what about its impressive number of client states, whose identities it would be impolitic to name? It also has fourteen formal dependencies, most of which are Pacific islands acquired before 1940: American Samoa, Baker Island, Guam, Howland Island, Jarvis Island, Johnston Atoll, Kingman Reef, Midway Islands, Navassa Island, the Northern Mariana Islands, Palmyra Atoll, Puerto Rico, the Virgin Islands and Wake Island.[2] If the American empire is compared to the British empire at its zenith, what is notable is the military power commanded by both. Concentrating on the United States, it is an arresting point that, at the beginning of the twenty-first century, the US by one account maintained just over 750 military installations in 130 countries, constituting what historian Brooke L. Blower calls 'the modern military base empire', with significant numbers of American troops stationed in sixty-five of these.[3] These numbers do not include several secret bases in Israel which seem not to have names.[4] Attached to these bases in 2001, even before the invasions of Afghanistan and Iraq, were 475,000 troops of various sorts.[5] As long as these countries can be protected without becoming protectorates, this American power will be welcomed, or at least tolerated. The question is, for how long will the United States continue to do so? The only thing truly predictable in international affairs is unpredictability.

Notes

INTRODUCTION: WHAT IS AN EMPIRE?

1. The 'Kingdom of Troy', for example, paid tribute to the Hittite Empire.
2. For an argument against the concept of the US as an empire see Anthony Pagden, *The Burdens of Empire: 1539 to the Present* (Cambridge: Cambridge University Press, 2015), pp. 35–7, and Elizabeth Cobbs Hoffman, *American Umpire* (Cambridge Mass Harvard University Press, 2013), *passim*.
3. For a brief and lucid description of and discussion about empires, see Stephen Howe, *Empire: A Very Short Introduction* (Oxford: Oxford University Press, 2002). He writes that at the peak of their strength European colonial powers plus the US ruled well over 80 per cent of the world's land, and effectively controlled all of the oceans as well (p. 62). For a thought-provoking discussion by an historical sociologist, see Julian Go, *Patterns of Empire: The British and American Empires, 1688 to the Present* (Cambridge: Cambridge University Press, 2011). For an analysis of the American Historiography about the American Empire, see Paul A. Kramer, 'Imperial Histories of the United States in the World, *The American Historical Review*, 114:5 (Dec. 2011), 1, 348–91.
4. But not everyone. See Brooke L. Blower, 'Nation of Outposts: Forts, Factories, Bases, and the Making of American Power, *Diplomatic History*, 41:3 (June 2017), 439–59.
5. For a rich discussion of the development of ideas about the early British empire, see David Armitage, *The Ideological Origins of the British Empire* (Cambridge: Cambridge University Press, 2000). For 1740, see Ian K. Steele, as quoted in *ibid.*, pp. 170–1.
6. *Ibid.*, p. 193.

7. Jefferson to George Rogers Clark, 25 Dec. 1780, in Julian P. Boyd, ed., *The Papers of Thomas Jefferson*, 42 vols (Princeton: Princeton University Press, 1951), IV, pp. 233–8, quote on pp. 237–8.

8. John C. Fitzpatrick, ed., *The Writings of George Washington from the Original Manuscript Sources 1745–1789: Prepared under the Direction of the United States Bicentennial Commission and Published by Authority of Congress*, 39 vols (Washington, DC: Government Printing Office, 1931–44), XXVIII, pp. 518–20.

9. Jefferson to Madison, 27 April 1809, J. Jefferson Looney, ed., *The Papers of Thomas Jefferson: Retirement Series*, 13 vols (Princeton: Princeton University Press, 2005), I, p. 169.

10. Jefferson to Monroe, 24 Oct. 1823, Paul Leicester Ford, ed., *The Writings of Thomas Jefferson*, 10 vols (New York: G. P. Putnam's Sons, 1892–9), X, pp. 277–8.

11. John Quincy Adams, *Memoirs of John Quincy Adams: Comprising Portions of his Diary from 1795 to 1848*, ed. Charles Francis Adams, 12 vols (Philadelphia: J. B. Lippincott, 1874–7), V, 249–53. For Canning's description of the argument, see Canning to Secretary of State, No. 3, 28 Jan. 1821, FO 5/47, The National Archive, Kew, London. See also Canning to Joseph Plante, Private, 6 Feb. 1821, FO 5/47.

12. The best example is Cobbs Hoffman, *American Umpire*, pp. 43, 119–20.

13. The divine-law doctrine derived from Roman law which refused to recognise lawful dominium by infidels without grace and considered their lands to be *terrae nullius*, or lands open to eminent domain seizure by a Christian sovereign.

14. William Bradford, *Bradford's History 'Of Plimoth Plantation'. From the Original Manuscript. With a Report of the Proceedings Incident to the Return of the Manuscript to Massachusetts* (Boston: Wright & Potter, 1898), pp. 32–3.

15. John Locke, *The Second Treatise of Government*, ed. Thomas P. Peardon (Upper Saddle River, NJ: Prentice Hall, 1997), p. 20.

16. And today, perhaps, ethnic cleansing?

17. Quoted in Wendy Hinde, *George Canning* (London: Collins, 1973), p. 345.

18. Howe, *Empire*, p. 24.

CHAPTER 1: IMPERIAL CLASHES OVER THE BORDER, 1783–1815

1. During the late nineteenth century, British soldiers risked their lives, and exercised considerable ingenuity, to explore and map the routes through Central Asia by which the Russians might threaten India.

2. Quoted from 'Transcript of Treaty of Paris' (1783), https://www.ourdocuments.gov, accessed 18 August 2013.

3. No – the river was to the south.

4. Quoted in John Lamberton Harper, *American Machiavelli: Alexander Hamilton and the Origins of U.S. Foreign Policy* (Cambridge: Cambridge University Press, 2004), p. 66.

5. Quoted in David McCullough, *John Adams* (New York: Simon & Schuster, 2001, pb edn 2002), p. 348.

6. Jerald A. Combs, *The Jay Treaty: Political Battleground of the Founding Fathers* (Berkeley: University of California Press, 1970), p. 14.

7. Samuel Flagg Bemis, *Jay's Treaty: A Study in Commerce and Diplomacy* (New Haven: Yale University Press, 1923, rev. edn 1962), pp. 3–4.

8. Combs, *The Jay Treaty*, p. 52.

9. *Ibid.*, p. 138.

10. Adams to Jay, 25 Aug. 1785, in John Adams, *The Works of John Adams, Second President of the United States, with a Life of the Author, Notes and Illustrations*, ed. Charles Francis Adams, 10 vols (Boston: Little, Brown, 1850–6), VIII, pp. 302–10, quote on p. 303.

11. Quoted in Charles R. Ritcheson, *Aftermath of Revolution: British Policy toward the United States 1783–1795* (Dallas: Southern Methodist University Press, 1969), p. 83.

12. *Ibid.*, p. 84.

13. *Ibid.*, pp. 186–227.

14. 'President George Washington's Proclamation of Neutrality', 22 April 1793, J. F. Watts and Fred L. Israel, eds, *Presidential Documents: The Speeches, Proclamations, and Policies that Have Shaped the Nation from Washington to Clinton* (London: Routledge, 2000), p. 12.

15. Bernard Mayo, ed., *Instructions to the British Ministers of the United States* (Washington, DC: Government Printing Office, 1941), p. 47, ref. 10.

16. Combs, *The Jay Treaty*, pp. 120–1; Ritcheson, *Aftermath of Revolution*, pp. 299–301.

17. As General Sir Guy Carleton, he had been Commander-in-Chief of all British forces in North America 1782–3; he was responsible for carrying out the British government's promise to grant freedom to slaves who joined the British during the American War of Independence and oversaw the evacuation of British forces, Loyalists and over 2,000 freemen from New York to a British colony.

18. Combs, *The Jay Treaty*, p. 138, for both quotes.

19. Quoted *ibid.*, p. 121.

20. Quoted *ibid.*, p. 147. (The citation given is Henry Dundas, Secretary of State for the Home Department, to Dorchester, 5 July 1794, CO 52/98, Colonial Office Papers, The National Archive, Kew. However, when I checked CO 52/98, it turned out to refer to the Cape of Good Hope, 1907.) A week later, Dundas became Secretary of State for War. Grenville wrote to the British Minister in Washington, George Hammond, on 8 Aug. 1794 that neither Dorchester's speech nor Simcoe's move to the foot of the Miamis Rapids had been approved by the King. Grenville to Hammond, No. 15, 8 Aug. 1794, ff. 59–64, Add MS 59084, Grenville Papers, British Library, London.

21. Grenville to Hammond, No. 15, 8 Aug. 1794, as in note 20.

22. Ritcheson, *Aftermath of Revolution*, pp. 54 and 262.

23. *Ibid.*, p. 238.

24. *Ibid.*, p. 310.

25. 'While Simcoe was preparing for the defences of Detroit against the expected attack of Wayne he received a dispatch from the Spanish Governor of Louisiana, Carondolet, who had sent a runner overland from New Orleans. Carondolet, alarmed at [French] intrigues in Kentucky and the projected descent of Kentucky riflemen on his capital, proposed common action of the colonial forces of the two European allies, Spain and England, in case of any attack on Louisiana. Simcoe, while expressing a hope that the alliance between the two countries might be strengthened to afford cooperation in case the United States should force a war, and stating that it was for the interest of Great Britain that Louisiana remain Spanish, replied that he could give no assistance at the moment, as he had his hands full with Wayne.' Bemis, *Jay's Treaty*, pp. 241–2 n. 40.

26. At least some of them were apparently white Canadians who had Indian mothers; there were also some Loyalists. Ritcheson, *Aftermath of Revolution*, p. 384.

27. Bemis, *Jay's Treaty*, pp. 247–8.

28. Quotations from Harper, *American Machiavelli*, pp. 133–4.

29. Hamilton to Washington, 14 April 1794, Alexander Hamilton, *The Papers of Alexander Hamilton*, ed. Harold C. Syrett and Jacob E. Cooke, 27 vols (New York: Columbia University Press, 1961–87), XVI, pp. 266–79, quote on p. 271.

30. Jay to Sally Jay, 19 April 1794, John Jay, *The Correspondence and Public Papers of John Jay*, ed. Henry P. Johnston, 4 vols (New York: G. P. Putnam's Sons, 1890–3), IV, p. 5.

31. Jay was to write to Randolph on 19 Nov. 1794, after agreement on the treaty had been reached, that 'great reserve and Delicacy has been observed respecting our Concerns with France:– The Stipulations in favour of existing Treaties was [sic] agreed to without hesitation: not an Expectation nor even a wish has been expressed that our conduct towards France should be otherwise than fair and friendly'. Despatches from U.S. Ministers to Great Britain, 1791–1906, Record Group 59 (State Department Papers), US National Archives, Washington, DC, Microfilm series 30 (hereafter M30), M30/2. All of the microfilm series used here are from Record Group 59.

32. Randolph to Jay, 6 May 1794, Diplomatic and Consular Instructions of the State Department, 1791–1801 (hereafter M28), M28/2.

33. When at one of their first meetings Jay described how British ships had seized and mistreated American ships and sailors, Grenville told him that 'not a single case under the instructions of [the Order of] November had been laid before him', and requested that some of the strongest of those cases be furnished him. Jay to Randolph, 6 July 1794, M30/3. Jay had a list of captures, but no statement of reasons for the condemnations. As it happened, H. C. Higginson, who had been sent to the West Indies to collect data, died of yellow fever while in the islands. The result was that Jay did not receive full and authoritative information in time to use it in the negotiations. Ritcheson, *After the Revolution*, p. 324.

34. Walter Stahr, *John Jay: Founding Father* (London: Hambledon & London, 2005), p. 320 for the Parisian deaths.

35. Bradford Perkins, *The First Rapprochement: England and the United States 1795–1805* (Philadelphia: University of Pennsylvania Press, 1955), p. 19.

36. Jay to Randolph, 6 July 1794, M30/3. Grenville and Jay 'soon became, and remained, firm friends'. John Ehrman, *The Younger Pitt: The Reluctant Transition* (London: Constable, 1983), p. 511.

37. Bemis, *Jay's Treaty*, p. 317.

38. Jay to Grenville, 16 Aug. 1794, f. 133, FO 95/512, Foreign Office Papers, The National Archive, Kew.

39. Grenville to Jay, Private, 17 Aug. 1794, Add MS 59084, Grenville Papers, British Library.

40. Jay to Randolph, 13 Sept. 1794, M30/2 contains Jay's 6 Aug. Note as well as a copy of Grenville's 30 Aug. Note; for a draft of the latter, which includes Grenville's marginal comments, see 'Projets of Heads of Proposals to be made to Mr Jay', n.d., ff. 141–51, FO 95/512.

41. Jay to Grenville, 4 Sept. 1794, ff. 212–15, FO 95/512.

42. 'Observations respecting the North Western Boundary of the United States of America', Grenville to [prob.] Hammond, 5 Sept. 1794, ff. 3–4, Add MS 59085, Grenville Papers, British Library.

43. Stahr, *John Jay*, p. 329.

44. Perkins, *The First Rapprochement*, p. 5.

45. The text of the treaty can be found in Bemis, *Jay's Treaty*, pp. 453–84.

46. Combs, *The Jay Treaty*, p. 156.

47. Bemis, *Jay's Treaty*, pp. 343–4, for an example, quote on p. 343.

48. Stahr, *John Jay*, p. 337.

49. New Brunswick was separated from Nova Scotia in 1794.

50. By 1803, St Andrews had nearly 500 inhabitants, and its harbour was one of the busiest north of Boston. David Demeritt, 'Representing the "True" St. Croix: Knowledge and Power in the Partition of the Northeast', *William and Mary Quarterly*, 3rd Series, 54:3 (July 1997), p. 516.

51. Geraldine Tidd Scott, *Ties of Common Blood: A History of Maine's Northeast Boundary Dispute with Great Britain 1783–1842* (Bowie, Md: Heritage Books, 1992), p. 11.

52. Demeritt, 'Representing the "True" St. Croix', p. 519.

53. T[homas] Pownall, *A Topographical Description of the Dominions of the United States of America*, ed. Lois Mulkearn (Pittsburgh: University of Pittsburgh Press, 1949), p. 68, quoted in Demeritt, 'Representing the "True" St. Croix', p. 519.

54. R. D. and J. I. Tallman, 'The Diplomatic Search for the St. Croix River, 1796–1798', *Acadiensis*, 1 (Spring 1972), p. 62.

55. *Ibid.* This was presumably Southack's *A Map of the Coast of NEW ENGLAND from Staten Island to the Island of Breton; as it was actually Survey'd by Capt. Cyprian Southack*. It provides numerous soundings as well as information on banks, shoals and other hazards, particularly in the waters off Nova Scotia and Cape Cod. 'The interior geography' was derived from Richard Daniel's *A Map of ye English Empire in ye Continent of America* (1679). https://collections.leventhalmap.org/search/commonwealth:3f462t67x, accessed on 4 March 2018.

56. Maine only became a state in 1820; until then, it was part of Massachusetts.

57. Tallman and Tallman, 'Diplomatic Search', pp. 61–2; Francis Carroll, *A Good and Wise Measure: The Search for the Canadian–American Boundary 1783–1842* (Toronto: University of Toronto Press, 2001), pp. 13–15.

58. Demeritt, 'Representing the "True" St. Croix', p. 522.

59. *Ibid.*, pp. 531–4, quote on p. 534.

60. John Bassett Moore, ed., *International Adjudications: Ancient and Modern ... Modern Series ... Saint Croix River Arbitration* (New York, 1929–33), vol. I, p. 289, quoted in Demeritt, 'Representing the "True" St Croix', p. 540.

61. Robert Pagan, 'Remarks on Captain Cyprian Southack's Plan of this Coast', 26 Oct. 1797, quoted in Tallman and Tallman, 'Diplomatic Search', p. 65.

62. *Ibid.*, p. 66.

63. Moore, *International Adjudications*, vol. II, p. 92, quoted in Demeritt, 'Representing the "True" St. Croix', p. 541.

64. Tallman and Tallman, 'Diplomatic Search', p. 68.

65. Demeritt, 'Representing the "True" St. Croix', p. 541.

66. Carroll, *A Good and Wise Measure*, pp. 16–19.

67. Demeritt, 'Representing the "True" St. Croix', pp. 543 and 548, quote from the latter.

68. Carroll, *A Good and Wise Measure*, pp. 19–20.

69. Perkins, *The First Rapprochement*, p. 12.

70. *Ibid.*

71. *Ibid.*, p. 15. Too big to fail, in current parlance?

72. *Ibid.*, pp. 90–9.

73. This was under a Tory or conservative government. A year later, a Whig coalition ministry, the 'Ministry of All the Talents', came to power; more sympathetic to American trading interests, it decided not to enforce the *Essex* decision. However, a year later the Tories returned to power, and American ships were again at risk. Troy Bickham, *The Weight of Vengeance: The United States, the British Empire, and the War of 1812* (New York: Oxford University Press, 2012), p. 26.

74. Perkins, *The First Rapprochement*, pp. 176–81, quotes on p. 180.

75. James Madison had written in his 'Political Observations' of 1795 that 'War is the parent of armies; from these proceed debts and taxes; and

armies, and debts, and taxes are the known instruments for bringing the many under the domination of the few.' James Madison, *The Papers of James Madison*, ed. Thomas Mason, Robert A. Rutland and Jeanne K. Sisson, 17 vols (Charlottesville: University of Virginia Press, 1962–91), XV, pp. 511–33, quote on p. 518. This may also be found in J. C. A. Stagg, ed., *The Papers of James Madison Digital Edition* (Charlottesville: University of Virginia Press, Rotunda, 2010), Congressional Series, XV (24 March 1793–20 April 1795), pp. 511–33, quote on p. 518.

76. Roger H. Brown, *The Republic in Peril: 1812* (New York: Columbia University Press, 1964), p. 18, quoted in Bickham, *The Weight of Vengeance*, p. 29.

77. Bradford Perkins, *Prologue to War: England and the United States 1805–1812* (Berkeley: University of California Press, 1968), p. 89.

78. *Ibid.*

79. The *Chesapeake* incident in the spring of 1807.

80. For the text of the 11 November Order, see Privy Council Register 1 Sept.–30 Nov. 1807, ff. 479–82, PC 174, Privy Council Papers, The National Archive, Kew.

81. Lloyds of London stopped quoting insurance rates entirely for voyages between Great Britain and the European continent, while the rates for Anglo-American voyages increased by 50 per cent. Denis Gray, *Spencer Perceval: The Evangelical Prime Minister 1762–1812* (Manchester: Manchester University Press, 1963), p. 171.

82. Burton Spivak, *Jefferson's English Crisis: Commerce, Embargo, and the Republican Revolution* (Charlottesville: University Press of Virginia, 1979), p. 158.

83. Garry Wills, *James Madison* (New York: Henry Holt, 2002), pp. 4–5.

84. Quoted in *ibid.*, p. 51.

85. Perkins, *Prologue to War*, pp. 160–1.

86. *Ibid.*, pp. 156–65.

87. Bickham, *The Weight of Vengeance*, p. 3.

88. Without, it must be said, the approval of all of their occupants. Bickham, *The Weight of Vengeance*, p. 38.

89. Gray, *Spencer Perceval*, pp. 214–74 and John Bew, *Castlereagh: Enlightenment, War and Tyranny* (London: Quercus, 2011), pp. 257–67.

90. Charles Esdaile, *The Wars of Napoleon* (London: Longman, 1995), p. 152.
91. Gray, *Spencer Perceval*, pp. 391–412.
92. Perkins, *Prologue to War*, p. 16 for the statistics.
93. *Ibid.*, p. 321.
94. For example, one petition introduced was from Liverpool. *Cobbett's Parliamentary Debates* (London: T. C. Hansard, 1812), vol. XXII, col. 1066.
95. J. E. Cookson, *Friends of Peace: Anti-War Liberalism in England 1793–1815* (Cambridge: Cambridge University Press, 1982), pp. 215–34.
96. For a very clear and useful discussion of 'the apparatus of early nineteenth-century warfare', see Jon Latimer, *1812: War with America* (Cambridge, Mass.: Harvard University Press, 2007), pp. 7–12.
97. John K. Mahon, *The War of 1812* (New York: Da Capo Press, 1991 pb edn, 1st pub. 1972), pp. 7–8. He adds that the US also had 200 gunboats for coastal waters.
98. J. C. A. Stagg, *The War of 1812: Conflict for a Continent* (Cambridge: Cambridge University Press, 2012), p. 10.
99. Indeed, historians of the War of 1812 sometimes describe their books as written from the British or the American perspective.
100. The (American) historian Bickham in *The Weight of Vengeance* argues that the Americans wanted Canada as a bargaining tool; the (British) historian Jon Latimer in *1812: War with America*, p. 3 argues that 'For the United States in 1812 the goal was to conquer Canada, and for more than two and a half years it tried and repeatedly failed to do so.' Stagg (American) in *The War of 1812*, p. 16 opts for the bargaining-tool argument, while Andrew Lambert (British) in *The Challenge: Britain against America in the Naval War of 1812* (London: Faber & Faber, 2012), pp. 32–3 states flatly that the goal was conquest. The (Canadian) historian Carl Benn in *The War of 1812* (Oxford: Osprey, 2002), p. 16 also believes that the Americans intended to conquer Canada.
101. Alan Taylor, *The Civil War of 1812: American Citizens, British Subjects, Irish Rebels, & Indian Allies* (New York: Alfred A. Knopf, 2010), p. 4.
102. Bickham, *The Weight of Vengeance*, pp. 103–4, p. 104 for the quotes; Mahon, *The War of 1812*, pp. 43–7.

103. Bickham, *The Weight of Vengeance*, p. 104 for the quotes; Mahon, *The War of 1812*, pp. 76–81, 93–5.

104. Jefferson to William Duane, 4 Aug. 1812, *Writings of Thomas Jefferson*, IX, pp. 365–7, quote on p. 366.

105. The battle came too late to have any legitimate influence on the New York election; however, Tompkins' supporters sent around victory proclamations regardless, and the American general kept the New York troops at home to vote for the Governor, who was re-elected by 3,606 votes. Benn, *The War of 1812*, p. 37. According to Wills, it was John Armstrong, Secretary of War, who decided that 'some victory, any victory, had to be scored by Dearborn's army before the April elections for congressional and state offices'. Wills, *Madison*, p. 123.

106. Mahon, *The War of 1812*, pp. 141–3; Benn, *The War of 1812*, pp. 78–80.

107. Benn, *The War of 1812*, pp. 78–80; Mahon, *The War of 1812*, pp. 141–3; Latimer, *1812*, pp. 132–3.

108. Mahon, *The War of 1812*, pp. 165–75, quotes on pp. 174, 175.

109. Perkins, *Prologue to War*, p. 426. Perkins (American) argues that the conquest of Canada was never a serious American war aim, citing this disbandment of the militia as evidence of the feeble desire for the permanent incorporation of Canada within the US. He argues elsewhere that both Madison and Monroe looked upon Canada as no more than a vulnerable target. Bradford Perkins, *Castlereagh and Adams: England and the United States 1812–1823* (Berkeley: University of California Press, 1964), p. 55.

110. Latimer, *1812*, pp. 224–7, 354–60.

111. Alfred Thayer Mahan, *Sea Power in its Relations to the War of 1812*, 2 vols (Boston: Little, Brown, 1905), I, pp. 328–35, 416–22; II, pp. 3–7. The *Guerrière* and the *Java* were both so damaged that they were burned at sea. The *Constitution* was blockaded in port for most of 1813 and 1814.

112. Lambert, *The Challenge*, p. 4.

113. The so-called *guerre de course*, commerce-destroying or plundering.

114. Benn, *The War of 1812*, p. 55; Henry Adams, *History of the United States of America during the Administrations of James Madison* (New York: Library of America, 1986, 1st pub. 1889–91), p. 1034.

115. Christopher D. Hall, *British Strategy in the Napoleonic War 1803–15* (Manchester: Manchester University Press, 1992), pp. 197–8; US

Bureau of the Census, *Historical Statistics of the United States: Colonial Times to 1957* (Washington, DC: Government Printing Office, 1960), pp. 563, 712; Benn, *The War of 1812*, pp. 55–61.

116. Bathurst to Ross, 20 May 1814, War Office Dispatches, The [National] Archives, now at Kew, cited as such and quoted in Adams, *History of the United States*, pp. 997–8, his comment p. 1000.

117. Cochrane to Prevost, 22 July 1814, C. 684, p. 221 and Orders of Vice-Admiral Cochrane, 18 July 1814, C. 684, p. 204, MSS, Canadian Archives, Ottawa, quoted in *ibid.*, pp. 998–1000.

118. There are masses of books covering these events. For an outline, see Kathleen Burk, *Old World, New World: The Story of Britain and America* (London: Little, Brown, 2007 or New York: Atlantic Books, 2008), pp. 236–41. For an extremely readable contemporary account, see An Officer Who Served in the Expedition [G. R. Gleig], *A Narrative of the Campaigns of the British Army at Washington and New Orleans under Generals Ross, Pakenham, and Lambert, in the Years 1814 and 1815; with Some Account of the Countries Visited* (London: John Murray, 1821).

119. Monroe to Gallatin, Adams and Bayard, 15 April 1813, Diplomatic Instructions of the State Department 1801–1906 (hereafter M77), M77/2, p. 239.

120. Perkins, *Castlereagh and Adams*, pp. 20–3.

121. In his diary for 1823, Adams referred to Gallatin's 'usual shrewdness and sagacity'. Adams, *Memoirs of John Quincy Adams*, VI, p. 193.

122. Adams, *History of the United States*, p. 1203.

123. Robert V. Remini, *John Quincy Adams* (New York: Henry Holt, 2002), p. 45.

124. Monroe to Gallatin, Adams and Bayard, 15 April 1813, when they expected negotiations to begin, but Great Britain refused, pp. 239–68, and Monroe to Adams, Bayard, Clay and Russell, 28 Jan. 1814, p. 313 for the quotation, both M77/2.

125. Monroe to Gallatin, Adams and Bayard, 23 June 1814, p. 98, M77/2.

126. Monroe to Adams, Bayard, Clay and Russell, 28 Jan. 1814, pp. 311–21, quote on p. 321, M77/2.

127. Perkins, *Castlereagh and Adams*, p. 60.

128. Those who read C. S. Forester's Hornblower series of novels might like to know that in *Flying Colours* (1938) Gambier was the model for the character Dismal Jimmy, who is devoted to religion.

129. Adams, *History of the United States*, p. 1193.

130. Perkins, *Castlereagh and Adams*, p. 61

131. Perkins in *ibid.*, p. 60, also considers that their talents were less.

132. Castlereagh to the Commissioners, 28 July 1814, Viscount Castlereagh, *Correspondence, Despatches, and Other Papers of Viscount Castlereagh, Second Marquess of Londonderry*, ed. Charles William Vane, Third Series, *Military and Diplomatic*, 4 vols (London: John Murray, 1853), II, pp. 67–72, and Gallatin to Monroe, 13 June 1814, quoted in Albert Gallatin, *The Writings of Albert Gallatin*, ed. Henry Adams, 3 vols (Philadelphia: J. B. Lippincott, 1879), I, pp. 627–9.

133. Adams, *History of the United States*, pp. 1195–9; Adams, *Memoirs of John Quincy Adams*, III, pp. 4–23.

134. Perkins, *Castlereagh and Adams*, p. 101.

135. Castlereagh to Liverpool, 28 Aug. 1814, Castlereagh, *Correspondence*, Third Series, II, pp. 100–2, quote pp. 101–2.

136. Liverpool to Wellington, 2 Sept. 1814, Duke of Wellington, *Supplementary Despatches, Correspondence, and Memoranda of Field Marshal Arthur Duke of Wellington, K.G.*, ed. Arthur R. Wellesley, 12 vols (London: John Murray, 1858–65), IX, pp. 211–13, quote on p. 213.

137. J. E. Cookson, *Lord Liverpool's Administration: The Crucial Years 1815–1822* (Edinburgh: Scottish Academic Press, 1975), p. 21 for government expenditure. See also Vansittart to Castlereagh, Confidential, 17 Oct. 1814, ff. 160–4, Add. MS 31231, Vansittart Papers, British Library. Thanks to Professor Thomas Otte for information on the subsidies.

138. Vansittart to Castlereagh, Confidential, 26 Nov. 1814, ff. 183–8, quote on ff. 184–5, Add. MS 31231, Vansittart Papers, British Library.

139. Liverpool to Castlereagh, 2 Nov. 1814, pp. 401–2, first quote on p. 402, and 28 Oct. 1814, pp. 382–83, second quote on p. 383, Wellington, *Supplementary Despatches*, IX, pp. 402, 383.

140. Vansittart to Castlereagh, Confidential, 26 Nov. 1814, ff. 183–8, quote on f. 185, Add. MSS 31231, Vansittart Papers, British Library.

141. Wellington to Liverpool, 9 Nov. 1814, Wellington, *Supplementary Despatches*, IX, pp. 424–6, quote on p. 426.

142. For a quite riveting account of the whole fisheries/Mississippi fight, see Adams, *History of the United States*, pp. 1212–19; Adams, *Memoirs of John Quincy Adams*, III, 70–118; Goulburn to

Bathurst, 10 Nov. and 25 Nov. 1814, Wellington., *Supplementary Despatches*, IX, pp. 427, 452–4.

143. Taylor, *The Civil War of 1812*, p. 10.

144. Richard Rush, American Minister to Great Britain 1817–25, wrote in his memoirs for 1818 that 'On the drop curtain at Covent Garden are seen the flags of nations with whom England has been at war. They are in a tattered state, and represented as in subjection to England. That of the United States is among them ... England has fame enough, military and of all kinds, without straining in small ways after what does not belong to her.' Richard Rush, *Memoranda of a Residence at the Court of London* (Philadelphia: Carey, Lea & Blanchard, 1833), p. 201.

CHAPTER 2: FROM SEA TO SHINING SEA, 1815–1903

1. Robert Frost, 'Mending Wall', https://www.poets.org/poetsorg/poem/mending-wall, accessed on 4 March 2018.

2. Rosemary Neering, *The Pig War: The Last Canada–US Border Conflict* (Victoria, BC: Heritage House, 2011), p. 62.

3. C. P. Stacey, 'The Myth of the Unguarded Frontier 1815–1908', *American Historical Review*, 56:1 (Oct. 1950), p. 4.

4. Kenneth Bourne, *Britain and the Balance of Power in North America 1815–1908* (London: Longmans, 1967), p. 5 n. 1.

5. Stacey, 'The Myth of the Unguarded Frontier 1815–1908', p. 9.

6. *Ibid.* The Act was approved on 27 Feb. 1815.

7. Bourne, *Britain and the Balance of Power*, p. 12. He further suggests on p. 13 that, while the government was concerned about the Lakes, this concern had probably been exaggerated in Parliament in order to secure its approval of the naval estimates.

8. There had been no British representative in Washington during the War of 1812. Bagot was appointed on 31 July 1815.

9. Monroe to Adams, 16 Nov. 1815, Diplomatic Instructions of the Department of State, 1801–1906), M77/3.

10. Quoted in Bradford Perkins, *The Cambridge History of American Foreign Relations*, vol. I: *The Creation of a Republican Empire 1776–1865* (Cambridge: Cambridge University Press, 1993), p. 208 for the quote, but, sadly, without giving a reference, beyond that it was written to 'a minister assigned to duty in Washington'.

11. Adams, *The Memoirs of John Quincy Adams*, III, pp. 287–8.

12. *Ibid.*, pp. 329–30; Adams to Castlereagh, 21 March 1816, FO 5/117; Castlereagh to Bagot, no. 7, 23 April 1816, FO 5/113.

13. Bagot to Castlereagh, no. 8, 3 May 1816, FO 5/114; Castlereagh to Bagot, no. 7, 23 April 1816, FO 5/113; Bagot to Castlereagh, no. 24, 12 Aug. 1816, FO 5/115. Perkins, *Castlereagh and Adams*, pp. 241–2; Bourne, *Britain and the Balance of Power*, p. 14.

14. Monroe to Bagot, 2 Aug. 1816, printed by the Avalon Project, Yale Law School, avalon.law.yale.edu/19th_century/br1817l2.asp, accessed 28 Aug. 2014.

15. Bagot to Monroe, 6 and 13 Aug. 1816, *ibid.*

16. Bagot to Monroe, 4 Nov. 1816, *ibid.*

17. Perkins, *Castlereagh and Adams*, p. 243.

18. An interesting title, given that Adams had in January 1816 referred to the 'Canadian Lakes' in his proposal to Castlereagh.

19. Stacey, 'The Myth of the Unguarded Frontier, 1815–71', p. 17.

20. Bourne, *Britain and the Balance of Power*, p. 269.

21. *Ibid.*, pp. 279–80, 291, 397, quotes on 391.

22. *Ibid.*, pp. 326–7 and 397, quote on p. 397.

23. Perkins, *Castlereagh and Adams*, pp. 245–58.

24. These were Dr William Adams, Fellow of Trinity Hall, Cambridge, a lawyer who specialised in Admiralty law, and Henry Goulburn, one of the negotiators for the Treaty of Ghent, who later became Chancellor of the Exchequer. They were soon joined by F. J. Robinson, Vice-President of the Board of Trade and the Plantations; he also became Chancellor of the Exchequer, when he became known as Prosperity Robinson. Rush, *Memoranda*, quote on p. 409.

25. R. B. Mowat, *The Diplomatic Relations of Great Britain and the United States* (London: Edward Arnold, 1925), p. 78; Rush, *Memoranda*, p. 345 for the list of topics handed to the British plenipotentiaries; Rush to Adams, no. 6, 4 Feb. 1818 and Rush to Adams, no. 7, 14 Feb. 1818, both M30/18; and Rush to Adams, no. 30, 25 July 1818, M30/19.

26. Rush, *Memoranda*, quotes on pp. 353 and 363–4; Gallatin and Rush to Adams, 20 Oct. 1818, M30/19.

27. *Ibid.*; Frederick Merk, *The Oregon Question: Essays in Anglo-American Diplomacy and Politics* (Cambridge, Mass.: Harvard University Press, 1967), pp. 33–43; Rush, *Memoranda*, p. 380 for the quote.

28. Carroll, *A Good and Wise Measure*, p. 35.

29. *Ibid.*

30. Thomas Barclay, *Selections from the Correspondence of Thomas Barclay*, ed. George Lockhart Rives (New York: Harper & Brothers, 1894), p. 359.

31. Barclay to Castlereagh, 10 Aug. 1816, in *ibid.*, pp. 370–1, quote on p. 371. Rives gives a good outline of the geographical issues, pp. 361–5.

32. Carroll, *A Good and Wise Measure*, pp. 37–40.

33. Barclay to Castlereagh, no. 4, 5 June 1817, ff. 257–8, FO 5/125.

34. Barclay to Castlereagh, 25 Oct. 1817, ff. 297–309, quote on ff. 303–4, FO 5/125.

35. Carroll, *A Good and Wise Measure*, p. 41.

36. Barclay to Castlereagh, 25 Oct. 1817, ff. 297–309, quote on f. 298, FO 5/125.

37. *Ibid.*, quotes on f. 306 and f. 307, FO 5/125.

38. *Ibid.*

39. Rush to Castlereagh, 24 Feb. 1818, M30/18.

40. Carroll, *A Good and Wise Measure*, p. 95.

41. *Ibid.*, p. 96 for the quote.

42. 'John Ogilvy', *Dictionary of Canadian Biography* [hereafter *DCB*], vol. V, pp. 635–6. http://www.biographi.ca/en/bio/ogilvy_john_5E.html, accessed 14 Sept. 2014.

43. John J. Bigsby, *The Shoe and the Canoe, or Pictures of Travels in the Canadas*, 2 vols (London: Chapman & Hall, 1850), I, p. 255. Latimer, *1812*, p. 148.

44. He is not, for example, in the *Dictionary of American Biography*.

45. 'David Thompson', *DCB*, vol. VIII, http://www.biographi.ca/en/bio/thompson_david_1770_1857_8E.html, accessed 14 Sept. 2014.

46. Adams to Peter Porter, 6 March 1819, quoted in Carroll, *A Good and Wise Measure*, p. 99.

47. 'Daniel Thompson', *DCB*, vol. VIII.

48. See, for example, Joseph Delafield, *The Unfortified Boundary: A Diary of the First Survey of the Canadian Boundary Line from St. Regis to the Lake of the Woods*, ed. Robert McElroy and Thomas Riggs (New York: privately printed, 1943), entry for 20 July 1818, pp. 201–2.

49. *Ibid.*, entries for 8 June and 10 June 1818, pp. 185–6; 27 June 1818, pp. 191–2; 3 July and 4 July 1818, pp. 194–5.

50. Carroll, *A Good and Wise Measure*, pp. 106–7.

51. *Ibid.*, pp. 102–3; Delafield, *Diary*, entries for 9 July through 20 July 1818, pp. 196–202, 22 Sept. 1818, p. 215.

52. Bigsby, *The Shoe and the Canoe*, I, pp. 249–50.

53. Porter to John Quincy Adams, 30 Sept. 1819, quoted in Carroll, *A Good and Wise Measure*, p. 104; Delafield, *Diary*, entry for 11 Aug. 1820, p. 293.

54. Castlereagh to Anthony Barclay, 11 Jan. 1820, ff. 2–3, FO 5/153.

55. Bigsby, *The Shoe and the Canoe*, I, p. 253.

56. Anthony Barclay to Castlereagh, 9 Nov. 1820, f. 164, FO 5/153.

57. Carroll, *A Good and Wise Measure*, p. 111; Delafield, *Diary*, entry for 28 June 1818, pp. 192–3.

58. Carroll, *A Good and Wise Measure*, pp. 111–15.

59. *Ibid.*, p. 118.

60. Bigsby, *The Shoe and the Canoe*, II, p. 266.

61. *Ibid.*, pp. 205–6.

62. Delafield, *Diary*, entry for 20 July 1823, pp. 411–12; the Lake in the Woods had several thousand islands. *Ibid.*, entry for 29 July 1823, pp. 424–6; Carroll, *A Wise and Good Measure*, p. 122.

63. Carroll, *A Wise and Good Measure*, p. 123.

64. *Ibid.*, pp. 131–41. Planta to A. Barclay, No. 1, 8 Jan. 1827, ff. 29–32, FO 5/240.

65. Carroll, *A Good and Wise Measure*, p. 49.

66. Thomas Barclay, *Correspondence*, p. 360.

67. The desired overland route from New Brunswick to Lower Canada (Quebec) was essentially up the St John River to the Madawaska River, across Lake Témiscouata, and over 'the height of land' to Rivière du Loup and the St Lawrence. Carroll, *A Good and Wise Measure*, p. 196.

68. Thomas Barclay, *Correspondence*, pp. 48–82.

69. Carroll, *A Good and Wise Measure*, pp. 85–6.

70. *Ibid.*, p. 80.

71. Barclay to Londonderry, Private, 6 Oct. 1821, rec. 5 Nov. 1821, f. 47, FO 5/164 and Stratford Canning to Londonderry, No. 58, 5 Nov. 1821, ff. 147–8, FO 5/159.

72. Adams to Rush, 5 Jan. 1822, M77/4.

73. Barclay to Londonderry, 11 July 1822, ff. 94–8, quote on f. 95, FO 5/170.

74. *Ibid.* According to Ward Chipman, the British agent, in a letter of 24 June 1820 to Lord Goulburn, the American agent would 'resist any

further demarcation of this part of the boundary however clearly ascertained'. *Ibid.*, f. 79.

75. *Ibid.*, f. 97.

76. Adams, *Memoirs of John Quincy Adams*, VI, p. 91.

77. Howard Jones, *To the Webster–Ashburton Treaty: A Study in Anglo-American Relations 1783–1843* (Chapel Hill: University of North Carolina Press, 1977), p. 13; Anna Lane Lingelbach, 'William Huskisson as President of the Board of Trade', *American Historical Review*, 43:4 (July 1938), pp. 759–74.

78. Jones, *To the Webster–Ashburton Treaty*, p. 13; Carroll, *A Good and Wise Measure*, pp. 154–5.

79. Carroll, *A Good and Wise Measure*, pp. 175–6.

80. This was to run due north from the St Croix River, along the middle of the St John River, to the St Francis River, along the middle of the St Francis to its north-westernmost branch and along the watershed line proposed by the US until it joined the line proposed by Great Britain, and thence until it reached the north-westernmost head of the Connecticut River. *Ibid.*, pp. 177–80. Essentially, it was impossible to locate the highlands as described in the treaty, and the Restigouche and the St John emptied not into the Atlantic, but into the Bay of Fundy. See Hunter Miller, ed., *Treaties and Other International Acts of the United States of America 1786–1863*, 8 vols (Washington, DC: US Government Printing Office, 1931–48), III, pp. 359–69.

81. Carroll, *A Good and Wise Measure*, pp. 177–80.

82. Herbert C. F. Bell, *Lord Palmerston*, 2 vols (Hamden, Conn.: Archon Books, 1966, 1st pub. 1936), I, p. 243.

83. Bagot to Palmerston, Private, from The Hague [where the King's decision had been given], 11 Jan. 1831, copy in ff. 1–3, Add. MS 43236, Aberdeen Papers, British Library.

84. Carroll, *A Good and Wise Measure*, p. 184.

85. Quoted in Jones, *To the Webster–Ashburton Treaty*, p. 17.

86. *Ibid.*, pp. 17–18.

87. Palmerston to Bankhead, No. 1, 30 Oct. 1835, ff. 49–65, FO 5/299.

88. Jones, *To the Webster–Ashburton Treaty*, p. 18.

89. Bell, *Palmerston*, I, p. 245. Palmerston to Bankhead, No. 1, 30 Oct. 1835, ff. 49–65, FO 5/299.

90. Quoted in Wilson P. Shortridge, 'The Canadian–American Frontier during the Rebellion of 1837–1838', *Canadian Historical Review*, 7:1 (March 1926), p. 15.

91. His sojourns in the US and France turned him into a republican, and he later supported the Montreal Annexation Manifesto that called for Canadian union with the US.

92. Sir Francis Head, Bart., Lieutenant-Governor of Upper Canada, to Henry S. Fox, British Minister to Washington, 8 Jan. 1838, Box 215, file 7 (Canadian Questions), Caleb Cushing Papers, Library of Congress, Washington, DC.

93. Quoted in Orrin Edward Tiffany, *The Relations of the United States to the Canadian Rebellion of 1837–1838* (Buffalo, NY: Buffalo Historical Society, 1st pub. 1905, POD 2014), pp. 29–30.

94. Leland H. Jenks, *The Migration of British Capital to 1875* (London: Thomas Nelson & Sons, 1963, 1st pub. 1927), pp. 86–8.

95. Tiffany, *Relations of the United States*, p. 30.

96. Jones, *To the Webster–Ashburton Treaty*, p. 22.

97. W. L. Marcy, 19 Dec. 1837, p. 59, FO 881/9. This file, containing all of the relevant documents on the *Caroline* episode, was printed for the Cabinet.

98. Lieut. John Elmsley, RN, to MacNab, 29 Dec. 1837 for being fired upon and Head to Fox, 8 Jan. 1838 for Chippewa and the horse, as well as for a description of events, both Box 215, f. 7, Cushing Papers. Jones, *To the Webster–Ashburton Treaty*, p. 24.

99. Jones, *To the Webster–Ashburton Treaty*, pp. 24 and 194. According to Jones, there was only one hotel in the area, and twenty-three passengers, along with the officer and nine crew members, slept on the boat.

100. Capt. Drew to Col. McNab, 30 Dec. 1837, p. 45, FO 881/9.

101. Tiffany, *Relations of the United States*, p. 35.

102. Jones, *To the Webster–Ashburton Treaty*, p. 24.

103. Quoted in *ibid.*, p. 25. The 'Fire, fire!' quote is from the Deposition of 30 Dec. 1837 of Gilman Appleby of Buffalo, who had commanded the *Caroline*, pp. 7–8, FO 881/9.

104. Jones, *To the Webster–Ashburton Treaty*, p. 25.

105. *Ibid.*, pp. 20–1.

106. Quoted in Scott Kaufman and John A. Soares, Jr, ' "Sagacious beyond Praise"? Winfield Scott and Anglo-American-Canadian Border Diplomacy, 1837–1860', *Diplomatic History*, 30:1 (Jan. 2006), p. 60.

107. Ulysses S. Grant, *Personal Memoirs of U.S. Grant*, 2 vols (New York: Charles R. Webster, 1885), I, p. 139., quoted in *ibid.*, p. 57.

108. http://www.presidency.ucsb.edu/ws/?pid=67317.

109. Jones, *To the Webster–Ashburton Treaty*, p. 28.
110. Howard Jones and Donald A. Rakestraw, *Prologue to Manifest Destiny: Anglo-American Relations in the 1840s* (Wilmington, Del.: SR Books, 1997), p. 39.
111. Quoted from Scott's instruction in Kaufman and Soares, Jr, 'Winfield Scott', p. 61.
112. Jones, *To the Webster–Ashburton Treaty*, p. 30.
113. Kaufman and Soares, Jr, 'Winfield Scott', p. 61.
114. Jones, *To the Webster–Ashburton Treaty*, p. 30.
115. Bourne, *Britain and the Balance of Power*, pp. 78–9.
116. According to Shortridge, 'The Canadian–American Frontier', p.19, 'The chief point to the obligation, by way of recognizing a brother Hunter, was not in any conceivable manner to make the shape or sign of the snow-shoe. If an individual claimed to be a member and could give the secret signs and pass word, the final test was to ask him to draw a picture of a snow-shoe. If he did, he was known not to be a member, for all Hunters were under obligation not to make it.'
117. *Ibid.*
118. *Ibid.*, pp. 19–21.
119. *Ibid.*, pp. 21–2, quote on p. 22.
120. *Ibid.*, pp. 20–4.
121. Jones, *To the Webster–Ashburton Treaty*, pp. 30–1.
122. Carroll, *A Good and Wise Measure*, p. 208.
123. Memorandum in the Stratford Canning Papers, f. 2, FO 352/59. This was possibly written as a response to Richard Rush, 'Informal Memorandum of the proposed heads of the Negotiations', 21 Jan. 1824, which is next to it in the file.
124. Jones and Rakestraw, *Prologue to Manifest Destiny*, pp. 8–10, quote on p. 10.
125. Carroll, *A Good and Wise Measure*, p. 209.
126. Quoted in *ibid.*
127. *Ibid.*, pp. 210, 373.
128. Scott, *Ties of Common Blood*, pp. 123–277.
129. Jones, *To the Webster–Ashburton Treaty*, pp. 44–7.
130. Palmerston to Fox, 8 April 1839, ff. 201–3, quote on f. 203, FO 97/19. FO 97/19 includes private intelligence gained by the US on the 1841 rebellion and given to the British Minister, who sent it to the Foreign Office and the Governor-General of British North America.

131. Jones, *To the Webster–Ashburton Treaty*, p. 49.

132. *Ibid.*, pp. 49–54.

133. Bourne, *Britain and the Balance of Power*, p. 86.

134. Palmerston to Fox, 9 Feb. 1841, quoted in *ibid.* Apparently not all of the 'British nation' were quite so certain about the legality of the British position. See the quotation from Greville's memoirs in Wilbur Devereux Jones, *The American Problem in British Diplomacy 1841–1861* (London: Macmillan, 1974), p. 5.

135. Bourne, *Britain and the Balance of Power*, p. 86.

136. Jones, *To the Webster–Ashburton Treaty*, pp. 54–5.

137. *Ibid.*, pp. 56–68.

138. Aberdeen to Clarendon, 5 Nov. 1854, ff. 245–6, quote on f. 246, Add. Ms 43189, Aberdeen Papers, British Library.

139. Edward Everett to Webster, No. 5, 21 Feb. 1842, enclosing Everett to Aberdeen, 21 Feb. 1842, M30/45. Jones, *To the Webster–Ashburton Treaty*, pp. 96–100.

140. Bourne, *Britain and the Balance of Power*, p. 70 for Ashburton quote. Mowat, *Diplomatic Relations*, pp. 112–15.

141. Ashburton to Aberdeen, No. 2, 25 April 1842, ff. 15–16, FO 5/379.

142. Ashburton to Aberdeen, No. 3, 25 April 1842, f. 24, FO 5/379.

143. *Ibid.*, ff. 26–7.

144. Mowat, *Diplomatic Relations*, p. 115.

145. *Ibid.*, pp. 114–15. Jones, *To the Webster–Ashburton Treaty*, pp. 102–13 for lots of interesting details about what Aberdeen in 1844 called 'the battle of the maps'.

146. The Treaty of Washington, 1842 is the more formal name for the Webster–Ashburton Treaty.

147. Everett to Buchanan, No. 302, 16 April 1845, M30/51.

148. Jones, *To the Webster–Ashburton Treaty*, pp. 170–1.

149. W. Jones, *The American Problem*, pp. 38–46. The claim had occasioned 'excitement' in London, but it was soon replaced by Irish problems. Everett to Buchanan, 3 March 1845, M30/51.

150. The 54° 40′ parallel had been fixed in the Convention of 1824 as the line dividing the claims of the US from those of Russia, which owned Alaska; the Anglo-Russian Treaty of 1825 used the same line as dividing the claims of Russia from those of Great Britain.

151. McLane to Buchanan, No. 34, 3 Feb. 1946, M30/52.

152. Bourne, *Britain and the Balance of Power*, p. 142; Stanley to Peel, 12 Aug. 1845, f. 338, Add. MS 40468, Peel Papers, British Library.

153. McLane to Buchanan, No. 35, 3 March 1846, M30/52.

154. James K. Polk, *The Diary of James K. Polk during his Presidency 1845–1849, Now First Printed from the Original Manuscript in the Collections of the Chicago Historical Society*, ed. M. M. Quaife, 4 vols (Chicago: A. C. McClurg, 1910), I, p. 241.

155. The number of Royal Navy ships was more impressive than the state of many of them, but the Americans probably did not realise this.

156. Bourne, *Britain and the Balance of Power*, pp. 147–61; John Seigenthaler, *James K. Polk* (New York: Henry Holt, 2003), pp. 122–8.

157. McLane to Buchanan, No. 44, 18 May 1846 and McLane to Buchanan, No. 58, 3 July 1846, both M30/52.

158. Merk, *The Oregon Question*, pp. 408–13. The text of the treaty can be found at http://avalon.law.yale.edu/19th_century/br-1846.asp, accessed on 2 Dec. 2014.

159. From the second American anthem, 'America the Beautiful'.

160. http://avalon.law.yale.edu/subject_menus/br1818m.asp.

161. http://avalon.law.yale.edu/19th_century/br-1846.asp.

162. Kaufman and Soares, Jr, 'Winfield Scott', p. 72.

163. *Ibid.*, p. 73.

164. E. C. Coleman, *The Pig War: The Most Perfect War in History* (Stroud: The History Press, 2009), pp. 41–56; Neering, *The Pig War*, p. 34.

165. Neering, *The Pig War*, p. 42.

166. *Ibid.*, p. 43.

167. Both quotes cited in *ibid.*, p. 50.

168. Kaufman and Soares, Jr, 'Winfield Scott', p. 73.

169. Both quotes cited in *ibid.*, p. 52.

170. *Ibid.*, p. 73.

171. Coleman, *The Pig War*, pp. 72–102; Neering, *The Pig War*, pp. 56–7.

172. Neering, *The Pig War*, p. 78.

173. This is widely quoted, but I have yet to see it cited with a reference.

174. Kaufman and Soares, Jr, 'Winfield Scott', p. 75.

175. *Ibid.*, p. 73.

176. *Ibid.*, p. 76.

177. Coleman, *The Pig War*, p. 65.

178. Kaufman and Soares, Jr, 'Winfield Scott', p. 81.

179. Quoted in Neering, *The Pig War*, p. 112.

180. *Ibid.*, pp. 110–25.

181. James Chambers, *Palmerston: The People's Darling* (London: John Murray, 2004), p. 491.

182. Mowat, *Diplomatic Relations*, p. 210.

183. *Ibid.*, p. 213.

184. *Ibid.*, pp. 213–20.

185. Neering, *The Pig War*, pp. 127–9.

186. Charles Callan Tansill, *Canadian–American Relations 1875–1911* (New Haven: Yale University Press, 1943), pp. 121–9.

187. http://avalon.law.yale.edu/19th_century/treatywi.asp.

188. Tansill, *Canadian–American Relations*, p. 131.

189. *Ibid.*, pp. 158–63, quotes on pp. 158 and 159.

190. *Ibid.*, p. 161.

191. William N. Tilchin, *Theodore Roosevelt and the British Empire: A Study in Presidential Statecraft* (Basingstoke: Macmillan Press, 1997), p. 36.

192. Tansill, *Canadian–American Relations*, p. 163.

193. Allan Nevins, *Henry White: Thirty Years of American Diplomacy* (New York: Harper & Brothers, 1930), p. 146.

194. Kenton J. Clymer, *John Hay: The Gentleman as Diplomat* (Ann Arbor: University of Michigan Press, 1975), p. 176.

195. Bradford Perkins, *The Great Rapprochement: England and the United States 1895–1914* (London: Victor Gollancz, 1969), p. 165.

196. Quoted in Tansill, *Canadian–American Relations*, p. 224.

197. Tilchin, *Theodore Roosevelt and the British Empire*, pp. 38–41, quotes from Roosevelt's instructions to the three American commissioners, 17 March 1903, pp. 40 and 41.

198. Perkins, *The Great Rapprochement*, p. 168.

199. Tansill, *Canadian–American Relations*, pp. 230–61.

200. David G. Haglund and Tudor Onea, 'Victory without Triumph? Theodore Roosevelt, Honour, and the Alaska Panhandle Boundary Dispute', *Diplomacy and Statecraft*, 19:1 (March 2008), pp. 20–41. These historians are Canadian, and they argue that, rather than bullying, Roosevelt and his administration were driven by a diplomacy of honour.

201. Quoted in Tansill, *Canadian–American Relations*, p. 264.

202. Perkins, *The Great Rapprochement*, p. 172. This was Sir Michael Herbert, the British Ambassador to Washington, who died on 30 Sept. 1903, three weeks before the award was made.

203. *Ibid.*, pp. 161–72, quote on p. 171.

204. A. J. P. Taylor, *The Struggle for Mastery in Europe 1848–1918* (Oxford: Oxford University Press, 1954), p. xxiv.

205. Andrew Lambert, 'Winning without Fighting: British Grand Strategy and its Application to the United States, 1815–65', in Bradford A. Lee and Karl F. Walling, eds, *Strategic Logic and Political Rationality: Essays in Honor of Michael I. Handel* (London: Frank Cass, 2003), pp. 164–95.

206. Howard Fuller, *Clad in Iron: The American Civil War and the Challenge of British Naval Power* (Westport, Conn.: Praeger, 2008), pp. 3–5, 128–31, 274–8.

207. Bourne, *Britain and the Balance of Power*, p. 275.

208. Lord Selborne, 'Distribution and Mobilization of the Fleet', Cabinet Memorandum, 6 Dec. 1904, Earl of Selborne, *The Crisis of British Power: The Imperial and Naval Papers of the Second Earl of Selborne 1895–1910*, ed. D. George Boyce (London: The Historians' Press, 1990), pp. 184–90, quote on pp. 184–5.

209. Quoted in Bourne, *Britain and the Balance of Power*, p. 362.

CHAPTER 3: CHINA AND THE BRITISH AND AMERICAN
BARBARIANS, 1783–1914

1. Lord Macartney, *An Embassy to China: Being the Journal kept by Lord Macartney during his Embassy to the Emperor Ch'ien-lung 1793–1794*, ed. J. L. Cranmer-Byng (London: Longmans, 1962), entry for 15 Sept. 1793, p. 125. The quotation is from John Milton, *Paradise Lost*, ed. Christopher Ricks (London: Penguin, 1968), Book IV, l. 35, p. 79 – 'Hide their diminisht heads', strictly speaking.

2. Macartney, *An Embassy to China*, 'An Edict from the Emperor Ch'ien-Lung to King George the Third of England', pp. 337–41, quotes on pp. 337 and 340. According to Cranmer-Byng, this was the first literal translation from the Chinese, the earlier translation having toned down the arrogance of the Chinese prose.

3. Frederick Wakeman, Jr, 'The Canton Trade and the Opium War', in John K. Fairbank, ed., *The Cambridge History of China*, vol. X: *Late Ch'ing 1800–1911, Part 1* (Cambridge: Cambridge University Press, 1978), p. 169; Foster Rhea Dulles, *The Old China Trade* (London: Macdonald & Jane's, 1974, 1st pub. 1930), pp. 1–12.

4. One example is the American historian George C. Herring, who uses the term 'hitch-hiking diplomacy' in *From Colony to Superpower: U.S. Foreign Relations since 1776* (New York: Oxford University Press, 2008), p. 210. 'Piggy-back diplomacy' is, as far as I know, mine.

5. H. B. Morse, ed., *The Chronicles of the East India Company Trading to China 1635–1834*, 4 vols (Oxford: Oxford University Press, 1926), I, pp. 3–4.

6. P. J. Marshall, 'The English in Asia to 1700', in Nicholas Canny, ed., *The Oxford History of the British Empire*, vol. I: *The Origins of Empire: British Overseas Enterprise to the Close of the Seventeenth Century* (Oxford: Oxford University Press, 1998), p. 268.

7. *Ibid.*, pp. 266–7.

8. *Ibid.*, p. 274.

9. *Ibid.*, p. 281; K. N. Chaudhuri, *The Trading World of Asia and the English East India Company 1660–1760* (Cambridge: Cambridge University Press, 1978), table on p. 538 for the import numbers, which do not include those for non-Company traders; William T. Rowe, *China's Last Empire: The Great Qing* (Cambridge, Mass.: Harvard University Press, 2009), pp. 136–7, 165.

10. *Ibid.*, p. 142.

11. Wakeman, 'The Canton Trade and the Opium War', pp. 163–5, quote on p. 163. James L. Hevia, *Cherishing Men from Afar: Qing Guest Ritual and the Macartney Embassy of 1793* (Durham, NC: Duke University Press, 1995), p. 49.

12. Morse, *Chronicles*, II, p. 162. The American spellings are as printed in the text of the document given here.

13. *Ibid.*, p. 155.

14. *Ibid.*, pp. 160–7, quote on p. 166.

15. Macartney, *An Embassy to China*, pp. 18–22, quote on p. 18.

16. Hevia, *Cherishing Men from Afar*, p. 74.

17. Morse, *Chronicles*, II, p. 215.

18. *Ibid.*, Appendix G, Henry Dundas, 'Instructions to Lord Macartney, Sept. 8, 1792', pp. 232–44.

19. Henrietta Harrison, 'The Qianlong Emperor's Letter to George III and the Early-Twentieth-Century Origins of Ideas about Traditional China's Foreign Relations', *American Historical Review*, 122:3 (July 2017), pp. 683–4.

20. Hevia, *Cherishing Men from Afar*, p. 136.

21. Macartney, *An Embassy to China*, entry for 6 Aug. 1793, p. 74.

22. *Ibid.*, p. 33.

23. *Ibid.*, p. 6.

24. Harrison, 'The Qianlong Emperor's Letter', p. 684.

25. Macartney, *An Embassy to China*, entry for 19 Aug. 1793, p. 90.

26. *Ibid.*, entry for 10 Sept. 1793, p. 119.

27. *Ibid.*, entry for 14 Sept. 1793, p. 122.

28. *Ibid.*, p. 128.

29. *Ibid.*, entry for 17 Sept. 1793, p. 134.

30. *Ibid.*, entry for 18 Sept. 1793, p. 137.

31. *Ibid.*, entry for 30 Sept. 1793, p. 145.

32. *Ibid.*, pp. 337 and 34.

33. Hevia, *Cherishing Men from Afar*, pp. 190–1, first quote on p. 190, second on p. 191.

34. Harrison, 'The Qianlong Emperor's Letter', pp. 684–5. This paragraph is based on and quotes from these pages.

35. Macartney, *An Embassy to China*, entry for 21 Oct. 1793, p. 168.

36. *Ibid.*, entry for 1 Jan. 1794, p. 209.

37. *Ibid.*, p. 29; Hevia, *Cherishing Men from Afar*, pp. 183–5.

38. Quoted in Hevia, *Cherishing Men from Afar*, p. 229.

39. Ritcheson, *Aftermath of Revolution*, p. 129.

40. Dulles, *The Old China Trade*, p. 4.

41. *Ibid.*

42. James R. Gibson, *Otter Skins, Boston Ships, and China Goods: The Maritime Fur Trade of the Northwest Coast 1785–1841* (Montreal: McGill-Queen's University Press, 1992, 1999 pb edn), p. 94.

43. Ibid., pp. 97–100.

44. Charles C. Stelle, 'American Trade in Opium in China, Prior to 1820', *Pacific Historical Review*, 9:4 (Dec. 1940), p. 427 n. 13.

45. This was Article 13 of the Jay Treaty of 1794. John Jay to Edmund Randolph, 19 Nov. 1794, M30/2.

46. Stelle, 'American Trade ... Prior to 1820', p. 431.

47. Charles C. Stelle, 'American Trade in Opium to China, 1821–39', *Pacific Historical Review*, 10:1 (March 1941), p. 62; Wakeman, 'The Canton Trade and the Opium War', p. 172.

48. Dulles, *The Old China Trade*, pp. 132–5; Jacques M. Downes, 'American Merchants and the China Opium Trade, 1800–1840', *Business History Review*, 42:4 (Winter 1968), pp. 427–8; Morse, *Chronicles*, IV, pp. 12–13.

49. *Ibid.*, p. 13.

50. Downes, 'American Merchants and the China Opium Trade', pp. 427–8.

51. *Ibid.*, pp. 428–9.

52. Sibing He, 'Russell and Company and the Imperialism of Anglo-American Free Trade', in Kendall Johnson, ed., *Narratives of Free Trade: The Commercial Cultures of Early US–China Relations* (Hong Kong: Hong Kong University Press, 2012), p. 96.

53. Michael H. Hunt, *The Making of a Special Relationship: The United States and China to 1914* (New York: Columbia University Press, 1983), pp. 10–11.
54. Michael Greenberg, *British Trade and the Opening of China 1800–42* (Cambridge: Cambridge University Press, 1951), pp. 18 for the quote and 196.
55. *Ibid.*, pp. 178 for the quote about diplomacy and 192–5; Wakeman, 'The Canton Trade and the Opium War', p. 173.
56. *Ibid.*, pp. 172–4.
57. Julia Lovell, *The Opium War: Drugs, Dreams and the Making of China* (London: Picador, 2011), p. 5.
58. *Ibid.*, pp. 6–7.
59. Wakeman, 'The Canton Trade and the Opium War', p. 175; Priscilla Napier, *Barbarian Eye: Lord Napier in China 1834: The Prelude to Hong Kong* (London: Brassey's, 1995).
60. Robert Erwin Johnson, *Far China Station: The U.S. Navy in Asian Waters 1800–1898* (Annapolis, Md: Naval Institute Press, 1979), pp. 5–9, 129.
61. Wakeman, 'The Canton Trade and the Opium War', p. 206.
62. *Ibid.*, pp. 178–9.
63. T. F. Tsiang, 'New Light on Chinese Diplomacy, 1836–49', *Journal of Modern History*, 3:4 (Dec. 1931), pp. 581–2. The article analyses the then newly published Chinese diplomatic documents from the Palace Museum at Peking.
64. Greenberg, *British Trade*, pp. 198–201, quote on p. 201.
65. *Ibid.*, p. 203.
66. Lovell, *The Opium War*, p. 66; Wakeman, 'The Canton Trade', p. 187.
67. Lovell, *The Opium War*, p. 66.
68. Tsiang, 'New Light on Chinese Diplomacy', p. 582.
69. Alexander Michie, *The Englishman in China during the Victorian Era as Illustrated in the Career of Sir Rutherford Alcock, K.C.B., D.C.L., Many Years Consul and Minister in China and Japan*, 2 vols (Taipei: Ch'eng-Wen Publishing, 1966, 1st pub. 1900), I, pp. 40–1.
70. Lovell, *The Opium War*, pp. 62–4.
71. *Ibid.*, pp. 170–1.
72. *Ibid.*, p. 101.
73. Wakeman, 'The Canton Trade and the Opium War', p. 191.
74. Muriel E. Chamberlain, *Lord Palmerston* (Cardiff: University of Wales Press, 1987), p. 56.
75. Hansard, HC Deb., 3rd Series, vol. 53, col. 940, 9 April 1840.

76. B. R. Mitchell, *British Historical Statistics* (Cambridge: Cambridge University Press, 1988), table on Gross Public Expenditure – United Kingdom 1801–1980, p. 587.

77. Wakeman, 'The Canton Trade and the Opium War', p. 194. In the House of Commons debate on 9 April as cited in note 75, Palmerston listed thirty firms which had signed a joint letter to him; cols 945–6.

78. Lovell, *The Opium War*, p. 168 for the first quote; Hunt, *The Making of a Special Relationship*, pp. 35–6 for the second.

79. Wakeman, 'The Canton Trade and the Opium War', p. 192.

80. Greenberg, *British Trade*, pp. 206–12.

81. Peter Ward Fay, *The Opium War 1840–1842: Barbarians in the Celestial Empire in the Early Part of the Nineteenth Century and the War by Which They Forced Her Gates Ajar* (Chapel Hill: University of North Carolina Press, 1975, 1997 pb edn), p. 362; Earl H. Prichard, 'The Origins of the Most-Favored-Nation and the Open Door Policies in China', *Far Eastern Quarterly*, 1:2 (Feb. 1942), pp. 168–70.

82. Tsiang, 'New Light on Chinese Diplomacy', p. 588.

83. Wakeman, 'The Canton Trade and the Opium War', p. 210.

84. Fay, *The Opium War*, pp. 80–127.

85. William J. Donahue, 'The Caleb Cushing Mission', *Modern Asian Studies*, 16:2 (1982), pp. 193–5.

86. http://www.presidency.ucsb.edu/ws/index.php?pid=67360, accessed 19 May 2015.

87. Stelle, 'American Trade ... 1821–39', p. 65.

88. Donohue, 'The Caleb Cushing Mission', pp. 196–9.

89. Webster to Cushing, 8 May 1843, US Senate, 28th Congress, 2nd sess., Message from the President, 'Copies of the instructions given to the late commissioner to China', 25 Feb. 1845, Doc. 138, pp. 1–5.

90. Cushing to Secretary of State, 26 Feb. 1844, Despatches from US Ministers to China, 1843–1906 (hereafter M92), M92/2.

91. Donohue, 'The Caleb Cushing Mission', p. 202 n. 45.

92. *Ibid.*, p. 203.

93. Pottinger, Government House, Victoria, Hong Kong, to Cushing, 6 March 1844, M92/2.

94. 2 March 1844, M92/2.

95. Cushing to Ching, 27 Feb. 1844, US Senate, 28th Congress, 2nd sess., Doc. 67, p. 2.

96. *Ibid.*, pp. 2–5.

97. Ching to Cushing, 8 May 1844, US Senate, 28th Congress, 2nd sess., Doc. 67, p. 28 for the first quote; Ping Chia Kuo, 'Caleb Cushing

and the Treaty of Wanghia, 1844', *Journal of Modern History*, 5:1 (March 1933), p. 39 n. 20 for the second.

98. Hunt, *The Making of a Special Relationship*, pp. 17–19, 31; John R. Haddad, *America's First Adventure in China: Trade, Treaties, Opium, and Salvation* (Philadelphia: Temple University Press, 2013), pp. 137–40.

99. Ping Chia Kuo, 'Caleb Cushing and the Treaty of Wanghia', p. 41.

100. Cushing to Ching, 22 April 1844, US Senate, 28th Congress, 2nd sess., Doc. 67, p. 18.

101. *Ibid.*, p. 20.

102. Tsiyeng is the name used in the Treaty of Wangxia (also called Wanghia), as well as in other documents.

103. Ping Chia Kuo, 'Caleb Cushing and the Treaty of Wanghia', pp. 46–7 n. 60.

104. *Ibid.*, pp. 47–51.

105. The Emperor to the Great Ministers of State to Kiying to Cushing, 12 May 1844, US Senate, 28th Congress, 2nd sess., Doc. 67, p. 30.

106. *Ibid.*, 27 May 1844, p. 32.

107. Cushing to Secretary of State, No. 69, 4 July 1844, M92/3.

108. Ping Chia Kuo, 'Caleb Cushing and the Treaty of Wanghia', p. 53.

109. http://en.wikisource.org/wiki/Treaty_of_Wanghia.

110. Haddad, *America's First Adventure in China*, p. 158.

111. Immanuel C. Y. Hsü, *The Rise of Modern China* (New York: Oxford University Press, 1990, 4th edn), p. 200.

112. John J. Nolde, 'The "False Edict" of 1849', *Journal of Asian Studies*, 20:3 (May 1961), p. 300.

113. Lovell, *The Opium War*, p. 247.

114. Nolde, 'The "False Edict" of 1849', p. 300.

115. Lovell, *The Opium War*, pp. 247–51.

116. *Ibid.*, p. 256.

117. J. W. Wong, *Deadly Dreams: Opium and the Arrow War (1856–1860) in China* (Cambridge: Cambridge University Press, 1998), p. xxii.

118. Hunt, *The Making of a Special Relationship*, p. 21.

119. *Ibid.*

120. Lovell, *The Opium War*, p. 252.

121. Wong, *Deadly Dreams*, pp. 90–1.

122. *Ibid.*, p. 163.

123. *Ibid.*, p. 293.

124. Hansard, HC Deb., 3rd Series, vol. 144, col. 1421 for the Resolution, cols 1393–4, 26 Feb. 1857.

125. Lovell, *The Opium War*, pp. 255–7.

126. *Ibid.*, p. 258.

127. James L. Hevia, *English Lessons: The Pedagogy of Imperialism in Nineteenth-Century China* (Durham, NC: Duke University Press, and Hong Kong: Hong Kong University Press, 2003), p. 39.

128. Johnson, *Far China Station*, p. 103.

129. *Ibid.*, p. 40.

130. *Ibid.*, pp. 104–5, one quotation on each page. Paul Kramer refers to the Tattnall quote as Anglo-Saxonism's 'chief origin myth, frequently recounted in clubs and social gatherings on both sides of the Atlantic in the late nineteenth century' in 'Empires, Exceptions, and Anglo-Saxons: Race and Rule between the British and United States Empires, 1880–1910', *Journal of American History*, 88:4 (March 2002), p. 1327. Anglo-Saxonism was meant to consolidate Anglo-American ties, but Kramer argues that it also 'legitimated U.S. overseas colonialism': pp. 1328–31, 1352, 1319 for the quote.

131. Johnson, *Far China Station*, pp. 42–6; Lovell, *The Opium War*, p. 262.

132. Hevia, *English Lessons*, pp. 47–8.

133. Odd Arne Westad, *Restless Empire: China and the World Since 1750* (London: Vintage, 2013, 1st pub. 2012), p. 54.

134. Rowe, *China's Last Empire*, pp. 214–19; Robert Bickers, *The Scramble for China: Foreign Devils in the Qing Empire 1832–1914* (London: Penguin Books, 2012), p. 192.

135. S. S. Kim, 'Burlingame and the Inauguration of the Co-operative Policy', *Modern Asian Studies*, 5:4 (1971), p. 340.

136. Rowe, *China's Last Empire*, p. 204.

137. Hunt, *The Making of a Special Relationship*, p. 182.

138. *Ibid.*, pp. 116–17.

139. Seward to Burlingame, No. 8, 6 March 1862, *Papers Relating to Foreign Affairs. Part II. Communicated to Congress December 1, 1862* (Washington, DC: Government Printing Office, 1862), p. 839, hereafter *Foreign Affairs, 1862, II*.

140. Bickers, *The Scramble for China*, p. 207.

141. Rowe, *China's Last Empire*, p. 203.

142. Haddad, *America's First Adventure in China*, pp. 213–14, quotes on p. 14.

143. Quoted in Kim, 'Co-operative Policy', p. 351, n. 62.

144. David L. Anderson, *Imperialism and Idealism: American Diplomats in China 1861–1898* (Bloomington: Indiana University Press, 1985), p. 20.

145. Kim, 'Co-operative Policy', pp. 347–9.

146. Burlingame to Seward, 14 Dec. 1867, Department of State, *Executive documents printed by order of the House of Representatives, during the third session of the fortieth Congress, 1868-'69*, vol. I: *1868–1869*, (Washington, DC: Government Printing Office, 1869), p. 494 for the quote; hereafter Executive Documents. Nathan A. Pelcovits, *Old China Hands and the Foreign Office* (New York: King's Crown Press, 1948), p. 46.

147. Pelcovits, *Old China Hands*, pp. 49–50.

148. Bickers, *The Scramble for China*, p. 212.

149. *Ibid.*, Burlingame to Clarendon, 1 Jan. 1869, rec. 13 Jan. 1869, No. 10, p. 4.

150. *Ibid.*, Clarendon to Alcock, 13 Jan. 1869, No. 11, p. 5.

151. *Ibid.*

152. Clarendon to Alcock, 28 Jan. 1869, ff. 70–1, FO 228/466.

153. Pelcovits, *Old China Hands*, pp. 5–6.

154. Bickers, *The Scramble for China*, p. 309.

155. Pelcovits, *Old China Hands*, pp. 5–8, quotes on p. 7.

156. Marius B. Jansen, *The Making of Modern Japan* (Cambridge, Mass.: Harvard University Press, 2000, 2002 pb edn), pp. 4–5.

157. Bickers, *The Scramble for China*, p. 324.

158. Quoted in T. G. Otte, *The China Question: Great Power Rivalry and British Isolation 1894–1905* (Oxford: Oxford University Press, 2007), p. 3.

159. Taylor, *The Struggle for Mastery in Europe*, p. 391.

160. A. E. Campbell, 'Great Britain and the United States in the Far East, 1895–1903', *Historical Journal*, 1:2 (1958), p. 160.

161. The whole of this quote is given in A. J. P. Taylor, 'Two Prime Ministers', in his *From Napoleon to Stalin: Comments on European History* (London: The Right Book Club, 1950), p. 115. Salisbury to Chamberlain, 30 Dec. 1897, quoted in J. L. Garvin, *The Life of Joseph Chamberlain*, 6 vols (London: Macmillan, 1932–69), III, p. 249.

162. United States Department of State, *Papers Relating to the Foreign Relations of the United States with the Annual Message of the President Transmitted to Congress December 5, 1899* (Washington, DC: Government Printing Office, 1901), pp. 131–43, hereafter *FRUS*.

163. Westad, *Restless Empire*, p. 131.
164. Bickers. *The Scramble for China*, pp. 338–40, quote on p. 338.
165. Campbell, 'Great Britain and the US', p. 163.
166. Bickers, *The Scramble for China*, pp. 338–44, quotes on pp. 338 and 344. The new base at Manila had 20,000 troops, 5,000 of whom were sent to China. This was, in fact, done without consulting Congress or declaring war, thereby creating a new presidential power. China had declared war on the US, but few in Washington seem to have paid it much attention.
167. Bickers, *The Scramble for China*, p. 346.
168. In the first relief force, the British provided over eight times as many soldiers as did the Americans, 915 vs 111. The Germans provided 512, the Russians 312 and the French 157. The three smallest forces were provided by the Japanese (54), the Italians (42) and the Austrians (26), making a total of 2,129. Frank J. Allston, 'U.S. Navy Paymaster: A Hero in the Boxer Rebellion', *Supply Corps Newsletter*, 0360716X, 63:4 (July/August 2000), Table 1.
169. Hevia, *English Lessons*, pp. 195–6.
170. Bickers, *The Scramble for China*, p. 346.
171. 'Remembering the Boxer Uprising: A righteous fist', *The Economist*, 16 Dec. 2010.
172. Otte, *The China Question*, p. 328.
173. Hunt, *The Making of a Special Relationship*, p. 199.
174. *Ibid.*, p. 182.
175. Rowe, *China's Last Empire*, pp. 253–83; Hsü, *The Rise of Modern China*, pp. 408–80.
176. The last First Lord not to be Prime Minister concurrently.
177. *The* (London) *Times*, 11 January 1898, p. 8, col. 3.
178. Pelcovits, *Old China Hands*, p. 214.
179. Bickers, *The Scramble for China*, pp. 359–60, quotes on p. 360.
180. Rowe, *China's Last Empire*, pp. 260–2.
181. Satow to Grey, 31 March 1906, f. 1, FO 800/44.
182. E. W. Edwards, *British Diplomacy and Finance in China 1895–1914* (Oxford: Oxford University Press, 1987), p. 149.
183. In a memorandum of 21 June 1909, C. S. Addis wrote that the claim was based on a letter from Chang to Satow (then British Minister to China), FO 371/624. Chang was Chang Chih-tung, Director-General of the railway. Alvey A. Adee, the Acting Secretary of State, in a note of 3 Aug. 1905 to the British Ambassador, H. M. Durand, refers to 'the promise made by the Chinese Government in 1903'. *FRUS, 1909*, p. 147.

184. Reid to Grey, 3 June 1909, f. 237, FO 371/624.
185. Quoted in Hunt, *The Making of a Special Relationship*, p. 210.
186. Quoted in *ibid.*, p. 209.
187. Knox to Reid to tell Grey, 2 June 1909, *FRUS, 1909*, p. 145; Reid to Grey, 8 June 1909, f. 300, FO 371/624.
188. Minute by Campbell, 14 Dec. 1908, f. 401, on Jordan to Grey, No. 199, 12 Dec. 1908, f. 402, FO 371/435.
189. Grey to Reid, 8 June 1909, *FRUS, 1909*, pp. 149–50.
190. Reid to Grey, 3 June 1909, f. 237, FO 371/624.
191. Minute by C. S. Addis, 22 June 1909, ff. 404–5, FO 371/624.
192. Minute by R.C., 15 June 1909, f. 326, referring to Reid to Grey, 12 June 1909, f. 330, FO 371/624.
193. Grey initialled a minute of 16 June 1909 drafted by Campbell, f. 366, FO 371/624.
194. Edwards, *British Diplomacy and Finance in China*, pp. 139 and 148.
195. Addis to Urbig, 24 June 1909, f. 438, FO 371/624.
196. Edwards, *British Diplomacy and Finance in China*, p. 141.
197. Hunt, *The Making of a Special Relationship*, p. 211.
198. *Ibid.*; Kathleen Burk, *Morgan Grenfell 1838–1988: The Biography of a Merchant Bank* (Oxford: Oxford University Press, 1989), pp. 65–6.
199. Hunt, *The Making of a Special Relationship*, p. 211.
200. Rowe, *China's Last Empire*, p. 236.
201. Quoted in Hunt, *The Making of a Special Relationship*, p. 211.
202. Edwards, *British Diplomacy and Finance in China*, p. 145.
203. Hunt, *The Making of a Special Relationship*, p. 213; Edwards, *British Diplomacy and Finance in China*, p. 146.
204. Hunt, *The Making of a Special Relationship*, p. 214.
205. *Ibid.*, pp. 214–15; Edwards, *British Diplomacy and Finance in China*, pp. 151–3.
206. Burk, *Morgan Grenfell*, p. 66.
207. Rowe, *China's Last Empire*, p. 282.
208. Campbell to Jordan, 3 Nov. 1911, f. 67, FO 350/1.
209. Campbell to Jordan, 15 Nov. 1911, f. 74, FO 350/1..
210. Grey to Jordan, No. 168, 14 Nov. 1911, f. 98, FO 371/1095.
211. Edwards, *British Diplomacy and Finance in China*, p. 158.
212. Hunt, *The Making of a Special Relationship*, p. 392 n. 31.
213. Bickers, *The Scramble for China*, pp. 368–9.
214. Hsü, *The Rise of Modern China*, pp. 472–7.
215. Bickers, *The Scramble for China*, p. 369 for first quote, p. 370 for the second.

216. Calhoun to Knox, 6 Dec. 1911, *FRUS, 1912*, p. 102.

217. Hunt, *The Making of a Special Relationship*, p. 218.

218. Reinsch to Bryan, 5 May 1914, *FRUS, 1914*, pp. 51–2.

CHAPTER 4: THE UNITED STATES, GREAT BRITAIN
AND JAPAN, 1854–1895

1. C. M. Conrad, Acting Secretary of State, to J. P. Kennedy, Secretary of the Navy, 5 Nov. 1852, 'Message of the President of the United States [Franklin Pierce], transmitting a report of the Secretary of the Navy, in compliance with a resolution of the Senate of December 6, 1854, calling for correspondence, &c., relative to the naval expedition to Japan', 31 January 1855, 33rd Congress, 2nd sess., 751 Senate Exdoc. 34, p. 8 (hereafter 751 Senate Exdoc. 34).

2. W. G. Beasley, *Great Britain and the Opening of Japan 1834–1858* (London: Luzac, 1951, Japan Library pb edn 1995), p. 90.

3. Burk, *Old World, New World*, pp. 311–24.

4. *Ibid.*, p. 87.

5. FO to Bowring, No. 30, 21 July 1852, ff. 158–9, quote on f. 158, FO 17/186.

6. Francis L. Hawks, *Narrative of the Expedition of an American Squadron to the China Seas and Japan: Performed in the Years 1852, 1853, and 1854, under the Command of Commodore M. C. Perry, by Order of the Government of the United States. Compiled from the Original Notes and Journals of Commodore Perry, United States Navy, and his Officers, at his Request and under his Supervision* (New York: D. Appleton, and London: Trubner, 1856), pp. 350–1.

7. Payson Jackson Treat, *The Early Diplomatic Relations between the United States and Japan 1853–1865* (Baltimore: The Johns Hopkins Press, 1917), p. 8.

8. Jansen, *The Making of Modern Japan*, pp. 80–1.

9. Samuel Eliot Morison, *'Old Bruin': Commodore Matthew C. Perry 1794–1858* (Boston: Atlantic Monthly Press, 1967), p. 263.

10. Engelbert Kaempfer, *The History of Japan*, trans. J. Scheuchzer (Glasgow: James MacLehose, 1906), III, 167–8, quoted in *ibid.*, pp. 83–4.

11. Michael R. Auslin, *Negotiating with Imperialism: The Unequal Treaties and the Culture of Japanese Diplomacy* (Cambridge, Mass.: Harvard University Press, 2004, pb edn 2006), p. 17.

12. Stephen Turnbull, *Tokugawa Ieyasu: Leadership, Strategy, Conflict* (Oxford: Osprey, 2012).

13. 'Shōgun' comes from the term current during the eighth to the twelfth centuries, *sei-i taishōgun*, or 'commander-in-chief of expeditions against the barbarians' or 'great general who subdues the eastern barbarians'.

14. Thus a *rōjū* was a member of the *rōjū*.

15. Treat, *Early Diplomatic Relations*, p. 18.

16. As it happens, 'in the year 1832, a Mr Roberts was appointed a special agent of the government, with authority to negotiate treaties with sundry nations in the east, and among others with Japan, but he died before he arrived at the island'. Conrad to Kennedy, 13 Nov. 1852, 751 Senate Exdoc. 34, p. 5.

17. 'Extension of American Commerce – Proposed Mission to Japan and Corea', Read and laid upon the table 15 Feb. 1845, House of Representatives, 28th Congress, 2nd sess., Doc. No. 138, pp. 1–2, quotes on p. 1.

18. David F. Long, *Sailor-Diplomat: A Biography of James Biddle 1783–1848* (Boston: Northeastern University Press, 1983), pp. 202–4; Merrill L. Bartlett, 'Commander James Biddle and the First Naval Mission to Japan, 1845–1846', *American Neptune*, 41 (Jan. 1981), p. 29.

19. Quoted in Long, *Sailor-Diplomat*, p. 209; Bartlett, 'Commander James Biddle', p. 31.

20. Quoted in Long, *Sailor-Diplomat*, p. 214.

21. Biddle to the Secretary of the Navy, 31 July 1846, quoted in *ibid.*, p. 14.

22. *Ibid.*, p. 215.

23. Quoted in *ibid.*, p. 219.

24. Beasley, *Great Britain and the Opening of Japan*, p. 69.

25. Quoted in Long, *Sailor-Diplomat*, p. 218.

26. Morison, *Perry*, pp. 273–8.

27. 751 Senate Exdoc. 34, pp. 5–9, quotes on pp. 6, 7, 8.

28. *Ibid.*, pp. 12–13.

29. *Ibid.*, p. 15.

30. Morison, *Perry*, p. 301.

31. *Ibid.*, p. 306.

32. *Ibid.*, pp. 308–11.

33. 751 Senate Exdeoc. 34, p. 85.

34. *Ibid.*, p. 31.

35. *Ibid.*, pp. 31–2, quote on p. 32.

36. Dobbin to Perry, 30 May 1854, *ibid.*, pp. 112–13.

37. According to contemporary Japanese prints, they were actually brown, but the Japanese called all foreign ships *kurofune* or black ships to differentiate them from the white ships of the Chinese traders. Jansen, *Modern Japan*, p. 277.

38. Morison, *Perry*, p. 267.

39. *Ibid.*, pp. 318–19.

40. 'Notes of events which transpired pending the preliminary negotiations of Commodore M. C. Perry with the authorities of Japan, in July, 1853', 751 Senate Exdoc. 34, pp. 45–6, quotes on p. 45.

41. Jansen, *Modern Japan*, p. 276.

42. 'Notes of events', 751 Senate Exdoc. 34, p. 47.

43. 'Millard Fillmore, President of the United States of America, to his Imperial Majesty, the Emperor of Japan', in *ibid.*, p. 10.

44. Jansen, *Modern Japan*, p. 277, based on Japanese documents.

45. 'Notes of events', 751 Senate Exdoc. 34, p. 47.

46. 'Your attention is particularly invited to the exploration of the coasts of Japan and of the adjacent continent and islands. You will cause linear or perspective views to be made of remarkable places, soundings to be taken at the entrances of harbors, rivers, &c., in and near shoals, and collect all the hydrographical information necessary for the construction of charts.' Secretary of the Navy Dobbin to Perry, 13 Nov. 1852, *ibid.*, p. 2.

47. *Ibid.*, p. 48.

48. *Ibid.*, p. 51.

49. Morison, *Perry*, p. 330.

50. *Ibid.*, p. 333.

51. *Ibid.*

52. 751 Senate Exdoc. 34, p. 51.

53. *Ibid.*, pp. 51–2.

54. *Ibid.*, p. 52.

55. *Ibid.*, p. 54.

56. *Ibid.*, p. 58.

57. *Ibid.*, pp. 57–8. The difficulty appears to have been that Congress prescribed by law the number of sailors in the US Navy, but presumably they could have been redeployed from their current ships if desired? Dobbin to Perry, 7 April 1853, p. 16.

58. Bonham to Perry, 22 Dec. 1853, 751 Senate Exdoc. 34, p. 82 and Perry to Bonham, 23 Dec. 1853, *ibid.*, p. 85.

59. *Ibid.*, p. 76.

60. *Ibid.*, pp. 106–7.

61. Paul E. Eckel, 'The Crimean War and Japan', *Far Eastern Quarterly*, 3:2 (Feb. 1944), pp. 109–11.

62. Hawks, *Narrative of the Expedition*, pp. 350–1.

63. Dobbin to Perry, 30 May 1854, 751 Senate Exdoc. 34, pp. 112–13. Perry's dispatch can be found in *ibid.*, Perry to Dobbin, No. 39, 25 Jan. 1854, pp. 108–11.

64. Henry Satoh, *Lord Hotta, the Pioneer Diplomat of Japan* (Tokio: Hakubunkan, 1908), p. 28.

65. Treat, *Early Diplomatic Relations*, p. 18.

66. Capt. F. Brinkley, with the collaboration of Baron Kikuchi, *A History of the Japanese People: From the Earliest Times to the End of the Meiji Era* (New York: Encyclopedia Britannica, 1915), p. 665. Brinkley was the editor of the *Japan Mail* and Kikuchi was the former president of the Imperial University at Kyōto.

67. Henry Satoh, *Agitated Japan: The Life of Baron Ii Kamon-no kami Naosuké (Based on the Kaikoku Shimatsu of Shimada Saburō)* [Summary of the Opening of Japan to Civilization], rev. William Elliot Griffis (New York: D. Appleton, 1896), pp. 129–40.

68. Brinkley, *Japanese People*, p. 666.

69. Treat, *Early Diplomatic Relations*, pp. 20–4.

70. Morison, *Perry*, p. 378.

71. Quoted in Peter Booth Wiley with Ichiro Korogi, *Yankees in the Land of the Gods: Commodore Perry and the Opening of Japan* (New York: Viking, 1990), p. 398.

72. Quoted in Morrison, *Perry*, p. 359.

73. Auslin, *Negotiating with Imperialism*, pp. 1–10.

74. Wiley, *Yankees*, p. 404.

75. Morison, *Perry*, pp. 379–80 for the terms of the treaty.

76. *Ibid.*, pp. 381–2, quote on p. 382.

77. *Ibid.*, pp. 383–99. Perry had strongly urged their acquisition on Washington, for reasons of coal, supplies and imperialistic rivalry – that is, to keep it out of the hands of the British and others.

78. See, for example, Aberdeen to Davis, 8 Aug. 1845, Separate and Secret, ff. 173–84, quote on f. 179, FO 17/96, in which a possible approach to Japan is partly conditioned by current problems in China, for example 'endeavour to expand as far as possible the advantages secured to us by our Treaties with China, by prevailing on the Japanese Government to open not Five but all the Great Ports of the Empire to our trade'.

79. Andrew Alexander Knox, 'Kaempfer's *Histoire de l'Empire du Japon*', *Edinburgh Review*, 96:196 (Oct. 1852), pp. 348–83, quote on p. 383.

80. Beasley, *Great Britain and the Opening of Japan*, pp. xiii–xv, 1–13.

81. Quoted in *ibid.*, p. 61.

82. *Ibid.*, pp. 55–68.

83. *Ibid.*, p. 102.

84. *Ibid.*, pp. 113–15; W. G. Beasley, 'From Conflict to Co-operation: British Naval Surveying in Japanese Waters, 1845–82', in Ian Nish and Yoichi Kibata, eds, *The History of Anglo-Japanese Relations*, vol. I: *The Political–Diplomatic Dimension 1600–1930* (London: Palgrave Macmillan, 2000), p. 94; Eckel, 'The Crimean War and Japan', pp. 109–18.

85. W. G. Beasley, 'The Language Problem in the Anglo-Japanese Negotiations of 1854', *Bulletin of the School of Oriental and African Studies*, 13:3 (1950).

86. Beasley, *Great Britain and the Opening of Japan*, pp. 116–30.

87. *Ibid.*, pp. 133–42, quote on p. 139.

88. Carl Crow, *He Opened the Door of Japan: Townsend Harris and the Story of his Amazing Adventures in Establishing American Relations with the Far East* (New York: Harper & Brothers, 1939), pp. 1–19, quote on p. 15. Townsend Harris, *The Complete Journal of Townsend Harris: First American Consul and Minister to Japan* ed. Mario E. Cosenza (Rutland, Vermont and Tokyo: Charles E. Tuttle, 1930, rev. edn 1959), p. 3.

89. Seward wrote to Harris on 21 Oct. 1861, No. 24, that 'You are perhaps now informed for the first time that your appointment as the first commissioner to Japan was made by President Pierce upon the joint recommendation of Commodore Perry and myself.' *Foreign Affairs, 1862, II*, p. 816.

90. Harris, *Journal*, pp. 9–10.

91. *Ibid.*, pp. 4–12; Crow, *Townsend Harris*, pp. 25–9, quote on p. 29.

92. Emily Hahn, 'A Yankee Barbarian at the Shogun's Court', *American Heritage*, 15:4 (June 1964), p. 29.

93. Harris, *Journal*, pp. 208–9. Moriyama was a constant presence in the conduct of relations with foreign powers.

94. *Ibid.*, pp. 219–22; William Maxwell Wood, *Fankwei; or, The San Jacinto in the Seas of India, China and Japan* (New York: Harper & Brothers, 1859), pp. 310–14.

95. Harris, *Journal*, pp. 231–2.

96. *Ibid.*, p. 242.

97. J. H. Gubbins, *The Progress of Japan 1853–1871* (Oxford: Oxford University Press, 1911), p. 69. Gubbins had been the Secretary of

Legation and the Japanese Secretary at the British Legation in Japan; at the time of the book, he was Lecturer in Japanese at Oxford.

98. Harris, *Journal*, p. 222 and n. 284a.

99. Shôzan Yashi, *Kinsé Shiriaku: A History of Japan from the First Visit of Commodore Perry in 1853 to the Capture of Hakodate by the Mikado's Forces in 1869*, trans. E. M. Satow (Yokohama: F. R. Wetmore, 1876), p. 6. This work resembles a chronicle, although some entries are longer than others.

100. He has a fascinating backstory; see Satoh, *Lord Hotta*, chs 1–4.

101. Harris to Secretary of State, No. 20, 25 Nov. 1856, rec. 9 March 1857, Despatches from US Ministers to Japan, 1855–1906 (hereafter M133), M133/1.

102. Satoh, *Lord Hotta*, pp. 33–5.

103. Yashi, *A History of Japan*, pp. 6–7.

104. Harris to Secretary of State, No. 13, 11 Sept. 1857, M133/1.

105. Harris to Secretary of State, No. 7, 18 June 1857, M133/1 – but it was not sent to Washington until September, because there was no ship available to carry it.

106. Yashi, *A History of Japan*, p. 7.

107. Harris to Secretary of State, No. 13, 11 Sept. 1857, M133/1.

108. Harris, *Journal*, pp. 411–43, quote on p. 443, ref. 526.

109. *Ibid.*, pp. 456–81, quote on p. 463; Harris to Secretary of State, No. 26, 10 Dec. 1857, M133/1.

110. Harris to Secretary of State, 4 March 1858, rec. 30 Nov. 1858, M133/1.

111. Satoh, *Lord Hotta*, pp. 50–5, quote on p. 55.

112. Harris, *Journal*, pp. 493–7, quote on p. 496.

113. *Ibid.*, pp. 497–500, first two quotes on p. 499, the third on p. 500.

114. Harris, *Journal*, pp. 527–30, quote on p. 527.

115. *Ibid.*, p. 537. According to Inouye, of the eighteen Great Daimyō, fourteen were opposed; of the 300 daimyō created by Iyeyasu, 210 were opposed. *Ibid.*, p. 543.

116. Satoh, *Lord Hotta*, pp. 64–9.

117. Treat, *Early Diplomatic Relations*, p. 97.

118. Harris, *Journal*, pp. 528–39 and 543–57.

119. *Ibid.*, p. 559 n. 629; Henry Heusken, *Japan Journal 1855–1861*, trans. and ed. Jeannette C. van der Corput and Robert A. Wilson (New Brunswick, NJ: Rutgers University Press, 1964), pp. 193–202.

120. Quoted in James L. McClain, *Japan: A Modern History* (New York: W. W. Norton, 2002), p. 141.

121. Satoh, *Lord Hotta*, pp. 72–103.

122. Harris to Secretary of State, No. 20, 31 July 1858, M133/1; Treat, *Early Diplomatic Relations*, p. 116 for the number of ships.

123. Quoted in William Elliot Griffis, *Townsend Harris, First American Envoy in Japan* (Boston: Houghton, Mifflin, 1895), p. 321.

124. Beasley, *Great Britain and the Opening of Japan*, pp. 184–5, quote on p. 185.

125. Captain Sherard Osborn, *A Cruise in Japanese Waters* (Edinburgh: W. Blackwood & Sons, 1859, reprint by General Books LLC), p. 32.

126. Treat, *Early Diplomatic Relations*, p. 117.

127. Beasley, *Great Britain and the Opening of Japan*, pp. 187–203.

128. Treat, *Early Diplomatic Relations*, pp. 116–18.

129. Jansen, *Modern Japan*, pp. 103, 203, 296.

130. *Ibid.*, p. 298.

131. Harris to Cass, 1 Aug. 1860, Harris Papers, Book 5, No. 7, quoted in John McMaster, 'Alcock and Harris: Foreign Diplomacy in Bakumatsu Japan', *Monumenta Nipponica*, 22:3/4 (1967), p. 347.

132. Alcock to Hammond, Private, 22 Feb. 1859, f. 61, FO 391/1.

133. Malmesbury to Alcock, No. 1, 1 March 1859, ff. 1–9, quote on f. 2, FO 46/2.

134. Michie, *The Englishman in China*, II, p. 14.

135. Harris to Cass, No. 8, 22 Feb. 1860, enclosing the letter from Alcock to Harris, M133/3.

136. Another two ports were scheduled to be opened in 1860 and 1863 respectively.

137. McMaster, 'Alcock and Harris', p. 313.

138. *Ibid.*, p. 314.

139. *Ibid.*, pp. 314–18, quote on p. 318.

140. Alcock to Malmesbury, No. 8, 9 July 1859, ff. 53–61, f. 57 for quote, FO 46/3.

141. Sir Ernest Mason Satow, *Diplomat in Japan: The Inner History of the Critical Years in the Evolution of Japan When the Ports were Opened and the Monarchy Restored, Recorded by a Diplomatist Who Took an Active Part in the Events of the Time, with an Account of his Personal Experiences of the Period* (Philadelphia: J. B. Lippincott, 1921, reprint by General Books LLC), p. 13.

142. Harris to Cass, No. 16, 16 May 1860, M133/3.

143. McMaster, 'Alcock and Harris', pp. 322–40; Satow, *A Diplomat in Japan*, pp. 5–6.

144. Treasury to FO, 9 July 1864, ff. 379–81, quote on f. 379, FO 46/49.
145. Harris to Cass, 22 Jan. 1861, printed in Heusken, *Japan Journal*, pp. 223–4, 226.
146. *Ibid.*, p. 224.
147. Alcock to Hammond, Private, 1 Jan. 1861, f. 83, FO 391/1.
148. McMaster, 'Alcock and Harris', pp. 350–1. By splitting away from the other foreign diplomats, Harris believed that he had made hostilities almost impossible. Harris to Seward, No. 112, 6 March 1861, Book 5, Harris Papers, cited in *ibid.*, p. 355.
149. Alcock to the Japanese Minister of Foreign Affairs, 26 Jan. 1861, *Parliamentary Papers 186, House of Lords 18, Correspondence Respecting Affairs in Japan. March and April, 1861. Presented to both Houses of Parliament by Command of Her Majesty. 1861*, pp. 7–10.
150. Yashi, *A History of Japan*, p. 18.
151. Harris to Cass, No. 8, 13 Feb. 1861, enclosing the documents exchanged between Harris and Alcock, M133/3.
152. Alcock to Harris, 25 Feb. 1861, included in Harris to Cass, No. 11, 6 March 1861, M133/3.
153. Harris to Alcock, 23 Feb. 1861, M133/3; also found in *Parliamentary Papers 186, House of Lords 18*, vol. 442, 162, p. 43.
154. Francis Hall, *Japan through American Eyes: The Journal of Francis Hall, Kanagawa and Yokohama 1859–1866*, ed. F. G. Notehelfer (Princeton: Princeton University Press, 1992), p. 288.
155. Rutherford Alcock, *The Capital of the Tycoon: A Narrative of Three Years' Residence in Japan*, 2 vols (New York: Harper & Brothers, 1868), I, pp. 195–201, especially pp. 199–200.
156. McMaster, 'Alcock and Harris', p. 354.
157. Examples are Alcock to Hammond, Confidential, 19 Aug. 1861, f. 127; 28 Nov. 1861, Private, f. 165; and 7 Feb. 1862, Private, f. 137, all FO 391/1.
158. Alcock to Russell, No. 3, 26 Jan 1861, FO 46/10.
159. Russell to Alcock, No. 37, 8 April 1861, ff. 80–4, f. 83 for the quote, FO 46/10.
160. McMaster, 'Alcock and Harris', pp. 354–5.
161. Alcock to Harris, 2 March 1861 and Harris to Alcock, 4 March 1861, both enclosed in Harris to Cass, No. 11, M 133/3.
162. Quoted in Jack L. Hammersmith, *Spoilsmen in a 'Flowery Fairyland': The Development of the U.S. Legation in Japan 1859–1906* (Kent, Ohio: Kent State University Press, 1998), p. 21.

163. Harris to Cass, No. 26, 1 Aug. 1860, M133/3.

164. Glyndon G. Van Deusen, *William Henry Seward* (New York: Oxford University Press, 1967), pp. 518–19.

165. 'Among Seward's lesser troubles was a chronic anxiety lest some contumacious Union naval officer insult the British flag in such flagrant fashion as to plunge the two countries into war.' Van Deusen, *Seward*, p. 350. See James D. Bulloch, *The Secret Service of the Confederate States in Europe or, How the Confederate Cruisers were Equipped* (New York: Sagamore Press, 1959, Random House Modern Library pb edn 2001).

166. McMaster, 'Alcock and Harris', p. 356.

167. *Ibid.*

168. Harris to Cass, No. 20, 8 May 1861, *Foreign Affairs, 1862, II*, pp. 794–7; McMaster, 'Alcock and Harris', p. 356.

169. Laurence Oliphant, 'The Attack on the British Legation in Japan in 1861', *Blackwood's Edinburgh Magazine*, 141:855 (Jan. 1887), pp. 45–57, quotes on pp. 53, 50. This was chapter 10 of Oliphant's memoir, *Episodes in a Life of Adventure or Moss from a Rolling Stone* (Edinburgh: William Blackwood & Sons, 1887). The quote is from p. 196, the numbers killed pp. 199–200.

170. McMaster, 'Alcock and Harris', pp. 359–63.

171. Hall, *Journal*, p. 423.

172. Recall Seneca and Nero.

173. 'To the victors belong the spoils,' so a change in a political party's control produces a changes in thousands of political appointees. American political term.

174. Hammersmith, *U.S. Legation in Japan*, p. 26.

175. *Ibid.*, p. 30.

176. Seward to Pruyn, No. 2, 15 Nov. 1861, *Foreign Affairs, 1862, II*, pp. 817–18, quote on p. 818.

177. Seward to Pruyn, No. 3, 19 Dec. 1861, *Foreign Affairs, 1862, II*, p. 819.

178. Hammersmith, *U.S. Legation in Japan*, p. 39.

179. Hugh Cortazzi, 'Lt Colonel St John Neale. Chargé d'Affaires at Edo/Yokohama, 1862–64', in Hugh Cortazzi, ed., *British Envoys in Japan 1859–1972* (Folkestone, Kent: Global Oriental for the Japan Society, 2004), p. 32.

180. He was the father of Shimazu Tadayoshi, who was the nominal daimyō of Satsuma; the father held the real power.

181. Neale to Russell, 15 & 16 Sept. 1862, quoted in Cortazzi, 'Neale', p. 25. Much more detail can be found in the *South Australian*

Register of 7 March 1863, which had received the information from the *Japan Herald* of 20 Sept. 1862.

182. Cortazzi, 'Neale', pp. 26–7.

183. FO Memorandum of 28 Nov. 1862, quoted in *ibid.*, p. 27.

184. Payson Jackson Treat, *Japan and the United States 1853–1921* (Boston and New York: Houghton Mifflin, 1921, Bibliolife Reproduction Series edn 2016), p. 66.

185. Quoted from Japanese documents in Auslin, *Negotiating with Imperialism*, p. 96.

186. Pruyn, 11 May 1863, cited in Treat, *Early Diplomatic Relations*, p. 260.

187. It was the news that Kyōto had decided to expel the foreigners that caused Pruyn, for the first time, to feel the necessity for the US to maintain a naval force in Japanese waters: 'I have not been anxious till recently for the presence of any of our naval force here. But my opinions have undergone a great change ... It was the presence of the British fleet and of other vessels-of-war in these waters, which has brought about a peaceful solution of the late complications.' Pruyn to Seward, 16 June 1863, pp. 1017–19, *Foreign Affairs, 1863, II*, quote on p. 1018.

188. Quoted in Cortazzi, 'Neale', pp. 29–30; Treat, *Early Diplomatic Relations*, pp. 268–72.

189. Quoted in Cortazzi, 'Neale', p. 31.

190. Hugh Cortazzi, 'The British Bombardment of Kagoshima, 1863', in Cortazzi, ed., *British Envoys in Japan*, Appendix I, pp. 271–80; Satow, *Diplomat in Japan*, pp. 28–30. Satow was on one of the smaller ships at the battle.

191. Quoted in Treat, *Early Diplomatic Relations*, p. 290 n. 22.

192. Jansen, *Modern Japan*, p. 320. The *bakufu* had led on this, sending eleven students to Leiden in 1862; however, they probably did not have the later political influence exercised by the students from Chōshū and Satsuma.

193. Yoshiyuki Kikuchi, 'Samurai Chemists, Charles Graham and Alexander William Williamson at University College London, 1863–1872', *Ambix*, 56:2 (July 2009), pp. 116–21.

194. Auslin, *Negotiating with Imperialism*, p. 98.

195. Russell to Alcock, No. 1, 17 Dec. 1863, ff. 190–2, FO 46/31.

196. Pruyn to Alcock, No. 45, 13 May 1864, *Foreign Affairs, 1864–5, III*, pp. 499–502, quote on p. 500.

197. Pruyn to Seward, No. 51, 10 Aug. 1864, *ibid.*, pp. 534–5.

198. Some of the sailors gave it 7 out of 10 that the students would lose their heads. The sailors were not to know that the students had been sent abroad by the daimyō, who would not then invoke the law requiring the execution of any Japanese leaving Japan.

199. Satow, *Diplomat in Japan*, pp. 31–2.

200. The failure to land forces at Kagoshima was believed by some to have been a mistake.

201. Treat, *Japan and the United States*, p. 66; Satow, *Diplomat in Japan*, pp. 33–41.

202. Russell to Alcock, No. 88, 26 July 1864, ff. 180–5, FO 46/42. Seen by the Cabinet and the Queen; Pruyn to Alcock, No. 45, 13 May 1864, in Alcock to Russell, No. 29, 14 May 1864, ff. 234–5, FO 46/44.

203. Extract from a letter, presumably from Russell (but it does not say) to Alcock, Private, 10 Aug. 1864, ff. 7–8, in the papers of Edward Hammond, the Permanent Under-Secretary of the Foreign Office, FO 391/1.

204. Russell to Alcock, No. 93, 8 Aug. 1864, ff. 209–10, FO 46/42. Seen by Palmerston and the Queen.

205. Alcock to Russell, No. 11, 31 March 1864, ff. 450–72, FO 46/43 for example.

206. Satow, *Diplomat in Japan*, p. 37.

207. Russell to Alcock, No. 131, 2 Dec. 1864, ff. 300–2, quote on f. 300, FO 46/42.

208. Some diplomats both then and now who were familiar with Japan were more accepting of Alcock's activities. These included Satow, Minister to Japan 1895–1900, and Cortazzi, Ambassador to Japan 1980–4.

209. Quoted in Cortazzi, 'Alcock Returns', p. 37.

210. Satoh, *Agitated Japan*, pp. 115–16.

211. Text of the order 'for the expulsion of the barbarians', *Foreign Affairs, 1863, II*, p. 1035.

212. Payson Jackson Treat, 'The Mikado's Ratification of the Foreign Treaties', *American Historical Review*, 23:3 (April 1918), pp. 541–2.

213. See the almost-no-warts-at-all biography by F. V. Dickins, *The Life of Sir Harry Parkes: Minister Plenipotentiary to Japan*, vol. II (London: Macmillan, 1894). Vol. I, by S. Lane-Poole, covers his life in China. Another example is in Brinkley's *A History of*

the Japanese People, p. 675, where he is referred to as 'a man of remarkably luminous judgement and military methods'.

214. See James Hoare, 'The Era of the Unequal Treaties, 1858–99', in Nish and Kibata, eds, *History of Anglo-Japanese Relations*, p. 11, where he says that Parkes' approach left a legacy of hostile feeling in Japan: the Japanese were tired of being lectured to on matters both British and Japanese. Hoare was, until 2003, a member of the UK Foreign and Commonwealth Office.

215. Plunkett to Rosebery, No. 35, Very Confidential, 1 March 1886, ff. 195–210, FO 46/343, quote of Plunkett f. 199, quote of Itō f. 202. He added to Rosebery that 'for her legitimate helpmate, she [Japan] must look either to England or America', because Germany was too far away from her base '& has no power except to cajole', f. 199.

216. There were one Dutch, three French and five British ships; there was no American man-of-war available, so the American Chargé d'Affaires, Mr Portman, joined the British frigate *Pelorus*. Treat, 'The Mikado's Ratification', p. 545. According to Auslin, Parkes 'browbeat' the French, Dutch and American ministers into accompanying him. *Negotiating with Imperialism*, p. 130.

217. Parkes to the Tycoon, on behalf of himself and the Representatives of France, the US and the Netherlands, 21 Nov. 1865, ff. 113–16, quote on f. 116, FO 46/58. Parkes to Russell, No. 69, 28 Nov. 1865, ff. 89–111, f. 95 for the sending of the Note, FO 46/58.

218. Parkes to Russell, No. 69, 28 Nov. 1865, f. 96, FO 46/58. The Japanese also agreed to another of the Treaty Powers' demands, which was a lowering of the tariff to 5 per cent; *ibid.*, f. 103.

219. *Ibid.*, ff. 105–6.

220. Parkes wrote to Foreign Secretary Clarendon, emphasising 'the proneness of this Government, in common with other Oriental states, to avoid, when they can do so, the execution of engagements which conflict with a traditional policy'. The Foreign Representatives will have to combine 'close watchfulness' with 'patient persuasion' to ensure that the Japanese would actually do what the Treaty required. No. 104, 18 July 1866, ff. 3–22, quotes on ff. 15–16, FO 46/69.

221. Auslin, *Negotiating with Imperialism*, p. 135; Grace Fox, *Britain and Japan 1858–1883* (Oxford: Oxford University Press, 1969), pp. 182–5. The Convention had an increasing importance: the Meiji government wanted to get rid of it, as one of the 'unequal

treaties', succeeding only in 1894 for the treaty with Britain and 1895 for the one with the US.

222. Van Valkenburgh to Seward, No. 59, 22 Dec. 1866, pp. 18–19, *Foreign Affairs, 1868, II*, quote on p. 19.

223. Jansen, *The Making of Modern Japan*, pp. 309–11; Treat, *Japan and the United States*, pp. 82–3, quote, which is from the Eight Point Plan, on p. 83; Satow, *Diplomat in Japan*, p. 101. Van Valkenburgh to Seward, No. 62, 7 Nov. 1867, pp. 67–8, *Foreign Affairs, 1868, II*. Parkes notified Stanley by telegram, 5 Dec. 1867; more details followed in No. 205, 5 Dec. 1867, ff. 5–9, FO 46/83.

224. Van Valkenburgh to Seward, No. 68, 2 Dec. 1867, pp. 76–8, *Foreign Affairs, 1868, II*, p. 76 for the announcement about the Tycoon. M. William Steele, 'The United States and Japan's Civil War', in his *Alternative Narratives in Modern Japanese History* (London: RoutledgeCurzon, 2003), p. 47.

225. Van Valkenburgh to Seward, No.7, 3 Feb. 1868, *Executive Documents 1868–'69*, vol. I: *1868–1869*, pp. 635–8.

226. Parkes to Stanley, No. 27, 1 Feb. 1868, f. 260, FO 46/91.

227. Parkes to Stanley, No. 29, 15 Feb. 1868, ff. 289–90, f. 289 for the quote, FO 46/91.

228. Van Valkenburgh to Seward, No. 12, 24 Feb. 1868, *Executive Documents 1868–'69*, I, pp. 671–2.

229. Auslin, *Negotiating with Imperialism*, p. 151.

230. *Ibid.*, pp. 151–2.

231. Parkes to Stanley, No. 62, Confidential, 19 March 1868, ff. 197–200, ff. 197–8 for the quote, FO 46/92.

232. Even had it been, he would soon receive instructions from Secretary of State Seward to assure the Tycoon and his government of the continued goodwill and esteem of the US. Seward to Van Valkenburgh, No. 45, 27 Feb. 1868, *Executive Documents 1868–'69*, I, p. 679.

233. Fox, *Britain and Japan*, pp. 228–9.

234. This was written to Vice-Admiral Keppel when Parkes asked him to assemble several vessels at Osaka. Quoted in *ibid.*, pp. 233–4.

235. Parkes to Stanley, No. 3, 13 Jan. 1869, ff. 9–10, FO 46/106.

236. Parkes to Stanley No. 5, 13 Jan. 1869, Confidential, ff. 32–5, quote on ff. 32–3, FO 46/106. Parkes' 'advice to the rulers of Japan ... was clearly sometimes delivered in a hectoring and aggressive tone ... Parkes was determined that Japan's new rulers should listen to

his advice, his interpretation of what was best for Japan, employ Britons wherever possible, and buy British.' Hoare, 'The Era of Unequal Treaties', p. 112.

237. Treat, *Japan and the United States*, p. 89; Dickins, *Harry Parkes*, p. 109.

238. Auslin, *Negotiating with Imperialism*, pp. 156–7.

239. Parkes to Granville, No. 72, 22 May 1871, ff. 122–5, FO 46/139. He also referred to it rather pointedly in his speech at his Private Audience with the Mikado on 18 May and then in the interview which followed with the Prime Minister and his government. Parkes' speech at the Private Audience, ff. 134–37. Auslin, *Negotiating with Imperialism*, pp. 167–8.

240. Marlene J. Mayo, 'A Catechism of Western Diplomacy: The Japanese and Hamilton Fish, 1872', *Journal of Asian Studies*, 26:3 (May 1967), pp. 395–8, 405–7.

241. *Ibid.*, pp. 396–7.

242. Auslin, *Negotiating with Imperialism*, p. 187.

243. Adams to Granville, No. 92, Confidential, 20 May 1872, ff. 407–14, quote on ff. 409–10, FO 46/153; Adams to Hammond, Private, 7 May 1872, ff. 198–200, f. 198 for the quote, FO 391/26.

244. Auslin, *Negotiating with Imperialism*, p. 188.

245. De Long to Fish, 19 Jan. 1871, quoted in *ibid.*, p. 183.

246. See the papers from the conference at the London School of Economics on 6 Dec. 1997 on 'The Iwakura Mission in Britain, 1872': http://eprints.lse.ac.uk/6908/1/The_Iwakura_Mission_in_Britain,_1872.pdf, accessed 4 March 2018.

247. Auslin, *Negotiating with Imperialism*, pp. 192–4.

248. J. Savile Lumley to Granville, No. 79, 27 Aug. 1862, ff. 15–16, FO 262/38.

249. Japan's feeling of hatred for China, 'which was the original cause [of the Sino-Japanese War] seems with every fresh success to be fast giving way to another feeling, namely, the ambition of Japan to prove herself equal to and to rank as one of the Great Powers, and this ambition seems in its turn to be making way to the conviction that Japan alone is well able to hold her own against any single European Power'. He adds that not everyone in Japan or the government believes this, although the war party, which is in the ascendancy, does. Power Trench, Minister to Japan, to Kimberley, No. 165, Secret, 14 Nov. 1894, quote on ff. 153–4, FO 46/438.

250. Auslin, *Negotiating with Imperialism*, pp. 198–9.

251. The Minister to Japan, Hugh Fraser, warned Salisbury, the Foreign Secretary, that, although Russia, Germany and the US had accepted Notes to be annexed to the Convention, he believed that one Note, dealing with the employment of foreign jurists, gave a fallacious guarantee, and England should not accept it. Fraser to Salisbury, No. 99, Confidential, 16 Aug. 1889, ff. 115–21, FO 46/387.

252. de Bunsen to Rosebery, No. 4, 12 Jan. 1894, ff. 17–23, f. 18 for the quote, FO 46/435.

253. M. de Bunsen, British Chargé d'Affaires in Tokyo, warned on 14 Jan. 1894 that Japan was really considering repudiation of the treaties; however, Mutsu Munemitsu, Minister for Foreign Affairs, and Itō separately reassured the British. Treat, *Japan and the United States*, p. 419.

254. John Curtis Perry, 'Great Britain and the Emergence of Japan as a Naval Power', *Monumenta Nipponica*, 21:3/4 (1966), pp. 305–21.

255. Gresham to Edwin Dun, US Minister to Japan, No. 66, 11 June 1894, ff. 166–70, M77/107; Dun to Gresham, No. 62, Confidential, 21 Feb. 1894, M133/17. No. 66 is in part Gresham's response to No. 62.

256. Treat, *Japan and the United States*, pp. 424–9.

CHAPTER 5: THE END OF THE (IMPERIAL) AFFAIR, 1895–1972

1. Justus D. Doenecke and Mark A. Stoler, *Debating Franklin D. Roosevelt's Foreign Policies 1933–1945* (Lanham, Md: Rowman & Littlefield, 2005), pp. 54–5.

2. Paul Kennedy, *The Rise and Fall of British Naval Mastery* (London: Macmillan, 1983 edn), p. 181.

3. Taylor, *The Struggle for Mastery in Europe*, p. xxx, Table IX.

4. The term comes from Rudyard Kipling's poem 'Mandalay': 'Ship me somewheres east of Suez, where the best is like the worst, Where there ain't no Ten Commandments an' a man can raise a thirst ...'

5. 'The Cat that Walked by Himself' is one of Rudyard Kipling's *Just So Stories*, published in 1902.

6. Aaron L. Friedberg, *The Weary Titan: Britain and the Experience of Relative Decline 1895–1905* (Princeton: Princeton University Press, 1988), p. 146.

7. See, for example, Peter Hopkirk, *The Great Game: On Secret Service in High Asia* (London: John Murray, 1990); Antony Wynn,

Persia in the Great Game: Sir Percy Sykes, Explorer, Consul, Soldier, Spy (London: John Murray, 2003); and Jennifer Siegel, *Endgame: Britain, Russia and the Final Struggle for Central Asia* (London: I. B. Tauris, 2002).

8. D. S. Richards, *The Savage Frontier: A History of the Anglo-Afghan Wars* (London: Macmillan, 1990, Pan pb edn 2003).

9. Hansard, HC Deb., 3rd Series, vol. 336, col. 1171 for the quote; for the passing of the Act, *ibid.*, p. 1609. Friedberg, *Weary Titan*, pp. 146–50. Although in 1889 the third-largest navy was Italian, not Russian, no one expected that Great Britain and Italy would go to war. Parliament authorised expenditure of £21,500,000 plus another £4,750,000 for dockyard work. See Jon Tetsuro Sumida, *In Defence of Naval Supremacy: Finance, Technology, and British Naval Power 1889–1904* (London: Routledge, 1993 pb edn), p. 13.

10. Walter LaFeber, *The New Cambridge History of American Foreign Relations*, vol. II: *The American Search for Opportunity 1865–1913* (Cambridge: Cambridge University Press, 1993), pp. 114–16.

11. Kennedy, *British Naval Mastery*, p. 201.

12. E. M. Spiers, *Army and Society 1815–1914* (London: Longman, 1980), p. 38; David Omissi, *The Sepoys and the Raj 1857–1940* (Basingstoke: Palgrave Macmillan, 1994), p. 133. Thanks to David French for the references.

13. US Bureau of the Census, *Historical Statistics of the United States*, pp. 736–7; Chris Cook and Brendan Keith, *British Historical Facts 1830–1900* (London: Macmillan, 1975), p. 185.

14. For an outline and analysis of the crisis see Burk, *Old World, New World*, pp. 382, 396–410.

15. E. J. Phelps, US Minister to Great Britain, to Salisbury, 8 Feb. 1887 and Salisbury to Phelps, 22 Feb. 1887, *Parliamentary Papers* [Blue Book], February 1896, Nos 1–2, Cmmd Paper United States, No. 1, 'Correspondence Respecting the Question of the Boundary of British Guiana', pp. 1–2.

16. David Brion Davis and Steven Mintz, *The Boisterous Sea of Liberty: A Documentary History of America from Discovery through the Civil War* (Oxford: Oxford University Press, 1998, 1989 pb edn), pp. 349–50.

17. Lincoln to Salisbury, 5 May 1890, Salisbury to Lincoln, 26 May 1890, Lincoln to Salisbury, 28 May 1890 and Salisbury to Pauncefote, 11 Nov. 1891, Nos 3–6, Cmmd Paper United States, No. 1, pp. 2–4.

18. John A. S. Grenville and George Berkeley Young, *Politics, Strategy, and American Diplomacy: Studies in Foreign Policy 1873–1917* (New Haven: Yale University Press, 1966), ch. 3, 'The Diplomat as Propagandist: William Lindsay Scruggs, Agent for Venezuela', pp. 125–57.

19. Quoted in Hinde, *George Canning*, p. 345.

20. George G. Eggert, *Richard Olney: Evolution of a Statesman* (University Park: Pennsylvania State University Press, 1974), pp. 198–9.

21. Gresham to Bayard, No. 657, 9 April 1895, enclosing the Joint Resolution of 20 Feb. 1895, ff. 110–11, M77/90. In 1893, Great Britain had upgraded its mission in Washington from a legation to an embassy and its representative from a minister to an ambassador. This had been a shrewd public relations move on London's part: the upgrade came in the knowledge, and in advance, of an impending congressional decision to raise US legations to embassies. Thanks to Thomas Otte.

22. Bayard to Gresham, No. 387, 16 Feb. 1895; Bayard to Gresham, No. 395, 9 March 1895; and Bayard to Gresham, No. 404, 5 April 1895, Memorandum of Conversation with Kimberley on 23 Jan. 1895 and Memo by Kimberley, 20 Feb. 1895, all M30/169. Eggert, *Olney*, p. 199.

23. Olney to Bayard, No. 222, 20 July 1895, ff. 291–9, M77/90; Salisbury to Gough, 7 Aug. 1895, No. 12, Cmmd Paper United States, No. 1, p. 21.

24. Olney to Bayard, No. 222, 20 July 1895, ff. 299, 304–7 for the quotations, M77/90. Olney's claim of 'entire impartiality' (f. 296) seems not to have taken account of Bayard's dispatch of 5 April 1895 (see note 22 above), which set out the attempts of Americans to secure mining concessions in the area under dispute. Despatch No. 222 can also be found as No. 11, Cmmd Paper United States, No. 1, pp. 7–21, quotes on pp. 17–18.

25. LaFeber, *The American Search for Opportunity*, p. 126.

26. Quoted in Eggert, *Olney*, p. 212.

27. Salisbury to Sir Julian Pauncefote, British Ambassador to the US, 26 Nov. 1895, No. 15, Cmmd Paper United States, No. 1, pp. 22–5, quote on p. 23.

28. Salisbury to Pauncefote, 26 Nov. 1895, No. 16, *ibid.*, pp. 25–32, quote on p. 31.

29. Henry F. Graff, *Grover Cleveland* (New York: Henry Holt, 2002), p. 125.

30. Watts and Israel, eds, *Presidential Documents*, pp. 181–4.
31. Graff, *Cleveland*, p. 125; R. B. Mowat, *The Life of Lord Pauncefote: First Ambassador to the United States* (London: Constable, 1929), p. 186 for the quote.
32. Andrew Roberts, *Salisbury: Victorian Titan* (London: Weidenfeld & Nicolson, 1999), p. 46.
33. *Ibid.*, p. 617.
34. Bayard to Salisbury, No. 18, 3 Feb., Salisbury to Bayard, No. 19, 7 Feb., and Bayard to Salisbury, No. 20, 10 Feb., all 1896, Cmmd Paper United States, No. 1, pp. 32–3.
35. Eggert, *Olney*, p. 238; Nevins, *Henry White*, pp. 114–15.
36. Mowat, *Pauncefote*, pp. 195–201.
37. Dean Rusk referring to the USSR and the 1962 Cuban Missile Crisis.
38. This was the Roosevelt Corollary to the Monroe Doctrine, part of his Annual Message to Congress. Watts and Israel, eds, *Presidential Documents*, p. 205.
39. David H. Burton, *British–American Diplomacy 1895–1914: Early Years of the Special Relationship* (Malabar, Fla.: Krieger, 1999), p. 20.
40. Anthony Trollope, *North America*, 2 vols (London: Chapman & Hall, 1862), II, p. 462; W. E. Adams, *Our American Cousins: Being Personal Impressions of the People and Institutions of the United States* (London: Walter Scott, 1883), p. iv; Matthew Arnold, *Civilization in the United States: First and Last Impressions of America* (Boston: Cupples & Hurd, 1888), p. 71; Arthur Conan Doyle, 'The Adventures of the Noble Bachelor', first published in *Strand* magazine in 1892, this quote from *Sherlock Holmes: His Adventures, Memoirs, Return, His Last Bow and The Case-Book: The Complete Short Stories* (London: John Murray, 1928), p. 246. Burk, *Old World, New World*, p. 299.
41. http://www.presidency.ucsb.edu/ws/?pid=103901.
42. LaFeber, *The American Search for Opportunity*, pp. 129–44; Robert L. Beisner, *From the Old Diplomacy to the New 1865–1900* (Arlington Heights, Ill.: Harlan Davidson, 1986 pb edn), pp. 120–30; Perkins, *The Great Rapprochement*, pp. 36–44.
43. Thomas A. Bailey, 'Dewey and the Germans at Manila Bay', *American Historical Review*, 45:1 (Oct. 1939), p. 59.
44. Perkins, *The Great Rapprochement*, p. 46.
45. Bailey, 'Dewey and the Germans', pp. 60–1.
46. www.rms-gs.de/phileng/history/kap02.html.

47. Bailey, 'Dewey and the Germans', pp. 63–5; the quote from Capt. Chichester's letter to Commodore Holland is on p. 65 n. 23. Ivan Musicant, *Empire by Default: The Spanish–American War and the Dawn of the American Century* (New York: Henry Holt, 1998), pp. 556–64.

48. Both quoted in Bailey, 'Dewey and the Germans', pp. 68–9.

49. *Ibid.*, pp. 76–7. Presumably the primary duty of the two cruisers was to escort the steamers full of British nationals leaving the Philippines.

50. Henry Cabot Lodge, *The War with Spain* (New York: Harper & Brothers, 1899), pp. 215–16.

51. Perkins, *The Great Rapprochement*, p. 47.

52. *Ibid.*, pp. 42–3, quote on p. 43.

53. LaFeber, *The American Search for Opportunity*, pp. 145–68.

54. Balfour to Lodge, 11 April 1905, ff. 175–6, Add. MS 49742, Balfour Papers, British Library.

55. One outcome of the troops' poor showing was a set of reforms of the army, the Haldane reforms, implemented in time to make a difference in 1914.

56. This was the origin of the term, but the intention was rather different – to concentrate the population in easily guarded places – from those of the Nazis.

57. A. N. Porter, 'The South African War (1899–1902): Context and Motive Reconsidered', *Journal of African History*, 31 (1990), pp. 43–57; Christopher Saunders and Iain R. Smith, 'Southern Africa, 1795–1910', in Andrew Porter, ed., *The Oxford History of the British Empire*, vol. III: *The Nineteenth Century* (Oxford: Oxford University Press, 1999), p. 617.

58. Henry S. Wilson, 'The United States and the War', in Peter Warwick and S. B. Spies, eds, *The South African War: The Anglo-Boer War 1899–1902* (London: Longman, 1980), pp. 318–19.

59. Quoted in Clymer, *John Hay*, p. 160.

60. *Ibid.*, pp. 158–66.

61. Tilchin, *Theodore Roosevelt and the British Empire*, e.g. pp. 19–20. For a short but incisive discussion of the Anglo-Saxon movement, see Kramer, 'Empires, Exceptions, and Anglo-Saxons', especially pp. 1318–19.

62. Wilson, 'The US and the War', pp. 322–4.

63. Stuart Anderson, *Race and Rapprochement: Anglo-Saxonism and Anglo-American Relations 1895–1904* (London: Associated University Press, 1981), p. 136.

64. Blaine to Lowell, US Minister to Great Britain, No. 270, 19 Nov. 1881, pp. 554–9, argued that the US needed to get rid of Clayton–Bulwer and would control any canal, and Blaine to Lowell, No. 281, 29 Nov. 1881, pp. 563–9, giving a history of the earlier discussions. https://uwdc.library.wisc.edu/collections/FRUS/. Mowat, *Pauncefote*, pp. 260–9; LaFeber, *The American Search for Opportunity*, pp. 72–4, p. 73 for the quote.

65. Hay to White, 13 Jan. 1899, private letter in the Hay Papers at the Library of Congress, quoted in Clymer, *John Hay*, p. 175. Nothing of the sort appears in *FRUS*.

66. Salisbury to Pauncefote, 15 Feb. 1899, FO 55/392; 'Memorandum respecting the Negotiations leading to Conclusion of the Hay–Pauncefote Treaty of November 18, 1901, superseding the Clayton–Bulwer Treaty of 1850', 31 March 1905, FO 881/8448 (hereafter 'Memorandum'); J. A. S. Grenville, *Lord Salisbury and Foreign Policy: The Close of the Nineteenth Century* (London: Athlone Press, 1970 pb edn), pp. 379–81.

67. Lansdowne to Pauncefote, No. 36, 22 Feb. 1901, FO 55/405; 'Memorandum', FO 881/8448; Lansdowne, 'Memorandum', 13 Dec. 1900 and Lansdowne to Pauncefote, 13 Dec. 1901, both FO 55/399; Grenville, *Lord Salisbury*, pp. 387–8; Mowat, *Pauncefote*, pp. 283–91.

68. Quoted in Lord Selborne, 'Memorandum', 26 Feb. 1904, CAB 23/22, Cabinet Papers, The National Archive, Kew.

69. Sumida, *In Defence of Naval Supremacy*, p. 10.

70. The last was arguably the Anglo-Portuguese Treaty of 1373. England/Great Britain was not keen on signing unnecessary treaties.

71. It was also to prevent what the British feared was an imminent Russo-Japanese rapprochement. George Monger, *The End of Isolation: British Foreign Policy 1900–1907* (Westport, Conn.: Greenwood Press, 1963), p. 47. Japan was to destroy the Russian Pacific and Baltic fleets in the 1904–5 Russo-Japanese War.

72. Bourne, *Balance of Power*, p. 362.

73. Chancellor of the Exchequer, 'Financial Difficulties: Appeal for Economy in Estimates', Oct. 1901, CAB 37/58, vol. 109, p. 8; Table 3-1, 'Gross Expenditures 1887–1907' in Friedberg, *Weary Titan*, p. 131.

74. Sumida, *In Defence of Naval Supremacy*, pp. 20–1, plus Figure 1, 'Expenditure on battleships and first-class cruisers, 1889–1904'.

Expenditure on new works, such as barracks, docks and other port facilities, increased five times from 1897 to 1904–5. *Ibid.*

75. Sir Edward Hamilton Diary, 16 May 1900, Add. MS 48676, British Library; Stephen Gladstone, Bank of England, to the Chancellor, 12 March 1900, T 168/87, Treasury Papers, The National Archive, Kew; Burk, *Morgan Grenfell*, pp. 118–20.

76. 'The Navy Estimates and the Chancellor of the Exchequer's Memorandum on the Growth of Expenditure', 16 Nov. 1901, in Boyce, ed., *The Crisis of British Power*, pp. 129–36, quote on p. 131.

77. Selborne, Memorandum for the Cabinet, 26 Feb. 1904, in *ibid.*, p. 171.

78. Bourne, *Balance of Power*, pp. 364–5.

79. Selborne, 'Cabinet Memorandum', 6 Dec. 1904, Boyce, ed., *The Crisis of British Power*, pp. 184–90, quote on pp. 184–5. For battleship and armoured cruiser numbers, Kennedy, *British Naval Mastery*, p. 183. After the destruction of the Russian fleet by Japan in May 1905 and the 1905 Moroccan Crisis, there was a further redistribution of the fleet to counter the German threat. Previously there were sixteen battleships deployed as part of the Channel and Home Fleets and seventeen in the Mediterranean and on the China Station. Afterwards, there were nine in the Mediterranean, none on the China Station, and twenty-four deployed with the Channel and Atlantic Fleets. David French, *The British Way in Warfare 1688–2000* (London: Unwin Hyman, 1990), p. 159.

80. E. C. Grenfell Correspondence 1900–36, p. 25, MS 21,799; Dawkins to H. Babington Smith, 26 March 1902, MS 21,800/1; Dawkins to Lansdowne, 12 Sept. 1902, Dawkins to Gewinner, 23 April 1903, and Dawkins to Babington Smith, 27 April 1903, all MS 21,800/2, Morgan Grenfell Papers, Guildhall Library, London. Hamilton Diary, 21 April 1903, Add. MS 48680, British Library. Karl Erich Born, *International Banking in the 19th and 20th Centuries* (Leamington Spa: Berg Publishers, 1983), pp. 142–3; Burk, *Morgan Grenfell*, pp. 124–5; Norman Rich, *Great Power Diplomacy 1814–1914* (Boston: McGraw-Hill, 1992), pp. 338–46.

81. David French to the author.

82. 'Minutes of the 7th Meeting of the War Policy Cabinet Committee', 19 June 1917, p. 14, CAB 27/6.

83. David French, *British Strategy and War Aims 1914–1916* (London: Allen & Unwin, 1986), p. 42.

84. Elizabeth Monroe, *Britain's Moment in the Middle East 1914–1971* (London: Chatto & Windus, 1981 rev. edn, 1st pub. 1963), p. 12 for the quote, and p. 25.

85. Robert Holland, 'The British Empire and the Great War, 1914–1918', in Judith M. Brown and Wm. Roger Louis, eds, *The Oxford History of the British Empire*, vol. IV: *The Twentieth Century* (Oxford: Oxford University Press, 1999), p. 123.

86. Howard M. Sachar, *The Emergence of the Middle East 1914–1924* (London: Allen Lane, 1970), p. 55.

87. *Ibid.*, pp. 223–6.

88. *Ibid.*, pp. 78–86, 223–6.

89. *Ibid.*, pp. 43–4.

90. Holland, 'The British Empire and the Great War', p. 133.

91. David L. Woodward, *Hell in the Holy Land: World War I in the Middle East* (Lexington, Ky.: University Press of Kentucky, 2006), p. 57.

92. John Darwin argues that ambitions in London had grown from small to large by 1918 when the British wanted to dominate all of the territory between Greece and Afghanistan, thereby eliminating the Ottoman Empire. John Darwin, *The Empire Project: The Rise and Fall of the British World-System 1830–1970* (Cambridge: Cambridge University Press, 2009), p. 314. On the other hand, David French argues that the motive of imperialists such as the former Viceroy of India, Lord Curzon, and Leo Amery in attacking Turkish territory in the Middle East was not a 'crude desire' to gain territory but a wish to safeguard the Indian Empire. David French, *Strategy of the Lloyd George Coalition 1916–1918* (Oxford: Oxford University Press, 1995), p. 175. Surely the desire to safeguard the empire did not preclude the desire to grab attainable spoils.

93. French, *Strategy of the Lloyd George Coalition*, p. 82.

94. Sachar, *The Emergence of the Middle East*, pp. 235–6, p. 235 for the first quote, pp. 235–6 for the second.

95. Monroe, *Britain's Moment in the Middle East*, p. 27; French, *British Strategy and War Aims*, pp. 144–7; and Sachar, *The Emergence of the Middle East*, pp. 137–43. According to Sachar, 'Feisal was unquestionably a charismatic personality who inspired fierce loyalty among his troops and nurtured and projected exalted political ambitions for his people. As a military leader, he was quite ineffective,' p. 137.

96. Milner to Lloyd George, 20 March 1918, Milner MS 355, Bodleian Library, cited in Darwin, *The Empire Project*, p. 313.
97. French, *Strategy of the Lloyd George Coalition*, p. 263.
98. Darwin, *The Empire Project*, p. 16.
99. Alan Sharp, *David Lloyd George: Great Britain: The Peace Conferences of 1919–23 and their Aftermath* (London: Haus Publishing, 2008), p. 155.
100. CAB 24/66/GT5976.
101. Lloyd George quote in Sharp, *Lloyd George*, p. 159.
102. French, *Strategy of the Lloyd George Coalition*, pp. 263–5.
103. CAB 23/14/WC489B.
104. J. C. Smuts, 'A Note on the Early Conclusion of Peace', 24 Oct. 1918, CAB 24/67/GT6091.
105. Woodrow Wilson, *The Papers of Woodrow Wilson*, ed. John F. Little and Arthur S. Link, 69 vols (Princeton: Princeton University Press, 1967–94), vol. XL: *November 20, 1916–January 23, 1917*, p. 537.
106. Godfrey Hodgson, *Woodrow Wilson's Right Hand: The Life of Colonel Edward M. House* (London: Yale University Press, 2006), p. 31.
107. House to Wilson, No. 8982, 30 Oct. 1918, *FRUS, 1918, Supplement 1, The World War (1918)*, p. 421.
108. Burk, *Old World, New World*, pp. 457–8.
109. Hodgson, *House*, p. 189; House to Wilson, No. 8983, 30 Oct. 1918, *FRUS, 1918, Supplement 1, The World War (1918)*, p. 424 for the quote.
110. Hodgson, *House*, pp. 187–91.
111. For some years there had been substantial numbers of American missionaries in Turkey, and their lobby in Washington was formidable, with close links to the White House, the Department of State and members of Congress. 'It was during Wilson's tenure in the White House that the missionary lobby reached perhaps the high-water mark of its influence in official government circles in Washington. Following American entry into the war, the missionary lobby influenced the President's decision not to intervene in the war in the Middle East, for such a declaration of war against Turkey would have resulted in Turkish reprisals against the missionaries who operated schools and hospitals.' Thomas A. Bryson, *Seeds of Mideast Crisis: The United States Diplomatic*

Role in the Middle East during World War II (Jefferson, NC: McFarland, 1981), pp. 4–6, quote on p. 6.

112. Edward M. House, *The Intimate Papers of Colonel House. Arranged as a Narrative by Charles Seymour, Professor of History at Yale University*, ed. Charles Seymour, 4 vols (London: Ernest Benn, 1928), vol. IV: *The Ending of the War June 1918–November 1919*, p. 263.

113. George W. Egerton, 'Ideology, Diplomacy and International Organisation: Wilsonism and the League of Nations in Anglo-American Relations, 1918–1920', in B. J. C. McKercher, ed., *Anglo-American Relations in the 1920s: The Struggle for Supremacy* (London: Macmillan, 1991), p. 32 for the first quote and David Reynolds, *Britannia Overruled: British Policy and World Power in the 20th Century* (London: Longman, 2000, 2nd edn) p. 110 for the second.

114. Akira Iriye, *The New Cambridge History of American Foreign Relations*, vol. III: *The Globalizing of America 1913–1945* (Cambridge: Cambridge University Press, 2013), p. 69.

115. Sharp, *Lloyd George*, p. 72.

116. House, *The Intimate Papers*, p. 53 n. 1.

117. Margaret MacMillan, *Peacemakers: The Paris Conference of 1919 and its Attempt to End War* (London: John Murray, 2001), p. 108.

118. *Ibid.*, pp. 109–12.

119. Arnold Toynbee, *Acquaintances* (London: Oxford University Press, 1967), pp. 211–12.

120. Sharp, *Lloyd George*, pp. 153–5.

121. Harold Nicolson, *Curzon: The Last Phase 1919–1925: A Study in Post-War Diplomacy* (London: Constable, 1934), p. 3.

122. *Ibid.*, p. 253.

123. Andrew Mango, *From the Sultan to Atatürk: Turkey: The Peace Conferences of 1919–23 and their Aftermath* (London: Haus Publishing, 2009), pp. 159–76; Sharp, *Lloyd George*, pp. 193–5; MacMillan, *Peacemakers*, p. 464 for the quote.

124. MacMillan, *Peacemakers*, p. 465.

125. Wm. Roger Louis, *Imperialism at Bay 1941–1945: The United States and the Decolonization of the British Empire* (Oxford: Oxford University Press, 1977), pp. 4–6, quote on p. 4.

126. Memorandum for the Cabinet, 'The Navy Estimates and the Chancellor of the Exchequer's Memorandum on the Growth of Expenditure', 16 Nov. 1901, in Boyce, ed., *Crisis of British Power*, p. 130.

127. Phillips Payson O'Brien, *British and American Naval Power: Politics and Policy 1900–1936* (Westport, Conn.: Praeger, 1998), p. 5.

128. Long to Lloyd George, 16 Feb. 1919, F/32/2, David Lloyd George Papers, House of Lords Record Office, London. In 1917 the Admiralty had estimated that the US spent £240 million (about $1,142.4 million) on new construction alone, an amount greater than the total Royal Navy budget. O'Brien, *British and American Naval Power*, p. 152.

129. By mid-July 1919, the short-term floating debt amounted to over £1 billion. 'The Financial Situation', 18 July 1919, T 171/170, Treasury Papers, The National Archive, Kew, circulated as CAB 24/84, GT 7729.

130. John R. Ferris, 'The Symbol and Substance of Seapower: Great Britain, the United States, and the One-Power Standard, 1919–1921', in McKercher, ed., *Anglo-American Relations in the 1920s*, pp. 57–61; O'Brien, *British and American Naval Power*, p. 162. In the severe depression of 1921, British GDP fell to 87.1 per cent of the 1913 level, a level which was not again achieved until 1925. G. C. Peden, *Arms, Economics and British Strategy: From Dreadnoughts to Hydrogen Bombs* (Cambridge: Cambridge University Press, 2007), p. 127. At the War Cabinet Finance Committee meeting on 11 Aug. 1919, it was suggested that the first step should be to stop all construction and to cut down the number of ships in commission to at least the pre-war standard. The suggestion was also made that the US should be approached about an arrangement for a reduction in the number of ships maintained in commission. The Committee agreed that the fighting services should be asked to draw up fresh estimates 'on the assumption that no great war is to be anticipated within the next ten years', f. 16, CAB 27/71. On 15 August, the full Cabinet agreed that 'it should be assumed, for forming revised Estimates, that the British Empire will not be engaged in any great war during the next ten years, and that no Expeditionary Force is required for that purpose'. War Cabinet 'A' Minutes, 15 Aug. 1919, CAB 23/15. The Chancellor of the Exchequer needed cuts in expenditure to balance the budget, and no war drums were sounding.

131. Donald J. Lisio, *British Naval Supremacy and Anglo-American Antagonisms 1914–1930* (Cambridge: Cambridge University Press, 2014), p. 8.

132. *Ibid.*, pp. 156–60. In addition, China, the Netherlands, Portugal, and Belgium were invited to take part in the discussions on Pacific

and Far Eastern questions because they had territorial or economic interests there. Stephen Roskill, *Naval Policy between the Wars*, vol. I: *The Period of Anglo-American Antagonism 1919–1929* (New York: Walker, 1968), p. 302; Ferris, 'The Symbol and Substance of Seapower', p. 72.

133. Lisio, *British Naval Supremacy*, p. 9.
134. Erik Goldstein, 'The Evolution of British Diplomatic Strategy for the Washington Conference', in Erik Goldstein and John Maurer, eds, *The Washington Conference 1921–22: Naval Rivalry, East Asian Stability and the Road to Pearl Harbor* (London: Frank Cass, 1994), pp. 26–8, quote on p. 27.
135. War Cabinet 'A' Minutes, 15 Aug. 1919, CAB 23/15. The term 'Ten Year Rule' irritates John Ferris, who argues that it should be termed the 'August 1919 principles', and the 'ten year period', depending on the use made of it; between 1925 and 1933, the term 'ten year rule' was used only once. John Ferris, 'Treasury Control, the Ten Year Rule and British Service Policies, 1919–1924', *Historical Journal*, 30:4 (1987), pp. 859–83.
136. Roskill, *Naval Policy between the Wars*, pp. 310–24, quote on p. 310; O'Brien, *British and American Naval Power*, p. 166.
137. McClain, *History of Japan*, p. 336.
138. Iriye, *The Globalizing of America*, p. 82; Roskill, *Naval Policy between the Wars*, pp. 300–30; B. J. C. McKercher, ' "The Deep and Latent Distrust": The British Official Mind and the United States, 1919–1929', in McKercher, ed., *Anglo-American Relations in the 1920s*, p. 223; O'Brien, *British and American Naval Power*, p. 181; Ryūji Hattori and Tosh Minohara, 'The 1920s: The Washington Treaty System and the Immigration Issue', in Makoto Iokibe and Tosh Minohara, eds, *The History of US–Japan Relations: From Perry to the Present* (Singapore: Palgrave Macmillan, 2017, 1st pub. in Japanese in Japan 2008), pp. 63–82; R. Craigie, 'Outstanding Problems Affecting Anglo-American Relations', 12 Nov. 1928, f. 178, FO 371/12812.
139. Great Britain also had considerably more cruisers and smaller ships under construction, 633,622 tons being built compared with the USA's 106,855 tons. O'Brien, *British and American Naval Power*, p. 187.
140. *Ibid.*, pp. 181–9.
141. *Ibid.*, quote on p. 189; Roskill, *Naval Policy between the Wars*, pp. 225–6, 498–502; B. J. C. McKercher, *The Second Baldwin Government and*

the United States 1924–1929: Attitudes and Diplomacy (Cambridge: Cambridge University Press, 1984), pp. 65–71.

142. Churchill, 'Reduction and Limitation of Armaments: The Naval Conference', 29 June 1927, CAB 24/187, f. 190.

143. O'Brien, *British and American Naval Policy*, pp. 192–5, p. 194 for 'dirty dog'; William Bridgeman, *The Modernisation of Conservative Politics: The Diaries and Letters of William Bridgeman 1904–1935*, ed. Philip Williamson (London: The Historians' Press, 1988), p. 209.

144. O'Brien, *British and American Naval Policy*, pp. 198–9, quote on p. 199.

145. Both he and his predecessor, Robert Vansittart, had American wives.

146. 'Outstanding Problems Affecting Anglo-American Relations', 12 Nov. 1928, FO 371/12812.

147. O'Brien, *British and American Naval Power*, pp. 201–12, quote on p. 201; B. J. C. McKercher, *Transition of Power: Britain's Loss of Global Pre-eminence to the United States 1930–1945* (Cambridge: Cambridge University Press, 1999), p. 33.

148. O'Brien, *British and American Naval Power*, pp. 210–12, quote on p. 212; Hattori and Minohara, 'The Washington Treaty System', pp. 80–2.

149. Burk, *Old World, New World*, pp. 473–5.

150. Minute on Sir J. Pratt, 'The Shanghai Situation', 1 Feb. 1921, in Rohan Butler, Douglas Dakin and M. E. Lambert, eds, *Documents on British Foreign Policy 1919–1939*, 2nd Series, vol. IX (London, Her Majesty's Stationery Office, 1955), No. 238, pp. 281–3, quote on p. 282; Norman Rose, *Vansittart: Study of a Diplomat* (London: Heinemann, 1978), pp. 105–8.

151. Lord Robert Cecil wrote to Baldwin on 12 Dec. 1932 that Simon 'seems to have given everybody the idea that he was a thick and thin supporter of Japan, or else that we are so afraid of her that we dare not say anything she dislikes'. Quoted in Keith Neilson, *Britain, Soviet Russia and the Collapse of the Versailles Order 1919–1939* (Cambridge: Cambridge University Press, 2006), p. 65.

152. McKercher, *Transition of Power*, pp. 118–20, quotes on pp. 118, 120.

153. Thomas Jones, *A Diary with Letters 1931–1950* (London: Oxford University Press, 1954), p. 30.

154. Minute on Pratt, 'The Shanghai Situation', quote on p. 282. However, Vansittart went on to write, 'I do not agree that this is necessarily so. The same was said of the US in the Great War. Eventually she was kicked in by the Germans. The Japanese may

end by kicking in the US too, if they go on long enough kicking as they are now.' *Ibid.* Iriye argues that the various American attempts to achieve some peaceful settlement of the crisis demonstrate the country's 'determination to retain a framework of international cooperation'. *The Globalizing of America*, p. 129.

155. Reynolds, *Britannia Overruled*, p. 120.

156. Comment on 22 June 1921, quoted in Goldstein, 'The Evolution of British Diplomatic Strategy for the Washington Conference', p. 12.

157. Elliott Roosevelt, *As He Saw It* (New York: Duell, Sloan & Pearce, 1946), p. 74.

158. Louis, *Imperialism at Bay*, pp. 19–21.

159. *Ibid.*, p. 26.

160. Roosevelt, *As He Saw It*, p. 206. Although Elliott conveys sympathy with what Great Britain was going through, particularly after he arrived in London during the closing stages of the Blitz, nevertheless the book is redolent with suspicion of Britain; what is not entirely clear is whether it is repeatedly emphasised by Elliott because of his own distrust of the British, or because it accurately conveys FDR's feelings and beliefs.

161. Louis, *Imperialism at Bay*, pp. 19–23, quotes on p. 21.

162. *Life*, 12 Oct. 1942 and *The Times*, 11 Nov. 1942.

163. Burk, *Old World, New World*, p. 505.

164. Kenton J. Clymer, 'The Education of William Phillips: Self-Determination and American Policy toward India, 1942–45', *Diplomatic History*, 8:1 (Winter 1984), p. 14.

165. Herring, *From Colony to Superpower*, p. 571 for 'major irritant'; Doenecke and Stoler, *Debating Franklin D. Roosevelt's Foreign Policies*, p. 53 for the other quotations. Roosevelt has been referred to as a man who liked specific dates or timetables in order to accomplish something. In May 1944, a Foreign Office document commented on this: 'The announcement that the Philippines would be independent in 1946, made before Pearl Harbour [sic], established the notion of a "time-table" and this is applied as a test of British policy.' 'American Relations with the British Empire', 1 May 1944, p. 25, 46(h), FO 371/38523/AN1577/16/45.

166. Wilson to House, 21 July 1917, Box 121, Edward M. House Papers, Yale University Library, New Haven, Conn.

167. David Reynolds, *The Creation of the Anglo-American Alliance 1937–1941: A Study in Competitive Co-operation* (London: Europa, 1981), p. 257.

168. Entry for Sunday, 10 Aug. 1941, Alexander Cadogan, *The Diaries of Sir Alexander Cadogan 1938–1945*, ed. David Dilks (London: Cassell, 1971), p. 398.

169. 'Third, they respect the right of all peoples to choose the form of government under which they will live; and they wish to see sovereign rights and self-government restored to those who have been forcibly deprived of them ...'

170. 'Eighth, they believe that all of the nations of the world, for realistic as well as spiritual reasons, must come to the abandonment of the use of force ...'

171. 'Fourth, they will endeavour, with due respect to their existing obligations, to further the enjoyment by all States, great or small, victor or vanquished, of access, on equal terms, to the trade and to the raw materials of the world which are needed for their economic prosperity ...'

172. 'Seventh, such a peace ['after the final destruction of Nazi tyranny' – from Clause 6] should enable all men to traverse the high seas and oceans without hindrance ...'

173. John Colville, *The Fringes of Power: Downing Street Diaries 1939–1955* (London: Hodder & Stoughton, 1985), entry for 12 Nov. 1940, pp. 291–2.

174. Henry Morgenthau Presidential Diary, vol. 3, f. 740, Franklin D. Roosevelt Presidential Library, Hyde Park, New York.

175. Kathleen Burk, 'American Foreign Economic Policy and Lend-Lease', in Ann Lane and Howard Temperley, eds, *The Rise and Fall of the Grand Alliance 1941–45* (Basingstoke: Macmillan, 1995), pp. 55–6; quote from 'Correspondence respecting the Policy of His Majesty's Government in connexion with the Use of Materials received under the Lend-Lease Act', *Parliamentary Papers, 1940–41*, vol. VIII: *United States No. 2 (10 September 1941)*, Cmd 6311, p. 424.

176. Winston Churchill and Franklin Roosevelt, *Churchill and Roosevelt: The Complete Correspondence*, ed. Warren F. Kimball, 3 vols (Princeton: Princeton University Press, 1984), vol. I: *Alliance Emerging: October 1933–November 1942*, p. 345.

177. Churchill to Halifax, 10 Jan. 1941, ff. 363–4, PREM 4/17/3, Prime Minister's Records, The National Archive, Kew; Halifax to Eden, No. 542, 30 Jan. 1942, ff. 326–7, PREM 4/17/3; Roosevelt to Churchill, 4 Feb. 1942, Churchill and Roosevelt, *The Complete Correspondence*, I, p. 345; Eden to Halifax, Private, 7 Jan. 1942, f. 369, PREM 4/17/3; Burk, 'American Foreign Economic Policy and Lend-Lease', pp. 56–7.

178. Burk, *Old World, New World*, pp. 565–74; Kathleen Burk, 'Britain and the Marshall Plan', in Chris Wrigley, ed., *Warfare, Diplomacy and Politics: Essays in Honour of A. J. P. Taylor* (London: Hamish Hamilton, 1986), pp. 210–30.

179. Randall Bennett Woods, *A Changing of the Guard: Anglo-American Relations 1941–1946* (Chapel Hill: The University of North Carolina Press, 1990), pp. 94–100; Woods considers that the fight was primarily over bureaucratic power. R. S. Sayers, *Financial Policy 1939–45* (London: Her Majesty's Stationery Office and Longmans, Green, 1956), pp. 427–37.

180. General B. Somervell, 'Lend-Lease Policy after the Defeat of Germany', 7 Sept. 1944, Box 335, Harry Hopkins Papers, Roosevelt Presidential Library, as summarised in Woods, *A Changing of the Guard*, p. 166; quote from Anne Orde, *The Eclipse of Great Britain: The United States and Imperial Decline 1895–1956* (Basingstoke: Macmillan, 1996), p. 143. Wanting unconditional freedom for US commercial aircraft to land at all British bases sounds pretty imperialistic to me. Presumably Somervell had Pan American Airways in mind, given their collaboration with the military. Blower, 'Nation of Outposts', p. 456.

181. Louis, *Imperialism at Bay*, pp. 18–19.

182. Roosevelt, *As He Saw It*, p. 72.

183. Louis, *Imperialism at Bay*, pp. 18–19.

184. I. C. B. Dear, ed., *The Oxford Companion to the Second World War* (Oxford: Oxford University Press, 1995), pp. 650–1, p. 651 for his daughter's comment; Mark A. Stoler, *Allies in War: Britain and America against the Axis Powers 1940–1945* (London: Hodder Arnold, 2005), p. 159, for the near-fight.

185. Christopher Thorne, *Allies of a Kind: The United States, Britain, and the War against Japan 1941–1945* (London: Hamish Hamilton, 1978), p. 725.

186. Louis, *Imperialism at Bay*, p. 3.

187. Herring, *From Colony to Superpower*, p. 570.

188. Roosevelt, *As He Saw It*, p. 115.

189. Quoted in Louis, *Imperialism at Bay*, p. 88.

190. P. J. Marshall, '1918 to the 1960s: Keeping Afloat', in P. J. Marshall, ed., *The Cambridge Illustrated History of the British Empire* (Cambridge: Cambridge University Press, 1996), p. 93.

191. Wm. Roger Louis and Ronald Robinson, 'The Imperialism of Decolonization', *Journal of Imperial and Commonwealth History*, 22:3 (1994), pp. 485–6.

192. Herring, *From Colony to Superpower*, p. 573.

193. Louis, *Imperialism at Bay*, p. 26.

194. Marshall, '1918 to the 1960s', p. 93.

195. According to John Lewis Gaddis, Roosevelt 'saw some possibility that the Soviet and American systems of government might, through evolution, become similar', a 'trend toward convergence'. John Lewis Gaddis, *The United States and the Origins of the Cold War 1941–1947* (New York: Columbia University Press, 1972 pb edn), p. 41.

196. 'The Essentials of American Policy', 21 March 1944, quote from pp. 1–2, FO 371/38523/AN1538/16/45. This is the original; it was decided that it should be circulated only in the FO, not to the Cabinet. A much longer version only went to the Cabinet after 3 November. According to the minutes, it was written by Graham Spry.

197. Martin H. Folly, 'Breaking the Vicious Circle: Britain, the United States, and the Genesis of the North Atlantic Treaty', *Diplomatic History*, 12:1 (Winter 1988), pp. 64–5. David French points out that there were also plans for an air offensive against southern Russia from the British base at Suez.

198. Chiefs of Staff Memorandum, 19 Dec. 1947, COS Paper (47)227(o) Annex A, DEFE 5/6, Ministry of Defence Records, the National Archive, Kew.

199. Burk, *Old World, New World*, pp. 580–7, especially pp. 584–5 for the June negotiations.

200. 'Department of State Policy Statement: Great Britain, 11 June 1948, *FRUS, 1948, Western Europe*, pp. 1091–1108, quotes on pp. 1092 and 1091.

201. Richard J. Aldrich, *The Hidden Hand: Britain, America and Cold War Secret Intelligence* (London: John Murray, 2001), p. 305, quoting from Kim Philby's memoirs, *Silent War*, p. 117.

202. Paper prepared for the Department of State, 'Essential Elements of US–UK Relations', 19 April 1950, quotes on pp. 870 and 878, *FRUS, 1950, Western Europe*.

203. *Ibid.*, p. 871.

204. Matthew Fallon Hinds, *The US, the UK and Saudi Arabia in World War II: The Middle East and the Origins of a Special Relationship* (London: I. B. Tauris, 2016), *passim*, pp. 12–13 for the quote.

205. For details of the dispute with emphasis on the Arab sides, see J. B. Kelly, *Eastern Arabian Frontiers* (London: Faber & Faber, 1964), pp. 142–260.

206. Tore Tingvold Petersen, 'Anglo-American Rivalry in the Middle East: The Struggle for the Buraimi Oasis, 1952–1957', *International History Review*, 14:1 (Feb. 1992), pp. 71–91, especially p. 72. Glubb was dismissed in March 1956. Michael S. Goodman, *The Official History of the Joint Intelligence Committee*, vol. I: *From the Approach of the Second World War to the Suez Crisis* (London: Routledge, 2014), pp. 378–9.

207. 'An Anglo-American Balance Sheet', 1 Aug. 1964, SC(64) 30 Revise, f. 119, FO 371/177830/PLA24/7A.

208. H. Duncan Hall, *History of the Second World War: North American Supply* (London: Her Majesty's Stationery Office and Longmans, Green, 1955), p. 60.

209. Petersen, 'Buraimi Oasis', pp. 73–4.

210. Eden to the Cabinet, 16 Feb. 1953, cited in *ibid.*, p. 73 n. 4.

211. Quoted in Petersen, 'Buraimi Oasis', p. 76.

212. Quoted in James R. Vaughan, *The Failure of American and British Propaganda in the Arab Middle East 1945–57: Unconquerable Minds* (London: Palgrave, 2005), p. 160.

213. Petersen, 'Buraimi Oasis', p. 78.

214. Goodman, *Joint Intelligence Committee*, pp. 355–62.

215. Petersen, 'Buraimi Oasis', p. 80; Aldrich to the State Dept., 23 April 1954, p. 2601, *FRUS, 1952–1954, The Near and Middle East*.

216. Petersen, 'Buraimi Oasis', pp. 82–3.

217. Hansard, HC Deb., 1953–4, vol. 531, col. 818; Kelly, *Eastern Arabian Frontiers*, p. 171.

218. Kelly, *Eastern Arabian Frontiers*, p. 175. They were using royalties from ARAMCO to finance this. Petersen, 'Buraimi Oasis', p. 86.

219. Evelyn Shuckburgh, *Descent to Suez: Diaries 1951–1956* (London: Weidenfeld & Nicolson, 1986), p. 278.

220. Petersen, 'Buraimi Oasis', pp. 84–5 for the quote. The Permanent Under-Secretary was Sir Ivone Kirkpatrick.

221. Quoted in *ibid.*, p. 85.

222. *Ibid.*

223. *Ibid.*

224. Wm. Roger Louis, *Ends of British Imperialism: The Scramble for Empire, Suez and Decolonization* (London: I. B. Tauris, 2006), p. 655.

225. David Dutton, *Anthony Eden: A Life and Reputation* (London: Arnold, 1997), pp. 240–1, 374, 422–3.

226. Shuckburgh, *Descent to Suez*, with examples on pp. 178, 327, 340 and 365.
227. Miles Copeland, Jr, *The Game Player: Confessions of the CIA's Original Political Operative* (London: Aurum Press, 1989), as cited in Hugh Wilford, *America's Great Game: The CIA's Secret Arabists and the Making of the Modern Middle East* (New York: Basic Books, 2013), pp. 221–5, quote on p. 225.
228. W. Scott Lucas, *Divided We Stand: Britain, the US and the Suez Crisis* (London: Hodder & Stoughton, 1996 pb edn), p. 27.
229. *Ibid.*, pp. 45–50; Louis, *Ends of British Imperialism*, pp. 641–7.
230. Aldrich, *Hidden Hand*, p. 478.
231. The Joint Intelligence Committee concluded that the arms deal had strengthened arguments in Israel for pre-emptive action. Goodman, *Joint Intelligence Committee*, p. 376.
232. United States Minutes of Meeting, Washington, The White House, 8 Jan. 1952, *FRUS, 1952–1954*, vol. IX: *The Near and Far East, Part 1*, p. 176.
233. Cabinet Conclusions, 4 Oct. 1955, quoted in Darwin, *The Empire Project*, p. 600.
234. The quote about Eisenhower is from Macmillan to Eden, f. 299; the quote about Dulles is Macmillan to Eden, 25 Sept. 1956, given to Eden on the 26th, ff. 302–3, both in PREM 11/1102.
235. Goodman, *Joint Intelligence Committee*, pp. 395 and 415.
236. This was the version given by Lloyd in his *Suez 1956: A Personal Account* (London: Jonathan Cape, 1978), p. 219. The version given in the official telegram is more subdued: 'He [Dulles] said that he had no complaint about our objectives in our recent operations. In fact they were the same as those of the United States but he still did not think that our methods of achieving them were the right ones. Even so he deplored that we had not managed to bring down Nasser.' Lloyd to Eden, Secret, 18 Nov. 1956, FO 371/118873/ JE1074/11.
237. Makins to Lloyd, No. 1849, 9 Sept. 1956, rec. 10 Sept. 1956, WO 32/16709, War Office and Successor Files, The National Archive, Kew.
238. Macmillan to Eden, 25 Sept. 1956, ff. 302–3, PREM 11/1102.
239. *New York Times*, 14 Sept. 1956, quoted in Louise Richardson, *When Allies Differ: Anglo-American Relations during the Suez and Falklands Crises* (New York: St Martin's Press, 1996), p. 51;

'Statement by the Secretary of State', 17 Sept. 1956, Box 10, file Suez Canal Second Conference, John Foster Dulles Papers, Princeton University Library, Princeton, New Jersey.

240. Shuckburgh, *Descent to Suez*, p. 365; Richardson, *When Allies Differ*, pp. 96–9. According to Denis Healey, Secretary of State for Defence 1964–70, Lord Mountbatten, then First Sea Lord (the head of the Royal Navy), opposed the Suez operation. Denis Healey, *The Time of my Life* (London: Michael Joseph, 1989), p. 257.

241. 'Memorandum of a Conference with the President', 30 Oct. 1956, *FRUS, 1955–1957*, vol. XVI: *Suez Crisis*, p. 854. Dulles suggested that 'their thinking might be that they will confront us with a de facto situation, in which they might acknowledge that they had been rash but would say that the U.S. could not sit by and let them go under economically.' *Ibid.*, p. 853.

242. At a meeting of the National Security Council on 1 November, Eisenhower asked Dulles to 'see what he could draft up in the way of the mildest things we could do in an effort to block the introduction of a really mean and arbitrary resolution in the UN General Assembly.' *Ibid.*, p. 912.

243. Diane B. Kunz, 'The Importance of Having Money: The Economic Diplomacy of the Suez Crisis', in Wm. Roger Louis and Roger Owen, eds, *Suez 1956: The Crisis and its Consequences* (Oxford: Oxford University Press, 1989), quotes on pp. 226–7.

244. Amin Hewedy, 'Nasser and the Crisis of 1956', in Louis and Owen, eds, *Suez 1956*, p. 167; Richardson, *When Allies Differ*, p. 95.

245. Richardson, *When Allies Differ*, pp. 107–8.

246. Richard E. Neustadt, *Alliance Politics* (New York: Columbia University Press, 1970 pb edn), p. 26.

247. Kunz, 'Economic Diplomacy', p. 227; Diane B. Kunz, *The Economic Diplomacy of the Suez Crisis* (Chapel Hill: University of North Carolina Press, 1991), *passim*.

248. 'Planning paper on interdependence: the effects of Anglo-American interdependence on the long-term interests of the United Kingdom', 27 Jan. 1958, Steering Committee SC (58) 8, p. 3, FO 371/132330/AU1051/3/G.

249. Piers Dixon, *Double Diploma: The Life of Sir Pierson Dixon* (London: Hutchinson, 1968), p. 278.

250. Caccia to Lloyd, 'The Present State of Anglo-United States Relations', 28 Dec. 1956, ff. 4–5, PREM 11/2189/AU1051/53. He

does, however, go on to say that 'I ... see no reason for despondency
... there is no other country with world interests which could take
our place as a "chosen ally"; and most countries, like individuals,
feel the need of a confidant.' *Ibid.*, ff. 5–6. On 10 Sept, 1957, Caccia
wrote to Hoyer Millar, the Permanent Under-Secretary, Foreign
Office, 'in American eyes the use of force by others is justifiable
in almost any circumstances when it can be shown to be directed
against communism; but ... conversely, when the connection cannot
be clearly shown, there are almost no circumstances in which they
can be counted on to support it openly.' Secret and Guard, FO
371/126888. On 19 Nov. 1956 Lord Harcourt, the UK Economic
Minister at the British Embassy, wrote to Sir Leslie Rowan, the head
of the Overseas Finance Division in the Treasury; in it he analysed
George Humphrey, the US Secretary of the Treasury, and other US
Treasury representatives with whom he was dealing. 'My own view
is that the feeling in the Administration is considerably more hostile
than it is amongst the general public. They are hurt and piqued at our
action which they look on as a blunder and they seem determined
to treat us as naughty boys who have got to be taught that they
cannot go off and act on their own without asking Nanny's permission first.' Quoted in Kunz, 'Economic Diplomacy', p. 228.

251. Percy Cradock, *Know your Enemy: How the Joint Intelligence
Committee Saw the World* (London: John Murray, 2002), p. 279.

252. Lloyd to Eden, No. 2307, 17 Nov. 1956, FO 371/118873/JE1074/
10.

253. Goodman, *Joint Intelligence Committee*, quote on p. 406.

254. *Ibid.*, quote on pp. 406–7.

255. 'Memorandum of Discussion at the 302d Meeting of the National
Security Council', 1 Nov. 1956, *FRUS, 1955–1957*, IX, p. 911,

256. Burk, *Old World, New World*, pp. 602–6.

257. Peter Golden, *Quiet Diplomat: A Biography of Max M. Fisher*
(New York: Cornwall Books, 1992), p. xviii, for Eisenhower's
regret. Henry Kissinger later wrote that the USSR noted America's
disavowal of its closest allies, while the Europeans drew the conclusion that the interests of the US and Europe did not always
run together. The French decided that Europe had to be united
in order to play a decisive role in world affairs, and both France
and Great Britain, according to Kissinger, decided that, because
they could not always count on US support, they needed to gain

and maintain their own nuclear deterrents. Kissinger, *Diplomacy* (New York: Simon & Schuster, 1994), pp. 536–8. The UK, of course, was already a nuclear power in 1956.

258. 'Most of the "British" Middle East became an Anglo-American concern after 1958.' Louis and Robinson, 'The Imperialism of Decolonization', p. 483.

259. The Sterling Area came to an end when the pound was floated in June 1972.

260. Kathleen Burk, 'Outline of Events, 1967 Devaluation Symposium', *Contemporary Record* (Winter 1988), pp. 44–5.

261. Healey, *The Time of my Life*, pp. 278–9.

262. *Ibid.*, pp. 280–1.

263. P. L. Pham, *Ending 'East of Suez': The British Decision to Withdraw from Malaysia and Singapore 1964–1968* (Oxford: Oxford University Press, 2010), pp. 150–94.

264. Quoted in C. J. Bartlett, *'The Special Relationship': A Political History of Anglo-American Relations since 1945* (London: Longman, 1992), p. 116.

265. Jonathan Colman, *A 'Special Relationship'? Harold Wilson, Lyndon B. Johnson and Anglo-American Relations 'at the Summit' 1964–68* (Manchester: Manchester University Press, 2004), p. 114.

266. Burk, '1967 Devaluation Symposium', pp. 45–51. In order to protect the US balance of payments in the summer of 1965, the Americans threated 'retaliatory action' against Great Britain if it devalued. Glen O'Hara, 'The Limits of US Power: Transatlantic Financial Diplomacy under the Johnson and Wilson Administrations, October 1964–November 1968', *Contemporary European History*, 12:3 (August 2003), p. 261.

267. Robert M. Hathaway, *Great Britain and the United States: Special Relations since World War II* (Boston: Twayne, 1990), pp. 81–2.

268. *Ibid.*, p. 90.

269. Harold Wilson, *The Labour Government 1964–70* (Harmondsworth: Penguin, 1974, 1st pub. 1971), p. 635 and quote on p. 341.

270. Louis Heren, *No Hail, No Farewell* (London: Harper & Row, 1970), p. 230.

271. Richard Crossman, *The Diaries of a Cabinet Minister*, vol. I: *Minister of Housing 1964–66* (London: Hamish Hamilton and Jonathan Cape, 1975), p. 95.

272. Healey, *The Time of my Life*, p. 299.

273. Burk, '1967 Devaluation Symposium', pp. 46 and 51.

274. Richard Crossman, *The Diaries of a Cabinet Minister*, vol. II: *Lord President of the Council and Leader of the House of Commons 1966–68* (London: Hamish Hamilton and Jonathan Cape, 1976), p. 639.

275. Their functions were taken over by the Foreign Office, which then became the Foreign and Commonwealth Office, or FCO.

276. Jeffrey Pickering, *Britain's Withdrawal from East of Suez: The Politics of Retrenchment* (London: Macmillan, 1998), pp. 168–86.

277. *Ibid.*, pp. 173–4, p. 173 for the quote.

278. Crossman, *The Diaries of a Cabinet Minister*, II, p. 639.

279. Walter Carruthers Sellar and Robert Julian Yeatman, *1066 and All That: A Memorable History of England. Comprising All the Parts You Can Remember Including One Hundred and Three Good Things, Five Bad Kings, and Two Genuine Dates* (London: Methuen, 1930), p. 115. This was classified as A Bad Thing.

ENVOI

1. Thanks to Michael Jewess, who also drew the map.

2. Niall Ferguson has conveniently listed them on p. 311 of *Colossus: The Rise and Fall of the American Empire* (London: Penguin, 2004).

3. *Ibid.*, p. 16; Blower, 'Nation of Outposts', p. 458.

4. Chalmers Johnson, *The Sorrows of Empire: Militarism, Secrecy, and the End of the Republic* (London: Verso, 2006 pb edn), p. 153.

5. *Ibid.*, pp. 156–60, for a table which sets out the deployment abroad of American military forces.

INDEX

1. Ralph Waldo Emerson, 'Self-Reliance', *Essays: First Series*, 1841.

Bibliography

PRIMARY SOURCES

Manuscripts – Government and Private Papers
Great Britain: Government
    The National Archive, Kew, London
        Cabinet Papers
        Colonial Office Papers
        Foreign Office Papers
        Ministry of Defence Papers
        Prime Ministers' Papers
        Privy Council Papers
        Treasury Papers

Great Britain: Private
    The British Library, London:
        Aberdeen Papers
        Balfour Papers
        Grenville Papers
        Hamilton Papers
        Peel Papers
        Vansittart Papers
    Lloyd George Papers, House of Lords Record Office
    Morgan Grenfell Papers, Guildhall Library, London

United States: Government
    State Department Papers

United States: Private
  Cushing Papers, Library of Congress
  Dulles Papers, Princeton University Library, Princeton, New Jersey
  House Papers, Yale University Library, New Haven, Connecticut
  Morgenthau Papers, Franklin D. Roosevelt Presidential Library,
    Hyde Park, New York

Printed Sources – Government and Private
Great Britain
Barclay, Thomas, *Selections from the Correspondence of Thomas
  Barclay*, ed. George Lockhart Rives (New York: Harper &
  Brothers, 1894)
Butler, Rohan, Douglas Dakin and M. E. Lambert, eds, *Documents on
  British Foreign Policy 1999–1939*, 2nd Series, vol. IX (London: Her
  Majesty's Stationery Office, 1955)
Cadogan, Alexander, *The Diaries of Sir Alexander Cadogan 1938–
  1945*, ed. David Dilks (London: Cassell, 1971)
Castlereagh, Viscount, *Correspondence, Despatches, and Other Papers
  of Viscount Castlereagh, Second Marquess of Londonderry*, Third
  Series, *Military and Diplomatic*, ed. Charles William Vane, 4 vols
  (London: W. Shoberl and John Murray, 1851–3)
Cobbett's Parliamentary Debates (London: T. C. Hansard, 1812)
Colville, John, *The Fringes of Power: Downing Street Diaries 1939–
  1955* (London: Hodder & Stoughton, 1985)
Cook, Chris and Brendan Keith, *British Historical Facts 1830–1900*
  (London: Macmillan, 1975)
Goodman, Michael S., *The Official History of the Joint Intelligence
  Committee*, vol. I: *From the Approach of the Second World War to
  the Suez Crisis* (London: Routledge, 2014)
Hall, H. Duncan, *History of the Second World War: North American
  Supply* (London: Her Majesty's Stationery Office and Longmans,
  Green, 1955)
Hansard, *Parliamentary Debates, House of Commons*, 3rd Series.
Jones, Thomas, *A Diary with Letters 1931–1950* (London: Oxford
  University Press, 1954)
Mitchell, B. R., *British Historical Statistics* (Cambridge: Cambridge
  University Press, 1988)
Morse, H. B., ed., *The Chronicles of the East India Company Trading
  to China 1635–1834*, 4 vols (Oxford: Oxford University Press, 1926)

Parliamentary Papers 186, House of Lords 18, Correspondence Respecting Affairs in Japan. March and April, 1861. Presented to Both Houses of Parliament by Command of Her Majesty, 1861

Parliamentary Papers. Correspondence Respecting the Relations between Great Britain and China, Cmmd 2168 (1869)

Parliamentary Papers, 1940–41, vol. VIII: *United States No. 2 (10 September 1941)*, Cmd 6311

Sayers, R. S., *Financial Policy 1939–45* (London: Her Majesty's Stationery Office and Longmans, Green, 1956) – official history

Selborne, Earl of, *The Crisis of British Power: The Imperial and Naval Papers of the Second Earl of Selborne 1895–1910*, ed. D. George Boyce (London: The Historians' Press, 1990)

Shuckburgh, Evelyn, *Descent to Suez: Diaries 1951 to 1956* (London: Weidenfeld & Nicolson, 1986)

Wellington, Duke of, *Supplementary Despatches, Correspondence, and Memoranda of Field Marshal Arthur Duke of Wellington, K.G.*, ed. Arthur R. Wellesley, 12 vols (London: John Murray, 1858–65)

United States

Adams, John, *The Works of John Adams, Second President of the United States, with a Life of the Author, Notes and Illustrations*, ed. Charles Francis Adams, 10 vols (Boston: Little, Brown, 1850–6).

Adams, John Quincy, *Memoirs of John Quincy Adams: Comprising Portions of his Diary from 1795 to 1848*, ed. Charles Francis Adams, 12 vols (Philadelphia: J. B. Lippincott, 1874–7)

Bradford, William, *Bradford's History 'Of Plimoth Plantation'. From the Original Manuscript. With a Report of the Proceedings Incident to the Return of the Manuscript to Massachusetts* (Boston: Wright & Potter, 1898)

Churchill, Winston and Franklin Roosevelt, *Churchill and Roosevelt: The Complete Correspondence*, ed. Warren F. Kimball, 3 vols (Princeton: Princeton University Press, 1984)

Davis, David Brion and Steven Mintz, *The Boisterous Sea of Liberty: A Documentary History of America from Discovery through the Civil War* (Oxford: Oxford University Press, 1998, 1999 pb edn)

Delafield, Joseph, *The Unfortified Boundary: A Diary of the First Survey of the Canadian Boundary Line from St. Regis to the Lake of the Woods*, ed. Robert McElroy and Thomas Riggs (New York: privately printed, 1943)

Department of State, *Executive Documents Printed by Order of the House of Representatives, during the Third Session of the Fortieth Congress, 1868–'69*, vol. I: *1868–1869* (Washington, DC: Government Printing Office, 1869)

Department of State, *Message of the President of the United States, and accompanying documents, to the two houses of Congress, at the commencement of the first session of the thirty-eighth Congress. Japan, Part II* (Washington, DC: Government Printing Office, 1863)

Department of State, *Papers Relating to Foreign Affairs. Part II. Communicated to Congress December 1, 1862* (Washington, DC: Government Printing Office, 1862)

Department of State, *Papers Relating to the Foreign Relations of the United States with the Annual Message of the President December 3, 1900* (Washington, DC: Government Printing Office, 1902)

Department of State, *Papers Relating to the Foreign Relations of the United States with the Annual Message of the President Transmitted to Congress December 5, 1899* (Washington, DC: Government Printing Office, 1901)

Department of State, *Papers Relating to the Foreign Relations of the United States with the Annual Message of the President Transmitted to Congress December 7, 1909* (Washington, DC: Government Printing Office, 1914)

Department of State, *Papers Relating to the Foreign Relations of the United States, 1918. Supplement 1, The World War (1918)* (Washington, DC: Government Printing Office, 1933)

Department of State, *Papers Relating to the Foreign Relations of the United States, 1948. Western Europe* (Washington, DC: Government Printing Office, 1974)

Department of State, *Papers Relating to the Foreign Relations of the United States, 1950. Western Europe* (Washington, DC: Government Printing Office, 1977)

Department of State, *Papers Relating to the Foreign Relations of the United States, 1952–1954*, vol. IX: *The Near and Middle East (in two parts)* (Washington, DC: Government Printing Office, 1986)

Department of State, *Papers Relating to the Foreign Relations of the United States, 1955–1957. Suez Crisis, July 26–December 31, 1956* (Washington, DC: Government Printing Office, 1990)

Gallatin, Albert, *The Writings of Albert Gallatin*, ed. Henry Adams, 3 vols (Philadelphia: J. B. Lippincott, 1879)

Hamilton, Alexander, *The Papers of Alexander Hamilton*, ed. Harold C. Syrett and Jacob E. Cooke, 27 vols (New York: Columbia University Press, 1961–87)

House, Edward M., *The Intimate Papers of Colonel House. Arranged as a Narrative by Charles Seymour, Professor of History at Yale University*, ed. Charles Seymour, 4 vols (London: Ernest Benn, 1928)

Jay, John, *The Correspondence and Public Papers of John Jay*, ed. Henry P. Johnston, 4 vols (New York: G. P. Putnam's Sons, 1890–3)

Jefferson, Thomas, *The Papers of Thomas Jefferson*, ed. Julian P. Boyd, 42 vols (Princeton: Princeton University Press, 1950–2016)

Jefferson, Thomas, *The Papers of Thomas Jefferson: Retirement Series*, ed. J. Jefferson Looney, 13 vols (Princeton: Princeton University Press, 2005–13)

Jefferson, Thomas, *The Writings of Thomas Jefferson*, ed. Paul Leicester Ford, 10 vols (New York: G. P. Putnam's Sons, 1892–9)

Madison, James, *The Papers of James Madison*, ed. Thomas Mason, Robert A. Rutland and Jeanne K. Sisson, 17 vols (Charlottesville: University Press of Virginia, 1962–91)

Madison, James, *The Papers of James Madison Digital Edition*, ed. J. C. A. Stagg (Charlottesville: University Press of Virginia, Rotunda, 2010)

Mayo, Bernard, ed., *Instructions to the British Ministers of the United States* (Washington DC: Government Printing Office, 1941)

Miller, Hunter, ed., *Treaties and Other International Acts of the United States of America, 1786–1863*, 8 vols (Washington, DC: Government Printing Office, 1931–48)

Polk, James K., *The Diary of James K. Polk during His Presidency, 1845–1849. Now First Printed from the Original Manuscript in the Collections of the Chicago Historical Society*, ed. M. M. Quaife, 4 vols (Chicago: A. C. McClurg, 1910)

Rush, Richard, *Memoranda of a Residence at the Court of London* (Philadelphia: Carey, Lea & Blanchard, 1833)

US Bureau of the Census, *Historical Statistics of the United States: Colonial Times to 1957* (Washington, DC: Government Printing Office, 1960)

United States House of Representatives, 28th Congress, 2nd Session, *Journal of the House of Representatives of the United States*, vol. 462 (Washington, DC: Blair & Rives, 1844–5)

United States House of Representatives, 28th Congress, 2nd Session,
Doc. No. 188, *Extension of American Congress-Proposed Mission to
Japan and Corea* [sic], 15 February 1845

United States Senate, 28th Congress, 2nd Session, *Message from
the President of the United States, communicating Copies of
the instructions given to the late commissioner to China*, 25
February 1845

United States Senate, 28th Congress, 2nd Session, *Journal of the
Executive Proceedings of the Senate of the United States. Documents
relating to and vote on the ratification of the treaty with the Ta Tsing
Empire (China)*, 16 January 1845

United States Senate, 33rd Congress, 2nd Session, Committee on
Foreign Relations, 751 Senate Exdoc. No. 34, *Message of the
President of the United States transmitting a Report of the
Secretary of the Navy, in compliance with a resolution of the
Senate of December 6, 1854, calling for correspondence, &c,
relative to the naval expedition to Japan* [no publisher given]

Washington, George, *The Writings of George Washington from
the Original Manuscript Sources, 1745–1789: Prepared under
the Direction of the United States Bicentennial Commission and
Published by Authority of Congress*, ed. John C. Fitzpatrick, 39 vols
(Washington, DC: Government Printing Office, 1931–44)

Watts, J. F. and Fred L. Israel, eds, *Presidential Documents: The
Speeches, Proclamations, and Policies that Have Shaped the Nation
from Washington to Clinton* (London: Routledge, 2000)

Wilson, Woodrow, *The Papers of Woodrow Wilson*, ed. John F. Little
and Arthur S. Link, 69 vols (Princeton: Princeton University Press,
1967–94)

Memoirs and Travels

Adams, W. E., *Our American Cousins: Being Personal Impressions of
the People and the Institutions of the United States* (London: Walter
Scott, 1883)

Alcock, Sir Rutherford, *The Capital of the Tycoon: A Narrative of
Three Years' Residence in Japan*, 2 vols (New York: Harper &
Brothers, 1868)

Arnold, Matthew, *Civilization in the United States: First and Last
Impressions of America* (Boston: Cupples & Hurd, 1888)

Bigsby, John J., *The Shoe and the Canoe, or Pictures of Travels in the
Canadas*, 2 vols (London: Chapman & Hall, 1850)

Bridgeman, William, *The Modernisation of Conservative Politics: The Diaries and Letters of William Bridgeman 1904–1935*, ed. Philip Williamson (London: The Historians' Press, 1988)

Conan Doyle, Arthur, *Sherlock Holmes: His Adventures, Memoirs, Return, His Last Bow and The Casebook: The Complete Short Stories* (London: John Murray, 1928)

Crossman, Richard, *The Diaries of a Cabinet Minister*, 3 vols (London: Hamish Hamilton and Jonathan Cape, 1975–7)

Dixon, Piers, *Double Diploma: The Life of Sir Pierson Dixon* (London: Hutchinson, 1968)

Grant, Ulysses S., *Personal Memoirs of Ulysses S. Grant*, 2 vols (New York: Charles R. Webster, 1885)

Hall, Francis, *Japan through American Eyes: The Journal of Francis Hall, Kanagawa and Yokohama 1859–1866*, ed. F. G. Notehelfer (Princeton: Princeton University Press, 1992)

Harris, Townsend, *The Complete Journal of Townsend Harris: First American Consul and Minister to Japan*, ed. Mario E. Cosenza (Rutland, Vermont and Tokyo: Charles E. Tuttle, 1930, rev. edn 1959)

Hawks, Francis L., *Narrative of the Expedition of an American Squadron to the China Seas and Japan: Performed in the Years 1852, 1853 and 1854, under the Command of Commodore M. C. Perry, by Order of the Government of the United States. Compiled from the Original Notes and Journals of Commodore Perry, United States Navy, and his Officers, at his Request and under his Supervision* (New York: D. Appleton, and London: Trubner, 1856)

Healey, Denis, *The Time of my Life* (London: Michael Joseph, 1989)

Heren, Louis, *No Hail, No Farewell* (London: Harper & Row, 1970)

Heusken, Henry, *Japan Journal 1855–1861*, trans. and ed. Jeannette C. van der Corput and Robert A. Wilson (New Brunswick, NJ: Rutgers University Press, 1964)

Lloyd, Selwyn, *Suez 1956: A Personal Account* (London: Jonathan Cape, 1978)

Macartney, Lord, *An Embassy to China: Being the Journal Kept by Lord Macartney during his Embassy to the Emperor Ch'ien-lung 1793–1794*, ed. J. L. Cranmer-Byng (London: Longmans, 1962)

An Officer Who Served in the Expedition [G. R. Gleig], *A Narrative of the Campaigns of the British Army at Washington and New Orleans under Generals Ross, Pakenham, and Lambert, in the Years 1814 and 1815; with Some Account of the Countries Visited* (London: John Murray, 1821)

Oliphant, Laurence, *Episodes in a Life of Adventure or Moss from a Rolling Stone* (Edinburgh: William Blackwood & Sons, 1887)

Osborn, Captain Sherard, *A Cruise in Japanese Waters* (Edinburgh: W. Blackwood & Sons, 1859; this edn Memphis, Tenn.: General Books, POD 2015)

Pownall, T[homas], *A Topographical Description of the Dominions of the United States of America*, 1784, ed. Lois Mulkearn (Pittsburgh: University of Pittsburgh Press, 1949)

Roosevelt, Elliott, *As He Saw It* (New York: Duell, Sloan & Pearce, 1946)

Satow, Ernest Mason, *Diplomat in Japan: The Inner History of the Critical Years in the Evolution of Japan When the Ports were Opened and the Monarchy Restored, Recorded by a Diplomatist Who Took an Active Part in the Events of the Time, with an Account of his Personal Experiences of the Period* (Philadelphia: J. B. Lippincott, 1921, reprint by General Books LLC)

Toynbee, Arnold, *Acquaintances* (London: Oxford University Press, 1967)

Trollope, Anthony, *North America*, 2 vols (London: Chapman & Hall, 1862)

Wilson, Harold, *The Labour Government 1964–70* (Harmondsworth: Penguin, 1974, 1st pub. 1971)

Wood, William Maxwell, *Fankwei; or, The San Jacinto in the Seas of India, China and Japan* (New York: Harper & Brothers, 1859)

General
Dictionary of Canadian Biography

Moore, John Bassett, ed., *International Adjudications: Ancient and Modern: History and Documents Together with Mediatorial Reports, Advisory Opinions, and the Decisions of Domestic Commissions on International Claims: Modern Series* (New York: Oxford University Press for the Carnegie Endowment for International Peace, 1929–33)

SECONDARY SOURCES

Books

Adams, Henry, *History of the United States of America during the Administrations of James Madison* (New York: Library of America, 1986, 1st pub. 1889–91)

Aldrich, Richard J., *The Hidden Hand: Britain, America and Cold War Secret Intelligence* (London: John Murray, 2001)

Anderson, David L., *Imperialism and Idealism: American Diplomats in China 1861–1898* (Bloomington: Indiana University Press, 1985)

Anderson, Stuart, *Race and Rapprochement: Anglo-Saxonism and Anglo-American Relations 1895–1904* (London: Associated University Press, 1981)

Armitage, David, *The Ideological Origins of the British Empire* (Cambridge: Cambridge University Press, 2000)

Auslin, Michael R., *Negotiating with Imperialism: The Unequal Treaties and the Culture of Japanese Diplomacy* (Cambridge, Mass.: Harvard University Press, 2004, pb edn 2006)

Bartlett, C. J., *'The Special Relationship': A Political History of Anglo-American Relations since 1945* (London: Longman, 1992)

Beasley, W. G., *Great Britain and the Opening of Japan 1834–1858* (London: Luzac, 1951, Japan Library pb edn 1995)

Beisner, Robert L., *From the Old Diplomacy to the New 1865–1900* (Arlington Heights, Ill.: Harlan Davidson, 1986 pb edn)

Bell, Herbert C. F., *Lord Palmerston*, 2 vols (Hamden, Conn.: Archon Books, 1966, 1st pub. 1936)

Bemis, Samuel Flagg, *Jay's Treaty: A Study in Commerce and Diplomacy* (New Haven: Yale University Press, 1923, rev. edn 1962)

Benn, Carl, *The War of 1812* (Oxford: Osprey, 2002)

Bew, John, *Castlereagh: Enlightenment, War and Tyranny* (London: Quercus, 2011)

Bickers, Robert, *The Scramble for China: Foreign Devils in the Qing Empire 1832–1914* (London: Penguin Books, 2012)

Bickham, Troy, *The Weight of Vengeance: The United States, the British Empire, and the War of 1812* (New York: Oxford University Press, 2012)

Born, Karl Erich, *International Banking in the 19th and 20th Centuries* (Leamington Spa: Berg Publishers, 1983)

Bourne, Kenneth, *Britain and the Balance of Power in North America 1815–1908* (London: Longmans, 1967)

Brinkley, Capt. F. and Baron Kikuchi, *A History of the Japanese People: From the Earliest Times to the End of the Meiji Era* (New York: Encyclopedia Britannica, 1915)

Brown, Roger H., *The Republic in Peril: 1812* (New York: Columbia University Press, 1964)

Bryson, Thomas A., *Seeds of Mideast Crisis: The United States Diplomatic Role in the Middle East during World War II* (Jefferson, NC: MacFarland, 1981)

Bulloch, James D., *The Secret Service of the Confederate States in Europe or, How the Confederate Cruisers were Equipped* (New York: Sagamore Press, 1959, Random House Modern Library pb edn 2001)

Burk, Kathleen, *Morgan Grenfell 1838–1988: The Biography of a Merchant Bank* (Oxford: Oxford University Press, 1989)

Burk, Kathleen, *Old World, New World: The Story of Britain and America* (London: Little, Brown, 2007 or New York: Atlantic Books, 2008)

Burton, David H., *British–American Diplomacy 1895–1914: Early Years of the Special Relationship* (Malabar, Fla.: Krieger, 1999)

Carroll, Francis, *A Good and Wise Measure: The Search for the Canadian–American Boundary 1783–1842* (Toronto: University of Toronto Press, 2001)

Chamberlain, Muriel E., *Lord Palmerston* (Cardiff: University of Wales Press, 1987)

Chambers, James, *Palmerston: The People's Darling* (London: John Murray, 2004)

Chaudhuri, K. N., *The Trading World of Asia and the English East India Company 1660–1760* (Cambridge: Cambridge University Press, 1978)

Cobbs Hoffman, Elizabeth, *American Umpire* (Cambridge Mass.: Harvard University Press, 2013)

Clymer, Kenton J., *John Hay: The Gentleman as Diplomat* (Ann Arbor: University of Michigan Press, 1975)

Coleman, E. C., *The Pig War: The Most Perfect War in History* (Stroud: The History Press, 2009)

Colman, Jonathan, *A 'Special Relationship'? Harold Wilson, Lyndon B. Johnson and Anglo-American Relations 'at the Summit' 1964–68* (Manchester: Manchester University Press, 2004)

Combs, Jerald A., *The Jay Treaty: Political Background of the Founding Fathers* (Berkeley: University of California Press, 1970)

Cookson, J. E., *Friends of Peace: Anti-War Liberalism in England 1793–1815* (Cambridge: Cambridge University Press, 1982)

Cookson, J. E., *Lord Liverpool's Administration: The Crucial Years 1815–1822* (Edinburgh: Scottish Academic Press, 1975)

Craddock, *Know your Enemy: How the Joint Intelligence Committee Saw the World* (London: John Murray, 2002)

Crow, Carl, *He Opened the Door of Japan: Townsend Harris and the Story of his Amazing Adventures in Establishing American Relations with the Far East* (New York: Harper & Brothers, 1939)

Darwin, John, *The Empire Project: The Rise and Fall of the British World-System 1830–1970* (Cambridge: Cambridge University Press, 2009)

Dear, I. C. B., ed., *The Oxford Companion to the Second World War* (Oxford: Oxford University Press, 1995)

Dickins, F. V., *The Life of Sir Harry Parkes: Minister Plenipotentiary to Japan* (London: Macmillan, 1894) – this is vol. II of his life; vol. I, by S. Lane-Poole, covers his life in China

Doenecke, Justus D. and Mark A. Stoler, *Debating Franklin D. Roosevelt's Foreign Policies 1933–1945* (Lanham, Md: Rowman & Littlefield, 2005)

Dulles, Foster Rhea, *The Old China Trade* (London: Macdonald & Jane's, 1974, 1st pub. 1930)

Dutton, David, *Anthony Eden: A Life and Reputation* (London: Arnold, 1997)

Edwards, E. W., *British Diplomacy and Finance in China 1895–1914* (Oxford: Oxford University Press, 1987)

Eggert, George G., *Richard Olney: Evolution of a Statesman* (University Park: Pennsylvania State University Press, 1974)

Ehrman, John, *The Younger Pitt: The Reluctant Transition* (London: Constable, 1983)

Esdaile, Charles, *The Wars of Napoleon* (London: Longman, 1995)

Fairbank, John K., ed., *The Cambridge History of China*, vol. X: *Late Ch'ing 1800–1911, Part 1* (Cambridge: Cambridge University Press, 1978)

Fay, Peter Ward, *The Opium War 1840–1842: Barbarians in the Celestial Empire in the Early Part of the Nineteenth Century and the War by Which They Forced Her Gates Ajar* (Chapel Hill: University of North Carolina Press, 1975, 1997 pb edn)

Ferguson, Niall, *Colossus: The Rise and Fall of the American Empire* (London: Penguin, 2004)

Fox, Grace, *Britain and Japan 1858–1883* (Oxford: Oxford University Press, 1969)

French, David, *British Strategy and War Aims 1914–1916* (London: Allen & Unwin, 1986)

French, David, *The British Way in Warfare 1688–2000* (London: Unwin Hyman, 1990)

French, David, *Strategy of the Lloyd George Coalition 1916–1918* (Oxford: Oxford University Press, 1995)

Friedberg, Aaron L., *The Weary Titan: Britain and the Experience of Relative Decline 1895–1905* (Princeton: Princeton University Press, 1988)

Fuller, Howard, *Clad in Iron: The American Civil War and the Challenge of British Naval Power* (Westport, Conn.: Praeger, 2008)

Gaddis, John Lewis, *The United States and the Origins of the Cold War 1941–1947* (New York: Columbia University Press, 1972 pb edn)

Garvin, J. L., *The Life of Joseph Chamberlain*, 6 vols (London: Macmillan, 1932–69) – vols 4–6 by Julian Amery

Gibson, James R., *Otter Skins, Boston Ships, and China Goods: The Maritime Fur Trade of the Northwest Coast 1785–1841* (Montreal: McGill-Queen's University Press, 1992, 1999 pb edn)

Go, Julian, *Patterns of Empire: The British and American Empires, 1688 to the Present* (Cambridge: Cambridge University Press, 2011)

Golden, Peter, *Quiet Diplomat: A Biography of Max M. Fisher* (New York: Cornwall Books, 1992)

Graff, Henry F., *Grover Cleveland* (New York: Henry Holt, 2002)

Gray, Denis, *Spencer Perceval: The Evangelical Prime Minister 1762–1812* (Manchester: Manchester University Press, 1963)

Greenberg, Michael, *British Trade and the Opening of China 1800–42* (Cambridge: Cambridge University Press, 1951)

Grenville, J. A. S., *Lord Salisbury and Foreign Policy: The Close of the Nineteenth Century* (London: Athlone Press, 1970 pb edn)

Grenville, John A. S. and George Berkeley Young, *Politics, Strategy, and American Diplomacy: Studies in Foreign Policy 1873–1917* (New Haven: Yale University Press, 1966)

Griffis, William Elliot, *Townsend Harris, First American Envoy in Japan* (Boston: Houghton, Mifflin, 1895, Miami: Hard Press pb edn)

Gubbins, J. H., *The Progress of Japan 1853–1871* (Oxford: Oxford University Press, 1911)

Haddad, John R., *America's First Adventure in China: Trade, Treaties, Opium, and Salvation* (Philadelphia: Temple University Press, 2013)

Hall, Christopher D., *British Strategy in the Napoleonic War 1803–15* (Manchester: Manchester University Press, 1992)

Hammersmith, Jack L., *Spoilsmen in a 'Flowery Fairyland': The Development of the U.S. Legation in Japan 1859–1906* (Kent, Ohio: Kent State University Press, 1998)

Harper, John Lamberton, *American Machiavelli: Alexander Hamilton and the Origins of U.S. Foreign Policy* (Cambridge: Cambridge University Press, 2004)

Hathaway, Robert, *Great Britain and the United States: Special Relations since World War II* (Boston: Twayne, 1990)

Herring, George C., *From Colony to Superpower: U.S. Foreign Relations since 1776* (New York: Oxford University Press, 2008)

Hevia, James L., *Cherishing Men from Afar: Qing Guest Ritual and the Macartney Embassy of 1793* (Durham, NC: Duke University Press, 1995)

Hevia, James L., *English Lessons: The Pedagogy of Imperialism in Nineteenth-Century China* (Durham, NC: Duke University Press, and Hong Kong: Hong Kong University Press, 2003)

Hinde, Wendy, *George Canning* (London: Collins, 1973)

Hinds, Matthew Fallon, *The US, the UK and Saudi Arabia in World War II: The Middle East and the Origins of a Special Relationship* (London: I. B. Tauris, 2016)

Hodgson, Godfrey, *Woodrow Wilson's Right Hand: The Life of Colonel Edward M. House* (London: Yale University Press, 2006)

Hopkirk, Peter, *The Great Game: On Secret Service in High Asia* (London: John Murray, 1990)

Howe, Stephen, *Empire: A Very Short Introduction* (Oxford: Oxford University Press, 2002)

Hsü, Immanuel C. Y., *The Rise of Modern China* (New York: Oxford University Press, 1990, 4th edn)

Hunt, Michael H., *The Making of a Special Relationship: The United States and China to 1914* (New York: Columbia University Press, 1983)

Iriye, Akira, *The New Cambridge History of American Foreign Relations*, vol. III: *The Globalizing of America 1913–1945* (Cambridge: Cambridge University Press, 2013)

Jansen, Marius B., *The Making of Modern Japan* (Cambridge, Mass.: Harvard University Press, 2000, 2002 pb edn)

Jenks, Leland H., *The Migration of British Capital to 1875* (London: Thomas Nelson & Sons, 1963, 1st pub. 1927)

Johnson, Chalmers, *The Sorrows of Empire: Militarism, Secrecy, and the End of the Republic* (London: Verso, 2006 pb edn)

Johnson, Robert Erwin, *Far China Station: The U.S. Navy in Asian Waters 1800–1898* (Annapolis, Md: Naval Institute Press, 1979)

Jones, Howard, *To the Webster–Ashburton Treaty: A Study in Anglo-American Relations 1783–1843* (Chapel Hill: University of North Carolina Press, 1977)

Jones, Howard and Donald A. Rakestraw, *Prologue to Manifest Destiny: Anglo-American Relations in the 1840s* (Wilmington, Del.: SR Books, 1997)

Jones, Wilbur Devereux, *The American Problem in British Diplomacy 1841–1861* (London: Macmillan, 1974)

Kelly, J. B., *Eastern Arabian Frontiers* (London: Faber & Faber, 1964)

Kennedy, Paul, *The Rise and Fall of British Naval Mastery* (London: Macmillan, 1983 edn)

Kissinger, Henry, *Diplomacy* (New York: Simon & Schuster, 1994)

Kunz, Diane B., *The Economic Diplomacy of the Suez Crisis* (Chapel Hill: University of North Carolina Press, 1991)

LaFeber, Walter, *The New Cambridge History of American Foreign Relations*, vol. II: *The American Search for Opportunity 1865–1913* (Cambridge: Cambridge University Press, 1993)

Latimer, Jon, *1812: War with America* (Cambridge, Mass.: Harvard University Press, 2007)

Lisio, Donald J., *British Naval Supremacy and Anglo-American Antagonisms 1914–1930* (Cambridge: Cambridge University Press, 2014)

Locke, John, *The Second Treatise of Government*, ed. Thomas P. Peardon (Uppersaddle River, NJ: Prentice Hall, 1997)

Lodge, Henry Cabot, *The War with Spain* (New York: Harper & Brothers, 1899)

Long, David F., *Sailor-Diplomat: A Biography of James Biddle 1783–1848* (Boston: Northeastern University Press, 1983)

Louis, Wm. Roger, *Ends of British Imperialism: The Scramble for Empire, Suez and Decolonization* (London: I. B. Tauris, 2006)

Louis, Wm. Roger, *Imperialism at Bay 1941–1945: The United States and the Decolonization of the British Empire* (Oxford: Oxford University Press, 1977)

Lovell, Julia, *The Opium War: Drugs, Dreams and the Making of China* (London: Picador, 2011)

Lucas, W. Scott, *Divided We Stand: Britain, the US and the Suez Crisis* (London: Hodder & Stoughton, 1996 pb edn)

McClain, James L., *Japan: A Modern History* (New York: W. W. Norton, 2002)

McCullough, David, *John Adams* (New York: Simon & Schuster, 2001)

McKercher, B. J. C., *The Second Baldwin Government and the United States 1924–1929: Attitudes and Diplomacy* (Cambridge: Cambridge University Press, 1984)

McKercher, B. J. C., *Transition of Power: Britain's Loss of Global Pre-eminence to the United States 1930–1945* (Cambridge: Cambridge University Press, 1999)

MacMillan, Margaret, *Peacemakers: The Paris Conference of 1919 and its Attempt to End War* (London: John Murray, 2001)

Mahan, Alfred Thayer, *Sea Power in its Relations to the War of 1812*, 2 vols (Boston: Little, Brown, 1905)

Mahon, John K., *The War of 1812* (New York: Da Capo Press, 1991 pb edn, 1st pub. 1972)

Mango, Andrew, *From the Sultan to Atatürk: Turkey: The Peace Conferences of 1919–23 and their Aftermath* (London: Haus Publishing, 2009)

Merk, Frederick, *The Oregon Question: Essays in Anglo-American Diplomacy and Politics* (Cambridge, Mass.: Harvard University Press, 1967)

Michie, Alexander, *The Englishman in China during the Victorian Era as Illustrated in the Career of Sir Rutherford Alcock, K.C.B., D.C.L., Many Years Consul and Minister in China and Japan*, 2 vols (Taipei: Ch'eng-Wen Publishing, 1966, 1st pub. 1900)

Monger, George, *The End of Isolation: British Foreign Policy 1900–1907* (Westport, Conn.: Greenwood Press, 1963)

Monroe, Elizabeth, *Britain's Moment in the Middle East 1914–1971* (London: Chatto & Windus, 1981 rev. edn, 1st pub. 1963)

Morison, Samuel Eliot, *'Old Bruin': Commodore Matthew C. Perry 1794–1858* (Boston: Atlantic Monthly Press, 1967)

Mowat, R. B., *The Diplomatic Relations of Great Britain and the United States* (London: Edward Arnold, 1925)

Mowat, R. B., *The Life of Lord Pauncefote: First Ambassador to the United States* (London: Constable, 1929)

Musicant, Ivan, *Empire by Default: The Spanish–American War and the Dawn of the American Century* (New York: Henry Holt, 1998)

Napier, Priscilla, *Barbarian Eye: Lord Napier in China 1834 – The Prelude to Hong Kong* (London: Brassey's, 1995)

Neering, Rosemary, *The Pig War: The Last Canada–US Border Conflict* (Victoria, BC: Heritage House, 2011)

Neilson, Keith, *Britain, Soviet Russia, and the Collapse of the Versailles Order 1919–1939* (Cambridge: Cambridge University Press, 2006)

Neustadt, Richard E., *Alliance Politics* (New York: Columbia University Press, 1970 pb edn)

Nevins, Allan, *Henry White: Thirty Years of American Diplomacy* (New York: Harper & Brothers, 1930)

Nicolson, Harold, *Curzon: The Last Phase 1919–1925* (London: Constable, 1934)

O'Brien, Phillips Payson, *British and American Naval Power: Politics and Policy 1900–1936* (Westport, Conn.: Praeger, 1998)

Omissi, David, *The Sepoys and the Raj 1857–1940* (Basingstoke: Palgrave Macmillan, 1994)

Orde, Anne, *The Eclipse of Great Britain: The United States and Imperial Decline 1895–1956* (Basingstoke: Macmillan, 1996)

Otte, T. S., *The China Question: Great Power Rivalry and British Isolation 1894–1905* (Oxford: Oxford University Press, 2007)

Pagden, Anthony, *The Burdens of Empire: 1539 to the Present* (Cambridge: Cambridge University Press, 2015)

Peden, G. C., *Arms, Economics and British Strategy: From Dreadnoughts to Hydrogen Bombs* (Cambridge: Cambridge University Press, 2007)

Pelcovits, Nathan A., *Old China Hands and the Foreign Office* (New York: King's Crown Press, 1948)

Perkins, Bradford, *The Cambridge History of American Foreign Relations*, vol. I: *The Creation of a Republican Empire 1776–1865* (Cambridge: Cambridge University Press, 1993)

Perkins, Bradford, *Castlereagh and Adams: England and the United States 1812–1823* (Berkeley: University of California Press, 1964)

Perkins, Bradford, *The First Rapprochement: England and the United States 1795–1805* (Philadelphia: University of Pennsylvania Press, 1955)

Perkins, Bradford, *The Great Rapprochement: England and the United States 1895–1914* (London: Victor Gollancz, 1969)

Perkins, Bradford, *Prologue to War: England and the United States 1805–1812* (Berkeley: University of California Press, 1968)

Pham, P. L., *Ending 'East of Suez': The British Decision to Withdraw from Malaysia and Singapore 1964–1968* (Oxford: Oxford University Press, 2010)

Pickering, Jeffrey, *Britain's Withdrawal from East of Suez: The Politics of Retrenchment* (London: Macmillan, 1998)

Remini, Robert V., *John Quincy Adams* (New York: Henry Holt, 2002)

Reynolds, David, *Britannia Overruled: British Policy and World Power in the 20th Century* (London: Longman, 2000, 2nd edn)

Reynolds, David, *The Creation of the Anglo-American Alliance 1937–1941: A Study in Competitive Co-operation* (London: Europa, 1981)

Rich, Norman, *Great Power Diplomacy 1814–1914* (Boston: McGraw-Hill, 1992)

Richards, D. S., *The Savage Frontier: A History of the Anglo-Afghan Wars* (London: Macmillan, 1990, Pan pb edn 2003)

Richardson, Louise, *When Allies Differ: Anglo-American Relations during the Suez and Falklands Crises* (New York: St Martin's Press, 1996)

Ritcheson, Charles R., *Aftermath of Revolution: British Policy towards the United States 1783–1795* (Dallas: Southern Methodist University Press, 1969)

Roberts, Andrew, *Salisbury: Victorian Titan* (London: Weidenfeld & Nicolson, 1999)

Rose, Norman, *Vansittart: Study of a Diplomat* (London: Heinemann, 1978)

Roskill, Stephen, *Naval Policy between the Wars*, vol. I: *The Period of Anglo-American Antagonism 1919–1929* (New York: Walker, 1968)

Rowe, William T., *China's Last Empire: The Great Qing* (Cambridge, Mass.: Harvard University Press, 2009)

Sacher, Howard M., *The Emergence of the Middle East 1914–1924* (London: Allen Lane, 1970)

Satoh, Henry, *Agitated Japan: The Life of Baron Ii Kamon-no kami Naosuké (Based on the Kaikoku Shimatsu of Shimada Saburō)* [Summary of the Opening of Japan to Civilization], rev. William Elliot Griffis (New York: D. Appleton, 1896)

Satoh, Henry, *Lord Hotta, the Pioneer Diplomat of Japan* (Tokio: Hakubunkan, 1908)

Scott, Geraldine Tidd, *Ties of Common Blood: A History of Maine's Northeast Boundary Dispute with Great Britain 1783–1842* (Bowie, Md: Heritage Books, 1992)

Seigenthaler, John, *James K. Polk* (New York: Henry Holt, 2003)

Sellar, Walther Carruthers and Robert Julian Yeatman, *1066 and All That: A Memorable History of England. Comprising All the Parts You Can Remember Including One Hundred and Three Good Things, Five Bad Kings, and Two Genuine Dates* (London: Methuen, 1930)

Sharp, Alan, *David Lloyd George: Great Britain: The Peace Conferences of 1919–23 and their Aftermath* (London: Haus Publishing, 2008)

Siegel, Jennifer, *Endgame: Britain, Russia and the Final Struggle for Central Asia* (London: I. B. Tauris, 2002)

Spiers, E. M., *Army and Society 1815–1914* (London: Longman, 1980)

Spivak, Burton, *Jefferson's English Crisis: Commerce, Embargo, and the Republican Revolution* (Charlottesville: University Press of Virginia, 1979)

Stagg, J. C. A., *The War of 1812: Conflict for a Continent* (Cambridge: Cambridge University Press, 2012)

Stahr, Walter, *John Jay: Founding Father* (London: Hambledon & London, 2005)

Stoler, Mark A., *Allies in War: Britain and America against the Axis Powers 1940–1945* (London: Hodder Arnold, 2005)

Sumida, Jon Tetsuro, *In Defence of Naval Supremacy: Finance, Technology, and British Naval Power 1889–1904* (London: Routledge, 1993 pb edn)

Tansill, Charles Callan, *Canadian–American Relations 1875–1911* (New Haven: Yale University Press, 1943)

Taylor, A. J. P., *The Struggle for Mastery in Europe 1848–1918* (Oxford: Oxford University Press, 1954)

Taylor, Alan, *The Civil War of 1812: American Citizens, British Subjects, Irish Rebels, & Indian Allies* (New York: Alfred A. Knopf, 2010)

Thorne, Christopher, *Allies of a Kind: The United States, Britain, and the War against Japan 1941–1945* (London: Hamish Hamilton, 1978)

Tiffany, Orrin Edward, *The Relations of the United States to the Canadian Rebellion of 1837–1838* (Buffalo, NY: Buffalo Historical Society, 1905, POD 2014)

Tilchin, William N., *Theodore Roosevelt and the British Empire: A Study in Presidential Statecraft* (Basingstoke: Macmillan Press, 1997)

Treat, Payson Jackson, *The Early Diplomatic Relations between the United States and Japan 1853–1865* (Baltimore: The Johns Hopkins Press, 1917)

Treat, Payson Jackson, *Japan and the United States 1853–1921* (Boston and New York: Houghton Mifflin, 1921, Bibliolife Reproduction Series edn 2016)

Turnbull, Stephen, *Tokugawa Ieyasu: Leadership, Strategy, Conflict* (Oxford: Osprey, 2012)

Van Deusen, Glyndon G., *William Henry Seward* (New York: Oxford University Press, 1967)

Vaughan, James R., *The Failure of American and British Propaganda in the Arab Middle East 1945–57: Unconquerable Minds* (London: Palgrave, 2005)

Westad, Odd Arne, *Restless Empire: China and the World since 1750* (London: Vintage, 2013)

Wiley, Peter Booth with Ichiro Korogi, *Yankees in the Land of the Gods: Commodore Perry and the Opening of Japan* (New York: Viking, 1990)

Wilford, Hugh, *America's Great Game: The CIA's Secret Arabists and the Making of the Modern Middle East* (New York: Basic Books, 2013)

Wills, Garry, *James Madison* (New York: Henry Holt, 2002)

Wong, J. W., *Deadly Dreams: Opium and the Arrow War (1856–1860) in China* (Cambridge: Cambridge University Press, 1998)

Woods, Randall Bennett, *A Changing of the Guard: Anglo-American Relations 1941–1946* (Chapel Hill: University of North Carolina Press, 1990)

Woodward, David L., *Hell in the Holy Land: World War I in the Middle East* (Lexington, Ky.: University Press of Kentucky, 2006)

Wynn, Antony, *Persia in the Great Game: Sir Percy Sykes, Explorer, Consul, Soldier, Spy* (London: John Murray, 2003)

Yashi, Shōzan [Ken Yamaguchi], *Kinsé Shiriaku: A History of Japan from the First Visit of Commodore Perry in 1853 to the Capture of Hakodate by the Mikado's Forces in 1869*, trans. E. M. Satow (Yokohama: F. R. Wetmore, 1876)

Articles and Chapters

Allston, Frank J., 'U.S. Navy Paymaster: A Hero in the Boxer Rebellion', *Supply Corps Newsletter*, 0360716X, 63:4 (July/Aug. 2000)

Bailey, Thomas A., 'Dewey and the Germans at Manila Bay', *American Historical Review*, 45:1 (Oct. 1939)

Bartlett, Merrill L., 'Commander James Biddle and the First Naval Mission to Japan, 1845–1846', *American Neptune*, 41 (Jan. 1981)

Beasley, W. G., 'From Conflict to Co-operation: British Naval Surveying in Japanese Waters, 1845–82', in Ian Nish and Yoichi Kibata, eds, *The History of Anglo-Japanese Relations*, vol. I: *The Political–Diplomatic Dimension 1600–1930* (London: Palgrave Macmillan, 2000)

Beasley, W. G., 'The Language Problem in the Anglo-Japanese Negotiations of 1854', *Bulletin of the School of Oriental and African Studies*, 13:3 (1950)

Burk, Kathleen, 'American Foreign Economic Policy and Lend-Lease', in Ann Lane and Howard Temperley, eds, *The Rise and Fall of the Grand Alliance 1941–45* (Basingstoke: Macmillan, 1995)

Blower, Brooke L., 'Nation of Outposts: Forts, Factories, Bases, and the Making of the American Power, *Diplomatic History*, 41:3 (June 2017)

Burk, Kathleen, 'Britain and the Marshall Plan', in Chris Wrigley, ed., *Warfare, Diplomacy and Politics: Essays in Honour of A. J. P. Taylor* (London: Hamish Hamilton, 1986)

Burk, Katheen, 'Outline of Events, 1967 Devaluation Symposium', *Contemporary Record* (Winter 1988)

Campbell, A. E., 'Great Britain and the United States in the Far East, 1895–1903', *Historical Journal*, 1:2 (1958)

Clymer, Kenton J., 'The Education of William Phillips: Self-Determination and American Policy toward India, 1942–45', *Diplomatic History*, 8:1 (Winter 1984)

Cortazzi, Hugh, 'The British Bombardment of Kagoshima, 1863', in Hugh Cortazzi, ed., *British Envoys in Japan 1859–1972* (Folkestone, Kent: Global Oriental for the Japan Society, 2004), Appendix I

Cortazzi, Hugh, 'Lt Colonel St John Neale. Chargé d'Affaires at Edo/Yokohama, 1862–64', in Hugh Cortazzi, ed., *British Envoys in Japan 1859–1972* (Folkestone, Kent: Global Oriental for the Japan Society, 2004)

Demeritt, David, 'Representing the "True" St. Croix: Knowledge and Power in the Partition of the Northwest', *William and Mary Quarterly*, 3rd Series, 54:3 (July 1997)

Donahue, William J., 'The Caleb Cushing Mission', *Modern Asian Studies*, 16:2 (1982)

Downes, Jacques M., 'American Merchants and the China Opium Trade, 1800–1840', *Business History Review*, 42:4 (Winter 1968)

Eckel, Paul E., 'The Crimean War and Japan', *Far Eastern Quarterly*, 3:2 (Feb. 1944)

Egerton, George W., 'Ideology, Diplomacy and International Organisation: Wilsonism and the League of Nations in Anglo-American Relations, 1918–1920', in B. J. C. McKercher, ed., *Anglo-American Relations in the 1920s: The Struggle for Supremacy* (London: Macmillan, 1991)

Ferris, John R., 'The Symbol and Substance of Seapower: Great Britain, the United States, and the One-Power Standard, 1919–1921', in B. J. C. McKercher, *Anglo-American Relations in the 1920s: The Struggle for Supremacy* (London: Macmillan, 1991)

Ferris, John, 'Treasury Control, the Ten Year Rule and British Service Policies, 1919–1924', *Historical Journal*, 30:4 (1987)

Folly, Martin H., 'Breaking the Vicious Circle: Britain, the United States, and the Genesis of the North Atlantic Treaty', *Diplomatic History*, 12:1 (Winter 1988)

Goldstein, Erik, 'The Evolution of British Diplomatic Strategy for the Washington Conference', in Erik Goldstein and John Maurer, eds, *The Washington Conference 1921–22: Naval Rivalry, East Asian Stability and the Road to Pearl Harbor* (London: Frank Cass, 1994)

Haglund, David and Tudor Onea, 'Victory without Triumph? Theodore Roosevelt, Honour, and the Alaska Panhandle Boundary Dispute', *Diplomacy and Statecraft*, 19:1 (March 2008)

Hahn, Emily, 'A Yankee Barbarian at the Shogun's Court', *American Heritage*, 15:4 (June 1964)

Harrison, Henrietta, 'The Qinglong Emperor's Letter to George III and the Early-Twentieth-Century Origins of Ideas about Traditional China's Foreign Relations', *American Historical Review*, 122:3 (July 2017)

Hattori, Ryūji and Tosh Minohara, 'The 1920s: The Washington Treaty System and the Immigration Issue', in Makoto Iokibe and Tosh Minohara, eds, *The History of US–Japan Relations: From Perry to the Present* (Singapore: Palgrave Macmillan, 2017, 1st pub. in Japanese in Japan 2008)

He, Sibing, 'Russell and Company and the Imperialism of Anglo-American Free Trade', in Kendall Johnson, ed., *Narratives of Free Trade: The Commercial Cultures of Early US–China Relations* (Hong Kong: Hong Kong University Press, 2012)

Hewedy, Amin, 'Nasser and the Crisis of 1956', in Wm. Roger Louis
    and Roger Owen, eds, *Suez 1956: The Crisis and its Consequences*
    (Oxford: Oxford University Press, 1989)
Hoare, James, 'The Era of the Unequal Treaties, 1858–99', in Ian
    Nish and Yoichi Kibata, eds, *The History of Anglo-Japanese
    Relations*, vol. I: *The Political–Diplomatic Dimension 1600–1930*
    (London: Palgrave Macmillan, 2000)
Holland, Robert, 'The British Empire and the Great War, 1914–1918',
    in Judith Brown and Wm. Roger Louis, eds, *The Oxford History of
    the British Empire*, vol. IV: *The Twentieth Century* (Oxford: Oxford
    University Press, 1999)
Kaufman, Scott and John A. Soares, Jr, '"Sagacious beyond Praise"?
    Winfield Scott and Anglo-American-Canadian Border Diplomacy,
    1837–1860', *Diplomatic History*, 30:1 (Jan. 2006)
Kikuchi, Yoshiyuki, 'Samurai Chemists, Charles Graham and
    Alexander William Williamson at University College London,
    1863–1872', *Ambix*, 56:2 (July 2009)
Kim, S. S., 'Burlingame and the Inauguration of the Co-operative
    Policy', *Modern Asian Studies*, 5:4 (1971)
Knox, Andrew Alexander, 'Kaempfer's *Histoire de l'Empire du Japon*',
    Edinburgh Review, 96:196 (Oct. 1852)
Kramer, Paul, 'Empires, Exceptions, and Anglo-Saxons: Race and Rule
    between the British and United States Empires, 1880–1910', *Journal
    of American History*, 88:4 (March 2002)
Kramer, Paul, 'Power and Connection: Imperial Histories of the United
    States in the World', *The American Historical Review*, Ibis (Dec. 2011)
Kunz, Diane B., 'The Importance of Having Money: The Economic
    Diplomacy of the Suez Crisis', in Wm. Roger Louis and Roger
    Owen, eds, *Suez Crisis: The Crisis and its Consequences* (Oxford:
    Oxford University Press, 1989)
Kuo, Ping Chia, 'Caleb Cushing and the Treaty of Wanghia, 1844',
    Journal of Modern History, 5:1 (March 1933)
Lambert, Andrew, 'Winning without Fighting: British Grand Strategy and
    its Application to the United States, 1815–65', in Bradford A. Lee and
    Karl F. Walling, eds, *Strategic Logic and Political Rationality: Essays in
    Honor of Michael I. Handel* (London: Frank Cass, 2003)
Lingelbach, Anna Lane, 'William Huskisson as President of the Board
    of Trade', *American Historical Review*, 43:4 (July 1938)
Louis, Wm. Roger and Ronald Robinson, 'The Imperialism of
    Decolonization', *Journal of Imperial and Commonwealth History*,
    22:3 (1994)

McKercher, B. J. B., ' "The Deep and Latent Distrust": The British
Official Mind and the United States, 1919–1929', in B. J. B.
McKercher, ed., *Anglo-American Relations in the 1920s: The
Struggle for Supremacy* (London: Macmillan, 1991)

McMaster, John, 'Alcock and Harris: Foreign Diplomacy in
Bakumatsu Japan', *Monumenta Nipponica*, 22:3/4 (1967)

Marshall, P. J., '1918 to the 1960s: Keeping Afloat', in P. J. Marshall,
ed., *The Cambridge Illustrated History of the British Empire*
(Cambridge: Cambridge University Press, 1996)

Marshall, P. J., 'The English in Asia to 1700', in Nicholas Canny, ed.,
The Oxford History of the British Empire, vol. I: *British Overseas
Enterprise to the Close of the Seventeenth Century* (Oxford: Oxford
University Press, 1998)

Mayo, Marlene J., 'A Catechism of Western Diplomacy: The
Japanese and Hamilton Fish, 1872', *Journal of Asian Studies*, 26:3
(May 1967)

Nolde, John J., 'The "False Edict" of 1849', *Journal of Asian Studies*,
20:3 (May 1961)

O'Hara, Glen, 'The Limits of US Power: Transatlantic Financial
Diplomacy under the Johnson and Wilson Administrations,
October 1964–November 1968', *Contemporary European History*,
12:3 (Aug. 2003)

Oliphant, Laurence, 'The Attack on the British Legation in Japan in
1861', *Blackwood's Edinburgh Magazine*, 141:855 (Jan. 1887)

Perry, John Curtis, 'Great Britain and the Emergence of Japan as a
Naval Power', *Monumenta Nipponica*, 21:3/4 (1966)

Petersen, Tore Tingvold, 'Anglo-American Rivalry in the Middle East:
The Struggle for the Buraimi Oasis, 1952–1957', *International History
Review*, 14:1 (Feb. 1992)

Porter, A. N., 'The South African War (1899–1902): Context and
Motive Reconsidered', *Journal of African History*, 31 (1990)

Pritchard, Earl H., 'The Origins of the Most-Favored-Nation and
the Open Door Policies in China', *Far Eastern Quarterly*, 1:2
(Feb. 1942)

Saunders, Christopher and Iain R. Smith, 'Southern Africa, 1795–1910',
in Andrew Porter, ed., *The Oxford History of the British Empire*,
vol. III: *The Nineteenth Century* (Oxford: Oxford University
Press, 1999)

Shortridge, Wilson P., 'The Canadian–American Frontier during the
Rebellion of 1837–1838', *Canadian Historical Review*, 7:1 (March
1926)

Stacey, C. P., 'The Myth of the Unguarded Frontier 1815–1908', *American Historical Review*, 56:1 (Oct. 1950)

Steele, M. William, 'The United States and Japan's Civil War', in M. William Steele, *Alternative Narratives in Modern Japanese History* (London: RoutledgeCurzon, 2003)

Stelle, Charles C., 'American Trade in Opium in China, Prior to 1820', *Pacific Historical Review*, 9:4 (Dec. 1940)

Stelle, Charles C., 'American Trade in Opium to China, 1821–39', *Pacific Historical Review*, 10:1 (March 1941)

Tallman, R. D. and J. I. Tallman, 'The Diplomatic Search for the St. Croix River, 1796–1798', *Acadiensis*, 1 (Spring 1972)

Taylor, A. J. P., 'Two Prime Ministers', in A. J. P. Taylor, *From Napoleon to Stalin: Comments on European History* (London: The Right Book Club, 1950)

The Times, 11 Jan. 1898

Treat, Payson Jackson, 'The Mikado's Ratification of the Foreign Treaties', *American Historical Review*, 23/3 (April 1918)

Tsiang, T. F., 'New Light on Chinese Diplomacy, 1836–49', *Journal of Modern History*, 3:4 (Dec. 1931)

Wakeman, Jr, Frederick, 'The Canton Trade and the Opium War', in John K. Fairbank, ed., *The Cambridge History of China*, vol. X: *Late Ch'ing 1800–1911, Part 1* (Cambridge: Cambridge University Press, 1978)

Wilson, Henry S., 'The United States and the War', in Peter Warwick and S. B. Spies, eds, *The South African War: The Anglo-Boer War 1899–1902* (London: Longman, 1980)

Newspapers

Japan Herald
National Intelligencer
New York Tribune
Niles' Register
Pall Mall Gazette
South Australian Register
The Times
Toronto News

Periodicals

Edinburgh Review
Life
Punch

Websites

http://avalon.law.yale.edu
http://www.biographi.ca/en/bio/ogilvy_john_5E.html
https://collections.leventhalmap.org/search/commonwealth:3f462t67x
http://en.wikisource.org/wiki/Treaty_of_Wanghia
http://eprints.lse.ac.uk/6908/1/The_Iwakura_Mission_in_Britain,_
    1872.pdf
https://www.ourdocuments.gov
https://www.poets.org/poetsorg/poem/mending-wall
http://www.presidency.ucsb.edu/ws/index.php?pid=67360
http://www.presidency.ucsb.edu/ws/?pid=67317
http://www.presidency.ucsb.edu/ws/?pid=103901
www.rms-gs.de/phileng/history/kap02.html
https://uwdc.library.wisc.edu/collections/FRUS/

Picture Credits

The American assault on York, Canada 27 April 1813
Painting by Owen Staples, 1914, courtesy of Toronto Public Library

The British burning of Washington, 24 August 1814
Photo by MPI/Getty Images

Combat between the USS *Constitution* and HMS *Guerrière*, 19 August 1812
Bettmann via Getty Images

Lake of the Woods
Photo by Dean Conger/National Geographic/Getty Images

John Quincy Adams
National Archives/Handout via Getty Images

General Winfield Scott
Encyclopaedia Britannica via Getty Images

British attack on the steamer the *Caroline*, 29 December 1837
Photo by Universal History Archive/UIG via Getty Images

Earl Macartney
Hulton Archive/Stringer via Getty Images

Caleb Cushing
Photo by © CORBIS/Corbis via Getty Images

Li Hung Chang
Photo by © Hulton-Deutsch Collection/CORBIS/Corbis via Getty Images

Yüan Chi-k'ai
Photo by Keystone-France/Gamma-Keystone via Getty Images

British bombardment of the treaty port of Canton
Woodcut, 1841. BPA2# 5375, Bettmann via Getty Images

A temple in the ruins of the Old Summer Palace
Photo by Hulton Archive/Getty Images

Townsend Harris
Photo by © CORBIS/Corbis via Getty Images

Sir Rutherford Alcock
Photo by the Print Collector/Print Collector/Getty Images

8th Earl of Elgin
Photo by Universal History Archive/UIG via Getty Image

Ïl Kamon no kami Naosuké
Wikimedia Commons

Tokugawa Yoshinobu
Photo by Adolphe-Eugene Disderi/ullstein bild via Getty Images

Anson Burlingame
Photo by Library of Congress/Corbis/VCG via Getty Images

Sir Harry Smith Parkes
Photo by Universal History Archive/UIG via Getty Images

The Chōshū Five
ref UGD172/4/2/1, A R Brown McFarlane & Co Ltd collection, the University of Glasgow Archive

Samurai
Photo by Historica Graphica Collection/Heritage Images/Getty Images

Itō Hirobumi
Photo by W. & D. Downey/Getty Images

Mutsuhito
Bettmann/Contributor via Getty Images

Commodore George Dewey
Hispanic Division, Library of Congress

John Hay
Photo by J.E./Library of Congress/Corbis/VCG via Getty Images

The American fleet at the Battle of Manila Bay
Photo12/UIG via Getty Images

William Waldegrave Palmer, 2nd Earl of Selborne
'Statesmen. No. 741.' by Sir Lesilie Ward © National Portrait Gallery, London

Sir Robert Craigie
Library of Congress Prints and Photographs Division, National Photo Company Collection (Reproduction Number: LC-DIG-npcc-02217)

General Sir Edmund Allenby
Photo by Universal History Archive/UIG via Getty Images

Henry J. Morgenthau, Jr
Photo by Library of Congress/Corbis/VCG via Getty Images

Cordell Hull
Photo by Thomas D. Mcavoy/The LIFE Picture Collection/Getty Images

Franklin Roosevelt and Sir Winston Churchill
Photo by Lt. L C Priest/ IWM via Getty Images

Henry L. Stimson
Photo by Library of Congress/Corbis/VCG via Getty Images

King Ibn Saud
Photo by ullstein bild/ullstein bild via Getty Images

Sir Ivone Kirkpatrick
Photo by Keystone-France\Gamma-Rapho via Getty Images

Harold Macmillan
Photo by Brian Seed/The LIFE Images Collection/Getty Images

Osbert Lancaster cartoon
Reproduced by kind permission of both Clare Hastings and the National Library of Scotland

Alexandria 1956
Photo by Keystone/Getty Images

Demonstration in Trafalgar Square
Photo by Mark Kauffman/The LIFE Picture Collection/Getty Images

John Foster Dulles and President Dwight D. Eisenhower
Photo by Ed Clark/The LIFE Picture Collection/Getty Images

Prime Minister Harold Wilson and President Lyndon Johnson
Bettmann via Getty Images

Roy Jenkins
Photo by Roger Jackson/Central Press/Getty Images

Denis Healey
Photo by Rolls Press/Popperfoto/Getty Images

Sir William Luce and the Trucial Oman Scouts
Photo by Comtos Bartholomew

The B-2 or stealth bomber
Photo by USAF/Getty Images

Index

'A foolish consistency is the hobgoblin of little minds'[1]

Abdullah bin al-Hussein 379
Abé Masahiro Ise no-kami 245,
    255–7, 270
Aberdeen, 4th Earl 128–34, 261–2, 474
Abu Dhabi 410–11
Adams, David P. 97
Adams, F.O. 322
Adams, Henry 64, 66
Adams, John 16, 18–9, 38, 71
Adams, John Quincy 4, 65–6, 71,
    80–2, 87, 97–8, 100, 101–2, 106–8
Adams, W.E. 348
Adams, William 67, 452
Adee, Alvey 469
Afghanistan 8, 210, 336, 361, 364, 367,
    371, 437
Africa 2, 51, 359, 365
Albany Iron and Saw Works 298
Alcock, Sir Rutherford 206, 281,
    284–5, 287–9, 291–3, 299, 300,
    303, 306–10, 314
Aldrich, Winthrop 413
Alexander, Sir William 38, 39
Allenby, General Sir Edmund ('Bull')
    369–71
Allen, William ('Foghorn Bill') 131
American Camp 142–3
American empire 1–9, 12, 16, 229, 294,
    359, 380, 497–8
    American Samoa 6, 331, 353, 391

British empire 269, 321, 329–30,
    332–5, 337–47, 349–50, 354–5,
    381–425
Caribbean 363
Central America 390–1
China trade 185–6, 188, 190, 232,
    244, 261, 320, 353, 390, 392
Chinese empire 158, 184–92, 194–5,
    201, 209, 211–15, 216–29, 238,
    251, 259, 265, 320
commercial and financial power
    151–2, 178, 189, 218–25, 331–2,
    397–8, 506
cooperation with British empire
    198, 203–4, 291, 294–5, 297,
    299, 327–8, 352–4, 406–9,
    411–12, 429–30, 432–3
cooperation with French empire
    203–4, 295, 299, 365–7, 387,
    421–2, 425
German empire 351–3, 396, 429
Guam 6, 59, 331, 391
Hawaiian Islands 6, 154, 244, 331,
    338, 353, 384, 391
informal empire 9, 158, 159
Japanese empire 231–328, 265,
    274–9, 290, 294, 300, 324–8,
    386, 389–90, 392–4, 400, 403
    reasons for forcing it open 232–2,
    269, 402

trade 232, 239–40, 320, 390
trade with Japan 259, 274, 320,
   322, 353
Legation in Edo 287, 291, 296
Middle East 375–7, 409–25
Midway Islands 6, 331
military and naval power 9, 152–4,
   187–8, 437
Moro Islands 6, 331
Open Door Notes 209, 215
Philippines 3, 6, 154, 210–11, 331,
   349–55, 390–1, 498
Puerto Rico 331
Russian empire 204, 333, 395,
   405–6, 408, 416
San Juan Island 73, 75, 137
Trade 172–4, 211–12, 228, 259, 316
Washington Territory 75, 136–7,
   141
American Formal Dependencies
   American Samoa 437
   Baker Island 437
   Guam 437
   Howland Island 437
   Jarvis Island 437
   Johnston Atoll 437
   Kingman Reef 437
   Midway Islands 437
   Navassa Island 437
   Northern Mariana Islands 437
   Palmyra Atoll 437
   Puerto Rico 437
   Virgin Islands 437
   Wake Island 437
American Revolution 3, 12, 17, 42, 76,
   86, 90, 171
   American private debts 18–19, 32
American states
   'states' rights' 77, 126
   Alaska 2, 78, 145–50, 154, 331, 357
   Arizona 6
   California 6, 258
   Colorado 6

Florida 12, 15, 43
Idaho 84–5
Illinois 5, 17
Indiana 5, 17, 50
Kentucky 75, 138
Maine 13, 32, 34–42, 71, 73, 77, 88,
   90, 91, 102–7, 109–11, 121–25,
   129–30, 136
   Aroostoock 121–5
Massachusetts 35, 43, 71, 91, 106–7,
   110, 129, 144, 150
Michigan 5, 17, 22, 58, 110, 119
Minnesota 13
Montana 84–5
Nevada 6
New Hampshire 105–6
New Mexico 6
New York 13, 17, 36, 59, 96, 106,
   115, 117, 119, 126–7, 142, 144,
   264, 298, 314, 321
North Dakota 84–5
Ohio 5, 17, 58, 60, 62, 119
Oregon 73, 77, 78, 86, 132, 139
Pennsylvania 17
Rhode Island 36–42, 172
Tennessee 139
Texas 131
Utah 6
Vermont 102, 106, 117
Virginia 5, 188
Washington 75, 78, 84–6,
   132–3
Wisconsin 5, 17
Amery, Leo 492
Ando Nobumasa 300
Anglo-American intelligence
   relationship 424, 433, 503
Anglo-American nuclear relationship
   406, 425, 433, 506–7
Anglo-American trade 18–20, 33–5,
   42–9, 52, 86–7, 102, 133, 151–2,
   172, 182–3
Anglo-Iranian Oil Company 411–13

Anglophobia 77, 86, 139, 186–7, 297, 348, 381, 395, 403
Aoki Shūzō 326
Appleby, Gilman 117
Arabia 364, 370–1
  Hejaz 370–1
Arabian-American Oil Company 410, 412–13
Armstrong, Commodore James 267
Arnold, Matthew 348–9
Arthur, Sir George 124
Atlantic Charter 398–9, 499
Austin, James T. 91–4
Australia 6, 377, 391, 406, 416, 427

Bagot, Charles 80–2, 106, 109–10
Bailey, Thomas A. 351
Baldwin, Stanley 386, 389, 393, 497
Balfour, Arthur James 216, 354, 385
Balkans 300
Bancroft, George 239–40, 249–50
Bankhead, Charles 111
Barbour, Walworth 414
Barclay, Anthony 98–9, 100, 101–2, 106
Barclay, Captain Robert 60
Barclay, Thomas 36–42, 88–94, 104
Bathurst, 3rd Earl 64, 68, 71
Battles
  Bull Run 294
  Fallen Timbers 25
  Gettysburg 139–40
  Kut-al-Amara 368–9
  Leipzig 65
  Montgomery's Tavern 114
  New Orleans 65
  Plattsburg Bay 61
  Put-in-Bay 60
  Queenston Heights 56, 58
  Thames 50, 69
  Third Battle of Gaza 369
  Tippecanoe 50
  Trafalgar 7, 43, 44

Waterloo 73
Windmill 119–20
Windsor 120–20
York, attack at 59–60
Bayard, James A. 66, 339–40
Bayly, C.A. 194
Baynes, Rear Admiral R. Lambert 140
Bays
  Cobscook 35
  Edo (Yedo, Tokyo) 231, 237, 245, 255, 274, 279
  Fundy 35, 91–2, 102
    Campobello Island 94
    Deer Island 94
    Grand Manan Island 90–4
  Garrison 142
  Kiaochow (Jiaozhou) 210, 351
  Manila 349–52
  Mirs 349–52
  Nagasaki 236
    Deshima 236, 259, 266, 287, 294
  Osaka 311
  Passamaquoddy 35, 38–41, 48, 71, 88–94, 104
    Dudley Island 93–4
    Frederick Island 93–4
    Moose Island 93–4
    West Quoddy Passage 92–3
  Puget Sound 78, 87, 131–3
    San Juan Channel 136
    San Juan Island(s) 136–7, 143–5
  San Francisco 108
  Yokohama 257, 293
Beasley, W.G. 279
Beechey, Captain Frederick William 244
Bellecourt, Duchesne de 289, 293–4, 303
Bellomont, 1st Earl (second creation) 172
Bemis, Samuel Flagg 17, 25, 442
Benson, Egbert 36
Bent, Lieutenant Silas 247

Bickers, Robert 227

Biddle, Commodore James 238–41, 245

Big navy party 387, 389

Bigsby, Dr John J. 96, 100–1
  The Shoe and the Canoe 96, 98, 100–1

Bingham, Senator William 128

Bismarck, Otto von 337

Blaine, James G. 147, 356

Blower, Brooke L. 437

Bonham, Sir George 251–2

Bourne, Kenneth 451

Bowring, Sir John 195, 271, 279, 292

Bradford, William 5

Bradley, William C. 102–4

Bretton Woods 429

Bridgeman, William 385–6

British Commonwealth 7, 400, 407

British empire 1–9, 16, 43, 66, 104, 154–5, 229, 307, 330, 333–5, 358–65, 380, 432, 495
  Aden 154, 333, 411, 414, 427, 429
  Africa 333, 359, 361, 365, 380, 404, 416, 425
  American empire 329–30, 337–53, 361–2, 365, 373, 376
  American empire as ally 154–5, 158, 174, 196–8, 200–1, 203–4, 219, 291, 327–8, 332–5, 348, 407–8, 432
  Antigua 333
  Australia 6, 154, 377, 391, 406, 416, 427
  Borneo 265, 391, 427, 431
  British Guiana 8, 154, 337
  Brunei 333, 431
  Burma 154, 264, 332, 391, 402–3
  Cape Colony 8, 51, 345, 354, 365
  Caribbean 154, 333, 363
  Ceylon 8, 264
    Bone Island 40

Chinese empire 8, 201, 206, 209–17, 247, 263, 280, 287, 309–10
  China trade 181, 193–4, 228
  Shantung (Shandong) Peninsula 210, 213
  Weihaiwei 210–11, 214
  commercial and financial power 7–8, 9, 33, 51, 151–2, 158, 178, 189, 218–25, 231, 330, 332, 339, 343, 381, 391–2, 426–32, 506

Cyprus 154, 333, 368, 411

East Asia 432

East of Suez 9, 333, 427, 429–32

Eastern Mediterranean 363–4, 367, 416

Egypt 154, 210, 335, 350, 364, 367–8, 371–2, 413, 416–25
  Suez Canal 336, 350, 367, 369, 378, 391, 411, 416, 431

Falkland Islands 333

French empire 320, 335–6, 345, 353, 359–61, 378

German empire 320, 345, 350–1, 353, 359, 391, 396, 430

Ghana 154

Gibraltar 333, 363, 428

Gold Coast 154

Grenada 7, 333

Guyana See British Guiana

Hong Kong 154, 181, 183, 184, 188, 194, 200, 247, 252, 253, 265, 271, 292, 301, 329, 333, 349–51, 396–7, 400, 430, 432, 435

India 7, 8, 42, 78, 161, 164, 173, 181, 193–7, 210, 263, 332–3, 335, 359, 361, 364, 367, 373, 378, 396–7
  North-West Frontier 335

Indian Army 152–4, 158, 196–200, 337, 368, 397

informal empire 8, 339
  China 8, 154, 158–229, 260, 339
  South America 8, 338–9, 339

Iraq 371, 373, 379
Japanese empire 231–3, 236–7,
    260–4, 271, 278–81, 302–3, 311,
    323–8, 332, 391
  Trade 232–3, 261–2, 271, 309
Kuwait 368, 371, 414, 427
Legation in Shinagawa 287, 295–6
Malaya 154, 391, 416, 430
Malta 154, 363, 411, 417, 421, 428
Middle East 332–3, 339, 371–3, 375,
    379–81, 402, 408–25, 431–2
Balfour Declaration 372
Suez Crisis 333, 415–25, 504
Natal 354
New Brunswick 121–5
New Zealand 6, 154, 265, 377, 391,
    416
Nigeria 154, 431
Palestine 364, 369–73, 378
Papua New Guinea 391, 431
Qatar 333
Russian empire 8, 223, 320, 333,
    335–6, 364, 370–1
Sandwich Islands 244
Singapore 154, 264, 333, 363, 384,
    391, 403, 425, 427–9
South Africa 210, 345, 354–6, 377
Transjordan 371, 379
Vancouver Island 73, 75, 87, 131–3,
    136–9
West Indies 7, 19–22, 26, 28, 42, 55,
    61, 171
British North America See Canada
British Overseas Territories
  Anguilla 435
  Ascension Island 435
  Bermuda 435
  British Antarctic Territory 435
  British Indian Ocean Territory 435
  British Virgin Islands 435
  Cayman Islands 435
  Cyprus - 2 sovereign bases 435
  Falkland Islands 435

  Gibraltar 435
  Montserrat 435
  Pitcairn Islands 435
  South Georgia 435
  South Sandwich Islands 435
  St Helena 435
  Tristan da Cunha 435
  Turks and Caicos Islands 435
Brooke, General Sir Alan 403
Brown, George 426
Bruce, Sir Frederick 197, 202, 205
Brumby, Lieutenant Thomas Mason
    352
Bryan, William Jennings 225, 228
Buchanan, James 131–2, 142
Bulgaria 372–3
Bunsen, Sir Maurice de 326, 485
Buraimi Oasis 410–15, 417, 419
Burke, Edmund 404
Burlingame, Anson 202–6
Burlingame Mission 205–7

Caccia, Sir Harold 424, 504–5
Cadogan, Sir Alexander 398
Calhoun, John C. 102
Callaghan, James 426, 429, 431–2
Cámara, Rear Admiral Manuel de la
    350
Campbell, Major (not Col.) William
    25–6
Campbell, Sir Francis A. 219, 225
Canada 19, 42, 48, 49, 70–3, 83–4,
    144–5, 154, 341, 344, 359, 365,
    400, 406
  Alberta 84–5
  American wish to acquire 4, 15, 16,
    31–2, 50, 67, 144, 327
  border with the US 34–42, 75–155
  boundary negotiations 1898–1903
    148–50, 357
  British Columbia 73, 77, 78, 85–6,
    132–3, 136–7, 147–50
    Fraser Canyon 137–8

British defences of 12, 16–18, 22–4, 50, 52, 53–5, 70, 76–9, 83–4, 104–5, 107, 109, 119, 121–5, 127, 132, 134, 136, 153, 344, 363

Canada Union Act 1840, 120

Canadian Pacific Railway 134

Canadian Rebellions 77, 83, 111–21
  Caroline incident 115–19, 125–8
  Hunters' Lodges 119–20

Confederation of Canada 134

Halifax 35, 59, 105, 123

Lower Canada 24, 53, 59, 60, 64, 76, 104–5, 113–14, 119

Manitoba 84–5

Maritime provinces 63, 76

New Brunswick 13, 22, 32, 34–42, 76, 77, 79, 90–4, 102–5, 107, 109, 121–5, 134, 136
  Grand Manan Island 90–4
  Madawaska River Valley 105, 25
  St John Valley 104

Newfoundland 361, 400

Nova Scotia 14, 22, 35–7, 76, 90–4, 104, 124, 134

Ontario 13, 76, 134

Prince Edward Island 76

Quebec 15, 59, 76, 79, 107, 109, 123, 134

Saskatchewan 84–5

Upper Canada 16, 24, 53–4, 56, 60, 61–2, 64, 76, 104, 113–14, 119–20, 126

War of 1812, 11, 17, 52–3, 88, 94, 96, 117, 121, 374

Yukon 148, 150

Canning, George 101

Canning, Stratford 4, 106–7, 121–3

Cape of Good Hope 144

Carmarthen, Marquess of, later 5th Duke of Leeds 18–19

Carroll, Francis 124

Cass, Lewis 142

Castlereagh, 1st Viscount 65, 68, 69, 81–2, 86, 91–4, 98–9, 104, 145

Cathcart, Lieutenant-Colonel Charles 163–4

Catholic Church 3, 353

Cecil, Lord Robert 377, 385–7, 497

Ch'ing Court See emperor of that date

Ch'ing (Qing) Yu-tsai 189, 190

Chamberlain, Joseph 148, 210, 345–6

Chamberlain, Sir Austen 385–6

Champlain, Samuel de 38–41

Chiang Kai-shek 392

Chichester, Captain Edward 350–2

China See Chinese Empire

China Question, the 214–15

Chipman, Ward 38–41, 90–2, 105, 454–5

Chipman, Ward, Jr 102

Chōshū Five 304–7, 311

Churchill, Winston 73, 385–9, 395–7, 400, 402, 411–13, 415–16, 419

Cities, towns, villages
  Albany 298
  Alexandria 350
  Alexandria 65
  Amoy (Xiamen) 185, 192
  Amsterdam 266
  Astoria 86
  Baghdad 364, 368–9
  Baltimore 65, 174
  Bangor 124
  Barcelona 43
  Basra 368–9
  Berlin 211, 364
  Boston 186
  Buffalo 61, 96, 114–15, 117, 126
  Cairo 210, 365, 370, 417
  Calcutta 264
  Canton (Guangzhou) 145, 158, 161–3, 165, 170, 172–3, 175–8, 184–6, 192–3, 195, 265, 271, 283, 310
  City of London 330

Cleveland 119
Constantinople 344, 372–3
Corinto 339
Damascus 371
Eastport 34
Edo (Yedo, Tokyo) 233, 237, 239,
    245, 248, 250, 256–8, 260, 266,
    270, 272–3, 275–6, 278, 280,
    286–7, 289–91, 293, 294, 297,
    300, 307, 317, 322, 325
Foochow (Fuzhou) 185, 192, 283
Fredericton 79
Geneva 144, 385–6, 392
Ghent 67, 69
Göteborg 67
Hagi 309
Haiphong 430
Hakodate 259, 263, 271
Hanoi 430
Havana 348
Ho-Hsi-Wu (Hexiwu) 199
Honolulu 232
Houlton 124
Hull 431
Hyōgo 315, 317
Jakarta 236
Jehol (Chengde) 168–9, 199
Jerusalem 369–70
Kagoshima 304–6
Kakamura 257
Kamchatka 262–4
Kanagawa 275, 279, 285–7, 301
Kurihama 248
Kyōto 233, 237, 276–8, 298, 302–3,
    311, 315–16
Liverpool 431
London 16, 18, 22, 26, 28, 41, 52–3,
    66, 67, 86, 107, 147, 164, 197,
    205, 309, 317, 348, 353, 368–9,
    374, 396, 420, 428, 431
Manchester 193, 208, 216, 431
Manila 264, 349–52, 357
Marseilles 127

Mecca 370
Montreal 59, 79, 105, 113
Moraviantown 61
Mosul 373
Mukden 392
Nagasaki 239, 240, 249, 254, 263,
    271–2, 286
Naha 260
New Delhi 397
New York City 30, 36, 46, 90, 99,
    172, 205, 264–6
Niagara 61
Ningpo (Ningbo) 165, 185,
    192, 265
Norfolk 188
Osaka 275, 294, 296–7, 316
Oswego 119
Ottawa 150
Pao-ting (Baoding) 213
Paris 70, 265
Peking (Beijing) 157, 163–6, 170,
    187, 190, 197, 199–202, 208,
    213–14, 228, 300
Penang 264
Petropavloski 254
Philadelphia 21, 26, 30
Port Fuad 422
Port Lloyd 244, 252
Port Said 422–3
Portsmouth 166
Prescott 119
Providence 36
Queenston 61
Rio de Janeiro 238
Riyadh 409
Salem 43
San Francisco 232, 321
Sault Ste Marie 99
Schlosser 115–16
Shanghai 185, 192, 197, 207, 208,
    227, 232, 239, 244, 252, 254,
    265, 280, 283, 293–4
Sheffield 193

Shimoda 259, 265–71, 273, 275, 277–80, 285, 294
Shimonoseki 308
Shinagawa 256
Smyrna 173
St Andrews 34, 38, 40, 90
St John 35
St Petersburg 67
The Hague 109, 295
Tientsin (Tianjin) 166, 197, 199
Tokyo *See Edo*
Toronto 114
Toulon 26
Tungchow (Tongzhou) 199
Uraga 245–6, 257
Washington 11, 20, 31, 33, 53, 65, 68–9, 106, 127, 141, 144, 205–6, 245–6, 265, 295, 307, 321, 358, 372, 387, 397, 410–11, 420, 428, 493
Watertown 120
Windsor 120
Yokohama 257, 286–7, 290–3, 296, 299, 301–2, 304, 308, 310, 316–17
York 11, 59–60
Clarendon, 4th Earl 206–7
Clarendon Declaration 206–8
Clay, Henry 66, 71, 102
Clemenceau, Georges 378
Cleveland, Grover 338–9, 342–4
Clymer, Kenyon J. 397
Cobden, Richard 195
Cochrane, Vice-Admiral Sir Alexander 65
Coffin, Captain Reuben 244
Coleman, E.C. 141
Colombia, President of, Simón Bolivar 108
Conan Doyle, Arthur 349
Conrad, C.M. 241–2
Coolidge, Calvin 384–8
Cooperative Policy 204–4

Copeland, Jr, Miles 417
Cornwallis, 2nd Earl 173
Cowpland, William 174
Craddock, Sir Percy 424
Craigie, Robert 387–8, 497
Crawford, William H. 102
Crossman, Richard 432
Crowley, Leo 401
Curzon, 1st Marquess 372, 379, 394, 492
Cushing, Caleb 186–92
Cushing Mission 186–92
Cushing, John P. 186
Cutler, Lyman 75, 138–9
Czechoslovakia 419

Daimyō
Daimyō fudai 238
    tozama 238, 313–14
Daimyō (domains)
    Awa 315
    Bizen 315
    Chōshū, 297–8, 303, 304–10, 313–15
    Geishiu 315
    Hikoné 256
    Mito 256, 276–7, 282, 296
    Sakura 270
    Satsuma 297–8, 302, 313–16
    Tosa 297, 313–15
Darby, William 98
Darwin, John 372, 492
Davis, Sir J.F. 262
Dawes, Charles G. 393
De Long, Charles 322
Dearborn, General Henry 58–9
Delafield, Major Joseph 97, 99, 101
Dewey, Commodore George 349–52
Diederichs, Vice-Admiral Otto von 351–2
Dixon, Sir Pierson 423
Dobbin, J.C. 250–3, 255, 473
Dominions 365, 391, 400, 408
Dorchester, 1st Baron 22, 24, 28

Dorr, Eben M. 287
Douglas, James 136–40
Drew, Captain Andrew 115–16
Drinkard, William 141
Drummond, Lieutenant-General
    Gordon 61
Du Gua de Monts (or Mons), Pierre
    39, 40
Duffield, W.W. 147
Dulles, Allen 419, 424
Dulles, John Foster 412–14, 416,
    419–22, 503–4
Dundas, Henry 24, 42
Durfee, Amos 116
Durham, 1st Earl 120
East Asia 384, 432

East India Company 159–62, 164, 173,
    175, 177–8, 261
Eden, Sir Anthony 411–13, 415–16,
    420, 424–5
Egypt 61, 350, 364, 413, 416,
    418–21
    Suez Canal 419, 431
Eight Powers, the 214
Eisenhower, Dwight D. 412, 420–3,
    425, 504
Elgin, 8th Earl 196–200, 279–81
Elizabeth I 161
Elliott, Captain Charles 181–2
Emerson, Ralph Waldo 535
Emperors, Japanese
    Kōkaku 1780–1817
    Kōmei 1846–67 231, 233, 238, 248,
        256, 270, 277–8, 281, 297–8,
        300–3, 307, 309–14
    Meiji 1867–1912 314–19
    Ninkō 1817–46
    Shōwa 1926–89
    Taishō 1912–26
Emperors, Qing dynasty
    Daoguang 1820–50 179–80, 181,
        187, 189–90, 192, 228–9

Guanghu 1875–1908 212–19
Jiaqing 1796–1820
Puyi 1908–12 219–29
Qinglong 1735–96 157, 165–71
Tongzhu 1861–75 205
Xianfeng 1850–61 197–201, 202,
    228–9
Empire
    See American Empire
    See British Empire
    'Empire for liberty' 3–4
    'Empire of liberty' 4
    Abyssinian 2
    Austro-Hungarian 1–2, 159, 214,
        262, 336, 345, 350, 359, 376
    Belgian 1–2, 20, 108–9, 495
    Chinese 2, 78, 125, 145, 155, 157–
        229, 234, 259, 336, 349, 384,
        495
    army 197–9
    Boxer Rebellion 209, 212–14
    Chihli (Zhili) 226
    Chinese Educational Mission 202
    concedes British embassy in
        Peking 200
    Hu-Huang (Huguang, later
        Hubei and Hunan) 180
    Mongolia 226
    Mongolian cavalry 199
    need for financial aid 217–25
    New Policies 217
    possible US support 202–3
    Prince Kung or Gong 199–201,
        205
    Prince Yi 199
    railways 217, 219–23
    revolution 1911–12, 225–6
    Self-Strengthening Movement 201
    Sinkiang (Xinjiang 226
    Summer Palace 168–9, 199–200
    Taiping Heavenly Kingdom 252
    Taiping Rebellion 252
    Tibet 226

trade - foreign factories 178,
180–2
trade with 161–3, 169–70, 177,
197
Tsungli Yamen 201–2, 213
unequal barbarians 165–67, 185,
190, 197
Danish 2
Danish Virgin Islands 2
Frederick VI 108
Greenland 2
definition 1–9
Dutch 1–2, 7–8, 20, 51, 66, 108–9,
159, 161, 184, 234–6, 239, 254,
261, 295, 299, 308–9, 342, 495
East Indies 159, 161, 172, 236
Japanese empire 236, 239, 245,
266, 276, 278, 289–90, 303,
311–12, 316–18, 320
William I 108–11, 130
French 2, 3, 7, 12, 16, 20–1, 41, 43,
44, 45–6, 49, 51, 94, 113, 128,
153, 154, 158–9, 196–7, 201–2,
209–12, 220–5, 228, 236, 262,
335–6, 359, 372–3, 377–9, 384,
391, 421, 506–7
Africa 210, 331, 354, 361
Cochin-China (Indo-China) 210,
331, 413
Japanese empire 279, 289–90,
302–3, 311–12, 317–18, 320
Navy 254, 308–9, 311–12, 330,
350, 360, 362–3, 372, 382–4
Algeria 421
Middle East 331, 365, 371, 378–9,
421–3
German 2, 153, 154, 158–9, 201,
209–15, 220–5, 330–1, 337, 353,
370–1, 376–7, 391, 413, 497–8
Africa 210, 331, 365
Japanese empire 236, 316, 320,
324–5
Kaiser Wilhelm I 144–5

Kaiser Wilhelm II 345, 348, 370
Kiaochow (Jiaozhou Bay) 210–11
Middle East 364, 371–2
Navy (High Seas Fleet) 210, 331,
350, 359, 362–3
Shantung 222
Informal 3, 7
Italian 2, 214, 299, 345, 359, 373,
379, 382–3, 391, 406
Japanese 2, 155, 159, 201–2, 209,
211–15, 220–5, 284, 286, 297,
313–17, 324–9, 359, 497–8
Age of Warring States 237
American empire 267–8, 326–8
bakufū 233–4, 238, 245, 247–8,
256, 266, 269–70, 272–3, 277,
281, 283, 286–7, 289, 292–3,
296, 298–304, 307–8, 480
Bingosama 236
British empire 263, 324
bugyō 266–7, 268, 269, 271–3
daimyō 237–8, 255–6, 276–8, 283,
286, 306, 308
diplomatic tactics 258–9, 266–9,
275–9, 293
Dutch empire 236, 239, 245, 266,
287
Einosuke 260
Fukien (Fujian) 222
Fukuyama 245
Hayashi 260
Imperial Navy 215, 326, 360,
382–7
Iwakura Mission 320–4
Korea 209, 215, 238, 324, 392
Liaotung (Liaodung) Peninsula
2009
Meiji Restoration 233, 281, 298,
305–6, 312–19
Navy 215, 256, 350
rōjū 237–8, 245–6, 255–7, 270,
274, 277, 279–81, 310–13
Taiwan 209

Talien (Dalien) 209
Tokugawa clan 237–8, 256, 316
Ottoman 2, 125, 173, 209, 262, 336,
    344, 364–8, 370–2, 375–8
Portuguese 2, 51, 66, 161, 176, 300,
    495
    Macao 166, 176, 181, 182, 185,
        188, 190, 253, 368
Russian 2, 8, 51, 65–6, 70, 125, 145–
    6, 153–4, 158–9, 198, 209–12,
    220–5, 254, 262, 329, 335–6,
    359, 365, 370, 377–8, 396,
    405–6, 422, 425
    Caucasus 371
    Central Asia 8, 331, 335, 359, 361
    Imperial Navy 215, 254, 259,
        262–4, 279, 330, 360, 362–3
    Japanese empire 236–7, 276, 317, 323
    Manchuria 210, 214–15, 222–3, 226
    Port Arthur 210–11
    Siberia 215
    Tsar Nicholas I 108
Spanish 2, 3, 6, 7, 12, 16, 25, 43, 44,
    51, 53, 300, 342, 349–52
English Camp 142–3
Eulenburg, Count Fredrich von 288–
    90, 294
European Economic Communty 423,
    431
European Free Trade Area 426
Evarts, William 324
Everett, Alexander Hill 238–9
Everett, Edward 186, 242
Extraterritoriality 163–4, 175–6, 191–
    2, 272, 320, 326

Fairfield, John 123–4
Far East 6, 132, 154, 159, 161, 264–5,
    298, 327–8, 332–3, 354, 359,
    384, 390, 392, 402
Farouk, King of Egypt 417
Federal Reserve Bank of New York
    429, 431

Feisal (Faisal) bin Hussein bin Ali al-
    Hashemi, Emir, then King of
    Iraq 370–1, 378–9
Ferguson, James 100
Ferris, John 496
Fillmore, Millard 231, 241–2, 246, 249,
    251, 255–6, 402
Finland 377
Fish, Hamilton 144,
    321–2
Forbes, Robert Bennett 182
Forrester, C.S. 449
Forsyth, John 124, 127
Forts
    Amherstberg 56
    Bellingham 140
    Dearborn 58
    Defiance 26
    Detroit 22, 25, 56, 58
    Erie 22
    Mackinac 58
    Miamis 24, 25
    Michilimachinac 22, 58
    Montgomery (Blunder) 105, 107,
        109–10
    Niagara 22, 61
    Ontario 22
    Oswegatchie 22
    Oswego 22
    Victoria 137
Fowler, Henry 428–9, 431
Fox, Henry S. 124–5, 127–8
Franklin, Benjamin 4, 129
Fraser, Hugh 485
Frederick William III, King of Prussia
    108
'freedom of the seas' See Neutral
    rights at sea
French, David 491–2, 501
Frost, Robert 75

Gaddis, John Lewis 501
Galapagos Islands 63

Gallatin, Albert 47–8, 66, 68, 71, 86–7, 107

Gambier, Admiral 1st Baron 67

General Agreement on Trade and Tariffs 426

Geneva Disarmament Conference 1927, 385–7

George III 42, 51, 157, 164–5

Gerry, Elbridge 91

Gladstone, William 195–6

Glover, Thomas Blake 305

Glubb, Sir John 411

Goderich, 1st Viscount 101

Goulburn, Henry 67–9, 452

Grand Falls 40

Grant, General James Hope 198

Grant, Ulysses S. 117

Granville, 2nd Earl 321–3

Gray, Colonel Charles 120

Great Britain 19, 83, 141
   Admiralty 46, 83, 153–4, 306–7, 309, 335, 357, 360, 362, 385, 495
   Army 54–5, 63–5, 108, 152, 199–200, 337
     Chiefs of Staff 408, 421
   Cabinet 30, 32–3, 51, 70–1, 82, 101, 126, 154, 308–9, 335–6, 344–5, 353–4, 357–9, 360, 362–3, 365, 368, 372–4, 382–4, 386, 388, 392–3, 400–1, 413, 415, 420–1, 423, 430–1, 495, 501
   Colonial Office 195, 404, 432
   Commonwealth Relations Office 432
   Foreign Office 41, 101, 106–7, 123, 130, 137, 181, 197, 208–9, 219, 221, 225–6, 262, 285, 288, 291, 293, 305, 311, 317, 322, 330, 346, 353–4, 357, 361, 378, 387–8, 392–3, 398, 398, 407, 411, 413–15, 418, 423, 498, 501, 507
   House of Commons 183, 195–6, 422, 430
   House of Lords 126–8
   Joint Intelligence Committee 503
   MI6, 417
   military forces 142
   Ministry of Defence 432
   Parliament 51–3, 80, 284, 306, 308, 336, 404, 413
   Regency Bill 51
   Royal Air Force 407–8, 427, 431–2, 501
   Royal Navy 7–8, 21, 26, 29–30, 43, 44, 49, 54, 56–8, 61, 80, 115–16, 121, 127, 133–4, 136, 140–2, 152–4, 223, 261, 284–5, 292, 299, 308–9, 311–12, 315, 318, 330, 332, 335–6, 338, 344–5, 350, 360–5, 372–5, 381–90, 415–16, 429, 495–6
     Base-Esquimalt 136, 363
     Base-Halifax 35, 59, 105, 123, 363
     Chinese empire 158, 193, 195–8, 207, 223, 261
     Impressment 12, 46–7, 66–7, 69, 72, 86
     War of 1812 54, 56–8, 61–3
   Sussex 430
   Treasury 143, 362, 423
   War Office 52, 153, 362, 368, 370
Great Lakes 13, 17, 31, 58, 60, 70, 77, 79–84, 96, 120–1
   Erie 14, 22, 24, 60–1, 98–9
   Gibraltar Island 60
   Huron 14, 22, 99
   Michigan 22, 96
   Ontario 14, 22, 60, 80, 82, 98–9
   Sacket's Harbor 60
   Superior 14, 22, 88, 94–7, 100–1
Greece 300, 379

Grenville, 1st Baron 26, 28–34, 42, 442–3

Grenville, George 29

Gresham, Walter Q. 326

Grey, Earl de Grey and Ripon 144

Grey, Sir Edward 217, 220–1, 223, 225–6, 360, 376
Griffin, Charles 75, 137–8
Gros, Baron Jean-Baptiste Louis 197, 200, 279
Gubbins, J.H. 269
Gulfs
    Alaska, Lynn Canal 146–7
    Mexico 144, 325, 327, 373
    Pei-chihli (Bohai) 166
    Persian 367–8, 410, 416, 422, 429–30
Gunboat diplomacy 7, 158, 284, 339

Hahn, Emily 266
Haldane reforms 489
Hall, Francis 292
Hamilton, Alexander 27, 33
Hamilton, Lord George 336, 419
Hammond, Edmund 284, 322
Hammond, George 31, 33
Harcourt, 2nd Viscount 505
Harding, Warren G. 382, 384
Hardinge, 1st Baron 367–8
Harney, Brigadier-General William Selby 139–42
Harris, Townsend 259, 264–83, 285–97, 478
Harrison, General William Henry 50, 60–1, 127
Harvey, Sir John 124–5
Hawkesbury, 1st Baron See Liverpool
Hawkins, Colonel Samuel 97
Hay, John 147–50, 203, 211–12, 355, 357
Hayes, Al 429, 431
Healey, Denis 427–8, 430, 432
Heren, Louis 430
Herring, George C. 461
Herschell, 1st Baron 148
Heusken, Henry 266, 270, 277, 280, 288–90, 295
Hevia, James L. 170
Hicks Beach, Sir Michael 344, 362
Higginson, H.C. 443

Hintze, Captain-Lieutenant Paul von 351–2
Hitler, Adolf 391
Hoare, James 482–3
Holland, Commodore Swinton 351
Holmes, John 88, 91
Hoover, Herbert 389, 393
Hope, Admiral James 197–8
Hopkins, Harry 399
Hornby, Captain Geoffrey 140
Hotta Bitchiu no kami Masayoshi (Sakura) 271–9, 476
House of Baring 128
House, Edward M. 374–5, 398
Howell, David 36–42
Howe, Stephen 439
Hudson's Bay Company 136–7, 139–40
Hughes, Billy 376
Hughes, Charles Evans 382–4
Hull, Cordell 401–2
Hull, General William 58–9
Humphrey, George 423, 505
Hungarian uprising 422
Hunt, Michael H. 215, 219
Husayn (Hussein) ibn Ali ibn Muhammad ibn Abd al-Mu'in ibn Awn, Sharif of Mecca 370–1
Huskisson, William 107

ibn Saud, King of Saudi Arabia (Abdul Aziz ibn Abdul Rahman ibn Faisal ibn Turki ibn Abdullah ibn Muhammad Al Saud) 410, 417
Iceland 2
Ignatyev, Count 197–200
Indian nations 8, 12, 16, 17–18, 20, 21–2, 24–6, 30, 32, 38–9, 49–51, 56, 58, 60, 62, 68–9, 71–2, 99–100, 139, 141
    Creek 55
    Shawnee 50, 61

India, Government of 367–8, 397
Indonesia 427
Inouye Shinano no kami 269–70, 273,
    275–6, 279
Iran 411, 413
Iraq 418, 425, 427
Ireland 3
Irish-Americans 343, 55
Iriye, Akira 498
Israel 418–19, 437
Ito, Dr Genboku 248–9
Itō Hirobumi 306–7, 311, 321
Iwakura, Tomomi 318–20, 322–3
Iwasay Higo no kami 279

Jackson, Andrew 102, 110
James I 38
Jameson Raid 345
Jansen, Marius B. 247
Japan See Japanese Empire
Jardine, Dr William 181
Jardine, Matheson & Company 305
Jay, John 18, 27–34, 38, 443
Jefferson, Thomas 4, 41–2, 45, 47–9,
    58, 59
Jenkins, Roy 431–2
Johnson, Lyndon B. 428–30, 431–2
Johnson, Samuel 164
Jones, Howard 456
Jordan 379, 411
    Arab Legion 411
Jordan, Sir John 225–6
Jōi movement 304–5
J. & T.H. Perkins, Boston 186
J.P. Morgan & Co. 222, 225

Kaoru Inoue 306–7, 324–5
Kearny, Commodore Lawrence 185–6
Kellogg, Frank B. 386–7
Kemal, Mustafa (Atatürk) 379
Khyber Pass 335
King, Admiral E.J. 403
King, Rufus 26–7, 41, 43

Kipling, Rudyard 353, 485
Kirkpatrick, Sir Ivone 414–15
Kissinger, Henry 505–6
Knox, Philander C. 219–25
Kowloon Peninsula 200
Kowtow (ketou) 166–8, 171
Kramer, Paul 467
Kruger, Paul 345
Kuper, Rear Admiral Sir Augustus
    301–2, 304, 309

Labour governments 1964–70 426–7
Lakes
    Champlain 56, 61, 80, 82, 123
        Rouse's Point 105, 107, 110, 130
    Chiputneticook 40
    Lake of the Woods 14–15, 31–2,
        84–5, 87, 88, 94, 100, 101
    Long Lake 14
    Saganaga 101
Lansdowne, 5th Marquess 357–9
Latimer, Jon 447
Latin America
    Brazil 144, 400
    Caribbean
        Bahamas 43
        Cuba 4, 6, 43, 348–9
        New Providence 6, 21, 43
        Puerto Rico 154
    Central America 6, 356, 39
        Haiti 6
        Nicaragua 7, 339–40
        Panama 6
        Santo Domingo 7
    Mexico 6, 12, 133–4
    Panama, isthmian canal 356–8
    South America 7, 341, 357
        Argentina 7, 8
        Cape Horn 356–7
        Chile 7, 341
        Colombia 7, 339
    Venezuela 149, 358
        Venezuelan Crisis 337–47, 358

Laurier, Sir Wilfrid 149
Lawrence, T.E. 370
League of Nations 374–9, 392–3, 404
    Mandates 377–9
Li Hung-chang (Li Hongzhang)
    202–3
Lin Tse-hsue (Lin Zexu) 180–2, 184
Lincoln, Abraham 294
Liverpool, 1st Earl 41, 43, 53, 69,
    70–3, 101
Livingston, Edward 110–11
Lloyd, Selwyn 400, 420, 423–4
Lloyd George, David 365, 369,
    371–8
Lloyds of London 446
Locke, John 5
Lodge, Henry Cabot 150, 352,
    354–6
    The War With Spain 352
London Naval Conference 1930 389
Long, Walter 382
Lothian, 11th Marquess 399
Louisiana Purchase 2, 12, 25, 41, 43,
    49, 81–2, 128
Louis, William Roger 380, 405

Macartney Embassy 157, 164–71
    objectives 164, 165–7
Macartney, 1st Earl 157, 164, 166–7,
    169–71
MacDonald, Ramsay 389
Mackenzie, William Lyon 114
MacLaughlin, James A. 124
MacLeod, Alexander 77
Macmillan, Harold 415–16, 420–1,
    423, 425
Madison, James 4, 41–2, 45, 47–8, 52–
    3, 59, 65, 68, 80, 97, 104, 445–6
Makins, Sir Roger 420–1
Malaysia 427–31
Malmesbury, 3rd Earl 233, 287
Manchurian Crisis 1931, 392–4
Manifest Destiny 6, 131, 232, 327

Marcy, W.L. 115, 117, 265–6, 272–3,
    285–6, 288
Marshall Plan 406–8
Marshall, George C. 406
Marshall, Humphrell 252–3
Marshall, Peter 404
Matheson, James 181
Matsdaïra Iga no kami 277
Maude, Lieutenant-General Sir
    Frederick 368–9
McIntire, Rufus 123–4
McKinley, William 147–8, 149, 203,
    212, 348–9, 353
McLane, Louis 132–3
McLane, R.M. 253
McLeod, Alexander 125–8
McMahon, Sir Henry 371
McMaster, John 290
McNab, Colonel Allan 115–16
McNamara, Rober 430
Melbourne, 2nd Viscount 113
Mesopotamia 364, 368–9, 371–3, 377
Mikado 237, 297–8
Milner, 1st Viscount 371
Missionaries 183–6, 193–4, 197, 206,
    213–14, 353, 493
Mitchell, John 36, 39
Monroe Doctrine 4, 338, 340, 343, 345
Monroe, James 42, 65–6, 80–3, 86–7,
    338
Morgenthau, Henry 395, 399, 401
Mori Arinori 306
Mori Daizen-no-Daibu (Chōshū) 303,
    310
Morison, Samuel Eliot 243–4
Moriyama Yenosuke 267, 475
Moro Islands 6
Morris, Robert 172
Morse, Lieutenant-Colonel Robert 35
Mountbatten, 1st Earl 504
Murray, Sir Archibald 369
Muscat and Oman 410, 414
Mussolini, Benito 391

Namamurgi Incident 300–2
Namibia 365
Naosuké, Ïi Kamon-no-kami
    Naosuké (Hikoné) 256, 270,
    279, 282, 286–7
Napier, 9th Baron 178, 181
Napoleon III 196
Nariaki, Tokugawa Nariaki (Mito)
    256, 276–7, 281–2, 296
Nasser, Colonel Gamal Abdel 417,
    420, 422, 503
Neale, Lieutenant-Colonel Edward St
    John 300–4
Near East 359, 368, 409
Neguib, General Muhammed 417
Nelson, Horatio, Admiral Lord 7, 44
Neustadt, Richard E. 423
Neutral rights at sea 21, 27, 32–3,
    43–9, 66, 72–3, 374–5, 386,
    397–9
    Rule of the War of 1756 21, 43–4
Newspapers 306, 343, 349, 353
    National Intelligencer 117
    New York Tribune 292
    Niles' Register 117
    Pall Mall Gazette 335
    The Times 200–200, 345
    Toronto News 150
Nicolson, Harold 378
Nixon, Lieutenant-General Sir John
    368
Nixon, Richard 425
North America 6
North Atlantic Treaty Organisation
    (NATO) 424, 433
Northwest Ordinance 1787 5
Northwest Territory 22, 49–51
Norway 400

Oceans
    Atlantic 14, 48, 55, 88, 104, 123,
        154, 333, 356
    Channel 361

    Indian 333, 429
    Pacific 6, 87–8, 131–2, 154, 231–2,
        244, 252, 332, 350, 356, 384,
        402
        Bonin Islands 242, 244, 251–2
Ogilvy, John 88, 98
O'Hara, Glenn 506
Oil 368, 373, 378, 409–13, 420, 422,
    431
Okinawa See Great Lew Chew Island
Old China Hands 208–9, 219
Oliphant,, Lawrence 279–80, 295–6
Olney, Richard 338–42, 487
Opium trade 164, 173–7, 182–4, 193,
    197, 261, 274
Orange Free State 345, 354
Orders-in-Council 46, 51–3
    26 December 1783 172
    6 November 1793 21, 26
    8 January 1794 21
    November 1807 47
Oregon Territory 73, 77, 86–7, 131–4,
    142, 151
Oregon Trail 131
Osborn, Captain Sherard 280
Oswald, Richard 130
Otte, Thomas 214–15, 335, 487
Oxford English Dictionary, definition
    of imperialism 158
Ōkuma Shigenobu 325

Pagan, Robert 40
Pakenham, Richard 131–3
Pakistan 335
Palmerston, 3rd Viscount 109–11,
    125–6, 130, 181–3, 194, 196,
    306
Pan American Airways 500
Panay Crisis 394
Panizzi, Sir Anthony 130
Papineau, Louis-Joseph 113, 456
Parkes, Harry 195–7, 199, 310–12,
    315–19, 324–5, 482–4

Pauncefote, Sir Julian 147–8, 342, 357
Peel, Sir Robert 128–31, 262
Pelcovits, Nathan A. 208
Pelham, Sir Henry 412
People's Republic of China 419
Perceval, Spencer 51, 53
Periodicals
 Edinburgh Review 260–1
 Life 396
 Punch 195
Perkings & Company, Canton 186
Perkins, Bradford 29, 448
Perry, Commodore Matthew C.
 231–2, 241–55, 262, 265, 271,
 274, 402, 474
Perry, Olive Hazard 60
Persia 8, 125, 361, 364, 367, 371, 378
Petersen, Tore Tingvold 415
Phelipeaux 14
Philby, Kim 408
Pickett, Captain George 139–43
Piedmont-Sardinia 365
Pierce, Franklin 265–6, 270, 272–3,
 285
Pilgrim Fathers 5
Pinckney, Thomas 26
Pitt the Younger, William 18–19, 26,
 28, 29
Platt Amendment 1901, 6
Plunkett, Sir Francis 311, 482
Poland 70, 377
Polk, James K. 131–3, 139
Porter, Peter 88, 96–8, 100
Portland, 3rd Duke 51–1
Pottinger, Major-General Sir Henry
 181, 188
Poutiatin, Vice-Admiral Yevfimiy
 254, 259
Pratt, Zadock 238
Preble, Lieutenant George Henry 258
Prévost, Sir George 65
Protectorates 6–7, 368
Prussia 184, 288–9, 316

Pruyn, Robert H. 297–301, 307–8, 480
Puerto Rico 6, 349

Railways
 South Manchurian Railway 392
 Trans-Aral Railway 335
 Orenburg-Tashkent branch 335
 Trans-Siberian Railway 335
Randolph, Edmund 27–8
Reagan, Ronald 7
Reed, William B. 195, 197
Reinsch, Paul S. 228
Republic of China 225–8, 329, 331,
 355, 360, 391–4, 396–7
 Nationalist Party (Kuomintang)
 226–7
 navy 227
 Progressive Party 227
Republic of the Transvaal 345, 354
Rhodes, Cecil 354
Richardson, Charles Lennox 301–2,
 304
Ritcheson, Charles 19, 24
Rivers
 Chiputneticook 40
 Columbia 78, 86, 132–3, 141, 151
 Connecticut 14, 41, 88, 96, 104–5,
 109
 Detroit 56, 99
 Glaize 26
 Klondike 148
 Magaguadavic 35, 38–41
 Maumee 24, 26, 28
 Mississippi 5, 15, 31–2, 41, 43, 50,
 56, 71–2
 Niagara 13, 56, 58, 61
 Grand Island 115
 Navy Island 114–18
 Niagara Falls 79
 North (Bei) 197
 Ohio 22, 25, 50
 Orange 354
 Orinoco 338

Oswego 22
Pearl (or Canton) 162–3, 174, 180,
    184
    Lintin (Nei Lingding) Island 176,
        179, 180
    Whampoa (Pazhou) Island,
        Whampoa Reach 174, 176, 189
Peiho (Haihe) 166, 190
Pigeon River Falls 13
Potomac 65
Richelieu 105
Schoodiac 35, 38–40
St Croix 14–15, 31–2, 35–42, 91,
    102, 104, 106, 111, 136
St Francis 110
St John 35, 39–40, 104, 110, 111,
    121–3, 129–30
St Lawrence 14, 22, 48, 56, 79, 94–6,
    102–4, 106–7, 123, 130, 144
    Thousand Islands 96
Thompson 137
Tigris 369
Vaal 354
Yangtze (Yangzi) 197, 222, 228, 394
Yellow 212
Robinson, F.J. ('Prosperity') 452
Roches, Léon 318
Rogers, Frederick 195
Roosevelt, Elliott 395, 402–4, 498
    As He Saw It 395
Roosevelt, Franklin Delano 329, 395–
    9, 402–3, 406, 498, 501
Roosevelt, Theodore 149–50, 347,
    355–6
Roosevelt, Theodore, Jr 383
Root, Elihu 220
Rosebery, 5th Earl 326
Ross, Major-General Robert 64
Rowan, Sir Leslie 505
Rowe, William T. 222, 225
Royal Isle 14
Rush, Richard 82, 86–7, 94, 106–7, 451
Rusk, Dean 430

Russell, Jonathan 66
Russell, Lord John 113, 293, 296,
    301–2, 306–9, 312
Ryūkyū Islands See Lew Chew
    Islands

Sachar, Howard M. 369–70
sakoku 307
Salisbury, 3rd Marquess 148, 210–11,
    338, 340, 342, 344–5, 357
Samurai 239, 246, 282–4, 287–8, 294,
    298, 313, 317–18
    bushidō, 282
    rōnin 284, 289, 295–6
San Remo Conference 378
Satow, Sir Ernest 217, 288, 307, 309
Saudi Arabia 409–10, 412–15, 418
Saxe-Weimar, Duke Karl August 108
Scott, General Winfield 117–19, 125,
    141–2
Scruggs, William, British Aggression
    in Venezuela 339
Seas
    'narrow seas'
        English Channel 360
        mouth of the Mediterranean at
            Gibraltar 360
        North Sea 360
        Suez Canal 360, 364, 367, 372,
            391
    Aegean 372
    Black 344, 368, 371–2
    Caribbean 4, 6, 21, 43
    East China
        Chusan (Zhoushan) Islands 165,
            170
        Great Lew Chew Island 243, 245,
            255, 258, 260
        Lew Chew Islands 242–4, 255
    Japan 275, 284
    Mediterranean 344, 367, 378, 416
    North 223, 360
    Okhotsk, Sakhalin Island 254, 262

Red 172
South China 223
Selborne, 2nd Earl 153, 360–3, 381
Sellar, W.C. and R.J. Yeatman, 1066
    and All That 433
Seward, William 83, 147, 203, 265,
    294–5, 297–9, 475, 479, 483
Seymour, Rear Admiral Sir Michael
    195
Shidehara, Admiral Kijūrō 384
Shimazu Hisamitsu (Satsuma) 300–4
Shimazu Tadayoshi (Satsuma) 479
Ships
    Alabama 143–4
        negotiation over claims 144–5,
        321
    Blossom
    Brandywine 189, 190
    Caroline 77, 115–20
    Chesapeake 62
    Columbus 239–40
    Constantine 254
    Constitution 62
    Emily 173–4
    Empress of China 172
    Encounter 293
    Endymion 62
    Essex 43, 62, 63, 445
    Favourite 43
    Furious 280
    Guerrière 62
    Hatteras 144
    Immortalité 350
    Iphigenia 352
    Iroquois 316
    Java 62
    Kaiserin Augusta 351
    Lee 280
    Linnet 350
    Lion 166, 170
    Macedonian 62
    Maine 348–9
    Michigan 83

    Mississippi 248, 278
    Monitor 153
    Oregon 356–7
    Panay 394
    Peacock 179
    Pembroke 303, 310
    Phoebe 62, 63
    Powhatan 279
    President 62
    Prince of Wales 398
    Princess Royal 312
    Retribution 280
    San Jacinto 267
    Shannon 62
    Stonewall Jackson 318–19
    Toey-Wan 198
    United States 62
    Vermont 251
    Victory 44
    Vincennes 239
    Warrior 153
    Winchester 263
Shortridge, Wilson P. 457
Shōguns 234, 237, 297–8
    Tokugawa Hitotsubashi Keiki
        (Yoshinobu) 1866–7 238,
        314–16, 318–19
    Tokugawa Iemochi 1858–66 238,
        281–2, 297–8, 300–3, 306, 308,
        311–14
    Tokugawa Ienari 1787–1837
    Tokugawa Ieoshi 1837–53 238, 239
    Tokugawa Iesada 1853–8 238, 245,
        249, 256, 258, 273, 280, 282,
        309
    Tokugawa Ieyasu 1603–5 237–8,
        277
    Tokugawa Tsunayoshi 1680–1709
        236
Shuckburgh, Evelyn 415
Siam 265
Simcoe, Lieutenant-General John
    22–5, 28

Simon, Sir John 392
Smuts, General Jan Christian 374, 377
    The League of Nations: A Practical
        Suggestion 377
Social Darwinist 209
Somervell, General Brehon 402–2, 500
South African Republic 354
South Vietnam 429–30
Southack, Captain Cyprian 36
Soviet Union *See Russian empire*
Sparks, Jared 129–30
Spring Rice, Thomas 182
Spry, Graham 501
St Croix Commission 36–42, 90
Stacey, C.P. 83–3
Stalin, Josef 395
Stanley, Lord, 14th Earl of Derby 132
Stanley, Oliver 329
Staunton, Master George 168–9
Staunton, Sir George 164–5
Stephen, James 44
    War in Disguise 43–4
Sterling Area 400–1
Stevenson, Andrew 126–7
Stimson Doctrine of Nonrecognition
    393
Stimson, Henry 389, 393
Stirling, Rear Admiral Sir James
    262–4, 271
Strachey, Henry 130
Straits
    Banka 164
    Behring 145
    Bosphorus 373, 379
    Dardanelles 344, 367, 372–3, 375,
        379
    Georgia 136–7
    Haro 136, 144
    Juan de Fuca 136–7
    Rosario 136
    Shimonoseki 303, 308
    Uraga 247–8, 250, 260
Sullivan, John 38–41

Sumner, Charles 144
Sun Yat-sen (Sun Yixian) 226–7
Sung Chiao-jen (Song Jiaoren) 227
Sweden 66
Syria 378, 418, 422

Taft, William Howard 219, 221, 225
Tanzania 365
Tateno Gozo 326
Tattnall, Commander-in-Chief Josiah
    198, 279
Taylor, A.J.P. 151–2, 209
Tea 161–2, 172–3, 181, 183
Tecumseh 50, 60–1, 69
Terrae nullius 440
Terranova, Francis 174–5, 177, 180
Thompson, David 97, 99, 100–1
Thorne, Christopher 403
Tibet 361
Tompkins, Daniel 59, 448
Townsend, Major-General Sir Charles
    368
Toynbee, Arnold 378
Tōkaidō 286, 301
Treaties
    American Loan Agreement 1946
        401
    Anglo-Egyptian 1936 417
    Anglo-Egyptian 1954 418, 421
    Anglo-French Agreement 1904
        360–1
    Anglo-Japanese 1858 280–1, 283,
        360
    Anglo-Japanese 1902 223, 306, 320,
        327, 382, 386
    Anglo-Japanese or Stirling
        Convention 1855 262–4, 271
    Anglo-Portuguese 1373 490
    Anglo-Russian Agreement 1907
        223, 361
    Anglo-Russian Convention 1825
        145
    Anglo-Venezuelan 1897 346

Aoki-Kimberley 1894 326
Baghdad Pact 1955 418–19
Brest-Litovsk 1918 370
Clayton-Bulwer 1850 356
Convention of 1818 86–7, 136
Convention of 1827 109
Convention of Kanagawa 1854 259, 267, 269, 272, 274
Convention of Peking, British 1858 200
Convention of Peking, France 1858 200
Convention of Peking, Russian 1858 197
Declaration of Washington 1954 413
Dutch-Japanese 1858 281
Edo Convention of Tariffs 1866 313, 324, 482–3
Four Power 1921 384
Franco-Japanese 1858 281
Franco-Russian Dual Alliance 1894 209–10, 221, 344, 359
Ghent 1814 13, 71–2, 73, 77, 88–9, 107
Hay-Herbert 1903 [Alaska] 150
Hay-Pauncefote 1901 357–8
Japanese-American 1894 326–7
Jay Treaty 1794 13, 27–34, 42–3, 71–2, 173
    British posts 12, 16–18, 27, 31–32
    neutral rights 27
Kanagawa 1858 274–9, 290, 292
Kellogg-Briand Pact 1928 393
Lausanne 1923 379
London Protocol 1862 296
Mediterranean Agreements 1887 345
Most Favoured Nation clause 185, 194
Naha 1854 260
Nanking (Nanjing) 184–6, 188, 192–4, 261

Nine-Power 1921 392
Oregon 1846 133–4
Paris 1783 12, 91, 104, 111, 129–30, 171
Protocol 1898 148
Rush-Bagot Agreement 1818 82–3, 86, 120–1
Russian-American 1867 145
Russo-Japanese 1858 281
Sevrès 1920 378–9
Sèvres Protocol 1965 421
Supplementary, the Bogue 1843 185, 188
Sykes-Picot Agreement 1916 371, 378
Tientsin, Anglo-Chinese 1858 197, 280
Tientsin, Sino-American 1858 197
Triple Alliance 1882 345, 359
Unequal Treaties 184–5, 200, 297, 313, 319–20, 482–3
Versailles 1919 393, 418
Wanghia (Wangxia) 191–2, 194, 239, 257
Washington 1868 206–7
Washington 1871 144
Washington Naval 1922 383
Webster-Ashburton 1842 88, 102, 111, 128–31
Trench, Power 484
Trollope, Anthony 348
Truman, Henry 419
Tsiyeng (Qiying) 190
Turkey 2, 364, 367–8, 372–3, 375, 378–9, 418, 493
Tycoon, Tykoon, Taikun See Shōguns
Tyler, John 127–8, 186

United Kingdom See Great Britain
United Nations 397, 402, 414, 422, 425, 504
    trusteeship 403–5

United States
  Army 54–5, 63–5, 133, 152, 203,
      337, 370–1, 417
    Joint Chiefs of Staff 405
  border with Canada 34–42, 76–155
  Cabinet 48, 342, 356
  CIA 408, 417, 419
  Congress 5, 16, 30, 49, 52–3, 77, 79,
      96, 104–5, 126, 133, 137, 141,
      251, 255, 262, 336, 342–3, 352,
      356–8, 375, 382, 387, 393, 399,
      429, 487, 493
  Embargo Act 1807 47–9
  Executive 77, 118, 123, 133, 140,
      307, 410–11, 415–16, 493, 505
  Foreign Economic Administration
      401
  House of Representatives 33, 66,
      102, 126, 238, 314, 339
  National Security Council 425, 504
  Navy 43, 54, 56–8, 80–4, 133, 152–3,
      179, 185–6, 198, 231–2, 231–2,
      234, 239–52, 253–5, 285, 300,
      315–16, 332, 336, 349–53, 357,
      363, 381–90, 394–5, 403, 421, 496
    War of 1812 54, 56–8, 61–3
  political institutions and culture
      106–7, 110, 405–6
  Rocky Mountains 87–8
  Senate 33, 83, 86, 110, 133, 150, 192,
      328, 339, 343, 356–8, 393
  State Department 41, 129–30,
      147–50, 186, 242, 245–7, 253,
      291, 339, 387, 400, 402, 408,
      413, 417–18, 428, 493, 505
  Treasury 395, 401–2, 431, 505
University Colege London 305
Urmston, James 175–6
USSR See Russian empire

Van Buren, Martin 102, 117–18, 125–7
Van Ness, Cornelius P. 88, 102–4

Van Rensselaer, Colonel Rensselaer
      114, 118
Van Valkenburgh, General Robert
      314–19
Vansittart, Nicholas 70
Vansittart, Robert 392–3, 497–8
Vaughan, Sir Charles 111
Vergennes, comte de 129
Versailles Peace Cnference 365, 375
Victoria 143, 244, 281, 308, 318
Vyse, Captain Francis Howard
      301–2

Wales 3
War Hawks 50–1
Ward, John E. 198
Wars
  American Civil War 1861–5 83, 88,
      139, 141, 143, 153, 203, 294–5,
      297–8, 307, 321, 327, 337
  Anglo-Afghan 1839–42 124
  Arab-Israeli 1948 419
  Arab-Israeli 1967 431
  Aroostook (Lumberjack) War 1839
      73, 77, 121–5
  Boxer Rebellion 1899–1901 209,
      212–15, 217, 226, 229
  Cold 1947–91 412
  Creek War 55
  Crimean 1853–6 254, 262, 365
  Crusades 370
  Egyptian crisis 1839–41 124
  First Anglo-Boer 1880 354
  First World War 1914–18 7, 8, 215,
      228, 330, 337–8, 350, 364–73,
      381, 385, 391, 394, 398, 404,
      409, 493, 497
  French War against Britain 1793–
      1802 20, 22, 28–9, 33, 34
  Indonesia-Malaysia 'Confrontation'
      1963–6 427
  Korean 1950–3 408

Mexican-American 1846–48 6, 133, 139, 329
Napoleonic War 1803–15 7, 42, 43, 45–6, 53, 56, 63, 64, 65, 70, 73, 374
  Berlin and Milan Decrees 46
Northwest Indian War 21–2, 30
Opium 1840–42 124, 179–85, 189, 228, 261, 280
Pig War 1859–72 73, 75, 78, 134–45
Quasi-War 1798–1800 43
Russo-Japanese 1904–5 215
Russo-Turkish 1877 367–8
Second Anglo-Boer 1899–1902 347–8, 354–7, 359
Second Opium (Arrow) 1856–60 185, 194–200, 228, 300, 310
  Taku (Dagu) forts 197–8, 214
Second World War 1939–45 9, 329–30, 390, 394–406, 409–10, 417
  Lend-Lease 332, 398–402
Seven Years' or French and Indian War 1756–63 15
Sino-French War 1884–5 209
Sino-Japanese 1894–5 202, 209, 214
Spanish-American 1898 337, 347–54, 356
Summer War 1866 313
Vietnam 1955–75 428–30, 432
War of 1812, 1812–14 1, 12, 17, 34–5, 45, 53–61, 76, 79
  attack on York 11
  burning of Washington 11

  causes 12–13, 15, 16
  Peace negotiations 65–73
  War aims 55
Washington Conference 1921 382–5, 496
Washington, George 4, 20, 22, 26, 30, 33, 65
Wayne, Major-General 'Mad Anthony' 22, 24–6
Webster, Daniel 127–31, 186–8
Wellington, 1st Duke 51, 69–71, 101
Western Hemisphere, American sphere of influence 338, 347, 358, 361, 363, 431
Weyler, General Valeriano ('the Butcher') 348–53
White, Henry 148, 357
Wilford, Hugh 417
Williamson, Professor Alexander William 305
Williams, Samuel Wells 258
Wilson, Harold 426, 430–2
Wilson, Woodrow 225, 365, 372–7, 380–2, 393, 398–9, 403, 493
Wisner, Frank 408
Wit, J.K. de 289, 294–4
Württemberg, King Karl I 108

Ye Ming-ch'en 195–7
Yüan Shih-k'ai (Yuan Shikai) 226–8

Zanzibar 365

A Note on the Author

Kathleen Burk is Professor Emerita of Modern and Contemporary History at University College London and a columnist and radio panellist. She is the author of several distinguished scholarly books on the US and its interventions in the rest of the world, and the definitive biography of A.J.P. Taylor, *Troublemaker: The Life and History of A.J.P. Taylor*.

She lives near Oxford.

A Note on the Type

The text of this book is set in Linotype Stempel Garamond, a version of Garamond adapted and first used by the Stempel foundry in 1924. It is one of several versions of Garamond based on the designs of Claude Garamond. It is thought that Garamond based his font on Bembo, cut in 1495 by Francesco Griffo in collaboration with the Italian printer Aldus Manutius. Garamond types were first used in books printed in Paris around 1532. Many of the present-day versions of this type are based on the Typi Academiae of Jean Jannon cut in Sedan in 1615.

Claude Garamond was born in Paris in 1480. He learned how to cut type from his father and by the age of fifteen he was able to fashion steel punches the size of a pica with great precision. At the age of sixty he was commissioned by King Francis I to design a Greek alphabet, and for this he was given the honourable title of royal type founder. He died in 1561.